Process

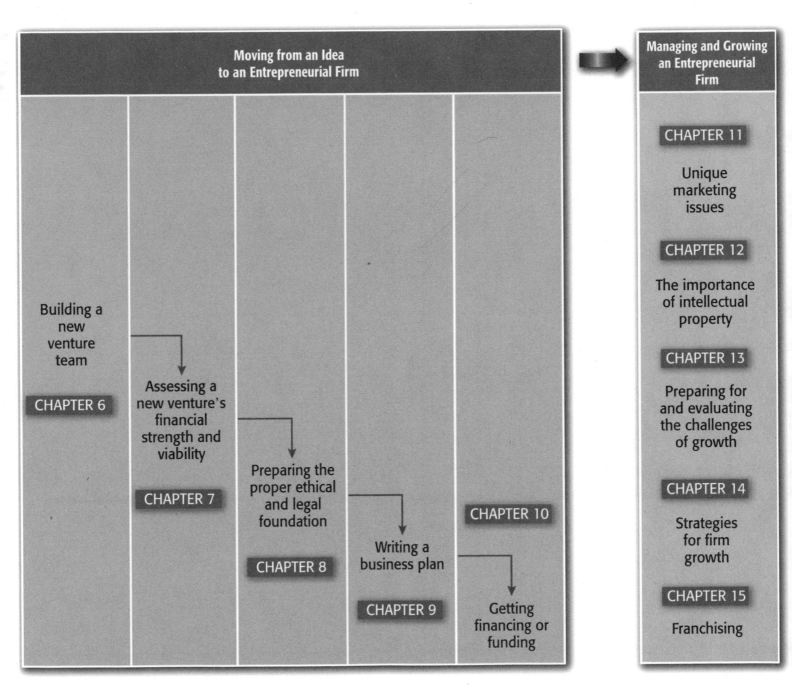

Moving from an Idea to an Entrepreneurial Firm					Managing and Growing an Entrepreneurial Firm
Building a new venture team **CHAPTER 6**	Assessing a new venture's financial strength and viability **CHAPTER 7**	Preparing the proper ethical and legal foundation **CHAPTER 8**	Writing a business plan **CHAPTER 9**	**CHAPTER 10** Getting financing or funding	**CHAPTER 11** Unique marketing issues **CHAPTER 12** The importance of intellectual property **CHAPTER 13** Preparing for and evaluating the challenges of growth **CHAPTER 14** Strategies for firm growth **CHAPTER 15** Franchising

Where a great idea meets a great process

entrepreneurship

successfully launching new ventures

Bruce R. Barringer
University of Central Florida

R. Duane Ireland
Texas A&M University

PEARSON

Prentice
Hall

Upper Saddle River, New Jersey 07458

Library of Congress Cataloging-in-Publication Data

Barringer, Bruce R.
    Entrepreneurship : successfully launching new ventures / Bruce R. Barringer, R. Duane Ireland.
        p. cm.
    Includes bibliographical references and index.
    ISBN 0-13-061855-1
        1. Entrepreneurship. 2. New business enterprises. I. Ireland, R. Duane. II. Title.

HB615.B374 2006
658.1′1—dc22

2004058696

Senior Acquisitions Editor: Jennifer Simon
VP/Editorial Director: Jeff Shelstad
Assistant Editor: Melissa Yu
Developmental Editor: Amy Whitaker
Senior Media Project Manager: Nancy Welcher
Marketing Manager: Anke Braun
Marketing Assistant: Patrick Danzuso
Senior Managing Editor (Production): Judy Leale
Production Editor: Mary Ellen Morrell
Permissions Coordinator: Charles Morris
Associate Director, Manufacturing: Vincent Scelta
Production Manager: Arnold Vila
Manufacturing Buyer: Diane Peirano
Design Director: Maria Lange
Designer: Michael Fruhbeis
Interior Design: Michael Fruhbeis
Cover Illustration/Photo: © Andre Judd/Masterfile
Illustrator (Interior): GGS Book Services, Atlantic Highlands
Photo Researcher: Rachel Lucas
Manager, Print Production: Christy Mahon
Composition/Full-Service Project Management: GGS Book Services, Atlantic Highlands
Printer/Binder: Courier/Kendallville

Credits and acknowledgments borrowed from other sources and reproduced, with permission, in this textbook appear on appropriate page within text. Photo credits appear on page 481.

Pearson Education LTD.
Pearson Education Singapore, Pte. Ltd
Pearson Education, Canada, Ltd
Pearson Education–Japan

Pearson Education Australia PTY, Limited
Pearson Education North Asia Ltd
Pearson Educación de Mexico, S.A. de C.V.
Pearson Education Malaysia, Pte. Ltd

10 9 8 7 6 5 4 3 2
ISBN 0-13-061855-1

To my wife, Jan, and our kids, John, Jennifer, and Emily.
Thanks for your encouragement and for your
enthusiastic support for this project.

— Bruce

To Mary Ann,
Your eyes continue to shine like a midnight sun,
lighting the path we're taking together. I love you.

— Duane

BRIEF CONTENTS

PREFACE   xvi
ABOUT THE AUTHORS   xxiii

part one   DECISION TO BECOME AN ENTREPRENEUR   2

1   INTRODUCTION TO ENTREPRENEURSHIP   2

part two   DEVELOPING SUCCESSFUL BUSINESS IDEAS   26

2   RECOGNIZING OPPORTUNITIES AND GENERATING IDEAS   26

3   FEASIBILITY ANALYSIS   50

4   INDUSTRY AND COMPETITOR ANALYSIS   74

5   DEVELOPING AN EFFECTIVE BUSINESS MODEL   98

part three   MOVING FROM AN IDEA TO AN ENTREPRENEURIAL FIRM   124

6   BUILDING A NEW VENTURE TEAM   124

7   ASSESSING A NEW VENTURE'S FINANCIAL STRENGTH AND VIABILITY   146

8   PREPARING THE PROPER ETHICAL AND LEGAL FOUNDATION   174

9   WRITING A BUSINESS PLAN   202

10   GETTING FINANCING OR FUNDING   228

part four   MANAGING AND GROWING AN ENTREPRENEURIAL FIRM   252

11   UNIQUE MARKETING ISSUES   252

12   THE IMPORTANCE OF INTELLECTUAL PROPERTY   276

13   PREPARING FOR AND EVALUATING THE CHALLENGES OF GROWTH   306

14   STRATEGIES FOR FIRM GROWTH   328

15   FRANCHISING   354

CASE APPENDIX   385

NOTES   441

GLOSSARY   459

NAME INDEX   468

SUBJECT INDEX   472

COMPANY INDEX   477

PHOTO CREDITS   481

CONTENTS

PREFACE   xv
ABOUT THE AUTHORS   xxii

part one   DECISION TO BECOME AN ENTREPRENEUR   2

chapter 1   INTRODUCTION TO ENTREPRENEURSHIP   2

Opening Profile—eBay   3
Introduction to Entrepreneurship   4
   What Is Entrepreneurship?   5
   Why Become an Entrepreneur?   6
   Characteristics of Successful Entrepreneurs   7
   Common Myths About Entrepreneurs   10
   ▬ *What Went Wrong?* ▬   11
   Types of Start-Up Firms   13
Entrepreneurship's Importance   14
   Economic Impact of Entrepreneurial Firms   14
   ▬ *Savvy Entrepreneurial Firm* ▬   15
   Entrepreneurial Firms' Impact on Society   16
   Entrepreneurial Firms' Impact on Larger Firms   16
   ▬ *Partnering for Success* ▬   17
The Entrepreneurial Process   17
   Decision to Become an Entrepreneur (Chapter 1)   18
   Developing Successful Business Ideas (Chapters 2–5)   18
   *Moving from an Idea to an Entrepreneurial Firm
   (Chapters 6–10)   19*
   *Managing and Growing an Entrepreneurial Firm
   (Chapters 11–15)   20*

   CHAPTER SUMMARY   20
   KEY TERMS   21
   REVIEW QUESTIONS   21
   APPLICATION QUESTIONS   21
   YOU BE THE VC   22
   CASE 1.1   23
   CASE 1.2   24

**part two   DEVELOPING SUCCESSFUL
BUSINESS IDEAS   26**

**chapter 2   RECOGNIZING OPPORTUNITIES
AND GENERATING IDEAS   26**

Opening Profile—BuyAndHold.com   27
Identifying and Recognizing Opportunities   28
   ▬ *What Went Wrong?* ▬   29
   Observing Trends   30

■ *Savvy Entrepreneurial Firm* ■   30
Solving a Problem   33
Personal Characteristics of the Entrepreneur   35
■ *Partnering for Success* ■   39

Techniques for Generating Ideas   39
Brainstorming   39
Focus Groups   41
Surveys   41
Other Techniques   42

Encouraging and Protecting New Ideas   42
Establishing a Focal Point for Ideas   42
Encouraging Creativity at the Firm Level   42
Protecting Ideas from Being Lost or Stolen   43

CHAPTER SUMMARY   44
KEY TERMS   45
REVIEW QUESTIONS   45
APPLICATION QUESTIONS   45
YOU BE THE VC   46
CASE **2.1**   47
CASE **2.2**   48

chapter 3   **FEASIBILITY ANALYSIS**   **50**

Opening Profile—Intuit   51

Feasibility Analysis   52
■ *What Went Wrong?* ■   53
Product/Service Feasibility Analysis   57
■ *Partnering for Success* ■   60
Industry/Market Feasibility Analysis   61
Organizational Feasibility Analysis   64
Financial Feasibility Analysis   65
■ *Savvy Entrepreneurial Firm* ■   66

CHAPTER SUMMARY   68
KEY TERMS   68
REVIEW QUESTIONS   68
APPLICATION QUESTIONS   69
YOU BE THE VC   70
CASE **3.1**   70
CASE **3.2**   71

chapter 4   **INDUSTRY AND COMPETITOR ANALYSIS**   **74**

Opening Profile—JetBlue   75

Industry Analysis   77

The Importance of Industry—Versus Firm-Specific Factors   77
The Five Competitive Forces That Determine Industry Profitability   78
The Value of the Five Forces Model   83
■ *Savvy Entrepreneurial Firm* ■   83
Industry Types and the Opportunities They Offer   85
■ *What Went Wrong?* ■   88

Competitor Analysis 89

    Identifying Competitors 89

    Sources of Competitive Intelligence 90

    — *Partnering for Success* — 90

    Completing a Competitive Analysis Grid 91

CHAPTER SUMMARY 92

KEY TERMS 93

REVIEW QUESTIONS 93

APPLICATION QUESTIONS 93

YOU BE THE VC 94

CASE 4.1 95

CASE 4.2 96

chapter 5   **DEVELOPING AN EFFECTIVE BUSINESS MODEL**   **98**

Opening Profile—Dell Inc. 99

Business Models 102

    The Importance of a Business Model 102

    How Business Models Emerge 104

    Potential Fatal Flaws of Business Models 106

    — *What Went Wrong?* — 107

Components of an Effective Business Model 107

    Core Strategy 108

    Strategic Resources 111

    Partnership Network 112

    — *Partnering for Success* — 113

    Customer Interface 114

    — *Savvy Entrepreneurial Firm* — 116

CHAPTER SUMMARY 117

KEY TERMS 118

REVIEW QUESTIONS 118

APPLICATION QUESTIONS 118

YOU BE THE VC 119

CASE 5.1 120

CASE 5.2 121

part three **MOVING FROM AN IDEA TO AN ENTREPRENEURIAL FIRM**   **124**

chapter 6   **BUILDING A NEW VENTURE TEAM**   **124**

Opening Profile—Waveset Technologies 125

Creating a New Venture Team 127

    — *Partnering for Success* — 127

    The Founder or Founders 128

    — *What Went Wrong?* — 130

    Recruiting and Selecting Key Employees 131

    The Roles of the Board of Directors 132

Rounding Out the Team: The Role of Professional
Advisers 134

  Board of Advisers 134

  ▬ *Savvy Entrepreneurial Firm* ▬ 137

  Lenders and Investors 138

  Other Professionals 139

CHAPTER SUMMARY 140
KEY TERMS 141
REVIEW QUESTIONS 141
APPLICATION QUESTIONS 141
YOU BE THE VC 142
CASE 6.1 143
CASE 6.2 144

chapter 7   **ASSESSING A NEW VENTURE'S FINANCIAL
               STRENGTH AND VIABILITY   146**

Opening Profile—LeapFrog, Inc. 147

Introduction to Financial Management 148

  Financial Objectives of a Firm 149

  The Process of Financial Management 150

  ▬ *Partnering for Success* ▬ 151

Financial Statements and Forecasts 152

  Historical Financial Statements 153

  ▬ *Savvy Entrepreneurial Firm* ▬ 156

  Forecasts 160

  ▬ *What Went Wrong?* ▬ 164

Pro Forma Financial Statements 164

  Pro Forma Income Statement 165

  Pro Forma Balance Sheet 165

  Pro Forma Statement of Cash Flows 166

  Ratio Analysis 168

CHAPTER SUMMARY 168
KEY TERMS 169
REVIEW QUESTIONS 169
APPLICATION QUESTIONS 170
YOU BE THE VC 171
CASE 7.1 171
CASE 7.2 172

chapter 8   **PREPARING THE PROPER ETHICAL AND
               LEGAL FOUNDATION   174**

Opening Profile—Getting Off to a Good Start 175

Initial Ethical and Legal Issues Facing a New Firm 176

  Ethically Departing from an Employer 177

  Choosing an Attorney for the New Firm 178

  Drafting a Founders' Agreement 180

  Avoiding Legal Disputes 181

  ▬ *What Went Wrong?* ▬ 181

Choosing a Form of Business Organization 184
  Sole Proprietorship 184
  Partnerships 186
  ▬ *Partnering for Success* ▬ 186
  Corporations 187
  ▬ *Savvy Entrepreneurial Firm* ▬ 189
  Limited Liability Company 190

The Legal Environment of the Internet 192
  The World Wide Web 192
  Trademarks and Domain Names 193
  Electronic Contracts and Digital Signatures 194
  ▬ *Savvy Entrepreneurial Firm* ▬ 195

CHAPTER SUMMARY 195
KEY TERMS 196
REVIEW QUESTIONS 196
APPLICATION QUESTIONS 197
YOU BE THE VC 198
CASE **8.1** 199
CASE **8.2** 200

chapter 9   WRITING A BUSINESS PLAN   **202**
  Opening Profile—Electronic Arts 203
  The Business Plan 205
    Why a Business Plan Is Important 205
    Who Reads the Business Plan—and What Are
    They Looking For? 206
    ▬ *What Went Wrong?* ▬ 208
    Guidelines for Writing a Business Plan 209
  Outline of the Business Plan 211
    Exploring Each Section of the Plan 213
    ▬ *Savvy Entrepreneurial Firm* ▬ 217
    ▬ *Partnering for Success* ▬ 219
  Presenting the Business Plan to Investors 221
    The Oral Presentation of a Business Plan 221
    Questions and Feedback to Expect from Investors 222

CHAPTER SUMMARY 222
KEY TERMS 223
REVIEW QUESTIONS 223
APPLICATION QUESTIONS 224
YOU BE THE VC 225
CASE **9.1** 225
CASE **9.2** 226

chapter 10   GETTING FINANCING OR FUNDING   **228**
  Opening Profile—Cisco Systems 229
  The Importance of Getting Financing or Funding 231
    Why Most Firms Need Funding 231
    Sources of Personal Financing 232
    Preparing to Raise Debt or Equity Financing 233
    ▬ *Savvy Entrepreneurial Firm* ▬ 234

Sources of Equity Funding 237

    Business Angels 237

    ▬ *Partnering for Success* ▬ 238

    Venture Capital 239

    Initial Public Offering 241

    ▬ *What Went Wrong?* ▬ 242

Sources of Debt Financing 243

    Commercial Banks 243

    SBA Guaranteed Loans 244

Creative Sources of Financing and Funding 244

    Leasing 244

    Government Grants 245

    Strategic Partners 246

CHAPTER SUMMARY 246
KEY TERMS 247
REVIEW QUESTIONS 247
APPLICATION QUESTIONS 247
YOU BE THE VC 248
CASE **10.1** 249
CASE **10.2** 250

part four MANAGING AND GROWING
AN ENTREPRENEURIAL FIRM **252**

chapter 11 UNIQUE MARKETING ISSUES **252**

Opening Profile—Curves 253

Selecting a Market and Establishing a Position 254

    Segmenting the Market 255

    Selecting a Target Market 256

    ▬ *What Went Wrong?* ▬ 257

    Establishing a Unique Position 258

Key Marketing Issues for New Ventures 258

    ▬ *Savvy Entrepreneurial Firm* ▬ 259

    Selling Benefits Rather Than Features 260

    Establishing a Brand 260

    ▬ *Partnering for Success* ▬ 263

The Four Ps of Marketing for New Ventures 263

    Product 264

    Price 265

    Promotion 266

    Place (or Distribution) 269

CHAPTER SUMMARY **270**
KEY TERMS 271
REVIEW QUESTIONS 271
APPLICATION QUESTIONS 272
YOU BE THE VC 273
CASE **11.1** 273
CASE **11.2** 274

chapter 12   THE IMPORTANCE OF INTELLECTUAL
              PROPERTY   276

Opening Profile—Switchboard, Inc. 277

The Importance of Intellectual Property 278

  Determining What Intellectual Property to Legally Protect 279

  ▬ Savvy Entrepreneurial Firm ▬ 281

  The Four Key Forms of Intellectual Property 282

Patents 282

  The Three Types of Patents 283
  Who Can Apply for a Patent? 284
  The Process of Obtaining a Patent 284

Trademarks 286

  The Four Types of Trademarks 287
  What Is Protected Under Trademark Law? 288
  Exclusions from Trademark Protection 288
  The Process of Obtaining a Trademark 289

Copyrights 290

  What Is Protected by a Copyright? 290
  Exclusions from Copyright Protection 291
  How to Obtain a Copyright 291
  Copyright Infringement 292
  Copyrights and the Internet 293

Trade Secrets 293

  ▬ What Went Wrong? ▬ 294
  What Qualifies for Trade Secret Protection? 295
  Trade Secret Disputes 295
  Trade Secret Protection Methods 296
  ▬ Partnering for Success ▬ 297

Conducting an Intellectual Property Audit 298

  Why Conduct an Intellectual Property Audit? 298
  The Process of Conducting an Intellectual
  Property Audit 299

CHAPTER SUMMARY 299
KEY TERMS 300
REVIEW QUESTIONS 300
APPLICATION QUESTIONS 301
YOU BE THE VC 302
CASE 12.1 302
CASE 12.2 304

chapter 13   PREPARING FOR AND EVALUATING
              THE CHALLENGES OF GROWTH   306

Opening Profile—Starbucks 307

Preparing for Growth 310

  Reasons for Firm Growth 311

  ▬ Savvy Entrepreneurial Firm ▬ 313

  Benchmarking Against Successful Growth Firms 314

Challenges of Growth 314
    Managerial Capacity 315
    Typical Challenges of Growing a Firm 316
    *Developing and Maintaining Professional
    Business Practices 317*
        ■ *What Went Wrong?* ■ *318*
    Myths About Growth 319
Attributes of Successful Growth Firms 320
    Growth-Related Firm Attributes 320
        ■ *Partnering for Success* ■ *322*

CHAPTER SUMMARY 322
KEY TERMS 323
REVIEW QUESTIONS 323
APPLICATION QUESTIONS 324
YOU BE THE VC 325
CASE 13.1 325
CASE 13.2 326

chapter 14   **STRATEGIES FOR FIRM GROWTH**   **328**
Opening Profile—Ask Jeeves 329
Internal Growth Strategies 330
    New Product Development 331
    Other Product-Related Strategies 333
        ■ *What Went Wrong?* ■ *334*
    International Expansion 335
        ■ *Savvy Entrepreneurial Firm* ■ *336*
External Growth Strategies 339
    Mergers and Acquisitions 340
    Licensing 343
    Strategic Alliances and Joint Ventures 345
        ■ *Partnering for Success* ■ *346*

CHAPTER SUMMARY 348
KEY TERMS 348
REVIEW QUESTIONS 349
APPLICATION QUESTIONS 349
YOU BE THE VC 350
CASE 14.1 351
CASE 14.2 352

chapter 15   **FRANCHISING**   **354**
Opening Profile—Cartridge World 355
What Is Franchising, and How Does It Work? 357
    What Is Franchising? 357
    How Does Franchising Work? 358
        ■ *Savvy Entrepreneurial Firm* ■ *359*
Establishing a Franchise System 360
    When to Franchise 360
    Steps to Franchising a Business 361
    Selecting and Developing Effective Franchisees 362

Advantages and Disadvantages of Establishing a Franchise System 362

— *Partnering for Success* — 365

Buying a Franchise 366

Is Franchising Right for You? 366

The Cost of a Franchise 366

Finding a Franchise 367

Advantages and Disadvantages of Buying a Franchise 368

Steps in Purchasing a Franchise 370

Watch Out! Common Misconceptions About Franchising 371

Legal Aspects of the Franchise Relationship 372

Federal Rules and Regulations 372

State Rules and Regulations 374

More About Franchising 374

Franchise Associations 375

Franchise Ethics 375

International Franchising 376

— *What Went Wrong?* — 377

The Future of Franchising 378

CHAPTER SUMMARY 378

KEY TERMS 379

REVIEW QUESTIONS 379

APPLICATION QUESTIONS 380

YOU BE THE VC 381

CASE 15.1 381

CASE 15.2 382

CASE APPENDIX 385

Case 1 *Hotmail: Delivering E-Mail to the World* 385

Case 2 *College Coach* 393

Case 3 *Jack Sprat's Restaurant* 400

Case 4 *AllAdvantage.com: An Internet Infomediary* 409

Case 5 *Jon Hirschtick's New Venture* 422

Case 6 *Meg Whitman—The Driving Force Behind eBay* 430

NOTES 441

GLOSSARY 459

NAME INDEX 468

SUBJECT INDEX 472

COMPANY INDEX 477

PHOTO CREDITS 481

Introduction

We are excited about this book and what it has to offer you. The main reason for this is that there has never been a more exciting time to study entrepreneurship. Across the world, young entrepreneurial firms are creating new products and services that make our lives easier, enhance our productivity at work, improve our health, and entertain us in new ways. Some of the most passionate and inspiring people you'll ever meet are entrepreneurs. This is why successful firms have started, literally in garages. It is typically the passion that an entrepreneur has about his or her business idea, rather than fancy offices or other material things, that is the number one predictor of a new venture's success. Conversely, a lack of passion often leads to entrepreneurial failure.

The purpose of this book is to provide you, our readers and students of entrepreneurship, a thorough introduction to the entrepreneurial process. Evidence suggests that it is important for entrepreneurs to thoroughly understand the entrepreneurial process. The facts that in the United States alone roughly 20% of new firms fail in the first year while another 20% fail in the second year of their existence is the type of evidence we have in mind. These failure rates show that while many people are motivated to start new firms, motivation alone is not enough; it must be coupled with good information, a solid business idea, an effective business plan and sound execution to maximize chances for success. In this book, we discuss many examples of entrepreneurial firms and the factors separating successful firms from unsuccessful ones.

This book provides a thoughtful, practical guide to the process of successfully launching and growing an entrepreneurial firm. To do this, the book provides you with a thorough analysis of the entrepreneurial process. We model this process for you in the first chapter and then use that model to frame the book's remaining parts. Because of its importance, we place a special emphasis on the beginnings of the entrepreneurial process—particularly opportunity recognition and feasibility analysis. We do this because history shows that many entrepreneurial firms struggle or fail not because the business owners weren't committed or didn't work hard, but because the idea they were pushing to bring to the marketplace wasn't the foundation for a vibrant, successful business.

How Is This Book Organized?

To explain the entrepreneurial process and the way this process typically unfolds, we chose to divide this book into four parts and 15 chapters. The four parts following the entrepreneurial process model are:

Part 1: Decision to Become an Entrepreneur

Part 2: Developing Successful Business Ideas

Part 3: Moving From an Idea to an Entrepreneurial Firm

Part 4: Managing and Growing an Entrepreneurial Firm

We believe that this sequence will make your journey to understand the entrepreneurial process both enjoyable and productive. This model is shown below. The step in the model that corresponds to the chapter being introduced is highlighted to help you, our readers, form a picture of where each chapter fits in the entrepreneurial process.

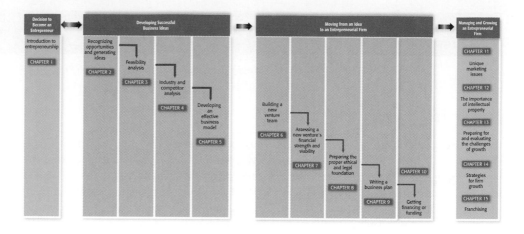

What Beneficial Features Does the Book Have?

To provide as thorough an introduction to the entrepreneurial process as possible, many features, as follows, are included in each chapter of this book.

Feature Included in Each Chapter	Benefit
Learning objectives	Help focus the reader's attention on the major topics in the chapter
Chapter opening case	Introduces the topic of the chapter
Boldfaced key terms	Draws the reader's attention to key concepts
Examples and anecdotes	Livens up the text and provides examples of both successful and unsuccessful approaches to confronting the challenges discussed in each chapter
End of chapter summary	Integrates the key topics and concepts included in each chapter
20 review questions	Allows students to test their recall of chapter material
10 application questions	Allows students to apply what they learned from the chapter material
Four application questions following each case	Allows students to apply the concepts learned in the chapter to help solve the challenges encountered by a real-life entrepreneurial firm

What Are Some Other Unique Features of This Book?

While looking through your book, we think you'll find several unique features, as presented next that will work to your benefit as a student of entrepreneurship and the entrepreneurial process.

Unique Feature of the Book	Explanation
Focus on opportunity recognition and feasibility analysis	The book begins with strong chapters on opportunity recognition and feasibility analysis. This is important, because opportunity recognition and feasibility analysis are key activities that must be completed early in the investigation of a new business idea.

What Went Wrong? boxed feature	Each chapter contains a boxed feature titled "What Went Wrong?" We use these features to explain the missteps of seemingly promising entrepreneurial firms. The purpose of these features, as you have no doubt already guessed, is to highlight the reality that sometimes things go wrong if the fundamental concepts in the chapters aren't adhered to.
Partnering for Success boxed feature	Each chapter contains a boxed feature titled "Partnering for Success." The ability to partner effectively with other firms is becoming an increasingly important attribute for successful entrepreneurial firms.
Savvy Entrepreneurial Firm boxed feature	Each chapter contains a boxed feature titled "Savvy Entrepreneurial Firm." These features illustrate the types of business practices that help entrepreneurial firms succeed. As such, these are practices you should strongly consider putting into play when you are using the entrepreneurial process.
You Be the VC end-of-chapter feature	A feature titled "You Be the VC" is provided at the end of each chapter. These features present a "pitch" for funding from an emerging entrepreneurial firm. The feature is designed to stimulate classroom discussion by sparking debate on whether a particular venture should or shouldn't receive funding. All of the firms featured are real-life entrepreneurial startups. Thus, you'll be talking about real—not hypothetical or fictitious—entrepreneurial ventures.
A total of 30 original end-of-chapter cases	Two medium-length cases are featured at the end of each chapter. The cases are designed to stimulate classroom discussion and illustrate the issues discussed in the chapter.
A total of six comprehensive cases	Six comprehensive cases, authored by leading entrepreneurship writers and scholars, are included at the end of the book. Each case touches on topics from several chapters. These cases are suitable for individual assignments, group assignments, or exams. A notation is made at the end of each chapter alerting you and your professor to the comprehensive cases that complement that particular chapter.

Instructor Support Material

A full package of support material for instructors is provided with the book to enhance the overall learning experience. *All of the instructor support material is prepared by the authors of the book.*

OneKey Online Courses

OneKey offers the best teaching and learning online resources all in one place. OneKey is all instructors need to plan and administer their course. OneKey is all students need for anytime, anywhere access to online course material. Conveniently organized by textbook chapter, these compiled resources help save time and help students reinforce and apply what they have learned. OneKey for convenience, simplicity, and success. *OneKey is available in three course management platforms: Blackboard, CourseCompass and WebCT.*

For the student:

- **Learning Modules**, which include section reviews, learning activities and pre- and post-tests
- **Student PowerPoints**
- **Research Navigator**–four exclusive databases of reliable source content to help students understand the research process and complete assignments
- **Feasibility Analysis Software**, which provides a step-by-step guide to completing a feasibility analysis for a new business idea

Instructor's Resource Center available online, in OneKey or on CD-ROM

The Instructor's Resource Center, available on CD, at www.prenhall.com, or in your OneKey online course, provides presentation and other classroom resources. Instructors can collect the materials, edit them to create powerful class lectures, and upload them to an online course management system. Using the Instructor's Resource Center on CD-ROM, instructors can easily create custom presentations. Desired files can be exported to the instructor's hard drive for use in classroom presentations and online courses.

With the Instructor's Resource Center, you will find the following faculty resources:

PowerPoint Slides (*Available on CD-ROM.*)

A full set of PowerPoint slides is provided. The slides are divided by chapter, and are suitable for leading class lectures and discussion. The slides contain the relevant material from each chapter along with reproductions of key tables and figures.

Instructor's Manual (*Print version also available.*)

An instructor's manual, which includes both traditional and new value-added material, includes the following:

- Chapter outlines
- Sample answers for each of the end-of chapter review questions, application questions, and questions following the cases
- A full analysis of the "You Be the VC" feature that appears at the end of each chapter
- An additional 10 "You Be the VC" features (that do not appear in the textbook) including full analysis
- Case notes for the six comprehensive cases included in the book
- A short summary of each video segment that is included in the video package that accompanies the book

Test Item File (*Word file*)

Test Gen (Test Generating) Software

The printed test bank contains approximately 75 questions per chapter including multiple-choice, true/false, and short-answer. Short-answer questions are questions that can be answered in one-to-five sentences. (Print version also available.)

Video

A collection of video segments is provided to supplement course material. There are also videos to supplement the "College Coach," "Jack Sprat's Restaurant," and "Jon Hirschtick's New Venture" cases which appear at the end of the book. A short summary of each video segment is provided in the Instructor's Manual.

Student and Instructor Web Site

The book's Web site, available at **www.prehall.com/barringer**, features:

- Chapter quizzes. These quizzes will be changed on an annual basis
- Web destinations. Links to additional sites of interest to entrepreneurship students and instructors
- Student PowerPoints

ACKNOWLEDGMENTS

There are three groups of people that we want to thank for helping make this book a reality.

The first group includes the professionals at Prentice Hall. These people have worked with us conscientiously and have fully supported our efforts to create a book that will work for both those studying and teaching the entrepreneurial process. From Prentice Hall, we want to extend our sincere appreciation to our editors Jennifer Simon, Jennifer Glennon, and David Parker, our marketing managers Shannon Moore and Eric Frank, and our Assistant Editor Melissa Yu. We would also like to thank Jeff Shelstad, Editorial Director, for his overall leadership of the project. Each individual provided us invaluable guidance and support and we are grateful for their contribution.

We would also like to thank our colleagues who participated in reviewing individual chapters of the book while they were being written. We gained keen insight from these reviews and incorporated many of the suggestions of our reviews into the final version of the book:

Thank you to these professors who participated in early manuscript reviews:

David C. Adams, *Manhattanville College*

Stephen Braun, *Concordia University*

Debbi Brock, *Berea College*

Jason Duan, *Midwestern State University*

Brooke Envick, *St. Mary's University*

Cathy Folker, *University of St. Thomas*

Eugene Fregetto, *University of Illinois at Chicago*

Connie Marie Gaglio, *San Francisco State University*

Michael Goldsby, *Ball State University*

Mihalis Halkides, *Bethune Cookman College*

John Lofberg, *South Dakota School of Mines and Technology*

Morgan Miles, *Georgia Southern University*

Nancy Upton, *Baylor University*

Monica Zimmerman-Treichel, *Temple University*

We thank this large group of professors whose thoughts about entrepreneurial education helped to shape this first edition:

Robert Tosterud, *University of South Dakota*

Andrea Hershatter, *Emory University*

Andrew Corbett, *Rensselaer Polytechnic Institute*

Chris McKinney, *Vanderbilt University*

Ashley Harmon, *Southeastern Technical College*

Lee Grubb, *East Carolina University*

Simone Cummings, *Washington University School of Medicine*

Bruce Lynskey, *Vanderbilt University*

Diana Wong, *Eastern Michigan University*

Allon Lefever, *Eastern Mennonite University*

Dee Cole, *Middle Tennessee State University*

Alec Johnson, *University of St. Thomas*

Brad Handy, *Springfield Technical Community College*

John Richards, *Brigham Young University*

Christo Robberts, *University of Minnesota-Twin Cities*

Alan Hauff, *University of Missouri-St. Louis*

Rob Mitchell, *Indiana University*

Doug WIlson, *University of Oregon*

Dana Fladhammer, *Phoenix College*

Doug WIlson, *University of Oregon*

John Pfaff, *University of the Pacific*

Richard Barker, *Upper Iowa University*

Jeffrey Alves, *Wilkes University*

Art Camburn, *Buena Vista University*

Gerald Segal, *Florida Gulf Coast University*

Jeffrey Martin, *University of Texas-Austin*

Roy Cook, *Fort Lewis College*

Joseph Stasio, *Merrimack College*

Gerry Scheffelmaier, *Middle Tennessee State University*

Barry Gilmore, *University of Memphis*

Cynthia Sheridan, *St. Edward's University*

Richard Hilliard, *Nichols College*

James Chrisman, *Mississippi State University*

Charles Fishel, *San Jose State University*

Gaylen Chandler, *Utah State University*

Jeffrey Alstete, *Iona College*

James Burke, *Loyola University-Chicago*

George Vozikis, *University of Tulsa*

Connie Nichols, *Odessa College*

Douglas Dayhoff, *Indiana University*

Dale Eesley, *University of Toledo*

Deborah Streeter, *Cornell University*

John Butler, *University of Texas-Austin*

Haesun Park, *Louisiana State University*

Gary Levanti, *Polytechnic University-LI Campus*

Alan Eisner, *Pace University*

John Callister, *Cornell University*

Frank Hoy, *University of Texas at El Paso*

Charlie Nagelschmidt, *Champlain College*

Cheryl Gracie, *Washtenaw Community College*

Caroline Glackin, *Delaware State University*

Frederick Greene, *Manhattan College*

Dara Szyliowicz, *Texas Tech University*

Anita Leffel, *University of Texas-San Antonio*

James M. Jones, *Univ. Incarnate Word, ERAU, Delmar College*

Charlene Williams, *Brewton Parker College*

Greg McCann, *Stetson University*

David Wilemon, *Syracuse University*

Henry Fernandez, *North Carolina Central University*

Jane Jones, *Mountain Empire Community College*

James Lang, *Virginia Tech University*

James J. Alling Sr., *Augusta Technical College*

Joseph Picken, *University of Texas at Dallas*

Jay Azriel, *Illinois State University*

Gary Nothnagle, *Nazareth College*

Delena Clark, *Plattsburgh State University*

Gordon Haym, *Lyndon State College*

Carol Carter, *Louisiana State University*

Sol Ahiarah, *SUNY—Buffalo State College*

David C. Adams, *Manhattanville College*

Joe Aniello, *Francis Marion University.*

Jenell Bramlage, *University of Northwestern Ohio*

Susan Jensen, *University of Nebraska-Kearney*

Brenda Flannery, *Minnesota State University*

Craig Tunwall, *Empire State College*

Dennis Hoagland, *LDS Business College*

Edward O'Brien, *Scottsdale Community College*

Jane Byrd, *University of Mobile*

Benyamin Lichtenstein, *Syracuse University*

Jo Hinton, *Copiah Lincoln Community College*

Bryant Mitchell, *University of Maryland-Eastern Shore*

Janice Rustia, *University of Nebraska Medical Center*

Suzanne D'Agnes, *Queensborough Community College*

Elizabeth McCrea, *Pennsylvania State-Great Valley*

Brian McKenzie, *California State University-Hayward*

Steve Harper, *University of North Carolina at Wilmington*

Barry Van Hook, *Arizona State University*

Barb Brown, *Southwestern Community College*

Dr. Jim Bell, *Texas State University*

Mary Avery, *Ripon College*

William Naumes, *University of New Hampshire*

Frank Demmler, *Carnegie Mellon University*

James Saya, *The College of Santa Fe*

Donald Shifter, *Fontbonne University*

William Scheela, *Bemidji State University*

Jeffrey Jackson, *Manhattanville College*

Grant Jacobsen, *Northern Virginia Community College-Woodbridge*

Frederic Aiello, *University of Southern Maine*

C.L.J. Spencer, *Kapi'olani Community College*

David Desplaces, *University of Hartford/Barney*

Janice Mabry, *Mississippi Gulf Coast Community College*

Edward Kuljian, *Saint Joseph's University*

George Roorbach, *Lyndon State College*

Carnella Hardin, *Glendale College*

Susan Everett, *Clark State Community College*

James Klingler, *Villanova University*

Lowell Busenitz, *University of Oklahoma*

Vern Disney, *University of South Carolina-Sumter*

Angela Mitchell, *Wilmington College*

John Friar, *Northeastern University*

Emmeline de Pillis, *University of Hawaii-Hilo*

Barbara Fuller, *Winthrop University*

Robert J. Berger, *SUNY Potsdam*

Joy Jones, *Ohio Valley College*

Elizabeth Kisenwether, *Penn State University*

Carol Reeves, *University of Arkansas*

Clint B. Tankersley, *Syracuse University*

Dale Meyer, *University of Colorado*

Steven C. Michael, *University of Illinois Urbana-Champaign*

Tom Kaplan, *Fairleigh Dickinson University-Madison*

Finally, we owe a debt of gratitude to our colleagues who have influenced our thinking and work over many years. Some have influenced us through their writing and teaching while others have guided us through their professional and ethical actions. We extend a heartfelt "thank you" to each person. We also want to express our appreciation to our home institutions (University of Central Florida and Texas A&M University) for creating environments in which ideas are encouraged and supported.

We wish you all the best in your study of the entrepreneurial process. And, of course, we hope that each of you will be successful entrepreneurs as you pursue the ideas you'll develop at different points in your careers.

Bruce R. Barringer

Bruce R. Barringer is an Associate Professor in the Department of Management at the University of Central Florida. He obtained his PhD from the University of Missouri and his MBA from Iowa State University. His research interests include feasibility analysis, firm growth, corporate entrepreneurship, and the impact of interorganizational relationships on business organizations. He also works closely with the University of Central Florida technology incubator.

He serves on the editorial review board of *Entrepreneurship Theory and Practice* and the *Journal of Small Business Management*. His work has been published in *Strategic Management Journal, Journal of Management, Journal of Business Venturing, Journal of Small Business Management, Journal of Developmental Entrepreneurship*, and *Quality Management Journal*.

His outside interests include running, swimming and reading.

R. Duane Ireland

R. Duane Ireland holds the Foreman R. and Ruby S. Bennett Chair in Business Administration in the Mays Business School, Texas A&M University. Previously, he has served on the faculties at University of Richmond, Baylor University, and Oklahoma State University. His research interests include strategic alliances, the effective management of organizational resources, corporate entrepreneurship, and strategic entrepreneurship.

He has served or is serving on the editorial review boards for *AMJ, AMR, AME, JOM, JBV, ETP, European Management Journal*, and *Journal of Business Strategy*. He has completed terms as an associate editor for *AME* and as a consulting editor for *ETP* and has served as a guest co-editor for special issues of *AMR, AME, SMJ, Journal of Engineering and Technology Management*, and *JBV* (forthcoming). Currently, he is an Associate Editor for *Academy of Management Journal*. He has been a member of the executive committee for the BPS division and served as the division's newsletter editor. Currently, Duane is serving as a member of the Academy's board of governors (as a representative-at-large).

His work has been published in journals such as *Academy of Management Journal, Academy of Management Review, Academy of Management Executive, Strategic Management Journal, Administrative Science Quarterly, Journal of Management, Human Relations, British Journal of Management*, and *Entrepreneurship Theory and Practice*. He is a co-author of both scholarly books and textbooks, including a best-selling Strategic Management textbook.

His outside interests include running, reading, and music.

entrepreneurship

successfully launching new ventures

CHAPTER
one

introduction to
entrepreneurship

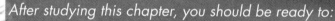

OBJECTIVES

After studying this chapter, you should be ready to:

1. Explain entrepreneurship and discuss its importance.

2. Describe corporate entrepreneurship and its use in established firms.

3. Discuss three main reasons that people become entrepreneurs.

4. Identify four main characteristics of successful entrepreneurs.

5. Explain the five common myths regarding entrepreneurship.

6. Explain how entrepreneurial firms differ from salary-substitute and lifestyle firms.

7. Discuss the economic impact of entrepreneurial firms.

8. Discuss the impact of entrepreneurial firms on society.

9. Identify ways in which large firms benefit from the presence of smaller entrepreneurial firms.

10. Explain the entrepreneurial process.

eBay: *the classic entrepreneurial story*

The founding of eBay, the Internet's largest auction site, offers a classic tale of an entrepreneurial firm's beginnings. Although eBay has achieved remarkable success, the story of how the company started is not extraordinary. It began with an entrepreneur who recognized an opportunity and, through passion, hard work, and a willingness to partner with others, built a successful entrepreneurial firm.[1]

Pierre Omidyar is a soft-spoken computer engineer. Born in France in 1967, he moved with his family to the United States as a young boy. Interested in computers from the time he was a child, Omidyar graduated from Tufts University with a computer science degree. After college, Omidyar worked for Claris and then left to cofound a firm called Ink Development, a developer of pen-based software. Ink eventually failed, but a computer system that Omidyar developed for Ink was salvaged. In turn, this system became the backbone of a new online retailer named eShop. Omidyar gained valuable experience helping eShop raise venture capital financing. Later, he left the company to take a position with General Magic. His experiences as a young entrepreneur, however, would prove invaluable to his ability to conceive, launch, and transform a new venture into a remarkably successful company.[2]

There are two versions of how eBay started. The romantic version is that over dinner one night, Omidyar's girlfriend (and now wife), a collector of Pez dispensers, asked him if there was any way he could set up a Web site for collectors like her. Pez dispensers are plastic tubes that dispense candy and are collector's items because they are made to look like different characters, such as movie stars and athletes. Although this is an appealing story, the truth is that Omidyar had been thinking about creating an online auction site for some time. The second and more accurate version of how eBay started is explained by Omidyar himself:

> The truth is, long before I clued in to [my wife's] Pezmania, I had been thinking about how to create an efficient marketplace—a level playing field, where everyone had access to the same information and could compete on the same terms as everyone else. As a software engineer, I worked for a couple of Silicon Valley companies, and I had even cofounded an early e-commerce site.
>
> This got me thinking that maybe the Internet was the place to create such an efficient market. Not just a site where big corporations sold stuff to consumers and bombarded them with ads, but rather one where people "traded" with *each other*. I thought, if you could bring enough people together and let them pay whatever they thought something was worth (in other words, have them bid in an auction format), real values could be realized and it could ultimately be a fairer system—a win-win for buyers and sellers.[3]

To get his idea rolling, Omidyar launched a Web site called AuctionWeb. The site was modest but offered a convenient auction format that allowed those wanting to buy and sell all kinds of items to meet one another. On Labor Day 1995, Omidyar announced his free service on the "What's New" Web page, a Yahoo directory of new Web sites. Before long, customers started showing up. Although Omidyar charged only a small fee to sellers, the venture was profitable from day one. Next, Omidyar took on a partner, Jeff Skoll, who had skills that Omidyar lacked. Unlike Omidyar, whose background was in computer science, Skoll had an MBA and substantial hands-on business experience.[4] The name "eBay" didn't come along until the fall of 1997. Omidyar liked the name "echo bay," but when he tried to register it, he found that the domain name *www.echobay.com* was already taken, so he shortened the name to eBay, and it seemed to fit.

In late 1997, eBay raised venture capital financing from the venture capitalists Omidyar met during the failure of his first firm. eBay never spent its venture capital funding, however. Instead, it asked its venture capitalists to help it round out its top management team, which led to the hiring of Meg Whitman, a seasoned executive. Whitman took the helm of eBay in March 1998. The company also developed a number of partnerships that fueled its growth. For example, eBay's Web-hosting function is provided by two companies invisible to the public, but they keep eBay's Web site up and running 24 hours a day, 7 days a week, in secure, state-of-the-art facilities.

Pierre Omidyar and his team have created a world-class entrepreneurial firm. The company now has 41 million active users, continues to grow, and is profitable.

Although their stories vary, all entrepreneurial firms start with one or more entrepreneurs, the recognition of an opportunity, and a plan for how to shape the opportunity into a viable business. The eBay example is particularly instructive because Pierre Omidyar managed this process very effectively and focused on start-up techniques that are emphasized throughout this book. He gained experience before he started eBay, launched it with minimal overhead, built a top-notch management team, won the trust of the investment community, and established partnerships with other firms to help the company grow. He also used information technology to its maximum potential. He took the basic process of a garage sale, put it in an auction format, and figured out a way to move it online.

In this chapter, we define entrepreneurship and discuss why people become entrepreneurs. We then look at successful entrepreneurs' characteristics, the common myths surrounding entrepreneurship, and the different types of start-up firms. Next, we examine entrepreneurship's importance, including the economic and social impact of new firms as well as the importance of entrepreneurial firms to larger businesses. To close the chapter, we introduce you to the entrepreneurial process. This process is the foundation we use to present the book's materials to you.

Introduction to Entrepreneurship

There is tremendous interest in entrepreneurship around the world. The Global Entrepreneurship Monitor (GEM), a joint research effort by Babson College and the London Business School, tracks entrepreneurship in 40 countries, including the United States. According to the GEM 2003 study, about 300 million, or 12.5 percent, of adults in the countries surveyed are involved in forming new businesses.[5]

The GEM report also identifies whether its respondents are starting new businesses to take advantage of attractive opportunities or out of necessity. In other words, it tracks whether people are becoming entrepreneurs because they have spotted an attractive opportunity or because they can find no better choice for work. Overall, about two-thirds of the individuals in the 40 countries surveyed reported they are starting a business to pursue an attractive opportunity. Unfortunately, in the United States, roughly 20 percent of new firms fail in the first year, while another 20 percent fail in the second year of their existence.[6] This statistic shows that while many people are motivated to start new firms, motivation alone is not enough; it must be coupled with good information, a solid business idea, and effective execution to maximize chances for success. In this book, we will discuss many examples of entrepreneurial firms and the factors separating successful firms from unsuccessful firms.

Many people see entrepreneurship as an attractive career path. Amazon.com currently lists over 5,800 books that deal with some facet of entrepreneurial behavior. The purpose of this book is to provide a thorough introduction to the entrepreneurial process.

What Is Entrepreneurship?

learning **objective**

1. Explain entrepreneurship and discuss its importance.

The word "entrepreneur" derives from the French words *entre*, meaning "between," and *prendre*, meaning "to take." The word was originally used to describe people who "take on the risk" between buyers and sellers or who "undertake" a task such as starting a new venture.[7] Inventors and entrepreneurs differ from each other. An inventor creates something new. An entrepreneur assembles and then integrates all the resources needed—the money, the people, the business model, the strategy, and the risk-bearing ability—to transform the invention into a viable business.[8]

Entrepreneurship is the process by which individuals pursue opportunities without regard to resources they currently control.[9] The essence of entrepreneurial behavior is identifying opportunities and putting useful ideas into practice.[10] The tasks called for by this behavior can be accomplished by either an individual or a group and typically requires creativity, drive, and a willingness to take risks. Pierre Omidyar, the founder of eBay, exemplified all these qualities. Omidyar saw an *opportunity* to create a marketplace where buyers and sellers could find each other online, he *risked* his career by quitting his job to work on eBay full time, and he *worked hard* to build a profitable company that delivers a *creative* and *useful* service to consumers.

In this book, we focus on entrepreneurship in the context of an entrepreneur or team of entrepreneurs launching a new business. However, ongoing firms can also behave entrepreneurially. Typically, established firms with an entrepreneurial emphasis are proactive, innovative, and risk taking. For example, 3M, one of the world's largest corporations, has a long history of entrepreneurial behavior, lasting through many chief executive officers (CEOs) and top management teams.[11] Similarly, a recent study on the rapid growth of Cisco Systems reveals a history of entrepreneurial behavior at multiple levels within the firm.[12] In addition, many of the firms traded on the NASDAQ, such as Microsoft, Oracle, Starbucks, and Qualcomm, are commonly thought of as entrepreneurial firms.

learning **objective**

2. Describe corporate entrepreneurship and its use in established firms.

Established firms with an orientation to behave entrepreneurially practice **corporate entrepreneurship**.[13] All firms fall along a conceptual continuum that ranges from highly conservative to highly entrepreneurial. The position of a firm on this continuum is referred to as its **entrepreneurial intensity**.[14] As we mentioned previously, entrepreneurial firms are typically proactive innovators and are not adverse to risk. In contrast, conservative firms take a more "wait and see" posture, are less innovative, and are risk adverse.

One of the most persuasive indications of the importance of entrepreneurship to an individual or to a firm is the degree of effort they undertake to behave in an entrepreneurial manner. Firms with higher entrepreneurial intensity regularly look for ways to cut bureaucracy. For example, Virgin Group, the large British conglomerate, works hard to keep its units small and instill in them an entrepreneurial spirit. Virgin is the third most recognized brand in Britain and is involved in businesses as diverse as airlines and music. In the following quote, Sir Richard Branson, the founder and CEO of Virgin, describes how his company operates in an entrepreneurial manner:

> Convention . . . dictates that "big is beautiful," but every time one of our ventures gets too big we divide it up into smaller units. I go to the deputy managing

3M is responsible for the creation of many different products—such as mailing supplies, ergonomic solutions, and Scotchgard™—that make our professional and personal lives easier. Inventors Spence Silver and Art Fry are responsible for perhaps 3M's most recognizable innovation, the Post-it™ Note.

director, the deputy sales director, and the deputy marketing director and say, "Congratulations. You're now MD [managing director], sales director and marketing director—of a new company." Each time we've done this, the people involved haven't had much more work to do, but necessarily they have a greater incentive to perform and a greater zeal for their work. The results for us have been terrific. By the time we sold Virgin Music, we had as many as 50 subsidiary record companies, and not one of them had more than 60 employees.[15]

Why Become an Entrepreneur?

learning **objective**

3. Discuss three main reasons that people become entrepreneurs.

The three primary reasons that people become entrepreneurs and start their own firms are to (1) be their own boss, (2) pursue their own ideas, and (3) realize financial rewards.

The first of these reasons—being one's own boss—is given most commonly. This doesn't mean, however, that entrepreneurs are difficult to work with or that they have trouble accepting authority. Instead, many entrepreneurs want to be their own boss because either they have had a long-time ambition to own their own firm or they have become frustrated working in traditional jobs. T. J. Rogers, the founder and longtime CEO of Cypress Semiconductor, an international supplier of computer chips, illustrates these points. Prior to founding Cypress, Rogers was on the fast track for promotion at Advanced Micro Devices (AMD), one of the world's largest semiconductor firms. When asked why he left AMD to start his own company, Rogers replied,

Actually, my mother asked me that. Her basic question was—rephrasing it negatively from my perspective—"Now that you're in the rat race and can scramble up the political ladder at Advanced Micro Devices, why give up the sure opportunities and start your own company?" I wanted to start a company since I graduated from college. It was one of my life goals, stated at age 21, that I would start a company by the age 35. Why do people start their own companies? The standard entrepreneurial answer is frustration. You see a company running poorly; you see that it could be a lot better. Like the freshman Congressman who's been around for six months, you realize that the other guys really aren't that good. All of a sudden you understand that you could go build something bigger and more important than where you are. That's a big deal.[16]

There are also people who long for independence, a desire that can be satisfied by owning their own business and being their own boss. Those who become entrepreneurs for only this reason typically do not grow their firms beyond their immediate control.[17] Recall that in the opening case, Omidyar knew that the potential of eBay would soon outpace his ability to lead it. So Omidyar hired Meg Whitman, a professional manager, to run the company. It is unlikely that Omidyar would have made this hire, however, if his primary and perhaps only motivation for starting eBay had been to be independent of the control of others.

The second reason people start their own firms is to pursue their own ideas. Some people are naturally alert, and when they recognize ideas for new products or services, they have a desire to see those ideas realized. Corporate entrepreneurs who innovate within the context of an existing firm typically have a mechanism for their ideas to become known. Established firms, however, often resist innovation. When this happens, employees are left with good ideas that go unfulfilled.[18] Because of their passion and commitment, some employees choose to leave the firm employing them in order to start their own business as the means to develop their own ideas.

This chain of events can take place in noncorporate settings, too. For example, some people, through a hobby, leisure activity, or just everyday life, recognize the need for a product or service that is not available in the marketplace. If the idea is viable enough to support a business, they commit tremendous time and energy to convert the idea into a part-time or full-time firm. How entrepreneurs spot ideas and determine whether ideas represent viable business opportunities is the focus of Chapters 2 and 3.

Finally, people start their own firms to pursue financial rewards. This motivation, however, is typically secondary to the first two and often fails to live up to its hype. The average entrepreneur does not make more money than someone with a similar amount of responsibility in a traditional job. For example, in 1997 (the most current year for which statistics are available), only 13.1 percent of the owners of small businesses in the United States made more than $50,000 a year.[19]

The financial lure of entrepreneurship is its upside potential. People such as Michael Dell of Dell Computer, Jerry Yang of Yahoo!, and Scott McNealy of Sun Microsystems made hundreds of millions of dollars building their firms. But these people insist that money wasn't their primary motivation. Marc Andreessen, founder of Netscape said, "[Money] is not the motivator or even the measure of my success."[20] Some entrepreneurs even report that the financial rewards associated with entrepreneurship can be bittersweet if they are accompanied by losing control of their firm. For example, Sir Richard Branson, after selling Virgin Records, wrote, "I remember walking down the street [after the sale was completed]. I was crying. Tears . . . [were] streaming down my face. And there I was holding a check for a billion dollars. . . . If you'd have seen me, you would have thought I was loony. A billion dollars."[21] For Branson, it wasn't just the money—it was the thrill of building the business and of seeing the success of their initial idea.

Characteristics of Successful Entrepreneurs

Although many behaviors have been ascribed to entrepreneurs, several are common to those who are successful. Those in new ventures and those who are already part of an entrepreneurial firm share these qualities, which are shown in Figure 1.1 and described in the following section.

learning **objective**

4. Identify four main characteristics of successful entrepreneurs.

Passion for the Business   The number one characteristic shared by successful entrepreneurs is a *passion for their business*, whether it is in the context of a new firm or an existing business. This passion typically stems from the entrepreneur's belief that the business will positively influence people's lives. Consider Benjamin Tregoe, cofounder of

Figure 1.1

Four Primary Characteristics of
Successful Entrepreneurs

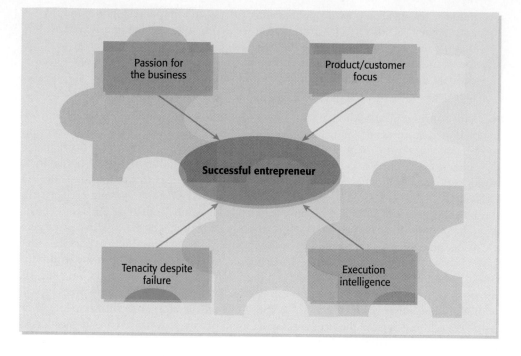

Kepner-Tregoe, a management consulting firm. In describing the purpose of his new venture, he said,

> Tremendously important to me was the feeling that we were doing something that had a significance far beyond building a company or what the financial rewards could be. I was convinced we were doing something that had tremendous importance in the world.[22]

This passion explains why people leave secure jobs to start their own firms and why billionaires such as Bill Gates of Microsoft, Michael Dell of Dell Computer, and Larry Ellison of Oracle continue working after they are financially secure. They strongly believe that the product or service they are selling makes a difference in people's lives and makes the world a better place to live in.

Passion is particularly important for entrepreneurs because, although rewarding, the process of starting and building a new firm is demanding. Entrepreneurship isn't for the person who is only partially committed. Investors watch like hawks to try to determine an entrepreneur's passion for his or her business idea. Michael Rovner, a partner in AV Labs, a venture capital firm in Austin, Texas, expresses this sentiment:

> Everyone has a different concept of what starting a business is like. We look for people who are highly motivated—people who are passionate about providing their solution to customers, people who really want to make a new company fly.[23]

A note of caution is in order here: While an entrepreneur should have passion, he or she should not wear rose-colored glasses. It is important to be enthusiastic about a business idea, but it is also important to understand its potential flaws and risks. An entrepreneur must also remain flexible enough to tweak the idea when it is necessary to do so.

Product/Customer Focus   A second defining characteristic of successful entrepreneurs is a ***product/customer focus***. This quality is exemplified by Steven Jobs, the cofounder of Apple Computer, who wrote, "The computer is the most remarkable tool we've ever built . . . but the most important thing is to get them in the hands of as many people as possible."[24] This sentiment underscores an understanding of the two most important elements in any business—products and customers. While it's important to think about management, marketing, finance, and the like, none of those functions makes any difference if a firm does not have good products with the capability to satisfy customers.

You might describe an entrepreneur as an independent thinker, an innovator, or perhaps a risk taker. These entrepreneurial employees are passionate enough to work out of their garage if that's what it takes to get the company up and running. Consider Bill Gates, who was so enthusiastic about computers that he dropped out of Harvard University to pursue his vision.

An entrepreneur's keen focus on products and customers typically stems from the fact that most successful entrepreneurs are, at heart, craftspeople. They are obsessed with making products that meet their customers' needs. This is an important point to remember, particularly in an era when it is tempting to envision new businesses resulting from every advance in technology. Michael Dell illustrated this point when he wrote, "We introduce technology that meets the needs of our customers, rather than introducing technology for its own sake."[25]

It is fascinating to watch entrepreneurs create products that meet unfilled needs. The idea for the Apple Macintosh, for example, originated in the early 1980s, when Steven Jobs and several other Apple employees took a tour of a Xerox research facility. They were astounded to see computers that displayed graphical icons and pull-down menus. The computers also allowed users to navigate desktops using a small, wheeled device called a mouse. Jobs decided to use these innovations to create the Macintosh, the first user-friendly computer. Throughout the two and a half years the Macintosh team developed this new product, it maintained an intense product/customer focus, creating a high-quality computer that is easy to learn, is fun to use, and meets the needs of a wide audience of potential users.[26]

Tenacity Despite Failure   Because entrepreneurs are typically trying something new, the failure rate associated with their efforts is naturally high. In addition, the process of developing a new business is somewhat similar to what a scientist experiences in the laboratory. A chemist, for example, typically has to try multiple combinations of chemicals before the optimal combination is found to accomplish a certain objective. In a similar fashion, developing a new business idea may require a certain degree of experimentation before a success is attained. Setbacks and failures inevitably occur during this process. The litmus test for entrepreneurs is their ability to persevere through setbacks and failures. Ken

Nickerson, the cofounder of iBinary, a wireless technology firm and a former Microsoft executive, exemplifies this quality. When asked in an interview, "What is the best thing you ever did?" Nickerson responded by saying, "Having high levels of tenacity. For example, bringing Hotmail to Microsoft Network took 18 months, and I just fought that deal through. It was arguably the best Internet thing Microsoft did."[27]

In actuality, a certain measure of fear is healthy when pursuing new ideas. Acknowledging, for example, that unforeseen circumstances or a competitor's aggressive action could ruin a company's plans produces vigilance in entrepreneurs that may help them succeed.[28] Andy Grove of Intel describes this type of fear in his book *Only the Paranoid Survive*. Grove argues that a company should remain alert about changes in market conditions, or competitors can quickly pass them by.[29]

Execution Intelligence   The ability to fashion a solid business idea into a viable business is a key characteristic of successful entrepreneurs. Rob Adams, a senior partner in AV Labs, calls this ability ***execution intelligence***.[30] In many cases, execution intelligence is the factor that determines whether a start-up is successful or fails. An ancient Chinese saying warns, "To open a business is very easy; to keep it open is very difficult."

The ability to effectively execute a business idea means developing a business model, putting together a new venture team, raising money, establishing partnerships, managing finances, leading and motivating employees, and so on. It also demands the ability to translate thought, creativity, and imagination into action and measurable results. As Jeff Bezos, the founder of Amazon.com, once said, "Ideas are easy. It's execution that's hard."[31]

To illustrate solid execution, let's look at Starbucks. Howard Schultz, the entrepreneur who purchased Starbucks in 1987, realized that most Americans didn't have a place to enjoy coffee in a comfortable, quiet setting. Seeing a great opportunity to satisfy customers' needs, Schultz attacked the marketplace aggressively to make Starbucks the industry leader and to establish a national brand. First, he hired a seasoned management team, constructed a world-class roasting facility to supply his outlets with premium coffee beans, and focused on building an effective organizational infrastructure. Then Schultz recruited a management information systems expert from McDonald's to design a point-of-sale system capable of tracking consumer purchases across 300 outlets. This decision was crucial to the firm's ability to sustain rapid growth over the next several years. Starbucks succeeded because Howard Schultz knew how to execute a business idea.[32] He built a seasoned management team, implemented an effective strategy, and used information technology wisely to make his business thrive.[33] In contrast to what Schultz has accomplished at Starbucks, the cost of ignoring execution is high, as explained by Bob Young, the founder of several entrepreneurial firms. When asked, "What was your hardest lesson or biggest mistake?" Young replied, "In my first two businesses, my interest was always in 'the new thing,' so I wasn't paying attention to details. As a result of my lack of interest in getting the repetitive stuff right, we never achieved the profitability we should have."[34]

To illustrate the importance of execution intelligence, as well as other factors that are critical in determining a firm's success or failure, we include a boxed feature titled "What Went Wrong?" in each chapter. The feature for this chapter shows how The Singing Machine, a maker of karaoke machines, got caught up in the excitement surrounding growth and started making careless decisions, leaving the firm's survivability in question. Indeed, evidence shows that the most successful companies learn how to manage their growth rather than letting growth manage the firm.[35]

learning objective

5. Explain the five common myths regarding entrepreneurship.

Common Myths About Entrepreneurs

There are many misconceptions about who entrepreneurs are and what motivates them to launch firms to develop their ideas. Some misconceptions are due to the media covering atypical entrepreneurs, such as a couple of college students who obtain venture capital to fund a small business that they grow into a multimillion-dollar company. Such articles rarely state that these entrepreneurs are the exception rather than the rule. Let's look at the most common myths and the realities about entrepreneurs.

   Myth 1: Entrepreneurs are born, not made. This myth is based on the mistaken belief that some people are genetically predisposed to be entrepreneurs. The consensus of

what went wrong?

The Singing Machine: How Success Can Breed Failure

Many entrepreneurs learn the hard way to be leery of quick success. If a firm's products catch on quickly, the ability to execute properly becomes doubly important. Success is fun—but if it comes too quickly, it's easy to get caught up in the euphoria and start making careless decisions. That is exactly what happened to The Singing Machine, a maker of karaoke machines.

The Singing Machine started out making karaoke machines for professional singers, a relatively small market. The company's products were made in China, so it had a fairly small staff and a modest overhead. Then the company had some good luck—karaoke caught on. Soon, it started selling its machines through Circuit City and Best Buy, and it looked as though the sky was the limit. In fact, *BusinessWeek* named The Singing Machine the number one hot growth company for 2002.

All of this sounds good, right? Wait till you read what happened. Expecting continued growth, The Singing Machine loaded up on karaoke machines for the 2002 Christmas season, getting as many machines as possible on retailers' shelves. But the big retailers were savvy, and protected their own self-interests, despite the popularity of karaoke machines. For example, one retailer demanded that The Singing Machine place their machines on its shelves on a consignment basis. It wouldn't actually buy the machines, it would only display and sell them, and if they sold, great! If not, The Signing Machine would have to take them back. Another retailer demanded that The Singing Machine provide it a guaranteed gross profit margin, essentially shielding itself from any risk.

As it turned out, the karaoke craze waned in late 2002. And, after the Christmas season was over, and The Singing

Machine was in trouble. Rather than helping it liquidate its inventory, the retailers it contracted with moved on to the next "hot" item and more than $30 million in karaoke machines ended up in The Singing Machine's warehouses. Reflecting on the agreements that his company entered into in its haste to get sales during the 2002 Christmas season, Y. P. Chan, the company's new CEO, said, "It's a classic business school case of growing pains. . . . One needs to be disciplined enough to walk away from a business deal which doesn't make sense."

Quick success—every entrepreneur's dream—can rapidly erode into failure if a business becomes overly optimistic about its products or services and starts chasing deals that don't make sense. Execution intelligence is as important in the good times as it is in the tough times.

Questions for Critical Thinking

1. As we've said in this chapter, execution intelligence is critical to entrepreneurial success. How did execution fall short for The Singing Machine? What would you have done differently to execute properly to ensure the early success of this entrepreneurial venture?

2. The Singing Machine's experiences suggest that the external (business) environment affects a venture's success. What could The Singing Machine have done to anticipate how the external environment would affect its business? Do you think The Singing Machine is unusual in its failure to carefully study and understand the effect of the external environment on its operations?

Source: J. Bailey, "Success Has Karaoke Maker Singing the Blues," Wall Street Journal, July 29, 2003, B7.

---

many hundreds of studies on the psychological and sociological makeup of entrepreneurs is that entrepreneurs are not genetically different from other people. No one is "born" to be an entrepreneur; everyone has the potential to become one. Whether someone does or doesn't is a function of environment, life experiences, and personal choices.[36] However, there are personality traits and characteristics commonly associated with entrepreneurs; these are listed in Table 1.1. These traits are developed over time and evolve from an individual's social context. For example, studies show that people with parents who were self-employed are more likely to become entrepreneurs.[37] After witnessing a father's or mother's independence in the workplace, a child is more likely to find independence appealing.[38] Similarly, people who personally know an entrepreneur are more than twice as likely to be involved in starting a new firm than those with no entrepreneur acquaintances or role models.[39]

Myth 2: Entrepreneurs are gamblers. A second myth about entrepreneurs is that they are gamblers and take big risks. The truth is, entrepreneurs are usually **moderate risk takers**, as are most people.[40] The idea that entrepreneurs are gamblers originates from two sources.

Table 1.1

Common Traits and Characteristics
of Entrepreneurs

Achievement motivated	Persuasive
Alert to opportunities	Promoter
Creative	Resource assembler/leverager
Decisive	Self-confident
Energetic	Self-starter
Has an internal locus of control	Has a strong work ethic
Is a moderate risk taker	Tenacious
Needs to achieve	Tolerant of ambiguity
Is a networker	Visionary

First, entrepreneurs typically have jobs that are less structured, and so they face a more uncertain set of possibilities than managers or rank-and-file employees.[41] For example, an entrepreneur who starts an e-business consulting service has a less stable job than a phone company employee. Second, many entrepreneurs have a strong need to achieve and often set challenging goals, a behavior that is sometimes equated with risk taking.

Myth 3: Entrepreneurs are motivated primarily by money. It is naive to think that entrepreneurs don't seek financial rewards. As discussed previously, however, money is rarely the primary reason entrepreneurs start new firms. Considering what motivated him to start Siebel Systems, a successful Silicon Valley firm, Tom Siebel wrote,

> [It] was never about making money. It was never about going public; it was never about the creation of wealth. This was about an attempt to build an incredibly high-quality company. I suppose if I was a great musician that maybe I would play the guitar, if I was a great golfer maybe I would go out on tour, but I can't play the guitar and my golf game is pretty horrible. So what I think, frequently under those circumstances, what you do is do what you do best. And I think that maybe what I do best is start and operate information technology companies.[42]

Some entrepreneurs warn that the pursuit of money can be distracting. Media mogul Ted Turner said, "If you think money is a real big deal . . . you'll be too scared of losing it to get it."[43] Similarly, Debbie Fields, the founder of Mrs. Fields Cookies, said that if you chase money, you'll never get it.[44] And Sam Walton, commenting on all the media attention that surrounded him after he was named the richest man in America by *Forbes* magazine in 1985, said,

> Here's the thing: money never has meant that much to me, not even in the sense of keeping score. . . . We're not ashamed of having money, but I just don't believe a big showy lifestyle is appropriate for anywhere, least of all here in Bentonville where folks work hard for their money. We all know that everyone puts on their trousers one leg at a time. . . . I still can't believe it was news that I get my hair cut at the barbershop. Where else would I get it cut? Why do I drive a pickup truck? What am I supposed to haul my dogs around in, a Rolls-Royce?[45]

Myth 4: Entrepreneurs should be young and energetic. The average entrepreneur is 35 to 45 years old and has 10 or more years of experience in a large firm.[46]

While it is important to be energetic, investors often cite the strength of the entrepreneur (or team of entrepreneurs) as their most important criterion in the decision to fund new ventures.[47] In fact, a sentiment that venture capitalists often express is that they would rather fund a strong entrepreneur with a mediocre business idea than fund a strong business idea and a mediocre entrepreneur. What makes an entrepreneur "strong" in the eyes of an investor is experience in the area of the proposed business, skills and abilities that will help the business, a solid reputation, a track record of success, and passion about the business idea. The first four of these five qualities favor

Clearly, Debbi Fields has come a long way since Mrs. Fields Chocolate Chippery, which opened in 1977. Today, there are hundreds of Mrs. Fields stores in the United States and she has even gone global with an international presence in 11 different countries.

older rather than younger entrepreneurs. In addition, many people turn to entrepreneurship in lieu of retirement. One study reported that 32 percent of early retirees who return to work start their own business.[48]

Myth 5: Entrepreneurs love the spotlight. While some entrepreneurs are flamboyant, the vast majority of entrepreneurs do not attract public attention. In fact, many entrepreneurs, because they are working on proprietary products or services, avoid public notice.

Consider that of the 3,300 companies listed on the NASDAQ, entrepreneurs, many of whom are still actively involved with their firms, launched these ventures. But how many of these entrepreneurs can you name? Maybe a half dozen? Most of us could come up with Bill Gates of Microsoft, Steven Jobs of Apple, and Michael Dell of Dell, Inc. Whether or not they sought attention, these are the entrepreneurs who are often in the news. But few of us could name the founders of Google, Nokia, or GAP even though we frequently use these firm's products and services. These entrepreneurs, like most, have either avoided attention or been passed over by the popular press. They defy the myth that entrepreneurs, more so than other groups in our society, love the spotlight.

Types of Start-Up Firms

As shown in Figure 1.2, there are three types of start-up firms: salary-substitute firms, lifestyle firms, and entrepreneurial firms.

Salary-substitute firms are small firms that afford their owner or owners a level of income similar to what they would earn in a conventional job. Examples of salary-substitute firms are dry cleaners, convenience stores, restaurants, accounting firms, retail stores, and hairstyling salons. The vast majority of small businesses fit into this category. Salary-

learning **objective**

6. Explain how entrepreneurial firms differ from salary-substitute and lifestyle firms.

Figure 1.2

Types of Start-Up Firms

substitute firms offer common products or services to customers and are not particularly innovative.

Lifestyle firms provide their owner or owners the opportunity to pursue a particular lifestyle and earn a living while doing so. Examples of lifestyle firms include ski instructors, golf pros, and tour guides. These firms are not innovative, nor do they grow quickly. Commonly, lifestyle companies promote a particular sport, hobby, or pastime and may employ only the owner or just a handful of people.

As we noted earlier in this chapter, the essence of entrepreneurship is the creation of value and the dissemination of value to customers. The word "*value*" refers to worth, importance, or utility. *Entrepreneurial firms* bring new products and services to market by creating and seizing opportunities. Google, eBay, and Starbucks are well-known, highly successful examples of entrepreneurial firms. Companies of this type create products and services that have worth, that are important to their customers, and that provide a measure of usefulness to their customers that they wouldn't have otherwise.

Entrepreneurship's Importance

Entrepreneurship has tremendous impact on the economy and on society. In 2002, a report by the Global Entrepreneurship Monitor stated that "the national level of entrepreneurial activity has a statistically significant association with the national level of economic growth."[49] Consistent with that finding, one scholar, commenting on the importance of entrepreneurship at the local level, noted that "entrepreneurship is still the best private vehicle we have to turn around and improve the economic health of a community."[50]

Entrepreneurship's importance to the economy and society was first articulated by in 1934 by Joseph Schumpeter, an Austrian economist who did the majority of his work at Harvard University. In his book *The Theory of Economic Development*, Schumpeter argued that entrepreneurs develop new products and technologies that over time make current products and technologies obsolete. Schumpeter called this process *creative destruction*. Because new products and technologies are typically better than those they replace and the availability of improved products and technologies increases consumer demand, creative destruction stimulates economic activity. The new products and technologies may also increase the productivity of all elements of society.[51]

The process of creative destruction is initiated most effectively by start-up ventures that improve on what is currently available. Small firms that practice this art are often called "innovators" or "agents of change." The process of creative destruction is not limited to new products and technologies; it can include new pricing strategies (e.g., discount brokers such as E*Trade), new distribution channels (such as FedEx or Amazon.com), or new retail formats (such as Staples in office supplies).

Now let's look more closely at the importance of entrepreneurship.

learning objective

7. Discuss the economic impact of entrepreneurial firms.

Economic Impact of Entrepreneurial Firms

For three reasons, entrepreneurial behavior has a strong impact on the strength and stability of the economy.

Innovation   *Innovation* is the process of creating something new, which is central to the entrepreneurial process.[52] Small entrepreneurial firms are responsible for 67 percent of all innovation in the United States[53] and have been responsible for 95 percent of radical innovations since World War II.[54] Many innovations help individuals and businesses work more smoothly and efficiently. An example of how one innovative firm, Nistevo, is helping large shippers work more efficiently is provided in the boxed feature titled "Savvy Entrepreneurial Firm." In each chapter, this feature will provide an illustration of the exemplary behavior of

Savvy entrepreneurial FIRM

Nistevo: Helping Shippers Become More Efficient Through Innovative Technologies

www.nistevo.com

When a manufacturer ships a truckload of products to a customer, it's the carrier's responsibility to find products to haul back on the return route. About 20 percent of the time, the carrier can't find a return load. That means that nationwide, about two out of every 10 trucks you see on the highway is running empty. Those empty miles translate into a 30 billion dollar inefficiency in the trucking system annually. A new startup, named Nistevo, has developed an innovative approach to tackling this problem.

Headquartered in Eden Prairie, Minnesota, Kevin Lynch founded Nistevo in 1997. The firm developed a collaborative logistics network that reduces the number of empty trucks on the road, and lowers the costs of shipping for both the shippers and the carriers. For large shippers such as General Mills and Georgia Pacific, shipping costs are a major portion of their annual expenses, so they are always on the lookout for ways to reduce this cost. Nistevo created a digital network that matches the routes of its customers, and essentially guarantees carriers full round-trips, which enables them to lower their costs and pass on a portion of the savings to their shippers.

The system works like this. When a company joins the Nistevo network at an annual fee of about $300,000, Nistevo identifies potential partners by comparing transportation routes of other members. This comparative analysis scores and ranks which companies would benefit from collaborating on common trucking lanes. After companies agree to collaborate, they form communities and negotiate ground rules, such as which carriers to use. Once a community is formed, Nistevo's software figures out how the companies can collaborate on loads to cut down on the number of empty trucks on the road.

For example, a community might consist of General Mills, Nestle, and Georgia Pacific. After Nistevo's software compares and matches the trucking routes of the community's companies, common routes are established.

Carrier A might complete the following three-legged route to move freight for General Mills, Nestle, and Georgia Pacific:

First leg: *move load from Minneapolis to Atlanta for General Mills.*

Second leg: *move load from Atlanta to Houston for Georgia Pacific.*

Third leg: *move load from Houston back to Minneapolis for Nestle.*

This arrangement produces a Minneapolis-Atlanta-Houston-Minneapolis round-trip for the carrier, with no empty loads. Without Nistevo, however, General Mills, Georgia Pacific, and Nestle wouldn't have known that this route was compatible for all three companies.

Today, Nistevo's network is growing, and the company estimates that it can save the average manufacturer 12 percent of its shipping costs. Although the company is young, it is enabling shippers and carriers to collaborate on over 4,000 daily shipments. The company's current customers include Baxter Healthcare, General Mills, Georgia Pacific, Kellogg's, Nestle, and Agilent Technologies.

Questions for Critical Thinking

1. We described for you some myths about entrepreneurship. Use the description of Nistevo's evolution to dispel one or more of these myths.

2. How does the process called "creative destruction" apply to the description of Nistevo?

3. In your opinion, what should this firm do to remain successful?

Sources: Nistevo, www.nistevo.com (accessed May 1, 2004), and P. Strozniak, "Sharing the Load," Industry Week, September 2001, 47–50.

one or more entrepreneurial firms or will provide an example of a tool or technique that well-managed entrepreneurial firms are using to improve their performance.

Job creation   In the past two decades, economic activity has moved increasingly in the direction of smaller entrepreneurial firms, possibly because of their unique ability to innovate and focus on specialized tasks. In 1970, for example, the *Fortune* 500 employed 20 percent of the U.S. labor force. By 1996, that number had dropped to 8.5 percent.[55] And between 1993 and 1996, fast-growth young companies, known as **gazelles**, created about two-thirds of all new jobs in the United States.[56] Large firms are increasingly focusing on what they do best, which is usually manufacturing, sales, and service, and are outsourcing the majority of their other tasks to smaller firms. In addition, former start-up ventures, which have grown as a result of their entrepreneurial activities, are serving the needs of consumers who were once serviced by larger firms.

Entrepreneurial firms that grow into large companies also provide substantial employment. An in-depth study of the 1997 *Fortune* 200 found that 197 of the 200 firms in the ranking could be traced back to one or more entrepreneurial founders.[57] Examples include Cisco Systems, Dell, and Microsoft.

Globalization   Today, over 97 percent of all U.S. exporters are small businesses with fewer than 500 employees. Between 1987 and 1997 the number of these small-company exporters tripled, and between 1992 and 1997 the value of small-company export dollars also tripled, to $171.9 billion.[58] Export markets are vital to the U.S. economy and provide outlets for the sale of U.S.-produced products and services.

Entrepreneurial Firms' Impact on Society

learning **objective**

8. Discuss the impact of entrepreneurial firms on society.

The innovations of entrepreneurial firms have a dramatic impact on society. Think of all the new products and services that make our lives easier, enhance our productivity at work, improve our health, and entertain us. For example, Amgen, an entrepreneurial firm that helped launch the biotech industry, has produced a number of drugs that have dramatically improved people's lives. An example is NEUPOGEN, a drug that decreases the incidence of infection in cancer patients who are undergoing chemotherapy treatment. Sensipar is another one of Amgen's important products. As a secondary treatment of hyperparathyroidism, patients with chronic kidney disease and who are on dialysis take this drug.[59] In addition to improved health care, consider cellular phones, personal computing, Internet shopping, overnight package delivery, digital photography, and microwave ovens. All these products are new to this generation, yet it's hard to imagine our world without them.

However, new innovations do create moral and ethical issues that societies are forced to grapple with. For example, bar-code scanner technology and the Internet have made it easier for companies to track the purchasing behavior of their customers, but this raises privacy concerns. Similarly, bioengineering has made it easier to extend the shelf life of many food products, but some researchers and consumers question the long-term health implications of bioengineered foods.

Entrepreneurial Firms' Impact on Larger Firms

learning **objective**

9. Identify ways in which large firms benefit from the presence of smaller entrepreneurial firms.

In addition to the impact that entrepreneurial firms have on the economy and society, entrepreneurial firms have a positive impact on the effectiveness of larger firms. For example, some entrepreneurial firms are original equipment manufacturers, producing parts that go into products that larger firms manufacture and sell. Thus, many exciting new products, such as DVD players, digital cameras, and improved prescription drugs, are not solely the result of the efforts of larger companies with strong brand names, such as Sony, Kodak, and Johnson & Johnson. They were produced with the cutting-edge component parts or research and development provided by entrepreneurial firms.

Many entrepreneurial firms have built their entire business models around producing products and services that help larger firms be more efficient or effective. For example, many international firms face the challenge of translating the content of their Web sites into other languages for the benefit of their foreign customers. Firms such as Avis, General Electric, and

Partnering for SUCCESS

Working Together: How Biotech Firms and Large Drug Companies Bring Pharmaceutical Products to Market

Large firms and smaller entrepreneurial firms play different roles in business and society and can often produce the best results by partnering with each other rather than acting as adversaries. The pharmaceutical industry is an excellent one to use to illustrate how this works.

It is well known that barriers to entry in the pharmaceutical industry are high. The average new product takes about seven years from discovery to market approval. The process of discovering, testing, obtaining approval, manufacturing, and marketing a new drug is long and expensive. How, then, do biotech start-ups make it? The answer is that few biotech firms actually take their products to market. Here's how it works.

Biotech firms specialize in discovering and patenting new drugs—it's what they're good at. In most cases, however, they have neither the money nor the know-how to bring the products to market. In contrast, the large drug companies, such as Pfizer and Merck, specialize in developing and marketing drugs and providing information to doctors about them. It's what they are good at. But these companies typically don't have the depth of scientific talent and the entrepreneurial zeal that the small biotech firms do. These two types of firms need one another to be as successful as possible. Often, but not always, what happens is this. The

biotech firms discover and patent new drugs, and the larger drug companies develop them and bring them to market. Biotech firms earn money through this arrangement by licensing or selling their patent-protected discoveries to the larger companies or by partnering with them in some revenue-sharing way. The large drug companies make money by selling the products to consumers.

The most compelling partnership arrangements are those that help entrepreneurial firms focus on what they do best, which is typically innovation, and that allow them to tap into their partners' complementary strengths and resources.

Questions for Critical Thinking

1. In your opinion, what factors in the business environment encourage firms to partner to compete?

2. What risks do small firms face when partnering with large, successful companies? What risks do large companies take when they rely on small firms as a source of innovation?

3. How might government policies affect partnering actions between small and large firms in the pharmaceutical industry?

Merrill Lynch rely on a small start-up named Convey Software to help them with this task. Similarly, many large firms occasionally need temporary labor to facilitate short-term personnel needs. A small start-up called IQNavigator has developed software to help *Fortune* 500 companies quickly hire reliable temporary labor through a network of sources.

In many instances, entrepreneurial firms partner with larger companies to reach mutually beneficial goals. Participation in business partnerships accelerates a firm's growth by giving it access to some of its partner's resources, managerial talent, and intellectual capacities. We examine the idea of partnering throughout this book. In each chapter, look for the boxed feature titled "Partnering for Success," which illustrates how entrepreneurial firms are using business partnerships to boost their chances for success. The feature in this chapter discusses how small, entrepreneurial biotech firms partner with large drug companies to bring their products to market. By working together rather than acting as adversaries, small biotech firms and large drug companies produce the best collective results.

The Entrepreneurial Process

The entrepreneurial process consists of four steps:

Step 1. Deciding to become an entrepreneur
Step 2. Developing successful business ideas
Step 3. Moving from an idea to an entrepreneurial firm
Step 4. Managing and growing the entrepreneurial firm

learning **objective**

10. Explain the entrepreneurial process.

Figure 1.3 models the entrepreneurial process. This process is the guide or framework we use to develop this book's contents. The double-headed arrow between the decision to become an entrepreneur and the development of successful business ideas indicates that sometimes the opportunity to develop an idea prompts a person to become an entrepreneur. Each section of Figure 1.3 is explained in the following sections.

Decision to Become an Entrepreneur (Chapter 1)

As discussed earlier, people become entrepreneurs to be their own boss, to pursue their own ideas, and to realize financial rewards. Usually, a ***triggering event*** prompts an individual to become an entrepreneur.[60] For example, an individual may lose her job and decide that the time is right to start her own business. Or a person might receive an inheritance and for the first time in his life have the money to start his own company. Lifestyle issues may also trigger entrepreneurial careers. For example, a woman may wait until her youngest child is in school before she decides to start her own firm.

Developing Successful Business Ideas (Chapters 2–5)

Many new businesses fail not because the entrepreneur didn't work hard but because there was no real opportunity to begin with. Developing a successful business idea includes opportunity recognition, feasibility analysis, industry analysis, and the development of an effective business model. Chapter 2 takes a scientific look at how entrepreneurs recognize

Figure 1.3 Basic Model of the Entrepreneurial Process

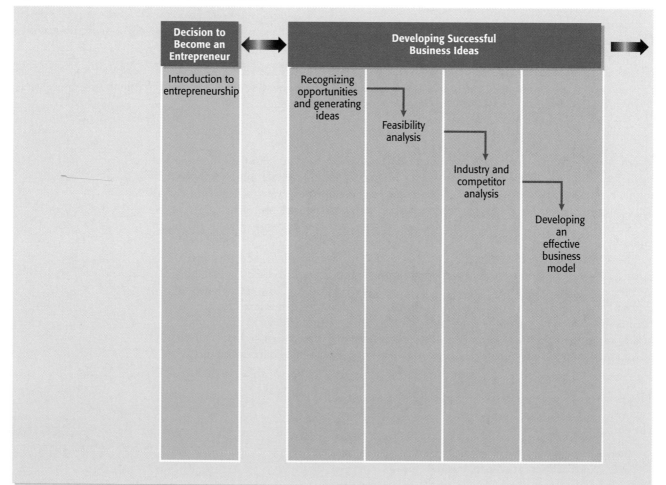

opportunities for business ideas, and describes how the opportunity recognition process typically unfolds. Chapter 3 focuses on feasibility analysis: the way to determine whether an idea represents a viable business opportunity. Industry and competitor analysis is our concern in Chapter 4. Knowing the industry in which a firm will choose to compete is crucial to an entrepreneur's success. Chapter 5 focuses on the important topic of developing an effective business model. A firm's **business model** is its plan for how it competes, uses its resources, structures it relationships, interfaces with customers, and creates value to sustain itself on the basis of the profits it generates. We'll study this topic using Dell, Inc.'s business model as an example.

Moving from an Idea to an Entrepreneurial Firm (Chapters 6–10)

The first step in turning an idea into reality is to build a new venture team. The actions taken here include assembling the firm's initial management team and selecting a board of directors and a board of advisers. This is discussed in Chapter 6. Chapter 7 deals with the important topic of assessing a new venture's financial strength and viability. Important information is contained in this chapter about completing and analyzing both historical and pro forma financial statements. Chapter 8 focuses on preparing a proper ethical and legal foundation for a firm, including selecting an appropriate form of business ownership. Chapter 9 describes how to write a business plan. A **business plan** is a written document that describes all the aspects of a business venture in a concise manner. It is usually necessary to have a written business plan to raise money and attract high-quality business partners.

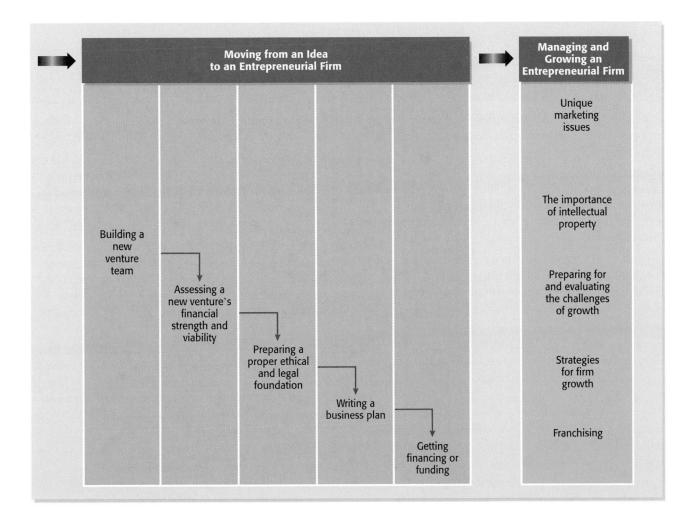

Some entrepreneurs are impatient and don't want to spend the time it takes to write a business plan. This approach is usually a mistake. Writing a business plan forces an entrepreneur to think carefully through all the aspects of a business venture. It also helps a new venture establish a set of milestones that can be used to guide the early phases of the business rollout. Chapter 10 focuses on the important task of getting financing or funding and identifies the options that a firm has for raising money.

Managing and Growing an Entrepreneurial Firm (Chapters 11–15)

Given today's competitive environment, all firms must be managed and grown properly to ensure their ongoing success. This is the final stage of the entrepreneurial process.

Chapter 11 focuses on the unique marketing issues facing entrepreneurial firms, including selecting an appropriate target market, building a brand, and the four Ps—product, price, promotion, and place (or distribution)—for new firms. Chapter 12 examines the important role of intellectual property in the growth of entrepreneurial firms. More and more, the value of "know-how" exceeds the value of a company's physical assets. In addition, we will talk about protecting business ideas through intellectual property statutes, such as patents, trademarks, copyrights, and trade secrets.

Preparing for and evaluating the challenges of growth is the topic of Chapter 13. We'll look at the characteristics and behaviors of successful growth firms. In Chapter 14, we'll study strategies for growth, ranging from new product development to mergers and acquisitions. We conclude with Chapter 15, which focuses on franchising. Not all franchise organizations are entrepreneurial firms, but franchising is a growing component of the entrepreneurial landscape.

CHAPTER SUMMARY

1. Entrepreneurship is the process by which individuals pursue opportunities without regard to resources they currently control.

2. Corporate entrepreneurship is the conceptualization of entrepreneurship at the firm level. Entrepreneurial firms are proactive, innovative, and risk taking. In contrast, conservative firms take a more "wait and see" posture, are less innovative, and are risk adverse.

3. Although reasons vary, the three primary reasons that people become entrepreneurs and start their own firms are as follows: to be their own boss, to pursue their own ideas, and to realize financial rewards.

4. The four main characteristics of successful entrepreneurs are passion for the business, product/customer focus, tenacity despite failure, and execution intelligence.

5. The five most common myths regarding entrepreneurship are that entrepreneurs are born, not made; that entrepreneurs are gamblers; that entrepreneurs are motivated primarily by money; that entrepreneurs should be young and energetic; and that entrepreneurs love the spotlight.

6. Entrepreneurial firms are the firms that bring new products and services to market by creating and seizing opportunities regardless of the resources they currently control. Entrepreneurial firms stress innovation, which is not the case for salary-substitute and lifestyle firms.

7. There is strong evidence that entrepreneurial behavior has a strong impact on economic stability and strength. The areas in which entrepreneurial firms contribute the most are innovation, job creation, and globalization.

8. The innovations produced by entrepreneurial firms have had a dramatic impact on society. It's easy to think of new products and services that have helped make our lives easier, that have made us more productive at work, that have improved our health, that have helped us better communicate with each other, and that have entertained us in new ways.

9. In addition to the impact that entrepreneurial firms have on the economy and society, entrepreneurial firms have a positive impact on the effectiveness of larger firms. There are many entrepreneurial firms that have built their entire business models around producing products and services that help larger firms become more efficient and effective.

10. The four distinct elements of the entrepreneurial process, pictured in Figure 1.3, are deciding to become an entrepreneur, developing successful business ideas, moving from an idea to an entrepreneurial firm, and managing and growing an entrepreneurial firm.

Business model, 19

Business plan, 19

Corporate
   entrepreneurship, 5

Creative destruction, 14

Entrepreneurial firms, 14

Entrepreneurial intensity, 5

Entrepreneurship, 5

Execution intellegience, 10

Gazelles, 16

Innovation, 15

Lifestyle firms, 14

Moderate risk takers, 11

Passion for their business, 7

Product/customer focus, 8

Salary-substitute firms, 13

Triggering event, 18

Value, 14

1. Entrepreneurship is growing around the world. Why do you think this is the case?

2. Which type of new business is more entrepreneurial: a business that is being started to pursue a unique opportunity or a business that is being started out of necessity? Explain your answer.

3. What is entrepreneurship? How can one differentiate an entrepreneurial firm from any other type of firm?

4. What are the three main attributes of firms that pursue high levels of corporate entrepreneurship? Would these firms score high or low on an entrepreneurial intensity scale?

5. What are the three primary reasons people become entrepreneurs?

6. Why is it that people who start their own firms to be independent typically do not grow their firms beyond their immediate control?

7. Some people start their own firms to pursue financial rewards. However, these rewards are often far fewer than imagined. Why is this so?

8. What are the primary traits and characteristics of successful entrepreneurs?

9. Why is passion such an important characteristic of successful entrepreneurs? What is it about passion that makes it particularly compatible with the entrepreneurial process?

10. Why is a product/customer focus an important characteristic of successful entrepreneurs?

11. What is meant by execution intelligence? Why is execution intelligence an important characteristic for entrepreneurs?

12. What are the five common myths of entrepreneurship?

13. What are the major differences between salary-substitute firms, lifestyle firms, and entrepreneurial firms?

14. Are entrepreneurs born or made? Defend your answer.

15. In general, are entrepreneurs high risk takers, moderate risk takers, or low risk takers?

16. What role does money play in motivating people to become entrepreneurs?

17. What did Joseph Schumpeter mean by the term "creative destruction"?

18. In general, what effect does entrepreneurship have on the U.S. economy?

19. To what extent do small entrepreneurial firms contribute to the amount of innovation that takes place in the United States?

20. Describe several examples of the impact that entrepreneurial firms have on society.

1. Reread the opening case, then list all the smart or effective moves Pierre Omidyar made in the early days of building eBay. Which three moves were most instrumental in eBay's early success?

2. Suppose that Kimberly-Clark, the large paper products firm, hired you to assess its level of entrepreneurial intensity. What three factors would you study to determine how entrepreneurial Kimberly-Clark is at this point in time? How would you determine if these factors were present?

3. Karen Jenkins has a good job working for the city of Charlotte, North Carolina, but is weary of 3 percent per year pay raises. Because she has read magazine articles about young entrepreneurs becoming extremely wealthy,

she decides to start her own firm. Do you think Karen is starting a firm for the right reason? Do you think the money she likely will earn will disappoint her?

4. Allison, a friend of yours, has always had a nagging desire to be her own boss. She has a good job with Microsoft but has several ideas for new products that she can't get Microsoft interested in. Allison just inherited $250,000 from an elderly relative and has the opportunity to start her own database software firm. She asks you, "Am I crazy for wanting to start my own firm to be my own boss and pursue my own ideas?" What would you tell her?

5. People are sometimes puzzled by the fact that entrepreneurs who have made millions of dollars still put in 60- to 80-hour weeks helping their companies innovate and grow. After reading the chapter, why do you think millionaire and multimillionaire entrepreneurs still get up and go to work everyday? If you were one of these entrepreneurs, do you think you would feel the same way? Why or why not?

6. Jim Chambers has always wanted to be an entrepreneur. He is intelligent, works hard, and has saved a substantial amount of money that would help him launch a firm. But Jim is hesitant to start his own company because a friend once told him, "Entrepreneurs are born, not made." Jim has never really known what to make of that statement. If he asked you about it, what would you tell him?

7. Yesterday in philosophy class, your professor said, "Give me one shred of evidence that demonstrates that entrepreneurship is good for the economy or has ever made a positive contribution to society." If you were to accept this challenge, what would you say?

8. A friend of yours just bought a Sony digital camera. While showing it to you, he said, "You think entrepreneurial firms are so smart, look at what Sony has done. It has produced a sophisticated digital camera that allows me to take pictures, download them to my PC, and e-mail them to family members. Sony's a big company, not a small entrepreneurial firm. What do you have to say to that?" If you were to defend of the role of entrepreneurial firms in developing new technologies, how would you respond?

9. Bill Williams was just laid off by Lucent Technologies and has decided to take his severance pay and open a small video rental store. He figures he'll make about the same running the video store as he made when he was with Lucent. Bill knows that you are taking a course in entrepreneurship and casually asks you, "If I open the video store, would you consider me to be an entrepreneur?" What would you tell him?

10. When Jill graduated from college, she opened a small ski shop near Jackson Hole, Wyoming. Although the shop sells some ski equipment, its primary purpose is to give lessons to people who want to learn to ski. Jill likes to tell her friends that she is a "true entrepreneur," just like her father, who started several technology businesses and patented more than 10 products. Do you consider Jill an entrepreneur? If not, what type of firm did she start?

you be the VC

Company: **Radar Golf** (*www.radargolf.com*)

Business Idea: Place a small electronic tag inside golf balls to make them easy to find when lost.

Pitch: What is more frustrating than losing a ball during a round of golf? Not only does a lost ball cost a player a two-stroke penalty, but looking for a ball slows down play on a golf course. Radar Golf offers a solution to these problems. The company has developed a small electronic tag that can be built into a golf ball during the manufacturing process. The tagged ball looks, feels, and performs like a regular golf ball. When a golfer hits a ball that is difficult to locate, she pulls out a handheld unit (that has also been developed by Radar Golf), turns it on, and points it in the direction of interest and begins walking towards the ball. By moving the unit from left to right, a pulsed audio tone (from the handheld unit) provides information on ball direction and distance. The golfer quickly walks in the direction of her ball, allowing it to be located within seconds. The Radar Golf ball system is intended to speed up play, improve the gofer's score, and provide an exciting new product to the $44 billion worldwide golf industry.

Q & A: Based on the material covered in this chapter, what questions would you ask this firm's founders before making your funding decision? What answers would satisfy you?

Decision: If you had to make your decision on just the information provided in the pitch and on the company's Web site, would you fund this firm? Why or why not?

Case 1.1

Launching the Palm Pilot: A Classic Tale of Tenacity Despite Failure
www.palmone.com

Every day, millions of people use Palm Pilots to organize their schedules. The story behind the founding of Palm, the leader in the handheld devices industry, is an intriguing tale of the tenacity it takes to pioneer a new technology and successfully bring it to market.

As a youngster, Jeff Hawkins, Palm's founder, helped his dad and brothers build boats. Hawkins remembers his father as a "consummate inventor" and believes the skills he acquired as a child helped him become an entrepreneur. "Learning to use shop tools, learning to use fiberglass and screws and stuff, is actually very useful in building little computers," Hawkins says. "Not many people in my business can get involved in as many aspects of product design as I do."

Hawkins graduated from Cornell in 1979 with a degree in electrical engineering and went to work for Intel. He stayed only three years and then took a job at GRiD Systems, a small Silicon Valley start-up whose goal was to design a computer that a person could carry—a crazy concept in the early 1980s. After a short stint at GRiD, where he became fascinated with how the brain functions, Hawkins went back to school—to Berkeley—to study how the human brain recognizes patterns. While there he developed "Palm-Print," a handwriting-recognition software.

After leaving graduate school short of a PhD, Hawkins returned to GRiD to see if he could develop pen-based hardware and software to complement his earlier invention. He developed a rudimentary handheld device, called the GriDPad, and launched it in 1990. Although it was slow, clunky, and ugly, it was a pen-based computer and was innovative for the time. The GRiDPad had a number of serious limitations, however, and eventually fizzled out. But Hawkins was determined to create a higher-quality pen-based computer that people could carry with them and that would give them the power of a PC at their fingertips.

To realize his dream, Hawkins left GRiD and founded his own company, Palm, in 1992. His first product was a handheld device for the consumer market called "Zoomer"—short for "consumer." Based on the strength of his reputation, Hawkins got venture-capital financing. He hired Donna Dubinsky, a former Apple Computer employee who was excited about what Hawkins was trying to accomplish. Dubinsky was a particularly good fit because she lent sales and management skills to Palm that Hawkins lacked. The first thing the two decided was that Palm would design only software and outsource Zoomer's hardware and operating system to others. While this sounded like a recipe for success, the plan didn't quite pan out. The Zoomer was eventually produced as a collaborative effort between Palm and a collection of its suppliers and was essentially "designed by committee." It had many interesting features but was slow, had bad text recognition, and was priced at $700, which was much too high for the consumer market. It quickly flopped.

Now, Hawkins was batting 0 for 2 regarding handheld devices. His first attempt at building a handheld computer, the GRiDPad, quickly fizzled. Strike one. His second attempt, the Zoomer, bombed. Strike two. Palm survived only because it was frugal and still had money in the bank.

Hawkins and Dubinsky went back to the drawing board and conducted in-depth surveys with people who had purchased the Zoomer, leading to two important realizations. First, consumers didn't want their handheld devices to be little PCs; they wanted them to *complement* their PCs. This would make the devices easier to design and produce. Second, because the biggest difficulty in building pen-based computers was getting the computers to recognize individual handwriting, Hawkins realized that instead of the handheld device learning everyone's handwriting, everyone would have to learn the handheld device's handwriting. From this insight, "Graffiti" was developed—the handwriting-recognition software that differentiated the Palm Pilot from other handheld devices. With Graffiti, each letter is made by writing in a standardized fashion; no individuality is allowed.

With this new understanding, Hawkins, Dubinsky, and a new partner, Ed Collins, rolled up their sleeves and pressed on. This time Palm would build the entire device. Strapped for cash, they sold the company to U.S. Robotics, with a strict understanding regarding the relative autonomy of Palm. Backed by the company's cash, manufacturing strength, and global presence, Palm introduced the original Palm Pilot in April 1996, and it became the fastest-selling consumer product in history—faster than the PC, the cell phone, the color television, and the VCR. When Palm Pilot was a clear winner, Jeff Hawkins was asked how the success of the product made him feel. He replied,

> It feels good. What really feels good is that people like the product. Since we're all product people here, there's nothing else that makes me happier than people saying, "Hey this is great, it's changed my life." That feels great.

Since the launch of the Palm Pilot, U.S. Robotics was acquired by 3Com, which eventually spun off Palm. Palm went public in 2000, becoming an independent corporation. As for Jeff Hawkins and Donna Dubinsky, they are apparently entrepreneurs at heart. They left Palm in 1998 and founded Handspring, a competing handheld device company that introduced an exciting line of products under the Visor brand name.

In late 2003, Palm and Handspring merged and formed a new company called palmOne to make handheld computers and other mobile gadgets. As part of that deal, Palm spun off the portion of its business that develops and licenses Palm's software for handheld computers and cell phones and created a company called palmsource. PalmOne and palmsource are separate legal entities.

1. Which of the characteristics of successful entrepreneurs, discussed in this chapter, do you see in Jeff Hawkins? To what extent do you believe these characteristics contributed to his success?

2. Which of the myths about entrepreneurs are dispelled by Jeff Hawkins's story?

3. It what ways do handheld devices have a positive impact on the economy, society, and the ability of businesses to increase their productivity? Do you think these factors contributed to the consumer's acceptance of handheld devices and their eventual success?

4. Although the Palm Pilot was "hot" when it was first introduced, handheld devices are waning in terms of consumer appeal. Why do you think this is the case?

Sources: S. Barnett, "Jeff Hawkins" (cover story), Pen Computing, 2001; PalmPower Magazine, no. 1, 1998; and D. D.Strauss, The Big Idea (New York: Dearborn Publishing, 2002).

Case 1.2

ChemConnect: Creating a New Kind of Marketplace Through Digital Technologies
www.chemconnect.com

Let's say you work in the purchasing department at Dow Chemical. Your job is to purchase the raw materials your company needs to produce its specialized chemical products. Of the following two approaches, which do you think is easier and more effective?

Approach A: Every time you get an order from one of your factories or refineries, you call your suppliers to see who has the grade of product you need at the best price. You might talk to 10 to 15 suppliers. Elapsed time: 3 hours. Best price for the product: $3.50 per kilogram.

Approach B: Every time you get an order from one of your factories or refineries, you log on to ChemConnect, an online exchange designed specifically for the chemical industry. Information about the availability and price of the chemical you want—not from 10 to 15 suppliers but from 50—appears in front of you. You complete a purchase online. Elapsed time: 30 minutes. Best price for the product: $3.44 per kilogram. Additional option: If you don't like the $3.44 price, you can set up an auction to try to get a better one.

ChemConnect was founded in 1995 as a bulletin board site and matured into an online exchange. In the late 1990s and early 2000s, online marketplaces existed for everything from eggs to gasoline. In fact, by April 2001, more than 1,700 exchanges were up and running, according to a study by Deloitte Consulting. As with many dot-com businesses that were based on shaky business models, many of these exchanges have either failed or been consolidated. But not ChemConnect. Today, the company is the leading online chemicals and plastics marketplace, with over 7,500 active members.

The key to success for ChemConnect has been its ability to provide value. Not only does the company help its customers save time and money, but it also offers a central marketplace in a fragmented industry. According to the American Chemical Council, over 89,000 companies around the world produce chemicals. ChemConnect, true to the nature of an effective online exchange, has allowed many of these companies to find suppliers for the raw materials they need or buyers for the products they sell that they would have never come into contact with otherwise.

ChemConnect was started by John Beasley and Jay Hall, an entrepreneur and a chemist, respectively. A third partner, Patrick van der Valk, an expert in the integration of Internet technology into the chemical industry, joined soon thereafter. Initially, the founders created a simple online bulletin board for the chemical industry. Based on the success of that service, they were able to raise $4 million in venture capital financing and took the company to the next level. Over the next couple of years, the founders worked long hours, moved the company to the Silicon Valley, added services, and established ChemConnect as a household name in the chemical industry. They were able to raise another $100 million in funding from industry players such as British Petroleum, Dow Chemical, Mitsubishi, and SAP. To add to its legitimacy, the company hired John Robison, an industry veteran, as its CEO. Prior to joining ChemConnect, Robinson was an executive with British Petroleum for 18 years. Robinson's experience and extensive network of professional contacts helped build the company beyond the start-up stage and lured customers who otherwise might have been skeptical of an Internet exchange as a venue for million-dollar deals.

Since ChemConnect was founded, the company has evolved to provide a full slate of products and services to its online customers, including the following:

- *Market information:* Up-to-the minute industry information is available in several formats, including an option to receive customized e-mail alerts for information pertaining to the products a customer sells and buys.

- *Commodity exchange:* A commodity exchange allows millions of metric tons of high-volume standardized commodity chemicals and plastics to be traded in real time.

- *Online auctions and reverse auctions:* These formats bring customers together in the same place at the same time to conduct private negotiations through the ChemConnect Trading Center.

- *Risk management:* Risk management solutions are provided to help customers minimize the effects of price volatility.
- *Fulfillment services:* ChemConnect provides a centralized hub for the electronic transfer of data among business partners after negotiations conclude.

ChemConnect is a model for successfully launching, growing, and maturing an online marketplace for specialty products.

Discussion Questions

1. One of the characteristics of successful entrepreneurial firms is execution intelligence. On a scale of 1 to 10 (with 10 being the highest), how would you rank ChemConnect in the area of execution intelligence? Justify your answer with examples from the case.

2. To what extent do you believe that ChemConnect has made itself important to other businesses? Do you think an entrepreneurial firm has a better chance of succeeding if its products or services are truly important to its customers? What is the definition of "value" in an entrepreneurial context? Do you think ChemConnect adds value for its customers? If so, in what ways?

3. What steps has ChemConnect taken to harness the power of the Internet to facilitate its business model? Explain your answer.

4. Many online marketplaces or business-to-business exchanges similar to ChemConnect have failed. Research the history of online marketplaces and provide a short explanation for why many of them have failed.

Sources: ChemConnect home page, www.chemconnect.com (accessed May 23, 2004), and R. Leuty, "Business to Business ChemConnect: Chemical Marketplace Getting a Reaction," San Francisco Business Times, October 23, 2000.

recognizing *opportunities* and generating ideas

OBJECTIVES

After studying this chapter, you should be ready to:

1. Explain the difference between an opportunity and an idea.

2. Describe the two general approaches entrepreneurs use to identify opportunities.

3. Explain why it's important to start a new firm when its "window of opportunity" is open.

4. Identify the four environmental trends that are most instrumental in creating business opportunities.

5. List the personal characteristics that make some people better at recognizing business opportunities than others.

6. Identify the five steps in the creative process.

7. Describe the purpose of brainstorming and its use as an idea generator.

8. Describe how surveys are used to generate new business ideas.

9. Explain the purpose of maintaining an idea bank.

10. Describe three steps for protecting ideas from being lost or stolen.

buyandhold.com: Filling a Void in the Online Investing Marketplace

When Geoffrey M. Tudisco graduated from college, he accepted a position with Shareholder Communication Corporation (SCC), a firm working with companies and their DRIP (Dividend ReInvestment Plan) programs. DRIP programs enable individuals to purchase stock directly from the company, with investments as low as $25. SCC offered a service called the Direct Purchase Plan Clearinghouse, which allowed investors to call and request enrollment materials for companies offering DRIP plans.

Soon after Tudisco was hired, SCC made an effort to offer the Clearinghouse's services over the Web through a partnership with a company called Netstockdirect.com. However, when Netstock redesigned its site, it removed all indications that Clearinghouse was a partner. Tudisco pointed this out to Peter Breen, his boss. Breen then gave Tudisco the green light to start working on a Web site for SCC. Built in only 30 days, Tudisco's first site made literature about DRIP plans available to investors over the Internet. What excited Tudisco, however, was the prospect of taking the site to the next level. He wanted to give DRIP investors the opportunity to enroll in the plan and purchase stock online.

Tudisco and Breen took the idea to their bosses, who simply weren't excited about their vision for what was being called a "buy and hold" type of brokerage service. (The idea behind the service was to make it easy for average people to **"buy"** small amounts of stock at a time and **"hold"** them to help secure their financial future.) Undeterred, Tudisco and Breen left SCC and started a new company, called BuyAndHold.com, to pursue their idea. "[SCC] failed to recognize that the Internet was revolutionizing the way business is done, and in turn failed to give us what we needed to make BuyAndHold.com a success,"[1] Tudisco later recalled. Peter Breen, who had a wealth of experience in the brokerage industry, became BuyAndHold.com's first chief executive officer (CEO).

Today, BuyAndHold.com is a vibrant online brokerage firm. Breen and Tudisco built the company quickly, thanks to Breen's experience, some smart hiring, the establishment of partnerships, and venture-capital backing. Today, investors can subscribe to the service for as little as $6.99 per month and make near real-time trades, with investments as low as $20 per trade. The company has a folksy appeal and has developed a strong rapport with its core customers. As evidence of this, on the Monday following the four-day halt in trading following the September 11, 2001, terrorist attacks, the buy-to-sell ratio was six to one in favor of buys, and the company, which is located near the World Trade Center, was swamped with e-mails asking if everyone was okay. The company interpreted the favorable buy-to-sell ratio as an act of patriotism on the part of their customers and the outpouring of support as an affirmation of the importance of the company to its customer's lives. "It was an awe-inspiring outpouring from customers," remarked CEO Breen.[2]

BuyAndHold.com didn't "just happen." Instead, it was built on the founders' recognition of an **opportunity gap**—which is a gap between what is currently on the market and the possibility for a new or significantly improved product, service, or business that results from emerging trends.

When Tudisco went to work for SCC in 1997, important economic, social, and technological changes were taking place in the United States that formed the seeds of an opportunity in the brokerage industry. The economy was strong and interest in the stock market growing, particularly among women, parents, and new investors. Society was changing. The rise in two-income families resulted in larger numbers of people having more money to invest, and a "do-it-yourself" mentality was becoming increasingly prevalent, suggesting that new investors might not require the same level of face-to-face support as traditional ones. Finally, the Internet was making it possible to move brokerage services online, dramatically reducing costs. E*Trade pioneered online brokerage services in the mid-1990s, with an astonishingly low flat commission of $14.95 per trade. E*Trade wasn't focused on the new types of investors, however; it targeted the customers of traditional brokers such as Merrill Lynch and Charles Schwab, which at the time were still charging commission rates of $60 per trade.

These events suggested that what was needed but wasn't available was a brokerage company that would (1) focus on women, parents, and new investors; (2) allow customers to invest a small amount of money at a time; and (3) make the service available online at a low cost. BuyAndHold.com filled this need.

Identifying and Recognizing Opportunities

Essentially, entrepreneurs recognize an opportunity and turn it into a successful business. An **opportunity** is a favorable set of circumstances that creates a need for a new product, service, or business. Most entrepreneurial firms are started in one of two ways. Some firms are externally stimulated. An entrepreneur decides to launch a firm, searches for and recognizes an opportunity, and then starts a business, as Jeff Bezos did when he created Amazon.com. In 1994, Bezos quit his lucrative job at a New York City investment firm and headed for Seattle with a plan to find an attractive opportunity and launch an e-commerce company.[3] Other firms are internally stimulated. An entrepreneur recognizes a problem or an opportunity gap and creates a business to fill it. This was the case with BuyAndHold.com.

Regardless of which of these two ways an entrepreneur starts a new business, opportunities are tough to spot. It is difficult to identify a product, service, or business opportunity that isn't merely a different version of something already available. Opportunity recognition is part art, part science. An entrepreneur must rely on instinct, which makes it an art, and on purposeful action and analytical techniques, which makes it a science.

An opportunity has four essential qualities: it is (1) attractive, (2) durable, (3) timely, and (4) anchored in a product, service, or business that creates or adds value for its buyer or end user.[4] For an entrepreneur to capitalize on an opportunity, its **window of opportunity** must be open.[5] The term "window of opportunity" is a metaphor describing the time period in which a firm can realistically enter a new market. Once the market for a new product is established, its window of opportunity opens. As the market grows, firms enter and try to establish a profitable position. At some point, the market matures, and the window of opportunity closes. This is the case with Internet search engines. Yahoo!, the first search engine, appeared in 1995, and the market grew quickly, with the addition of Lycos, Excite, AltaVista, and others. Google entered the market in 1998, sporting advanced search technology. Since then, the search engine market has matured, and the window of opportunity has essentially closed. Today, it would be very difficult for a new start-up search engine firm to be successful unless it was extraordinarily well funded and offered compelling advantages over already established competitors.

It is important to understand that there is a difference between an opportunity and an idea. An **idea** is a thought, impression, or notion.[6] It may or may not meet the criteria of an opportunity. This is a critical point because, as we noted in Chapter 1, many businesses fail

learning **objective**

1. Explain the difference between an opportunity and an idea.

what went **wrong?**

Online Postage: An Idea Instead of an Opportunity

If a seemingly attractive new product or service idea turns out to be more trouble than good for its customers, it's almost sure to fail. The story of two Internet companies trying to sell stamps online provides a vivid example of the importance of one of the four qualities of an attractive opportunity; namely, the opportunity must be anchored in a product or service that adds value for its buyer or end user.

Until recently, buying stamps was a chore for small businesses and for people who work from their homes. Because of the cost, most small firms don't have postal meters, which are devices that store prepaid postage. So the only choice for most of these businesspeople had been to stand in line at the post office.

Then, the Internet came along, and two start-ups, E-Stamps and Stamps.com, offered a solution to the problem. The companies, with the U.S. Postal Service's blessing, rolled out services that allowed customers to purchase stamps over the Internet and print them out from their PCs. The media was captivated. "Now there's a new way to go postal," exclaimed ABC News. Investors were equally enthralled. Collectively, the two companies raised more than half a billion dollars from investors and through initial public offerings.

But regrettably, both E-Stamps and Stamps.com fell flat. One of the most important reasons for their failure is that their service didn't deliver sufficient "value" to attract the interest of enough paying customers. In fact, for many businesses, the service turned out to be more trouble than benefit. Here's why.

First, although the idea of avoiding trips to the post office sounded good, there was no price break for buying postage online. In fact, in most cases, it cost more to buy postage online because of the service fee charged by the online providers. Both E-Stamps and Stamps.com lobbied the Postal Service to allow them to offer their customers stamps at

a discount. Their argument was that online postage relieves congestion at post offices and makes the mail easier to sort. But the Postal Service didn't agree. Second, downloading postage turned out to be a hassle, largely because of security provisions required by the Postal Service. A downloaded stamp doesn't look like an actual stamp. Instead, it is a tamper-proof bar code that is affixed to a letter in place of a regular stamp. To download stamps, a customer had to jump through several hoops, making the process somewhat awkward. Finally, other complications made the service cumbersome, at least initially. For example, in some instances, businesses had to buy special hardware to attach to the computer that stored the downloaded postage.

As this story shows, the services offered by E-Stamps and Stamps.com failed one of the key tests of an opportunity: the idea wasn't anchored in a product or service that created enough value for its buyers to represent a legitimate opportunity.

Questions for Critical Thinking

1. From an entrepreneurial perspective, does the initial idea to delivery stamps via the Internet make sense? Are you surprised that entrepreneurs weren't able to convert this idea into an opportunity? Why or why not?

2. What should the entrepreneurs in their respective companies have tried to do to gain the cooperation of the U.S. Postal Service? Do these firms' experiences suggest tough times for entrepreneurs needing to work with government agencies to successfully launch and operate their ventures?

Source: J. Bailey, "Tepid Response Routs Two Postage Pioneers," Wall Street Journal, www.startupjournal.com (accessed October 20, 2003).

not because the entrepreneurs that started them didn't work hard but rather because there was no real opportunity to begin with. Before getting excited about a business idea, it is crucial to understand whether the idea fills a need and meets the criteria for an opportunity. When it doesn't, it can lead to a disappointing outcome, as illustrated in the boxed feature titled "What Went Wrong?"

Now let's look at the two ways to identify an opportunity.

Observing Trends

learning **objective**

2. Describe the two general approaches entrepreneurs use to identify opportunities.

learning **objective**

3. Explain why it's important to start a new firm when its "window of opportunity" is open.

The first approach to identifying opportunities is to observe trends and study how they create opportunities for entrepreneurs to pursue. Economic factors, social factors, technological advances, and political action and regulatory changes are the most important trends to follow. There are two ways entrepreneurs can get a handle on these trends. First, they can carefully study and observe them. Some entrepreneurs are better at this than others, depending on their personal characteristics and levels of motivation. Entrepreneurs who have industry experience, who have a well-established social network, who are creative, and who are, in general, alert are more likely to spot trends and interpret them correctly.[7] The second way entrepreneurs understand emerging trends is to purchase customized forecasts and market analyses from independent research firms. These tools allow for a fuller understanding of how specific trends create opportunities. Forrester Research, Gartner Group, and Yankee Group are some of the research firms that produce these reports, as illustrated in the boxed feature "Savvy Entrepreneurial Firm."

Savvy entrepreneurial FIRM

Getting High-Quality Advice on Emerging Trends

Savvy entrepreneurs realize they don't have the time and resources to know everything about emerging trends. This is particularly true of the entrepreneurs in the area of technology, where changes occur daily. So how do entrepreneurs keep up with the latest developments in their industry? Entrepreneurial firms can take advantage of the services offered by professional research firms, such as Forrester Research, Gartner, and Yankee Group. These companies provide conventional consulting services but also provide a variety of other products and services that may be more affordable to young entrepreneurial firms. For example, Forrester Research, which specializes in the area of emerging technologies, offers the following:

- Annual memberships that provide access to research on specific business and technology topics

- Advisory services similar to consulting services

- One- and two-day conferences on technology related topics

- Interactive assessment tools that help businesses make technology-related decisions

Other companies (e.g., Gartner) offer publications on emerging trends that can be downloaded from the Internet.

The research is cutting edge and may give a firm important insight that it never would have generated internally.

For entrepreneurial firms, an added benefit of using the services of consulting companies is getting an outside perspective on their current and potential operations. Prudent firms know that their time and field of vision is limited and that investing in a fresh perspective on business trends and developments can often be money well spent.

Questions for Critical Thinking

1. What disadvantages might an entrepreneurial firm experience by relying on outside firms as the basis for understanding emerging trends? Are some of these disadvantages more relevant in the short term while others are more relevant for the long term?

2. Is it possible for aspiring entrepreneurs to become overwhelmed by the rapid pace of environmental changes? What advice would you offer to the person believing that change is too difficult to predict and understand?

Sources: Forrester Research home page, www.forrester.com (accessed June 1, 2004); Gartner home page, www.gartner.com (accessed June 1, 2004).

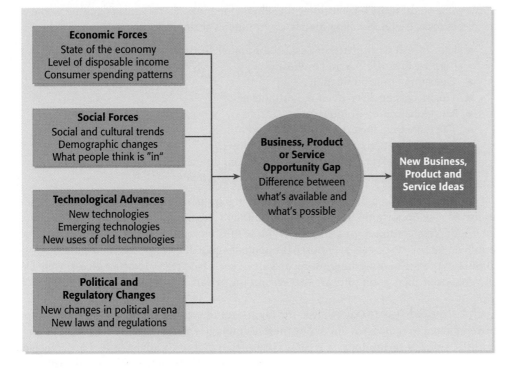

Figure 2.1 provides a summary of the relationship between the environmental factors mentioned previously and identifying opportunity gaps. Next, let's look at how each of these factors helps entrepreneurs spot product opportunity gaps.

Economic Forces   Economic forces affect consumers' level of disposable income. When incomes are high, people are more willing to buy products and services that enhance their lives. Individual sectors of the economy have a direct impact on consumer buying patterns. For example, a drop in interest rates typically leads to an increase in new home construction and furniture sales. Conversely, a rapid decline in the stock market, such as the one in the late 1990s and early 2000s, may lead to a reduction in the demand for luxury goods.

When studying how economic forces affect opportunities, it is important to evaluate who has money to spend. For example, an increase in the number of women in the workforce and their related increase in disposable income was one of the factors that led the founders of BuyAndHold.com to target women as one of their potential customers. Similarly, as more teens enter the workforce, demand increases for products they buy, such as designer clothing, compact discs, and concert tickets. Companies such as CD Warehouse, for example, which expanded from one store to more than 280 in just over 10 years, grew so rapidly because teenagers had increasing levels of cash to spend during the same period.

Another trend that is affected by economic factors is pressure on firms to improve their economic performance. In a recent PricewaterhouseCoopers survey of fast-growth firms, which are companies identified in the media as the fastest-growing U.S. businesses over the past five years, 74 percent reported that cost control is one of their top priorities.[8] Many entrepreneurs have taken advantage of this trend by starting firms that help other firms control costs. In the chemical industry, for example, ChemConnect provides an online marketplace to make it less expensive for chemical companies to buy and sell chemicals on a global scale.[9]

Social Forces   An understanding of the impact of social forces on trends and how they affect new product, service, and business ideas is a fundamental piece of the opportunity recognition puzzle. The persistent proliferation of fast-food restaurants, for example, isn't due primarily to people's love of fast food but rather to the fact that people are busy: the number of households with both parents working remains high. Similarly, the Sony Walkman was developed not because consumers wanted smaller radios but because people wanted to listen to

learning objective

4. Identify the four environmental trends that are most instrumental in creating business opportunities.

music while on the move—while riding the subway, for example, and while exercising. Some of the recent social trends that allow for new opportunities are the following:

- Family and work patterns (e.g., the number of two-income households and the number of single-parent families)
- The aging of the population
- The increasing diversity in the workplace
- The globalization of industry
- The increasing focus on health care and fitness
- The proliferation of computers and the Internet
- The continual increase in the number of cell phone users
- New forms of music and other types of entertainment

There is an ebb and flow pertaining to how much each of these trends affects the availability of new opportunities. For example, although the number of households that have Internet access continues to grow, the window of opportunity to launch a new Internet search engine, as discussed previously, is essentially closed. Conversely, substantial opportunities may exist in other Internet-related areas, such as wireless Internet access, Web TV, and enhanced encryption software that secures the privacy of computer networks.

Technological Advances   Given the rapid pace of technological change, it is vital for entrepreneurs to remain on top of how new technologies affect current and future opportunities. Once a technology is created, products emerge to advance it. For example, RealNetworks was created to add video capabilities to the Internet, which took the Internet to the next level. The following quote from RealNetwork's Web site explains the impact that it is having on Internet users.

> In 1995, RealNetworks pioneered the entire Internet media industry, and continues to fuel its exponential growth. Because the Internet was built to handle text-based information, not audio and video and other rich media, Real Networks foresaw the need for specific solutions that could handle the creation, delivery and consumption of media via the Internet. Today, hundreds of millions of unique individuals throughout the world take advantage of RealNetworks world-class media creation, delivery, and playback technology.[10]

Advances in technology frequently dovetail with economic and social changes to create opportunities. For example, the creation of the cell phone is a technological achievement, but it was motivated by an increasingly mobile population that found many advantages to having the ability to communicate with its coworkers, customers, friends, and families from anywhere. Similarly, many e-commerce sites are technological marvels, allowing a customer to order products, pay for them, and choose how quickly they're shipped. But again, it isn't so much the technology that makes e-commerce so attractive. The ultimate reason most people buy online is because they are busy and prefer to shop when they have free time rather than being restricted to traditional store hours.

Political Action and Regulatory Changes   Political and regulatory changes also provide the basis for opportunities. For example, new laws create opportunities for entrepreneurs to start firms to help companies comply with these laws. RMS Systems, for example, designed a product called Compliance Suite, which helps its customers track their compliance with Environmental Protection Agency and Occupational Safety and Health Administration regulations. Another example is CHH Incorporated. Although CHH has been in business since 1913, it has remained innovative and now features a software product called SEC Compliance Desktop, which enables firms to be sure that their stock option plans and employee stock purchase programs comply with Security and Exchange Commission regulations.

Political change also engenders new business and product opportunities. For example, global political instability and the threat of terrorism have resulted in many firms becoming more security conscious. These companies need new products and services to protect their physical assets and intellectual property as well as protect their customers and employees. The backup data storage industry, for example, is expanding because of this

new trend in that firms now feel the need for their data to be more protected than in the past. Companies such as Protect-Data.com and EMC provide data storage services that allow companies to back up their computer data in a secure offsite location.

Table 2.1 offers additional examples of changes in environmental trends that provided fertile soil for opportunities and subsequent concepts to take advantage of them.

Solving a Problem

Sometimes identifying opportunities simply involves noticing a problem and finding a way to solve it. These problems can be pinpointed through observing trends and through more simple means, such as intuition, serendipity, or chance.[11] There are many problems that have yet to be solved. Commenting on this issue and how noticing problems can lead to the recognition of business ideas, Philip Kotler, a marketing expert, said,

> Look for problems. People complain about it being hard to sleep through the night, get rid of clutter in their homes, find an affordable vacation, trace their family origins, get rid of garden weeds, and so on. As the late John Gardner, founder of Common Cause, observed: "Every problem is a brilliantly disguised opportunity."[12]

Some business ideas are clearly gleaned from the recognition of problems in emerging trends. For example, Symantec Corporation created Norton antivirus software to rid computers of viruses, and computer firewall firms such as McAfee develop software to secure computer systems and guard them against attack from hackers or unauthorized users. These companies took advantage of the problems that surface when new technology is introduced.

At other times, the process is less deliberate. An individual may set out to solve a practical problem and realize that the solution may have broader market appeal. The most romantic example of this is the founding of Cisco Systems:

> The Cisco legend is the tale of two inhibited sweethearts at Stanford University in the late 1970s. Sandra Lerner of the Stanford University Business School and

Changing Environmental Trend	Resulting New Business, Product and Service Opportunities	Companies that Resulted
Economic Trends		
Teenagers with more cash and disposal income	Designer cloths, compact discs, DVD players, games consoles, handheld computers	GAP, Banana Republic, MTV, Sega, Palm
Increased interest in the stock market	Online brokerage services, stock research services, magazines for investors	BuyAndHold.com, Motley Fool, The Street.com, *Red Herring* magazine
Social Trends		
Increasing predominance of dual-income families leaves less time to cook at home	Restaurants, microwavable dinners, food delivery services	McDonald's, Kentucky Fried Chicken, Olive Garden, Healthy Choice Frozen Dinners, Domino's Pizza
Increased interest in fitness, as the result of new medical information warning of the hazards of being overweight	Fitness centers, in-house exercise equipment, weight-loss-centers, health food stores	Curves International, Stair Master Fitness Equipment, GNC Nutrition Center, Whole Foods Market
Increased mobility of the population, as the result of better transportation and increased disposable income	Cell phones, laptop computers, handheld computers, phone cards	Nokia, Palm, Handspring, Research In Motion
Technological Trends		
Development of the Internet	E-commerce, improved supply chain management, improved communications	Yahoo, Amazon.com, America Online, ChemConnect, AutoDirect, Eudora
Advances in biotechnology	Biotech-related pharmaceutical products, food products, veterinary products, information services	Genetech, Amgen, Genzyme, BioInform, Bio Online
Political and Regulatory Trends		
Increased EPA and OSHA standards	Consulting companies, software to monitor compliance, products to help ensure compliance	RMS Systems, PrimaTech, Compliance Consulting Services, Inc.

Leonard Bosack of the computer science department wanted to send love letters to each other via e-mail, but their respective departments used different computer networks. So Len and Sandy, impassioned and determined, invented the router—a mysterious black box consisting of a twist of cable and some agile software. Then they conceived Cisco (which is the last syllable in San Francisco, the city near where they lived). The router made Cisco the fastest growing company ever. In 2004, 20 years after its founding, Cisco was worth $162 billion.[13]

At still other times, someone may simply notice a problem that others are having and think that the solution might represent an opportunity. Often, however, when you get the whole story, it turns out that the discovery wasn't quite so unanticipated. A **serendipitous discovery** is a chance discovery made by someone with a prepared mind.[14]

Newgistics, an entrepreneurial firm specializing in helping consumers return merchandise they order online and through catalogs, is a good example of the serendipity that sometimes surrounds the launching of a new business. The firm was started by Phil Siegel, who had worked at Boston Consulting Group for a decade, where he had acquired a thorough understanding of consumer and retail businesses. Rod Adams, the venture capitalist who provided the early funding for the firm, tells of the auspicious conversation that led to the founding of Newgistics:

> Phil's idea for Newgistics grew out of a conversation with his wife, Lauren, a dedicated Internet and catalog shopper who relished the convenience of online buying. She'd just ordered a blouse from a well-known Internet retailer, and it didn't fit. Now, she'd have to e-mail the site, pack and ship the blouse, and wait until the merchant received it before getting credit toward another order. Why, Lauren lamented, did returning or exchanging these goods have to be so inconvenient? Why wasn't there a way to do it as easily as with a bricks-and-mortar retailer? Phil had a hunch that millions of online and catalog shoppers would second her concern. He resolved to start a company that would streamline the complex product return process,—not just for the end consumer but for online and catalog retail merchants as well.[15]

Newgistics offers Return Valet, a returns service that provides catalog and online shopping customers a physical location to hand off returns and get instant credit for their purchases. Among the first retailers to sign up for the service were Eddie Bauer, Spiegel, and J. Crew.

Newgistics received funding primarily because the company solves a specific problem. Many other colorful examples of people who launched businesses to solve problems are shown in Table 2.2.

Personal Characteristics of the Entrepreneur

learning **objective**

5. List the personal characteristics that make some people better at recognizing business opportunities than others.

How did Michael Dell come up with the idea of a "build it yourself" computer company? How did Charles Schultz, the founder of Starbucks, figure out how to turn a 50-cent cup of coffee and a little skimmed milk into a $3 plus cappuccino?

Researchers have identified several characteristics that tend to make some people better at recognizing opportunities than others. Before we talk about them, there is an important yet subtle difference between two key terms pertaining to this topic. We've already defined opportunity: a favorable set of circumstances that create the need for a new product, service, or business. But, the term **opportunity recognition** refers to the process of *perceiving* the possibility of a profitable new business or a new product or service. That is,

Table 2.2 Businesses Created to Solve a Problem

Entrepreneur(s)	Year	Problem	Solution	Name of Business That Resulted
Rob Glaser	1995	No way to play audio and video on the Internet	Developed software to play audio and video on the "Net"	RealNetworks
Jerry Yang and David Filo	1994	No method to find or organize favorite Web sites	Created online directories to find and store favorites	Yahoo!
Scott Cook	1982	Frustration over traditional process of paying bills and keeping track of personal finances	Developed a software program (Quicken) to make the task easier	Intuit
Anthony Desio	1980	Impatience with U.S. Postal Service's long lines, short hours, and limited services	Started a company to provide an alternative to the post ofice	Mail Boxes Etc.
Anita Roddick	1976	Unable to find small amounts of cream or lotion to sample before buying a larger bottle	Started a company to, in part, provide smaller quantities of bath and body products	The Body Shop
Fred Smith	1973	Inability to get spare parts delivered on a timely basis for his company, a jet-aircraft sales firm	Started a new company to help others get packages delivered in a timely manner	Federal Express

an opportunity cannot be taken until it's *recognized*. Now let's look at some specific characteristics shared by those who excel at recognizing opportunity.

Prior Experience Several studies show that prior experience in an industry helps entrepreneurs recognize business opportunities.[16] For example, a 1989 report of the Inc. 500 founders revealed that 43 percent of those studied got the idea for their new businesses while working for companies in the same industries.[17] This finding is consistent with research conducted by the National Federation of Independent Businesses.[18] There are several explanations. By working in an industry, an individual may spot a market niche that is underserved. This was the case in the BuyAndHold.com example, where founder Geoffrey M. Tudisco felt that there wasn't an attractive brokerage service that targeted women, parents, and new investors. It is also possible that while working in an industry, an individual builds a network of social contacts in that industry who may provide insights that lead to opportunities.

Once an entrepreneur starts a firm, new venture opportunities become apparent. This is called the **corridor principle**, which states that once an entrepreneur starts a firm, he or she begins a journey down a path where "corridors" leading to new venture opportunities become apparent.[19] The insight provided by this principle is simply that once someone starts a firm and becomes immersed in an industry, it's much easier for that person to see new opportunities in the industry than it is for someone looking in from the outside.

Cognitive Factors Opportunity recognition may be an innate skill or a cognitive process.[20] There are some who think that entrepreneurs have a "sixth sense" that allows them to see opportunities that others miss. This sixth sense is called **entrepreneurial alertness**, which is formally defined as the ability to notice things without engaging in deliberate search.[21] Most entrepreneurs see themselves in this light, believing they are more "alert" than others.[22] Alertness is largely a learned skill, and people who have more knowledge of an area tend to be more alert to opportunities in that area than others. A computer engineer, for example, would be more alert to needs and opportunities within the computer industry than a lawyer would be.

The research findings on entrepreneurial alertness are mixed. Some researchers conclude that alertness goes beyond noticing things and involves a more purposeful effort.[23]

Google's founders, Larry Page and Sergey Brin, are true entrepreneurs. Why? Because they identified a problem and solved it. Frustrated with what existing search engines such as Yahoo! and Lycos had to offer, these two Stanford University students created a new and improved search engine. In fact, today Google is known for its speed, reliability, and ease of use. Google is now a publicly owned company listed on the NASDAQ.

For example, one scholar believes that the crucial difference between opportunity finders (i.e., entrepreneurs) and nonfinders is their relative assessments of the marketplace.[24] In other words, entrepreneurs may be better than others at sizing up the marketplace and inferring the likely implications.

Social Networks   The extent and depth of an individual's social network affects opportunity recognition.[25] People who build a substantial network of social and professional contacts will be exposed to more opportunities and ideas than people with sparse networks.[26] This exposure can lead to new business starts.[27] In a survey of 65 start-ups, half the founders reported that they got their business ideas through social contacts.[28] A similar study examined the differences between **solo entrepreneurs** (those who identified their business ideas on their own) and **network entrepreneurs** (those who identified their ideas through social contacts). The researchers found that network entrepreneurs identified significantly more opportunities than solo entrepreneurs but were less likely to describe themselves as being particularly alert or creative.[29]

An important concept that sheds light on the importance of social networks to opportunity recognition is the differential impact of strong-tie versus weak-tie relationships. All of us have relationships with other people that are called "ties." **Strong-tie relationships** are characterized by frequent interaction and form between coworkers, friends, and spouses. **Weak-tie relationships** are characterized by infrequent interaction and form between casual acquaintances. According to research in this area, it is more likely that an entrepreneur will get a new business idea through a weak-tie than a strong-tie relationship[30] because strong-tie relationships, which typically form between like-minded individuals, tend to reinforce insights and ideas the individuals already have. Weak-tie relationships, on the other hand, which form between casual acquaintances, are not as apt to be between like-minded individuals, so one person may say something to another that sparks a completely new idea.[31] An example might be an electrician explaining to a restaurant owner how he solved a business problem. After hearing the solution, the restaurant owner might say, "I would never have heard that solution from someone in my company or industry. That insight is completely new to me and just might help me solve my problem."

One way that entrepreneurs network with one another is through membership in industry trades associations, as illustrated in the boxed feature "Partnering for Success."

Creativity   **Creativity** is the process of generating a novel or useful idea. Opportunity recognition may be, at least in part, a creative process.[32] For example, Long and McMullen described opportunity recognition as a process involving iterations of creative thinking.[33] On a more anecdotal basis, it is easy to see the creativity involved in the formation of many products, services, and businesses.

For an individual, the creative process can be broken into five stages, as shown in Figure 2.2.[34] Let's examine how these stages relate to the opportunity recognition process.[35] In the figure, the horizontal arrows that point from box to box suggest that the creative process progresses through five stages. The vertical arrows suggest that if at any stage an individual gets "stuck" or doesn't have enough information or insight to continue, the best choice is to return to the preparation stage—to obtain more knowledge or experience before continuing to move forward.

learning **objective**

6. Identify the five steps in the creative process.

Preparation. Preparation is the background, experience, and knowledge that an entrepreneur brings to the opportunity recognition process. Just as an athlete must practice to excel, an entrepreneur needs experience to spot opportunities. Studies show that 50 to 90 percent of start-up ideas emerge from a person's prior work experience.[36]

Incubation. Incubation is the stage during which a person considers an idea or thinks about a problem; it is the "mulling things over" phase. Sometimes incubation is a conscious activity, and sometimes it is unconscious and occurs while a person is engaged in another activity. One writer characterized this phenomenon by saying that "ideas churn around below the threshold of consciousness."[37]

Insight. Insight is the flash of recognition—when the solution to a problem is seen or an idea is born. It is sometimes called the "eureka" experience. In a business context,

Figure 2.2

Five-Steps to Generating Creative Ideas

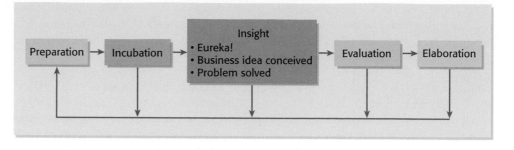

this is the moment an entrepreneur recognizes an opportunity. Sometimes this experience pushes the process forward, and sometimes it prompts an individual to return to the preparation stage. For example, an entrepreneur may recognize the potential for an opportunity but may feel that more knowledge and thought is required before pursuing it.

Evaluation. Evaluation is the stage of the creative process during which an idea is subjected to scrutiny and analyzed for its viability. Many entrepreneurs mistakenly skip this step and try to implement an idea before they've made sure it is viable. Evaluation is a particularly challenging stage of the creative process because it requires an entrepreneur to take a candid look at the viability of an idea.[38] The process of evaluating the feasibility of new business ideas is discussed in Chapter 3.

Elaboration. Elaboration is the stage during which the creative idea is put into a final form: the details are worked out, and the idea is transformed into something of value, such as a new product, service, or business concept. In the case of a new business, this is the point at which a business plan is written.

Figure 2.3 illustrates the opportunity recognition process. As shown in the figure, there is a connection between an awareness of emerging trends and the personal characteristics of the entrepreneur because the two facets of opportunity recognition are interdependent. For example, an entrepreneur with a well-established social network may be in a better position to recognize emerging technological trends than an entrepreneur with a poorly established social network. Or the awareness of an emerging technology trend, such as digitization, may prompt an entrepreneur to attend conferences or workshops to learn more about the topic, expanding her social network.

Figure 2.3

The Opportunity Recognition Process

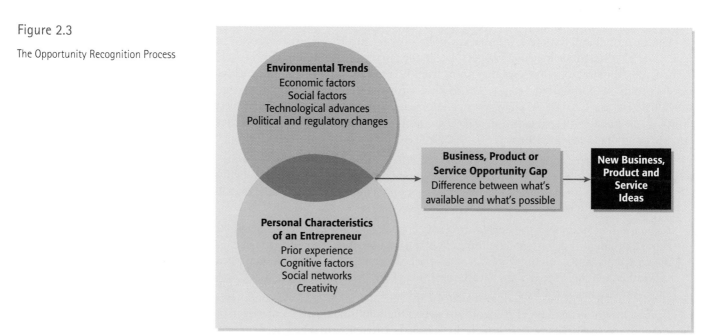

Partnering for SUCCESS

Networking: The Importance of Industry Trade Associations

Trade associations are typically nonprofit organizations formed by firms in the same industry to collect and disseminate information, offer legal and technical advice, furnish industry-related training, and provide a forum for the people in the industry to network and discuss industry-related issues. Many trade associations organize annual meetings and trade shows. For example, the Internet Society (ISOC) is a professional trade association with more than 150 companies and 16,000 individual members. Members of the association meet in local chapters and come together once a year for an annual conference to discuss issues related to the Internet. The Electronic Industries Alliance, which has over 2,300 members from all fields of electronics, is another example. The association hosts an annual "legislative roundtable" to provide its members an opportunity to discuss current and pending legislation pertinent to the electronics industry.

For many people, the biggest advantage to belonging to a trade association is the opportunity to network with industry peers. This is one reason busy CEOs and entrepreneurs are willing to donate their time to serve on the board of directors of their respective associations. Serving on the board or on an association committee gives them the opportunity to exchange ideas with their peers.

Recognizing the benefits of networking, some associations have even created online forums. For example, the American Booksellers Association (which restricts its membership to independent bookstores, thus eliminating the potential divergent interests of bookstore chains like Borders and Barnes & Noble), hosts an online forum on its Web site

called Idea Exchange. This is a password-protected portion of the Web site that is set up in a bulletin board format and allows members to ask each other questions and share information. Another example is the Smart Card Alliance, which is the global trade association for the smart card industry. A smart card is a plastic card about the size of a credit card with an embedded microchip that can be loaded with data. This association provides its members a password-protected online discussion forum that facilitates an ongoing, free-flowing discussion of the smart card industry.

Questions for Critical Thinking

1. As an entrepreneur, what would you do to establish more weak-tie relationships?

2. Does an entrepreneurial firm accept any risks as a member of a trade association? Are there risks, for example, associated with the decision to share information with other trade association members about how you as an entrepreneur compete? If so, name some examples of those risks.

Sources: B. R. Barringer and J. S. Harrison, "Walking a Tightrope: Creating Value through Interorganizational Relationships," Journal of Management 26, no. 3 (2000): 367–403; Internet Society home page, www.isoc.org (accessed June 1, 2002); Electronic Industries Alliance home page, www.eia.org (accessed June 1, 2004); American Booksellers Association home page, www.bookweb.com (accessed June 1, 2004); and Smart Card Alliance home page, www.scia.org (accessed June 1, 2004).

Techniques for Generating Ideas

In general, entrepreneurs identify more ideas than opportunities[39] because many ideas are typically generated to find the best way to capitalize on an opportunity. Several techniques can be used to stimulate and facilitate the generation of new ideas for products, services, and businesses. Let's take a look at some of them.

Brainstorming

Brainstorming is used to generate a number of ideas quickly. It is not used for analysis or decision making—the ideas generated during a brainstorming session need to be filtered and analyzed, but this is done later.

A brainstorming "session" is targeted to a specific topic about which a group of people are instructed to come up with ideas. The leader of the group asks the participants to share their ideas. One person shares an idea, another person reacts to it, another person reacts to the reaction, and so on. A flip chart is typically used to record all the ideas.

learning **objective**

7. Describe the purpose of brainstorming and its use as an idea generator.

Brainstorming sessions may target a specific topic and should be casual, freewheeling, and lively. The main objective is to create an atmosphere of enthusiasm where many ideas can be generated. The results of a brainstorming session may be an inspiration for an innovative new product or even a vision for a new company.

A productive session is freewheeling and lively. The main objective is to create an atmosphere of enthusiasm and originality where lots of ideas are generated.[40] However, there are four strict rules for conducting brainstorming sessions. If they are not adhered to, it is unlikely that the participants will feel comfortable openly sharing ideas:

- No criticism is allowed, including chuckles, raised eyebrows, or facial expressions that express skepticism or doubt. Criticism stymies creativity and inhibits the free flow of ideas.
- Freewheeling, which is the carefree expression of ideas free of rules or restraints, is encouraged; the more ideas, the better. Even crazy or outlandish ideas may lead to a good idea or a solution to a problem.
- The session moves quickly, and nothing is permitted to slow down its pace. For example, it is more important to capture the essence of an idea than to take the time to write it down neatly.
- Leapfrogging is encouraged. This means using one idea as a means of jumping forward quickly to other ideas. (The word "leapfrogging" comes from the child's game of Leapfrog, in which one player kneels over while the next in line leaps over him or her.)

There are two reasons brainstorming generates ideas that might not arise otherwise. First, because no criticism is allowed, people are more likely to offer ideas than they would in a traditional setting. Criticism is the act of passing judgment and typically stems from intolerance. For example, the manager of a retail store may be skeptical of the Internet. In a normal meeting, he might criticize any suggestion regarding its use. But if the store held a brainstorming session focused on ways to improve customer service, ideas about ways to use the Internet may surface and be discussed. Of course, an employee may be reluctant to suggest an idea that is directly counter to a known position of the boss even though no criticism in the brainstorming session is permitted. To avoid this complication, some firms conduct electronic brainstorming sessions that are supported by **group support system (or GSS) software**, which allows participants to submit ideas anonymously.

Second, brainstorming sessions can generate more ideas than a traditional meeting because brainstorming focuses on creativity rather than evaluation. Think about a typical meeting. One person suggests an idea, and immediately the rest of the group begins to evaluate it. This happens because most people are better at criticizing ideas than they are at suggesting new ones. The sole purpose of a brainstorming session is to generate ideas, with no evaluation permitted. So if a two-hour brainstorming session is held, the group will spend two hours generating ideas, which almost never happens outside a brainstorming context.[41]

Most brainstorming sessions involve the employees of an organization, but Kodak, for example, hosts pizza-video parties where groups of customers meet with the company's technical people to discuss problems and needs and to brainstorm potential solutions. Similarly, some companies make brief brainstorming sessions a routine part of facility tours.[42]

Focus Groups

A **focus group** is a gathering of 5 to 10 people who are selected because of their relationship to the issue being discussed. Although focus groups are used for a variety of purposes, they can be used to help generate new business ideas.

The strength of focus groups is that they help companies uncover what's on their customers' minds through the give-and-take nature of a group discussion.[43] The weakness is that because the participants do not represent a random sample, the results cannot be generalized to larger groups. Usually, focus groups are conducted by trained moderators. The moderator's primary goals are to keep the group "focused" and to generate lively discussion. It is also important that the moderator fully understand the underlying objectives of the study. Much of the effectiveness of a focus group session depends on the moderator's ability to ask questions and keep the discussion on track.

For example, a coffee shop, such as Starbucks, might conduct a focus group consisting of 7 to 10 frequent customers and ask the group, "What is it that you *don't* like about our coffee shop?" A customer may say, "You sell one-pound bags of your specialty ground coffees for people to brew at home. That's okay, but I often run out of the coffee in just a few days. Sometimes it's a week before I get back to the shop to buy another bag. If you sold three-pound or five-pound bags, I'd actually use more coffee because I wouldn't run out so often. I guess I could buy two or three one-pound bags at the same time, but that gets a little pricey. I'd buy a three- or five-pound bag, however, if you'd discount your price a little for larger quantities." The moderator may then ask the group, "How many people here would buy three-pound or five-pound bags of our coffee if they were available?" If five hands shoot up, the coffee shop may have just uncovered an idea for a new product line.

Surveys

A **survey** is a method of gathering information from a sample of individuals. The sample is usually just a fraction of the population being studied. Surveys can be conducted over the telephone, by mail, online, or in person. The most effective surveys sample a "random" portion of the population, meaning that the sample is not selected haphazardly or only from people who volunteer to participate. Instead, the sample is chosen in a way that ensures that everyone in the population has an equal chance of being chosen, making the results of the survey generalizable to the larger population.

Surveys are taken in a standardized way so that every participant is asked the same questions in the same manner. The intention of a survey is not to describe the experiences or opinions of a particular individual but rather to obtain a composite profile of the entire population. The quality of survey data is determined largely by the purpose of the survey and how it is conducted. For example, most call-in television surveys or magazine write-in polls are highly suspect because the participants represent what's called a **self-selected opinion poll**. Most people who take the time to participate in a self-selected opinion poll do so because they have either strong positive or strong negative feelings about a particular product or topic.[44]

Surveys generate new product, service, and business ideas because they ask specific questions and get specific answers. For example, a company such as palmOne might administer a survey to a randomly selected sample of owners of Palm Pilots and ask the participants which of the following enhancements they would pay extra for if they were

learning **objective**

8. Describe how surveys are used to generate new business ideas.

added to Palm Pilots: voice capabilities (e.g., a cell phone), text messaging, Internet access, paging, GPS capability, and so on. The survey might also ask how much extra the participants would be willing to pay for each enhancement and how likely it is that they would buy an enhanced product. Some surveys also include open-ended questions to provide the participants an opportunity to add information. For example, at the end of the survey, palmOne might ask, "Is there any other product that our company might be uniquely capable of providing that we currently don't provide?" Although the answers to this question won't represent a scientific sample, they sometimes produce interesting leads to new product or service ideas.

Other Techniques

Firms use a variety of other techniques to generate ideas. Some companies set up **customer advisory boards** that meet regularly to discuss needs, wants, and problems that may lead to new ideas.[45] Some of these advisory boards are conducted online to make it easier for the participants to meet. Other companies conduct varying forms of anthropological research, such as **day-in-the-life research**. A company that practices a variation of this technique is Chaparral Steel, which is an entrepreneurial-minded steel minimill. To make sure its customers are satisfied and to probe for new product ideas, the company routinely sends employees to the facilities of their customers.[46]

Some companies attend trade shows, conferences, and gatherings of industry personnel and approach them as intelligence missions to learn what their competition is doing and then use the information to stimulate new product and service ideas. Another technique for generating ideas is to set up an idea or suggestion program for employees. Important attributes of successful suggestion programs are processing suggestions rapidly, giving quality feedback, reacting to useful suggestions and ideas, and offering cash incentives. Suggestion programs vary in terms of their complexity, ranging from simple suggestion boxes to complex programs where ideas are placed in an idea bank for peer review and evaluation.

Encouraging and Protecting New Ideas

In many firms, idea generation is a haphazard process. However, there are some concrete steps a firm can take to build an organization that encourages and protects new ideas.

Establishing a Focal Point for Ideas

Some firms meet the challenge of encouraging, collecting, and evaluating ideas by designating a specific person to screen and track them—for if it's everybody's job, it may be no one's responsibility.[47] Another approach is to establish an **idea bank** (or vault), which is a physical or digital repository for storing ideas. An example of an idea bank would be a password-protected location on a firm's **intranet** that is available only to qualified employees. It may have a file for ideas that are being actively contemplated and a file for inactive ideas. Other firms do not have idea banks but instead encourage employees to keep journals of their ideas.

Encouraging Creativity at the Firm Level

There is an important distinction between creativity and innovation. Innovation, as mentioned in Chapter 1, refers to the successful introduction of new outcomes by a firm. In contrast, creativity is the process of generating a novel or useful idea but does not require implementation. In other words, creativity is the raw material that goes into innovation. A team of employees may come up with a hundred legitimate creative ideas for a new product or service, but only one may eventually be implemented. Of course, it may take a hundred creative ideas to discover the one that ideally satisfies an opportunity.

Creativity Enhancers

Organizational Level	Individual Supervisory Level
• Elevating creativity's importance throughout the organization	• Listening attentively in order to acknowledge and provide early support to ideas
• Offering tangible rewards to those generating new ideas	• Dealing with employees as equals to show that status isn't very important
• Investing in resources that help employees sharpen their creative skills	• Speculate, be open, and build on others' ideas
• Hiring people different from those currently working in the company	• Protecting people who make honest mistakes and are willing to learn from them

Creativity Detractors

Organizational Level	Individual Supervisory Level
• Not attempting to hire creative people	• Being pessimistic, judgmental, and critical
• Maintaining a "stiff" organizational culture with no room for different behaviors	• Punishing mistakes or failed ideas
• Pigeonholing employees; keeping them in the same job for years	• Being cynical or negative and insisting on early precision
• Promoting a mentality suggesting that the best solutions to all problems have already been found	• Being inattentive, acting distant, and remaining silent when employees want to discuss new ideas

Source: Adapted from I. S. Servi, *New Product Development and Marketing* (New York: Praeger, 1990).

An employee may exhibit creativity in a number of ways, including solving a problem or taking an opportunity and using it to develop a new product or service idea. Although creativity is typically thought of as an individual attribute, it can be encouraged or discouraged at the firm level.[48] The extent to which an organization encourages and rewards creativity affects the creative output of its employees.[49] Table 2.3 provides a list of actions and behaviors that both encourage and discourage creativity at both the organizational level and the individual supervisor level.

Protecting Ideas from Being Lost or Stolen

Intellectual property is any product of human intellect that is intangible but has value in the marketplace. It can be protected through tools such as patents, trademarks, copyrights, and trade secrets, which we'll discuss in depth in Chapter 12. As a rule, a mere idea or concept does not qualify for intellectual property protection; that protection comes later when the idea is translated into a more concrete form. At the opportunity recognition stage, however, there are three steps that should be taken when a potentially valuable idea is generated:

Step 1. The idea should be put into a tangible form—either entered into a physical idea logbook or saved on a computer disk—and dated. When using a physical logbook, be sure that it is bound so that it cannot be alleged that a page was added. Make all entries in ink and have them witnessed. If an idea has significant potential, the signature of the person who entered the idea into the logbook and the witness should be notarized.

Putting the idea into tangible form is important for two reasons. First, if the idea is in concrete form, is original and useful, and is kept secret or is disclosed only in a situation where compensation for its use is contemplated, the

learning **objective**

10. Describe three steps for protecting ideas from being lost or stolen.

idea may qualify as a "property right" or "trade secret" and be legally protected under a variety of statutes.

Second, in the case of an invention, if two inventors independently come up with essentially the same invention, the right to apply for the patent belongs to the first person who invented the product. A properly maintained idea log provides evidence of the date that the idea for the invention was first contemplated.

Once an invention demonstrates feasibility, a form called a "Disclosure Document," which describes an invention, can be filed with the U.S. Patent and Trademark Office. The purpose of the form is to provide evidence of the date of an invention's conception.[50]

Step 2. The idea, whether it is recorded in a physical idea logbook or saved in a computer file, should be secured. This may seem like an obvious step but is one that is often overlooked. The extent to which an idea should be secured depends on the circumstances. On the one hand, a firm wants new ideas to be discussed, so a certain amount of openness in the early stages of refining a business idea may be appropriate. On the other hand, if an idea has considerable potential and may be eligible for patent protection, access to the idea should be restricted. In the case of ideas stored on a computer network, access to the ideas should be at a minimum password protected.

Step 3. Avoid making an inadvertent or voluntary disclosure of an idea in a way that forfeits your claim to its exclusive rights. In general, the intellectual property laws seek to protect and reward the originators of ideas as long as they are prudent and try to protect the ideas. For example, if two coworkers are chatting about an idea in an elevator in a public building and a competitor overhears the conversation, the exclusive rights to the idea are probably lost.

In summary, opportunity recognition is a key part of the entrepreneurial process. As mentioned, many firms fail not because the entrepreneurs didn't work hard but because there was no real opportunity to begin with.

CHAPTER SUMMARY

1. An idea is a thought, impression, or notion. An opportunity is an idea that has the qualities of being attractive, durable, and timely and is anchored in a product or service that creates value for its buyers or end users. Not all ideas are opportunities.

2. Observing trends and solving a problem are the two general approaches entrepreneurs use to identify an opportunity.

3. Once recognized, an opportunity's window of opportunity opens, and the market to fill the opportunity grows. At some point, the market matures and becomes saturated with competitors, and the window of opportunity closes.

4. Economic forces, social forces, technological advances, and political action and regulatory changes are the four environmental trends that are most instrumental in creating opportunities.

5. The personal characteristics that researchers have identified that tend to make some people better at recognizing business opportunities than others are prior experience, cognitive factors, social networks, and creativity.

6. For an individual, the five steps in the creative process are preparation, incubation, insight, evaluation, and elaboration.

7. Brainstorming is a technique used to quickly generate a large number of ideas and solutions to problems. One reason to conduct a brainstorming session is to generate ideas that might represent product, service, or business opportunities.

8. A focus group is a gathering of 5 to 10 people who have been selected on the basis of their common characteristics relative to the issue being discussed. One reason to conduct a focus group is to generate ideas that might represent product or business opportunities.

9. An idea bank is a physical or digital repository for storing ideas.

10. The three main steps that can be taken to protect ideas from being lost or stolen are putting the idea into tangible form by means such as entering it in a logbook or saving it in a computer file, securing the idea, and avoiding making an inadvertent or voluntary disclosure of an idea in a manner that forfeits the right to claim exclusive rights to it if it falls into someone else's hands.

Brainstorming, 39

Corridor principle, 36

Creativity, 37

Customer advisory boards, 42

Day-in-the-life research, 42

Entrepreneurial alertness, 36

Focus group, 41

Group support system (or GSS) software, 40

Idea, 29

Idea bank, 42

Intellectual property, 43

Intranet, 42

Network entrepreneurs, 37

Opportunity, 28

Opportunity gap, 28

Opportunity recognition, 35

Self-selected opinion poll, 41

Serendipitous discovery, 34

Solo entrepreneurs, 37

Strong-tie relationships, 37

Survey, 41

Weak-tie relationships, 37

Window of opportunity, 28

1. What is a product opportunity gap? How can an entrepreneur tell if a product opportunity gap exists?

2. What is an opportunity? What are the qualities of an opportunity, and why is each quality important?

3. What four environmental trends are most instrumental in creating business opportunities? Provide an example of each environmental trend and the type of business opportunity that it might help create.

4. Explain how "solving a problem" can create a business opportunity. Provide an example that was not mentioned in the chapter of a business opportunity that was created in this way.

5. What is meant by the term "serendipitous discovery"? How does a serendipitous discovery differ from a discovery by mere chance?

6. What is meant by opportunity recognition?

7. In what ways does prior industry experience provide an entrepreneur an advantage in recognizing business opportunities?

8. What is the corridor principle? How does this corridor principle explain why the majority of business ideas are conceived at work?

9. What is entrepreneurial alertness?

10. In what ways does an extensive social network provide an entrepreneur an advantage in recognizing business opportunities?

11. Describe the difference between strong-tie relationships and weak-tie relationships. Is an entrepreneur more likely to get new business ideas through strong-tie or weak-tie relationships? Why?

12. Define creativity. How does creativity contribute to the opportunity recognition process?

13. Briefly describe the five stages of the creative process.

14. Explain the difference between an opportunity and an idea.

15. Describe the brainstorming process. Why is "no criticism" the number one rule for brainstorming?

16. Describe how a focus group is set up and how it is used to generate new business ideas.

17. Describe how the use of surveys can be used to generate new business ideas.

18. What is a self-selected opinion poll? Are self-selected opinion polls an effective or an ineffective way to collect data to help generate new business ideas?

19. What is the purpose of an idea bank? Describe how an idea bank can be set up in a firm.

20. What are the three main steps to protect ideas from being lost or stolen?

1. Kevin, a software engineer, plans to write a memo to his boss describing an idea he has for a new software product. Kevin wants to convince his boss that his idea represents an opportunity the firm should pursue. In your opinion, what should Kevin put in the memo?

2. Melanie is very perceptive and believes she has identified an opportunity for a new business in the fashion industry. She wants to make sure, however, that she isn't just following a hunch—that the opportunity is sound. What criteria can Melanie use to determine whether she has identified an attractive opportunity?

3. Matrix Industries is interested in producing handheld devices similar to the products sold by palmOne. Jim Ryan, the founder of Matrix, remembers hearing about a

concept called "window of opportunity." He asks you to explain the concept and how he can use it to help him make his decision. What do you tell him?

4. Kim is the founder of a small firm that produces highly specialized components for the semiconductor industry. Sales reps from both Forrester Research and Gartner have called to set up appointments with her to explain how their firms could help identify emerging opportunities that might translate into new product ideas for Kim's company. Keeping on top of emerging trends is important to Kim, and she knows that new product ideas are the lifeblood of high-tech firms. However, her busy schedule causes her reluctance to sit through two sales pitches. Kim explains this dilemma to you and asks whether you think she should take the time to meet with the sales reps. What is your answer?

5. Marshall Hanson, the founder of Santa Fe Hitching Rail, a chain of nine steak restaurants in New Mexico, is considering expanding his menu, which is currently restricted to steak, hamburger, potatoes, and fries. He has just read a book about entrepreneurship and learned that entrepreneurs should study social trends to help identify new product opportunities. List the social trends that might help Martin choose items to add to his menu. Given the trends you list, what items do you suggest Martin add?

6. Recognizing a problem and proposing a solution to it is one way entrepreneurs identify opportunities. Think about your current activities as well as others in which you have an interest. Identify a problem with the activity you are considering and recommend a business to solve the problem.

7. Megan Jones owns a small chain of fitness centers in Kansas City. In general, her centers are successful, but she feels they are getting "stale" and could benefit from new ideas. Suggest to Megan some ways she could generate new ideas for her centers.

8. Tom Garrett, the manager of a midsize advertising agency, is conducting brainstorming sessions to identify new ideas for products and services to offer his clients. The first session is tomorrow, and Tom remembers from your résumé that you took an entrepreneurship class. He calls you in his office to ask you whether you know anything about how to conduct brainstorming sessions. Using materials in this chapter, prepare an answer to Tom's question.

9. Delores Jones owns a company that produces a fat-free peanut butter named "Best Choice Peanut Butter." To learn of people's feelings about her product, she stamps an invitation on each jar that reads, "If you'd like to tell me your opinion of Best Choice, send me a message at the following e-mail address." Is this an effective way to receive quality feedback from customers? In addition, Delores wants to know what other fat-free products her customers would be interested in and is considering sending a survey to 100 of her customers. Provide Delores advice about how to structure and administer the survey.

10. Freedom Electronics is a start-up with about 20 sales representatives. The company has a solid product line but knows that to remain competitive, it must continue recognizing opportunities for new products and services. The firm has not developed a systematic way for its sales staff to report new ideas. Suggest some ways that Freedom can record and protect the idea of its sales representatives.

you be the VC

Company: TVEyes (www.tveyes.com)

Business idea: Build a service that monitors all programming on the major broadcast and cable networks and sends customers alerts when a key word or phrase the customer preselects is mentioned.

Pitch: All companies are interested in what the news media are saying about their products, about their competitors' products, and about emerging technologies and social trends. TVEyes will monitor ABC, CBS, NBC, CNN, CNNfn, CNBC, MSNBC, FOX News, C-SPAN, ESPN, and major stations in New York, Chicago, Los Angeles, Houston, and Miami. Customers pay for a key word or phrase. If it is mentioned on any of these networks,

an e-mail alert will be sent to the customer, who then can log on to the TVEyes Web site to read a full transcript of the report. TVEyes sees itself as the perfect 24-hour-a-day business intelligence tool.

Q&A: On the basis of the material covered in this chapter, what questions would you ask the founders of this firm before making your funding decision? What answers would satisfy you?

Decision: If you had to make your decision on just the information provided in the pitch and on the company's Web site, would you fund this firm? Why or why not?

Case 2.1

ParentWatch: Providing Comfort to Working Parents
www.parentwatch.com

For parents worrying about how their kids are doing at day care, ParentWatch has the answer. The company, which is headquartered in New York City, makes small video cameras that are deployed at child care centers, giving parents the ability to watch their youngsters throughout the day on the Internet. For $25 a month, a father who drops off his fussy child at 7:00 A.M. can check on the child when he gets to work 30 minutes later and be comforted by the fact that the child has calmed down. Similarly, if a mother knows that her child will be involved in a special activity at 2:00 P.M., she can log on and watch.

Adam Aronson, who is not a parent himself, founded ParentWatch in 1998. Prior to launching the company, the 31-year-old had been a trader at Credit Suisse First Boston and a money manager at AC Capital Management in Greenwich, Connecticut. He often heard friends talking about how badly they felt about not seeing their children enough. When several of them said that they would readily pay for a monitoring device that would allow them to see their kids during the day, a light went on, and ParentWatch was conceived.

ParentWatch's service is free to the child care center, as are the cameras, Internet access, and a customized Web site called the ParentWatch Community Site. The service is tailored to each center and can be used to post announcements, upcoming events, lunch menus, and other items of particular interest to parents of children at the center. The company's main source of revenue is the subscription fees from parents. Discounts are provided for kids who are at a center only a few days a week.

ParentWatch did not pioneer the child care Webcam idea, although it was an early entrant and is now one of the stronger industry participants. In the beginning, according to Mr. Aronson, it was a struggle to get day care centers to sign on. Privacy and security were particular concerns. Some centers also worried that parents might misinterpret scenes they saw online, leading to complaints or litigation. To dispel these worries, Mr. Aronson calls ParentWatch a "keeping families connected tool" rather than a "watch your kid" monitoring tool. Since the service was launched, it has been used by day care centers and working parents and grandparents in the United States, Taiwan, Venezuela, and Russia and by military personnel overseas.

The service works like this. Each classroom in a day care center is equipped with a minimum of two Webcams that are strategically positioned in the classroom and focused on places where children normally congregate, such as tables or rugs. Care is taken to avoid filming private locations, such as diaper-changing areas and restrooms. The system then delivers live streaming video images to users, who are typically parents logged on at work.

ParentWatch has been successful because it helps parents feel more connected with their kids and gives them a sense of security about their child's care. Parents write testimonials, some of which are posted on the company's Web site. Here is an example:

> I do not believe I would be able to work all day and not have the ability to peek at him periodically. He is the baby of four children, and we truly are enjoying these years. Today I was able to catch him during his time at show-and-tell. . . . I think watching ParentWatch is the next best thing to being a stay-at-home mom. Your service is what gets me through the day. Thank you!

ParentWatch is also attracting investors; it received $10 million in venture capital in 2000 from Oak Street Investments. And the market for child care Webcams remains huge. As of early 2000, less than 1 percent of the nation's more than 100,000 licensed child care centers featured Webcam services. In addition, the number of two-income families who will need day care services is increasing.

Day care centers also benefit from ParentWatch and similar services. They experience the following:

- *Increased enrollment:* Because of the availability of online streaming video and related services, enrollments at centers that offer ParentWatch increase.

- *Cost savings:* ParentWatch helps centers defer costs by providing them a Web site and Internet access.

- *Insurance savings:* Installing a video service can help a center lower its insurance costs.

- *Enhanced parental trust:* The service provides a sense that a participating center is open and transparent and is glad to have parents watch how their kids are treated.

With ParentWatch everyone wins—the company, the parents, the investors, and the day care centers.

Discussion Questions

1. What environmental trends contributed to creating the opportunity for ParentWatch? Which trend do you believe was the most significant? Why?

2. In the chapter, an opportunity is defined as having the qualities of being (1) attractive, (2) durable, (3) timely, and (4) anchored in a product or service that creates value for its buyer or end user. To what extent does ParentWatch meet each of these tests of an opportunity? Along with your written explanation for each of the tests,

rank the extent to which ParentWatch meets the test as excellent, good, fair, or poor.

3. Does Adam Aronson seem like a likely founder or an unlikely founder for a company like ParentWatch? What personal characteristics does Mr. Aronson have that most likely assisted him in recognizing the opportunity for ParentWatch?

4. Can you think of any other ways that technology could help link children to their parents when they are physically apart?

Sources: E. Schibsted, "Parental Peekaboo," Business 2.0, March 2000, and D. Sessa, "Day-Care TV: ParentWatch Keeps Eye on Kids," Wall Street Journal, December 7, 2000, B16; ParentWatch home page, www.parentwatch.com (accessed June 3, 2004).

Case 2.2

Align Technology: Making Braces More Bearable
www.invisalign.com

Do you wish you had straighter teeth but can't imagine getting braces? If you're reluctant because of the way braces look, you'll be happy to hear that Align Technology has devised a treatment plan called Invisalign that straightens teeth without braces. Invisalign requires patients to wear a series of clear plastic snap-in aligners. They're a bit more expensive than traditional braces, but the appliances are nearly invisible when worn.

Align Technology was founded in 1997 by Zia Chishti and Kelsey Wirth, who were MBA students together at Stanford University. The story of the firm's conception is a classic entrepreneurial tale. While working in investment banking for Morgan Stanley, Chishti was fitted with braces that he felt were awkward and embarrassing. After his braces were removed, he wore a clear plastic retainer. He noticed that when he forgot to wear his retainer for a couple of days, his teeth would move a bit, and when he resumed wearing the retainer, they would shift back into place. Through this observation, he started wondering whether teeth could be straightened through the use of clear plastic devices instead of braces. His background in computer science lead him to believe that it was possible to design and manufacture an entire series of clear orthodontic devices, similar to the retainer he wore, using three-dimensional computer graphics technology.

The combination of these factors led to the creation of a business plan. Chishti added Wirth as a partner, raised venture-capital financing, and Align Technology was born. Today, Align is the largest manufacturer of custom orthodontic products in the world, and has certified over 24,000 orthodontists to use its product. These orthodontists now have over 155,000 patients using the Invisalign approach to orthodontic treatment.

The market potential for Invisalign appears to be huge. In the United States alone, over 200 million people have some form of teeth misalignment, and the American Academy of Cosmetic Dentistry says that 50 percent of adults are not satisfied with how their teeth look. Yet less than 1 percent of these adults obtain braces, primarily because braces are unattractive and uncomfortable during the treatment period. In addition, most people associate braces with adolescence. The Invisalign treatment plan is designed to remove inhibitions about wearing braces. The big advantage, of course, is that aligners are nearly invisible when worn, eliminating the aesthetic concerns. Another advantage is that the devices can be removed for eating and brushing, improving dental hygiene. The scientific concept behind using a series of customized removable appliances was discussed in orthodontic journals as early as the 1940s, but Align was the first company to bring the concept to market and already has won industry awards.

Although Invisalign has been fairly well received, some orthodontists have reservations about the new approach; they are unsure whether it will match the results they have with traditional braces. To mitigate some of this hesitancy, Align restricts its patients to those who are at least 18 years old and have a fully matured facial structure. Patients with severe alignment or dental problems are also not considered good candidates. The hope is that Align, along with similar companies that are sure to follow, will encourage people who wouldn't do so otherwise to get orthodontic treatment.

Align Technology went public on January 26, 2001, with an offering of 10 million shares of its common stock. The company trades on the NASDAQ under the ticker symbol ALGN. The company has grown from two employees in 1997 to more than 1,100 employees.

Discussion Questions

1. What environmental trends contributed to creating the opportunity that made Align Technology possible?

2. As mentioned in the case, the scientific concept behind using a series of customized removable appliances has been around since the 1940s. Why do you think this concept hadn't been translated into a business until now? Why didn't a practicing orthodontist run with this concept long before Align Technology was founded?

3. Give five reasons for Align's rapid growth.

4. Look at the model of the opportunity recognition process (see Figure 2.3). Re-create the figure, inserting in the boxes labeled "Environmental Trends" and "Personal Characteristics of an Entrepreneur" the specific environmental trends and personal characteristics of Zia Chishti that contributed to the recognition of the invisible braces business opportunity. What does this re-created figure teach you? Explain your answer.

Sources: Align Technology home page, www.invisalign.com (accessed June 24, 2004); K. T. L. Tran, "Innovator Is Hoping for a Bite of Braces Market," Wall Street Journal, *October 28, 1999, B10; and T. D. Reeves, "New Device Makes Braces More Bearable,"* St. Petersburg Times, *October 12, 2000.*

three

feasibility analysis

After studying this chapter, you should be ready to:

1. Explain what a feasibility analysis is and why it's important.

2. Discuss the proper time to complete a feasibility analysis when developing a business venture.

3. Explain a concept statement and its contents.

4. Describe the purpose of a product/service feasibility analysis and the two primary issues that a proposed business should consider in this area.

5. Identify three primary purposes for concept testing.

6. Define the term usability testing and explain why it's important.

7. Describe the purpose of industry/market feasibility analysis and the three primary issues to consider in this area.

8. Explain the difference between primary research and secondary research.

9. Describe the purpose of organizational feasibility analysis and list the two primary issues to consider in this area.

10. Explain the importance of financial feasibility analysis and list the most important issues to consider in this area.

intuit: the value of validating business ideas

Intuit is the leading provider of financial management software and related services in the United States. Its flagship products, Quicken, QuickBooks, and Quicken TurboTax, simplify personal finance, small-business management, payroll processing, and tax preparation.

Intuit's founding is an excellent example of how a strong business idea, coupled with properly executed feasibility analysis, leads to business success. Scott Cook, a business consultant, started the company in 1983. After watching his wife painstakingly pay bills by hand, Cook wondered whether a software product could be developed to help people manage their personal finances. He drew up a preliminary business plan and

partnered with Tom Proulx, a computer science student at Stanford University, to found Intuit and develop a product that was to be named Quicken.

Cook's background in consumer marketing was a true advantage during the product's development. Cook spent several years as a brand manager with Procter & Gamble earlier in his career and had a thorough understanding of feasibility analysis and marketing research. Cook insisted that he and Proulx first determine exactly what consumers wanted in a personal finance program. When asked how he approached this task, Cook answered,

The only way to find that information out was to talk to households. So I'd make calls and I got my sister-in-law to call households. We asked upper-income consumers—they were the only people buying computers—about their financial lives. We did this to build a real gut knowledge about how real people did their finances: their behaviors, their likes, and their dislikes. We looked at behavioral data as well. It became very clear to us that people wanted a way to take the hassle out of doing their finances. Who likes to pay bills and write in checkbooks?[1]

An important component of Cook's approach was a keen understanding that because personal financial management software was a product that consumers hadn't seen before, it wouldn't work to simply ask them what they would like in this type of product. So, in addition to the phone interviews, Cook and Proulx actually watched people managing their finances. Quicken was developed only after they were confident that they knew what consumers needed to make personal financial management easier. Cook said this about understanding a customer's needs:

> The key to business success is knowing your customer cold. We had spent time understanding the customer. We clearly understood customer behavior and had data showing that our solution was vastly better according to customers' decision-making criteria.[2]

Following Quicken, Intuit developed several other software products using a variety of techniques to determine customers' needs. Along with interviews, Intuit employs usability testing, which entails sitting consumers down in front of early versions of Intuit products and observing how they interact with the software. Intuit also uses "follow-me-home" testing. Company programmers travel to the businesses and homes of their customers to observe how their products are used. Both of these techniques are designed to help Intuit get their products right—before rather than after they are introduced to the marketplace.

Intuit was reminded of the value of feasibility analysis and marketing research when it developed QuickBooks, its popular accounting program. Initially, the company targeted the personal consumer market, assuming that because businesses have accountants, they wouldn't need a basic accounting software program. In follow-up research, however, Intuit found that about 98 percent of all U.S. businesses have 50 or fewer employees and that most don't have their own accountants. QuickBooks was repositioned to appeal to the small-business market and today is the top-selling small-business accounting program in the United States.

The Intuit case illustrates a set of activities that is fundamental to the launch of a successful business—determining if the business idea is feasible, what niche market the business will serve, and the initial product or service's characteristics. Although these activities seem obvious, feasibility analysis is often given very little attention. Rather than engaging in the type of research that Scott Cook did before rolling out Quicken, many entrepreneurs take a business idea and race ahead with the development of a product or service that they "know" will sell in the marketplace and then spend precious resources tweaking or redoing products or services on the basis of negative customer feedback.[3] This scenario is often referred to as the "ready, fire, aim" approach to launching a business, implying that the business is launched or "fired" before its aim is certain.

In this chapter, we'll discuss the importance of feasibility analysis and look at its four key areas: product/service feasibility, industry/market feasibility, organizational feasibility, and financial feasibility. Failure to conduct a feasibility analysis can result in disappointing outcomes, as illustrated in the boxed feature titled "What Went Wrong?" about satellite phones.

Feasibility Analysis

learning objective

1. Explain what a feasibility analysis is and why it's important.

Feasibility analysis is the process of determining if a business idea is viable. As a preliminary evaluation of a business idea, a feasibility analysis is completed to determine if an idea is worth pursuing and to screen ideas before spending resources on them. It follows the opportunity recognition stage but comes before the development of a business plan, as illustrated in Figure 3.1. When a business idea is deemed unworkable, it should be dropped or rethought. If it is rethought and a slightly different version of the original idea emerges, the new idea should be subjected to the same level of feasibility analysis as the original idea.

what went *wrong?*

Satellite Phones: How Feasible Were They?

When Bary Bertiger's wife couldn't reach her clients via her cell phone while vacationing in the Caribbean, the Motorola engineer had an idea. He envisioned placing a constellation of 66 low-earth-orbiting satellites in space that would allow subscribers to make phone calls from anywhere on earth. Although satellite phones were already available while Bertiger was considering this idea, there were problems: they used satellites at high altitudes, they were heavy, and they involved annoying quarter-second voice delays. By using low-altitude satellites, the phones could be smaller, and the voice delay would be imperceptible. Bertiger called his solution Iridium.

Sound like a good idea? Unfortunately, it wasn't. Here's what happened.

To build the satellites and put them in orbit, Motorola established Iridium LLC as a separate company in 1991. The cost of putting the satellites in orbit was enormous, meaning that the company started with significant debt. The service was launched on November 1, 1998, in a ceremony at which Vice President Al Gore made the first call using Iridium. Iridium charged $3,000 for a handset and $3 to $8 per minute for a call. Iridium knew that its phone would be too large (they were the size of a brick) and that its service would be too expensive to compete with traditional cellular service, so its target market was people who traveled or worked in areas where cellular wasn't available. This group included international business travelers, construction workers in remote areas, ships at sea, military forces around the world, and offshore oil rig workers. Iridium's chief executive officer (CEO), Edward Staiano, predicted that by the end of 1999, the company would have 500,000 subscribers.

But by July 1999, the company had only 20,000 subscribers. It needed 52,000 subscribers just to meet its loan obligations. The next month, Iridium defaulted on $1.5 billion in loans and filed for bankruptcy. What went wrong?

Well, several things. First, because of the complexity of its technology, it took 11 years for the Iridium concept to be fully developed, and traditional cell phone service spread much more quickly than Iridium had anticipated. By the time Iridium was available, a good share of its target market

could meet its needs via traditional cell phones—which were cheaper and lighter and worked better in most areas. Second, because Iridium's technology depended on line of sight between the phone's antenna and an orbiting satellite, the functionality of the phone was limited. It couldn't be used inside moving cars, inside buildings, or in many urban areas where tall buildings obstructed the line of sight between the phone and the satellite. Dartmouth College professor Sydney Finkelstein, who wrote about Iridium in his book *Why Smart Executives Fail*, said that in studying the failure of Iridium, a top industry consultant told him, "You can't expect a CEO traveling on business in Bangkok to leave a building, walk outside to a street corner, and pull out a $3,000 phone." Iridium had other annoying limitations. For example, in remote areas where electricity wasn't available, the battery charger required special solar-powered accessories, which made it unappealing to busy travelers.

One has to wonder what type of feasibility analysis Iridium engaged in before it spent billions of dollars to so spectacularly fail. Another passage from Professor Finkelstein's book, quoting Iridium's second CEO, John Richardson, makes one wonder further:

We're a classic MBA case study in how not to introduce a product. First we created a marvelous technological achievement. Then we asked how to make money on it.

Questions for Critical Thinking

1. Why do you think that those who were leading Iridium continued to push the concept forward despite all the difficulties being encountered in the early stages of the venture's life? Would you have pulled the plug on this venture sooner than actually happened? If so, at what point?

2. One of Iridium's problems was rapidly advancing cell phone technologies. As an entrepreneur, what would you do to remain abreast of technological developments and to monitor their meaning?

Source: S. Finkelstein, Why Executives Fail (New York: Penguin Group, 2003).

Although the sequence pictured in Figure 3.1 makes perfect sense, statistics show that the majority of entrepreneurs do not follow this pattern before launching their ventures.[4] Several studies have investigated why this is the case. The consensus of the research is that entrepreneurs tend to underestimate the amount of competition there will be in the marketplace and tend to overestimate their personal chances for success.[5]

Once a business idea is determined to be feasible, much work remains to be done to completely flesh out the idea when preparing to write the business plan and launch the

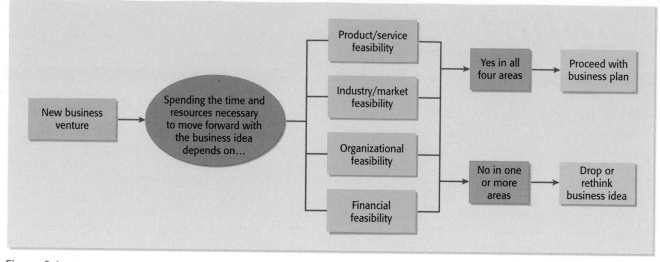

Figure 3.1 Role of Feasibility Analysis in Developing Successful Business Ideas

venture. Table 3.1 shows where we offer a more complete discussion on each of the components of feasibility analysis is this book. A positive feasibility analysis gives the green light to pursue a business idea. Each area of the feasibility analysis must then be completely explored in anticipation of launching the new venture.

A business idea developed by Trakus, Inc. provides an example of the importance of conducting a feasibility analysis. Unlike Iridium, the company we looked at in the "What Went Wrong?" feature, Trakus effectively used feasibility analysis to determine that a business idea wasn't feasible before spending a lot of time and effort on it.

Originally named Retailing Insights, Trakus was founded in 1997. The company's business idea was to build computerized shopping carts for grocery stores called Videocarts. Using wireless technologies, Videocarts would know where each cart was in a store and would alert shoppers to specials and provide other useful information on a video display attached to the cart. If a shopper were in the cereal aisle, for example, the Videocart would show advertisements for cereals and let the shopper know what brands were on sale. The Videocart had other useful features, too. The cart could provide recipes and locate items in the store.

Another company's earlier attempt to build a Videocart failed, primarily because of poor execution. Retailing Insights vowed to do it right and equipped its carts with all the latest technology. The company obtained $50,000 of seed money from an angel investor. **Seed money** is the initial investment made in a firm. The investor insisted that Retailing Insights conduct a feasibility analysis of the market for the product before using resources for product development. In response to this request, the company developed a very detailed description of the Videocart, which included all the benefits of the cart for both

learning objective

2. Discuss the proper time to complete a feasibility analysis when developing a business venture.

Table 3.1

Where Additional Information about Each Component of Feasibility Analysis Is Located

Component of Feasibility Analysis	More Complete Discussion of Topic
Product/service feasibility	Chapter 3 (this chapter)
Industry/market feasibility	Chapter 4: Industry and Competitor Analysis
Organizational feasibility	Chapter 5: Developing an Effective Business Model
	Chapter 6: Building a New Venture Team
Financial feasibility	Chapter 7: Assessing a New Venture's Financial Strength and Viability
	Chapter 10: Getting Financing or Funding

Ever wonder if a wide receiver runs his pattern in the fourth quarter as fast as he did in the first? Trakus Inc., can provide broadcasters with real-time performance data that can make your football-watching experience a little more entertaining. Trakus is also working with the NHL, PGA, and NASCAR.

the grocery store retailers and the grocery products' manufacturers. They showed this description to both retailers and manufacturers and were surprised by what they found. Neither was interested. The previous cart's bad reputation was a major concern for retailers, who were wary of trying another version of something that had already failed. Retailing Insights knew then that it would have to establish multiple test sites (at its own expense) to convince retailers that the carts were reliable. Manufacturers told the company that they would be willing to consider a new medium of advertising only if sufficient scale were established to justify the cost of producing ads and incurring related expenses. This stipulation led Retailing Insights to realize that they would have to sign up a significant portion of all grocery stores in the United States to get manufacturers excited about its product.

After considering these obstacles, the idea for the Videocart was abandoned. The company still thought it had core competencies, however, and after a brainstorming session decided to go in a completely different direction. A **core competency** is a resource or capability that serves as a source of a firm's competitive advantage over its rivals.[6] A new idea was conceived, based on Retailing Insight's core competency in the area of miniature electronics, to build rugged little transmitters that could be put on athletes (in their helmets or on their clothing) that, together with a set of antennas in a stadium, could determine where every athlete was at any given time during a sports contest. The devices would generate real-time statistics during the course of a game, such as the percentage of time that a defensive lineman spent on his opponent's side of the line of scrimmage during a football game. Such data could be fed to broadcasters to liven up the information they provided during the game's broadcast. To test the product feasibility of the idea, Research Insights changed its name to Trakus and showed a detailed description and simulation of the device to its potential clientele. This time, the reception the company received was overwhelmingly positive. The only real concern was whether the device could actually be built. Trakus has since received venture capital financing; has tested its devices in National Hockey League games; has been discussed in *Sports Illustrated*,[7] *USA Today*,[8] and the *Wall Street Journal*;[9] and is developing its systems for several sports.

Trakus could have spent millions of dollars fully developing the Videocart only to find that the product had no real value in the marketplace. The feasibility analysis accomplished exactly what it was supposed to—it gave the company a candid assessment of the viability of its business idea *before* it consumed resources such as money. To its credit, the company responded by shifting to a different and viable product, causing the firm to be moving in a more promising direction.[10]

Before a company undertakes a feasibility analysis, a concept statement should be developed. A **concept statement** is a preliminary description of a business and includes the following:

- *A description of the product or service being offered:* This section details the features of the product or service and may include a sketch of it as well. A computer-generated simulation of the functionality of the product or service is also helpful.
- *The intended target market:* This section lists the businesses or people who will buy the product or service.
- *The benefits of the product or service:* This section describes the benefits of the product or service and includes an account of how the product or service adds value and/or solves a problem.
- *A description of how the product will be positioned relative to similar ones in the market:* A company's position describes how it is situated relative to its competitors.
- *A description of how the product or service will be sold and distributed:* This section specifies whether the product will be sold directly by the manufacturer or through distributors or franchisees.

Figure 3.2 is the concept statement for a fictitious company named New Venture Fitness Drinks, which sells a line of nutritional fitness drinks and targets sports enthusiasts. Its strategy is to place small restaurants, similar to smoothie restaurants, near large sports

Figure 3.2

New Venture Fitness Drinks' Concept Statement

New Business Concept
New Venture Fitness Drinks Inc.

Product

New Venture Fitness Drinks will sell delicious, nutrition-filled, all-natural fitness drinks to thirsty sports enthusiasts. The drinks will be sold through small storefronts (600 sq. ft.) that will be the same size as popular smoothie restaurants. The drinks were formulated by Dr. William Peters, a world-renowned nutritionist, and Dr. Michelle Smith, a sports medicine specialist, on behalf of New Venture Fitness Drinks and its customers.

Target Market

In the first three years of operation, New Venture Fitness Drinks plans to open three or four restaurants. They will all be located near large sports complexes that contain soccer fields and softball diamonds. The target market is sports enthusiasts.

Why New Venture Fitness Drinks?

The industry for sports drinks continues to grow. New Venture Fitness Drinks will introduce exciting new sports drinks that will be priced between $1.50 and $2.50 per 16-ounce serving. Energy bars and other over-the-counter sports snacks will also be sold. Each restaurant will contain comfortable tables and chairs (both inside and outside) where sports enthusiasts can congregate after a game. The atmosphere will be fun, cheerful, and uplifting.

Special Feature—No Other Restaurant Does This

As a special feature, New Venture Fitness Drinks will videotape select sporting events that take place in the sports complexes nearest its restaurants and will replay highlights of the games on video monitors in their restaurants. The "highlight" film will be a 30-minute film that will play continuously from the previous day's sporting events. This special feature will allow sports enthusiasts, from kids playing soccer to adults in softball leagues, to drop in and see themselves and their teammates on television.

Management Team

New Venture Fitness Drink is led by its cofounders, Jack Petty and Peggy Wills. Jack has 16 years of experience with a national restaurant chain, and Peggy is a certified public accountant with seven years of experience at a Big 4 accounting firm.

complexes. Most concept statements look like product brochures or print ads and are relatively short in hopes that they will be read.

Now let's turn our attention to the four areas of feasibility analysis. The first area we'll discuss is product/service feasibility.

Product/Service Feasibility Analysis

Product/service feasibility analysis is an assessment of the overall appeal of the product or service being proposed. Before rushing a prospective product or service into development, a firm should be confident that it's what customers want and that the product or service will have an adequate market. In launching a new firm, it is easy for an entrepreneur to get caught up in activities such as raising money, hiring employees, buying computer equipment, signing leases, writing press releases, and so on. For most firms, however, the number one success factor is delivering a superior product or service.[11] The importance of knowing the feasibility of a new product or service idea is affirmed by R. G. Cooper, a widely published author in the area of product development, who wrote,

> New product success or failure is largely decided in the first few plays of the game—in those critical steps and tasks that precede the actual development of the product. The upfront homework defines the product and builds the business case for development.[12]

Table 3.2 provides a summary of the benefits of conducting a detailed and thorough product/service feasibility analysis. As shown in the table, the benefits and rewards of conducting the analysis are well worth the effort.

Two primary tests—concept testing and usability testing—constitute product/service feasibility analysis.

Concept Testing   A **concept test** entails showing a representation of the product or service to prospective users to gauge customer interest, desirability, and purchase intent.[13] It was after the concept test that Retailing Insights abandoned its plans to build the Videocart.

learning **objective**

4. Describe the purpose of a product/service feasibility analysis and the two primary issues that a proposed business should consider in this area.

learning **objective**

5. Identify three primary purposes for concept testing.

Table 3.2

Benefits of Conducting a Product/Service Feasibility Analysis

Benefit	Explanation
Getting the product right the first time	You know what customers want because you asked them. You also tested a product's usability and the quality of the user experience.
A beta (or early adopter) community emerges	The firms or individuals that participate in the feasibility analysis often become a company's first customers or "adopters." These early customers provide additional feedback as the product or service rolls out.
Avoiding any obvious flaws in product or service design	By asking prospective customers to test the usability of a product or the ease of use of a service, obvious design flaws are usually uncovered.
Using time and capital more efficiently	Because you have a better idea of what customers want, you won't spend as much time or money chasing ideas that customers don't want.
Gaining insight into additional product and service offerings	Often, conducting a feasibility analysis for one product or service prompts the recognition of the need for additional products or services.

There are three primary purposes for a concept test, the first one being to validate the underlying premises of a product or service idea that an entrepreneur thinks is compelling. To test his idea, an entrepreneur must ask prospective customers and key industry participants what they think. This can be accomplished via phone interviews, personal interviews, and focus groups and simply by watching people perform relevant tasks. In some instances, it is also important for firms to do basic research to make sure that they fully understand the behaviors and attitudes of their potential clientele. An example of this type of basic research is a recent study that Cheskin, a marketing firm, performed for PepsiCo. (Pepsi is one of the units of PepsiCo.) Pepsi wanted to have a better understanding of the teen market to guide development of its soft drinks. The following describes the way that Cheskin went about helping Pepsi accomplish its objective:

> We designed an approach that looked at teens the way they look at themselves. We sent cameras out to hundreds of teens, asking them to photograph their lives as they really are. We interviewed friends together, asking them about their dreams, fears, cares and concerns. We talked to experts who built careers understanding the teen psyche, and we visited common teen hang-outs, observing how they acted when away from adults. As a result, we were able to create a model that accurately explains the five main types of teenagers, tracks their relative influence over time, and accurately predicts how trends move through the teen population.[14]

Pepsi used the model and teen learnings to ensure that their perspective on teens was always up to date. This information will undoubtedly direct the firm's product development efforts of its soft drinks for the teen market and may provide it with an advantage over its competitors. While most new firms can't afford a study as elaborate as Pepsi's, a firm must understand its customers before it can create products and services that truly meet their needs.

The second purpose of a concept test is to help develop an idea. For example, a firm may show a product idea to prospective customers, get feedback, and tweak the idea. Then, in an iterative manner, they'll show it to more potential customers, get feedback and tweak the idea some more, and so on. The objective is to emerge from the concept test with a product or service that is refined to the point that the entrepreneur is confident that it satisfies a defined need and with one that prospective customers have said that they like and may be willing to buy.

The third purpose of a concept test is to estimate the potential market share the product or service might command. Some type of buying intention question appears in almost every concept test, usually in the form of survey questionnaire that looks something like this:

How likely would you be to buy a product like this, if we make it?[15]

1. Definitely would buy
2. Probably would buy
3. Might or might not buy
4. Probably would not buy
5. Definitely would not buy

The number of people who definitely would buy and probably would buy are typically combined and used as a gauge of customer interest. One caveat is that people who say that they intend to purchase a product don't always follow through, so the numbers resulting from this activity are almost always optimistic. Nonetheless, the numbers do give a business an indication of the degree of consumer interest in a firm's product or service.

learning objective

6. Define the term usability testing and explain why it's important.

Usability Testing   A concept test is usually followed by the development of a prototype or model of the product or service. **Prototyping** is iterative, meaning that the mock-up is refined and refined again until the customer and designer agree on the final design.[16] Typically, a basic prototype is developed and is used to gauge customer interest and to conduct usability testing.

Usability testing requires that users of a product perform certain tasks in order to measure the product's ease of use and the user's perception of the experience. Usability tests are sometimes called user tests, beta tests, or field trials, depending on the circumstances involved. Again, while it is tempting to rush a new product or service to market, conducting a usability test is a good investment of an entrepreneur's or a firm's resources. Many products that consumers find frustrating to work with have been brought to market too quickly.

There are many forms of usability tests. Some entrepreneurs, working within limited budgets, develop a fairly basic prototype and ask friends and colleagues to use the product, then complete an evaluation form or give verbal feedback. While fairly rudimentary, this approach is better than no testing. Other companies have elaborate usability testing programs and facilities. For example, in Intuit's usability-testing lab at its California headquarters, participants are seated in front of PCs and then asked to work with software programs that are being developed. A soundproof room is attached to the lab, where Intuit programmers and designers observe the participants. A "logger" is typically assigned to record usability problems or any comments participants make during the test, and the sessions are taped for further review. As mentioned in the opening case, Intuit also has a **follow-me-home testing** methodology, in which the company sends teams of testers to the homes of users to see how its products are working. A team typically consists of three Intuit employees, including someone from the User Experience Group, someone from Quality Assurance, and someone from Engineering or Technical Documentation.

Usability testing is particularly important for software and Web site design. According to one survey, 36 percent of all Web site owners in the United States conduct usability research.[17] Figure 3.3 illustrates the way in which concept and usability testing unfolds at Activision, a maker of electronic games. Activision calls the process the "greenlight process." As a product passes through the various stages of testing, it must receive a "green light" before it is allowed to progress to the next stage. At any point in the process, a

Companies such as Activision, known for games such as Tony Hawk's Underground, appreciate the importance of usability testing. Activision understands that if it wants to remain competitive and increase sales, it needs to tap into its potential customers' needs to improve its products before they hit the market.

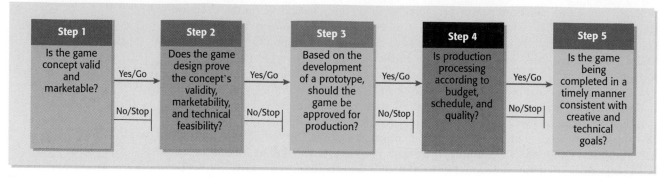

Step 1		Step 2		Step 3		Step 4		Step 5
Is the game concept valid and marketable?	Yes/Go ─── No/Stop	Does the game design prove the concept's validity, marketability, and technical feasibility?	Yes/Go ─── No/Stop	Based on the development of a prototype, should the game be approved for production?	Yes/Go ─── No/Stop	Is production processing according to budget, schedule, and quality?	Yes/Go ─── No/Stop	Is the game being completed in a timely manner consistent with creative and technical goals?

Figure 3.3   Role of Feasibility Analysis in the Development of Successful Business Ideas at Activision

product can also receive a "red light" and be terminated or sent back for further development and review.

The boxed feature titled "Partnering for Success" describes an approach to usability testing employed at Apple Computer.

Apple Computer: Partnering with Customers to Produce Software Products That Work

www.appleseed.apple.com

Typically, firms don't consider their customers "partners." But Apple Computer has implemented a program called "Apple Software Customer Seeding" in an effort to partner with its customers to develop software products that work. The program allows customers to test prerelease software products and then provide Apple software engineers with real-world quality and usability feedback. It is a hands-on program that facilitates a dialogue between Apple users and Apple software engineers during rather than after the development of a software product.

The program works like this. An Apple user can express interest in the program by completing a customer profile that is available on Apple's Web site. The program is voluntary, and there is no compensation. When the development of a software product begins, the development team selects volunteers from the customer profiles on the basis of customer skill level, demographics, and computing environment. Selected volunteers are then provided access to a software product that is under development and are asked to provide feedback through Web forums, discussion lists, mailing lists, engineering questionnaires, and bug reporting tools. Each participant signs a confidentiality agreement because software products are usually expensive to develop and Apple doesn't want to lose trade secrets or proprietary information to competitors.

The Customer Seeding Program is important to Apple because it helps the company test the usability of its products and keeps it attuned to the needs, preferences, and desires of its users. It also sends a message to customers that the company cares about their input and suggestions. Participants like the program because it gives them a first look at new and upcoming software programs. It also gives them the unique opportunity to interact directly with Apple engineers. The Customer Seeding Program is a good example of how companies can "partner" with their customers. It is also a savvy approach to product feasibility analysis.

Questions for Critical Thinking

1. If you owned an entrepreneurial venture, would you want to partner with Apple as described in this "Partnering for Success" feature? Why or why not?

2. Do you think Apple would be willing to reciprocate with its partners? In other words, if your small entrepreneurial venture developed a prototype of a product, would Apple be interested in partnering with you to test its feasibility? What would you do to try to convince Apple to work with you in this manner if the firm's initial response to your request was negative?

Sources: Apple Computer home page, www.apple.com (accessed July 13, 2002), and AppleSeed home page, http://appleseed. apple.com (accessed July 13, 2002).

Industry/Market Feasibility Analysis

Industry/market feasibility analysis is an assessment of the overall appeal of the market for the product or service being proposed. For feasibility analysis, there are three primary issues that a proposed business should consider: industry attractiveness, market timeliness, and the identification of a niche market.[18]

Industry Attractiveness   Industries vary considerably in terms of their growth rate, as shown in Table 3.3. Typically, an industry that is growing is more attractive because it is more receptive to new entrants and new product introductions. A primary determinant of a new venture's feasibility is the attractiveness of the industry it chooses. This is why many venture capitalists, such as Don Valentine of Sequoia Capital, first assess the attractiveness of a start-up's industry when considering funding a new venture.[19] In general, the most attractive industries are characterized as the following:

- Being large and growing (with growth being more important than size).
- Being important to the customer. These markets typically sell products or services that customers "must have" rather than "would like to have."
- Being fairly young rather than older and more mature. These markets tend to be early in their product life cycle, when price competition is not intense.
- Having high rather than low operating margins. These markets are simply more profitable for entry and competition purposes.
- Not being crowded. A crowded market, with lots of competitors, is typically characterized by fierce price competition and low operating margins.

Although this is admittedly an ideal list, the extent to which a new business's proposed industry's growth possibilities satisfy these criteria should be taken seriously. For example, an entrepreneur may have an idea for a new product or service that would ideally suit the needs of a particular customer. The market may not be big enough, however, to support a business. This was part of the problem experienced by Iridium, as mentioned earlier in this chapter. Its product fit a defined need—people who traveled or worked in areas where cellular service was unavailable. The market just wasn't big enough to support the company's cost structure, at least in the company's original form.

In addition to evaluating an industry's growth potential, a new venture will want to know more about the overall attractiveness of the industry it plans to enter. This can be accomplished through both primary and secondary research. **Primary research** is research that is original and is collected by the entrepreneur. In assessing the attractiveness of a market, this typically involves an entrepreneur talking to potential customers and key industry participants. **Secondary research** probes data that are already collected, such as those

Table 3.3

Three-Year Industry Growth in Revenues (1999–2002)

Industry	Three-Year Revenue Growth
Application software	1.9%
Biotechnology	21.1%
Communications equipment	5.1%
Drug manufacturers	5.4%
Electronics stores	7.7%
Internet Information providers	4.5%
Investment brokerage	0.8%
Medical instruments	13.1%
Multimedia/graphics software	1.0%
Personal computers	5.8%
Restaurants	10.2%
Semiconductors	5.1%
Specialty eateries	21.8%
Sporting goods	0.1%
Toys and games	4.2%

Source: Adapted from Hoovers Online, *www.hoovers.com* **(accessed November 1, 2003).**

shown in Table 3.3. The sources of secondary research include industry-related publications, government statistics, competitors' Web sites, and industry reports from respected research firms, such as Forrester Research. There are also many authoritative sources of industry related data available online or in hard copy, as shown in Table 3.4. Most universities buy licenses or subscriptions to these resources and provide access to them to their students, faculty, and staff for free. As evidence that primary and secondary research has been completed, an entrepreneur should have concrete numbers relative to the market size and projected growth rate of the industry that he or she plans to enter. When looking for funding, for example, it is not enough for an entrepreneur to simply say that the research supports that the firm will be participating in a "large and growing market." Instead, an entrepreneur should have hard data to support such a claim.

A caveat to this discussion is that it is impossible to analyze markets that don't exist. This is a challenge confronting entrepreneurs trying to bring breakthrough products or services to market. **Breakthrough products and services** establish new markets or new market segments.[20] Most new products and services feature incremental improvements to existing ones, such as a slightly better DVD player or computer program, while examples of breakthrough products and services include Yahoo and Internet search engines, eBay and online auctions, and Intuit and personal finance software. Each of these companies pioneered the market it entered. In these instances, it is particularly important that a firm conduct primary research to determine if there is a sufficient market for its product or service.

Market Timeliness   A second consideration in regard to the industry/market feasibility of a business idea is the timeliness of the introduction of a particular product or service. The factors to consider vary, depending on whether a prospective business is planning to introduce a breakthrough new product or service or one that is an improvement on those currently available.

If the product or service is an improvement on those already available in the marketplace, the first consideration is to determine whether the window of opportunity for the

Table 3.4

Resources to Facilitate an Industry Analysis

Source	Description
ABI-Inform	Articles covering a wide variety of business- and industry-related issues.
Dun & Bradstreet Industry Handbook	Provides a complete analysis (including an overview, ratios, and statistics) of select industries
Hoovers Online	Brief histories and financial information on companies, industries, people, and products
LexisNexis	Business news along with Securities and Exchange Commission filings
MultexNET	Provides real-time and full-text investment, corporate, and industry reports supplied by over 700 brokerage firms, investment banks, and independent research providers
Reuters Business Insight	Market research and business reports covering a wide range of industries
Standard & Poor's Industry Surveys	Provides 53 industry surveys running 30 to 40 pages each
Value-Line Investment Survey	Provides stock information along with a concise one- to two-page industry commentary at the beginning of each industry section
Wall Street Journal	Financial newspaper offering in-depth coverage of financial markets along with business and industry news

product or service is open or closed. As explained in Chapter 2, some markets, such as the one for Internet search engines, are either saturated with competitors or dominated by competitors with sufficient market power that they are essentially closed to new entrants. Other markets, such as specialty eateries, are characterized by windows of opportunity that are wide open and are receptive to new entrants. The second consideration is to study the simple economics of a marketplace to determine the current dynamics of the industry and whether the timing for a new business is good. For example, the personal computer industry is currently consolidating—look at Hewlett-Packard's acquisition of Compaq and Dell's increasing market dominance. When an industry consolidates, a handful of large firms in the industry acquire or force out of business the smaller firms in the industry and take over the majority of the business. This trend in the personal computer industry suggests that it is not a good time to launch a new personal computer firm.

For new businesses that are developing a potential breakthrough product or service, the issue of whether to try to capture a first-mover advantage is vitally important. A **first-mover advantage** is a sometimes insurmountable advantage gained by the first significant company to move into a new market.[21] Whether getting to market first is truly an advantage remains an active topic for debate. Proponents of first-mover advantage argue that first movers can set the standard for an industry and typically have an advantage in terms of brand recognition and market power.[22] There are many examples of first movers who have captured these advantages, including Palm, Yahoo, and Nokia. Others argue that there are an equal number of disadvantages to being first to market, such as high research-and-development costs, the risk of seeing whether the product or service will catch on, and the risk that a competitor will study the first-mover's product or service and quickly come out with a slightly better version of essentially the same thing.[23] This last disadvantage is compelling. In fact, the term **second-mover advantage** is used to describe the advantage that the second rather than the first entrant has in entering a market. The second mover has the advantage of studying all the mistakes that were made by the first mover, something that observers believe helps the second mover build a better product or service.[24]

A well-crafted feasibility analysis gives a new firm an edge, just like good coaching and hard work allow one runner to outpace others. The key is to complete all four steps in the feasibility analysis process. It's hard work but a carefully executed feasibility analysis can pay rich dividends down the road for a startup firm.

Identifying a Niche Market   The final step in industry/market feasibility analysis is identifying a niche market in which the firm can participate. A **niche market** is a place within a larger market segment that represents a narrower group of customers with similar interests.[25] Most successful entrepreneurial firms do not start by selling to broad markets. Instead, most start by identifying an emerging or underserved niche with a larger market, as discussed in more detail in Chapter 11.[26]

For a new firm, selling to a niche market makes sense for at least two reasons. First, it allows a firm to establish itself within an industry without competing against major participants head on. For example, as discussed in Chapter 2, BuyAndHold.com appeals to new investors who want to invest relatively small amounts of money at a time. With this strategy, BuyAndHold.com avoids competing directly with industry heavyweights Charles Schwab, Merrill Lynch, and Fidelity Investments, among others. Second, a niche strategy allows a firm to focus on serving a specialized market very well instead of trying to be everything to everybody in a broad market, which is nearly impossible for a new entrant. An example is Prometheus Laboratories, a firm selling diagnostic services to the 15,000 doctors in the United States specializing in gastroenterology and rheumatology. Explaining his firm's strategy of developing world-class expertise in a specialized area, Prometheus CEO Michael Walsh said, "We want to be an inch wide and a mile deep."[27]

The challenge in identifying an attractive niche market is that it must be large enough to support a proposed business yet small enough to avoid initial direct head-to-head competition with industry leaders. If a clearly defined niche market cannot be identified, it is difficult to envision the industry/market feasibility of a new business venture.

Organizational Feasibility Analysis

Organizational feasibility analysis is conducted to determine whether a proposed business has sufficient management expertise, organizational competence, and resources to successfully launch its business. There are two primary issues to consider in this area: management prowess and resource sufficiency.

Management Prowess   A firm should candidly evaluate the prowess, or ability, of its management team. Requiring detailed introspection, this means that the entrepreneur must complete a self-assessment. Two of the most important factors in this area are the passion that the solo entrepreneur or the management team has for the business idea and the extent to which the management team or solo entrepreneur understands the markets in which the firm will participate.[28] There are no practical substitutes for strengths in these areas.[29] Although financing, for example, is important, it is not as important as passion for the business and knowledge of the customer. Scott Cook, the founder of Intuit, makes this point:

> Financing is really not the most important issue. If you have a great business, know your customer, and know that what you are doing is superior to what's on the market—that's what it takes to win. But if you have a lousy business idea, financing won't turn it into a good one. Getting money is a necessary requirement, but I really wouldn't focus on the financing. I would focus on knowing the customer cold.[30]

An example of a company that suffered by having a management team that was unfamiliar with the industry it entered is illustrated in "What Went Wrong?" feature in Chapter 6. The feature focuses on an Internet start-up named Garden.com, which was started in 1995 to sell gardening supplies on the Internet. None of Garden.com's three founders had any experience in garden retailing, nor were they knowledgeable gardeners. The firm failed after losing many millions of dollars of its investors' money.

Several other factors should be considered regarding management prowess. Managers with extensive professional and social networks have an advantage in that they are able to reach out to colleagues and friends to help them plug experience or knowledge gaps. In addition, a potential new venture should have an idea of the type of new venture team that it can assemble. A **new venture team** is the group of founders, key employees, and advisers that either manage or help manage a new business in its start-up years. If the founder or

learning **objective**

9. Describe the purpose of organizational feasibility analysis and list the two primary issues to consider in this area.

founders of a new venture have identified several individuals they believe will join the firm after it is launched and these individuals are highly capable, that knowledge lends credibility to the organizational feasibility of the potential venture. The same rationale applies for highly capable people who a new venture believes would be willing to join its board of directors or board of advisers.

Resource Sufficiency   The second area of organizational feasibility analysis is to determine whether the potential new venture has sufficient resources to move forward to successfully develop a product or service idea. The focus in organizational feasibility analysis should be on nonfinancial resources in that financial feasibility is considered separately. Several areas should be examined, including the availability of office space, the quality of the labor pool in the area where the business will be located, and the possibility of obtaining intellectual property protection on key aspects of the new business (intellectual property is discussed in detail in Chapter 12). Some start-ups are able to minimize their initial facility expenses and gain access to resources that they wouldn't have access to otherwise by locating themselves in a community- or university-sponsored business incubator. The advantages of launching a new venture in a business incubator is the subject of the boxed feature titled "Savvy Entrepreneurial Firm."

One resource sufficiency issue that new firms should consider is their proximity to similar firms. There are well-known **clusters** of high-tech firms, for example, in the Silicon Valley of California, on Route 128 around Boston, and in the Cambridge region in the United Kingdom. Clusters arise because they increase the productivity of the firms participating in them. Because these firms are located near one another, it is easy for their employees to network with each other, and it is easy for the firms to gain access to specialized suppliers, scientific knowledge, and technological expertise indigenous to the area. A semiconductor start-up that decided to locate in Kansas City, Missouri, for example, would be at a significant disadvantage to a semiconductor start-up in the Silicon Valley, which already has a cluster of semiconductor firms. Researchers have found that small manufacturing firms benefit more than larger firms by being physically close to a cluster of similar firms.[31]

To test resource sufficiency, it is suggested that a prospective firm list the 6 to 12 most critical nonfinancial resources that will be needed to move its business idea forward and to assess the feasibility of securing those resources for the business. If critical resources are not available in key areas, it may be impracticable to proceed with a business idea.

Financial Feasibility Analysis

Financial feasibility analysis is the final stage of a comprehensive feasibility analysis. For feasibility analysis, a quick financial assessment is usually sufficient. More rigor at this point is typically not required because the specifics of the business will inevitably evolve, making it impractical to spend a lot of time early on preparing detailed financial forecasts. The most important issues to consider at this stage are capital requirements, financial rate of return, and overall attractiveness of investment. If a proposed new venture moves beyond the feasibility analysis stage, it will need to complete pro forma (or projected) financial statements that demonstrate the firm's financial viability for the first one to three years of its existence. In Chapter 7, we'll provide you with specific instructions for preparing these statements.

Capital Requirements   An assessment of the feasibility of raising enough money to fund the capital requirements for the business is necessary. New firms typically need money for a host of purposes, including the hiring of personnel, office or manufacturing space, equipment, training, research and development, marketing, and the initial product rollout. At the feasibility analysis stage, it is not necessary for this number to be exact. However, the number should be fairly accurate and give an entrepreneur an idea of the dollar amount that will be needed to launch the firm.

We fully discuss the topic of raising capital in Chapter 10. In the feasibility analysis stage, what's important is that an entrepreneur has a sense of what the capital requirements will be. The figure that is determined provides important information about the rate of return that can be anticipated from the business and about the type of financing or funding that will be needed.

learning **objective**

10. Explain the importance of financial feasibility analysis and list the most important issues to consider in this area.

Savvy entrepreneurial FIRM

Incubators: An Affordable Choice for Entrepreneurial Start-Ups

Imagine the challenge faced by the average high-tech start-up when it moves into its first facility. Not only is it working hard to develop a technology, but it needs to conduct a feasibility analysis, write a business plan, raise capital, and hire key employees. Along with these critical activities are the more mundane tasks that all businesses face when moving into a new building, such as installing a phone and computer system and ordering office supplies. And what about other considerations that often aren't made until a firm starts looking at office space? Who will answer the phone? Where will the company meet clients or hold staff meetings if it can afford only two or three small offices? Where will the mail be sorted? And where will the money come from? If a start-up is cash strapped and wants to invest every penny it has in a feasibility analysis and product development, can it really afford a receptionist?

These hurdles are precisely why many high-tech start-ups are launched in a business incubator rather than in a stand-alone space. An incubator is a facility that is dedicated to helping new businesses get off the ground in an affordable manner. The first incubator opened in 1942 at Cornell University in Ithaca, New York, to nurture student-run companies. The idea spread as other schools and, later, communities set up facilities to try to encourage entrepreneurship in their local areas. There are now both nonprofit and for-profit incubators throughout the United States as well as in some European nations. Nonprofit incubators are typically sponsored by a local community, university, or research park. Their goal is to identify start-ups with promising ideas and give them the support they need to get up and running. For-profit incubators have a similar mission but usually take an equity stake in the start-ups involved in exchange for their services.

To help a business enjoy a successful launch, most incubators provide their clients subsidized office space and light research-and-development or manufacturing space if necessary. Incubators may also provide office furniture, access to a phone system, access to a computer network, a common conference room, a receptionist that is shared with other incubator clients, and consulting on topics of interest to start-ups. There are now over 900 small-business or new venture incubators in the United States. On a global scale, incubators are growing in popularity as more communities try to attract promising start-ups.

The Valley Technology Park Incubator at the University of Minnesota, Crookston, is an example of an interesting nonprofit incubator. Located in the small community of Crookston (population 8,900) in northwestern Minnesota, this incubator opened in 1999 with an emphasis on emerging companies with technology-oriented products and services. It is funded through a joint effort of the City of Crookston, Polk County (Minnesota), the University of Minnesota, and several other nonprofit organizations. The incubator, which currently has 15 clients, offers the following services:

- Office, laboratory, technology, and light manufacturing space
- Affordable rental rates, including basic utilities
- Business planning and development assistance
- Conference room
- Shared secretarial and reception services
- Shared access to copiers, fax machines, and other office equipment
- On-site postal and freight services
- Ample, free parking
- Access to the University of Minnesota's facilities and services, including child care, library, audio/visual resources, conference facilities, and cafeteria
- Counseling regarding topics of interest to small-business start-ups

This list of support services illustrates the cost savings associated with launching a business in an incubator. Added benefits of locating in an incubator include the networking opportunities associated with being in close proximity to other incubator clients. These networking opportunities allow firms to develop contacts with other people and companies that may help them both at the time of launch and in the future. There are several important questions the new firm must ask before enrolling in an incubator program, particularly if the incubator is new:

1. How long has the incubator been in operation?

2. What percentage of the companies that have been in the incubator graduated successfully? (A company "graduates" when it can afford to move out of the incubator and make it on its own.)

3. How long, on average, have clients remained in the incubator program?

4. What are the qualifications of the incubator staff?

5. What are the services offered, and how much do they cost?

Financial Rate of Return   Return on assets, return on equity, and return on investment are examples of the many ways the rate of return expected from a new business can be projected. This is another topic that is discussed in Chapter 7. In the feasibility analysis stage, it is important to determine whether the projected return is adequate to justify the business. Adequate is a relative term and depends on one or more of the following factors:

- The amount of capital invested
- The amount of time required to earn the return
- The risks assumed in launching the business
- The existing alternatives for the money being invested
- The existing alternatives for the entrepreneur's time and efforts

Although situations vary, several considerations can be made to determine the rate of return that is necessary to justify investing in a business. Opportunities demanding substantial capital, requiring long periods of time to mature, and having a lot of risk involved make little sense unless they provide high rates of return. For example, it simply makes no economic sense for a group of entrepreneurs to invest $10 million in a capital-intense risky start-up that offers a 3 percent rate of return. Three percent interest can be earned through a money market fund, with essentially no risk. The adequacy of returns also depends on the alternatives the individuals involved have. For example, an individual who is thinking about leaving a $150,000-per-year job to start a new firm requires a higher rate of return than the person thinking about leaving a $50,000-per-year job.[32]

Overall Attractiveness of the Investment   A number of other financial factors are associated with promising business opportunities. In the feasibility analysis stage, the extent to which a business opportunity is positive relative to each factor is based on an estimate or forecast rather than actual performance. Table 3.5 provides a list of the factors that pertain to the overall financial feasibility of a business opportunity.[33]

In summary, feasibility analysis is a vital step in the process of developing successful business ideas. Many entrepreneurs, in their haste to get their idea to market, neglect to conduct a thorough feasibility analysis. This approach is almost always a mistake and, more often than not, results in failure.

Table 3.5

Financial Feasibility

- Steady and rapid growth in sales during the first five to seven years in a clearly defined market niche
- High percentage of recurring revenue—meaning that once a firm wins a client, the client will provide recurring sources of revenue
- Ability to forecast income and expenses with a reasonable degree of certainty
- Internally generated funds to finance and sustain growth
- Availability of an exit opportunity (such as an acquisition or an initial public offering) for investors to convert equity into cash

1. Feasibility analysis is the process of determining whether a business idea is viable. It is a preliminary evaluation of a business idea, conducted for the purpose of determining whether the idea is worth pursuing.

2. The proper time to conduct a feasibility analysis is early in thinking through the prospects for a new business idea. It follows opportunity recognition but comes before the development of a business plan.

3. The feasibility analysis should be preceded by the development of a concept statement. A concept statement is a preliminary description of a business. The concept statement should include a description of the product or service being offered, the intended target market, the benefits of the product or service, and a description of how the product or service will be sold and distributed.

4. Product/service feasibility analysis is an assessment of the overall appeal of the product or service being proposed. Concept testing and usability testing are the two primary issues that a proposed business should consider in this area.

5. There are three primary purposes for concept testing: to validate the underlying premises behind a product or service idea, to help develop an idea rather than just test it, and to estimate the potential market share the potential product or service might command.

6. Usability testing is a method by which users of a product or service are asked to perform certain tasks in order to measure the product's ease of use and the user's perception of and satisfaction with the experience.

7. Industry/market feasibility analysis is an assessment of the overall appeal of the market for the product or service being proposed. For feasibility analysis, there are three primary issues that a proposed business should consider: industry attractiveness, market timeliness, and the identification of a niche market.

8. Primary research is research that is original and is collected by the entrepreneur. In assessing the attractiveness of a market, this typically involves an entrepreneur talking to potential customers and/or key industry participants. Secondary research is examined to discover meaning in or from data that are already collected.

9. Organizational feasibility analysis is conducted to determine whether a proposed business has sufficient management expertise, organizational competence, and resources to successfully launch its business. There are two primary issues to consider in this area: management prowess and resource sufficiency.

10. Financial feasibility analysis is a preliminary financial analysis of whether a business idea is prudent. The most important issues to consider are capital requirements, financial rate of return, and overall attractiveness of the investment.

breakthrough products and services, 62

clusters, 65

concept statement, 56

concept test, 57

core competency, 55

feasibility analysis, 52

financial feasibility analysis, 65

first-mover advantage, 63

follow-me-home testing, 59

industry/market feasibility analysis, 61

new venture team, 64

niche market, 64

organizational feasibility analysis, 64

primary research, 61

product/service feasibility analysis, 57

prototyping, 58

secondary research, 61

second-mover advantage, 63

seed money, 54

usability testing, 58

1. What is a feasibility analysis? What is it designed to accomplish?

2. Briefly describe each of the four areas that a properly executed feasibility analysis explores.

3. What is a concept statement? Why is it important to develop a concept statement before initiating a feasibility analysis?

4. What is product/service feasibility analysis?

5. What is a concept test, and what does it accomplish? What are the three primary purposes for it?

6. What is a usability test, and what does it accomplish?

7. Define prototyping.

8. Describe Intuit's "follow-me home" testing methodology.

9. What is industry/market feasibility analysis?

10. Describe the attributes of an attractive industry for a new venture.

11. Describe the difference between primary and secondary research. Provide an example of each.

12. What is a breakthrough new product or service? Provide several examples.

13. Identify the pluses and minuses of trying to capture a first-mover advantage.

14. Why is it important for a new venture to identify a niche market in which it can participate?

15. What is organizational feasibility analysis?

16. Briefly describe each of the two primary issues to consider when conducting an organizational feasibility analysis.

17. What is the purpose of a business incubator?

18. Why is it usually to a firm's advantage to be located near similar firms in its industry?

19. What is financial feasibility analysis?

20. Briefly describe the three primary issues to consider when conducting a financial feasibility analysis.

1. Jason Palmer has an idea for a new approach to personal finance software. He plans to use the $200,000 inheritance he recently received to produce the product and bring it to market. When you ask Jason if he has conducted a feasibility analysis, he acts alarmed and says, "I knew I'd have to write a business plan, but I'm not familiar with what you are calling a feasibility analysis. I don't want to blow the $200,000 I just inherited, so if a feasibility study is necessary, I'm game. Can you tell me how to conduct one?" What would you tell Jason?

2. A good friend of yours, Abby Franklin, has decided to open a sporting goods store geared toward adults 55 years of age and older. As far as she knows, her store will be the only sporting goods store in the United States focused specifically on older adults. Using your imagination, write a concept statement for Abby's proposed venture.

3. Ann O'Neil, who has considerable experience in the home security industry, is planning to launch a firm that will sell a new line of home security alarms that she believes will be superior to anything currently on the market. She is weighing whether to take the time to conduct a product/service feasibility analysis, given the amount of industry experience that she has. If she asked you for your advice, what would you tell her are the benefits of conducting a product/service feasibility analysis?

4. Marc is planning to open a fitness center that will feature a set of exercise machines that he designed himself. He would like to do some usability testing of the machines but doesn't know how to go about it. If Marc asked you for your advice, what would you tell him?

5. Carrie Wells is planning to open a store to sell DVDs in Nashville. As part of her feasibility study, she hands out a questionnaire to 500 people in her trade area, asking them to indicate whether they would shop at her store. Carrie is pleased to find that 75 percent of the people surveyed said they would either "definitely" or "probably" shop in her store at least once a month. Should Carrie plan her business based on the 75 percent figure? Why or why not?

6. Recently, you were telling a friend about Intuit, in particular about the company's "follow-me-home" usability testing methodology. Your friend, who plans to launch a business to sell and make modifications on all-terrain vehicles (ATVs), was intrigued by the story. Describe how your friend could use the follow-me-home methodology to improve the quality of usability testing for his business.

7. Steve Ambrose, who is a physical therapist, is thinking about starting a firm in the medical instruments industry. He would like to know more about the industry, however, before proceeding. Provide Steve with suggestions for conducting primary and secondary research on the industry.

8. Kate Wilson has developed an innovative suite of software products for K–12 schools. She is wondering if now is a good time to launch a business to sell her products. What factors should Kate consider in making this determination?

9. Wayne Baker has invented a new type of skateboard. He is anxious to get it to market to capture first-mover advantages. Wayne seemed somewhat puzzled when you told him that there are both advantages and disadvantages of capturing a first-mover advantage. Explain to Wayne what you meant by your statement.

10. Pam Berry is launching a laser-optics firm in Orlando and has the opportunity to occupy space in the University of Central Florida Technology Incubator. Pam asked you whether you're acquainted with incubators and, if so, whether you know what the advantages of locating in an incubator are for new firms. What would you tell Pam?

you be the VC

Company: Air-Grid Networks (www.air-grid.com)

Business idea: Rent handheld wireless devices to the patrons of sporting events such as Major League Baseball. The devices are to provide live video and play-by-play audio of the game on the field, featuring a selection of camera angles. The devices will also have access to the Internet, e-mail, and television and radio broadcasts of simultaneously occurring sports events.

Pitch: Air-Grid's product will get fans closer to the action, allow them to surf the Web, and provide them the opportunity to place an order at a concession stand, all from the comfort of their seats. For sports teams, it provides a new way to generate revenues. The cost to a fan would be roughly $25 per game. Air-Grid Networks and the sponsoring sporting event would share the revenues.

Q&A: Based on the material covered in this chapter, what questions would you ask the firm's founders before making your funding decision? What answers would satisfy you?

Decision: If you had to make your decision on just the information provided in the pitch and the company's Web site, would you fund this firm? Why or why not?

Case 3.1

Knowing Your Customers: Why Instant Messaging Is More Popular at Home Than at the Office

High-tech firms face the challenge of creating products driven by customer need rather than those driven by the capabilities of technology. The "ready, fire, aim" approach to product development takes place when firms design products first and then try to determine whether there is demand among the target audience. A more preferable approach to product development is "ready, aim, fire," which is characterized by understanding customers' needs first and then developing products to fill the need.

An interesting example of the importance of understanding customer need is instant messaging, a tool that allows a PC user to maintain a list of people—called contacts or "buddies"—that he or she communicates with and to send a message to anyone on the list, provided that person is online and is using the same program. Sending a message opens up a small window that allows the two parties to communicate with each other. Several windows can be open at the same time, allowing the user to simultaneously engage in several conversations. The most popular instant messaging programs provide the following benefits to users:

- *Instant messages:* The ability to send notes back and forth with a friend or coworker
- *Chat:* The ability to create your own custom chat rooms with friends or coworkers
- *Web links:* The ability to share your favorite Web links with friends or coworkers

- *Images:* The ability to look at an image stored on your friend's or coworker's computer
- *Sounds:* The ability to play sounds for friends or coworkers
- *Data:* The ability to send data (such as a Microsoft Word document) to a friend or coworker's computer

Instant messaging is widely popular. According to Nielsen, a media research firm, more than 41 million people were using instant messaging in their homes, and 12.6 million were using it in the workplace in 2002. What's interesting about these figures, aside from their size, is that instant messaging has caught on in a much more pervasive way at home than at work. To understand why, we need to look at who uses instant messaging and the reasons they do so.

Teenagers are one of the largest demographic groups of instant messaging. For most teens, the ideal form of communication is a face-to-face meeting, but they also enjoy talking to one another in groups. This behavior can easily be seen by watching interactions among teens in a mall or at school. Because it mimics their natural behavior, instant messaging is a comfortable way of communicating for teens. A teen may have three or four friends whom he or she talks to regularly, and instant messaging allows the user to talk to all of them simultaneously. For teens, this ability to talk to more than one person at the same time also gives instant messaging an edge over e-mail. This sentiment is expressed in a research report by Cheskin, a marketing research firm that interviewed a number of teens about e-mail and instant messaging usage:

> Ethan is a 19-year-old from the Chicago area. He says, "I'm not really a big fan of e-mail—I like to IM [instant message] people more than e-mail. When you IM it's like talking to a person face-to-face and e-mail is like just leaving a message on the machine. It's like being at home with a friend or in a coffee shop and just catching up on stuff on what is going on and stuff like that.

Instant messaging is also popular among young adults and is growing in popularity for older users. Adults use instant messaging primarily to keep in touch with relatives, their children at college, and friends who have moved. Again, instant messaging is successful in these contexts because it mimics the behaviors that people perform naturally. Imagine a mom chatting with her daughter on a weekend the daughter is home from college. The mom might ask the daughter a hundred questions, such as, "Is the food good?" "How are your classes going?" and "Whatever happened to that guy named Steve you were dating?" Via instant messaging, these are exactly the types of questions that a mom can ask her daughter who is perhaps thousands of miles away in school. And she can do so any time of day or night. Understanding these needs and behaviors, companies featuring instant messaging as part of their Internet service, such as America Online, MSN, and Yahoo, have marketed the service heavily to teens and families.

Now consider instant messaging in a business context. In the fall of 2000, a prominent marketing research firm predicted that 70 percent of all corporations would make instant messaging available to their employees by early 2002. It was believed that employees would use instant messaging to chat with each other during the workday and even to chat with key customers or suppliers. But as it turns out, the usage rates among businesspeople are not anywhere close to the 70 percent figure. Why? Because businesspeople behave differently than teens and PC users at home. Instant messaging just isn't as appropriate in a business setting. It has nothing to do with the technology and everything to do with the way that businesspeople think and behave. Some businesspeople are reluctant, for example, to let everyone on their buddy list know when they are or aren't online. Imagine one coworker saying

to another, "I checked my buddy list three times last week at 4:30 P.M. , and you weren't online any of those times. Where were you?" Or consider an employee who is urgently trying to complete an important project being distracted by repeated instant messaging requests from an important customer. What does the employee do? Stop working on the project, or ignore the customers? Security is another important issue. A sales manager may encourage her employees to talk freely about an upcoming sales campaign in a secure conference room. But is it secure to let employees chat about the strategy online? Future generations of instant messaging products are working to provide solutions to these dilemmas, such as disguising whether a user is online and his or her instant messaging program is open. However, the solutions aren't perfected yet.

In its current form, instant messaging is simply more appealing to users at home than to users at work. This product provides an excellent example of the importance of knowing your customer; and it's knowing their customers that allows firms to take the "ready, aim, fire" approach to product development.

Discussion Questions

1. Do you think the instant messaging companies understand business users as well as they understand teens and at home PC users? If so, why haven't they worked harder to overcome some of the limitations that instant messaging has in a business context?

2. How would you conduct a product/service feasibility analysis for instant messaging in a business context?

3. How would you conduct a product/service feasibility analysis for wireless applications of instant messaging (such as making instant messaging available on cell phones and/or handheld computers) for the teen market?

4. What appropriate applications for instant messaging do you see in the business market? What would influence you to use instant messaging in a business setting, and what factors would discourage you from doing so?

Source: R. Perera, "Instant Messaging Gets Down to Business," IDG News Service, November 15, 2001, www.pcworld.com (accessed July 15, 2002), and Cheskin Web site, "Designing Digital Experiences for Youth," www.cheskin.com (accessed July 5, 2002).

Case 3.2

iRobot: Proving the Feasibility of a Consumer Robotics Product
www.irobot.com

Your best friend just called to say she's on her way over with her new boyfriend. Your apartment is a mess! There are dirty dishes in the sink, and the carpet is covered with cat hair. Your guests will be here in half an hour. Which chore should you tackle?

Thanks to Roomba, you can accomplish both. Roomba is a small robot that vacuums by itself. It even turns itself off when it's finished! So while you wash the dishes, it'll pick up the cat hair.

Roomba was created by iRobot, a firm launched in 1990 by Colin Angle, Helen Greiner, and Rod Brooks. Both Angle and Greiner were students of Brooks, who heads the Artificial Intelligence Laboratory at the Massachusetts Institute of Technology. While working together at the lab, the three shared a vision of creating robots that would improve people's everyday lives.

Once iRobot was launched, the first idea the entrepreneurs concentrated on was a wireless massager that could climb up a person's back and, with thermal sensors, detect and rub sensitive areas. That idea was eventually scrapped as being too expensive. Over the next 10 years, the company worked on a number of consumer robotics products, with limited success. It was able to stay afloat only by getting contracts to build specialized robots for the military, such as roving search robots used in Afghanistan. In the late 1990s, it pushed harder to crack the consumer marketplace. In 2000, it created a doll called My Real Baby, which giggled when its feet were tickled and displayed other human characteristics. The Roomba came along in 2001. Initially, it was designed to be a mechanical carpet sweeper. The project's direction changed as the result of a focus group that urged the company to make the product a vacuum cleaner, even if the price had to increase.

Sensing that it was on to something, iRobot fully committed itself to making a robot vacuum cleaner. The potential market for the product included seniors, the disabled, and anyone wanting relief from the task of vacuuming carpets or floors. Designing the product turned out to be harder than anticipated. It went through about 20 iterations before it was ready for market and ended up having over 100 parts. When the prototype was shipped to its contract manufacturer in China for production, the kinks took four months to work out rather than the anticipated two weeks. Recalling this hectic period in the development of the product, iRobot cofounder Angle said, "Every day, there'd be a list of problems 50 items long. The minutiae were terrifying."

Proving that hard work pays off, Roomba, which is the product that emerged, turned out to be pretty nifty. It looks like an oversize Frisbee that crawls around on the floor gobbling up dust and crumbs. The only controls are an "on" switch and three buttons to specify whether the room is small, medium, or large. When it's turned on, it starts moving around the room, vacuuming the carpet or floor. In about half an hour or so, depending on the size of the room, it declares victory and stops. The device works on a battery that is rechargeable. The dirt ends up in a plastic cartridge. Roomba has special sensors that help it navigate and prevent it from falling down a set of stairs or leaving a room. It bumps into objects without disrupting or damaging them.

The market response to Roomba has been mostly positive. It was initially sold through retailers such as Target, Linens 'n Things, Brookstone, and Sharper Image. At first, "people were enamored with the whole idea of the Jetsons becoming real," Brookstone CEO Michael Anthony said. While the reviews of the functionality of Roomba have been generally positive,

some kinks have tempered the initial enthusiasm for the product. One review of Roomba, from an author writing in *Scientific American*, said,

> I tried Roomba on low-pile carpets and hardwood floors in rooms both empty and full. It didn't damage or topple anything, and it did remarkably well at extricating itself from power and phone cords, either by shifting direction or temporarily shutting off the brush. . . . Much as I tried, I couldn't entice Roomba to fall down a flight of stairs. I even put it on a table and let it clear off the crumbs. . . . Roomba slurped up most of the filth, but it didn't replace the need for manual vacuuming or sweeping, and iRobot is wise not to claim it does. The real Achilles' heel of the robot, though, is the wire that is supposed to keep rug corners from jamming the brush. It got yanked off within a couple runs, and the company had to send me a new one. . . . And even though it was usually able to free itself from cords, "usually" was not good enough: it got hung up at least once per run. You don't have to watch Roomba continuously, but you had better be nearby to help it.

One of the most common complaints involving the original Roomba (alluded to in the previous quote) is that it isn't a substitute for a regular vacuum cleaner. It was meant to keep floors clean between regular vacuuming, so many buyers who tried to use Roomba as a substitute for their regular vacuum cleaner were disappointed. To counter this disappointment, iRobot is planning to market new versions of Roomba that will have sufficient power to replace regular vacuuming for all but the deepest carpets. "We didn't realize for many people [Roomba] was going to start replacing the upright as the primary vacuum," iRobot CEO Angle said.

iRobot is currently working on additional products for the consumer marketplace. After 10 years of waiting and hard work, the company feels as though it is finally realizing its vision of creating robots that enhance people's lives. Especially when company's coming!

Discussion Questions

1. Based on the information continued in the case, develop a concept statement for the Roomba.

2. Look at iRobot's Web site at www.irobot.com. Study the backgrounds of its three cofounders. On the basis of these backgrounds, do you think it was easy or difficult for iRobot to convince potential investors and business partners that the firm had sufficient "management prowess" to be a serious player in the robotics industry?

3. As mentioned in the case, some of the original buyers of the Roomba were disappointed because it isn't a substitute for a regular vacuum cleaner. iRobot cofounder Colin Angle seemed to be surprised by this development,

as shown in the following quotation: "We didn't realize for many people [the Roomba] was going to start replacing the upright as the primary vacuum." What could iRobot have done to better anticipate this complication and to be prepared to deal with it quickly?

4. Come up with a household chore, other than vacuuming, that could potentially be done by a robot. Let's say you suggest your idea to iRobot, and they ask you to plan a product/service feasibility study for the idea. List all the steps that would be included in your study.

Source: J. Saranow, "Robot Vacuum Nips at Uprights," Wall Street Journal, August 27, 2003, D4; L. Buchanan, "Death to Cool," Inc., July 1, 2003; "How the Roomba Was Realized: iRobot's Vacuum Is a Hit—But It Took Plenty of Trial and Error to Get There," BusinessWeek, October 6, 2003, 10; and G. Musser, "Robots That Suck," Scientific American, February 2003, 84

four

industry and competitor *analysis*

OBJECTIVES

After studying this chapter, you should be ready to:

1. Explain the purpose of an industry analysis.

2. Identify the five competitive forces that determine industry profitability.

3. Explain the role of "barriers to entry" in creating disincentives for firms to enter an industry.

4. Identify the nontraditional barriers to entry that are especially associated with entrepreneurial firms.

5. List the four industry-related questions to ask before pursuing the idea for a firm.

6. Identify the five primary industry types and the opportunities they offer.

7. Explain the purpose of a competitor analysis.

8. Identify the three groups of competitors a new firm will face.

9. Describe ways a firm can ethically obtain information about its competitors.

10. Describe the reasons for completing a competitive analysis grid.

jetblue: occupying a unique position in a difficult industry—and thriving!

The airline industry may well be the worst possible industry in which to start a new firm. It is plagued by high fixed costs, low profit margins, and fierce competition—factors that have created a poor environment for start-ups. In fact, since the airline industry was deregulated in 1978, over 100 new entrants have failed.

So how has JetBlue, an airline launched in 1998, posted profits since it was founded while its rivals have lost billions? Did JetBlue simply beat the odds? Not at all. First, through founder David Neeleman's leadership, JetBlue staked out a favorable position in the airline industry. Next, he tested the feasibility of what he planned to do, and finally he crafted a business model that

works. Despite the perception that the airline industry was one of the toughest to enter, Neeleman believed that the window of opportunity was open for a new airline that offered both low fares and a distinctive style.

To understand how JetBlue came together, a little background information on its founder is in order. In 1984, Neeleman cocreated Morris Air, the Salt Lake City–based airline that devised the concept of ticketless travel. Nine years later, Southwest Airlines acquired Morris. Although Neeleman took a job with Southwest, he lasted only six months. An engineer at heart, he was appalled by the lack of automation. "When I got to Southwest, you couldn't even make a reservation on the phone. You were instructed to go to the airport to buy your ticket," Neeleman later remembered.[1] As part of his severance package from Southwest, he signed a five-year agreement that barred him from starting a competing airline.

After leaving Southwest, Neeleman cofounded a company called Open Skies that sold an accounting and reservation system to airlines. The system tightly integrated electronic ticketing, electronic booking, and revenue management tools. The lore that surrounds Neeleman is that he spent every day from the time he left Southwest until the day he launched JetBlue thinking about what it would take to operate a successful airline. "We tested a lot of technologies during that time," Neeleman said. "Open Skies became a great test laboratory for JetBlue."[2]

In 1998, Neeleman's noncompete agreement with Southwest expired, and he began to put together JetBlue. From the outset, he decided that JetBlue would occupy a unique position in the airline industry: it would offer discount fares and a unique flying experience by avoiding the industry's largest negatives. In pursuit of that goal, the following decisions were made. These decisions formed the underlying strategy and distinctive nature of the start-up venture.

- JetBlue decided to serve handpicked markets rather than compete head to head with the major carriers nationwide. In this way, the company did not have to support a costly hub-and-spoke system (such as United and American), which is necessary to reach all markets. Instead, it offered point-to-point service in high-volume corridors, such as New York to South Florida. "We didn't want to be all things to all people. We wanted to go where we could make money," Neeleman said.[3]

- The company decided to avoid travel agents (average cost: $14 per ticket). Instead, its reservation agents answer calls from their homes (average cost: $4.50 per ticket). The company also pushes online ticket sales (average cost: 50 cents per ticket).

- The company decided to build efficiency into everything it does and use state-of-the-art technology. For example, JetBlue created the first paperless cockpit, which equips pilots with laptops that speed maintenance checks and turnaround times at gates. The company also uses only one type of airplane, the Airbus 320, to minimize maintenance and training expenses.

- The company decided to offer a unique flying experience. In Neeleman's mind, the airline industry suffered from a product opportunity gap. What travelers resented most about airlines, Neeleman believed, was being herded around and stuck in cramped cabins for hours with few if any choices. To keep its seats full, JetBlue offered an alternative to that experience: individual television monitors and choice of channels for each passenger, efficient check-in, leather seats, more leg room than other airlines, direct routes, and an affordable price.

The most impressive thing about JetBlue's business model is that it is self-reinforcing. Its planes are full because it offers amenities, low fares, and flies direct routes in attractive markets. At the same time, it is able to offer amenities and low fares because its planes are full and it is highly efficient. The results of Jet Blue's efforts are striking. The airline's on-time arrival rate of nearly 80 percent leads the airline industry, and JetBlue's profitability from its beginning is a rarity in the airline industry.

JetBlue is a success because of Neeleman's ability to analyze the airline industry and precisely position JetBlue within it. In this chapter, we'll look at industry analysis and competitor analysis. The first section of the chapter considers **industry analysis**, which is business research that focuses on the potential of an industry. An **industry** is a group of firms producing a similar product or service, such as airlines, fitness drinks, or electronic games. Once it is determined that a new venture is feasible in regard to the industry and market in which it will compete, a more in-depth analysis in needed to learn the ins and outs of the industry the firm plans to enter. This analysis helps a firm determine if the niche markets it identified during its feasibility analysis are accessible and which ones represent the best point of entry for a new firm.

The second section of the chapter focuses on competitor analysis. A **competitor analysis** is a detailed evaluation of a firm's competitors. Once a firm decides to enter an industry and chooses a market in which to compete, it must gain an understanding of its competitive environment. We'll look at how a firm identifies its competition and the importance of completing a competitive analysis grid.

Industry Analysis

learning **objective**

1. Explain the purpose of an industry analysis.

When studying an industry, an entrepreneur must answer three questions before pursuing the idea of starting a firm. First, is the industry accessible—in other words, is it a realistic place for a new venture to enter? Second, does the industry contain markets that are ripe for innovation or are underserved? Third, are there positions in the industry that will avoid some of the negative attributes of the industry as a whole? It is useful for a new venture to think about its **position** at both the company level and the product or service level. At the company level, a firm's position determines how the entire company is situated relative to its competitors. For example, JetBlue has positioned itself as a short- to medium-haul airline that services heavily traveled routes, primarily in the eastern United States. Northwest Airlines, in comparison, has positioned itself as a medium- to long-haul airline that serves both domestic and international markets. Sometimes, through savvy positioning, a firm can enter an unattractive industry and do well. Because it found an attractive niche market and has nicely positioned itself in that market, JetBlue is profitable even though it competes in an unattractive industry.

The importance of knowing the competitive landscape, which is what an industry is, may have been first recognized in the fourth century B.C. by Sun-tzu, a Chinese philosopher. Reputedly, he wrote *The Art of War* to help generals prepare for battle. However, the ideas in the book are still used to help managers prepare their firms for the competitive wars of the marketplace. The following quote from Sun-tzu's work points out the importance of industry analysis:

> We are not fit to lead an army on the march unless we are familiar with the face of the country—its pitfalls and precipices, its marshes and swamps.[4]

These words serve as a reminder to entrepreneurs that regardless of how eager they are to start their businesses, they are not adequately prepared until they are "familiar with the face of the country"—that is, until they understand the industry or industries they plan to enter.

The Importance of Industry— Versus Firm-Specific Factors

To illustrate the importance of the industry a firm chooses to enter, research has shown that both firm- and industry-specific factors contribute to a firm's profitability.[5] Firm-level factors include a firm's assets, products, culture, teamwork among its employees, reputation, and other resources. Industry-specific factors include the threat of new entrants, rivalry among existing firms, the bargaining power of suppliers, and other factors discussed in this chapter. A number of studies have tried to determine if firm specific- or industry-specific factors are more important. Virtually all the studies have concluded that firm-specific factors are the most important, although the industry a firm chooses is important too.[6] In various studies, researchers have found that from 8[7] to 30[8] percent of the variation in firm profitability is directly attributable to the industry in which a firm competes. In a recent study, Harvard University professor Michael Porter, the author of the five competitive forces framework discussed in the next section, found that 19 percent of the variation in firm profitability is attributable to stable industry effects. Commenting on the 19 percent figure, Porter concluded, "This result provides strong support for the idea that industry membership has an important influence on [firm] profitability."[9]

Because both firm- and industry-level factors are important in determining a firm's profitability, there are firms that do well in unattractive industries, as illustrated in the JetBlue case. Still, the overall attractiveness of an industry should be part of the equation when an entrepreneur decides whether to pursue a particular business opportunity. A new venture can use the five forces to assess the overall attractiveness of the industry it plans to enter and to determine if a favorable position to occupy exists in that industry.

The Five Competitive Forces That Determine Industry Profitability

learning **objective**

2. Identify the five competitive forces that determine industry profitability.

The five competitive forces model is a framework for understanding the structure of an industry and was developed by Harvard professor Michael Porter. Shown in Figure 4.1, the framework is comprised of the forces that determine industry profitability.[10] These forces—the threat of substitutes, the entry of new competitors, rivalry among existing firms, the bargaining power of suppliers, and the bargaining power of buyers—determine the average rate of return for the firms in an industry.

Each of Porter's five forces impacts the average rate of return for the firms in an industry by applying pressure on industry profitability. Well-managed companies try to position their firms in a way that avoids or diminishes these forces—in an attempt to beat the average rate of return for the industry. For example, the rivalry among existing firms in the airline industry is high. JetBlue diminished the impact of this threat to its profitability by avoiding head-to-head competition with the major carriers in most markets. This is part of the reason that JetBlue outperforms the average profitability of the airline industry.

In his book *Competitive Advantage*, Porter points out that industry profitability is not a function of a product's features. Although it was written in 1985 and the dynamics of the industries mentioned have changed, Porter's essential point remains correct:

> Industry profitability is not a function of what the product looks like or whether it embodies high or low technology but of industry structure. Some very mundane industries such as postage meters and grain trading are extremely profitable, while some more glamorous, high-technology industries such as personal computers and cable television are not profitable for many participants.[11]

The five competitive forces that determine industry profitability are described next.

Threat of Substitutes The price that consumers are willing to pay for a product depends in part on the availability of substitute products. For example, there are few if any substitutes for prescription medicines, which is one of the reasons the pharmaceutical industry is so profitable. When a person is sick, he or she typically doesn't quibble with the pharmacist about the price of a medicine. In contrast, when close substitutes for a product do exist, industry profitability is suppressed because consumers will opt not to buy when the price is too high. Consider the price of movie tickets. If the price gets too high, consumers can easily switch to watching rented videos or pay-per-view.

The extent to which substitutes suppress the profitability of an industry depends on the propensity for buyers to substitute alternatives. This is why the firms in an industry

Figure 4.1

Forces That Determine Industry Profitability

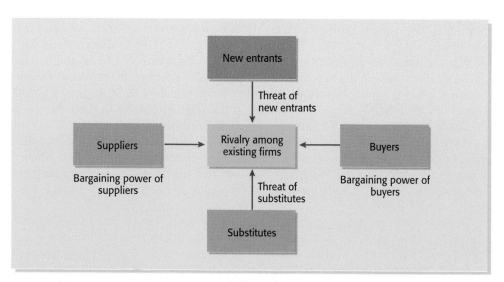

Source: M. Porter, *Competitive Strategy: Techniques for Analyzing Industries and Competitors* (New York: Free Press, 1980)

often offer their customers amenities to reduce the likelihood of their switching to a substitute product, even in light of a price increase. Let's look at the coffee restaurant industry as an example of this. The coffee sold at Starbucks is relatively expensive. A consumer could easily find a less expensive cup of coffee at a donut shop or brew coffee at home rather than pay more at Starbucks. To decrease the likelihood that customers will choose either of these alternatives, Starbucks offers high-quality fresh coffee, a pleasant atmosphere, and good service. Some Starbucks restaurants even offer their customers access to computers and the Internet as a way of motivating them to remain loyal to Starbucks. Starbucks doesn't do this just so its customers don't go to a different coffee restaurant. It offers the service so its customers won't switch to substitute products as well.

Threat of New Entrants   If the firms in an industry are highly profitable, the industry becomes a magnet to new entrants. Unless something is done to stop this, the competition in the industry will increase, and average industry profitability will decline. There are a number of ways that firms in an industry can keep the number of new entrants low. These techniques are referred to as barriers to entry. A **barrier to entry** is a condition that creates a disincentive for a new firm to enter an industry. Let's look at the six major sources of barriers to entry:

learning **objective**

3. Explain the role of "barriers to entry" in creating disincentives for firms to enter an industry.

- *Economies of scale:* Industries that are characterized by large economies of scale are difficult for new firms to enter, unless they are willing to accept a cost disadvantage. **Economies of scale** occur when mass-producing a product results in lower average costs. For example, Intel has huge microchip factories that produce vast quantities of chips, thereby reducing the average cost of a chip. It would be difficult for a new entrant to match Intel's advantage in this area.
- *Product differentiation:* Industries such as the soft drink industry that are characterized by firms with strong brands are difficult to break into without spending heavily on advertising. For example, imagine how costly it would be to compete head to head against Pepsi or Coca-Cola.
- *Capital requirements:* The need to invest large amounts of money to gain entrance to an industry is another barrier to entry. The airline industry is characterized by large capital requirements, although JetBlue was able to overcome this barrier by winning the confidence of investors through the strength of its business model and its management team. Similarly, it currently takes about two years and $4 million to develop a single electronic game (such as those sold by Electronic Arts and Activision).[12] Many new firms do not have the capital to compete at this level.
- *Cost advantages independent of size:* Entrenched competitors may have cost advantages not related to size that are not available to new entrants. Commonly, these advantages are grounded in the firm's history. For example, the existing competitors in an industry may have purchased land and equipment in the past when the cost was far less than new entrants would have to pay for the same assets today.
- *Access to distribution channels:* Distribution channels are often hard to crack. This is particularly true in crowded markets, such as the convenience store market. For a new sports drink to be placed on a convenience store shelf, it has to displace a product that is already there.
- *Government and legal barriers:* In knowledge-intensive industries, such as biotechnology and software, patents, trademarks, and copyrights form major barriers to entry. Other industries, such as banking and broadcasting, require the granting of a license by a public authority.

When a new firm tries to enter an industry with powerful barriers to entry, it must have a plan to overcome those barriers. Scott McNealy, the cofounder of Sun Microsystems, says that Sun was able to overcome the barriers to entry in many of its industries primarily through a program of partnering with other firms:

> Initially, Sun's business model was no different from that of its rivals. We wanted to beat our competitors, grow internally, build manufacturing plants, create new

When you see the Krispy Kreme logo, chances are your craving for one of their doughnuts kicks in—which is exactly what the company wants. The strength of the Krispy Kreme brand is a barrier to entry. Imagine how difficult it would be for another doughnut shop startup to match that Krispy Kreme craving.

distribution channels, acquire promising new startups, and so on. What happened was that we realized we couldn't do it alone. The markets were vast, our competitors were huge, barriers to entry to some segments were overwhelming, we didn't have enough cash, and the pace of change in the industry was too fast. What we did was purely instinctive. We reached out to other companies that could help us. We leveraged their expertise and specialty products by forming strategic alliances.[13]

learning objective

4. Identify the nontraditional barriers to entry that are especially associated with entrepreneurial firms.

When start-ups create their own industries or create new niche markets within existing industries, they must create barriers to entry of their own to reduce the threat of new entrants. It is difficult for start-ups to create barriers to entry that are expensive, such as economies of scale, because money is usually tight. The biggest threat to a new firm's viability, particularly if it is creating a new market, is that larger, better-funded firms will step in and copy what it is doing. The ideal barrier to entry is a patent, trademark, or copyright, which prevents another firm from duplicating what the start-up is doing. Apart from these options, however, start-ups have to rely on nontraditional barriers to entry to discourage new entrants, such as assembling a world-class management team that would be difficult for another company to replicate. For example, JetBlue's David Neeleman put together an unparalleled team to launch his airline, consisting of Neeleman; David Barger, who led the turnaround at Continental Airlines; and several executives from Southwest Airlines. The fact that this unique group of people heads JetBlue may lead potential rivals to reconsider competing against this firm in the niche market it has established. A list of nontraditional barriers to entry, which are particularly suited to start-up firms, is provided in Table 4.1.

Rivalry Among Existing Firms In most industries, the major determinant of industry profitability is the level of competition among the firms already competing in the industry. Some industries are fiercely competitive to the point where prices are pushed below the level of costs. When this happens, industry-wide losses occur. In other industries, competition is much less intense and price competition is subdued. For example, the personal com-

Table 4.1

Nontraditional Barriers to Entry

Barrier to Entry	Explanation	Example
Strength of management team	If a start-up puts together a world-class management team, it may give potential rivals pause in taking on the start-up in its chosen industry.	JetBlue
First-mover advantage	If a start-up pioneers an industry or a new concept within an existing industry, the name recognition the start-up establishes may create a formidable barrier to entry.	Yahoo!
Passion of management team and employees	If the key employees of a start-up are highly motivated by the unique culture of a start-up, are willing to work long hours because of their belief in what they are doing, and anticipate large financial gains through stock options, this is a combination that cannot be replicated by a larger firm. Think of the employees of a biotech firm trying to find a cure for a disease.	Amgen
Unique business model	If a start-up is able to construct a unique business model and establish a network of relationships that make the business model work, this set of advantages create a barrier to entry.	Dell Inc.
Inventing a new approach to an industry and executing the idea in an exemplary fashion	If a start-up invents a new approach to an industry and executes it in an exemplary fashion, these factors create a barrier to entry for potential imitators.	Starbucks

puter industry is so competitive that profit margins are extremely thin. In contrast, the market for specialized medical equipment is less competitive, and profit margins are higher.

There are four primary factors that determine the nature and intensity of the rivalry among existing firms in an industry:

- *Number and balance of competitors:* The more competitors there are, the more likely it is that one or more will try to gain customers by cutting its prices. Price-cutting causes problems throughout the industry and occurs more often when all the competitors in an industry are about the same size and when there is no clear market leader. In industries where there is a clear market leader, such as Intel in the semiconductor industry, the leader maintains price discipline and keeps the industry from engaging in destructive price wars.

- *Degree of difference between products:* The degree to which products differ from one producer to another affects industry rivalry. For example, commodity industries such as paper products producers tend to compete on price because there is no meaningful difference between one manufacturer's products and another's.

- *Growth rate of an industry:* The competition among firms in a slow-growth industry is stronger than among those in fast-growth industries. Slow-growth industry firms, such as insurance, must fight for market share, which may tempt them to lower prices or increase quality to get customers. In fast-growth industries, such as pharmaceutical products, there are enough customers to go around to fill the capacity of most firms, making price-cutting less likely.

- *Level of fixed costs:* Firms that have high fixed costs must sell a higher volume of their product to reach the break-even point than firms with low fixed costs. Once the break-even point is met, each additional unit sold contributes directly to a firm's bottom line. Firms with high fixed costs are anxious to fill their capacity, and this anxiety may lead to price-cutting.

Bargaining Power of Suppliers   In some cases, suppliers can suppress the profitability of the industries to which they sell by raising prices or reducing the quality of the components they provide. If a supplier reduces the quality of the components it supplies, the quality of the finished product will suffer, and the manufacturer will eventually have to lower its price. If the suppliers are powerful relative to the firms in the industry to which they sell, industry profitability can suffer.[14] For example, Intel, with its Pentium chip, is a powerful supplier to the PC industry. Because most PCs feature Pentium chips, Intel can command a premium price from the PC manufacturers, thus directly affecting the overall profitability of the PC industry. Several factors have an impact on the ability of suppliers to exert pressure on buyers and suppress the profitability of the industries they serve. These include the following:

- *Supplier concentration:* When there are only a few suppliers that supply a critical product to a large number of buyers, the supplier has an advantage. This is the case in the pharmaceutical industry, where relatively few drug manufacturers are selling to thousands of doctors and their patients.
- *Switching costs:* Switching costs are the fixed costs that buyers encounter when switching or changing from one supplier to another. If switching costs are high, a buyer will be less likely to switch suppliers. For example, suppliers often provide their largest buyers with specialized software that makes it easy to buy their products. After the buyer spends time and effort learning the supplier's ordering and inventory management systems, it will be less likely to want to spend time and effort learning another supplier's system.
- *Attractiveness of substitutes:* Supplier power is enhanced if there are no attractive substitutes for the products or services the supplier offers. For example, there is little the computer industry can do when Microsoft and Intel raise their prices, as there are simply no practical substitutes for these firms' products.
- *Threat of forward integration:* The power of a supplier is enhanced if there is a credible possibility that the supplier might enter the buyer's industry. For example, Microsoft's power as a supplier of computer operating systems is enhanced by the threat that it might enter the PC industry if PC makers balk too much at the cost of its software or threaten to use an operating system from a different software provider.

Bargaining Power of Buyers   Buyers can suppress the profitability of the industries from which they purchase by demanding price concessions or increases in quality. For example, the automobile industry is dominated by a handful of large automakers that buy products from thousands of suppliers in different industries. This enables the automakers to suppress the profitability of the industries from which they buy by demanding price reductions. Similarly, if the automakers insisted that their suppliers provide better-quality parts for the same price, the profitability of the suppliers would suffer. Several factors affect buyers' ability to exert pressure on suppliers and suppress the profitability of the industries from which they buy. These include the following:

- *Buyer group concentration:* If the buyers are concentrated, meaning that there are only a few large buyers, and they buy from a large number of suppliers, they can pressure the suppliers to lower costs and thus affect the profitability of the industries from which they buy.
- *Buyer's costs:* The greater the importance of an item is to a buyer, the more sensitive the buyer will be to the price it pays. For example, if the component sold by the supplier represents 50 percent of the cost of the buyer's product, the buyer will bargain hard to get the best price for that component.
- *Degree of standardization of supplier's products:* The degree to which a supplier's product differs from its competitors affects the buyer's bargaining power. For example, a buyer who is purchasing a standard or undifferentiated product from a supplier, such as the corn syrup that goes into a soft drink, can play one supplier against another until it gets the best combination of price and service.

- **Threat of backward integration:** The power of a buyer is enhanced if there is a credible threat that the buyer might enter the supplier's industry. For example, the PC industry can keep the price of computer monitors down by threatening to make its own monitors if the price gets too high.

The bargaining power of buyers is such a pervasive threat that some new ventures opt out of particular industries when the extent of the bargaining power of buyers becomes clear. This scenario changed the course of history for the Sony Corporation, as explained in the boxed feature titled "Savvy Entrepreneurial Firm."

The Value of the Five Forces Model

Along with helping a firm understand the dynamics of the industry it plans to enter, the five forces model can be used in two ways to help a firm determine whether it should enter a particular industry and whether it can carve out an attractive position in that industry.

Savvy entrepreneurial FIRM

How the Bargaining Power of Buyers Changed the Fate of Sony in Its Start-Up Years

www.sony.com

There are many variables that shape a company in its start-up years, but perhaps none are as powerful as Porter's five forces. Many companies, for example, establish strong brands or differentiate themselves in creative ways, primarily to establish barriers to entry and stem the tide of new entrants. Other companies, such as Starbucks, offer amenities in their places of business to discourage customers from switching to less expensive substitute products. The story of Sony, however, tops them all. When Sony was a start-up, it changed its entire approach to doing business as the result of the bargaining power of buyers. In fact, if Sony hadn't responded to this threat in the way it did, it wouldn't be a household name today.

Sony was established in 1946 by Masaru Ibuka and Akio Morita, two Japanese businessmen, to make communication equipment for the reconstruction of Japan after World War II. One thing Ibuka and Morita learned quickly was that to make a sale, they had to win the confidence of the purchasing officers in the government agencies with whom they were dealing. This task often proved difficult, but the hard work typically paid off in orders from these purchasing officers. One day, however, early in the life of Sony, a purchasing agent who Morita had worked particularly hard to win over was transferred to a new position. This was frustrating to Morita because he had to start from square one to win the confidence of the purchasing officer's replacement.

After this scenario repeated itself several times, Morita considered the problem. While he liked the fact that large orders could be granted by the purchasing agents of government agencies and large firms, he was leery of the fact that Sony's sales hinged on the decisions of such a small number of people. After discussing this concern with Ibuka, Morita decided to take Sony in a different direction. Instead of placing the future of Sony in the hands of a few purchasing agents, Morita decided that Sony would go after the consumer market. "In other words, we decided to do business with unspecified millions of individuals instead of with a specific few. On this basis we started to produce the first tape recorders and tapes in Japan," Morita later recalled.

This remarkable story illustrates the compelling nature of the real bargaining power of buyers. This clout is most formidable when there are only a few buyers and many sellers. Morita redirected Sony's entire future to avoid this threat. Today, as it has throughout the majority of its history, Sony's future lies in the hands of the millions of people who buy its products rather than in the hands of just a few powerful buyers.

Questions for Critical Thinking

1. If Sony had been able to reduce the bargaining power of its buyers, which of the remaining five forces do you believe has the strongest negative effect on Sony's profitability today? Justify your answer.

2. How is Sony's industry changing? What are the main causes of these changes? What should Sony do to successfully deal with these changes?

Source: A. Morita, "Moving Up in Marketing by Getting Down to Basics," in The Book of Entrepreneurs' Wisdom, ed. Peter Krass, 315–23 (New York: John Wiley & Sons, 1999).

First, the five forces model can be used to assess the attractiveness of an industry or a specific position within an industry by determining the level of threat to industry profitability for each of the forces, as shown in Table 4.2. This analysis of industry attractiveness should be more in-depth than the cursory analysis conducted during feasibility analysis. For example, if a firm filled out the form shown in Table 4.2 and several of the threats to industry profitability were high, the firm may want to reconsider entering the industry or think carefully about the position it will occupy in the industry. In the restaurant industry, for example, the threat of substitute products, the threat of new entrants, and the rivalry among existing firms are high. For certain restaurants, such as fresh-seafood restaurants, the bargaining power of suppliers may also be high (the number of seafood suppliers is relatively small compared to the number of beef and chicken suppliers). Thus, a firm that enters the restaurant industry has several forces working against it simply because of the nature of the industry. To help sidestep or diminish these threats, it must establish a favorable position. One firm that has accomplished this is Panera Bread, as discussed in Case 4.1 in this chapter. By studying the restaurant industry, Panera found that some consumers have tired of fast food but don't always have the time to patronize a sit-down restaurant. To fill the gap, Panera pioneered a new category called "fast casual," which combines relatively fast service with high-quality food. Panera has been very successful in occupying this unique position in the restaurant industry. You'll learn more about Panera Bread's success while reading Case 4.1.

The second way a new firm can apply the five forces model to help determine whether it should enter an industry is by using the model to answer several key questions. By doing so, a new venture can assess the thresholds it may have to meet to be successful in a particular industry:

learning **objective**

5. List the four industry-related questions to ask before pursuing the idea for a firm.

Question 1: Is the industry a realistic place for our new venture to enter? This question can be answered by looking at the overall attractiveness of an industry, as depicted in Table 4.2, and by assessing whether the window of opportunity is open. It is up to the entrepreneur to determine if the window of opportunity for the industry he or she plans to enter is open or closed.

Question 2: If we do enter the industry, can our firm do a better job than the industry as a whole in avoiding or diminishing the impact of the forces that suppress industry profitability? A new venture can enter an industry with a fresh brand, innovative ideas, and a world-class management team and perform better than the industry incumbents. This was the case when Google entered the Internet search engine industry and displaced Yahoo! as the market leader. Outperformance of industry incumbents can also be achieved if a new venture brings an attractive new product to market that is patented, preventing others from duplicating it for a period of time.

Table 4.2

Determining the Attractiveness of an Industry Using the Five Forces Model

Competitive Force	Threat to Industry Profitability		
	Low	Medium	High
Threat of substitutes			
Threat of new entrants			
Rivalry among existing firms			
Bargaining power of suppliers			
Bargaining power of buyers			

Instructions:

Step 1	Select an industry
Step 2	Determine the level of threat to industry profitability for each of the forces (low, medium, or high)
Step 3	Use the table to get an overall feel for the attractiveness of the industry
Step 4	Use the table to identify the threats that are most often relevant to industry profitability

Panera Bread offers a variety of alternatives to the typical burger and fries offered at many fast food restaurants. In addition to a selection of fresh baked breads, Panera is also known for bagels, pastries, soups, sandwiches, salads, and coffee.

Question 3: Is there a unique position in the industry that avoids or diminishes the forces that suppress industry profitability? As we've described, this is the advantage that both JetBlue and Panera Bread have captured.

Question 4: Is there a superior business model that can be put in place that would be hard for industry incumbents to duplicate? Keep in mind that the five forces model provides a picture of an industry "as is," which isn't necessarily the way a new venture has to approach it. Sometimes the largest firms in an industry are trapped by their own strategies and contractual obligations, providing an opening for a start-up to try something new. For example, when Dell started selling computers directly to consumers, its largest rivals—Hewlett-Packard, Compaq, and IBM—were not able to respond. They were locked into a strategy of selling through retailers. If they had tried to mimic Dell and sell direct, they would have alienated their most valuable partners—retailers such as Sears, Circuit City, and Best Buy.

The steps involved in answering these questions are pictured in Figure 4.2. If the founders of a new firm believe that a particular industry is a realistic place for their new venture, a positive response to one or more of the questions posed in Figure 4.2 increases the likelihood that the new venture will be successful.

Industry Types and the Opportunities They Offer

Along with studying the factors discussed previously, it is helpful for a new venture to study industry types to determine the opportunities they offer. The five most prevalent industry types, depicted in Table 4.3, are emerging industries, fragmented industries, mature industries, declining industries, and global industries.[15] There are unique opportunities offered by each type of industry.

learning **objective**

6. Identify the five primary industry types and the opportunities they offer.

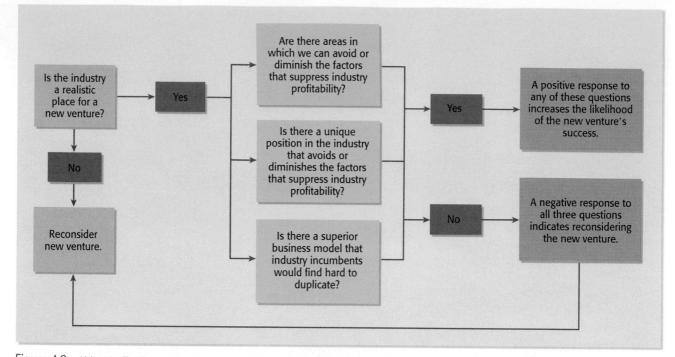

Figure 4.2   Using the Five Forces Model to Pose Questions to Determine the Potential Success of a New Venture

Emerging Industries   An **emerging industry** is new industry in which standard operating procedures have yet to be developed. The firm that pioneers or takes the leadership of an emerging industry often captures a first-mover advantage, which is a sometimes insurmountable advantage gained by the firm initiating the first significant move into a new market, as explained in Chapter 3.[16]

Because a high level of uncertainty characterizes emerging industries, any opportunity that is captured may be short lived. Still, many new ventures enter emerging industries in that barriers to entry are usually low and there is no established pattern of rivalry.

Table 4.3   Industry Structure and Opportunities

Industry Type	Industry Characteristics	Opportunities	Examples of Entrepreneurial Firms Exploiting These Opportunities
Emerging industries	Recent changes in demand or technology; new industry standard operating procedures have yet to be developed	First-mover advantage	• Cisco Systems in routers • eBay in Internet auctions • Intuit in personal finance software
Fragmented industries	Large number of firms of approximately equal size	Consolidation	• Starbucks in coffee restaurants • Kinko's in copying and printing • Krispy Kreme in doughnuts
Mature industries	Slow increases in demand, numerous repeat customers, and limited product innovation	Emphasis on service and process innovation	• Wal-Mart in retailing • JetBlue in airlines • ServiceMaster in janitorial services
Declining industries	Consistent reduction in industry demand	Leaders, niche, harvest, and divest	• Nucor in steel
Global Industries	Significant international sales	Multinational and global	• Nike in athletic shoes • EDS in computer services

Fragmented Industries   A **fragmented industry** is one that is characterized by a large number of firms of approximately equal size. The primary opportunity existing for start-ups in fragmented industries is to consolidate the industry and establish industry leadership as a result of doing so. In **industry consolidation**, the smaller companies are typically acquired or go out of business to give way to a handful of larger companies that take over the majority of the business. This is what Blockbuster did in the video rental industry. Prior to Blockbuster's arrival, thousands of small video stores were scattered throughout the United States. Through internal growth and acquisitions, Blockbuster grew quickly, consolidating a previously fragmented industry.

There are risks associated with trying to consolidate an industry, as highlighted in the boxed feature titled "What Went Wrong?" on the PurpleTie Company. The primary risks are that a firm either will overestimate its ability to consolidate an industry or will be successful in its early efforts to consolidate an industry and will grow so quickly that it exceeds its ability to properly manage growth.

Mature Industries   A **mature industry** is an industry that is experiencing slow or no increase in demand, has numerous repeat (rather than new) customers, and has limited product innovation. Occasionally, entrepreneurs introduce new product innovations to mature industries, surprising industry incumbents who thought nothing new was possible in their industries. An example is Steve Demos, the founder of White Wave, a company that makes vegetarian food products. In 1996, the company introduced Silk Soymilk, which has quickly become the best-selling soymilk in the country. Soymilk isn't really milk at all—it's a soybean-based beverage that looks like milk and has a similar texture. Still, it has made its way into the dairy section of most supermarkets in the United States and has positioned itself as a healthy substitute for milk. Who would have thought that a major innovation was possible in the milk industry?

Declining Industries   A **declining industry** is an industry that is experiencing a reduction in demand. Typically, entrepreneurs shy away from declining industries because the firms in the industry do not meet the tests of an attractive opportunity described in Chapter 2. There are occasions, however, when a start-up will do just the opposite of what conventional wisdom would suggest and, by doing so, stake out an industry position that isn't being hotly contested.

Entrepreneurial firms employ three different strategies in declining industries. The first is to adopt a **leadership strategy**, in which the firm tries to become the dominant player in the industry. This is a rare strategy for a start-up in a declining industry. The second is to pursue a **niche strategy**, which focuses on a narrow segment of the industry that might be encouraged to grow through product or process innovation. The third is a **cost reduction strategy**, which is accomplished through achieving lower costs than industry incumbents through process improvements. Nucor Steel, a small steel company that revolutionized the steel industry through the introduction of the "minimill" concept, is an example of an entrepreneurially minded firm that pursued this strategy. Most steel mills in the United States use large blast furnaces that produce a wide line of products and require enormous throughput in order to be profitable. Nucor's minimills are smaller and produce a narrower range of products. They are, however, energy efficient and make high-quality steel.[17] Nucor proved its concept and quickly found growth markets within the largely declining U.S. steel industry.

Global Industries   A **global industry** is an industry that is experiencing significant international sales. Many start-ups enter global industries and from day one try to appeal to international rather than just domestic markets. The two most common strategies pursued by firms in global industries are the multidomestic strategy and the global strategy. Firms that pursue a **multidomestic strategy** compete for market share on a country-by-country basis and vary their product or services offerings to meet the demands of the local market. In contrast, firms pursuing a **global strategy** use the same basic approach in all foreign markets. The choice between these two strategies depends on how similar consumers' tastes are from market to market. For

what went **wrong?**

PurpleTie: A Failed Attempt to Consolidate the Dry Cleaning Industry

Few industries are as fragmented as the dry cleaning industry. Most dry cleaners are small, family-owned businesses that appeal to a local clientele. In the late 1990s, one company, PurpleTie, set out to change that. Payam Zamani, a 29-year-old with no prior experience in the dry cleaning industry, founded PurpleTie. Despite his youth and lack of experience, Zamani had an impressive résumé. In 1994, he cofounded AutoWeb, an online auto retailer that remains in business. Zamani's ambition was to consolidate the dry cleaning industry by building state-of-the art dry cleaning processing centers and serving a national clientele. In fact, the company's initial goal was to be in the 25 largest metropolitan markets in the United States by 2003.

Although there are few hard numbers on the dry cleaning industry, the 1997 United States Economic Census indicated there are about 30,000 dry cleaners in the United States, generating a total of roughly $7 billion in revenue. PurpleTie thought the number was more like 100,000 shops generating $32 billion in annual revenue. In any event, PurpleTie felt that the dry cleaning industry was ripe for consolidation. Typically, when a market consolidates, the smaller companies are acquired or run out of business by a handful of larger companies that take over the majority of the business.

To accomplish its objective, PurpleTie burst on the scene in 2000 with $8 million in venture-capital funding to prove its concept. The company's initial base was the San Francisco Bay Area. Here is how PurpleTie's service worked. Customers registered online to create an itemized list of garments to be cleaned and shoes to be shined. They then selected one-hour pickup and next-day delivery windows from their homes or places of business. Similar to FedEx's "hub" system, the driver would take the items to a place that PurpleTie called its "central sort and data capture center" near San Francisco. Once tagged with bar codes, items were whisked away to dry cleaning processing centers. After being cleaned, the process was reversed to route items back to the customer.

The system worked, but there were too many things PurpleTie didn't know, ultimately leading to its failure. The first thing the company realized was that it wasn't practical to build state-of-the art dry cleaning facilities. There was already excess dry cleaning capacity in the market, and there was simply no need for more. Unfortunately, the company spent $1 million on its own facility before it realized this and ultimately shut the facility down. The second thing the company learned is that consumers don't change their behavior easily. Just because an idea makes perfect sense—an idea such as having your dry cleaning picked up at your home and delivered back to you the next day—doesn't mean that consumers will buy into it. And

some people like dealing with mom-and-pop shops. Partly for these reasons, PurpleTie never got the numbers it needed. Finally, the company, by its own admission, tried to grow too fast. Rather than winning the confidence of customers in one neighborhood before moving to the next, PurpleTie attacked the entire San Francisco Bay Area all at once. This approach necessitated a regional advertising campaign and a fleet of delivery trucks. "We had grand visions and we built too much infrastructure too fast," says David Kallery, PurpleTie's former chief operating officer, who spent 25 years with sturdy companies such as UPS and Visa before joining the start-up. "We should have grown the business organically brick by brick, or as one investor said, route by route. Had we taken that approach, we would've made the $8 million (in venture capital funding) last for several years and built a very successful business."

When PurpleTie closed its doors in February 2001, it was serving 10,000 residential customers in the San Francisco area. Ironically, another San Francisco–based dry cleaner named CleanSleeves acquired the company's assets, including its name and its Web address. CleanSleeves started about the same time as PurpleTie, also offering home pickup service. Unlike PurpleTie, however, CleanSleeves never got venture-capital funding and has grown slowly rather than rapidly. When asked what it plans to do with PurpleTie's assets, Kay Madegarian, chief executive officer (CEO) of CleanSleeves, said, "We have big plans, but ours is a self-funded approach and a much more traditional bootstrapping kind of thing."

It will be interesting to see whether the dry cleaning industry can be successfully consolidated. Along with CleanSleeves (which is now operating under the PurpleTie name), two other companies, Zoots and Hangers Cleaners, are flirting with the idea. The key for these companies will be to learn from PurpleTie's mistakes and manage their consolidation efforts in a more thoughtful and deliberate manner.

Questions for Critical Thinking

1. Describe the bargaining power of buyers as a force affecting the profitability of the dry cleaning industry as well as the ability of PurpleTie to be profitable in this industry.

2. PurpleTie started its business in San Francisco. Do you think this product idea would have been more favorably received in another part of the United States? If so, where and why?

Sources: M. Hofman, "An Opportunity to Clean Up," Inc., January 30, 2001, 21, and S. Overby, "This Spotcom Is Now a Notcom," CIO Online, March 15, 2001.

example, food companies typically are limited to a multidomestic strategy because food preferences vary significantly from country to country. Firms that sell more universal products, such as athletic shoes, have been successful with global strategies. A global strategy is preferred because it is more economical to sell the same product in multiple markets.[18]

Competitor Analysis

learning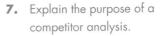

7. Explain the purpose of a competitor analysis.

After a firm has gained an understanding of the industry and the market in which it plans to compete, the next step is to complete a competitor analysis. A competitor analysis is a detailed analysis of a firm's competition. It helps a firm understand the positions of its major competitors and the opportunities that are available to obtain a competitive advantage in one or more areas. These are important issues, particularly for new ventures.[19] In the words of Sun-tzu, quoted earlier in this chapter, "Time spent in reconnaissance is seldom wasted."

First we'll discuss how a firm identifies its major competitors, and then we'll look at the process of completing a competitive analysis grid, which is a tool for organizing the information a firm collects about its primary competitors.

Identifying Competitors

The first step in a competitive analysis is to determine who the competition is. This is more difficult than one might think. For example, take a company such as 1-800-FLOWERS. Primarily, the company sells flowers. But 1-800-FLOWERS is not only in the flower business. Because flowers are often given for gifts, the company is also in the gift business. If the company sees itself in the gift business rather than just the flower business, it has a broader set of competitors—and opportunities—to consider.

The different types of competitors a business will face are shown in Figure 4.3. The challenges associated with each of these groups of competitors are described here:

learning

8. Identify the three groups of competitors a new firm will face.

- *Direct competitors:* These are businesses that offer products identical or similar to the products of the firm completing the analysis. These competitors are the most important because they are going after the same customers as the focal firm. A new firm faces winning over the loyal followers of its major competitors, which is difficult to do, even when the new firm has a better product.
- *Indirect competitors:* These competitors offer close substitutes to the product the firm completing the analysis sells. These firms' products are also important in that they target the same basic need that is being met by the focal firm's product. For example, when people told Roberto Goizueta, the late CEO of Coca-Cola, that Coke's market share was at a maximum, he countered by saying that Coke accounted for less than 2 percent of the 64 ounces of fluid that the average person drinks each day. "The enemy is coffee, milk, tea [and] water," he once said.[20]
- *Future competitors:* These are companies that are not yet direct or indirect competitors but could move into one of these roles at any time. Firms are always concerned about strong competitors moving into their markets. For example, think of how the world has changed for Barnes & Noble since Amazon.com was founded.

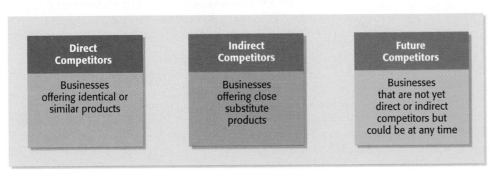

Figure 4.3

Types of Competitors New Ventures Face

It is impossible for a firm to identify all its direct and indirect competitors, let alone its future competitors. However, identifying its top 5 to 10 direct competitors and its top 5 to 10 indirect and future competitors makes it easier for the firm to complete its competitive analysis grid.

Although most of the time the firms in an industry compete against one another, there are occasions when competitors unite for the good of the industry as a whole. On these occasions, it is typically to the advantage of a new venture to cooperate. If it doesn't, it may find itself trying to sell a product or service that doesn't comply with evolving industry norms. The boxed feature titled "Partnering for Success" offers an example of this scenario. As you'll see, this segment deals with Digital Home Working Group.

Sources of Competitive Intelligence

learning objective

9. Describe ways a firm can ethically obtain information about its competitors.

To complete a meaningful competitive analysis grid, a firm must first understand the strategies and behaviors of its competitors. The information that is gathered by a firm to learn about its competitors is referred to as **competitive intelligence**. Obtaining sound competitive intelligence is not always a simple task. If a competitor is a publicly traded firm, a description of the firm's business and its financial information is available through annual reports filed with the Securities and Exchange Commission (SEC). These reports are public record and are available at the SEC's Web site (*www.sec.gov*). If one or more of the competitors is a private company, the task is more difficult. Private companies are not required to divulge information to the public.

Partnering for SUCCESS

Tech Industry Unites to Create Common Standards for Home Networks

www.dlna.org

Although most of the time firms in an industry compete with one another, there are occasions when firms unite for the good of the industry as a whole. An example is the creation of Digital Living Network Alliance, which is a nonprofit organization founded to create a set of rules aimed at making gadgets communicate better with each other through home networks. Gateway, Hewlett-Packard, Intel, Microsoft, Sony, Nokia, and 11 other firms that create products for home networks created the organization.

Many people have a growing collection of electronic devices in their homes and would like to network them together. They want to share music, pictures, and video, for example, among their PCs, televisions, sound systems, and mobile devices. However, it is often difficult to network these different devices together because they are seldom perfectly compatible. To make the problem more difficult, many forms of digital music and movies are based on proprietary formats that work on some devices but not on others.

The purpose of the Digital Living Network Alliance is to solve this problem. The belief is that all tech firms will benefit if their devices easily network with each other and if consumers can feel confident that when they buy a new device, it will seamlessly integrate with the other devices in

their homes. The Digital Living Network Alliance has established guidelines to ensure that these goals will be met. For example, a cell phone with a digital camera that adheres to the guidelines will be able to transmit pictures wirelessly to PCs or television sets.

Philip Kotler, the marketing expert and highly respected business professor who we spoke about in Chapter 2, has made the statement that for a firm to be an effective competitor, it must also be "an effective cooperator." The firms that established the Digital Living Network Alliance adhere to the spirit of Professor Kotler's remarks.

Questions for Critical Thinking

1. What do you think Professor Kotler means when he says that "firms must be effective cooperators to be effective competitors"? Given what you've read in this book and learned from your other courses, do you agree with Kotler's statement? Why or why not?

2. In general, is it easier for direct competitors or indirect competitors to cooperate? Explain your answer.

Sources: P. Kotler, Marketing Insights from A to Z (New York: John Wiley & Sons, 2002), 24, and "Tech Giants Unite on Gadget Standard for Home Networks," Wall Street Journal, 2003, B4.

There are a number of ways that a firm can ethically obtain information about its competitors:

- *Attend conferences and trade shows:* Most industries have conferences at which firms talk about the latest trends in the industry and display their products.
- *Read industry related books, magazines, and Web sites, along with general business magazines, such as* Inc. *and* BusinessWeek: In addition, many industries and associations publish magazines and newsletters that contain information about competitors.
- *Talk to customers about what motivated them to buy your product as opposed to your competitors':* Customers can provide a wealth of information about the advantages and disadvantages of competing products.
- *Purchase competitors' products to understand their features, benefits, and shortcomings:* The process of purchasing the product will also provide data about how the competitor treats its customers.
- *Study competitors' Web sites:* Many companies put a lot of information on their Web sites, including their company's history, profiles of their management teams, product information, and the latest news about the company.
- *Study Web sites that provide information about companies:* Several sites on the Internet provide information about public and private firms. Hoover's Online (*www.hoovers.com*), Thomas Register (*www.thomasregister.com*), and Quicken (*www.quicken.com*) are three of the most valuable and useful of these types of sites.

Completing a Competitive Analysis Grid

As we mentioned previously, a **competitive analysis grid** is a tool for organizing the information a firm collects about its competitors. It can help a firm see how it stacks up against its competitors, provide ideas for markets to pursue, and, perhaps most importantly, identify its primary sources of competitive advantage. To be a viable company, a new venture must have at least one clear competitive advantage over its major competitors.

An example of a competitive analysis grid is provided in Table 4.4. This grid is for Activision, a company that makes electronic games. The company's products cover the

learning **objective**

10. Describe the reasons for completing a competitive analysis grid.

Table 4.4 Competitive Analysis Grid for Activision

Name	Activision	Electronic Arts	Infograms	LucasArts	Eidos	THQ
Product features						
Brand-name recognition						
Compatibility of products with popular platforms						
Access to distribution channels						
Quality of products						
Ease of use						
Price						
Marketing support						
Quality of Customer service						

action, adventure, action sports, racing, role-playing, simulation, and strategy games categories. These products operate on both PCs and game consoles such as the Nintendo GameCube. According to Activision, the main competitive factors in the electronics games industry are product features, brand-name recognition, compatibility of products with popular platforms (e.g., GameCube), access to distribution channels, quality of products, ease of use, price, marketing support, and quality of customer service.[21] These factors are placed on the vertical axis of Activision's competitive analysis grid. The horizontal axis contains Activision and its five main competitors. In each box, Activision would rate itself compared to its main competitors. The purpose of this exercise is for a company to see how it stacks up against its competitors and to determine if any opportunities exist that it may have overlooked. For example, if Activision judged itself superior to its competitors in the category "ease of use," it might use this knowledge to highlight this advantage in its advertising and promotions.

In summary, it is extremely important for a new venture to have a firm grasp on the industry it plans to enter and on the companies it will be competing against on a day-to-day basis. By carefully studying these important areas, a new venture can position itself correctly in its industry and be fully aware of its competitors' strengths and weaknesses as its makes its own product-related decisions.

CHAPTER SUMMARY

1. Industry analysis is business research that focuses on an industry's potential. The knowledge gleaned from an industry analysis helps a firm decided whether to enter an industry and if it can carve out a position in the industry that will provide it a competitive advantage.

2. The threat of substitutes, the threat of new entrants, rivalry among existing firms, the bargaining power of suppliers, and the bargaining power of buyers are the five competitive forces that determine an industry's profitability.

3. One of the five forces that determine industry profitability is threat of new entrants. Firms try to keep other firms from entering their industries by erecting barriers to entry. A barrier to entry is a condition that creates a disincentive for a new firm to enter an industry. Economies of scale, product differentiation, capital requirements, cost advantages independent of size, access to distribution channels, and government and legal barriers are examples of barriers to entry.

4. The nontraditional barriers to entry that are particularly well suited for entrepreneurial firms include strength of the management team, first-mover advantage, passion of the management team and employees, unique business model, and inventing a new approach to an industry and executing the approach in an exemplary manner.

5. The four industry-related questions that a firm should ask before entering an industry are the following: Is the industry a realistic place for a new venture? If we do enter the industry, can our firm do a better job than the industry as a whole in avoiding or diminishing the threats that suppress industry profitability? Is there a unique position in the industry that avoids or diminishes the

forces that suppress industry profitability? Is there a superior business model that can be put in place that would be hard for industry incumbents to duplicate?

6. The five primary industry types and the opportunities they offer are as follows: emerging industry/first mover advantage; fragmented industry/consolidation; mature industry/emphasis on service and process innovation; declining industry/leadership, niche, harvest and divest; and global industry/multidomestic strategy or global strategy.

7. A competitor analysis is a detailed analysis of a firm's competition. It helps a firm understand the positions of its major competitors and the opportunities that are available to obtain a competitive advantage in one or more areas.

8. The three groups of competitors a new firm will face are direct competitors, indirect competitors, and future competitors.

9. There are a number of ways a firm can ethically obtain information about its competitors, including attending conferences and trade shows; reading industry-related books, magazines, and publications; talking to customers about what motivated them to buy your product opposed to those of your competitors; purchasing competitors' products to understand their features, benefits, and shortcomings; and studying competitors' Web sites.

10. A competitive analysis grid is a tool for organizing the information a firm collects about its competitors. This grid can help a firm see how it stacks up against its competitors, provide ideas for markets to pursue, and, perhaps most importantly, identify its primary sources of competitive advantage.

barrier to entry, 79

competitive analysis grid, 91

competitive intelligence, 90

competitor analysis, 76

cost reduction strategy, 87

declining industry, 87

economies of scale, 79

emerging industry, 86

fragmented industry, 87

global industry, 87

global strategy, 87

industry, 76

industry analysis, 76

industry consolidation, 87

leadership strategy, 87

mature industry, 87

multidomestic strategy, 87

niche strategy, 87

position, 77

1. What is an industry? Provide an example of an industry and several firms in it.

2. What is the purpose of industry analysis?

3. Identify the five competitive forces that determine industry profitability.

4. Describe how the threat of substitute products has the potential to suppress an industry's profitability.

5. How does the threat of new entrants have the potential to suppress an industry's profitability?

6. What is meant by the term "barrier to entry"? Describe the six major sources of barriers to entry that firms use to restrict entry into their markets.

7. Identify the nontraditional barriers to entry that are particularly suitable for entrepreneurial firms.

8. Describe the four primary factors that play a role in determining the nature and intensity of rivalry among an industry's existing firms. How does rivalry among existing firms have the potential to suppress an industry's profitability?

9. Describe how the bargaining power of suppliers has the potential to suppress an industry's profitability.

10. Describe the four major factors that affect suppliers' ability to exert pressure on buyers and suppress the profitability of the industries to which they sell.

11. In what way does bargaining power of buyers have the potential to suppress an industry's profitability?

12. Describe the four major factors that affect buyers' ability to exert pressure on suppliers and suppress the profitability of the industries from which they buy materials.

13. Describe the characteristics of a fragmented industry. What is the primary opportunity for new firms in fragmented industries?

14. Describe the characteristics of a mature industry. What is the primary opportunity for new firms in a mature industry?

15. What is a global industry? Describe the two most common strategies pursued by firms in global industries.

16. Describe the purpose of a competitor analysis. Make your answer as complete as possible.

17. Describe the differences between direct competitors, indirect competitors, and future competitors.

18. What is meant by the term "competitive intelligence"? Why is it important for firms to collect intelligence about their competitors?

19. Identify three sources of competitive intelligence.

20. What is the purpose of completing a competitive analysis grid?

1. Linda Williams is thinking about starting a firm in the electronic games industry. When asked by a potential investor if she had studied the industry, Linda replied, "The electronic games industry is so full of potential, it doesn't need formal analysis." Will Linda's answer satisfy the investor? In what ways will Linda limit her potential if her current attitude about the importance of industry analysis doesn't change?

2. Your friend Lisa Ryan is opening a smoothie shop that will sell a variety of smoothie drinks in the $3 to $4 price range. When you ask her if she was worried that the steep price of smoothies might prompt potential customers to buy a soda or a sports drink instead of a smoothie, Lisa answers, "You're right. Someone could substitute a soda or a sports drink for a smoothie and save a lot of money. Is there anything I can do to discourage that?" What do you tell her?

3. Jose Gonzales has been investigating the possibility of starting a package delivery service but is frustrated by the amount of money it takes to get into the industry. He is particularly concerned about getting the cash to buy the trucks he would need. Which of the five forces in Porter's five forces model is strongly affecting Jose's potential business? How can Jose overcome this obstacle?

4. Peter Jones is in the process of starting a business in the restaurant industry. In a recent *Fortune* magazine article, he read that in industries where the bargaining power of suppliers is high, industry profitability suffers. What criteria can Peter use to determine if the bargaining power of suppliers is high in the industry in which he has an interest?

5. As mentioned in this chapter, White Wave Inc. produces Silk Soymilk, a product that has done surprisingly well in the mature milk industry. Based on the material we've covered so far, why do you think Silk Soymilk has been so successful?

6. Troy Pearson is starting a medical products business in Albany, New York. He knows he should put together a competitor analysis but doesn't know how to go about it. If Troy turned to you for advice, what would you tell him?

7. Susan Willis is planning to launch an advertising agency in Tampa, Florida. She knows that she needs to complete a competitor analysis but doesn't know where to obtain information about her competitors. Provide Susan with several suggestions on how to proceed.

8. M. B. Jenkins is the founder of a new firm in the electronics industry. A friend of his owns an electronic business in a neighboring state and has invited him to be his guest at a large electronics industry trade show. M. B. can't decide whether to take the time to attend the trade show. In the context of the material presented in this chapter, what are the arguments in favor of attending the trade show?

9. Dana Smith will soon be opening a fitness club in Tucson, Arizona. Having identified his competitors, he wants to display the information he has collected in a way that will help him determine how he'll stack up against his competitors and pinpoint his sources of competitive advantage. Describe to Dana a technique that he could use to help achieve his objectives.

10. Complete Activision's competitive analysis grid, which is pictured in Table 4.4.

you be the VC

Company: Cold Fusion Foods (www.coldfusionfoods.com)

Business idea: Produce the first frozen energy bar.

Pitch: Many athletes and health food enthusiasts like to eat energy bars and drink energy shakes. However, these products are often tasteless concoctions that don't encourage mass consumption. This is where Cold Fusion Foods comes in. Cold Fusion has taken the nutritional value of a power bar or shake and made it into a frozen nutritional product that resembles an ice cream bar. The company has significantly improved the taste of consuming a highly nutritious product for fitness-conscious consumers, dieters, and people interested in healthy snacking. The company currently sells protein bars and protein juice bars. Cold Fusion is ready to expand.

Q&A: Based on the material covered in this chapter, what questions would you ask this firm's founders before making your funding decision? What answers would satisfy you?

Decision: If you had to make your decision on just the information provided in the pitch and the company Web site, would you fund this firm? Why or why not?

Case 4.1

Panera Bread: Occupying a Favorable Position in a Highly Competitive Industry

www.panera.com

If you analyzed the restaurant industry using Porter's five forces model, you wouldn't be favorably impressed. Three of the threats to profitability—the threat of substitutes, the threat of new entrants, and rivalry among existing firms—are high. And recently, restaurants have been suffering financially. For example, in late 2002, McDonald's posted its first-ever quarterly loss. Other restaurant chains have posted losses as well. According to one investment analyst, "Restaurant stocks got eaten alive in 2002, punished by a slow economy and a discount war." Although things improved a bit for restaurants in 2003 and 2004, profits were still hard to earn.

At least one restaurant chain, however, has held fast against the trend. St. Louis–based Panera Bread Company, a chain of specialty bakery-cafés, has grown from 369 company owned and franchised units in 2001 to over 630 today. In 2003 alone, its sales increased by 38.1 percent and its net income increased by 39.4 percent. So what's Panera's secret? How is it that this company flourishes while its industry as a whole is in decline? As we'll see, Panera Bread's success can be explained in two words: positioning and execution.

Panera's roots go back to 1981, when it was founded under the name of Au Bon Pain Co. and consisted of three Au Bon Pain bakery-cafés and one cookie store. The company grew slowly until the mid-1990s, when its owners noticed two significant changes in the restaurant industry. First, they observed that people were increasingly looking for products that were "special"—that were a departure from run-of-the-mill restaurant food. Second, they noted that although consumers were tiring of standard fast-food fare, they didn't want to give up the convenience of quick service. This trend led the company to conclude that consumers wanted the convenience of fast food combined with a higher-quality experience. In slightly different words, they wanted good food served quickly in an enjoyable environment.

From these conclusions, which were made by other restaurant owners too, a new category in the restaurant industry, called "fast-casual," emerged. This category provided consumers the alternative they wanted by capturing the advantage of both the fast-food category (speed) and the casual dining category (good food), with no significant disadvantages, as presented in the graphic titled "Positioning Strategy of Various Restaurant Chains." A market positioning grid provides a visual representation of the positions of various companies in an industry. About Panera's category, industry expert T. J. Callahan said, "I don't think fast-casual is a fad; I think it's a structural change starting to happen in the restaurant industry."

To establish itself as the leader in the fast-casual category and to distinguish itself from its rivals, Panera (which is Latin for "time for bread") added a bonus to the mix—specialty food. The company has become known as the nation's bread expert and offers a variety of artisan and other specialty breads, along with bagels, pastries, and baked goods. Panera Bread's restaurants are open for breakfast, lunch, and dinner and also offer hand-tossed salads, signature sandwiches, and hearty soups served in edible sourdough bread bowls, along with hot and cold coffee drinks. Its restaurants also provide an inviting neighborly atmosphere, adding to their appeal. The company even suggests a new time of day to eat specialty foods, calling the time between lunch and dinner "chill-out" time.

With high hopes for future expansion, Panera Bread is now the acknowledged leader in the fast-casual category. Systemwide sales were $355 million in 2003. Its unique blend of fast-casual service and specialty foods also continues to gain momentum. This sentiment is captured in the following quote from Mark von Waaden, an investor and restaurateur who recently signed an agreement to open 20 Panera Bread restaurants in the Houston, Texas, area. Commenting on why he was attracted to Panera Bread as opposed to other restaurant chains, Mr. von Waaden said,

> My wife, Monica, and I fell in love with the fresh-baked breads and the beautiful bakery-cafés. We think the Panera Bread concept of outstanding bread coupled with warm, inviting environment is a natural fit with the sophistication that the Houston market represents.

The spirit of von Waaden's statement captures the essence of Panera's advantage. It isn't just another restaurant. By observing trends and listening to customers, its leaders helped the firm carve out a unique and favorable position in a difficult industry.

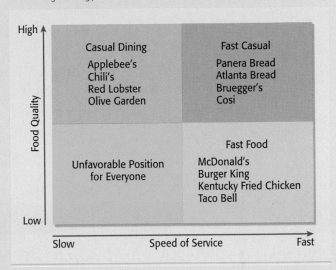

Positioning Strategy of Various Restaurant Chains

Casual Dining	**Fast Casual**
Applebee's	Panera Bread
Chili's	Atlanta Bread
Red Lobster	Bruegger's
Olive Garden	Cosi
Unfavorable Position for Everyone	**Fast Food**
	McDonald's
	Burger King
	Kentucky Fried Chicken
	Taco Bell

Food Quality: High / Low — Speed of Service: Slow / Fast

1. How has Panera Bread established a unique position in the restaurant industry? How has this unique position contributed to its success?

2. Analyze the restaurant industry using Porter's five forces model. In what ways has Panera Bread successfully positioned itself against the forces that are suppressing the profitability of the restaurant industry as a whole?

3. What barriers to entry has Panera Bread created for potential competitors? How significant are these barriers?

4. What are Panera Bread's primary sources of competitive advantage? In your judgment, are these sources of advantage sustainable? Why or why not?

Sources: "Industry by Industry: A Look at the Start, Their Stocks—and Their Latest Picks," Wall Street Journal, May 12, 2003, R8; "Panera Bread Annual Report" (2003).

Case 4.2

UpLink: An Attractive Niche in the GPS Industry Helps Golfers Improve Their Scores
www.uplinkgolf.com

On the eighth fairway of your favorite golf course, you look at the green and wonder whether to use a seven or an eight iron. The last time you played the course, you were in roughly the same spot and misjudged the distance to the hole, coming up 20 yards short. Today, you walk back to your cart and glance at the monitor hanging from the roof. It tells you you're 132 yards from the hole. You select your eight iron, loft a shot 125 yards in the air, and watch your ball roll 10 inches from the hole. To say the least, you are thrilled with this shot!

At the same time, the club pro is looking at a computer screen in the clubhouse. He sees a digital map of the course, along with 28 dots, which represent the exact positions of the golf carts on the course. On the sixth fairway is cart number 16. This cart is holding up play and has four carts stacked up behind it. The club pro radios the course ranger and asks him to drive out to the sixth fairway to politely ask the players who are using cart number 16 to let the faster golfers play through.

How is all this possible? Through the implementation of a Global Positioning Satellite (GPS) golf course management system developed by Uplink. Uplink traces its roots to 1994, when two inventors, Darryl Cornish and Chad Huston, patented the use of the GPS system for distance measurement and cart tracking on golf courses, carving out an interesting niche in the GPS systems industry. Uplink is the fastest-growing provider of GPS-based golf course management systems to the golf industry. In addition, it has differentiated itself from its competitors by developing an integrated system that offers attractive features to golf courses and their patrons.

From the golfer's point of view, the biggest amenity offered by Uplink is golf carts equipped with monitors that provide precise distance information. When a golfer is in the middle of a fairway and glances up at the monitor, he or she sees a screen that looks something like this:

- 183 Back of Green
- 170 Yards to Pin (the "hole")
- 160 Front of Green
- 122 Front of Water

The distances change as the cart moves. The monitors can also be equipped to display additional information, such as messages from the clubhouse; real-time leader boards for tournaments, providing up-to-the-minute information on who's leading the tournament; and food and beverage menus. The food and beverage menus are typically activated on the eighth hole and provide golfers the opportunity to "order ahead" and have a snack waiting for them when they pass the clubhouse between the 9th and 10th holes.

An integral part of the system is the "Course Management Computer," which is housed in the clubhouse and is networked with the monitors in the carts. As mentioned earlier, this system permits clubhouse personnel to track carts and monitor the pace of play. The system also helps clubhouse personnel spot a cart that has strayed into a restricted area, such as an environmentally protected area on the course, and allows a message to be sent to the cart driver instructing him to exit the area.

Most courses charge a small fee for the use of the monitors, providing the course with additional income, and many courses are finding that the digital menus cause an increase in food and beverage sales.

Because Uplink is a private company, it doesn't release financial information, so its financial progress is unknown. It's clear from the company's press releases, however, that it is signing up golf courses and building a top-flight management team. For example, Rodney Bond, a seasoned executive in the videoconferencing industry, was recently hired as Uplink's chief financial officer, and the company recently added Dick Bermingham and Clayton Reed to its board of directors. Bermingham is the former chairman of American Golf Inc., and Reed is a former vice president for Cisco Systems.

One particularly interesting feature of Uplink's Web site is an online competitor analysis grid that allows interested parties to compare Uplink's offerings to its competitors. An abbreviated version of the competitor analysis is shown in the table titled "Competitor Analysis."

Competitor Analysis: Grid Designed to Facilitate a Comparison Between Uplink and Its Competitors

Decision Factor	Uplink	Competitor
Golfer Features		
Precise pin placement (not quadrants)	Yes	Yes or No
Easy to read and use	Yes	Yes or No
Food and beverage ordering	Yes	Yes or No
On-cart scoring	Yes	Yes or No
On-cart leaderboard	Yes	Yes or No
Course Management Features		
Management reporting tailored to course's needs	Yes	Yes or No
Message forwarding to marshall and beverage carts	Yes	Yes or No
"Restricted zones"	Yes	Yes or No
Positionally relevant warnings	Yes	Yes or No
Advertising Programs		
Local programs for immediate revenue	Yes	Yes or No
National program	Yes	Yes or No

The present challenge for Uplink is to maintain its momentum and to defend its position as the leader in the niche market it pioneered. Only 4 percent of all golf courses in the United States feature GPS-equipped golf carts. For Uplink, this statistic represents both good news and bad news. The good news is that the company has tremendous upside potential. The bad news is that if the GPS market for golf courses takes off, Uplink is sure to attract serious competitors.

Discussion Questions

1. What is the definition of a niche market? In your judgment, has Uplink identified an attractive niche market in the GPS industry? Why or why not?

2. What barriers to entry exist in Uplink's niche in the GPS industry? Are the barriers to entry sizable or small? How does this affect the attractiveness of Uplink's niche market?

3. Do you think the profitability of Uplink's industry is suppressed by the bargaining power of its buyers (i.e., golf courses)? Explain your answer.

4. Do you like Uplink's competitor analysis? How meaningful is this analysis to potential golf course customers or buyers? Do you think that putting the competitor analysis on its Web site is a good idea? Why or why not?

5. If the GPS market for golf courses takes off, what actions can Uplink take now to prevent the loss of its leadership position as it attracts competitors?

Sources: Uplink home page, www.uplinkgolf.com (accessed May 10, 2003); "UpLink Corporation Ensures Scalability with Key Additions to Its Board and Senior Management Team," PR Newswire, August 10, 2001; and "UpLink Corporation Enhances Its Credibility with Addition of Rodney Bond as CFO," PR Newswire, September 18, 2001.

developing an *effective* business model

After studying this chapter, you should be ready to:

1. Describe a business model.

2. Explain the concept of business model innovation.

3. Discuss the importance of having a clearly articulated business model.

4. Discuss the concept of the value chain.

5. Identify a business model's two potential fatal flaws.

6. Identify a business model's four major components.

7. Explain the meaning of the term "business concept blind spot."

8. Define the term "core competency" and describe its importance.

9. Explain the concept of supply chain management.

10. Define the term "target market."

dell inc.: eliminating the middleman

At its simplest, a business model is the story of how a company operates. As with all good stories, it has characters, a setting, motivation, and a plot. For the plot of a business model to be convincing, the characters must be precisely laid out, their motivations must be clear, and the plot must turn on how the business ultimately creates value and earns a profit.[1]

Dell Inc. (formerly known as Dell Computer) is one of the best examples of both a good story and an excellent business model. When Michael Dell was in high school, he bought an Apple II, took it apart, and figured out how to adapt it to suit his needs. The ability to customize a computer struck Dell as an interesting business idea, so he set up a bulletin board to advertise his service and earned extra income by customizing the computers of his friends.

As a college student, Dell began selling computers out of his dorm room. He realized that the computer industry was extremely inefficient. First, he looked at the way computers were sold and saw that by the time a computer passed through the hands of a manufacturer, a distributor, and a retailer, a machine that contained only about $600 worth of parts cost the customer $2,000. Second, he realized that it was impossible to buy a computer with the latest technology because it took about a year for a new technology to be integrated into the computers that were sold in stores.

Remembering his frustration regarding these issues, Dell later wrote, "I would read in the industry publications that Intel had this new superfast processor, but the best one that I could buy in the store was only half that speed. It was just gross inefficiency in the inventory and supply chain."[2]

In May 1984, Dell dropped out of University of Texas and set up a 1,000-square-foot office in Austin, Texas. At that time, PCs didn't come with hard drives. The initial business of Dell Computer was the selling of kits to PC owners. The owners then used the kits to equip their computers with hard drives. The company grew quickly and moved again and again into progressively larger facilities.

Michael Dell was young and made mistakes. Drawing both customers and investors to the young company, however, was the fact that the firm's premise was perfectly sensible. Instead of forecasting demand, building computers, shipping them to retailers, and hoping they would sell, Dell took a customer's order, bought and assembled the components, and then shipped the product directly to the customer's doorstep. Dell didn't need plants and equipment to build the components, and it didn't have to invest a large sum in research and development. Most important, the customer got exactly the computer that he or she wanted, with all the latest technology.[3]

By making products to order, Dell eliminated most of the costs and risks associated with carrying inventories of finished goods. Unlike its rivals, Dell didn't have to *hope* that someone would buy its PCs; its PCs were sold before they were made. Commenting on the early years of Dell Computer and its direct-sales approach, Michael Dell wrote, "We screwed up all kinds of things, but there was so much inherent value in what we were doing that it masked all the mistakes we made. Still, we didn't make a lot of the same mistakes over and over again. We learned from the mistakes and figured out how we could progress."[4]

It's easy to see how Dell stands apart by looking at Figure 5.1, which contrasts the way Dell sells PCs with the way its main competitors sell them. Its computers never sit in warehouses because they are built when they are ordered, so Dell has virtually no inventory, its products are always up to date, its customers get the configurations they want, and Dell gets its money up front. This approach is roughly Dell's "business model"—its core logic for creating value.

How does the business model perform? The results speak for themselves. Dell is the world's #1 direct-sale computer vendor and competes with Hewlett-Packard (which acquired Compaq in 2002) for the worldwide PC title. Why had Dell surpassed so many of its industry peers? Because Dell offers customers a better deal compared to the deals available from its competitors. How? Because Dell's cost structure is lower. And the cost structure is lower because of the way its business model is configured. At different times, other firms (e.g., Gateway) have tried to imitate Dell's business model. But, to date, no company has been able to come close to doing so.

This chapter introduces the business model and explains why it's important for a new venture to develop a business model early in its life. In everyday language, a model is a plan that's used to make or describe something. A **business model** is a firm's plan or diagram for how it competes, uses its resources, structures its relationships, interfaces with customers, and creates value to sustain itself on the basis of the profits it earns. As you'll see later in this chapter, a successful business model has four components.

The term "business model" first came into use with the advent of the PC and the spreadsheet. The spreadsheet made sensitivity analysis possible, giving managers the ability to ask "what-if" questions. A manager could sit at a computer, manipulate an item such as sales, and see how a shortfall or an upswing in sales would affect every other aspect of the business. In other words, a manager could "model" the behavior of the business.[5] Today, the term "business model" is used in a much broader context to include all the activities that define how a firm competes in the marketplace.[6]

It's important to understand that a firm's business model takes it beyond its own boundaries. Almost all firms partner with others to make their business models work. In Dell's case, it needs the cooperation of its suppliers, shippers, customers, and many others to make its business model possible. For example, if Dell's suppliers weren't willing to deliver up-to-date parts to the company on a just-in-time basis, Dell would have higher inventory costs and wouldn't be able to ship its customer's state-of-the-art products or be as price competitive. Dell works closely with its suppliers and keeps them motivated to participate. Working with Dell this way can also help a supplier operate profitably in that the size of Dell's orders may account for a major portion of a supplier's production. This could

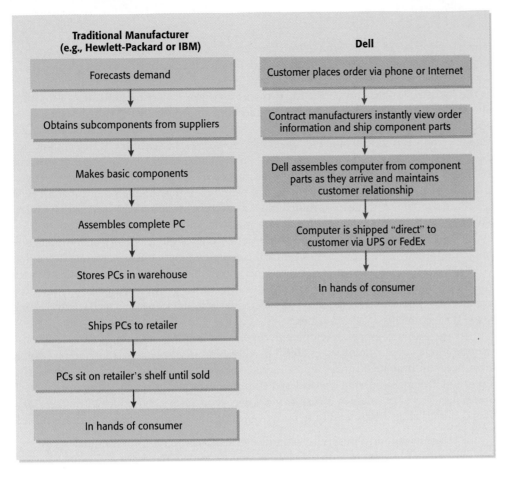

be significant in that Dell is known to be loyal to its suppliers and to help their cash flow by paying them quickly for their delivered products.

A company's business model involves its network of partners along with its products. It encompasses the capabilities of multiple firms, all of which must be willing and motivated to play along. Some early e-commerce firms that had plausible business models on paper failed because they couldn't get key partners to participate. An example is online beauty retailer Eve.com. The company struggled largely because many of the high-profile suppliers of women's beauty products wouldn't sell their products on its Web site. The suppliers were concerned that if they sold through Eve.com, they would offend their traditional channel partners, such as Nordstrom and Saks. Eve.com's business model never coalesced, and the firm eventually went out of business.

Some business models are configured so that others, especially competitors, won't be able to understand how the firm makes money. This tactic may make the business model itself part of a firm's competitive advantage. For example, look at Google's Web site (*www.google.com*) and try to figure out how the firm generates income. It isn't obvious. Google makes money through (1) carefully placing discreet ads that run alongside search results (type in "Ford truck" and see what happens), (2) licensing its search technology to portals such as America Online, (3) licensing its search technology to companies for internal search engines, and (4) whatever else Google is up to that's hard for even informed observers to discern. Google keeps its business model secret to keep other firms from successfully duplicating what it is doing. It may be harder for Google to maintain the secrecy of its business model now that it's a publicly traded firm. However, the longer the details of Google's effective business model remain a mystery to others, the longer it will be able to earn significant returns on its investments.

In this chapter, we'll first discuss business models and their importance. Then we'll look at how they emerge and examine some potential "fatal flaws" of business models. Finally, we'll examine the components of effective business models.

Business Models

learning **objective**

1. Describe a business model.

There is no standard business model, no hard-and-fast rules that dictate how a firm in a particular industry should compete. In fact, it's dangerous for a company to assume that it can be successful by simply copying the business model of another firm—even if that other firm is the industry leader. This is true for two reasons. First, it may be difficult to determine specifically what another firm's business model is, as illustrated by the Google example we talked about earlier. Second, a firm's business model is inherently dependent on the collection of resources it controls and the capabilities it possesses. For example, if Dell employs the best group of supply chain managers in the country and has established long-term trusting relationships with key suppliers, it may be the only company in the world that can effectively implement its business model. No other firm would have this unique set of capabilities, at least initially. The term **business model innovation** refers to initiatives such as that undertaken by Michael Dell that revolutionize how products are sold in an industry.[7]

learning **objective**

2. Explain the concept of business model innovation.

The development of a firm's business model follows the feasibility analysis stage of launching a new venture but comes before the completion of a business plan. If a firm has conducted a successful feasibility analysis and knows that it has a product or service with potential, the business model stage addresses how to surround it with a core strategy, a partnership model, a customer interface, distinctive resources, and an approach to creating value that represents a viable business.

At the business model development stage, it is premature for a new venture to raise money, hire a lot of employees, establish partnerships, or implement a marketing plan. A firm needs to have its business model in place before it can make additional substantive decisions. Failure to develop a well-designed business model generally stems from a naive understanding of business or a rush to get a new product or service idea to market. Matt Ragas, a marketing expert, said this about neglecting to design a thorough business model:

> A killer new product or service without a well-thought out business model is a lot like a sailor lost at sea without navigational charts. Think about it. Suppose we packed a dream team of yachtsmen onto a ship and told them to set sail and find a new route to Asia. Being pros, they'd give it their best shot, but without charts to guide their journey, they'd end up drifting on the oceans endlessly. Eventually they'd run out of supplies and more than likely not survive. Companies that create innovative products or services without well-crafted business models act much the same way. [They] believe they can succeed in the marketplace merely by throwing their new product or service over the side and hoping it will swim.[8]

Entrepreneurs must do much more than "hope their new ideas can swim." Indeed, a great product or service idea that isn't supported by a carefully crafted business model will likely become an unfulfilled promise of success. Now, let's look specifically at why a business model is important.

The Importance of a Business Model

Having a well-thought-out business model is important for several reasons. While some models are better than others, it is dangerous to link the performance of a firm solely to the configuration of its business model. In most cases, performance is a function of both the *choice* of a business model and how effectively a firm *uses* its chosen model. The problem that befell many of the early e-commerce companies was that they thought that by selecting an Internet-based business model, they could sit back and watch the money roll in. But entrepreneurship is not that simple. These companies neglected to pay attention to *how they performed* within that business model. A company must craft a strategy, use resources efficiently, develop a partnership model, and interface with customers effectively to be successful.

learning **objective**

3. Discuss the importance of having a clearly articulated business model.

Having a clearly articulated business model is important because it does the following:

- Serves as an ongoing extension of feasibility analysis (a business model continually asks the question, Does the business make sense?)
- Focuses attention on how all the elements of a business fit together and constitute a working whole

- Describes why the network of participants needed to make a business idea viable is willing to work together
- Articulates a company's core logic to all stakeholders, including the firm's employees

A good way to illustrate the importance of these points is to describe a business model that *didn't* work. WebHouse Club was launched by Priceline.com founder Jay Walker in the fall of 1999 and failed just a year later after eating up nearly $350 million of its investors' money. Priceline.com allows customers to "bid" for airline tickets, hotel rooms, and home mortgages. WebHouse was set up to mimic Priceline.com's business model and extend it to grocery store items. WebHouse worked like this: A shopper obtained a plastic card with a unique number and a magnetic strip from a local grocery store or a newspaper insert. The card was used to activate an account on the WebHouse Internet site. Once an account was established, the shopper could then make a bid for a supermarket item, say $3.75 for a box of toasted corn flakes cereal. The shopper could specify the price but not the brand. In seconds, the shopper would learn whether a maker of toasted corn flakes cereal was willing to accept the price. If so, the shopper would pay WebHouse for the cereal with a credit card and would then pick up the cereal at a participating store using the WebHouse card. The cereal could be Kellogg's, General Mills, or any other brand.

Behind the scenes, WebHouse followed the same formula that Priceline.com had invented to sell airline tickets and hotel rooms. By aggregating shopper demand for products such as cereal, tuna, or diapers, WebHouse could go to producers such as Kellogg's and General Mills and negotiate discounts. The company could then pass along the discounts to consumers and take a small fee for bringing buyers and sellers together.[9]

Why didn't this business model work for WebHouse? For several reasons. First, it assumed that companies such as Kellogg's would be willing to participate—not a wise assumption when you consider that Kellogg's has spent millions of dollars convincing consumers that Kellogg's Corn Flakes is better than competing brands. The WebHouse model teaches consumers to select products strictly on the basis of price rather than brand identity. So why would Kellogg's or any other producer want to help WebHouse do that? Second, the WebHouse model assumed that millions of shoppers would take the time to sit down at their computers and bid on grocery store items. It's easy to see why a consumer might take the time to get a better deal on an airline ticket or a stay in a four-star hotel room. But how many people have the time to sit down, log on to their computer, and interact with a Web site to save 50 cents on a box of cereal without even being able to choose the brand? As it turned out, not many.

Ultimately, WebHouse failed because its business model was flawed. The company just couldn't motivate its suppliers or customers to participate at a sufficient scale to support the overhead of the business. WebHouse was asking suppliers to act against their self-interest and was asking shoppers to take too much time to save too little money. As busy as people are today, shoppers want to make the very best use of their limited time, meaning that they'll likely reject a time-consuming process that doesn't create obvious value for them.

WebHouse illustrates the importance of articulating a business model in the early life of a new venture. Once the model is clearly determined, the entrepreneur should diagram it on paper (to the extent possible), examine it, and ask the following questions:

- Does my business model make sense?
- Will the businesses I need as partners participate?
- If I can get partners to participate, how motivated will they be? Am I asking them to work for or against their self-interest?
- How about my customers? Will it be worth their time to do business with my company?
- If I do get customers, how motivated will they be?
- Can I motivate my partners and customers at a sufficient scale to cover the overhead of my business and make a profit?
- How distinct will my business be? If I'm successful, will it be easy for a larger competitor to step in and steal my idea?

If the answer to each of these questions isn't satisfactory, then the business model should be revised or abandoned. Ultimately, a business model is viable only insofar as the buyer, the seller, and the partners involved see it as an appropriate method of selling a product or service.[10]

How Business Models Emerge

The value chain is a model developed by an academic researcher[11] that many businesses and entrepreneurs use to identify opportunities to enhance their competitive strategies. The value chain also explains how business models emerge and develop. The **value chain** is the string of activities that moves a product from the raw material stage, through manufacturing and distribution, and ultimately to the end user. Depicted in Figure 5.2, the value chain consists of primary activities and support activities. The primary activities have to do with the physical creation, sale, and service of a product or a service, while the support activities provide reinforcement for the primary activities. As a product moves through the different stages of the value chain, separate parts of the firm add value (or don't add value) at each stage. The final product or service is an aggregate of the value contributions made to it.

By studying a product's or service's value chain, an organization can identify ways to create additional value and assess whether it has the means to do so. For example, Dell learned that it has customers who want technical support available on a 24-hour-per-day basis, seven days a week (24/7), and that these customers are willing to pay extra to get it. Dell realized that it could "add value" to the value chain for selling computers by beefing up the "service" segment to include 24/7 technical support. This would work, however, only if Dell has enough trained personnel to offer the 24/7 support and can make money doing so. Additionally, if Dell can offer the 24/7 support and its competitors can't, the 24/7 service becomes a point of profit-generating differentiation between Dell and its competitors. This example illustrates why the value chain has been widely adopted as a tool for developing firm strategy and analyzing firm competitiveness.

Value chain analysis is also helpful in identifying opportunities for new businesses and in understanding how business models emerge. Many scholars now have a wider view of the value chain than the original conceptualization pictured in Figure 5.2. A key reason

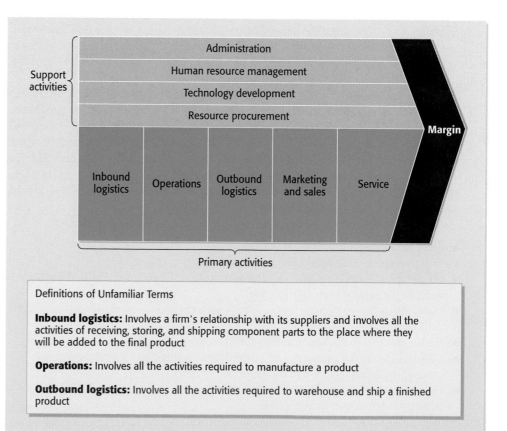

Figure 5.2

The Value Chain

Definitions of Unfamiliar Terms

Inbound logistics: Involves a firm's relationship with its suppliers and involves all the activities of receiving, storing, and shipping component parts to the place where they will be added to the final product

Operations: Involves all the activities required to manufacture a product

Outbound logistics: Involves all the activities required to warehouse and ship a finished product

Source: *Competitive Advantage: Creating and Sustaining Superior Performance* by Michael E. Porter. © 1995, 1998 by Michael E. Porter. All rights reserved. Reprinted with permission of The Free Press, a Division of Simon & Schuster Adult Publishing Group.

this expanded view has evolved is that most products and services are produced in a complex supply chain that involves many companies rather than a single firm. Variations of the value chain have been created to depict the production of goods and services through "value networks" or "value systems" rather than a single firm value chain.[12] Because of this, a value *chain* tends to be identified more with a product (e.g., a computer) or service (e.g., tax preparation) than a particular company (e.g., Dell or tax preparation firm Jackson Hewitt).

Entrepreneurs look at the value chain of a product or a service to pinpoint where the value chain can be made more effective or to spot where additional "value" can be added in some meaningful way. This type of analysis may focus on (1) a single primary activity of the value chain (such as marketing and sales), (2) the interface between one stage of the value chain and another (such as the interface between operations, which are the activities required to manufacture a product, and outbound logistics, which are the activities require to warehouse and ship it), or (3) one of the support activities (such as human resource management). If a product's value chain, like a computer, can be strengthened in any one of these areas, it may represent an opportunity for the formation of a *new* firm to perform that activity. Table 5.1 provides examples of entrepreneurial firms that have enhanced the value chain

Table 5.1 Firms Founded to Enhance the Value Chain of an Existing Product or Service

New Venture's Name (at time of founding)	Value Chain Activity	Reason New Venture was Started
Primary Activities		
Airborne Logistics, Excel, Maersk Logistics	Inbound logistics	To provide efficient material management, warehousing, and inventory control
Celestica, Flextronics, Solectron	Operations	To provide efficient contract manufacturing services for companies such as IBM, Microsoft, and Ericsson
Bax Global, FedEx, UPS	Outbound logistics	To provide new ways to warehouse and move goods effectively to the end user
Costco, Home Depot, Wal-Mart	Marketing and sales	To provide new ways to market and sell products
CyberRep, Inktel Direct, TellMe	Service	To provide efficient call center, e-mail, and Web-based customer contact services
Support Activities		
Accenture, Booz Allen, Boston Consulting Group	Firm infrastructure	To provide management support
Administaff, Ceridan, Paychex	Human resource management	To provide payroll, tax, benefits administration, and other human resource services
EDS, Razorfish, Scient	Technological	To help firms integrate emerging technologies into existing business systems
Hughes Supply, W. W. Grainger	Procurement	To help firms procure the raw materials and supplies needed for their production processes
The Interface Between One Stage of the Value Chain and Another		
Ariba, ChemConnect, i2 Technologies	Inbound logistics/operations	To help firms with the interface between inbound logistics and operations
CNF, DHL Worldwide Express, UPS	Operations/outbound logistics	To help firms with the interface between operations and outbound logistics
Interstate Cold Storage, Specialized Warehousing Services	Outbound logistics/marketing and Sales	To help firms with the interface between outbound logistics and marketing and sales
ExpressScripts, Liberty Medical	Marketing and sales/service	To help firms with the interface between marketing and sales/service

of an existing product or service by focusing on one of the three previously mentioned areas.

A firm can be formed to strengthen the value chain for a product, however, only if a viable business model can be created to support it. For example, Michael Dell's idea of selling computers directly to end users wouldn't have been possible if it weren't for low-cost shippers, such as UPS, and manufacturers of computer components who were willing to sell their products to him.

Start-ups can choose to enhance or improve an area in a product's value chain only if they can put together a value chain or value network that brings their own product or service to market (even if their "market" is enhancing only a small portion of the value chain of an existing product). Typically, this involves developing core competencies in one or more areas and developing multiple partnerships to do the rest. Dell's core competencies are supply chain management, assembling computers, and selling computers online or on the phone. Dell lets its partners do the rest, such as manufacturing parts and delivering the final product.

Potential Fatal Flaws of Business Models

learning **objective**

5. Identify a business model's two potential fatal flaws.

Two fatal flaws can render a business model untenable from the beginning: a complete misread of the customer and utterly unsound economics. Business models that fall victim to one of these two flaws have lost the race before leaving the starting gate.

In plain terms, a product must have customers to be successful. In the previously mentioned WebHouse example, the savings that were possible by bidding on grocery store items just weren't large enough to make it worthwhile for enough people to participate. The product had no customers. A similar misread of the customer sank Pets.com, a high-profile e-commerce flameout. Although it was convenient for consumers to have pet food and supplies delivered directly to their homes, the orders took several days to arrive—too long for customers who have access to the same products at the grocery store and at pet superstores such as PetSmart. Pets.com didn't realize that fast delivery was essential to its customers.

Pets.com was known for its "spokespuppet," which appeared in Super Bowl ads and even in the Macy's Thanksgiving Day parade in New York City. The company's ads were larger than life, but when it came down to basic customer satisfaction Pets.com missed the mark, revealing fatal flaws in the company's business model. Pets.com closed its doors in early 2001.

what went wrong?

MobileStar's Mistaken Belief: "If We Build It, They Will Come"

In 1997, MobileStar was launched to manufacture, sell, and install wireless "hot spot" networks. A hotspot is in an area in which high-speed wireless Internet connectivity is available. The idea behind MobileStar was to install hot spots in public places, such as hotel lobbies and restaurants, where business travelers and others could log on to the Internet via their laptop computers.

To capture first-mover advantages, MobileStar moved quickly to secure venues for its networks. It struck deals with a number of companies, including Hilton Hotels, American Airlines Admirals Clubs, Columbia Sussex Hotels, and its biggest prize, Starbucks, which allowed it to install networks in 500 of its locations. A key element of MobileStar's business model was its formula for making money. Rather than charging the restaurants and hotels in which it built its networks, it charged the end users of its service. The price of its service was $15.95 to $59.95 for a monthly subscription (the nature of the subscriptions varied by location) and around $2.95 per hour for people who bought prepaid minutes cards.

Unfortunately, in late 2001, MobileStar failed. What went wrong? As it turned out, MobileStar's business model just wasn't viable. Here's why.

First, by taking on all the costs associated with installing the networks, MobileStar incurred substantial up-front expenditures. This meant that it needed to entice a large number of people to use its service to cover its overhead. By adopting this approach, critics say that MobileStar engaged in a classic "If we build it, they will come" mentality. But the customers didn't come. In its eagerness to get into prized locations, it didn't ask companies such as Starbucks or Hilton to share any of the costs or risk. When its numbers fell below their projections, it ended up with huge costs and meager income.

Second, by charging the end user for its service rather than the locations that the service was placed in, MobileStar didn't motivate the owners or employees of the locations to sell the service. The number of customers of Starbucks who used the MobileStar network had no effect on the profits of Starbucks. Starbucks agreed to host MobileStar as a service to its customers, but it didn't have a financial stake in whether the service succeeded or failed. This factor turned out to be MobileStar's fatal flaw in many of its locations.

The hot spot industry is still alive, and an increasing number of restaurants, hotels, airports, and other public places are offering wireless Internet connectivity. The new companies, however, are sporting new business models that avoid MobileStar's miscues. The companies are charging the venues in which they place their networks a fee for their services and are letting the venues themselves charge the end users.

Questions for Critical Thinking

1. First-mover advantages are thought to benefit firms. Was MobileStar's first-mover advantage beneficial for the firm? If not, why not?

2. Who is MobileStar's primary customer? Is it the end user, or is it the companies in which the service can be placed? What could those leading MobileStar have done to better identify the firm's customers and their needs?

3. Make a list of the lessons you've learned from reading about MobileStar's experiences.

The second fatal flaw is pursuing unsound economics, as shown by the failure of Iridium, the satellite telephone company that was featured in Chapter 3. The idea behind Iridium was to target people who traveled to or worked in areas where traditional cellular service was unavailable. Unfortunately, the cost of putting satellites into orbit was so high that literally hundreds of thousands of people would have had to subscribe to Iridium's service to make it economically viable. As you'll recall, this never happened. Although satellite telephone service is still available, skeptics wonder if it will ever be economically viable. Another firm that failed because of a business model based on unsound economics was MobileStar, as described in the boxed feature titled "What Went Wrong?"

Components of an Effective Business Model

Although not everyone agrees precisely about the components of a business model, many agree that a successful business model has a common set of attributes. For example, one team of academics thinks of a business model as a coordinated plan to design strategy

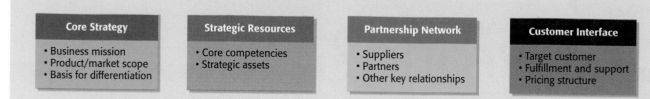

Core Strategy	Strategic Resources	Partnership Network	Customer Interface
• Business mission • Product/market scope • Basis for differentiation	• Core competencies • Strategic assets	• Suppliers • Partners • Other key relationships	• Target customer • Fulfillment and support • Pricing structure

Figure 5.3   Components of a Business Model

learning **objective**

6. Identify a business model's four major components.

along three vectors: customer interaction, asset configuration, and knowledge leverage.[13] Similarly, a noted business professor and writer, Gary Hamel, believes that a business model consists of four components: core strategy, strategic resources, customer interface, and value network.[14] We'll adopt a similar view and talk about a business model consisting of the following components:

- Core strategy (how a firm competes)
- Strategic resources (how a firm acquires and uses its resources)
- Partnership network (how a firm structures and nurtures its partnerships)
- Customer interface (how a firm interfaces with its customers)

Each of these components has several subcomponents that we'll explore. We provide a summary of each component and its respective subcomponents in Figure 5.3.

Core Strategy

The first component of a business model is the **core strategy**, which describes how a firm competes relative to its competitors.[15] The firm's mission statement, the product/market scope, and the basis for differentiation are the primary elements of a core strategy.

Mission Statement   A firm's mission, or **mission statement**, describes why it exists and what its business model is supposed to accomplish.[16] Table 5.2 provides examples of the mission statements of three firms from very different industries. To varying degrees, the statements articulate the overarching priorities of the firms and set criteria to measure performance. It is fairly easy to discern the intent of all three organizations by looking at their mission statements. The statement of Southwest Airlines is more concise than the others, and even provides a clear sense of what the company is about and how it intends to compete.

It is important that a firm's mission not be defined too narrowly. If it is, the business model that evolves may become too singularly focused and resistant to change. Take Xerox, for example. The firm styled itself as "The Document Company," with an implicit mission that focused on copiers and copying. This mission created what some call a **business concept blind spot**, which prevents a firm from seeing an opportunity that might fit its business model. Xerox viewed itself as a company that *reproduced* documents that already existed, causing the firm to be a late entrant into the market for computer printers, which print original documents stored electronically. This narrow focus allowed Hewlett-Packard to gain control of the printer market.[17]

learning **objective**

7. Explain the meaning of the term "business concept blind spot."

Product/Market Scope   A company's **product/market scope** defines the products and markets on which it will concentrate. First, the choice of product has an important impact on a firm's business model. For example, Amazon.com started out as an online bookseller but has evolved to sell other product lines, including CDs, DVDs, jewelry, and apparel. Its business model has expanded to now include the challenge of managing relationships with a number of vendors and partners beyond those connected with books. Similarly, Yahoo started as a company offering free Internet search services in an attempt to generate enough traffic to sell advertising space on its Web site. This business model worked until the e-commerce bubble burst in early 2000 and advertising revenues declined. Yahoo is revising its business model to include more subscription services to generate a more consistent income stream.

Table 5.2

Examples of Firm Mission Statements

Dell Inc.

Dell's mission is to be the most successful computer company in the world at delivering the best customer experience in markets we serve. In doing so, Dell will meet customer expectations of the following:
- Highest quality
- Leading technology
- Competitive pricing
- Individual and company accountability
- Best-in-class service and support
- Flexible customization capability
- Superior corporate citizenship
- Financial stability

Starbucks

Establish Starbucks as the premier purveyor of the finest coffee in the world while maintaining our uncompromising principles as we grow. The following six guiding principles will help us measure the appropriateness of our decisions:
- Provide a great work environment and treat each other with respect and dignity
- Embrace diversity as an essential component in the way we do business
- Apply the highest standards of excellence to the purchasing, roasting, and fresh delivery of our coffee
- Develop enthusiastically satisfied customers all the time
- Contribute positively to our communities and our environment
- Recognize that profitability is essential to our future success

Southwest Airlines

The mission of Southwest Airlines is dedication to the highest quality of customer service delivered with a sense of warmth, friendliness, individual pride, and company spirit.

The markets on which a company focuses are also an important element of its core strategy. For example, Dell targets business customers and government agencies, while Gateway targets individuals, small businesses, and first-time computer buyers. For both firms, their choices have had a significant impact on the shaping of their business models.

Because 80 percent of Dell's customers are corporations and government agencies, Dell has built into its business model sophisticated forms of customer support. For example, Dell has set up a "Premier Pages" program, which includes Web pages that are tailor-made for individual corporate customers. These pages allow customers to search for products, place orders, and configure products online. In contrast, Gateway's business model is geared more toward individual consumers, small businesses, and first-time computer buyers, which account for 66 percent of its business. Gateway has learned that the majority of first-time buyers want to see and touch a computer prior to purchase, leading to the creation of Gateway Country stores. The Gateway stores, which have since been closed, provided customers the opportunity to try computers and talk with a salesperson.[18] They also opened a new market for Gateway: computer training. In early 2004, Gateway closed its stores, indicating that it hadn't had the success with them that it had intended. This failure suggests that Gateway's business model will continue to evolve in efforts to find a product/market scope through which it can generate value for customers.

New ventures should be particularly careful not to expand their product/market offerings beyond their capabilities. Even Dell had to resist this temptation, as illustrated by Michael Dell in his book *Direct from Dell:*

Growing a company much faster than the industry is growing is great, but when your company grows by as much as 127 percent in one year, you can quickly outstrip your ability to manage it effectively. Our problem was not that Dell was in serious decline or that our customers didn't want to buy our products. Quite the opposite, we learned that it was possible to grow too quickly. The problem was that we had been overenthusiastically pursuing every opportunity that presented itself. We needed to learn that not only did we not have to jump at each and every one, as we once did—but that we couldn't or shouldn't, for our overall well-being.[19]

Basis for Differentiation   It is important that a new venture differentiate itself from its competitors in some way that is important to its customers. If a new firm's products or services aren't different from those of its competitors, why should anyone try them?

From a broad perspective, firms typically choose one of two generic strategies (cost leadership and differentiation) to position themselves in their marketplaces. Firms that have a **cost leadership strategy** strive to have the lowest costs in the industry, relative to competitors' costs, and typically attract customers on that basis. In contrast, firms using a **differentiation strategy** compete on the basis of providing unique or different products and typically compete on the basis of quality, service, timeliness, or some other important dimension.[20] In most instances, it is difficult for a new venture to feature a cost leadership strategy because cost leadership typically requires economies of scale that take time to develop.

Firms within the same industry often use different generic strategies. In the retail clothing industry, for example, Ross has a cost leadership strategy by offering slightly out-of-date merchandise at a deep discount. In contrast, Abercrombie & Fitch uses a differentiation strategy. It rarely cuts prices and instead competes on the basis that its products are different and stylish enough that they should command a premium price.

The strategy that a firm chooses greatly affects its business model. A cost leadership strategy requires a business model that is focused on efficiency, cost minimization, and large volume. As a result, a cost leader's facilities typically aren't fancy, as the emphasis is on keeping costs low rather than on comfort. Conversely, a differentiation strategy requires a business model focused on developing products and services that are unique and that command a premium price. In addition, differentiators typically work hard to create **brand loy-**

Prices may be high and the discount rack may be bare, but image is everything and Abercrombie & Fitch knows this. A&F targets young adults who are willing to pay for the Abercrombie look. A&F is looking to lure even young consumers with the introduction of Abercrombie Kids (ages 7–14) and Hollister Co. (ages 14–18).

alty, wherein customers become loyal to a particular company's product, such as Levis jeans or Apple computers. Brand loyalty is a valuable asset in that it causes customers to buy a firm's product or service time and time again.

Strategic Resources

A firm is not able to implement a strategy without resources, so the resources a firm has affects its business model substantially. For a new venture, its strategic resources may initially be limited to the competencies of its founders, the opportunity they have identified, and the unique way they plan to service their market. The two most important resources are a firm's core competencies and its strategic assets.

Core Competencies   As defined in Chapter 3, a **core competency** is a resource or capability that serves as a source of a firm's competitive advantage over its rivals. It is a unique skill or capability that transcends products or markets, makes a significant contribution to the customer's perceived benefit, and is difficult to imitate.[21] Examples of core competencies include Sony's competence in miniaturization, Dell's competence in supply chain management, and 3M's competence in managing innovation. A firm's core competencies determine where it creates the most value. In distinguishing its core competencies, a firm should identify the skills it has that are (1) unique, (2) valuable to customers, (3) difficult to imitate, and (4) transferable to new opportunities.[22]

A firm's core competencies are important in both the short and the long term. In the short term, it is a company's core competencies that allow it to differentiate itself from its competitors and create unique value. For example, Dell's core competencies include supply chain management, efficient assembly, and serving corporate customers, so its business model of providing corporate customers computers that are price competitive, are technologically up to date, and have access to after-sale support makes sense. If Dell suddenly started assembling and selling musical instruments, analysts would be skeptical of the new strategy and justifiably ask, "Why is Dell pursuing a strategy that is outside its core competency?"

In the long term, it is important to have core competencies to grow and establish strong positions in complementary markets. For example, Dell has taken its core competencies in the assembly and sale of PCs and has moved them into the market for computer servers and other electronic devices. This process of adapting a company's core competencies to exploit new opportunities is referred to as **resource leverage**.

There is growing evidence that firms benefit from developing core competencies and focusing their efforts on core businesses. This trend means that firms are concentrating on smaller and smaller segments of a product or service's value chain and becoming experts at servicing their respective segments. A recent Bain and Company study of over 1,800 public companies in seven countries found that 80 percent of the companies that sustained both value creation and at least 5.5 percent annual growth over 10 years had one core business with clear market leadership. This evidence validates the belief that it's better to be really good at one or two things than mediocre at many things.[23]

Strategic Assets   **Strategic assets** are anything rare and valuable that a firm owns. They include plant and equipment, location, brands, patents, customer data, a highly qualified staff, and distinctive partnerships. A particularly valuable strategic asset is a company's brand, which will be discussed in detail in Chapter 11. Starbucks, for example, has worked hard to build the image of its brand, and it would take an enormous effort for another coffee retailer to achieve this same level of brand recognition. Companies ultimately try to combine their core competencies and strategic assets to create a **sustainable competitive advantage**. This factor is one to which investors pay close attention when evaluating a business.[24] A sustainable competitive advantage is achieved by implementing a value-creating strategy that is unique and not easy to imitate.[25] This type of advantage is achievable when a firm has strategic resources and the ability to use them.[26]

learning **objective**

8. Define the term "core competency" and describe its importance.

Partnership Network

A firm's network of partnerships is the third component of a business model. New ventures, in particular, typically do not have the resources to perform all the tasks required to make their businesses work, so they rely on partners to perform key roles. In most cases, a business does not want to do everything itself because the majority of tasks needed to build a product or deliver a service are not core to a company's competitive advantage.[27] For example, Dell differentiates itself from its competitors through its expertise in assembling computers but buys chips from Intel. Dell could manufacturer its own chips, but it doesn't have a core competency in this area. Similarly, Dell relies on UPS and FedEx to deliver its products because it would be silly for Dell to build a nationwide system to deliver its computers. Firms also rely on partners to supply intellectual capital needed to produce complex products and services, as illustrated in the following observation from two authorities on business partnerships:

> Neither Boeing nor Airbus has one tenth of the intellectual capital or coordination capacity to cost effectively mine metals, create alloys, make fasteners, cast and machine parts, design avionics, produce control systems, make engines, and so on. The complex systems we call airplanes come together through the voluntary agreements and collaborations of thousands of companies operating in the global marketplace.[28]

A firm's partnership network includes suppliers and other partners. Let's look at each of them.

Suppliers

A **supplier** (or vendor) is a company that provides parts or services to another company. Intel is Dell's supplier for computer chips, for example. A **supply chain** is the network of all the companies that participate in the production of a product, from the acquisition of raw materials to the final sale. Almost all firms have suppliers who play vital roles in the functioning of their business models.

Traditionally, firms maintained an arm's-length relationship with their suppliers and viewed them almost as adversaries. Producers needing a component part would negotiate with several suppliers to find the best price. Over the past two decades, however, firms have increasingly moved away from contentious relationships with their suppliers and are now partnering with them to achieve mutually beneficial goals.[29] This shift resulted from competitive pressures that motivated managers to look up and down their value chains to find opportunities for cost savings, quality improvement, and improved speed to market. More and more, managers are focusing on **supply chain management**, which is the coordination of the flow of all information, money, and material that moves through a product's supply chain. The more efficiently an organization can manage its supply chain, the more effectively its entire business model will perform.[30]

Firms are developing more collaborative relationships with their suppliers, finding ways to motivate them to perform at a higher level. Many firms are reducing the number of their suppliers and working more closely with a smaller group. For example, 20 suppliers account for 90 percent of the $5 billion in annual spending by Sun Microsystems. To leverage its relationship with this group of select companies, Sun formed a special council with its top five suppliers to jointly attack important problems.[31] Similarly, Dell maintains close relationships with its suppliers and uses sophisticated software to enhance the performance of its supply chain. Dell has accomplished a level of rigor in its supply chain that supports its core strategy of offering technologically up-to-date computers at affordable prices. The following comes from a case study about Dell, posted on the Web site of i2 Technologies, Dell's provider of supply chain management software:

> Every 20 seconds, Dell aggregates its orders, analyzing the material requirements. i2 SCM [a computer program] compares Dell's on-hand inventory with its suppliers' inventory, then creates a supplier bill of material to meet its order needs. Dell's suppliers have 90 minutes to pull the needed materials and drive them to Dell's factory. Dell then takes 30 minutes to unload the truck and place the material—in the precise order in which they will be manufactured—onto the assembly line. Since the company pulls only the materials it needs for its on-hand orders, Dell operators with an extremely small seven hours' worth of inventory.[32]

learning **objective**

9. Explain the concept of supply chain management.

Partnering for SUCCESS

Want to Get Noticed by Potential Partners? Do Something Impressive

www.insitugroup.com

Many small firms want to partner with larger companies but find that it's hard to get noticed. But on September 10, 2001, Insitu, a small engineering firm, managed this feat. It signed a 15-month partnership with Boeing, a *Fortune 500* company, to codevelop its most important product. The product is the Scan Eagle, an unmanned aircraft that will be sold to the U.S. Department of Defense.

Insitu was founded in 1994 to develop unmanned weather airplanes. Since that time, it has developed a specialty for building lightweight, long-range, radio-controlled aircraft. In 1998, one of Insitu's products, the Aerosonde, became the first unmanned aircraft to make a transatlantic flight. The news media called attention to the firm, and Boeing took notice. A partnership between the two firms began in September of 2001, and two months later, Boeing announced a new unmanned-aircraft division that included Insitu.

Working together, Insitu and Boeing will develop the Scan Eagle. The 33-pound plane will be able to fly 5,000 miles nonstop over three days, doing reconnaissance, search and rescue, and military missions. Insitu will also license Boeing technology for some of its other projects in which its planes are used for wildlife monitoring.

Insitu proved that one way for a small firm to get noticed by a larger potential partner is to do something impressive. There are many win-win partnerships between larger and smaller firms, in which the smaller firm, like Insitu, stands to benefit enormously. The first step in making this happen, however, is to get the attention of the larger firm.

Questions for Critical Thinking

1. Given the information in this feature, describe what you believe is Insitu's core strategy.

2. Does Insitu face risks with its partnership with Boeing? If so, what are those risks, and what should the firm do to control them?

Sources: Fortune Small Business, *November 2002, and S. Wilhelm,* "Boeing Contract Puts Wind under Insitu's Wings," *Puget Sound Business Journal, May 31, 2002.*

In regard to partnerships in general, one challenge that new ventures have is establishing relationships with high-quality partners. One way to get the attention of high-quality partners is by doing something impressive, as illustrated in the boxed feature titled "Partnering for Success."

Other Key Relationships   Along with its suppliers, firms partner with other companies to make their business models work. As described in Table 5.3, strategic alliances, joint ventures, networks, consortia, and trade associations are common forms of these partnerships. A recent survey by PricewaterhouseCoopers found that over the past three years, more than half of America's fastest-growing companies have formed multiple partnerships to support their business models. According to the research, these partnerships have "resulted in more innovative products, more profit opportunities, and significantly high growth rates" for the firms involved.[33]

An entrepreneur's ability to launch a firm that achieves a sustainable competitive advantage may hinge as much on the skills of the partners that are involved as the skills within the firm itself. Partnerships also help firms stay nimble and focus on their core competencies, as mentioned earlier in this chapter. And top-notch firms are able to choose the best partners. These are the reasons Dell decided to form partnerships early on, as explained by Michael Dell:

> Leveraging our suppliers [who Dell early on described as alliance partners] has allowed us to scale our business very quickly without having to become an expert in surface-mount technology, semi-conductor manufacturing, or building mother-boards and other electrical assemblies, all of which would require an enormous commitment of intellectual and monetary capital. Traditional industry mentality dictates that if you don't build your own components, you'll never have enough control over the process. But by working with outside suppliers, we've found that you actually gain more control over the quality of your products than if you were to do everything yourself. How? You can choose among the best providers in the world.[34]

Table 5.3

The Most Common Types of Business
Partnerships

Partnership Form	Description
Joint venture	An entity created by two or more firms pooling a portion of their resources to create a separate, jointly owned organization
Network	A hub-and-wheel configuration with a local firm at the hub organizing the interdependencies of a complex array of firms
Consortia	A group of organizations with similar needs that band together to create a new entity to address those needs
Strategic alliance	An arrangement between two or more firms that establishes an exchange relationship but has no joint ownership involved
Trade associations	Organizations (typically nonprofit) that are formed by firms in the same industry to collect and disseminate trade information, offer legal and technical advice, furnish industry-related training, and provide a platform for collective lobbying

Source: B. Barringer and J. Harrison, "Walking a Tightrope: Creating Value through Interorganizational Relationships," *Journal of Management* 26, no. 3 (2000): 367–403.

There are other important motivations for firms to partner with each other. These include gaining economies of scale, risk and cost sharing, gaining access to foreign markets, learning, speed to market, flexibility, and neutralizing or blocking competitors.[35]

There *are* risks involved in partnerships, particularly if a single partnership is a key component of a firm's business model. Many partnerships fall short of meeting the expectations of the participants for a variety of reasons. In recent years, the international accounting firms of PricewaterhouseCoopers[36] and KPMG,[37] through studies they have conducted, have estimated that the failure rate for business alliances is 50 percent and 60 to 70 percent, respectively. Many of the failures result from poor planning or the difficulties involved with meshing the cultures of two or more organizations to achieve a common goal. There are also potential disadvantages to participating in alliances, including loss of proprietary information, management complexities, financial and organizational risks, risk of becoming dependent on a partner, and partial loss of decision autonomy.[38]

Customer Interface

Customer interface—how a firm interacts with its customers—is the fourth component of a business model. The type of customer interaction depends on how a firm chooses to compete. For example, Amazon.com sells books solely over the Internet, while Barnes & Noble sells both through its traditional bookstores and online. In the computer industry, there are several customer interface models. Dell sells strictly online and over the phone, while Hewlett-Packard and IBM sell primarily through retail stores. Gateway, like Dell, sells primarily online and over the phone.

For a new venture, the customer interface that it chooses is central to how it plans to compete and where it is located in the value chain of the products and services it provides. The three elements of a company's customer interface are target customer, fulfillment and support, and pricing model. Let's look at each of these elements closely.

learning **objective**

10. Define the term "target market."

Target Market   A firm's **target market** is the limited group of individuals or businesses that it goes after or tries to appeal to, as discussed earlier in this book. The target market a firm selects affects everything it does, from the strategic assets it acquires to the partnerships it forges to its promotional campaigns. For example, the clothing retailer Abercrombie & Fitch targets 18- to 22-year-old men and women who are willing to pay full price for trendy apparel. So the decisions it makes about strategic assets, partnerships, and

advertising will be much different from the decisions made by Chico's, a clothing store that targets 30- to 60-year-old women.

Typically, a firm greatly benefits from having a clearly defined target market. Because of the specificity of its targeted customer, Abercrombie & Fitch can keep abreast of the clothing trends for its market, it can focus its marketing and promotional campaigns, and it can develop deep core competencies pertaining to its specific marketplace. A company such as Gap has a larger challenge because its stores appeal to a broader range of clientele. In fact, when a retailer such as Gap starts offering too many products, it typically begins breaking itself down into more narrowly focused markets so that it can regain the advantages that are enjoyed by a singularly focused retailer such as Abercrombie & Fitch. Gap has done this successfully and now has a more diversified collection of stores, including Gap, GapKids, BabyGap, GapBody, Banana Republic, Old Navy and Gap Outlet stores.

For firms that sell primarily to other businesses, it is important not only to select a target market but also to know who the decision makers in the target market are so that a firm's sales efforts can be focused appropriately. This point is illustrated in the boxed feature titled "Savvy Entrepreneurial Firm."

Fulfillment and Support

Fulfillment and support describes the way a firm's product or service "goes to market" or how it reaches its customers. It also refers to the channels a company uses and what level of customer support it provides.[39] All these issues impact the shape and nature of a company's business model.

Firms differ considerably along these dimensions. Suppose that a new venture developed and patented an exciting new cell phone technology. In forming its business plan, the firm might have several options regarding how to take its technology to market. It could (1) license the technology to existing cell phone companies such as Nokia and Ericsson, (2) manufacture the cell phone itself and establish its own sales channels, or (3) partner with a cell phone company such as Motorola and sell the phone through

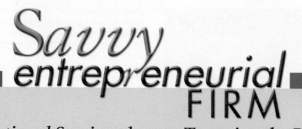

Savvy entrepreneurial FIRM

National Semiconductor: Targeting the Right Customer

www.national.com

Sometimes a firm reaches its target customer most effectively not by interfacing directly with the customer but by interfacing with the people who influence the purchase decision. For example, minivans are advertised in magazines for teenagers not because advertisers think the teenagers will buy the minivans but because families with teenagers buy minivans and kids influence the purchase decisions of their parents. Marketing experts even have a term for this influence—pester power.

A firm that uses this logic is National Semiconductor. When the design engineers for National Semiconductor's customers are designing new or improved products, they have to locate all the available parts they'll need. To do so, they consult parts catalogs, Web sites, and other sources to get all the information they can about the competing parts that are available. Once a part has been specified into a product design, the purchasing department takes over to place the order.

National Semiconductor understands this process. It knows that the person with the most influence over the actual purchase decision is not the purchasing agent but the design engineer. As a result, the company focuses its customer interface efforts on the design engineers rather than on the purchasing agents.

Questions for Critical Thinking

1. As this feature shows, it is important for firms to precisely recognize the decision makers in their target markets. Think of your university or college. What is your school's target market, and who is or are the key decision makers in that market?

2. Think of a firm in your local community. What is that firm's target market, and how does the firm go about interfacing with the customers in that market?

Source: P. Seybold, Customers.com (New York: Random House, 1998).

---

partnerships with the cell phone service providers such as Cingular and Verizon. The choice a firm makes about fulfillment and service has a dramatic impact on the type of company that evolves and the business model that develops. For example, if the company licenses its technology, it would probably build a business model that emphasized research and development to continue to have cutting-edge technologies to license to the cell phone manufacturers. In contrast, if it decides to manufacture its own cell phones, it needs to establish core competencies in the areas of manufacturing and design and needs to form partnerships with cell phone retailers such as Cingular, Sprint, and Verizon.

The level of customer support a firm is willing to offer also impacts its business model. Some firms differentiate their products or services and provide extra value to their customers through high levels of service and support. Customer service can include delivery and installation, financing arrangements, customer training, warranties and guarantees, repairs, layaway plans, convenient hours of operation, convenient parking, and information through toll-free numbers and Web sites.[40] Dell, as mentioned earlier, has a broad menu of tiered services available to provide its corporate clients the exact level of support they need and for which they are willing to pay. Making this choice of services available is a key component of Dell's business model.

Pricing Structure   A third element of a company's customer interface is its pricing structure, a topic that will be discussed in more detail in Chapter 11. Pricing models vary, depending on a firm's target market and its pricing philosophy. For example, some rental car companies charge a daily flat rate, while other charge so much per mile. Similarly, some consultants charge a flat fee for performing a service (e.g., helping an entrepreneurial venture write a business plan), while others charge an hourly rate. In some instances, a company must also choose whether to charge its customers directly or indirectly through a service provider. For example, most long-distance carriers charge their services through a local phone company's billing system so that their customers won't have to write separate checks every month for their local and long-distance telephone services.

Firms differentiate themselves on the basis of their pricing structure in both common and unusual ways. In general, it is difficult for new ventures to differentiate themselves on price, which is a common strategy for larger firms with more substantial economies of scale. There are exceptions, such as Amazon.com in books and Domino's in pizza, which have been price leaders since their inception. In contrast, there are several examples of firms that have started primarily on the basis of featuring innovative pricing models. The most noteworthy is Priceline.com, which pioneered the practice of letting customers explicitly set prices they are willing to pay for products and services. Another example is Carmax, which features a "no-haggle" pricing policy and sells new and used cars through its showrooms and Web site. The company's slogan is "The Way Car Buying Should Be." Carmax offers its customers a low-stress environment by presenting them with what it believes to be a fair price, with no negotiations.

In summary, it is very useful for a new venture to look at itself in a holistic manner and understand that it must construct an effective "business model" to be successful. Everyone that does business with a new firm, from its customers to its partners, does so on a voluntary basis. As a result, a firm must motivate its customers and partners to play along. The primary elements of a firm's business model are its core strategy, strategic resources, partnership network, and customer interface. Close attention to each of these elements is essential for a new venture's success.

CHAPTER SUMMARY

1. A firm's business model is its plan or diagram for how it intends to compete, use its resources, structure relationships, interface with customers, and create value to sustain itself on the basis of the profits it generates.

2. Business model innovation refers to initiatives such as those undertaken by Michael Dell that revolutionize how products are sold in an industry.

3. The main reasons that having a clearly articulated business model is important are as follows: it serves as an ongoing extension of feasibility analysis, it focuses attention on how all the elements of a business fit together, it describes why the network of participants who are needed to make a business idea viable would be willing to work together, and it articulates the core logic of a firm to all its stakeholders.

4. The value chain shows how a product moves from the raw-material stage to the final consumer. The value chain helps a firm identify opportunities to enhance its competitive strategies and to recognize new business opportunities.

5. A complete misread of the customer and utterly unsound economics are the two fatal flaws that can make a business model a failure from the outset.

6. Core strategy, strategic resources, partnership networks, and customer interface are the four major components of a firm's business model.

7. A business concept blind spot prevents a firm from seeing an opportunity that might fit its business model.

8. A core competency is something that a firm does particularly well. It is a resource or capability that serves as a source of a firm's competitive advantage over its rivals.

9. Supply chain management refers to the flow of all information, money, and material that moves through a product's supply chain. The more efficiently an organization can manage its supply chain, the more effectively its entire business model will perform.

10. A firm's target market is the limited group of individuals or business that it goes after or tries to appeal to at a point in time.

brand loyalty, 110

business concept blind
    spot, 108

business model, 100

business model
    innovation, 102

core competency, 111

core strategy, 108

cost leadership strategy, 110

customer interface, 114

differentiation strategy, 110

fulfillment and
    support, 115

mission statement, 108

product/market scope, 108

resource leverage, 111

strategic assets, 111

supplier, 112

supply chain, 112

supply chain
    management, 112

sustainable competitive
    advantage, 111

target market, 114

value chain, 104

REVIEW QUESTIONS

1. Define the term "business model." How can entrepreneurial firms benefit by developing and using a business model?

2. Explain what business model innovation means. Provide an example of business model innovation other than the Dell Inc. example given in this chapter.

3. Why is it dangerous for a company to assume that it can be successful by simply copying the business model of the industry leader?

4. Briefly describe the value chain concept. How does the value chain help firms identify business opportunities?

5. How does an understanding of the value chain help explain how business models emerge?

6. What are the two fatal flaws that can render a business model untenable?

7. What are the four primary components of a firm's business model? Briefly describe the importance of each component.

8. Describe what is meant by the term "core strategy" and why it is important.

9. Describe the purpose of a mission statement.

10. What is meant by the term "business model blind spot"? Provide an original example of a firm that suffered as the result of having a business model blind spot.

11. What is a firm's product/market scope? Why is the concept of product/market scope important in regard to crafting a successful business model?

12. Why is it important for firms to differentiate themselves from competitors?

13. In what ways does a focus on a cost leadership strategy lead to a very different business model than a focus on a differentiation strategy?

14. Define the term "core competency" and describe why it's important for a firm to have one or more core competencies. How do a company's core competencies help shape its business model?

15. What is meant by the term "resource leverage"? How does an understanding of this term help a firm exploit new product or service opportunities?

16. What is meant by the term "strategic asset"? Provide examples of the strategic assets of three well-known firms.

17. Why do firms typically need partners to make their business models work?

18. What is meant by the term "supply chain management"?

19. What is meant by the term "customer interface"? Explain how Dell and Gateway differ from each other on this core dimension.

20. Describe the impact of a firm's pricing structure on its business model.

APPLICATION QUESTIONS

1. Given the information in this chapter about Dell Inc., write a brief description of Dell's business model.

2. Jim Payne is a writer for the business section of a major newspaper in Colorado. Recently, he wrote an article with the following headline: "Why Bother with Business Models?" The gist of the article was that most firms exist in such competitive environments that any business

model put in place today will probably be outdated tomorrow. Do you agree or disagree with Jim's assessment? Explain the rationale for your answer.

3. Carol Schmidt plans to open a company that will make accessories for cell phones. She has read that having a clearly articulated business model will help "all the elements of her business fit together." Carol isn't quite

sure what that statement means. If Carol asked you to explain it to her, what would you say?

4. Jane Rowan is an experienced business consultant. Through working with clients, she has noticed that many companies have "business concept blind spots." How can having a business concept blind spot affect the strength of a firm's business model?

5. Select one of the following companies: Amazon.com, Google, or eBay. For the company you selected, identify its core competency and explain how its core competency strengthens its business model and contributes to its competitive advantage.

6. Using the same firm as you selected for question 5, make a list of the firm's strategic assets. How does each of its strategic assets strengthen its business model?

7. Rich Matthews has a successful electronics company that makes components for DVD and MP3 players. In fact, in the past several years, Rich's company has won several awards for manufacturing excellence. Rich wants to expand his business to increase revenues. He has heard about "resource leverage" but doesn't really understand what it means. If Rich asked you to explain this concept to him and how he could use it in his business, what would you tell him?

8. Six months ago, Peter Wilcox retired as an engineer with NASA and used some of his retirement savings to open a chain of three video stores near the Kennedy Space Center in Florida. Peter had never been in the video store business before but likes the retail environment and enjoys watching videos. So far, the business hasn't done very well. Peter recently went to a bank to get a loan for the business and was startled when the banker told him, "It's no wonder your business isn't thriving. As far as I can tell, it doesn't have a core competency." Peter can't figure out what the banker means by this comment. What would you tell Peter if he asked you to interpret the banker's comment? What core competencies might be particularly important for Peter's type of business?

9. Jill Hopkins just received an e-mail message from an investor who has agreed to listen to her pitch her business idea. The investor said, "Your timing is good—I just happen to be sitting on $500,000 that I'm anxious to invest. One thing I'll warn you about ahead of time, however, is that you must show me that your business has the potential to achieve a sustainable competitive advantage. If you can't show me that, I won't invest." Jill has read about sustainable competitive advantage but is still a little hazy about the concept. Can you explain the concept to Jill?

10. Tom Sanders is a software engineer for Orbitz, the online reservation service for airlines and hotels. He is planning to leave Orbitz to sell a software product that he has developed for the travel industry. Tom's goal is to create a business that achieves a sustainable competitive advantage. Of the four main components of a business model, the area with which Tom is the least acquainted is "customer interface." Based on Tom's business idea, explain the choices that he has available in this area.

Company: **AuctionDrop**
(www.auctiondrop.com)

Business idea: Provide an easy and convenient way for people to sell their stuff on eBay.

Pitch: Many people have items they would like to sell on eBay but are unable to because they lack Internet access, because they don't own a digital camera (to send eBay a picture of the item), or because they are simply too busy to follow an auction. AuctionDrop provides a solution to these problems. To take advantage of AuctionDrop's service, a seller simply takes the item he or she would like to auction to an AuctionDrop store. AuctionDrop takes a digital photo of the item, writes a detailed description of it, lists it on eBay, and handles the shipping and correspondence. After the item sells, the customer receives a check in the mail for the selling price of the item, minus AuctionDrop's commission of roughly 35 percent. To maintain a high positive feedback rating on eBay, AuctionDrop doesn't accept all items. The company has proprietary systems in place to avoid listing stolen goods. It also does not accept items in poor condition. Items that don't sell are either held for pickup by the owner or donated to charity at the owner's discretion.

Q&A: Based on the material covered in this chapter, what questions would you ask the founders of this firm before making your funding decision? What answers would satisfy you?

Decision: If you had to make your decision on just the information provided in the pitch and the company's Web site, would you fund this firm? Why or why not?

Case 5.1

Bright Horizons Family Solutions: A Business Model That Works for Everyone
www.brighthorizons.com

> But we knew that in order to succeed we had to come up with a viable business model.—Roger Brown, cofounder, Bright Horizons Family Solutions

When Roger Brown and Linda Mason met in business school, it seemed as though their life was destined for corporate America. But after graduation and before entering the corporate world, the two traveled to Cambodia to spend the summer working in refugee camps. They were so taken by the crowds of malnourished children that they stayed for two years. After a short stint back in the states at consulting jobs, the two were drawn to Sudan and spent two more years doing relief work. When they finally left, they decided to put their résumés away and make a career of working with children.

Roger and Linda decided they would like to open a child care center. After briefly examining and rejecting the idea of a nonprofit, parent cooperative model, the couple concluded that to realize their vision they would need to build a for-profit organization. At the suggestion of a colleague, they decided to enter the emerging business of providing child care at work sites and in 1986 launched what's now known as Bright Horizons Family Solutions. At that time, child care in the United States was run like a commodity business. In fact, the largest company in the industry was trying to imitate the fast-food business and labeled itself the "McDonald's of child care." That philosophy, which engendered an environment of high employee turnover and plain vanilla curricula, was the opposite of Brown and Mason's dream. They wanted to build a high-quality child care network with low employee turnover and exciting surroundings for the children.

But the couple knew that they needed more than a vision; they needed a viable business model to succeed. If they were going to introduce a new type of child care center, they had to have a good story to tell and a business model that would motivate everyone involved to participate. The first thing the pair did was recruit three industry experts to help them refine their ideas. They also spent a lot of time talking to child care center teachers and directors in the Boston area. They decided that they would partner with employers to offer on-site centers so that they would have an immediate supply of potential customers. This meant that they wouldn't have to advertise or try to sell their services to one parent at a time.

More important, the idea made sense for employers. There was evidence to suggest that on-site day care reduced employee turnover at the firm, lowered unscheduled absences, and increased employee morale. There were lots of reasons to think that a company's new parents would like the service. By having their children down the hall, they could reduce their commute time and drop by to see their kids on breaks. In addition, companies could use the availability of on-site day care as a way of differentiating themselves from their competitors to potential employees.

Another piece of the puzzle was thinking through how Bright Horizons would recruit teachers to staff its centers. The child care industry is notorious for low pay, insufficient training, limited supplies and resources, and high turnover. There is also an ongoing battle between child care providers and regulators in many states over a variety of issues, and many centers get cited for violating regulations. Brown and Mason intuitively knew that high-quality employers, such as the ones they wanted to partner with, would never align themselves with a child care provider that paid minimum wage, hired run-of-the mill teachers, and fought with regulators. As a result, the founders vowed from day one to offer a high-quality product, attract the best teachers available, pay above-average wages, and strictly adhere to state child care regulations. They also vowed to create a warm and inviting atmosphere for the children, rich with educational activity and healthy fun.

Prudential was the firm's first customer. In August 1987, the firm opened its first child care center in Prudential's downtown Boston complex. The going was rough early on, and Brown and Mason made many cold calls. Most companies were afraid of the liability they might incur by having a child care center on their property. Bright Horizons eventually overcame that obstacle by securing insurance 50 times above the industry standard and by indemnifying their clients. The revenue side of the business model evolved as the company gained partners, and two revenue models emerged. In the first model, Bright Horizons assumed the financial risk for a center that opened in a partner's workplace and earned its profit out of the operating budget. In the second model, the client simply paid Bright Horizons a management fee. In either case, the employer supplied the capital for building and outfitting the centers.

Today, Bright Horizons Family Solutions is the nation's leading provider of employer-sponsored child care centers. It currently manages over 380 child care centers for the world's leading employers, including IBM, General Electric, Universal Studios, and Cisco Systems. It also works with many of the nation's leading universities, such as John Hopkins, Duke, Georgia Tech, and Iowa State.

The business model of Bright Horizons hasn't changed much since its inception in the late 1980s. Even during the early 1990s, when the company was struggling to manage its growth, it never backed off its commitment to quality.

The commitment to quality and its steadfast execution of its business model have served the company well since its inception, and the company continues to be committed to offering high-quality on-site child care centers in the future.

1. How does Bright Horizons Family Solution's business model motivate its customers, its employees, and its partners (such as Prudential and the other companies that host its day care centers) to participate with its business? On a scale of 1 to 5 (with 5 being high), rate how motivated you think each group is to do business with Bright Horizon's Family Solutions and help it succeed.

2. At the beginning of this chapter, the statement is made that "at its simplest level, a business model is a story of how a company operates." Do you think Bright Horizons has a good story to tell? When it goes to a company to try to solicit business (to open an on-site day care center), do you think it's easy or hard for employees of Bright Horizons to clearly explain to an employer why having an on-site child care center is a good idea?

3. Write a mission statement for Bright Horizons Family Solutions.

4. Describe Bright Horizons Family Solution's strategic resources. Discuss the importance of its strategic resources in supporting its business model.

5. Suppose that you are the chief operating officer of Bright Horizons Family Solutions. You just received an e-mail from Brad Jennings, the chief executive officer of a company that is interested in opening an on-site child care center. In his e-mail message to you, Mr. Jennings asks the following of you: "Describe to me your business model. Convince me that your organization has a good story." How would you respond to Mr. Jennings's message?

Sources: "Providing the Killer Perk," BusinessWeek, *June 10, 2002, and R. Brown, "How We Built a Strong Company in a Weak Industry,"* Harvard Business Review 79, *no. 2, February 2001.*

Case 5.2

Netflix: Great Idea, but Will the Business Model Work?
www.netflix.com

While cleaning up your living room, you discover a three-week-overdue DVD from Blockbuster. When you return it the next day, you find out that with the late fees you've incurred, you could have *bought* the movie. To add insult to injury, you never even watched it!

When Reed Hastings returned a copy of *Apollo 13* to a video store and was charged $40 in late fees, he thought, "There has to be a better way," and started Netflix.

When it was founded in 1997, Netflix was similar to the traditional movie rental model, except that customers selected their rentals online and movies were delivered to their homes. After watching a movie, a customer would return it in a pre-paid envelope via the United States Postal Service (USPS). Reed hadn't eliminated late fees, but he did limit them to $2 per week.

Two years later, Netflix changed its approach to a subscriptions service that offered unlimited DVD rentals with no late fees. For a flat monthly fee of $17.99, you get three DVDs. Here's how it works. On the Netflix Web site, you list the DVDs you would like to watch, choosing from Netflix's menu of over 12,000 movies. The DVDs are shipped to your home via the USPS. You can keep the DVDs as long as you want, with no late fees. When you return one, the next selection on your movie priority list is mailed out. You are always entitled to have three DVDs as long as you're willing to pay the monthly fee.

The result of Netflix's new approach has been rapid subscription growth, particularly among customers who hate paying late fees. Netflix now claims to have over two million active subscribers and is adding new subscribers every month. To minimize risk and reduce overhead, the company has a number of interesting twists to its business model. One is that it does not pay for much of its inventory. Instead, the company has risk-sharing alliances with the major movie studios, including DreamWorks SKG, 20th Century Fox, Universal Studios, and several others, in exchange for a share of the rental revenues and a stake in its business. In return, 80 percent of the 3.3 million DVDs in Netflix's inventory were acquired from the studios without any up-front payment. These partnerships with the studios also allow Netflix to offer its subscribers movies within 90 days of release, which is quicker than traditional video stores.

Netflix raised $82 million in an initial public offering (IPO) of shares of it stock in May 2002. The IPO, which was led by Merrill Lynch, was one of the most successful of the year. Despite its success, however, and its ability to go public, several questions linger about the strength and ultimate viability of Netflix's business model. Some observers still aren't sold on Netflix's ability to achieve a sustainable competitive advantage and believe that viewers will eventually tire of paying $17.99 per month. In addition, other observers believe that Blockbuster, Hollywood Video, or even Wal-Mart will eventually imitate what Netflix is doing and will squash the smaller rival.

The accompanying figure lists the most compelling strengths and weaknesses of Netflix's business model. As for the future of Netflix, time will tell.

Strengths and Weaknesses of Netflix's Business Model

Strengths	Weaknesses
Convenience: No more trips to the video store. Netflix's products are ordered online and shipped and returned via the U.S. Postal Service.	**Can Netflix remain the most convenient?** If convenience is an issue, what about movies on demand provided by cable companies? If Netflix continues to be a hit, will Time Warner and the other cable operators try to offer a similar service? What if Time Warner offered unlimited pay-per-view movies a month for $17.99 without the hassle of the mail?
DVDs rather than videotapes: Netflix's product offering is built around DVDs rather than videotapes. DVDs are cheaper to ship and are steadily replacing videos as the medium of choice for viewing movies.	**Netflix's rivals have DVDs too:** An intense battle may be shaping up among Netflix, Blockbuster, and Wal-Mart for the home DVD subscription market. Certainly, Blockbuster will not simply stand back and allow Netflix to take its customers.
Bigger selection than video stores: The average Blockbuster store carries roughly 1,500 movie titles. Netflix, which isn't limited by physical space, carries more than 12,000 titles, including hard-to-find old movies and documentaries.	**User fatigue:** How many people will continue paying the monthly fee after they watch their 50 favorite movies? At some point, will subscribers tire of the service and start dropping out?
No late fees: With Netflix, there are no late fees. Analysts estimate that 18 percent of Blockbuster's $5 billion in revenue comes from late fees. Late fees are annoying, even to the most loyal video store customer.	**Fulfillment challenges:** Even though Netflix doesn't have late fees, users have to wait for videos to arrive in the mail. They can't impulse shop. In addition, as its subscriber base increases, skeptics wonder if Netflix can maintain acceptable turnaround times for its DVDs.
Strong partnership network: Netflix has strong partnership arrangements with the U.S. Postal Service, the movie studios, and several retailers to help drive potential customers to its Web site.	**Are the partnerships unique?** To what extent are Netflix's partnership agreements unique? If approached, would the studios offer Blockbuster and Hollywood Video the same deals they are offering Netflix?
Good Web site: Netflix's Web site is simple to use. It has a clean design, a strong search engine, and a simple queuing mechanism for ordering. Most customer interactions are handled via e-mail, reducing Netflix's expense.	**Who does the work?** Netflix does have a Web site that automates its ordering, but it also incurs a higher handling cost than a traditional video store. In a physical store, customers pick up and drop off their rentals—in other words, they do a lot of the work. Netflix's model results in it doing all the work. It pays for shipping rentals and also pays for their return.
Personalization: On its Web site, Netflix presents its subscribers recommendations for movies they might like based on their past selections. In fact, it provides more than 18 million personal recommendations a day. No video store can do that.	**Do customers care?** Personalized services, like movie recommendations, are an intangible, and it's hard to know how much difference they make.

Discussion Questions

1. Does Netflix have a good story? Are its strengths sufficiently compelling to offset its weaknesses? If a debate were held between the proponents and critics of Netflix's business model, who would win? Why?

2. What is Netflix's core competency? What are its strategic assets? Is there anything in Netflix's business model that makes what the company is doing hard to replicate? Explain your answer.

3. Describe Netflix's partnership network. Describe how each of Netflix's major partnerships supports its business model.

4. If you were advising Netflix, what would you tell it to do to make its business model more financially viable for the long term?

5. Describe how Netflix interfaces with its customers. To what extent to you believe that this component of Netflix's business model contributes to its sustainable competitive advantage.

6. A company named TriggerFingers has a business model very similar to Netflix. Its product is electronic games rather than DVDs. Visit TriggerFinger's Web site at www.triggerfingers.com. Do you think TriggerFingers will be successful? Why or why not?

Sources: E-Business Strategies, "Netflix: Transforming the DVD Rental Business," www.ebstrategy.com (accessed November 10, 2002); L. Walker, "Now Showing, in Your Mailbox," Washington Post, August 11, 2002, H01; and J. Ellis, "Strategy," Fast Company, November, 2002, 66.

building a *new venture* team

After studying this chapter, you should be ready to:

1. Identify the primary elements of a new venture team.

2. Explain the term "liabilities of newness."

3. Discuss the difference between heterogeneous and homogeneous founding teams.

4. Identify the personal attributes that strengthen a founder's chances of launching a successful new firm.

5. Explain the actions of an executive-search firm.

6. Identify the two primary ways in which the nonemployee members of a start-up's new venture team help the firm.

7. Describe a board of directors and explain the difference between inside directors and outside directors.

8. Describe the concept of signaling and explain why it's important.

9. Discuss the purpose of forming an advisory board.

10. Explain why new venture firms use consultants for help and advice.

waveset: hitting the ground running

In the late 1990s, Mark McClain, Mike Turner, Kevin Cunningham, and Bill Kennedy had plans to start a new company. Previously, these four men worked together at Tivoli (now a division of IBM), a software company helping firms manage their computer networks. Although committed to launching a venture, these entrepreneurs had yet to settle on a business idea.

As they researched business concepts, the four were disappointed time and time again when they learned that someone else had already come up with their ideas.[1] Their initial plan was to create a tool that would help companies manage their computer firewalls, but they discarded this scheme when they discovered that several other companies were already doing this.

But as idea after idea fizzled, the four kept returning to the firewall tool, mostly because it was within their area of expertise. In 2000, the group settled on a concept very close to their original idea. They launched Waveset Technologies, a company that sells identity management software, which allows corporations to provide outsiders access to data in their information technology systems in a controlled and secure way.

The turning point in their decision to found Waveset came during a meeting with John Thornton, a venture capitalist at Austin Ventures, a venture-capital firm based in Austin, Texas. In the meeting, Thornton helped the four realize that the greatest asset that entrepreneurs bring to a new venture isn't an idea; it's their experience and know-how. Rob Adams, one of Thornton's partners, talked about this meeting and Waveset in a book he wrote about the start-up process:

> The day he talked with Mark, Mike, Bill, and Kevin, John made a particularly shrewd observation. Mark recalls it quite vividly. "We were describing the various areas we were thinking about," he says. "We thought we wanted a real challenge, something brand new, something far away from what we'd already done. So we'd sort of been avoiding the one idea that had a lot of relevance to the team's background and experience. When we first mentioned what turned out to be our final concept (the firewall idea), John just looked at us for a minute, then pounded his hand on the table as he said, 'With your experience and credibility, you're actually thinking about not doing this? You're missing the picture!' " That's when we started to get it.[2]

What Mark McClain and the other founders of Waveset finally started to "get" was that it wasn't so much the uniqueness of their idea that would prove the worth of their new venture but rather the uniqueness of their ability to execute it. McClain and his team of founders were uniquely qualified to tackle the challenges posed by their original business idea. Here's how that original idea can serve customers.

As companies grow, one of the key difficulties they face is opening up their information technology systems to a growing number of users without sacrificing security and control. Another difficulty is figuring out how to safely open their systems to customers and suppliers—even on a limited basis. Through their experiences with Tivoli and other companies, McClain and his cofounders understood the problems their customers were trying to solve and knew how to approach them.

The foursome's efforts have been successful. Since Waveset was launched in 2000, its management team has remained intact, it has raised several rounds of venture-capital funding, it has hired new personnel, and it was acquired by Sun Microsystems in December 2003.[3] Its final round of venture capital funding came in September 2002, when the company obtained $13 million from Lightspeed Venture Partners, one of its original backers. Commenting on why Lightspeed offered Waveset additional funding, Ravi Mhatre, a Lightspeed general partner, said,

> We believe that Waveset has what it takes to be a long-term leader in the security industry and are proud to continue backing this management team. Waveset's executives leverage decades of experience from industry leaders such as IBM, BMC, Microsoft and Novell and continue to demonstrate technology leadership and business acumen—both vital to success in today's extremely competitive marketplaces.[4]

Note that in these remarks, Mhatre said very little about Waveset's products or industry. Instead, he focused on the strength of Waveset's management team and on the experience its founders and other leaders have for operating in their industry.

Although Waveset is now a division of Sun Microsystems, the majority of its managers remain, largely due to their industry experience and expertise. The same qualities that prompted the venture capitalists to invest in the company have prompted Sun Microsystems to retain the founders of Waveset and provide them exciting opportunities within the context of the larger firm.

learning **objective**

1. Identify the primary elements of a new venture team.

In this chapter, we'll focus on how the founders of a business build a new venture team as well as the importance of the team to the overall success of the firm. A **new venture team** is the group of founders, key employees, and advisers that move a new venture from an idea to a fully functioning firm. Usually, the team doesn't come together all at once. Instead, it is built as the new firm can afford to hire additional personnel.

The team also involves more than paid employees. Many firms have boards of directors, boards of advisers, and professionals on whom they rely for direction and advice. For instance, Bright Horizons Family Solutions, the company introduced in Chapter 5, has a nine-person board of directors (including seven outsiders) and an 18-member advisory board. While the individuals that serve on these boards play different roles, they all have one thing in common: a vested interest in Bright Horizon's success. This interest means that Bright Horizon's can call on each individual to seek counsel, support, and advice.

In this chapter's first section, we discuss the role of the founder or founders of a firm and emphasize the substantial effect that founders have on their firm's future. The section then talks about how the founders build a new venture team, including the recruitment and selection of key employees and the forming of a board of directors. The second section of the chapter discusses the important role of advisers in shaping and rounding out a new venture team. Specifically, the role of a board of advisers, lenders and investors, and other professionals are examined and discussed.

As we note throughout this book, new ventures have a high propensity to fail. The high failure rate is due in part to what researchers call the **liability of newness**, which refers to the fact that companies often falter because the people who start the firms can't adjust quickly enough to their new roles and because the firm lacks a "track record" with outside buyers and suppliers.[5] Assembling a talented and experienced new venture team is one path that firms can take to overcome these limitations. Indeed, experienced management teams that get up to speed quickly are much less likely to make a novice's mistakes. In addition, firms able to persuade high-quality individuals to join them as directors or advisers quickly gain legitimacy. In turn, legitimacy opens doors that otherwise would be closed.

Affiliating with peer groups to provide them access to high-quality advice and emotional support is another way entrepreneurs overcome the liability of newness problem. One such group, the Young Entrepreneurs' Organization, is highlighted in the boxed feature titled "Partnering for Success."

learning **objective**

2. Explain the term "liabilities of newness."

Creating a New Venture Team

The group of people who start a firm is an important part of the firm's business concept. A well-conceived business plan cannot get off the ground unless a firm has the leaders and personnel to carry it out. As one expert put it, "People are the one factor in production . . .

Partnering for**SUCCESS**

Peer Groups: Bringing Entrepreneurs Together

www.yeo.com

Peer groups bring entrepreneurs together to learn from each other's successes and failures. They also provide entrepreneurs the opportunity to share their toughest business and personal problems in a confidential setting with people who have experienced similar challenges.

The Young Entrepreneurs' Organization (YEO) is a global, nonprofit organization for business owners under age 40 who are leading companies with annual sales of $1 million or more. The founders of venture-backed start-ups may also join if they have raised $2 million or more in investment capital and plan to reach at least $1 million in sales within three years. There are 120 YEO chapters in the United States and abroad. Worldwide, YEO currently has 5,300 members in 38 countries. Membership is by invitation only, although interested candidates can submit an application.

The purpose of the YEO is to provide entrepreneurs access to a network of their peers. Most chapters organize their members in "forums," which are groups of 12 entrepreneurs who meet on a monthly basis to confidentially discuss the business and personal issues that are of the greatest importance to them. It's always the same group, and attendance is mandatory. The topics in these groups

range from specific business issues to how to strike an appropriate balance between work and family. Workshops and educational programs are examples of additional services that most YEO chapters offer.

There are other similar peer groups, such as the Young Presidents' Organization, that may suit the needs of a particular entrepreneur. There are also industry-specific peer groups, such as Premier PEN, which is a peer group for printing executives.

Questions for Critical Thinking

1. Assume that you live in a community without a YEO chapter. As an entrepreneurial opportunity, what actions would you take to establish a YEO chapter? What problems would you anticipate facing to establish this chapter, and what would you do to deal with those problems?

2. If you were a young entrepreneur, would you enjoy belonging to an organization such as the YEO? What benefits would you hope to gain from membership in YEO or a similar organization?

Source: Young Entrepreneurs' Organization home page, www. yeo.org (Accessed June 23, 2004).

that animates all the others."[6] Often, several start-ups develop what is essentially the same idea at the same time. When this happens, the key to success is not the idea but rather the ability of the initial founder or founders of the firm to put together a team that can execute the idea better than anyone else.

The way a founder builds his or her new venture team sends an important signal to potential investors, partners, and employees. Some founders like the feeling of control and are reluctant to bring on partners or hire managers who are more experienced than they are. In contrast, other founders are keenly aware of their own limitations and work hard to find the most experienced people available to bring on board. Similarly, some new firms never form an advisory board, while others persuade the most important people they can find to provide them with counsel and advice. In general, the way to impress potential investors, partners, and employees is to put together as strong a team as possible.[7] Investors and others know that experienced personnel and access to good-quality advice contributes greatly to a new venture's success.

The elements of a new venture team are shown in Figure 6.1. Firms vary in the way they use these elements. Let's look at each of these elements closely.

The Founder or Founders

The characteristics of the founder or founders of a firm and their early decisions have a significant impact on the way a firm is received and the manner in which the new venture team takes shape. The size of the founding team and the qualities of the founder or founders are the two most important issues in this matter.

Size of the Founding Team   The first decision that most founders face is whether to start a firm on their own or whether to build an initial **founding team**. Studies show that more than one individual starts 50 to 70 percent of all new firms.[8] It is generally believed that new ventures started by a team have an advantage over those started by an individual because a team brings more talent, resources, ideas, and professional contacts to a new venture than does a sole entrepreneur. In addition, the psychological support that cofounders of a new business can offer one another is an important element in the firm's success.[9]

Several factors affect the value of a team that is starting a new firm. First, teams that have worked together before, as opposed to teams that are working together for the first time, have an edge. If people have worked together before and have decided to partner to start a firm together, it usually means that they get along personally and trust one another.[10] They also tend to communicate with one another more effectively than people

Figure 6.1

Elements of a New Venture Team

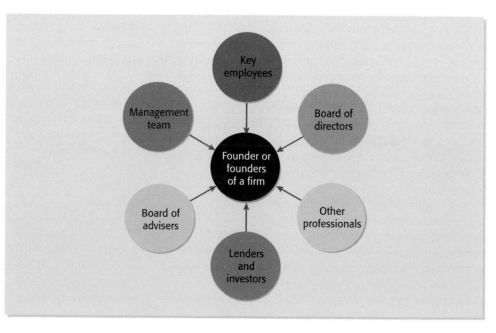

who are new to one another.[11] Second, if the members of the team are **heterogeneous**, meaning that they are diverse in terms of their abilities and experiences, rather than **homogeneous**, meaning that their areas of expertise are very similar to one another, they are likely to have different points of view about technology, hiring decisions, competitive tactics, and other important activities. These different points of view are likely to generate debate and constructive conflict among the founders, reducing the likelihood that decisions will be made in haste or without the airing of alternative points of view.[12] A founding team can be too big, causing communication problems and an increased potential for conflict. A founding team larger than four people is typically too large to be practical.[13]

There are two potential pitfalls associated with starting a firm as a team rather than as a sole entrepreneur. First, the team members may not get along. This is the reason investors favor teams consisting of people who have worked together before. It is simply more likely that people who have gotten along with one another in the past will continue to get along in the future. Second, if two or more people start a firm as "equals," conflicts can arise when the firm needs to establish a formal structure and designate one person as the chief executive officer (CEO). If the firm has investors, the investors will usually weigh in on who should be appointed CEO. In these instances, it is easy for the founder that wasn't chosen as the CEO to feel slighted. This problem is exacerbated if multiple founders are involved and they all stay with the firm. At some point, a hierarchy will have to be developed, and the founders will have to decide who reports to whom. Some of these problems can be avoided through the development of a founder's agreement, which is described in Chapter 8.

Qualities of the Founders   The second major issue pertaining to the founders of a firm is the qualities they bring to the table. The past several chapters have illustrated the importance that investors and others place on the strength of the firm's founders and initial management team. One reason the founders are so important is that in the early days of a firm, their knowledge, skills, and experiences are the most valuable resource the firm has. Because of this, new firms are judged largely on their "potential" rather than their current assets or current performance. In most cases, this results in people judging the future prospects of a firm by evaluating the strength of its founders and initial management team.

Several features are thought to be significant to a founder's success. The level of a founder's education is important because it's believed that entrepreneurial abilities such as search skills, foresight, creativity, and computer skills are enhanced through obtaining a college degree. Similarly, some observers think that higher education equips a founder with important business-related skills, such as math and communications. In addition, specific forms of education, such as engineering, computer science, management information systems, physics, and biochemistry, provide the recipients of this education an advantage if they start a firm that is related to their area of expertise.[14]

Prior entrepreneurial experience, relevant industry experience, and networking are other attributes that strengthen the chances of a founder's success. One study singled out **prior entrepreneurial experience** as one of the most consistent predictors of future entrepreneurial performance.[15] Because launching a new venture is a complex task, entrepreneurs with prior start-up experience have a distinct advantage. The impact of **relevant industry experience** on an entrepreneur's ability to successfully launch and grow a firm has also been studied, as illustrated in the boxed feature titled "What Went Wrong?" on Garden.com.[16] Entrepreneurs with experience in the same industry as their current venture, which wasn't the case with the founders of Garden.com, will have a more mature network of industry contacts and will have a better understanding of the subtleties of their respective industries.[17] The importance of this factor is particularly evident for entrepreneurs who start firms in technical industries such as biotechnology. The demands of biotechnology are sufficiently intense that it would be virtually impossible for someone to start a biotech firm while at the same time learning biotechnology. The person must have an understanding of biotechnology prior to launching a firm through either relevant industry experience or an academic background.

A particularly important attribute for founders or founding teams is the presence of a mature network of social and professional contacts.[18] Founders must often "work" their

what went **wrong?**

Garden.com: Why Experience Counts

Launching a new venture is a complex task. Research shows that founders with experience in the industry in which they are starting a firm have a distinct advantage. There is no better story illustrating the importance of this point than Garden.com.

In May 1995, three new MBAs, Cliff Sharples, Lisa Sharples, and Jamie O'Neill, each in their early 30s, met in one of their homes. They were all working for Trilogy, a software firm in Austin, Texas. They wanted to start a company together but didn't know what to do. Though none of them had any experience in garden retailing, they picked the gardening industry and decided to launch a gardening e-commerce site: Garden.com. At that time, Amazon.com and Yahoo! were new, and there was a lot of excitement surrounding the Internet. The $50 billion gardening industry was fragmented, and no one was selling gardening supplies on the Internet. Garden.com wanted to offer a way for gardeners to purchase plants and supplies online.

The company launched its Web site in March 1996. Over the next four years, as the dot-com bubble expanded, Garden.com raised over $50 million in funding. Soon, in addition to gardening supplies, it was selling furniture, candles, cookware, soap, tea, perfume, and Christmas ornaments. In September 1999, the company went public. Two years later, it was out of business. What went wrong?

Well, several things. First, its business model may have been fundamentally flawed. Its only means of attracting customers to its Web site was advertising, which made it extremely expensive to get people to look at its offerings. In fact, the company spent 56.7 percent of the money it raised through its initial public offering on various forms of advertising, including glossy catalogs and full-page magazine advertisements. Commenting on Garden.com's high customer acquisition costs, John Thornton, a member of the company's board of directors, later said, "They [Garden.com's management team] did not understand what it would cost to attract the traffic."

Second, the Internet bubble burst in early 2000, making it impossible for Garden.com to raise additional funds. Because the company wasn't even close to being profitable (it lost $19 million in its fiscal year that ended June 30, 1999), it couldn't continue without raising money. The company's plan was to drive costs down and increase revenues to the point where it was profitable and wouldn't need any more investment capital, which it felt it was within two years of achieving. But after the Internet bubble burst, investors closed their checkbooks. This series of events left the company with no way to continue financially.

Third, the entrepreneurs behind Garden.com had no background in gardening or retailing and had no prior entrepreneurial experience. Although it's hard to know how much difference this made, it is a point worth serious consideration. For example, after studying the demise of Garden.com for a book titled *Buy, Lie, and Sell High: How Investors Lost Out on Enron and the Internet Bubble*, D. Quinn Mills, a Harvard Business School professor, wrote,

> Gardeners for this book observed that the Garden.com Web site was difficult to use, and offered the opinion that the people running the company seemed to know little or nothing about gardening.

In making his own assessment, Professor Mills observed that Garden.com's business premise hinged not on gardening products but on trying to introduce a new way for people to buy gardening products and supplies. Yet its founders didn't have any background in the gardening industry or have any prior knowledge about customer behavior as it relates to gardening products. The traditional criterion that investors use when funding a venture is that the founders have some experience in the area in which they are working or at least related experience. In the excitement that surrounded the Internet bubble, this criterion wasn't applied in the case of Garden.com.

Garden.com's failure is a vivid reminder of the importance of relevant industry experience for the founders of a new venture.

Questions for Critical Thinking

1. Based on information contained in this feature, would you classify Cliff Sharples, Lisa Sharples, and Jamie O'Neill as a homogeneous founding team or as a heterogeneous founding team? Given your choice, how do you believe the founding team's diversity or lack of diversity affected the firm's ability to succeed?

2. In your opinion, is it possible for entrepreneurs to overcome the problems that surface when they lack experience in the industry in which they intend to launch a new venture? Even more particularly, what could Garden.com's three entrepreneurs have done to reduce the negative effect their lack of industry experience created for their venture?

Sources: D. Q. Mills, Buy, Lie and Sell High: How Investors Lost Out on Enron and the Internet Bubble *(Upper Saddle River, N.J.: Prentice Hall, 2002), and "Wilted,"* Texas Monthly, *February 1, 2001.*

social and personal networks to raise money or gain access to critical resources on behalf of their firms.[19] **Networking** is building and maintaining relationships with people whose interests are similar or whose relationship could bring advantages to a firm. The way this might play out in practice is that a founder calls a business acquaintance or friend to ask for an introduction to a potential investor, business partner, or customer. For some founders, networking is easy and is an important part of their daily routine. For others, it is a learned skill.

Table 6.1 shows the preferred attributes of the founder or founders of a firm. Start-ups that have founders or a team of founders with these attributes have the best chances of early success.

Recruiting and Selecting Key Employees

Once the decision to launch a new venture has been made, building a management team and hiring key employees begins. Start-ups vary in terms of how quickly they need to add personnel. In some instances, the founders work alone for a period of time while the business plan is being written and the firm starts to take shape. In other instances, employees are hired immediately.

Founders differ in terms of how they approach the task of recruiting and selecting key employees. Some founders draw on their network of contacts to identify candidates for key positions, while others use executive-search firms. An **executive-search firm** is a company that specializes in helping other companies recruit and select key personnel. There are two reasons a new venture might take this route. First, the process of recruiting and screening job candidates is time consuming, reducing the amount of time founders have to spend on other critical tasks. Second, the initial hires that firms make are often critical to their eventual success. For example, some founders may decide to hire a CEO rather than give this position to one of the founding members and may need someone with a unique set of attributes and skills. It may take the experience and network of contacts of an executive-search firm to find the right candidate.

learning **objective**

5. Explain the actions of an executive-search firm.

Table 6.1

Preferred Attributes of the Founder or Founders of a Firm

Attribute	Explanation
Firm started by a team	New ventures that are started by a team can provide greater resources, a broader diversity of viewpoints, and a broader array of items than ventures started by individuals.
Higher education	Evidence suggests that important entrepreneurial skills are enhanced through higher education.
Prior entrepreneurial experience	Founders with prior entrepreneurial experience are familiar with the entrepreneurial process and are likely to avoid costly mistakes than founders new to the rigors of the entrepreneurial process.
Relevant industry experience	Founders with experience in the same industry as their new venture will most likely have better-established professional networks and more applicable marketing and management expertise than founders without relevant industry experience.
Broad social and professional network	Founders with broad social and professional networks have potential access to additional know-how, capital, and customer referrals.

Many founders worry about hiring the wrong person for a key role. Because most new firms are strapped for cash, every team member must make a valuable contribution, so it's not good enough to hire someone who is well intended but who doesn't precisely fit the job. Alisa Nessler, the founder of Lane15, a software start-up, emphasizes this point in the following remarks:

> One of the first things you learn in a startup is that it's very expensive to make a bad hire. In a large company, people sometimes tend to think that when you have somebody who fits into the bucket labeled "Heart's in the right place," or the one labeled "Good attitude but just not getting it done," you can work around it. Maybe it's because in an established organization, it's easier to lose sight of an individual's value-adds. In a startup, you simply can't do that. Everyone is important. Every team member's work has to have a direct impact on value, or the person has to go.[20]

On some occasions, key hires work out perfectly and fill the exact roles that the founders of the firm need. For example, one of the first hires of Starbucks founder Howard Schultz was Dave Olsen, the owner of a popular coffeehouse in the university district of Seattle, the city where Starbucks was born. In his autobiography, Schultz recalls the following about the hiring of Olsen:

> On the day of our meeting, Dave and I sat on my office floor and I started spreading the plans and blueprints out and talking about my idea. Dave got it right away. He had spent ten years in an apron, behind a counter, serving espresso drinks. He had experienced firsthand the excitement people can develop about espresso, both in his café and in Italy. I didn't have to convince him that this idea had big potential. He just knew it in his bones. The synergy was too good to be true. My strength was looking outward: communicating the vision, inspiring investors, raising money, finding real estate, designing the stores, building the brand, and planning for the future. Dave understood the inner workings: the nuts and bolts of operating a retail café, hiring and training baristas (coffee brewers), ensuring the best quality coffee.[21]

Dave Olsen went on to become a key member of the Starbucks new venture team and remains with the company today.

Some founders approach the task of hiring by creating a formal hiring plan. Others approach the task more informally and hire personnel as funds become available and opportunities emerge. One attribute investors value in founders is a willingness to be flexible and assume the role that makes the most sense for them in their firm rather than insisting on being the CEO. This is a difficult task for some founders who become entrepreneurs to "be their own boss" or put their distinctive stamp on a firm. Founders who do remain flexible, however, often have an easier time obtaining financing or funding. The way many founders look at this issue is that it is better to be the vice president of a $100 million firm than the CEO of a $10 million firm. An example of a group of founders who decided at the outset to hire an outside CEO is provided in Case 6.2 in this chapter.

The Roles of the Board of Directors

If a new venture organizes as a corporation, it is legally required to have a **board of directors**—a panel of individuals who are elected by a corporation's shareholders to oversee the management of the firm.[22] A board is typically made up of both inside and outside directors. An **inside director** is a person who is also an officer of the firm. An **outside director** is someone who is not employed by the firm.

A board of directors has three formal responsibilities: appoint the officers (the key managers) of the firm, declare dividends, and oversee the affairs of the corporation. In the wake of the Enron and WorldCom scandals, there is growing emphasis on the board's role in making sure the firm is operating in an ethical manner. One outcome of this movement is a trend toward putting more outsiders on boards of directors because people who do not work for the firm are usually more willing to scrutinize the behavior of management than insiders who work for the company. Most boards meet formally three or four times a year. Large firms pay their directors for their service. New ventures are more likely to pay their directors in company stock or ask them to serve without direct compensation—at least

learning **objective**

6. Identify the two primary ways in which the nonemployee members of a start-up's new venture team help the firm.

learning **objective**

7. Describe a board of directors and explain the difference between inside directors and outside directors.

As a new venture matures, it may reorganize into a corporation. If it does, it must have a board of directors, who provide advice and legitimacy to the growing business.

until the company is profitable. The boards for publicly traded companies are required by law to have audit and compensation committees. Many boards also have nominating committees to select stockholders to run for vacant board positions.

If handled properly, a company's board of directors can be an important part of its new venture team. Two ways a board of directors can help a new firm get off to a good start and develop what, it is hoped, will become a sustainable competitive advantage are providing guidance and lending legitimacy.

Provide Guidance   Although a board of directors has formal governance responsibilities, its most useful role is to provide guidance and support to the firm's managers. Many CEOs interact with their board members frequently and obtain important input. The key to making this happen is to pick board members who are skilled and experienced and are willing to give advice and ask insightful and probing questions. An illustration of what can happen when a board functions in this way is provided by Sam Eichenfield, the CEO of the FINOVA Group:

> An effective board is one that is available to me and other members of the management team when we have questions that their expertise could assist in. Also, when we contemplate certain kinds of strategic activities, I want them to be available for consultation. . . . I also value the questions the board asks. We're in the finance business, but our board members are from manufacturing, insurance, academia. Very often their questions will open our eyes to a different way of looking at things.[23]

Because managers rely on board members for counsel and advice, the search for outside directors should be purposeful, with the objective of filling gaps in the experience and background of the executives of the firm and the other directors. For example, if two computer programmers started a software firm and neither one of them had any marketing experience, it would make sense to place a marketing executive on the board of directors. Indeed, a board of directors has the foundation to effectively serve its organization when its members represent many important organizational skills (e.g., manufacturing, human resource management, and financing) involved with running a company. Sometimes companies err by not being thoughtful enough about the people they place on their boards. Bob Weissman, a former executive of several companies, makes this point in the following statement:

> Let's assume I am the CEO of Netscape and I'm dealing with the typical mix of business issues—changes in the marketplace, the competitive mix, changes in cost dynamics being driven externally. If I have on my board five experienced, intelligent people, all of whom have spent thirty years working in a slow-moving, regulated industry, they won't be able to help me much. Not that they're incompetent or disinterested. They just won't understand my market, my customers, or the dynamics of a highly fragmented and competitive marketplace simply because they have no experience with it.[24]

This complication can be avoided by carefully selecting board members who have experience in the areas in which the firm needs guidance and advice the most.

learning **objective**

8. Describe the concept of signaling and explain why it's important.

Lend Legitimacy   Another important function of a board of directors is to lend legitimacy to a firm. Well-known and respected board members bring instant credibility to the firm. For example, just imagine the positive buzz a firm could generate if it could say that John Chambers of Cisco Systems or Larry Ellison of Oracle had agreed to serve on its board of directors. This phenomenon is referred to as **signaling**. Without a credible signal, it is difficult for potential customers, investors, or employees to identify high-quality start-ups. Presumably, a high-quality individual would be reluctant to serve on the board of a low-quality firm because that would put his or her reputation at risk. So when a high-quality individual does agree to serve on a board of a firm, the individual is in essence "signaling" that the company has potential to be successful.[25]

Achieving legitimacy through high-quality board members can result in other positive outcomes. Investors like to see new venture teams, including the board of directors, that have people with enough clout to get their foot in the door with potential suppliers and customers. Board members are also often instrumental in helping young firms arrange financing or funding. As we will discuss in Chapter 10, it's almost impossible for a firm's founders to get the attention of an investor without a personal introduction. One way firms deal with this challenge is by placing individuals on their boards who are acquainted with people in the investment community.

Table 6.2 contains a list of guidelines for putting together an effective board of directors.

Rounding Out the Team: The Role of Professional Advisers

Along with the new venture team members we've already identified, founders often rely on the professionals with whom they interact for important counsel and advice. In many cases, these professionals become an important part of the new venture team. Next, we discuss the roles that boards of advisers, lenders, investors, and other professionals play in rounding out new venture teams.

Board of Advisers

learning **objective**

9. Discuss the purpose of forming an advisory board.

A growing number of start-ups are forming advisory boards to provide them direction and advice. An **advisory board** is a panel of experts who are asked by a firm's managers to provide counsel and advice on an ongoing basis. Unlike a board of directors, an advisory board possesses no legal responsibility for the firm and gives nonbinding advice.[26] An advisory board can be established for general purposes or can be set up to address a specific issue or need. For example, some firms have customer advisory boards specifically to help identify new product and service ideas. Other companies have advisory boards to help them enter international markets or deal with an emerging challenge, such as how to make better use of the Internet.

Table 6.2

Guidelines for Forming an Effective
Board of Directors

Guideline	Explanation
Aim high	Select directors with the following characteristics: • Have run successful companies • Have competencies the new venture needs • Are well known and respected in their fields
Composition	Select a board with the following characteristics: • Is diverse • Is in tune with the technology and the markets in which the new venture will participate • Is composed of both inside and outside directors
Establish ground rules pertaining to decisions	Establish the following ground rules: • Routine decisions will be handled by the firm's managers • Significant personnel, operational, and financial decisions will be taken to the board for approval
Share information	Practice the following communication protocols: • Consistently update the board about the firm's activities • Do not blindside the board with bad news (one thing board members loathe is being blindsided by unexpected bad news that management has withheld from them)
Use committees	Implement the following approach to committees: • Recognize that boards do their best work in committees • Maintain statutory committees, such as the audit, compensation, and nomination committees • Establish additional committees on an "as needed" basis
Motivate board members	Motivate board members to provide exemplary service through the following: • Some form of financial incentive, such as company stock or stock options • The opportunity to be part of an exciting new project
Address liability issues	Disclose to board members the following: • Advise members that they have a fiduciary duty to the new venture's shareholders • Verify that the members are aware of their points of potential liability • Make legal and accounting experts available to board members for counsel and advice

The fact that a corporation has a board of directors does not preclude it from establishing one or more advisory boards. For example, Akamai, a well-known Internet company, has a board of directors, a board of advisers, a customer advisory board, and a public sector advisory board (which includes individuals who provide the company advice on market opportunities in the public sector).[27] Many people are more willing to serve on a company's board of advisers than its board of directors because it requires less time and there is no potential legal liability involved. In this way, they can still provide a company's managers counsel and advice and can lend credibility to the firm.[28]

Boards of advisers interact with each other and with a firm's managers in several ways. Some advisory boards meet three or four times a year at the company's headquarters or in another location. Other advisory boards meet in an online environment. In some cases, a firm's board of advisers will be scattered across the country, making it more cost effective for a firm's managers to interact with the members of the board on the telephone or via e-mail rather than to bring them physically together. In these situations, board members

Entrepreneurs often meet with a member of their advisory board on a personal basis to obtain valuable business advice. With a carefully structured and diverse advisory board, entrepreneurs can tap into a wide range of experience and expertise.

don't interact with each other at all on a face-to-face basis yet still provide high levels of counsel and advice.

Most boards of advisers have between five and 15 members. Companies typically pay the members of their board of advisers a small honorarium for their service either annually or on a per-meeting basis.

BeautyBuys.com is an e-commerce company selling cosmetics, jewelry, hair care products, perfume, and gifts online. The company has a five-person advisory board that consists of the following members:

- *Chazz Palminteri—Hollywood actor, writer, and director.* Mr. Palminteri received an Academy Award nomination for his performance in Woody Allen's *Bullets over Broadway.* He also starred with Robert De Niro, Billy Crystal, and Lisa Kudrow in *Analyze This.*
- *Lawrence K. Fleischman—president of Capital Vision Group, a financial consulting firm.* Mr. Fleischman is also managing director of the Cappello Group and Cappello Capital Group.
- *Kim Lockerbie—vice president of business development at Kopf Zimmerman Schultheis Advertising.* Ms. Lockerbie has earned numerous international awards including honors from the International Association of Business Communicators.
- *Dr. Helen Flamenbaum—a medical doctor specializing in dermatology.* Dr. Flamenbaum is associated with Long Island Jewish Medical Center and North Shore University Hospital.
- *KZS Advertising—A full-service advertising and marketing firm that was founded in 1980.* The agency's clients include leading companies such as Computer Associates, InterBiz Solutions, North Fork Bank, Winthrop-University Hospital, the Long Island Convention and Visitor's Bureau, and Synergy Brands.

This example provides an illustration of the breadth of talent and expertise that a firm can have available when it creates a board of advisers. Imagine the combined network of friends and acquaintances that BeautyBuy.com's board of advisers has and the number of referrals they can make to BeautyBuy.com's Web site.

There are several guidelines to organizing a board of advisers. First, a board of advisers should not be organized just so a company can boast of it. Advisers will become quickly disillusioned if they don't play a meaningful role in the firm's development and growth. Second, a firm should look for board members who are compatible and complement one another in terms of experience and expertise. Unless the board is being set up for a specific purpose, a board that includes members with varying backgrounds is preferable to a board of people with similar backgrounds. Finally, when inviting a person to serve on its board of advisers, a company should carefully spell out to the individual the rules in terms of access to confidential information.[29] Some firms ask the members of their advisory board to sign nondisclosure agreements, which are described in Chapter 8. This type of requirement varies on a firm-to-firm basis.

One of the biggest challenges in managing an advisory board is finding a time when all the board members can meet. To deal with this challenge, entrepreneurial companies must often find innovative ways to make it more convenient for the board members to meet. An example is using the Internet as a vehicle for getting board members together, as illustrated in the boxed feature titled "Savvy Entrepreneurial Firm."

Savvy entrepreneurial FIRM

Can't Get Your Advisory Board Together? Move the Meeting Online

One of the challenges in maintaining an active board of advisers is finding a convenient time and place for the board to meet. Because the members are volunteers and are usually either unpaid or paid a modest honorarium, it's not easy to ask them to travel long distances or take too much time from their schedules to meet. Conducting meetings online is one way to bring the board together. Some firms tried this approach early in the development of the Internet and were disappointed by the somewhat tacky appearance of the first generation of chat rooms and discussion boards. Fortunately, there are now extremely good collaboration software tools available that provide firms a number of options when conducting online meetings.

Facilitate.com., for example, is one of many companies selling software that helps companies conduct effective meetings over the Internet. Here's what an advisory board meeting might look like using Facilitate.com 8.0, the company's latest iteration of collaboration software. This particular board is a customer advisory board that meets to brainstorm new product ideas and to discuss customer service issues.

On the day of the meeting, the participants sign on to a designated Web site that combines a Web conferencing service and the collaboration software. To start the meeting, you share a PowerPoint presentation that sets the agenda for the meeting. The first item on the agenda is to brainstorm new product ideas. Each board member is asked to contribute ideas that flow onto an electronic flip chart that everyone can

see. After a few minutes, you lead the group in a verbal discussion of the ideas and assign them to categories that are displayed in real time on everyone's screen. You now quickly change the flip chart to a ranking system and ask the group to rank the ideas according to profit potential and feasibility. The results are immediately shown in both numeric and graphic form. The same type of approach is used to discuss customer service issues and to reach a consensus among the group on each of them. At the end of the meeting, each participant receives a complete set of meeting notes.

Questions for Critical Thinking

1. Imagine that you are a member of a board of advisers using Facilitate.com's software to conduct a meeting. How would you react to this type of experience? Do you feel that you could be effective using this technology? Why or why not?

2. Choose two or three entrepreneurial firms or start-up ventures in your local community. Set up a meeting with each firm's top manager. During the meeting, ask your contact person if his or her venture has established one or more board of advisers. If such boards have been formed, ask for feedback about how effective they've been for the venture. If such boards haven't been formed, ask why they haven't been established. Finally, ask all your managers to comment about their view of the effectiveness of having a board of advisers meet online to conduct business.

Lenders and Investors

As emphasized throughout this book, lenders and investors have a vested interest in the companies they finance, often causing them to become very involved in helping the firm's they fund. It is rare that a lender or investor will put money into a new venture and then simply step back and wait to see what happens. In fact, the institutional rules governing banks and investment firms typically require that they monitor new ventures fairly closely, at least during the initial years of a loan or an investment.[30]

The amount of time and energy a lender or investor dedicates to a new firm depends on the amount of money involved and how much help the new firm needs. For example, a lender with a well-secured loan may spend very little time with a client, while a venture capitalist may spend an enormous amount of time helping a new venture refine its business model, recruit management personnel, and meet with current and prospective customers and suppliers. In fact, one study found that the average venture capitalist visits each company in his or her portfolio 19 times a year.[31] This number denotes a high level of involvement and support.

As with the other nonemployee members of a firm's new venture team, lenders and investors help new firms by providing guidance and lending legitimacy and assume the natural role of providing financial oversight.[32] In some instances, lenders and investors also work hard to help new firms fill out their management teams. Sometimes this issue is so important that a new venture will try to obtain investment capital not only to get access to money but also to get help hiring key employees.

For example, during eBay's beginning stages, eBay's partners, Pierre Omidyar and Jeff Skoll, decided to recruit a CEO. They wanted someone who was not only experienced but also had the types of credentials that Wall Street investors value. They soon discovered that every experienced manager they tried to recruit asked if they had venture-capital backing—which at that time they did not. For a new firm trying to recruit a seasoned executive, venture-capital backing is a sort of seal of legitimacy. To get a seal of legitimacy, Omidyar and Skoll obtained funding from Benchmark Venture Capital, even though eBay didn't really need the money. Writer Randall Stross recalls this event as follows:

> eBay was an anomaly: a profitable company that was able to self-fund its growth and that turned to venture capital solely for contacts and counsel. No larger lesson can be drawn. When Benchmark wired the first millions to eBay's bank account, the figurative check was tossed into the vault—and there it would sit, unneeded and undisturbed.[33]

This strategy worked for eBay. Soon after affiliating with Benchmark, Bob Kagle, one of Benchmark's general partners, led eBay to Meg Whitman, an executive who had experience working for several top firms, including Procter & Gamble, Disney, and Hasbro. Meg Whitman remains eBay's chairman and CEO today.

Experienced investors can also assist new ventures in the hiring process by helping them structure compensation packages that are fair to both the firm and the new hires. An illustration of this advantage is provided by Alisa Nessler, CEO of Lane15, a firm backed by venture capital:

> If you're looking to recruit that all-important CEO, investors can be a particular boon. They know how much a CEO should earn, cash- and stock-wise. They can help you negotiate a package that fits your capital and equity structures, while also motivating the CEO to build a world-class company.[34]

Bankers also play a role in establishing the legitimacy of new ventures and their initial management teams. Some studies show that the presence of bank loans is a favorable signal to other capital providers.[35] Investors often take a seat on the boards of directors of the firms they fund to provide oversight and advice. It is less common for a banker to take a seat on the board of directors of a new firm, primarily because bankers provide operating capital rather than large amounts of investment capital to new firms.

There are additional ways that lenders and investors add value to a new firm beyond financing and funding. These roles are highlighted in Table 6.3.

Meg Whitman, a seasoned executive, joined eBay in March 1998. Since she took the reins, eBay has rocketed to the top rankings of e-commerce Web sites. Even more impressive, she was able to accomplish this feat at an uncertain time in the industry.

Other Professionals

At times, other professionals assume important roles in a new venture's success. Attorneys, accountants, and business consultants are often good sources of counsel and advice. The role of lawyers in helping firms get off to a good start is discussed in Chapter 8, and the role of accountants is discussed in Chapter 7. So here, let's take a look at the role consultant may play.

Consultants   A **consultant** is an individual who gives professional or expert advice. New ventures vary in terms of how much they rely on business consultants for direction. In some ways, the role of the general business consultant has diminished in importance as businesses seek specialists to get advice on complex issues such as patents, tax planning, and security laws.[36] In other ways, the role of general business consultant is as important as ever; it is the general business consultant who conducts in-depth analyses on behalf of a firm, such as preparing a feasibility study or an industry analysis. Because of the time it

learning **objective**

10. Explain why new venture firms use consultants for help and advice.

Table 6.3

Beyond Financing and Funding: Ways Lenders and Investors Add Value to a New Venture

- Help identify and recruit key management personnel
- Provide insight into the industry and markets in which the firm intends to participate
- Help the firm fine-tune its business model
- Serve as a sounding board for new ideas
- Provide introductions to additional sources of capital
- Recruit customers
- Help the firm arrange business partnerships
- Serve on the firm's board of directors or board of advisers
- Provide a sense of calm in the midst of the emotional roller-coaster ride that many new venture teams experience

would take, it would be inappropriate to ask a member of a board of directors or board of advisers to take on one of these tasks on behalf of a firm. These more time-intensive tasks must be performed by the firm itself or by a paid consultant.

A new firm often turns to consultants for help and advice because while large firms can afford to employ experts in many areas, new firms typically can't. If a new firm needs help in a specialized area, such as building a product prototype, it may need to hire an engineering consulting firm to do the work. The fees that consultants charge are typically negotiable. If a new venture has good potential and offers a consulting firm the possibility of repeat business, the firm will often be willing to reduce its fee or work out favorable payment arrangements.

Consultants fall into two categories: paid consultants and consultants who are made available for free or at a reduced rate through a nonprofit or government agency. The first category includes large international consulting firms, such as Bearing Point (formerly KPMG), Accenture, IBM Global Services, and Bain & Company. These firms provide a wide array of services but are beyond the reach of most start-ups because of budget limitations. But there are many smaller, localized firms. The best way to find them is to ask around for a referral.

Consultants are also available through nonprofit or government agencies. SCORE, for example, is a nonprofit organization that provides free consulting services to small businesses. SCORE currently has over 10,500 volunteers, who are typically retired business owners and who counsel in areas as diverse as finance, operations, and sales.[37] And the Small Business Administration, a government agency, provides a variety of consulting services to small businesses and entrepreneurs throughout the United States.

In summary, putting together a new venture team is one of the most critical activities that a founder or founders of a firm undertake. Many entrepreneurs suffer by not thinking broadly enough or carefully enough about this process. Ultimately, people must make any new venture work. New ventures benefit by surrounding themselves with high-quality employees and advisers to tackle the challenges involved with launching and growing an entrepreneurial firm.

CHAPTER SUMMARY

1. A new venture team is the group of people who move a new venture from an idea to a fully functioning firm. The primary elements of a new venture team are the company founders, key employees, the board of directors, the board of advisers, lenders and investors, and other professionals.

2. The liability of newness refers to the fact that firms often falter because the people who start the firms can't adjust quickly enough to their new roles and because the firm lacks a "track record" with customers and suppliers. These limitations can be overcome by assembling a talented and experienced new venture team.

3. A heterogeneous founding team has members who have diverse abilities and experiences. A homogeneous founding team has members who are very similar to one another.

4. The personal attributes that affect a founder's chances of launching a successful new firm include level of education, prior entrepreneurial experience, relevant industry experience, and the ability to network. Networking is building and maintaining relationships with people who are similar or whose friendship could bring advantages to the firm.

5. An executive-search firm is a company specializing in helping other companies recruit and select key personnel.

6. The two primary ways in which the nonemployee members of a start-up's new venture team help the firm are by providing guidance and lending legitimacy.

7. A board of directors is a panel of individuals who is elected by a corporation's shareholders to oversee the management of the firm. It is typically made up of both inside and outside directors. An inside director is a person who is also an officer of the firm. An outside director is someone who is not employed by the firm.

8. When a high-quality individual agrees to serve a company's board of directors, the individual is in essence expressing his or her opinion that the company has potential (why else would the individual agree to serve?). This phenomenon is referred to as signaling.

9. An advisory board is a panel of experts who are asked by the management of a firm to provide counsel and advice on an ongoing basis.

10. The primary reason that new ventures turn to consultants for help and advice is that while large firms can afford to employ experts in many areas, new firm typically can't. Consultants can be paid or can be part of a nonprofit or government agency and provide their services for free or for a reduced rate.

advisory board, 134

board of directors, 132

consultant, 139

executive-search firm, 131

founding team, 128

heterogeneous team, 129

homogeneous team, 129

inside director, 132

liability of newness, 127

networking, 131

new venture team, 126

outside director, 132

prior entrepreneurial experience, 129

relevant industry experience, 129

signaling, 134

1. What is a new venture team? Who are the primary participants in a start-up's new venture team?

2. What is liability of newness? What can a new venture do to overcome the liability of newness?

3. Describe the difference between a heterogeneous and a homogeneous founding team.

4. List several factors that enhance the value of a new venture team.

5. Describe the two potential pitfalls of using a team to start a firm.

6. What are the personal attributes that affect a founder's chances of launching a successful new firm? In your judgment, which of these attributes are the most important. Why?

7. Explain why having prior entrepreneurial experience helps the founder of a firm.

8. Define the term "networking." Why is it important for an entrepreneur to have a vibrant social and professional network?

9. What are the two reasons that prompt new ventures to use executive-search firms to help them identify and screen key employees?

10. What is a board of directors? What is the difference between inside and outside directors?

11. Describe the three formal responsibilities of a board of directors.

12. Explain why recruiting a well-known and highly respected board of directors lends legitimacy to a firm.

13. Define the term "signaling."

14. Discuss the purpose of forming an advisory board. If you were the founder of an entrepreneurial firm, would you set up an advisory board? Why or why not?

15. Describe the different ways that advisory boards meet and conduct their business.

16. Describe several of the guidelines to setting up a board of advisers.

17. In what ways do lenders and investors lend legitimacy to a firm?

18. Explain why new ventures often turn to consultants for advice.

19. Describe the purpose of SCORE. What type of advice and counsel do SCORE volunteers provide?

20. What is a peer group? If you were the founder of a firm, would you join a peer group, such as the Young Entrepreneurs' Organization? Why or why not?

1. Reread the opening case. List the decisions made by the founders of Waveset in the early days of building their firm. In what ways did each decision contribute to the firm's success?

2. Bill Carroll plans to start a chain of fitness clubs in Virginia. He has considered establishing a board of directors and a board of advisers but has decided to shield himself from the advice of others so that he can stay focused on his objectives. Why is Bill making a poor decision?

3. Amy Snell works for Coldwater Creek, a catalog retailer for women's apparel in Sandpoint, Idaho. She is thinking about leaving Coldwater Creek to move to Boise to open a store that sells hiking, fishing, and camping gear. She

wants to find a partner to help her start the firm. What qualities should Amy look for in a potential partner or "cofounder" for her new firm?

4. Tom Ryan is part of a group of four individuals who recently left IBM to launch a computer consulting firm. They are trying to recruit a CEO but haven't had any luck finding someone with the credentials they want. Tom has suggested to his partners that they hire an executive-search firm to help, but his partners think that executive-search firms are too expensive. If you were Tom, what arguments would you use to persuade your cofounders that hiring an executive-search firm might be money well spent?

5. Peggy Armstrong is in the process of starting an educational software company. She has incorporated the business and has 22 stockholders. She next needs to set up a board of directors but doesn't know how to proceed. How would you advise Peggy?

6. Andrew Powell recently launched a tutoring service to help high school students prepare for college entrance exams. Andrew is very ambitious and plans to have 100 centers open within two years. He recently put together his board of directors. The board consists of himself, his cofounder, his chief financial officer, and two college buddies with whom he plays golf occasionally. Do you think Andrew has formed a board with a high chance of being effective? If not, what would be a better approach for Andrew?

7. Examine the board of advisers set up by BeautyBuys.com, the company described in this chapter. Briefly comment on the potential of each board member to help this firm.

8. Pamela Smith, a professional investor, was having lunch with a colleague recently and said, "Do you remember Phil Moore, the entrepreneur we met the other day, who has invented a new kind of computer keyboard? I checked up on him, and he has all the right personal attributes to be a successful entrepreneur." Pamela's dinner companion said, "Really, tell me about him." What do you think Pamela would say if she were describing a person who had all the right personal attributes to be a successful entrepreneur?

9. Jim Lane is an executive with General Motors. A former coworker of his recently started a company and raised $3 million from a well-known investor even through he didn't need the money to launch the business. Jim thinks his friend is foolish and can't think of one reason to take money from an investor if you don't need it. If you were talking to Jim, what would you tell him about this situation?

10. Melanie Atkins is preparing to launch a software firm near Minneapolis. She is very capable but is worried about the amount of money she'll need to spend paying consultants to help her launch and grow her business. Does Melanie have to rely strictly on paid consultants to help her launch and grow her business? If not, what alternatives does Melanie have?

you be the VC

Company: Smart Safety Systems, Inc. (www.kidsmartdetector.com)

Business idea: Produce fire safety devices, such as smoke detectors, that permit parents of young children or adult children of elderly parents to record customized messages to be played during a fire emergency.

Pitch: When a fire emergency occurs, young children are often afraid of the very things and the people who could save them: the sound of smoke detectors, fire alarms, fire engine sirens, and firefighters. During a fire, children often wait for their parents to rescue them or even hide in closets or under beds to avoid the fire. Sometimes children even stay in their "hiding places" when firefighters, who they see as dressed in strange and intimidating gear, try to locate them. Sadly, an average of three children under the age of 15 die in a residential fire somewhere in the United States every day. Although children often become confused or frightened when they hear a firm alarm or the piercing

sound of a smoke detector, they will usually respond to the voices of their parents. Recognizing this, Smart Safety Systems invented the KidSmart smoke alarm, which permits parents of young children or adult children of elderly parents to record customized messages to be played during a fire emergency. The messages are intended to convey simple, understandable instructions to children in the voices of their parents or another trusted adult during a fire emergency.

Q&A: Based on the material covered in this chapter, what questions would you ask this firm's founders before making your funding decision? What answers would satisfy you?

Decision: If you had to make your decision on just the information provided in the pitch and the company's Web site, would you fund this firm? Why or why not?

Case 6.1

Wherify Wireless: Progressively Strengthening Its New Venture Team
www.wherifywireless.com

The worst nightmare of a young child's parents is to be with the child, leave the child alone for just a minute, and find that the child is missing upon their return. An equally worrisome possibility confronts the caregivers of Alzheimer's patients. Alzheimer's causes memory loss. As a result, if an Alzheimer's patient becomes separated from her caregiver, it may be difficult for the patient to find her way safely home.

Wherify Wireless, a Silicon Valley startup, was launched in 1998 with an invention and subsequent business model through which worries of these kinds could be eased. The company has invented a device that can be secured to the wrist of a child or an adult. Using GPS technology, the device, which looks like a wristwatch, provides parents or other authorities the location of the wearer. Although its value is most apparent in the case of an emergency, it is also designed to give parents and caregivers simple peace of mind. For example, if a child goes on a school field trip, a parent can check the child's location to make sure that the bus arrived at its intended location safely.

The initial target market for the device, called a GPS locator, is the parents of young children. Here's how it works. Once secured to a child's wrist, the product communicates with global positioning satellites and Sprint's wireless network. Parents can communicate with the device, and locate their children, by either calling Wherify's toll free number or accessing the company's Web site. In a reverse sequence, a child can simultaneously press two buttons to send an emergency page. The device is locked into place on the child's wrist and is virtually impossible to remove without a key. The device cost about $400. The parents must also pay a monthly subscription fee of $24.95 to $49.95 (the price varies depending on the features involved) to access Wherify's 24/7 location services.

Timothy J. Neher is Wherify's founder. Prior to starting Wherify, Neher spent more than a decade developing and marketing new consumer products for several companies. His most recent position was vice president of marketing and sales for CTH Consumer Plastic.

Shortly after Wherify was founded, Neher started hiring personnel. His first three key hires were as follows:

Anthony L. LaRochelle, Chief Technical Officer. LaRochelle is in charge of product design, manufacturing, and distribution. He is a seasoned engineer who has managed the design of hundreds of products. Prior to joining Wherify, LaRochelle worked for Westinghouse, Loral Fairchild Sensors, and Harris Semiconductor.

Matthew J. Neher, Vice President. Neher is in charge of business development. Prior to joining Wherify, Neher was the executive vice president of Windy City Products, where he managed the company's growth.

Robert Jacobsen, Chief Information Officer. Jacobsen was hired to lead the development of Wherify's Location Service Center. Prior to accepting his current position, Jacobsen worked for Compaq, Tandem, and Sprint Communications.

The initial tasks that Neher and his group tackled revolved around refining Wherify's business model and proving that the GPS tracking device and location system could be built. In late 1998, Wherify was awarded its first patent, which was a major milestone for the nascent company. On the strength of that development, in early 1999 Neher and his team started hiring additional personnel to further develop the company's product and its unique tracking system.

At the same time that Neher was making his initial hires, he was working to build additional elements of his company's new venture team. Wherify is incorporated and has a board of directors. Since its inception, several notable individuals have joined the board, including former Best Buy executive Wade Fenn. The company has investors—although Wherify is mum about their identity. Wherify has a number of business partners with whom it has worked with to develop its product. Its major partners include AMD, LSI Logic, and Sirf. Both AMD and LSI Logic make semiconductors, and Sirf is a GPS technology firm.

To bolster Wherify's legitimacy and get the word out about its product, Neher is actively working to form additional partnerships with organizations promoting child safety. Presently, Wherify has partnerships with about 55 child safety groups to help disseminate child safety information. An example is the company's partnership with the Lost Children's Network (www.lostchildren.org), an organization dedicated to aid in the search for lost and abducted children. Both Wherify and the Lost Children's Network have similar goals—the protection of children. By providing financial support to the Lost Children's Network and helping it achieve its objectives, Wherify gains an ally in helping it get the word out about its GPS locator device.

Wherify is now shipping its initial GPS locator devices to consumers, and the early response has been extremely positive. New versions of the product are on the drawing boards, including a version specifically designed for Alzheimer's patients and a sports model designed for women joggers.

Discussion Questions

1. Do you think Neher has done a good job building Wherify's new venture team? Do you believe there are any omissions in the team's composition? If so, what are they, and how would you suggest that the omissions be corrected?

2. Has Neher done a good job of building a new venture team that can both (1) provide guidance to the firm's

managers and (2) lend legitimacy to the firm's products and business model? Explain your answer.

3. Only sketchy information is provided in the case about the composition of Wherify's board of directors. If you had been providing advice to Timothy Neher when Wherify was selecting its initial directors, what types of individuals would you have urged him to include on the board? What about the composition of the board, in regard to insiders versus outsiders?

4. As Wherify diversifies and starts producing GPS locator devices that are targeted specifically to Alzheimer's patients and sports enthusiasts (e.g., female joggers), to what extent will its new venture team need to change to reflect these changes?

Source: Wherify Wireless home page, www.wherifywireless.com (accessed July 2, 2004). W.S. Mossberg, "Putting Junior Under Surveillance," Wall Street Journal, September 17, 2003.

Case 6.2

S2io Technologies: What Comes First—The CEO or the Funding?
www.s2io.com

S2io is a promising start-up that hopes to develop and market an integrated circuit, or chip, that will boost the processing power of servers for data networks. Five former Nortel Networks employees launched S2io in September 2001, and on August 19, 2002, it named Dave Zabrowski its new president and CEO.

Zabrowski is the type of executive who confidently takes the reins of a company such as S2io. He is 39 years old and has 16 years of broad experience with Hewlett-Packard, working in both its marketing and its finance departments. More important, he has "connections" and knows his way around Silicon Valley. There are few things more coveted in the start-up world than landing an executive who already has a network of acquaintances among investors, suppliers, and potential customers.

The steps that led up to Zabrowski's hiring provide a glimpse into the dilemmas facing start-ups when building their new venture teams. From the outset, the founders knew they would have to attain venture-capital funding and hire an outside CEO to gain the traction needed to be a player in their industry. But which goal should they pursue first? Should they hire a CEO and then go after funding? Or should they get funding first and then seek a high-quality CEO?

Let's look at each of the possible approaches.

Approach 1: Hiring a CEO before getting funding: Hiring a well-known CEO first would give S2io more credibility with lenders and investors. "Back then, our biggest challenge was getting someone to pay attention to us," said Ed Roseberry, one of the company's founders. "Start-up companies don't have any clout." The founders realized that having a first-rate CEO would bring legitimacy to the firm and open doors that wouldn't open otherwise, exposing them to a broader range of funding choices. By hiring a CEO first, the business plan presented to investors could be strengthened.

In addition, a well-connected CEO brings a broad network of industry-related contacts, so a strong CEO might gain commitments from initial customers and might enable partnerships to be struck. These types of initiatives could strengthen S2io's business plan and increase the likelihood of obtaining favorable funding.

Approach 2: Getting funding before hiring a CEO: The second approach provided seemingly equal advantages. To attract a high-quality CEO, a start-up needs all the positive attributes it can muster, and a firm with access to funding would certainly make it more attractive to a potential CEO. Getting funding not only provides a firm the capital it needs but also is a seal of legitimacy, suggesting that a firm is a serious contender. One downside to this approach is that the founders knew that once they got funding, pressure to perform would become more acute. This meant that they would have progressively less time to devote to a search for a CEO.

In the end, the decision of whether to hire a CEO and then get funding or whether to get funding and then hire a CEO boiled down to the age-old "what comes first, the chicken or the egg?" type of quandary. Hiring an experienced CEO would help S2io get funding, while at the same time having funding would help S2io get an experienced CEO. So, which approach should be adopted?

The decision: S2io's founders decided to get funding first and then hire an experienced CEO, primarily to make the firm more attractive to CEO candidates. In November 2001, the company received $9 million in venture-capital funding after the founders worked hard to obtain funding on their own. Then the founders geared up to find an experienced CEO. Time was of the essence. The founders wanted to land a high-quality CEO quickly so that they could focus on product development and so that the new CEO could lead the search for a second round of funding. Before initiating the search, the founders agreed on the type of CEO they wanted and, with the help of a human resources consulting firm, established the overall structure of a compensation package.

The search: At first, the founders conducted their own search and mined their individual networks of acquaintances to identify viable candidates. The search turned up empty. Then they elicited the help of several executive-search firms to identify and screen candidates. After interviewing a number of candidates but finding no one, a small executive-search firm, Cross Creek System, introduced the founders to Dave Zabrowski, who had most recently been vice president and general manager for business personal computers at Hewlett-Packard. More important, he had the types of connections the founders felt could help take S2io to the next level. Zabrowski was hired, and in December 2002 he helped the company close its second round of funding, which brought in an additional $18 million. Since then, he has been active in recruiting new executives to round out S2io's management team and in the day-to-day management of the firm.

This case illustrates why the process of building a new venture team should be approached carefully, with the timing of key hires made in a thoughtful manner. The individual hired to lead a new firm is of paramount importance. In the case of S2io, the founders wanted someone who had a broad range of experience and a network of contacts that could help take the firm to the next level. Another lesson is that at times, finding the ideal candidate for a job may exceed the capacities of the founders of a firm. This is the point at which an executive-search firm is often employed. Although costly, using an executive-search firm may be a company's best avenue to finding the right individual to fill a key role.

Discussion Questions

1. Do you think the decision to get funding before hiring a CEO was the correct decision? What risks did S2io's founders take in making this decision?

2. Rather than hiring a CEO, one of the founders of S2io could have moved into the CEO position. Do you think this would have been a good alternative for S2io? Why or why not?

3. Go online and find three executive-search firms. Write a brief summary of the services that each firm offers. Do you think using an executive-search firm was a good choice for S2io? Why or why not?

4. Go to S2io's Web site and look at the composition of its board of directors. Write a short critique of its board on the basis of the preferred attributes of directors discussed in this chapter.

Sources: S2io home page, www.S2io.com (accessed April 15, 2003), and J. Sterline, "How Do You Know whether to Hire a CEO?," Wall Street Journal, March 17, 2003, R6.

seven

assessing a new venture's *financial strength* and viability

OBJECTIVES

After studying this chapter, you should be ready to:

1. Explain the two functions of the financial management of a firm.

2. Identify the four main financial objectives of entrepreneurial firms.

3. Explain the difference between historical and pro forma financial statements.

4. Explain the purpose of an income statement.

5. Explain the purpose of a balance sheet.

6. Explain the purpose of a statement of cash flows.

7. Discuss how financial ratios are used to analyze and interpret a firm's financial statements.

8. Discuss the role of forecasts in projecting a firm's future income and expenses.

9. Explain what a completely new firm bases its forecasts on.

10. Explain what is meant by the term "percent of sales method."

leapfrog: keeping a sharp eye on the financials

Next time you see a group of grade school kids waiting for their bus, notice if any are carrying LeapPads—colorful devices that look like laptop computers. LeapFrog Inc. makes LeapPads, which help schoolkids learn reading, math, spelling, science, and music. The gadgets are brought to life by an audio cartridge and book that are sold separately. To use a LeapPad, the user pops in a cartridge, places the book on top of the device, and touches a page with an interactive pen. The pen elicits a verbal response when it is pointed at a particular area on the page.[1]

Mike Wood, who developed the idea for LeapFrog while trying to teach his son to read, founded his firm in 1995. In part, the idea was prompted by the fact that Wood was having a difficult time helping his three-year-old realize that letters represent sounds and that, taken together, sounds become words.[2] An attorney, Wood once represented a "talking" greeting card company. Recalling how he relied on previous knowledge as the foundation for putting two and two together to come up with the idea for LeapFrog, Wood said,

I was fascinated by this audio chip embedded in their cards that played these little musical messages. And I thought, "What if I put chips inside a set of squeezable letters, so that when kids touch a certain letter, they would hear its phonetic sound?"

Even after founding LeapFrog, Wood wasn't sure his idea was viable, so he focused on three questions. First, was there a market for the product? Second, could the device he imagined be built at an affordable price? And third, could the company cut it financially? Wood knew that there would be considerable product development and testing expense before his invention could be sold. He also knew that he would have to hire staff and a sales force and set up an office before any revenue came in. From day one, Wood was sharply focused on the financial aspects of the business.

As LeapFrog took shape, the answers to the first two questions became clear. Through working with focus groups and industry experts, Wood learned that there was indeed a market for his product, and he figured out a way to build his original product at an affordable price.[3] The company's first break came in the late 1990s, when Toys "R" Us agreed to stock LeapFrog's products.

In regard to the financials, a sharp focus on costs and a conservative approach to raising money helped LeapFrog meet its early goals. In its first three years, the company operated with a survival mentality and knew that success or failure hinged on its ability to execute its financial plan. The company's first round of funding came from Wood's family and friends. LeapFrog's first office was a mere 1,000 square feet, where Wood and three colleagues worked at desks laid across sawhorses. Reflecting on this period in his company's history, Wood said,

We're in the business of putting products on store shelves, where either they sell or they don't sell.

There's no halfway. You execute, and you get to do next year's plan. You fail, and next year's plan is irrelevant. At every turn, that fact forced us to focus on the bottom line.[4]

For LeapFrog, focusing on the bottom line meant keeping close tabs on how its strategies affected its income statement, balance sheet, and cash flow. Every decision was weighed in light of how it affected the company's cash position, its net income, and its ability to strengthen its overall financial posture.

LeapFrog made it through the hectic start-up years. Today, it is one of the fastest-growing educational companies in the United States.[5] In 2002, it staged a successful initial public offering and raised $115 million for product development and expansion. Despite its success, the company still focuses on the bottom line. Its headquarters, which is very simple, is located in a renovated warehouse near Oakland, California. The company works hard to leverage the value of the educational content it produces. For example, the company now has six different versions of its LeapPad product that target different age-groups so that content that is created for one age-group, such as a science cartridge, can be revised and repositioned for other age-groups, resulting in considerable cost savings. This product development approach helps conserve the company's cash and increase its net income.

learning **objective**

1. Explain the two functions of the financial management of a firm.

In this chapter, we'll look at how new ventures assess their financial strength and viability. For the purposes of completeness, we'll look at how both existing ventures and start-up firms assess their financial strength and viability. First, we'll consider general financial management and discuss the financial objectives of a firm and the steps involved in the financial management process. **Financial management** deals with two things: raising money and managing a company's finances in a way that achieves the highest rate of return.[6] We cover the process of raising money in Chapter 10. This chapter focuses on how a company manages its finances in an effort to increase its financial strength and earn the highest rate of return. Next, we'll examine how existing firms track their financial progress through preparing, analyzing, and maintaining past financial statements. Finally, we'll discuss how both existing firms and start-up ventures forecast future income and expenses and how the forecasts are used to prepare pro forma (i.e., projected) financial statements. Pro forma financial statements, which include the pro forma income statement, the pro forma balance sheet, and the pro forma statement of cash flows, are extremely helpful to firms in financial planning.

Introduction to Financial Management

An entrepreneur's ability to pursue an opportunity and turn the opportunity into a viable entrepreneurial firm hinges largely on the availability of money. Regardless of the quality of a product or service, a company can't be viable in the long run unless it is successful financially. Money either comes from external sources (such as investors or lenders) or is internally generated by the firm through earnings. It is important for a firm to have a solid grasp of how it is doing financially.

It is also vital for a firm to be aware of how much money it has in the bank and whether it will be able to meet its obligations. Just because a firm is successful doesn't mean that it doesn't face financial challenges. For example, many of the small firms that sell to larger companies, such as IBM, General Electric, and Home Depot, don't get paid for 30 to 60 days from the time they make a sale. Think about the difficulty this scenario creates. The small firm must buy parts, pay its employees, pay its routine bills, ship its products, and then wait for one to two months for payment. Unless a firm manages its money carefully, it is easy to run out of cash, even if its products or services are selling like hotcakes.

The financial management of a firm deals with questions such as the following on an ongoing basis:

- How are we doing? Are we making or losing money?
- How much cash do we have on hand?
- Do we have enough cash to meet our short-term obligations?
- How efficiently are we utilizing our assets?
- How does our growth and net profits compare to those of our industry peers?
- Where will the funds we need for capital improvements come from?
- Are there ways we can partner with other firms to share risk and reduce the amount of cash we need?
- Overall, are we in good shape financially?

A properly managed firm stays on top of these questions through the tools and techniques that we'll discuss in this chapter.

Financial Objectives of a Firm

Most entrepreneurial firms—whether they have been in business for several years or they are start-ups—have four main financial objectives: profitability, liquidity, efficiency, and stability. Understanding these objectives sets a firm on the right financial course and helps it track the answers to the previously posed questions. Figure 7.1[7] describes each of these objectives.

Profitability is the ability to earn a profit. Many start-ups are not profitable during their first one to three years while they are training employees and building their brands, but a firm must become profitable to remain viable and provide a return to its owners.

Liquidity is a company's ability to meet its short-term financial obligations. Even if a firm is profitable, it is often a challenge to keep enough money in the bank to meet its routine obligations in a timely manner. To do so, a firm must keep a close watch on accounts receivable and inventories. A company's **accounts receivable** is money owed to it by its customers. Its **inventory** is its merchandise, raw materials, and products waiting to be sold. If a firm allows the levels of either of these assets to get too high, it may not be able to keep sufficient cash on hand to meet its short-term obligations.

Efficiency is how productively a firm utilizes its assets relative to its revenue and its profits. Southwest Airlines, for example, uses its assets very productively. Its turnaround

learning **objective**

2. Identify the four main financial objectives of entrepreneurial firms.

Figure 7.1

Primary Financial Objectives of Entrepreneurial Firms

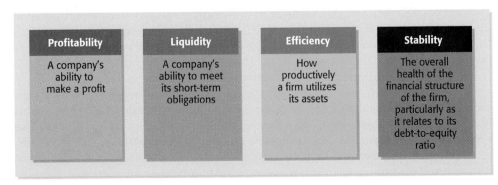

Profitability	Liquidity	Efficiency	Stability
A company's ability to make a profit	A company's ability to meet its short-term obligations	How productively a firm utilizes its assets	The overall health of the financial structure of the firm, particularly as it relates to its debt-to-equity ratio

Many high-tech entrepreneurial firms use state-of-the-art manufacturing technology to increase efficiency and reduce costs. Intel, for example, has been known since its entrepreneurial beginnings for its strong manufacturing capability, which is one reason why the company has succeeded for 35 years.

time, or the time that its airplanes sit on the ground while they are being unloaded and reloaded, is the lowest in the airline industry. As Southwest is quick to point out, "Our planes don't make any money sitting on the ground—we have to get them back into the air."[8]

Stability is the strength and vigor of the firm's overall financial posture. For a firm to be stable, it must not only earn a profit and remain liquid but also keep its debt in check. If a firm continues to borrow from its lenders and its **debt-to-equity ratio**, which is calculated by dividing its long-term debt by its shareholders' equity, gets too high, it may have trouble meeting its obligations and securing the level of financing needed to fuel its growth.

Some firms improve their financial position on all four of these dimensions through strategic partnership arrangements that enable them to minimize the assets they need to generate sales. An example of this is provided by Blimpie Subs and Salads, which minimizes costs and increases revenue by locating in nontraditional locations, as illustrated in the boxed feature titled "Partnering for Success."

The Process of Financial Management

To assess whether its financial objectives are being met, firms rely heavily on analysis of financial statements, forecasts, and budgets. A **financial statement** is a written report that quantitatively describes a firm's financial health. The income statement, the balance sheet, and the statement of cash flows are the financial statements entrepreneurs use most commonly. **Forecasts** are an estimate of a firm's future income and expenses, based on its past performance, its current circumstances, and its future plans.[9] New ventures typically base their forecasts on an estimate of sales and then on industry averages or the experiences of similar start-ups regarding the cost of goods sold (based on a percentage of sales) and on other expenses. **Budgets** are itemized forecasts of a company's income, expenses, and capital needs and are also an important tool for financial planning and control.[10]

Blimpie Subs and Salads: Minimizing Costs and Increasing Revenues by Locating in Nontraditional Locations

www.blimpie.com

If you're familiar with Blimpie sub shops, you've noticed that they are frequently located in nontraditional locations, such as gasoline stations, convenience stores, hospitals, and high schools. The idea behind selling food in nontraditional locations is to establish minirestaurants in places that attract a lot of foot traffic and to economize on building or lease expenses by partnering with companies that already have buildings and are looking for ways to differentiate themselves from their competitors. Blimpie is a pioneer in the development of nontraditional locations for quick-service food.

A classic example of how nontraditional locations work is illustrated by Blimpie's aggressive efforts to establish partnerships and cobranding relationships with petroleum companies. Currently, Blimpie has partnerships with BP Oil, Mobil, Exxon, Amerada Hess, Williams Express, and Tosco. These partnerships work like this. A Blimpie franchisee strikes a deal with say a Mobil gas station to lease space within the station for a reduced-in-scale Blimpie sub shop. To maintain its image, Blimpie typically insists that the interior of the gas station take on the Blimpie ambiance, including the company's distinctive logos and familiar green, yellow, and red color schemes. The relationship is meant to benefit both parties. Blimpie benefits by opening another location without incurring the cost of constructing a freestanding building or leasing expensive shopping mall space. The Mobil station benefits by having a quality branded food partner to help draw in road traffic and by collecting lease income. Having a Blimpie sub shop inside its store also helps the Mobil station become a "destination stop" for regular customers rather than simply another gas station servicing passing cars.

By partnering with companies such as Mobil Oil, Blimpie is able to minimize costs and boost revenues simultaneously.

Questions for Critical Thinking

1. As described in this feature, Blimpie's partnerships with oil companies are successful. What conditions or factors could signal to Blimpie that one of its partnerships is in trouble? Viewed in a slightly different fashion, what indicators or conditions would you counsel Blimpie to observe to identify potential problems with individual partnerships?

2. Go to Blimpie's Web site (www.blimpie.com) to study its financial performance. Given the information available at the Web site, how do you assess Blimpie's performance in terms of profitability, liquidity, efficiency, and stability?

The process of a firm's financial management is shown in Figure 7.2. It begins by tracking the company's past financial performance through the preparation and analysis of financial statements. These statements organize and report the firm's financial transactions. They tell a firm how much money it is making or losing (income statement), the structure of its assets and liabilities (balance sheet), and where its cash is coming from and going (statement of cash flows). The statements also help a firm discern how it stacks up against its competitors and industry norms. Most firms look at two to three years of past financial statements when preparing forecasts.

The next step is to prepare forecasts for two to three years in the future. Then forecasts are used to prepare a firm's pro forma financial statements, which, along with its more fine-tuned budgets, constitute its financial plan.

The final step in the process is the ongoing analysis of a firm's financial results. **Financial ratios**, which depict relationships between items on a firm's financial statements, are used to discern whether a firm is meeting its financial objectives and how it stacks up against its industry peers. These ratios are also used to assess trends. Obviously, a completely new venture would start at step 2 in Figure 7.2. It is important that a new venture be familiar with the entire process, however. Typically, new ventures prepare financial statements quarterly so that as soon as the first quarter is completed, the new venture will have historic financial statements to help prepare forecasts and pro forma statements for future periods.

Figure 7.2 The Process of Financial Management

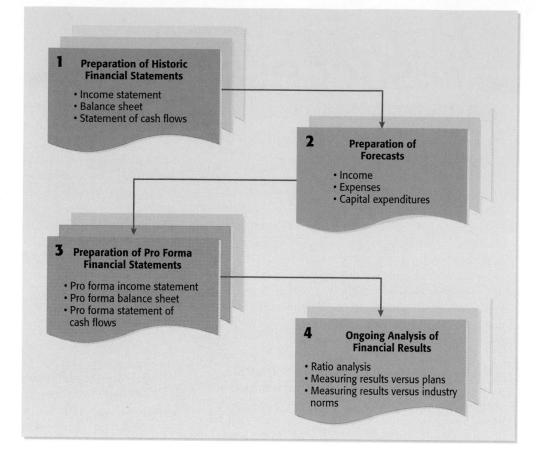

It is important for a firm to evaluate how it is faring relative to its industry. Sometimes raw financial ratios that are not viewed in context are deceiving. For example, a firm's past three years' income statements may show that it is increasing its sales at a rate of 15 percent per year. This number may seem impressive—until one learns that the industry in which the firm competes is growing at a rate of 30 percent per year, showing that the firm is steadily losing market share.

Many experienced entrepreneurs stress the importance of keeping on top of the financial management of a firm. In the competitive environments in which most firms exist, it's simply not good enough to shoot from the hip when making financial decisions. Reinforcing this point, Bill Gates, the founder of Microsoft, said,

> The business side of any company starts and ends with hard-core analysis of its numbers. Whatever else you do, if you don't understand what's happening in your business factually and you're making business decisions based on anecdotal data or gut instinct, you'll eventually pay a big price.[11]

Financial Statements and Forecasts

learning **objective**

3. Explain the difference between historical and pro forma financial statements.

Historical financial statements reflect past performance and are usually prepared on a quarterly and annual basis. Publicly traded firms are required by the Securities and Exchange Commission (SEC) to prepare financial statements and make them available to the public. The statements are submitted to the SEC through a number of required filings. The most comprehensive filing is the **10-K**, which is a report similar to the annual report except that it contains more detailed information about the company's business.[12] The 10-K for any publicly traded firm is available through the SEC Edgar database on the Web (*www.sec.gov/edgar*).

Many entrepreneurs work with financial analysts and accountants to better understand their financial progress. Entrepreneurs who keep on top of the financial aspects of their company make strong decisions. Bill Gates would not be the success he is today had he not made the time to watch the numbers. His net worth is $46.6 billion, and he has been #1 on the Forbes list of richest people every year since 1999.

Pro forma financial statements are projections for future periods based on forecasts and are typically completed for two to three years in the future. Pro forma financial statements are strictly planning tools and are not required by the SEC. In fact, most companies consider their pro forma statements to be confidential and reveal them to outsiders, such as lenders and investors, only on a "need-to-know" basis.

To illustrate how these financial instruments are prepared, let's look at New Venture Fitness Drinks, a fictitious sports drink company first introduced in Chapter 3. New Venture Fitness Drinks has been in business for five years. Targeting spots enthusiasts, the company sells a line of nutritional fitness drinks. It opened a single location in 1999, added a second location in 2004, and plans to add a third in 2005. The company's strategy is to place small restaurants, similar to smoothie restaurants, near large outdoor sports complexes. The company is profitable and is growing at a rate of 25 percent per year.

Historical Financial Statements

Historical financial statements include the income statement, the balance sheet, and the statement of cash flows. The statements are usually prepared in this order because information flows logically from one to the next. In start-ups, financial statements are typically scrutinized closely to monitor the financial progress of the firm. On the rare occasion when a company has not used financial statements in planning, it should prepare and maintain them anyway. If a firm goes to a banker or investor to raise funds, the banker or investor will invariably ask for copies of past financial statements to analyze the firm's financial history. If a firm does not have these statements, it may be precluded from serious consideration for an investment or a loan. Let's look at each of these statements.

Income Statement

The **income statement** reflects the results of the operations of a firm over a specified period of time.[13] It records all the revenues and expenses for the given period and shows whether the firm is making a profit or is experiencing a loss (which is why the income statement if often referred to as the "profit-and-loss statement"). Income statements are typically prepared on a monthly, quarterly, and annual basis. Most income statements are prepared in a multiyear format, making it easy to spot trends.

The consolidated income statement for the past three years for New Venture Fitness Drinks is shown in Table 7.1. The value of the multiperiod format is clear. It's easy to see that the company's sales are increasing at the rate of about 25 percent per year, it is profitable, and its net income is increasing. The numbers are used to evaluate the effect of past strategies and to help project future sales and earnings.

The three numbers that receive the most attention when evaluating an income statement are the following:

- *Net sales:* **Net sales** consist of total sales minus allowances for returned goods and discounts.
- *Cost of sales (or cost of goods sold):* **Cost of sales** includes all the direct costs associated with producing or delivering a product or service, including the material costs and direct labor. In the case of New Venture Fitness Drinks, this would include the ingredients that go into the fitness drinks and the labor needed to produce them.
- *Operating expenses:* **Operating expenses** include marketing, administrative costs, and other expenses not directly related to producing a product or service.

One of the most valuable things that entrepreneurs and managers do with income statements is to compare the ratios of cost of sales and operating expenses to net sales for different periods. For example, the cost of sales for New Venture Fitness Drinks, which includes the ingredients for its fitness drinks and the labor needed to make them, has been 55, 49, and 46 percent of sales for 2002, 2003, and 2004, respectively. This is a healthy trend. It shows that the company is steadily decreasing its material and labor costs per dollar of sales. This is the type of trend that can be noticed fairly easily by looking at a firm's multiyear income statements.

One ratio of particular importance in evaluating a firm's income statements is profit margin. A firm's **profit margin**, or return on sales, is computed by dividing net income by net sales. For the years 2002, 2003, and 2004, the profit margin for New Venture Fitness Drinks has been 13.6, 17.9, and 22.3 percent, respectively. This is also a healthy trend. A firm's profit margin tells it what percentage of every dollar in sales contributes to the bottom line. A rising profit margin means that a firm is either boosting its sales without

Table 7.1

Consolidated Income Statements for New Venture Fitness Drinks, Inc. (all data in dollars)

	December 31, 2004	December 31, 2003	December 31, 2002
Net sales	586,600	463,100	368,900
Cost of sales	268,900	225,500	201,500
Gross profit	317,700	237,600	167,400
Operating expenses			
Selling, general, and administrative expense	117,800	104,700	90,200
Depreciation	13,500	5,900	5,100
Operating income	186,400	127,000	72,100
Other income			
Interest income	1,900	800	1,100
Interest expense	(15,000)	(6,900)	(6,400)
Other income (expense), net	10,900	(1,300)	1,200
Income before income taxes	184,200	119,600	68,000
Income tax expense	53,200	36,600	18,000
Net income	131,000	83,000	50,000
Earnings per share	1.31	0.83	0.50

increasing its expenses or that it is doing a better job of controlling its costs. In contrast, a declining profit margin means that a firm is losing control of its costs or that it is slashing prices to maintain or increase sales.

One ratio that will not be computed for New Venture Fitness Drinks is price-to-earnings ratio, or P/E ratio. New Venture Fitness Drinks is incorporated, so it has stock, but its stock is not traded on a public exchange such as the NASDAQ or the New York Stock Exchange. **P/E** is a simple ratio that measures the price of a company's stock against its earnings. Generally, the higher a company's price-to-earnings ratio goes, the greater the market thinks it will grow. In 2004, New Venture Fitness Drinks earned $1.31 per share. If it was listed on the NASDAQ and its stock was trading at $20 per share, its P/E would be 15.3. This is what is meant when you hear that a company is selling for "15 times earnings."

The importance of looking at several years of income statement rather than just one is illustrated in the boxed feature titled "Savvy Entrepreneurial Firm."

learning **objective**

5. Explain the purpose of a balance sheet.

Balance Sheet   Unlike the income statement, which covers a specified *period* of time, a **balance sheet** is a snapshot of a company's assets, liabilities, and owners' equity at a specific *point* in time. The left-hand side of a balance sheet (or the top, depending on how it is displayed) shows a firm's assets, while the right-hand side (or bottom) shows its liabilities and owners' equity. The assets are listed in order of their "liquidity," or the length of time it takes to convert them to cash. The liabilities are listed in the order in which they must be paid. A balance sheet must always "balance," meaning that a firm's assets must always equal its liabilities plus owners' equity.

The major categories of assets listed on a balance sheet are the following:

- *Current assets:* **Current assets** include cash plus items that are readily convertible to cash, such as accounts receivable, marketable securities, and inventories.
- *Fixed assets:* **Fixed assets** are assets used over a longer time frame, such as real estate, buildings, equipment, and furniture.
- *Other assets:* **Other assets** are miscellaneous assets, including accumulated goodwill.

The major categories of liabilities listed on a balance sheet are the following:

- *Current liabilities:* **Current liabilities** include obligations that are payable within a year, including accounts payable, accrued expenses, and the current portion of long-term debt.
- *Long-term liabilities:* **Long-term liabilities** include notes or loans that are repayable beyond one year, including liabilities associated with purchasing real estate, buildings, and equipment.
- *Owners' equity:* **Owners' equity** is the equity invested in the business by its owners plus the accumulated earnings retained by the business after paying dividends.

Balance sheets are somewhat deceiving. First, a company's assets are recorded at cost rather than fair market value. A firm may have invested $500,000 in real estate several years ago that is worth $1 million today, but the value that is reflected on the firm's current balance sheet is the $500,000 purchase price rather than the $1 million fair market value. Second, intellectual property, such as patents, trademarks, and copyrights, receive value on the balance sheet in some cases and in some cases they don't, depending on the circumstances involved. In many cases, a firm's intellectual property will receive no value on its balance sheet even though it may be very valuable from a practical standpoint.[14] Third, intangible assets, such as the amount of training a firm has provided to its employees and the value of its brand, are not recognized on its balance sheet.

The consolidated balance sheet for New Venture Fitness Drinks is shown in Table 7.2. Again, multiple years are shown so that trends can be easily spotted. When evaluating a balance sheet, the two primary questions are whether a firm has sufficient short-term assets to cover its short-term debts and whether it is financially sound overall. There are two calculations that provide the answer to the first question. In 2004, the **working capital** of New Venture Fitness Drinks, defined as its current assets minus its current liabilities, was $82,500. This number represents the amount of liquid assets the firm has available. Its **current ratio**, which equals the firm's current assets divided by its current liabilities,

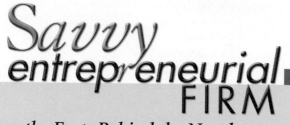

Savvy entrepreneurial FIRM

Know the Facts Behind the Numbers

Let's say that New Venture Fitness Drinks was interested in hiring a new chief executive officer (CEO) and was interviewing the CEOs of three small restaurant chains. To get a sense of how savvy each candidate was at managing a firm's finances, the board of directors of New Venture Fitness Drinks asked each person to submit the 2004 financial statements for his or her current firm. An analysis of an abbreviated version of each firm's income statement is shown here. (If this were an actual case, balances sheets and statement of cash flows would be analyzed too.)

	Candidate 1: CEO of New Venture Soup and Salad	Candidate 2: CEO of New Venture Beef	Candidate 3: CEO of New Venture Sea Food
Net sales	$326,400	$281,200	$486,700
Cost of sales	150,500	143,900	174,700
Gross profit	175,900	137,300	312,000
All expenses, including taxes and depreciation	114,200	112,400	150,000
Net income	61,700	24,900	162,000

By glancing at these statements, it would appear that the shrewdest financial manager of the three is the CEO of New Venture Sea Food. The company's net income is more than double that of the other two firms. In addition, New Venture Sea Food's costs of sales were 35.9 percent of net sales in 2004, compared to 46.1 percent for New Venture Soup and Salad and 51 percent for New Venture Beef. Similarly, New Venture Sea Food's expenses were 30.9 percent of sales, compared to 35.0 percent for New Venture Soup and Salad and 40 percent for New Venture Beef.

Fortunately, one of the board members of New Venture Fitness Drinks asked a series of questions during the personal interviews of the candidates and uncovered some revealing information. As it turns out, New Venture Sea Food was in the hottest segment of the restaurant industry in 2004. Seafood restaurants of comparable size produced about 1.5 times as much net income as New Venture Seafood did. So if candidate 3 had done his job properly,

his company's net income should have been in the neighborhood of $240,000 instead of $162,000. New Venture Soup and Salad was in a slow-growth area and at midyear feared that it might not meet its financial targets. So the CEO pulled several of his best people off projects and reassigned them to marketing with the charge to develop new menu items. In other words, the company borrowed from its future to make its numbers work today.

As for New Venture Beef, the CEO found herself in a market that was losing appeal. Several reports that gained national publicity were published early in the year, warning consumers of the risks of eating red meat. To compensate, the CEO quickly implemented a productivity improvement program and partnered with a local beef promotion board to counter the bad press with more objective research results about beef's nutritional value. The company also participated in several volunteer efforts in its local community to raise the visibility of its restaurants in a positive manner. If the CEO of New Venture Beef hadn't moved quickly to take these actions, its 2004 performance would have been much worse.

Ultimately, New Venture Fitness Drinks decided that candidate 2, the CEO of New Venture Beef, was the best candidate for its job. This example illustrates the need to look at multiple years of an income statement rather than a single year to fairly assess how well a firm is performing financially. It also illustrates the need to look beyond the numbers and understand the circumstances that surround a firm's financial results.

Questions for Critical Thinking

1. Show the income statements for the three candidates to two or three friends who are majoring in business. Ask them to select the best CEO from among these three people on the basis of these income statements. In addition, ask your friends to explain their choices to you. Did your friends choose the same candidate? If not, what caused the differences in their choices?

2. What are the three most important insights you gained from studying this feature? Which of these insights surprised you, and why?

provides another picture of the relationship between its current assets and current liabilities and can tell us more about whether the firm can pay its short-term debts.

New Venture Fitness Drink's current ratio is 3.06, meaning that it has $3.06 in current assets for every $1.00 in current liabilities. This is a healthy number and provides confidence that the company will be able to meet its current liabilities. The company's trend in

Assets	December 31, 2004	December 31, 2003	December 31, 2002
Current assets			
Cash and cash equivalents	63,800	54,600	56,500
Accounts receivable, less allowance for doubtful accounts	39,600	48,900	50,200
Inventories	19,200	20,400	21,400
Total Current Assets	**122,600**	**123,900**	**128,100**
Property, plant, and equipment			
Land	260,000	160,000	160,000
Buildings and equipment	412,000	261,500	149,000
Total property, plant, and equipment	672,000	421,500	309,000
Less: accumulated depreciation	65,000	51,500	45,600
Net property, plant and equipment	**607,000**	**370,000**	**263,400**
Total Assets	**729,600**	**493,900**	**391,500**
Liabilities and shareholders' equity			
Current liabilities			
Accounts payable	30,200	46,900	50,400
Accrued expenses	9,900	8,000	4,100
Total current liabilities	**40,100**	**54,900**	**54,500**
Long term liabilities			
Long-term debt	249,500	130,000	111,000
Long-term liabilities	**249,500**	**130,000**	**111,000**
Total liabilities	**289,600**	**184,900**	**165,500**
Shareholders' equity			
Common stock (100,000 shares)	10,000	10,000	10,000
Retained earnings	430,000	299,000	216,000
Total shareholders' equity	440,000	309,000	226,000
Total liabilities and shareholders' equity	729,600	493,900	391,500

this area is also positive. For the years 2002, 2003, and 2004, its current ratio has been 2.35, 2.26, and 3.06, respectively.

Computing a company's overall debt ratio will give us the answer to the second question, as it is a means of assessing a firm's overall financial soundness. A company's debt ratio is computed by dividing its total debt by its total assets. The present debt ratio for New Venture Fitness Drinks is 39.7 percent, meaning that 39.7 percent of its total assets are financed by debt and the remaining 60.3 percent by owners' equity. This is a healthy number for a young firm. The trend for New Venture Fitness Drinks in this area is also encouraging. For the years 2002, 2003, and 2004, its debt ratio has been 42.3, 37.4, and 39.7 percent, respectively. These figures indicate that, over time, the company is relying less on debt to finance its operations. In general, less debt creates more freedom for the entrepreneurial firm in terms of taking different actions.

The numbers across all the firm's financial statements are consistent with one another. Note that the $131,000 net income reported by New Venture Fitness Drinks on its 2004 income statement shows up as the difference between its 2004 and 2003 retained earnings on its 2004 balance sheet. This number would have been different if New Venture Fitness Drinks had paid dividends to its stockholders, but it paid no dividends in 2004. The company retained all of its $131,000 in earnings.

Statement of Cash Flows   The **statement of cash flows** summarizes the changes in a firm's cash position for a specified period of time and details why the change occurred. The statement of cash flows is similar to a month-end bank statement. It reveals how much cash

learning objective

6. Explain the purpose of a statement of cash flows.

is on hand at the end of the month as well as how the cash was acquired and spent during the month.

The statement of cash flows is divided into three separate activities: operating activities, investing activities, and financing activities. These activities, which are explained in the following list, are the activities from which a firm obtains and uses cash:

- *Operating activities:* **Operating activities** include net income (or loss), depreciation, and changes in current assets and current liabilities other than cash and short-term debt. A firm's net income, taken from its income statement, is the first line on the corresponding period's cash flow statement.
- *Investing activities:* **Investing activities** include the purchase, sale, or investment in fixed assets, such as real estate, equipment, and buildings.
- *Financing activities:* **Financing activities** include cash raised during the period by borrowing money or selling stock and/or cash used during the period by paying dividends, buying back outstanding stock, or buying back outstanding bonds.

Interpreting and analyzing cash flow statements takes practice. On the statement, the *uses* of cash are recorded as negative figures (which are shown by placing them in parentheses) and the *sources* of cash are recorded as positive figures. An item such as depreciation is shown as a positive figure on the statement of cash flow because it was deducted from net income on the income statement but was not a cash expenditure. Similarly, a decrease in accounts payable shows up as a negative figure on the cash flow statement because the firm used part of its cash to reduce its accounts payable balance from one period to the next.

The statement of cash flows for New Venture Fitness Drinks is shown in Table 7.3. As a management tool, it is intended to provide perspective on the following questions: Is the firm generating excess cash that could be used to pay down debt or returned to stockholders in the form of dividends? Is the firm generating enough cash to fund its investment

Table 7.3

Consolidated Statement of Cash Flows for New Venture Fitness Drinks, Inc. (all data in dollars)

	December 31, 2004	December 31, 2003
Cash flows from operating activities		
Net income	131,000	83,000
Additions (sources of cash)		
Depreciation	13,500	5,900
Decreases in accounts receivable	9,300	1,300
Increase in accrued expenses	1,900	3,900
Decrease in inventory	1,200	1,000
Subtractions (uses of cash)		
Decrease in accounts payable	(16,700)	(3,500)
Total adjustments	9,200	8,600
Net cash provided by operating activities	**140,200**	**91,600**
Cash flows from investing activities		
Purchase of building and equipment	(250,500)	(112,500)
Net cash flows provided by investing activities	**(250,500)**	(112,500)
Cash flows from financing activities		
Proceeds from increase in long-term debt	119,500	19,000
Net cash flows provided by financing activities		19,000
Increase in cash	9,200	(1,900)
Cash and cash equivalents at the beginning of year	54,600	56,500
Cash and cash equivalents at the end of the year	**63,800**	**54,600**

activities from earnings, or is it relying on lenders or investors? Is the firm generating sufficient cash to pay down its short-term liabilities, or are its short-term liabilities increasing as the result of an insufficient amount of cash?

Again, a multiperiod statement is created so that trends can easily be spotted. A large increase in a firm's cash balance is not necessarily a good sign. It could mean that the firm is borrowing heavily, is not paying down its short-term liabilities, or is accumulating cash that could be put to work for a more productive purpose. On the other hand, it is almost always prudent for a young firm to have a healthy cash balance.

Table 7.3 shows the consolidated statement of cash flows for New Venture Fitness Drinks for two years instead of three because it takes three years of balance sheets to produce two years of cash flow statements. The statements show that New Venture Fitness Drinks is funding its investment activities from a combination of debt and earnings while at the same time it is slowly decreasing its accounts receivable and inventory levels (which is good—these items are major drains on a company's cash flow). It is also steadily increasing its cash on hand. These are encouraging signs for a new venture.

Ratio Analysis   The most practical way to interpret or make sense of a firm's historical financial statements is through ratio analysis. Table 7.4 is a summary of the ratios used to evaluate New Venture Fitness Drinks during the time period covered by the previously provided financial statements. The ratios are divided into profitability ratios, liquidity ratios, and overall financial stability ratios. These ratios provide a means of interpreting the historical financial statements for New Venture Fitness Drinks and provide a starting point for forecasting the firm's financial performance and capabilities for the future.

Comparing a Firm's Financial Results to Industry Norms   Comparing its financial results to industry norms helps a firm determine how it stacks up against its competitors and if there are any financial "red flags" requiring attention. This type of comparison work best for firms that are of similar size so the results should be interpreted with caution by new firms. Many sources provide industry-related information. For example, Hoovers provides industry norms to which a new firm can compare itself, and is typically

learning **objective**

7. Discuss how financial ratios are used to analyze and interpret a firm's financial statements.

Table 7.4   Ratio Analysis for New Venture Fitness Drinks, Inc.

Profitability ratios: associate the amount of income earned with the resources used to generate it

Ratio	Formula	2004	2003	2002
Return on assets	ROA = net income/average total assets[a]	21.4%	18.7%	14.7%
Return on equity	ROE = net income/average shareholders' equity[b]	35.0%	31.0%	24.9%
Profit margin	Profit margin = net income/net sales	22.3%	17.9%	13.6%

Liquidity ratios: measures the extent to which a company can quickly liquidate assets to cover short-term liabilities

Ratio	Formula	2004	2003	2002
Current	Current assets/current liabilities	3.06	2.26	2.35
Quick	Quick assets/current liabilities	2.58	1.89	1.96

Overall financial stability ratio: measure the overall financial stability of a firm

Ratio	Formula	2004	2003	2002
Debt	Total debt/total assets	39.7%	37.4%	42.3%
Debt to Equity	Total liabilities/owners' equity	65.8%	59.8%	73.2%

[a] Average total assets = beginning total assets + ending total assets ÷ 2.

[b] Average shareholders' equity = beginning shareholders' equity + ending shareholders' equity ÷ 2.

free of charge if accessed from a university library that subscribes to Hoover's premium service. To access this information, simply go to *www.hoovers.com*. Hoovers also provides comparison data for publicly traded firms. For example, the comparison data for LeapFrog (discussed at the beginning of this chapter) for the 2003–2004 fiscal year is listed at Hoovers as follows:

Comparison Data (2003–2004 Fiscal Year)	LeapFrog	Industry Norms[a]	Market Norms[b]
Gross profit margin	50.78%	52.60%	49.42%
Net profit margin	9.16%	7.89%	5.26%
Return on equity (ROE)	15.1%	14.8%	10.6%
Return on assets (ROA)	12.0%	8.5%	1.8%
Current ratio (CR)	6.17%	2.33%	1.48%
12-month revenue growth	22.6%	5.4%	14.6%

[a] Industry: toys and games.
[b] All firms listed on the major stock exchanges.

These data cast LeapFrog in a favorable light and raise no immediate red flags. Reliable data are harder to come by for private firms. One source is BizStats (*http://bizstats.com*), a Web site that provides industry data in a variety of formats. Using information gleaned from BizStats, the owners of New Venture Fitness Drinks could make the following comparisons for its most current reporting period:

Comparison Data (Most Current Data Available)	New Venture Fitness Drinks	All LLCs and Partnerships[a]	Profitable Only
Sales	100%	100%	100%
Cost of sales	45.8%	40.0%	39.3%
Net operating income	22.3%	0.1%	9.6%
Current ratio	3.05%	0.9%	1.3%
Debt-to-equity ratio	0.65%	3.2%	1.7%

[a] Industry: eating and drinking establishments.

Note the comparison is for firms organized as LLCs (limited liability companies) and partnerships rather than publicly traded corporations (forms of business ownership are discussed in Chapter 8). These firms are more similar to New Venture Fitness Drinks than publicly traded firms. The comparisons cast New Venture Fitness Drinks in a positive light and raise no immediate red flags. Cost of sales is higher than industry norms, which may be attributed to the nutritionally laden ingredients that New Venture Fitness Drinks uses in its products. By collecting this information on a periodic basis, New Venture Fitness Drinks could keep track of how its numbers compare to industry norms over time. This type of analysis may be particularly important to New Venture Fitness Drinks as it grows, and the firm must continually assess how its growth is affecting its financials.

Forecasts

learning **objective**

8. Discuss the role of forecasts in projecting a firm's future income and expenses.

learning **objective**

9. Explain what a completely new firm bases its forecasts on.

As depicted in Figure 7.2, the analysis of a firm's historical financial statement is followed by the preparation of forecasts. Forecasts are predictions of a firm's future sales, expenses, income, and capital expenditures. A firm's forecasts provide the basis for its pro forma financial statements. A well-developed set of pro forma financial statements helps a firm create accurate budgets, build financial plans, and manage its finances in a proactive rather than a reactive manner.

As mentioned earlier, completely new firms typically base their forecasts on a good-faith estimate of sales and on industry averages (based on a percentage of sales) or the experiences of similar start-ups for cost of goods sold and other expenses. As a result, a completely new firm's forecast should be preceded in its business plan by an explanation of the sources of the numbers for the forecast and the assumptions used to generate them. This explanation is called an **assumption sheet**. Investors typically study assumption sheets like hawks to make sure the numbers contained in the forecasts and the resulting financial projections are realistic. For example, the assumption sheet for a new venture may say that its forecasts are based on selling 500 units of its new product the first year, 1,000 units the second year, and 1,500 units the third year and that its cost of goods sold will remain stable (meaning that it will stay fixed at a certain percentage of net sales) over the three-year period. It's up to the reader of the plan to determine if these numbers are realistic. If the reader feels they are not, then the credibility of the entire plan is called into question.

Sales Forecast A **sales forecast** is a projection of a firm's sales for a specified period (such as a year), though most firms forecast their sales for two to five years into the future.[15] It is the first forecast developed and is the basis for most of the other forecasts.[16] A sales forecast for an existing firm is based on (1) its record of past sales, (2) its current production capacity and product demand, and (3) any factor or factors that will affect its future production capacity and product demand. To demonstrate how a sales forecast works, Figure 7.3 is a graph of the past sales and the forecasted future sales for New Venture Fitness Drinks. The company's sales increased at a rate of about 26 percent per year from 2002 to 2004 as the company became established and more people became aware of its brand. In forecasting its sales for 2005 and 2006, the company took into consideration the following factors:

- The fitness craze in America continues to gain momentum and should continue to attract new people to try its fitness drinks.
- The interest in intramural sports, especially soccer, baseball, and softball, should continue to provide a high level of traffic for its restaurants, which are located near large intramural sports complexes.
- The company expanded from a single location in 2003 to two locations 2004 (the second restaurant was added in November of 2004), and this should increase its capacity to serve fitness drinks by approximately 50 percent. The second restaurant is smaller than the first and is located in an area where the company is not as well known. The company will be actively promoting the new restaurant but knows it will take time to win market share.
- The general economy in the city where the company is located is flat—it is neither growing nor shrinking. However, there are layoffs rumored by a larger employer near the location of the new restaurant.

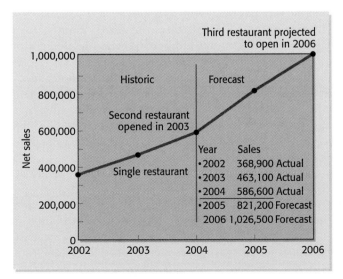

Figure 7.3

Historical and Forecasted Annual Sales for New Venture Fitness Drinks

The combination of these factors results in a forecast of 40 percent increase in sales from 2004 to 2005 and a 25 percent increase in sales from 2005 to 2006. It is extremely important for a company such as New Venture Drinks to forecast future sales as accurately as possible. If it overestimates the demand for its products, it might get stuck with excess inventory and spend too much on overhead. If it underestimates the demand for its product, it might have to turn away business, and some of its potential customers might get into the habit of buying other firms' fitness drinks.

Note that sophisticated tools are available to help firms project future sales. One approach is to use **regression analysis**, which is a statistical technique used to find relationships between variables for the purpose of predicting future values.[17] For example, if New Venture Fitness Drinks felt that its future sales were a function of its advertising expenditures, the number of people who participate in intramural sports at the sports complexes near its restaurants, and the price of its drinks, it could predict future sales using regression analysis as long as it had historical data for each of these variables. If the company used simpler logic and felt that its future sales would increase a certain percentage over its current sales, regression analysis could be used to generate a more precise estimate of future sales than was predicted from the information contained in Figure 7.3. For a new firm that has limited years of "annual data," monthly data could be used to project sales.

learning **objective**

10. Explain what is meant by the term "percent of sales method."

Forecast of Costs of Sales and Other Items

Once a firm has completed its sales forecast, it must forecast its cost of sales (or cost of goods sold) and the other items on its income statement. The most common way to do this is to use the **percent-of-sales method**, which is a method for expressing each expense item as a percentage of sales.[18] For example, in the case of New Venture Fitness Drinks, its cost of sales has averaged 47.5 percent of sales over the past two years. In 2004, its sales were $586,600, and its cost of sales was $268,900. The company's sales are forecast to be $821,200 in 2005. Therefore, based on the percent-of-sales method, its cost of sales in 2005 will be $390,000, or 47.5 percent of projected sales. The same procedure could be used to forecast the cost of each expense item on the company's income statement.

Once a firm completes its forecast using the percent-of-sales method, it usually goes through its income statement on an item-by-item basis to see if there are opportunities to make more precise forecasts. For example, a firm can typically closely estimate its depreciation expenses, so it might not use the percent-of-sales method to make a forecast for this item. In addition, some expense items are not tied to sales. For those items, reasonable estimates are made.

Obviously, a firm must apply common sense in using the percent-of-sales method. If a company is implementing cost-cutting measures, for example, it might be able to justify projecting a smaller percentage increase in expenses as opposed to sales. Similarly, if a firm hires an administrator, such as a chief financial officer, toward the end of the year and plans to pay the person $75,000 the next year, that $75,000 may have no immediate impact on sales. In this case, the firm's forecast for administrative expenses may have to be adjusted upward beyond what the percent-of-sales method would suggest.

If a firm determines that it can use the percent-of-sales method and it follows the procedure described previously, then the net result is that each expense item on its income statement (with the exception of those items that may be individually forecast, such as depreciation) will grow at the same rate as sales. This approach is called the **constant ratio method of forecasting**. This approach will be used in preparing the pro forma financial statements for New Venture Fitness Drinks in the next section.

A summary of the forecasts used to prepare the pro forma financial statements for New Venture Fitness Drinks is provided in Table 7.5.

One thing a new venture should guard itself against is becoming overly optimistic about cutting costs by switching to a supplier that promises to deliver the same quality at a lower cost or by buying supplies through a B2B (business-to-business) exchanges. Often, these tactics represent false hopes for cost savings, as illustrated in the boxed feature titled "What Went Wrong?"

Table 7.5

Forecasts Used to Prepare Pro Forma Financial Statements for New Venture Fitness Drinks, Inc.

Pro Forma Income Statements

Net sales
Historic	Average sales increase of 25% per year
2005	Increase to 40% as the result of increased brand awareness and the opening of a second service location
2006	Increase 25% as the result of increased brand awareness (a third service location will be opened late in the year)

Cost of goods sold (COGS)
Historic	Average of 47.5% of sales the past two years
2005	47.5% of sales
2006	47.5% of sales

Selling, general, and administrative expense
Historic	Average 22% of sales the past two years
2005	Increase to 25% of sales as the result of the opening of a second service location (the increase will not be any larger as the result of increased operating effiencies)
2006	25% of sales

Interest expense
Historic	6% to 7% of long-term debt
2005	7% of long-term debt
2006	7% of long-term debt

Other income
Historic	Licensing income of $10,900 per year
2005	Licensing income will increase to $20,000 as the result of the renegotiation of the licensing contract
2006	Licensing income will be $20,000

Pro Forma Balance Sheets

Accounts receivable
Historic	Accounts receivable have trended down to 7% of sales in 2003 from 13.6% of sales in 2001
2005	7% of sales
2006	7% of sales

Inventories
Historic	Inventories have trended down to 3.3% of sales in 2003 from 5.8% of sales in 2002
2005	4% of sales (reflecting slight increase over 2003 as the result of the opening of a second service location)
2006	4% of sales

Land, buildings, and equipment
2005	$100,000 in equipment purchases and capital improvements made to existing buildings
2006	$275,000 in capital improvements, including a $100,000 real estate purchase and $175,000 in buildings and equipment

Accounts payable
Historic	Accounts payable have trended down to 5% of sales in 2003 from 13.6% of sales in 2001 because of the implementation of more effective collection methods (a slightly higher level of accounts payable will be projected for the future)
2005	7% of sales
2006	7% of sales

Long-term debt
2005	$75,000 reduction in long-term debt from earnings
2006	$150,000 will be borrowed to finance $275,000 acquisition of land, equipment, and buildings (the balance of the acquisition costs will be funded from earnings)

what went **wrong?**

B2B Exchanges: A False Hope for Cost Savings?

A B2B (business-to-business) exchange is an online marketplace that connects the buyers and the sellers in an industry. The goal of these connections is to improve the efficiency of the supply chain and save money for everyone. ChemConnect, the company featured in Case 1.2 in Chapter 1, is an example of a B2B exchange. ChemConnect helps companies that purchase chemicals locate the suppliers they need and negotiate a favorable price. Over 89,000 companies around the world produce chemicals. True to the nature of an effective online exchange, ChemConnect has helped many companies find suppliers for the raw materials they need and buyers for the products they sell that they would never reach otherwise.

In the early days of e-commerce, experts predicted that B2B exchanges would change the way companies interacted with their buyers and suppliers. Unfortunately, the majority of online exchanges have not worked out as well as ChemConnect. In fact, a study conducted by George Day, Adam Fein, and Gregg Ruppersberger tracked the number of B2B exchanges from 1,500 in 2001 to fewer than 700 in 2002 to an estimated 180 in 2003. The study notes that this kind of shakeout has occurred in new technology markets before, but usually over a 20- to 30-year period. So what went wrong, so fast, with B2B exchanges?

Well, several things. First, even though many B2B exchanges were proficient in helping firms find the supplier with the lowest price, price isn't everything. Most suppliers want to establish a relationship with the companies they sell to rather than make a one-time sale motivated strictly by price. In fact, many advisers counsel firms to limit the number of their suppliers to develop trusting relationships and ensure the delivery of high-quality products or parts. B2B exchanges encourage just the opposite by emphasizing price as the most important buying criterion.

Second, rather than seeing B2B exchanges as making the supply chain more efficient, many firms see the exchanges as adding one more layer of cost. Once a supplier and seller get together and start doing business with each other, they can easily avoid the exchange and eliminate the exchange's commission. As Art Jahnke, writing in *CIO* magazine, put it,

Neither (the buyer and the seller) is prepared to dance to the tune of an intermediary who had a bright idea a few years back, and who wants to sit back and take a percentage forever.

Third, the technology involved with B2B exchanges seldom lived up to the promise. A common complaint from both buyers and sellers was the functionality of B2B Web sites.

Although some exchanges, such as ChemConnect, are doing well, the jury is still out on the future of B2B exchanges. The majority of the exchanges have not been able to overcome the obstacles described here and, in the end, have represented a false hope for cost savings.

Questions for Critical Thinking

1. Choose two companies in your community with which you are familiar. Make an appointment with a top-level manager in each company. Ask the managers to describe the criteria they deem most important when working with their suppliers. Is price the most important criterion for the people you are interviewing? If so, why? If not, are relationships important? If relationships are important to your interviewees, how do they go about establishing and maintaining those relationships?

2. Given the knowledge you've acquired from studying this book as well as from other academic courses and work experience, develop a list of advantages and disadvantages associated with entrepreneurs deciding to rely on B2B transactions. For entrepreneurs, do the advantages of B2B transactions outweigh the disadvantages, or is the reverse true, and why?

Sources: G. S. Day, A. J. Fein, and G. Ruppersberger, "Shakeouts in Digital Markets: Lessons from B2B Exchanges," California Management Review 45, no. 2 (winter 2003): 131–50, and A. Jahnke, "What Was Wrong with B2B Exchanges?," CIO, June 20, 2002.

Pro Forma Financial Statements

A firm's pro forma financial statements are similar to its historical financial statements except that they look forward rather than track the past. New ventures typically offer pro forma statements, but well-managed established firms also maintain these statements as part of their routine financial planning process and to help prepare budgets. The preparation of pro forma statements also helps firms rethink their strategies and make adjustments if necessary. For example, if the pro forma statements predict a downturn in prof-

	2004 Actual	2005 Projected	2006 Projected
Net sales	586,600	821,200	1,026,500
Cost of sales	268,900	390,000	487,600
Gross profit	317,700	431,200	538,900
Operating expenses			
Selling, general, and administrative expense	117,800	205,300	256,600
Depreciation	13,500	18,500	22,500
Operating income	186,400	207,400	259,800
Other income			
Interest income	1,900	2,000	2,000
Interest expense	(15,000)	(17,500)	(17,000)
Other income (expense), net	10,900	20,000	20,000
Income before income taxes	184,200	211,900	264,800
Income tax expense	53,200	63,600	79,400
Net income	131,000	148,300	185,400
Earnings per share	1.31	1.48	1.85

itability, a firm can make operational changes, such as increasing prices or decreasing expenses, to help prevent the decrease in profitability from actually happening.

A firm's pro forma financial statements should not be prepared in isolation. Instead, they should be created in conjunction with the firm's overall planning activities. The following sections explain the development of pro forma financial statements for New Venture Fitness Drinks.

Pro Forma Income Statement

Once a firm forecasts its future income and expenses, the creation of the **pro forma income statement** is merely a matter of plugging in the numbers. Table 7.6 shows the pro forma income statement for New Venture Fitness Drinks. Recall that net sales for New Venture Fitness Drinks' are forecast to increase by 40 percent from 2004 to 2005 and by 25 percent from 2005 to 2006 and that its cost of sales has averaged 47.5 percent of net sales. In the pro forma income statement, the constant ratio method of forecasting is used to forecast the cost of sales and general and administrative expense, meaning that these items are projected to remain at the same percentage of sales in the future as they were in the past (which is the mathematical equivalent of saying that they will increase at the same rate of sales). Depreciation, other income, and several other items that are not directly tied to sales are figured separately—using reasonable estimates. The most dramatic change is "other income," which jumps significantly from 2004 to 2005. New Venture Fitness Drinks anticipates a significant increase in this category as the result of the renegotiation of a licensing agreement for one of its fitness drinks that is sold by another company.

Pro Forma Balance Sheet

The **pro forma balance sheet** provides a firm a sense of how its activities will affect its ability to meet its short-term liabilities and how its finances will evolve over time. It can also quickly show how much of a firm's money will be tied up in accounts receivable, inventory, and equipment. The pro forma balance sheet is also used to project the overall financial soundness of a company. For example, a firm may have a very aggressive set of pro forma income statements that project rapidly increasing growth and profitability. However, if this rapid growth and profitability pushes the firm's debt ratio to 75 percent (which is extremely high), investors may conclude that there is too much risk involved for the firm to be an attractive investment.

The pro forma balance sheet for New Venture Fitness Drinks is shown in Table 7.7. Note that the company's projected change in retained earnings each year is consistent

Table 7.7

Assets	December 31, 2005	2005 Projected	2006 Projected
Current assets			
Cash and cash equivalents	63,800	53,400	80,200
Accounts receivable, less allowance			
for doubtful accounts	39,600	57,500	71,900
Inventories	19,200	32,900	41,000
Total current assets	**122,600**	**143,800**	**193,100**
Property, plant and equipment			
Land	260,000	260,000	360,000
Buildings and equipment	412,000	512,000	687,000
Total property, plant, and equipment	672,000	772,000	1,047,000
Less: accumulated depreciation	65,000	83,500	106,000
Net property, plant, and equipment	**607,000**	**688,500**	**941,000**
Total assets	**729.600**	**832,300**	**1,134,100**
Liabilities and shareholders' equity			
Current liabilities			
Accounts payable	30,200	57,500	71,900
Accrued expenses	9,900	12,000	14,000
Total current liabilities	**40,100**	**69,500**	**85,900**
Long-term liabilities			
Long-term debt	249,500	174,500	274,500
Total long-term liabilities	**249,500**	**174,500**	**274,500**
Total liabilities	**289,600**	**244,000**	**360,400**
Shareholders' equity			
Common stock (100,000 shares)	10,000	10,000	10,000
Retained earnings	430,000	578,300	763,700
Total shareholders' equity	440,000	588,300	773,700
Total liabilities and shareholders' equity	729,600	832,300	1,134,100

with its projected net income for the same period on its pro forma income statements. The same approach was used to construct the pro forma balance sheets as the pro forma income statements. For each item listed under current assets and current liabilities, the item's historical percentage of sales was used to project its future percentage of sales. Several of the numbers were adjusted slightly upward, such as inventory levels and accounts payable, to reflect the potential impact of the opening of the second restaurant.

In regard to property, plant, and equipment, New Venture Fitness Drinks plans to invest $100,000 in 2005 and $275,000 in 2006. The pro forma balance sheet shows a corresponding increase in valuation in this category for 2005 and 2006, respectively. The company's projected long-term debt for 2005 and 2006 reflects changes resulting from principal reductions from cash flow and increased borrowing to fund the property, plant, and equipment purchases just mentioned. These transactions are reflected in the pro forma statement of cash flows for New Venture Fitness Drinks.

Pro Forma Statement of Cash Flows

The **pro forma statement of cash flows** shows the projected flow of cash into and out of the company during a specified period. The most important function of the pro forma statement of cash flow is to project whether the firm will have sufficient cash to meet its needs. As with the historical statement of cash flows, the pro forma statement of cash flows is broken into three activities: operating activities, investing activities, and financing activities. Close attention is typically paid to the section on operating activities because it shows how changes in the company's accounts receivable, accounts payable, and inventory levels affect the cash that it has available for investing and finance activities. If any of these items

	December 31, 2004	Projected 2005	Projected 2006
Cash flows from operating activities			
Net income	131,000	148,300	185,400
Changes in working capital			
Depreciation	13,500	18,500	22,500
Increase (decrease) in accounts receivable	9,300	(17,900)	(14,400)
Increase (decrease) in accrued expenses	1,900	2,100	2,000
Increase (decrease) in inventory	1,200	(13,700)	(8,100)
Increase (decrease) in accounts payable	(16,700)`	27,300	14,400
Total adjustments	9,200	16,300	16,400
Net cash provided by operating activities	**140,200**	**164,600**	**201,800**
Cash flows from investing activities			
Purchase of building and equipment	(250,500)	(100,000)	(275,000)
Net cash flows provided by investing activities	**(250,500)**	**(100,000)**	**(275,000)**
Cash flows from financing activities			
Proceeds from increase in long-term debt	119,500	—	100,000
Principle reduction in long-term debt		(75,000)	
Net cash flows provided by financing activities			
Increase in cash	9,200	(10,400)	26,800
Cash and cash equivalents at the beginning of the year	54,600	63,800	53,400
Cash and cash equivalents at the end of the year	**63,800**	**53,400**	**80,200**

increases at a rate that is faster than the company's annual increase in sales, it typically raises a red flag. For example, an increase in accounts receivable, which is money that is owed to a company by its customers, decreases the amount of cash that it has available for investment or finance activities. If accounts receivable gets out of hand, it may jeopardize a company's ability to fund its growth or service its debt.

The pro forma consolidated statement of cash flows for New Venture Fitness Drinks is shown in Table 7.8. The figures appearing on the statement come directly, or are calculated directly, from the pro forma income statement and the pro forma balance sheet. The one exception is that the last line of each statement of cash flows, which reflects the company's cash balance at the end of the period, becomes the first line of the company's balance sheet for the next period. The pro forma statement of cash flows for New Venture Fitness Drinks shows healthy cash balances at the end of each projected period and shows that investment activities are being funded more by earnings than by debt. This scenario reflects a company that is generating sufficient cash flow to fund the majority of its growth without overly relying on debt.

In regard to dividends, the pro forma statement of cash flows shows that New Venture Fitness Drinks is not planning to pay a dividend to its stockholders in 2005 and 2006. Recall that New Venture Fitness Drinks is incorporated and has stockholders even through it is not traded on an organized exchange. If New Venture Fitness Drinks were planning to pay a dividend, the projected dividend payments would show up under financing activities and would reduce the amount of cash available for investing and financing activities. It is common for a new firm to invest the majority of its cash in activities that fund its growth, such as property, plant, and equipment purchases, rather than pay dividends.

Table 7.9

Ratio Analysis of Historical
and Pro Forma Financial Statements
for New Venture Fitness Drinks, Inc.

| | Historical | | | Projected | |
Ratio	2002	2003	2004	2005	2006
Profitability ratios					
Return on assets	14.7%	18.7%	21.4%	19.0%	18.9%
Return on equity	24.9%	31.0%	35.0%	28.9%	27.2%
Profit margin	13.6%	17.9%	22.3%	18.1%	18.1%
Liquidity ratios					
Current	2.35	2.26	3.05	2.07	2.24
Quick	1.96	1.89	2.58	1.60	1.78
Overall financial stability ratios					
Debt	42.3%	37.4%	39.7%	29.3%	31.8%
Debt to equity	73.2%	59.8%	65.8%	41.5%	46.6%

Ratio Analysis

The same financial ratios used to evaluate a firm's historical financial statements should be used to evaluate the pro forma financial statements. This work is completed so the firm can get a sense of how its projected financial performance compares to its past performance and how its projected activities will affect its cash position and its overall financial soundness.

The historical financial ratios and projected ratios for New Venture Fitness Drinks are shown in Table 7.9. The profitability ratios show a slight decline from the historical period to the projected. This indicates that the projected increase in assets and corresponding sales will not produce income quite as efficiently as has been the case historically. Still, the numbers are strong, and no dramatic changes are projected.

The liquidity ratios show a consistently healthy ratio of current assets to current liabilities, suggesting that the firm should be able to cover its short-term liabilities without difficulty. The overall financial stability ratios indicate promising trends. The debt ratio drops from an actual of 39.7 percent in 2004 to a projected 31.8 percent in 2006. The debt-to-equity ratio shows an even more dramatic drop, indicating that an increasing portion of the firm's assets is being funded by equity rather than debt.

In summary, it is extremely important for a firm to understand its financial position at all times and for new ventures to base their financial projections on solid numbers. As mentioned earlier, regardless of how successful a firm is in other areas, it must succeed financially to remain strong and viable.

CHAPTER SUMMARY

1. Financial management deals with two things: raising money and managing a company's finances in a way that achieves the highest rate of return.

2. Profitability, liquidity, efficiency, and stability are the four main financial objectives of entrepreneurial firms.

3. Historical financial statements reflect past performance. Pro forma financial statements are projections for expected performance in future periods.

4. An income statement reflects the results of a firm's operations over a specified period of time. It records all the revenues and expenses for the given period and shows whether the firm is making a profit or is experiencing a loss.

5. A balance sheet is a snapshot of a company's assets, liabilities, and owners' equity.

6. A statement of cash flows summarizes the changes in a firm's cash position for a specified period of time.

7. Financial ratios depict relationships between items on a firm's financial statement and are used to discern whether a firm is meeting its financial objectives and how it stacks up against its competitors.

8. Forecasts are predictions of a firm's future sales, expenses, income, and capital expenditures. A firm's forecasts provide the basis for its pro forma financial statements.

9. Completely new firms typically base their forecasts on a good-faith estimate of sales and on industry averages (based on a percentage of sales) or the experiences of similar start-ups for cost of goods sold and other expenses.

10. Once a firm has completed its sales forecast, it must forecast its costs of sales as well as the other items on its income statement. The most common way to do this is to use the percent-of-sales method, which is a method for expressing each expense item as a percentage of sales.

KEY TERMS

accounts receivable, 149

assumption sheet, 161

balance sheet, 155

budgets, 150

constant ratio method of forecasting, 162

cost of sales, 154

current assets, 155

current liabilities, 155

current ratio, 155

debt-to-equity ratio, 150

efficiency, 149

financial management, 148

financial ratios, 151

financial statements, 150

financing activities, 158

fixed assets, 155

forecasts, 150

historical financial statements, 152

income statement, 154

inventory, 149

investing activities, 158

liquidity, 149

long-term liabilities, 155

net sales, 154

operating activities, 158

operating expenses, 154

other assets, 155

owners' equity, 155

P/E, 155

percent-of-sales method, 162

pro forma balance sheet, 165

pro forma financial statements, 153

pro forma income statement, 165

pro forma statement of cash flows, 166

profit margin, 154

profitability, 149

regression analysis, 162

sales forecast, 161

stability, 150

statement of cash flows, 157

10-K, 152

working capital, 155

REVIEW QUESTIONS

1. What are the two primary functions of the financial management of a firm?

2. What are the four main financial objectives of a firm?

3. Why is it important for a company to focus on its liquidity? What special challenges do entrepreneurial firms have in regard to remaining liquid?

4. What is meant by the term "efficiency" as it relates to the financial management of a firm?

5. What is meant by the term "stability" as it relates to the financial management of a firm?

6. What is the purpose of a forecast? What factors does a firm use to create its forecasts of future income and expenses?

7. On what factors or conditions do completely new firms base their forecasts?

8. What is the purpose of an income statement? What are the three numbers that receive the most attention when

evaluating an income statement? Why are these numbers important?

9. How does a firm compute its profit margin? What is the significance of this ratio?

10. How does a firm compute its price-to-earnings ratio? Why does a high price-to-earnings ratio indicate that the stock market thinks the firm will grow?

11. What is the purpose of a balance sheet?

12. What are the major categories of assets and liabilities on a balance sheet? Briefly explain each category.

13. What is meant by the term "working capital"? Why is working capital an important consideration for entrepreneurial firms?

14. How does a firm compute its current ratio? Is this a relatively important or unimportant financial ratio? Explain your answer.

15. What is the purpose of a statement of cash flows?

16. What are the three separate categories of activities that are reflected on a firm's statement of cash flows? Briefly explain the importance of each activity.

17. What is the purpose of financial ratios? Why are financial ratios particularly useful in helping a firm interpret its financial statements?

18. What is the purpose of an assumption sheet?

19. Describe why a firm's sales forecast is the basis for most of the other forecasts.

20. Explain what is meant by the percentage of sales method as it relates to forecasts.

APPLICATION QUESTIONS

1. Trevor Smith has developed a new wireless application that he feels will revolutionize the communications industry. He has been turned down by several potential investors who seemed to like his idea but who insisted on seeing pro forma financial statements as part of a business plan. Trevor doesn't think it's a good use of time to develop pro forma financial statements. He believes, "If the product is good enough, the financials will take care of themselves." Why is Trevor's thinking unwise? In your opinion, how common is the position Trevor is taking about financial statements?

2. Kirsten, a friend of yours, plans to start a business in the advertising industry. She told you that she leafed through several books on how to prepare forecasts and pro forma financial statements but that the books were geared toward existing firms that have several years of historical financial statements on which to base their projections. If Kirsten asked you your advice for how to prepare forecasts for a completely new firm in the advertising industry, what would you tell her?

3. Dustin Berg is the owner of a company, located in Oxford, Mississippi, that sells security systems to the owners of luxury cars. He keeps good records but has never completed financial statements. He wants to expand his business and has been told that he'll need both historical and pro forma financial statements to complete a business plan. Dustin isn't sure he understands the difference between historical and pro forma financial statements. If he asked you to explain the distinction, what would you tell him?

4. Sheila Clark just retired from a career with British Petroleum, cashing out a sizable retirement fund at the time of doing so. To start a second career, she is looking at the possibility of buying three different businesses. She has the historical financial statements for each business and has been poring over the numbers. She was puzzled when she read this footnote attached to one of the balance sheets: "Assets are valued at purchase price rather than fair market value." If Sheila asked you to explain this statement, what would you tell her?

5. Jarrett Baker is the founder of an enterprise software company located in Philadelphia. By looking at the income statements for Jarrett's business over the past three years, you see that its working capital has declined

from $42,400 in 2002 to $17,900 in 2003 to $3,100 in 2004. If this trend continues, in what ways could it jeopardize the future of Jarrett's business?

6. Casey Cordell is the owner of a digital photography service in Madison, Wisconsin. The company has been profitable every year of its existence. Its debt ratio is currently 68 percent, its current ratio is 1.1, and its debt-to-equity ratio is 72.2 percent. Do these financial numbers cause any reason to be concerned? Why or why not?

7. Go to Hoovers (*www.hoovers.com*) and analyze how the financials of Panera Bread, the company that is the focus of Case 4.1 in Chapter 4, compare to other firms in the restaurant industry in the same manner as LeapFrog was compared to other firms in the toy industry in this chapter. Evaluate the financial performance of Panera Bread as it compares to industry norms.

8. Megan Mesker owns a company that is in the health services industry. She is planning to expand her business and is working on a business plan to present to investors. A friend of Megan's suggested that she compare the past financial results of her firm to industry norms. Megan is not sure why her friend made that suggestion and doesn't know where to start to find the relevant information. If Megan asked you for your assistance, how would you help her?

9. Josh Lee has owned a fitness center for the past four years. He has historical financial statements but has never put together a set of pro forma financial statements. He just applied for a bank loan and has been told he needs a set of pro forma financial statements for the next two years. If Josh asked you to help him, how would you tell him to proceed?

10. Brenda Wilson owns a restaurant chain named Rhapsody Cuisine. She is planning to expand her chain from nine restaurants to 15. Brenda is now working to put together a set of pro forma financial statements for an investor who expressed interest in her expansion project. Brenda used a combination of common sense and industry norms to project her future income and expenses. Shortly after she submitted the financial statement, she received them back, with a handwritten note from the investor, who wrote, "I'm comfortable with your sales forecasts but think you would be on firmer ground if you used the percent-of-sales method to forecast expenses. Please redo the statements." If Brenda asked you what the investor was talking about, what would you tell her?

you be the VC

Company: Teeccino
(www.teeccino.com)

Business idea: Produce an herbal drink that brews, smells, and tastes like coffee but is caffeine free.

Pitch: Many people love the taste and aroma of coffee but can't tolerate caffeine and don't care for the taste of decaffeinated coffee. Even for people who can tolerate caffeine, there is increasing evidence that caffeine can have undesirable side effects, such as stress, fatigue, blood sugar swings, acid indigestion, and trouble sleeping. Many people tolerate these side effects, however, because they don't want to give up coffee. Teeccino (which is a takeoff on the word "cappuccino") produces a caffeine-free herbal coffee that the company says is the world's first caffeine-free match for robust, roasted coffee. Teeccino's herbal coffee drips and brews just like regular coffee and has a rich, Mediterranean flavor. The caffeine-free herbal coffee is sold

online and through health food stores and other retail outlets. Teeccino is a very socially conscious firm. The company was launched in the mid-1990s and is now in the growth stage of its life cycle. It sells its products online, through health food stores, and through other retail outlets. All of Teeccino's beverages are made from ingredients that are natural and sugar free.

Q&A: Based on the material covered in this chapter, what questions would you ask the founders of this firm before making your funding decision? What answers would satisfy you?

Decision: If you had to make your decision on just the information provided in the pitch and the company's Web site, would you fund this firm? Why or why not?

Case 7.1

Dell Inc.: How Its Business Model Sweetens Its Financial Statements
www.dell.com

As we've mentioned in other chapters, there are many reasons that Dell Inc.'s sales approach has been so successful. One of the most profound is the impact that selling directly to the end user has had on Dell's financial structure. Conventionally, a business forecasts its demand and then schedules its production. The sales forecast that it sets reverberates throughout the supply chain. A company such as Hewlett-Packard (HP) shares its forecasts with its component manufacturers, which set their production schedules accordingly. If sales fall short, everyone gets stuck with inventory that's hard to unload. If fact, an often-told joke in the PC industry is that unsold inventory is like unsold vegetables—it spoils quickly. If sales go better than expected, everyone has to scramble to meet demand. Think of the financial implications that this way of doing business has for computer manufacturers and their suppliers. Forecasting, inventory levels, and unsold, obsolete products are just some of the challenges.

Dell's business model sidesteps these problems through its direct-sales approach. Building to order means producing a unit after the customer's order is transmitted to the factory floor. There's not much forecasting to do because the tempo of sales is determined in real time. Component suppliers who also build

to order get information electronically from Dell as customers place orders. They deliver parts that Dell quickly places into production. Shippers, such as UPS and FedEx, eagerly cart the products away as soon as they exit the production process. This process compresses the amount of time it takes from order to delivery and forces everyone in the supply chain to be extremely efficient. Dell can take an order, build a computer, and have it to its customer within a week. Now think about the financial implications of doing business *this* way. Dell has very little forecasting to do and has little inventory to worry about. It gets its money before rather than after the sale. And it can focus its attention on manufacturing and customer service rather than trying to find ways to unload stale inventory.

As an added benefit, Dell's model significantly improves its inventory turnover, which is an important financial metric for an assembly company. Inventory turnover is determined by the following formula:

$$\text{Inventory Turnover} = \frac{\text{Cost of Good Sold}}{\text{Average Inventories}}$$

A high inventory turnover means that a company is converting its inventory into cash quickly. Dell turns its inventory over about 80 times a year, compared with about 60 to 70 times a year for its competitors. This advantage enables Dell to generate a tremendous amount of cash that it uses to fund its growth.

Along with crunching numbers, savvy managers assess the impact of their financial strategies on their overall goals and levels of customer satisfaction. Ultimately, it doesn't matter that a company has pretty financial statements if its customers are starting to go elsewhere. Dell's business model shines in this area too. Because it turns its inventory over quickly, it offers its customers the latest technologies rather than saddling them with products that are going out of date. It can also pass along the advantages of falling component costs quicker than its competitors can.

It's hard to quantify how much long-term benefit a firm receives by passing along advantages to its customers. Positive "buzz" is a hard thing to put a price tag on. If you were the CEO of HP or IBM, it would also be hard to know how to respond. Companies such as HP can't simply scrap unsold inventory just because it's getting a little out of date. And Dell doesn't have unsold inventory sitting at Best Buy or Circuit City to worry about.

Dell's business model illustrates how the financial management of a firm is intimately tied to what the firm is doing in its other areas. In Dell's case, its business model sweetens its financials, making its most compelling customer satisfaction measures feasible.

Discussion Questions

1. To what extent do you think it is difficult for PC manufacturers to forecast future sales?

2. Investigate the financial ratio of inventory turnover. Find current information about Dell (www.hoovers.com is a good starting place) and report whether its inventory turnover is still as impressive as the number mentioned in the case. How does Dell's current inventory turnover ratio compare to that of its competitors?

3. Locate Dell's most recent 10-K and compute the financial ratios for Dell that are shown in Table 7.4. Comment on Dell's strength or weakness as suggested by these ratios.

4. If you were the CEO of HP, how would you respond to Dell's direct approach to selling?

Case 7.2

Managing the Left Side as Well as the Right Side of the Balance Sheet

Many firms focus on managing their liabilities, or the right side of their balance sheet. By closely managing its liabilities, a firm can build a healthy working capital balance, keep its overall debt ratio low, and make sure its accounts payable are paid on time. Along with managing the right side of their balance sheets, however, firms must manage the left side, or the assets side, too. By reducing the assets they need to produce a dollar of sales, firms can reduce their need for debt, improve their cash flow, and increase their overall profitability.

There are many ways firms do this, and the possibilities are limited only by the imagination. For example, Netflix, the online DVD subscription service, stocks almost every title available on DVD—one of the most appealing aspects of its business model. Paradoxically, the company doesn't own a large inventory of DVDs. Instead, it has revenue sharing agreements with over 50 studios and distributors that provide DVDs in exchange for a share of the subscription revenue. Similarly, eBags, an online retailer of name-brand bags, sells nearly 8,000 different backpacks, suitcases, and other bags. The company, however, stocks very little of what it sells. When it receives an order, it is electronically transmitted to the manufacturer or the distributor of the product who ships the item directly to the purchaser through a process called "drop shipping." The product is even shipped in boxes with the eBags logo. This approach lets eBags offer a huge selection of products without the cost and risk of maintaining a large inventory. "It's probably one of the most important reasons why we survived," says eBags cofounder Peter Cobb.

Other firms have been equally creative in finding ways to minimize the amount of assets they need to grow their operations. For example, the reservation agents for airlines JetBlue and Midwest Air work out of their homes instead of in company facilities. This approach allows JetBlue and Midwest Air to avoid the cost of building, purchasing, or leasing office space for these employees. Sometimes the insights into how to minimize expenses come more by accident than by deliberate planning. For example, in the mid-1990s, Cisco Systems started using an Internet-based system that provided its customers the opportunity to post technical problems and questions for the Cisco tech staff to answer. What the company didn't expect was that as soon as the posting capability was made available, its customers started responding to each other's questions. A single posting would often prompt several suggestions, solutions, and work-arounds without ever involving a Cisco engineer. As a result of this phenomenon, Cisco was able to get through its explosive growth years without significantly bolstering its call center staff. In fact, if it weren't for this site, a Cisco executive once determined, the company would have had to hire up to 10,000 engineers to maintain pace with answering the volume of questions that its customers answered for each other. Similarly, eBay doesn't have to hire a staff of people to monitor the performance of its buyers and sellers. Buyers and sellers rate each other, and the cumulative ratings are posted on eBay's Web site.

There is also a large amount of outsourcing that is done by entrepreneurial firms, in part to reduce the amount of staff and assets they have to maintain. Outsourcing is work done by someone other than a firm's full-time employees. According to a recent PricewaterhouseCoopers survey of fast-growing firms, 70 percent of the firms that participated in the survey reported that they save money outsourcing. The most common activities that are outsourced are administrative activities, such as payroll and benefits management, and internal operations, such as building maintenance and information technology services. Most companies, according to the survey, outsource to save money and to gain access to technical expertise. Although a controversial practice in the United States, largely because many jobs are being outsourced to companies in other nations, outsourcing can contribute to an entrepreneurial firm's success, especially during its infancy.

Finally, firms reduce the amount of assets they need through alliances and other types of partnerships. By partnering with a larger firm, a smaller firm can in effect co-opt a portion of the larger firm's resources and managerial expertise. An example is Pixar's former alliance with Disney. At the time Pixar made *Toy Story* (its first full-length animated film), it needed money to finance production costs. Disney provided the money for the production of *Toy Story* in exchange for a percentage of the profits. Although Disney and Pixar have ended their partnership, the partnership played an important role in Pixar's success during the 1990s. Similar arrangements are common in the biotech industry. In fact, the vast majority of biotech firms would never be able to fund the years of research and development it takes to develop a new drug without access to the financial resources of large drug companies through revenue-sharing agreements. Firms in all industries can often benefit as much by managing their assets as they do by managing their liabilities.

Discussion Questions

1. Describe the items that receive the most scrutiny on the left side and the right side of a firm's balance sheet. In regard to each of these items, what are the most important factors that a new venture should focus on to maintain its overall financial health?

2. Make a list of the ways that the firms mentioned in the case have saved money by minimizing the amount of assets they need to produce revenues or maintain customer satisfaction. Next to each item in your list, briefly comment on how important this item is to the overall competitive advantage of the firm.

3. Make a list of the advantages and disadvantages of Netflix's strategy of avoiding the cost of owning DVDs through revenue-sharing agreements with major studios and distributorships.

4. What are the potential downsides of eBag's strategy of acting strictly as a storefront and allowing the manufacturers and distributors of the products it sells to ship the products to its customers?

Sources: Netflix, 10-K (filed with the SEC on March 31, 2003); D. Fuscaldo, Looking Big: How Can Online Retailers Carry So Many Products?," Wall Street Journal, April 28, 2003; Wolff, The Biotech Investor's Bible (New York: John Wiley & Sons, 2001); D. Bunnell, Making the Cisco Connection (New York: John Wiley & Sons, 2000); and A. Deutschman, The Second Coming of Steve Jobs (New York: Broadway Books, 2000).

eight

preparing the proper
ethical and legal
foundation

After studying this chapter, you should be ready to:

1. Identify the two most important issues to consider when leaving an employer.

2. Discuss the importance of nondisclosure and noncompete agreements.

3. Explain the criteria important in selecting an attorney for a new firm.

4. Discuss the importance of a founders' agreement.

5. Provide several suggestions for how new firms can avoid litigation.

6. Discuss techniques entrepreneurs use to promote high standards of business ethics in their firms.

7. Discuss the differences between sole proprietorships, partnerships, corporations, and limited liability companies.

8. Explain why most fast-growth entrepreneurial firms organize as corporations or limited liability companies rather than sole proprietorships or partnerships.

9. Explain double taxation.

10. Explain the importance of the Electronic Signatures in Global and International Commerce Act.

getting off to a good start:
ethical and legal considerations in launching a new firm

Tom, Jennifer, and Taylor work for Nokia, the international cell phone company. The three have developed a plan to produce handheld devices designed for college students. The devices would be similar to Palm Pilots but would have special capabilities for students, such as the ability to download PowerPoint slides and a voice recognition program to use to transcribe classroom lectures. The devices, which would be called Study Pals, would also include a wireless option that would enable students to send and receive e-mail and instant message with classmates and friends. All three entrepreneurs are eager to leave Nokia to start the firm. The name they have picked for the company is Pegasus Computing. The logo, which has yet to be designed, will resemble Pegasus,

the mythical winged horse from Greek mythology.

On the advice of a colleague, the three decide to see an attorney before proceeding further with their idea and intentions to form an entrepreneurial firm. They contact a highly reputable law firm and are directed to an attorney specializing in business start-ups. The attorney, Jim Branson, listens to their idea and tells them that he is glad they came in, as there are at least three issues to be addressed before they go further. He also advises them not to quit their jobs before resolving these issues.

First, Mr. Branson tells them that if they leave Nokia, it will be important to leave in an ethical manner to protect their reputations and to avoid putting the new venture in jeopardy. In addition, he tells them that their legal right to work on their new product idea while at Nokia (or even for a period of time after they quit) will depend on the written agreements they have with Nokia and how closely their new handheld device resembles products on which they are working at Nokia. To investigate these issues, Mr. Branson asks Tom, Jennifer, and Taylor to obtain copies of their employment contracts, including any noncompete and nondisclosure agreements they have signed, for his review. When asked by Jennifer, "Do you think we have a problem in this area?" Mr. Branson replies, "It's impossible to know without reading the agreements you have signed. I have noticed that cell phones and handheld devices look more like one another every day. That might work to your disadvantage. Most technology companies require their employees to sign noncompete agreements, meaning that you can't compete with your former employer for a specific period of time after you quit your job. If it looks like your device will compete against something that you've been working on at Nokia, you may have a problem."

Second, Mr. Branson asks Tom, Jennifer, and Taylor if they have discussed how they plan to split the ownership and the responsibilities associated with the new firm. He tells them that when more than one person launches a firm, he recommends that a "founders' agreement" be drafted. A founders' agreement specifies how the equity in the firm will be split and how things will be handled if one founder dies or leaves the firm. He also tells them that if they pro-ceed, he will need to talk to them about the legal form of business ownership most appropriate for their firm. Tom interjects, "We plan to incorporate from day one." Mr. Branson answers, "That's probably a good idea, but let's take it one step at a time. There are different forms of corporations, and there are other alternatives, such as a limited liability company, that achieve many of the same objectives. When we get to that point, I'll explain to you your options, and you can make an informed decision."

Finally, Mr. Branson tells the three not to get too committed to Pegasus Computing, the name they have selected for the company, or to Study Pal, the name they have chosen for their first product. The reason for these cautions, he notes, is that he will have to conduct a trademark search to see if the names are available for an electronics company. He also tells them that there are many intellectual property issues they need to talk about in their next meeting regarding patents, trademarks, copyrights, and trade secrets. Taylor, acting a little surprised, says, "I never realized there were so many legal issues involved with starting a firm." Mr. Branson looks up from his legal pad and says, "You don't know the half of it, but at least you're here. I had a client in a couple of weeks ago who had quit his job at PeopleSoft, only to find out that his noncompete agreement will prevent him from starting the company he's interested in for 18 months. He was heartsick. At least we're getting started early. I can guide you through the process and help you avoid any costly mistakes."

The ethical and legal challenges involved with starting a firm are complicated. It is extremely important that entrepreneurs understand these issues and avoid costly mistakes. This chapter begins by discussing the most important initial ethical and legal issues facing a new firm, including ethically departing from an employer, choosing a lawyer for the new firm, drafting a founders' agreement, and avoiding litigation. The chapter next discusses the different forms of business organization, including sole proprietorships, partnerships, corporations, and limited liability companies. The chapter concludes with a focus on the legal environment surrounding the Internet.

Chapter 12 discusses the protection of intellectual property through patents, trademarks, copyrights and trade secrets. This topic, which is also a legal issue, is becoming increasingly important as entrepreneurs rely more on intellectual property rather than physical property to gain a competitive advantage.

Initial Ethical and Legal Issues Facing a New Firm

As the opening case suggests, new ventures must deal with important ethical and legal issues at the time of their launching. Ethical and legal errors made early on can be extremely costly for a new venture down the road. And there is a tendency for entrepreneurs to overestimate their knowledge of the law. In one study, researchers examined the information that some 279 early-stage entrepreneurs sought from a Small Business Student

Legal Clinic. They concluded that entrepreneurs underestimate the amount of legal support they will need in the early stages of launching a business. In fact, 44 percent of the new ventures in the study altered or abandoned their original business strategy after they obtained a fuller understanding of the legal issues involved.[1] In a similar study, 254 small retailers and service company owners were asked to judge the legality of several business practices.[2] A sample of the practices included in the survey is shown next. Which practices do you think are legal, and which ones do you think aren't legal?

- Avoiding social security payments for independent contractors
- Hiring only experienced help
- Preempting potential competition with prices below costs
- Agreeing to divide market with rivals

The first two practices are legal, while the second two are illegal. How did you do? For comparison purposes, you might want to know that the participants in the survey were wrong 35 percent of the time about these four practices.

Neither of these studies implies that entrepreneurs break the law intentionally or that they do not have ethical intentions. What the studies do imply is that entrepreneurs tend to overestimate their knowledge of the legal complexities involved with starting and running a business. Against this backdrop, the following sections discuss several of the most important ethical and legal issues facing the founders of new firms.

Ethically Departing from an Employer

Although some entrepreneurial firms are started by students or by self-employed individuals, people holding traditional jobs start the majority of new ventures. After leaving a job to start a new firm, many entrepreneurs are surprised to find themselves in the midst of a dispute with their former employer. Recall the situation in the opening case. If Tom, Jennifer, and Taylor left Nokia to start a company to make handheld devices, Nokia might see the new company as a potential competitor and try to stop them from proceeding. Nokia might point to noncompete agreements signed by the founders or, worse, argue that the founders developed the technology for their new product in Nokia labs during their employment. Both claims would pit Tom, Jennifer, and Taylor against Nokia, which is probably the last thing they want. A better approach for the three would be to avoid an argument with Nokia by carefully laying the groundwork for departing their employer in an ethical manner. The following are the two most important guidelines when leaving an employer.

learning **objective**

1. Identify the two most important issues to consider when leaving an employer.

Behave in a Professional Manner   First, it is important that an employee give proper notice of an intention to quit and that the employee perform all assigned duties until the day of departure. Quitting on a moment's notice typically doesn't sit well with an employer. In addition, an employee shouldn't spend the last few days on a job making arrangements for the launch of the new venture. This type of behavior is unprofessional and is an improper use of the current employer's time and resources.

If an employee is leaving a job to start a firm in the same industry, it is vital that he or she not take information that belongs to the current employer. Employers have a right to protect their trade secrets (e.g., client lists, marketing plans, product prototypes, and acquisition strategies) from theft or from inappropriate transfer by an employee from the office to his or her home. In addition, an employee should be aware of the general spirit of the law regarding loyalty and employer–employee relationships. According to the legal principle referred to as the **corporate opportunity doctrine**, key employees (such as officers, directors, or managers) and skilled employees (such as software engineers, accountants, and marketing specialists) owe a special duty of loyalty to their employer.[3] The corporate opportunity doctrine most often kicks in when an employee diverts to him- or herself an opportunity that rightfully belongs to the employer. An employee may make plans to compete with an employer while still on the job (on off-duty time) but may not divert opportunities, solicit employees to work for the new business, or actually start a competing business until the employment relationship has ended.[4]

To leave a job ethically and pleasantly and to avoid any suspicion of inappropriate behavior, a departing employee should follow the practices shown in Table 8.1.

Table 8.1

Practices to Follow When Leaving a Job

1. Give notice of an intention to leave a job at least two weeks in advance.
2. Remain committed to your current job until you leave. Do not spend time on your current job making arrangements for your new venture.
3. Don't talk to coworkers about joining your new firm until you have left your job and get the go-ahead from your attorney.
4. Don't redirect business opportunities that belong to your current employer to your new firm while you are still employed by your current employer.
5. Don't actually start your new firm while you are still employed by your current employer, especially if your new firm competes in any way with your current employer.
6. Take nothing with you except your personal belongings. Don't spend a lot of time at the copy machine or in your office after hours regardless of how innocent your activity may be.
7. Don't use the e-mail account provided by your current employer to make arrangements for the new business even if you're using the account after hours.
8. Do everything you can to prevent the impression that you're taking any information from your current employer. Don't do anything out of the ordinary.

learning **objective**

2. Discuss the importance of nondisclosure and noncompete agreements.

Honor All Employment Agreements   It is also important that an employee be fully aware of the employment agreements that he or she has signed and honor them. In most cases, key employees have signed nondisclosure and noncompete agreements. A **nondisclosure agreement** is a promise made by an employee or another party (such as a supplier) to not disclose the company's trade secrets. An employee should strictly adhere to this document during employment and after he or she leaves a firm. Many employees have also signed a **noncompete agreement**, which prevents an individual from competing against a former employer for a specific period of time. In making an ethical departure from a firm, an employee should adhere to this agreement if one has been signed.

Sometimes, regardless of how careful an individual is to make an ethical departure from a former employer, disputes arise. An example might be someone who leaves a personal finance software company to start a company that makes financial management software for small businesses. The personal software company may sue the former employee for violation of his or her noncompete agreement on the basis of the argument that some small businesses use its personal finance software rather than more expensive business software. An attorney can help an entrepreneur anticipate and avoid such claims and help mount a defense if one is necessary.

A sample nondisclosure and noncompete agreement is shown in Figure 8.1.

Choosing an Attorney for the New Firm

learning **objective**

3. Explain the criteria important in selecting an attorney for a new firm.

It is important for an entrepreneur to select an attorney as early as possible when developing a business venture. Table 8.2 provides guidelines to consider when selecting an attorney. It is critically important that the attorney be familiar with start-up issues and that he or she has successfully shepherded entrepreneurs through the start-up process before. It is not wise to select an attorney just because she is a friend or because you were pleased with the way she prepared your will.

Entrepreneurs often object to the expense of hiring an attorney when there are many books, Web sites, and other resources that can help entrepreneurs address legal issues on their own. However, these alternatives should be chosen with extreme caution. Reflect on the contents of the opening case. What if the three Nokia employees hadn't gone to an attorney and it never occurred to them to check their noncompete agreements before proceeding with their new venture idea? They could have quit their jobs, hired employees, raised money, and started producing handheld devices, only to be sued by Nokia for violating their noncompete agreements. But their attorney alerted them to this possibility. After reviewing the agreements, the attorney may tell them that it's not a problem, tell them to drop the idea, or help them position their new venture in a way that is unlikely to prompt a negative response from Nokia.

Figure 8.1

Sample Nondisclosure and Noncompete Agreement

Nondisclosure and Noncompetition. (a) At all times while this agreement is in force and after its expiration or termination, [employee name] agrees to refrain from disclosing [company name]'s customer lists, trade secrets, or other confidential material. [Employee name] agrees to take reasonable security measures to prevent accidental disclosure and industrial espionage.

(b) While this agreement is in force, the employee agrees to use [his/her] best efforts to [describe job] and to abide by the nondisclosure and noncompetition terms of this agreement; the employer agrees to compensate the employee as follows: [describe compensation]. After expiration or termination of this agreement, [employee name] agrees not to compete with [company name] for a period of [number] years within a [number] mile radius of [company name and location]. This prohibition will not apply if this agreement is terminated because [company] violated the terms of this agreement.

Competition means owning or working for a business of the following type: [specify type of business employee may not engage in]

(c) [Employee name] agrees to pay liquidated damages in the amount of $[dollar amount] for any violation of the covenant not to compete contained in subparagraph (b) of this paragraph.

IN WITNESS WHEREOF, [company name] and [employee name] have signed this agreement.

_____
[company name]

_____
[employee's name]
Date: _____

Source: Office Depot

Figure 8.1

Sample Nondisclosure and Noncompete Agreement

Many attorneys recognize that start-ups are short on cash and will work out an installment plan or other payment arrangement to get the firm the legal help it needs without starving it of cash. This is particularly true if the attorney senses that the new venture has good potential and may develop into a steady client in the future. There are also ways for entrepreneurs to save on legal fees and to increase the value of their

Table 8.2

How to Select an Attorney

1. Contact the local bar association and ask for a list of attorneys who specialize in business start-ups in your area.

2. Interview several attorneys. Check references. Ask your prospective attorney whom he or she has guided through the start-up process before and talk to the attorney's clients. If an attorney is reluctant to give you the names of past or present clients, select another attorney.

3. Select an attorney who is familiar with the start-up process. Make sure that the attorney is more than just a legal technician. Most entrepreneurs need an attorney who is patient and is willing to guide them through the start-up process.

4. Select an attorney who can assist you in raising money for your firm. This is a challenging issue for most entrepreneurs, and help in this area can be invaluable.

5. Make sure your attorney has a track record of completing his or her work on time. It can be very frustrating to be prepared to move forward with a business venture, only to be stymied by delays on the part of an attorney.

6. Talk about fees. If your attorney won't give you a good idea of what the start-up process will cost, keep looking.

7. Trust your intuition. Select an attorney who you think understands your business and with whom you will be comfortable spending time.

8. Learn as much about the process of starting a business yourself as possible. It will help you identify any problems that may exist or any aspect that may have been overlooked. Remember, it's your business start-up, not your attorney's. Stay in control.

relationship with their attorney. The following are several ways for entrepreneurs to achieve these dual objectives:

- **Group together legal matters:** It is typically cheaper to consult with an attorney on several matters at one time rather than schedule several separate meetings. For example, in one conference, a team of start-up entrepreneurs and their attorney could draft a founders' agreement, decide on a form of business organization, and discuss how to best draft nondisclosure and noncompete agreements for new employees.
- **Offer to assist the attorney:** There are excellent resources available to help entrepreneurs acquaint themselves with legal matters. An entrepreneur could help his or her attorney save time by writing the first few drafts of a founders' agreement or a contract or by helping gather the documents needed to deal with a legal issue.
- **Ask your attorney to join your advisory board:** Many start-ups form advisory boards (discussed in Chapter 6). Advisory board members typically serve as volunteers to help young firms get off to a good start. An attorney serving on an advisory board becomes a coach and a confidant as well as a paid service provider. However, entrepreneurs must be careful not to give the attorney the impression that he or she was asked to serve on the advisory board as a way of getting free legal advice.
- **Use nonlawyer professionals:** Nonlawyer professionals can perform some tasks at a much lower fee than a lawyer would charge. Examples include management consultants for business planning, tax preparation services for tax work, and insurance agents for advice on insurance planning.

Drafting a Founders' Agreement

learning **objective**

4. Discuss the importance of a founders' agreement.

It is important to ensure that founders are in agreement regarding their interests in the venture and their commitment to its future. It is easy for a team of entrepreneurs to get caught up in the excitement of launching a venture and fail to put in writing their initial agreements regarding the ownership of the firm. A **founders' agreement** (or shareholders' agreement) is a written document that deals with issues such as the relative split of the equity among the founders of the firm, how individual founders will be compensated for the cash or the "sweat equity" they put into the firm, and how long the founders will have to remain with the firm for their shares to fully vest.[5] The items typically included in a founders' agreement are shown in Table 8.3.

An important issue addressed by most founders' agreements is what happens to the equity of a founder if the founder dies or decides to leave the firm. Most founders' agreements include a **buyback clause**, which legally obligates the departing founder to sell to the remaining founders his or her interest in the firm if the remaining founders are interested.[6] In most cases, the agreement also specifies the formula for computing the dollar value to be paid. The presence of a buyback clause is important for at least two reasons. First, if a

Table 8.3

Items Included in a Founders' (or Shareholders') Agreement

- Nature of the prospective business
- A brief business plan
- Identity and proposed titles of the founders
- Legal form of business ownership
- Apportionment of stock (or division of ownership)
- Consideration paid for stock or ownership share of each of the founders (may be cash or "sweat equity")
- Identification of any intellectual property signed over to the business by any of the founders
- Description of the initial operating capital
- Buyback clause, which explains how a founders' shares will be disposed of if a founder dies, wants to sell, or is forced to sell by court order

founder leaves the firm, the remaining founders may need his or her shares to offer to a replacement person. Second, if a founder leaves because he or she is disgruntled, the buy-back clause provides the remaining founders a mechanism to keep the shares of the firm in the hands of people who are fully committed to the future of the venture.

Avoiding Legal Disputes

Most legal disputes are the result of misunderstandings, sloppiness, or a simple lack of knowledge of the law. Getting bogged down in legal disputes is something that an entrepreneur should work hard to avoid. It is important early in the life of a new business to establish practices and procedures to help avoid legal disputes. Legal snafus, particularly if they are coupled with management mistakes, can be extremely damaging to a new firm, as illustrated in the boxed feature titled "What Went Wrong?"

learning **objective**

5. Provide several suggestions for how new firms can avoid litigation.

what went **wrong?**

How Legal and Management Snafus Can Kill a Business

In 1990, Jambia Juice started in San Luis Obispo, California. The company, which sells smoothie drinks, got off to a good start, opened two more cafés in 1993, and now has hundreds of outlets all the way from Hawaii to Boston. In fact, Jambia Juice is somewhat unusual in that at one point during its growth, it obtained venture-capital funding, which is normally reserved for high-tech or biotech firms. Apparently, Benchmark Capital, the venture-capital firm involved, felt that smoothie drinks were a good bet.

In 1994, two entrepreneurs, Sean Nicholson and Aaron Souza, who had watched Jambia Juice grow, decided to try their own hands at opening a smoothie restaurant and started Green Planet Juicery. Nicholson and Souza were impressed with Jambia Juice and followed its lead in several areas. For example, Jambia Juice located its cafés near college campuses, where smoothie drinks were popular, so Green Planet's first café opened near the University of California, Davis. The café was a hit. In months, it was earning a profit, and its first year had sales of more than $500,000.

Three years later, Green Planet Juicery was broke. What went wrong? It wasn't the market for smoothie drinks. In fact, Jambia Juice is growing faster than ever. Instead, what killed Green Planet were legal and management snafus. Here's what happened.

First, Green Planet tried to grow too quickly. Unlike Jambia Juice, which waited three years to open its second café, Green Planet moved more quickly and opened three additional cafés within two years of its founding. In the process, it abandoned the idea of locating near college campuses and opened all its new outlets in nearby Sacramento. Two of the three new outlets struggled and, in hindsight, were poorly located. The first was located near a high school (where the students were not allowed to leave the premises during lunchtime), and the second was opened near a discount store. The third outlet was a hit and rivaled the sales of the original café. To open it, though, Green Planet had to form a partnership with an investor and received only a portion of the café's profits.

Second, at the same time Green Planet was struggling with its growth, Jambia Juice sued Green Planet for copyright infringement. According to Jambia Juice, Green Planet copied from its menu or other literature descriptions of such nutritional smoothie additives as algae, tofu, bee pollen, and brewer's yeast. Jambia Juice also alleged that Green Planet copied its promotional slogan for nutritional additives: "If you're green inside, you're clean inside." Green Planet admitted guilt and settled with Jambia Juice for an undisclosed sum.

Green Planet Juicery never fully recovered from these blunders and eventually went out of business. Its story provides a vivid reminder of the damage that can be caused by legal and management snafus, especially early in the life of a venture.

Questions for Critical Thinking

1. If you had been one of the entrepreneurs founding Great Planet Juicery, what would you have done differently compared to the actions described in this segment?

2. Go to Jambia Juice's Web site (www.jambiajuice.com). Does it appear to you that Jambia Juice is still a successful firm? If so, given what you've studied at the Web site, what do you believe accounts for the firm's continuing success?

Source: M. Selz, "Starting Too Fast: Green Planet Rushed to Add More Stores—Often in the Wrong Places," Wall Street Journal, September 25, 2000, 18.

There are several steps entrepreneurs can take to avoid legal disputes and complications:

- *Meet all contractual obligations:* It is important to meet all contractual obligations on time. This includes paying vendors, contractors, and employees as agreed and delivering goods or services as promised. If an obligation cannot be met on time, the problem should be communicated to the affected parties as soon as possible. It is irritating to a vendor, for example, not only to not get paid on time but also to have no explanation for the delay. Commenting on this issue, David Preiser, the managing director of an investment banking company in Los Angeles, says, "Credibility and confidence are built slowly but destroyed rapidly."[7] Preiser recommends being forthright with vendors or creditors if an obligation cannot be met and providing the affected party or parties a realistic plan for repaying the money as a way of retaining their confidence.

- *Avoid undercapitalization:* If a new business is starved for money, it is much more likely to experience financial problems that will lead to litigation.[8] A new business should raise the money it needs to effectively conduct business or should stem its growth to conserve cash. Many entrepreneurs face a dilemma regarding this issue. It is the goal of most entrepreneurs to retain as much of the equity in their firms as possible, but equity must often be shared with investors to obtain sufficient investment capital to support the firm's growth.

- *Get everything in writing:* Many business disputes arise because of the lack of a written agreement or because poorly prepared written agreements do not anticipate potential areas of dispute. While it is tempting to try to show business partners or employees that they are "trusted" by downplaying the need for a written agreement, this approach is usually a mistake. Disputes are much easier to resolve if the rights and obligations of the parties involved are in writing. For example, what if a new business agreed to pay a Web design firm $5,000 to design its Web site? The new business should know what it's getting for its money, and the Web design firm should know when the project is due and when it will receive payment for its services. In this case, a dispute could easily arise if the parties simply shook hands on the deal and the Web design firm promised to have a "good-looking Web site" done "as soon as possible." The two parties could easily later disagree over the quality and functionality of the finished Web site and the project's completion date.

learning **objective**

6. Discuss techniques entrepreneurs use to promote high standards of business ethics in their firms.

- *Promote business ethics:* There are many things a new business can do to establish an ethical culture and to promote ethical behavior on the part of its employees. Some companies have a formal code of ethics or a set of core values. A **code of ethics** describes the firm's general value system, moral principles, and specific ethical rules that apply.[9] The advantage of having a code of ethics or a set of core values is that it provides specific guidance to managers and employees regarding what is expected of them in terms of ethical behavior. Consider TManage, an Austin, Texas-based start-up based in Austin, Texas, that helps firms connect remote workers, mobile workers, and branch offices to corporate resources. Its company's core values follow.[10]

TManage core values represent "what we stand for" and are the foundation of our success. These are values and principles that we do not compromise.

Passion —What we do and how we deliver

Responsibility —Smart decisions and accountability

Respect —Open communication and integrity

Success —Growing and winning

Opportunity —Embracing change and striving for a better way

Partnership —Teamwork and synergy

These values help set the competitive and ethical tone at TManage, providing guidance to employees in terms of their behavior. Many organizations also have formal **ethics training programs** that teach employees how to respond to the types of ethical dilemmas that might arise on their jobs.[11] Ethics training programs often involve role plays, where employees are confronted with a tough ethical situation and are challenged to think quickly about how to respond to it. The role plays are typically videotaped so that employees can observe themselves and gain insights they need to sharpen their skills in handling tough ethical situations.

There are four common types of ethical problems that tend to flare up in business organizations and have the highest potential of leading to a lawsuit. An awareness of these common trouble spots can help a new business put policies and procedures in place to avoid trouble and to ensure adherence to high ethical standards. The four types of ethical problems most common in businesses are the following:[12]

- *Human resource ethical problems:* These problems relate to the equitable and just treatment of current and prospective employees. Unethical behavior here can range from asking an inappropriate question in a job interview to treating people unfairly because of their gender, color, religion, ethnic background, and so on.
- *Conflicts of interest:* These problems relate to situations that divide the loyalty of employees. For example, it would be inappropriate for an employee of a company to award a business contract to a friend or family member because of their personal relationship rather than for legitimate business reasons.
- *Customer confidence:* Problems in this area flare up when a company behaves in a way that shows a lack of respect for customers or a lack of concern with public safety. Examples include misleading advertising and the sale of a product that a company knows is unsafe.
- *Inappropriate use of corporate resources:* Problems in this area typically arise when an employee uses corporate resources for personal gain beyond what is customary and reasonable. For example, an employee who spends two hours of every eight-hour workday surfing the Internet is guilty of excessive or inappropriate use of corporate resources.

A final issue important in promoting business ethics involves the manner in which entrepreneurs and managers demonstrate accountability to their investors and shareholders. This issue, which we discuss in greater detail in Chapter 10, is particularly important given the rash of corporate scandals in the early 2000s.

A vision statement articulates a company's vision for its future. Many startups are so passionate about their vision that they take extraordinary steps to keep it on their employees' minds. Ortho Biotech feels so strongly about its vision statement that it's imprinted on the company's conference room tables.

Choosing a Form of Business Organization

When a business is launched, a form of legal entity must be chosen. The most common legal entities are sole proprietorship, partnerships, corporations, and limited liability companies. Choosing a legal entity is not a one-time event. As a business grows and matures, it is necessary to periodically review whether the current form of business organization remains appropriate. In most cases, a firm's form of business entity can be changed without triggering adverse tax implications.

There is no single form of business organization that works best in all situations. It's up to the owners of a firm and their attorney to select the legal entity that best meets their needs. The decision typically hinges on several factors, including the cost of setting up and maintaining the legal form, the extent to which an entrepreneur can shield his or her personal assets from the liabilities of the business, tax considerations, and the ease of raising capital. It is important to be careful in selecting a legal entity for a new firm because each form of business organization involves trade-offs among these factors and because an entrepreneur wants to be sure to achieve the founders' specific objectives.

This section describes the four forms of business organization and discusses the advantages and disadvantages of each. A comparison of the four legal entities, based on the factors that are typically the most important in making a selection, is provided in Table 8.4.

learning **objective**

7. Discuss the differences between sole proprietorships, partnerships, corporations, and limited liability companies.

learning **objective**

8. Explain why most fast-growth entrepreneurial firms organize as corporations or limited liability companies rather than sole proprietorships or partnerships.

Sole Proprietorship

The simplest form of business entity is the sole proprietorship. A **sole proprietorship** is a form of business organization involving one person, and the person and the business are essentially the same. Sole proprietorships are the most prevalent form of business organization. According to statistics collected within the past five years, there are over 14 million sole proprietorships in the United States, compared with 3.5 million corporations and 1.6 million partnerships.[13] The two most pervasive advantages of a sole proprietorship is that the owner maintains complete control over the business and that business losses can be deducted against the owner's personal tax return.

Setting up a sole proprietorship is cheap and relatively easy compared to the other forms of business ownership. The only legal requirement, in most states, is to obtain a license to do business. If the business is a retail business, the state will also require a sales tax license. Starting up gets more complicated if the business will deal with hazardous material, such as asbestos, or if it wants to sell alcoholic beverages or tobacco products. In these instances, additional licenses are required. In some cases, primarily because of government regulations, obtaining these licenses can be difficult and time consuming.

If the business will be operated under a trade name (e.g., Top-Flight Consulting) instead of the name of the owner (say, Melanie Smith), the owner will have to file an assumed or fictitious name certificate with the appropriate local government agency. This step is required to ensure that there is only one business in an area using the same name and provides a public record of the owner's name.

A sole proprietorship is not a separate legal entity. For tax purposes, the profit or loss of the business flows through to the owner's personal tax return, and the business ends at the owner's death or loss of interest in the business. The sole proprietor is responsible for all the liabilities of the business, and this is a significant drawback. If a sole proprietor's business is sued, the owner could theoretically lose all the business's assets along with his or her personal assets. The liquidity of an owner's investment in a sole proprietorship is typically low. **Liquidity** is the ability to sell a business or other asset quickly at a price that is close to its market value.[14] It is usually difficult for a sole proprietorship to raise investment capital because the ownership of the business cannot be shared. Unlimited liability and difficulty raising investment capital are the primary reasons entrepreneurs typically form corporations or limited liability companies as opposed to sole proprietorships. Most sole proprietorships are salary-substitute or lifestyle firms (as described in Chapter 1) and are typically a poor choice for an aggressive entrepreneurial firm.

Table 8.4 Comparison of Forms of Business Ownership

Factor	Sole Proprietorship	Partnership		Corporation		Limited Liability Company
		General	Limited	C-Corporation	S-Corporation	
Number of owners allowed	1	Unlimited number of general partners allowed	Unlimited number of general and limited partners allowed	Unlimited	Up to 75	Unlimited number of "members" allowed
Cost of setting up and maintaining	Low	Moderate	Moderate	High	High	High
Personal liability of owners	Unlimited	Unlimited for all partners	Unlimited for general partners; limited partners only to extent of investment	Limited to amount of investment	Limited to amount of investment	Limited to amount of investment
Continuity of business	Ends at death of owner	Death or withdrawal of one partner unless otherwise specified	Death or withdrawal of general partner	Perpetual	Perpetual	Typically limited to a fixed amount of time
Taxation	Not a taxable entity; sole proprietor pays all taxes	Not a taxable entity; each partner pays taxes on his or her share of income and can deduct losses against other sources of income	Not a taxable entity; each partner pays taxes on his or her share of income and can deduct losses against other sources of income	Separate taxable entity	No tax at entity level; income/loss is passed through to the shareholders	No tax at entity level if properly structured; income/loss is passed through to the members
Management control	Sole proprietor is in full control	All partners share control equally, unless otherwise specified	Only general partners have control	Board of directors elected by the shareholders	Board of directors elected by the shareholders	Members share control or appoint manager
Method of raising capital	Must be raised by sole proprietor	Must be raised by general partners	Sale of limited partnerships, depending on terms of operating agreement	Sell shares of stock to the public	Sell shares of stock to the public	It's possible to sell interests, depending on the terms of the operating agreement
Liquidity of investment	Low	Low	Low	High, if publicly traded	Low	Low
Subject to double taxation	No	No	No	Yes	No	No

To summarize, the primary advantages and disadvantages of a sole proprietorship are as follows:

Advantages of a Sole Proprietorship
- Creating one is easy and inexpensive.
- The owner maintains complete control of the business.
- Business losses can be deducted against the sole proprietor's other sources of income.
- It is not subject to double taxation (explained later).

Disadvantages of a Sole Proprietorship
- Liability on the owner's part is unlimited.
- The business relies on the skills and abilities of a single owner to be successful. Of course, the owner can hire employees who have additional skills and abilities.
- Raising capital can be difficult.
- The business ends at the owner's death or loss of interest in the business.
- The liquidity of the owner's investment is low.

Partnerships

If two or more people start a business, they must organize as a partnership, corporation, or limited liability company. Partnerships are organized as either general or limited partnerships. In the business world, people merging their skills and interests to form a company is a common occurrence. The founding of Honest Tea, as illustrated in the boxed feature titled "Partnering for Success," is an example of this type of activity.

Partnering for SUCCESS

Student and Former Professor Collaborate to Found Honest Tea

www.honesttea.com

In 1995, Seth Goldman, a second-year master's student at the Yale School of Management, was doing a case study on the beverage industry. Goldman was struck by the fact that the beverage industry consisted primarily of high-calorie, sugary drinks on one end and no-calorie bottled water at the end, with little in between. "What if we created a beverage that had a few calories, so that it had taste, but didn't have all the junk in it?" he wondered at the time. Goldman shared his idea with Barry Nalebuff, one of his professors. Although Nalebuff was intrigued, neither he nor Goldman followed through at the time.

Two years later, Goldman remembered his idea after a jog through New York City's Central Park. He was thirsty but couldn't find a drink that appealed to him. So Goldman dropped an e-mail message to Nalebuff, his former professor, to rekindle his interest in the idea. The two met and hit on the beverage they felt the market lacked: bottled tea. The two decided to start a company to produce organic bottled tea and call it Honest Tea—a name that fit well with Goldman's personal interests in social causes.

In early 1998, Goldman left his job with a mutual fund company and started working on Honest Team full time. Nalebuff kept his teaching job but contributed $200,000 in investment capital and used his contacts to find additional funds. Goldman refined the initial Honest Tea flavors in his kitchen, working hard to find retailers who would stock his product while doing so. An early break came through a meeting that Goldman had with the marketing director of Fresh Fields, a food chain in the Washington, D.C., area that agreed to stock Honest Tea's drinks. Not coincidentally, the marketing director was also a former student of Barry Nalebuff, Goldman's partner.

In the ensuing years, Honest Tea has done extremely well and is now the best-selling and fastest-growing organic bottled tea company in the United States; it is available in all 50 states. Goldman remains the company's president and TeaEO (as he calls it). The company is known not only for the quality of its drinks but also for its socially responsible mission and its willingness to give back a portion of its profits to the foreign nations from which it purchases its tea leaves.

Questions for Critical Thinking

1. Think of all the teachers or professors from whom you've taken classes during your educational process. From the list you've generated, select the one with whom you would be most likely to form a partnership. What are that person's traits or characteristics that make him or her an attractive partner for a business venture?

2. As explained in this feature, ethical business practices are important to Seth Goldman as he serves as Honest Tea's TeaEO. Earlier in this chapter, we listed the values of TManage, a start-up venture located in Austin, Texas. Given what you've read about Honest Tea and Seth Goldman, develop a list of values you believe are important to him as he leads his company.

Sources: J. Yang, "On the Steep Path to Success: Honest Tea's Journey from Business School to Store Shelves," Washington Post, March 11, 1999, E01, and J. Hyman, "Honest Team Company Fills Niche with Natural Low-Cal Alternative," Washington Times, September 14, 1998, D8.

General Partnerships   A **general partnership** is a form of business organization where two or more people pool their skills, abilities, and resources to run a business. The primary advantage of a general partnership over a sole proprietorship is that the business isn't dependent on a single person for its survival and success. In fact, in most cases, the partners have equal say in how the business is run. Most partnerships have a partnership agreement, which is a legal document that is similar to a founders' agreement. A **partnership agreement** details the responsibilities and the ownership shares of the partners involved with an organization. The business created by a partnership ends at the death or withdrawal of a partner, unless otherwise stated in the partnership agreement. General partnerships are typically found in service industries. In many states, a general partnership must file a certificate of partnership or similar document as evidence of its existence. Similar to a sole proprietorship, the profit or loss of a general partnership flows through to the partner's personal tax returns. If a business has four general partners and they all have equal ownership in the business, then one-fourth of the profits or losses would flow through to each partner's individual tax return.[15] The partnership files an informational tax return only.

The primary disadvantage of a general partnership is that the individual partners are liable for all the partnership's debts and obligations. If one partner is negligent while conducting business on behalf of the partnership, all the partners may be liable for damages. Although the nonnegligent partners may later try to recover their losses from the negligent one, the joint liability of all partners to the injured party remains. It is typically easier for a general partnership to raise money than a sole proprietorship simply because more than one person is willing to assume liability for a loan. One way a general partnership can raise investment capital is by adding more partners. Investors are typically reluctant to sign on as general partners, however, because of the unlimited liability that follows each one.

In summary, the primary advantages and disadvantages of a general partnership are as follows:

Advantages of a General Partnership
- Creating one is relatively easy and inexpensive compared to a corporation or limited liability company.
- The skills and abilities of more than one individual are available to the firm.
- Business losses can be deducted against the partners' other sources of income.
- It is not subject to double taxation (explained later).

Disadvantages of a General Partnership
- Liability on the part of each general partner is unlimited.
- The business relies on the skills and abilities of a fixed number of partners. Of course, similar to a sole proprietorship, the partners can hire employees who have additional skills and abilities.
- Raising capital can be difficult.
- The business ends at the death or withdrawal of one partner unless otherwise stated in the partnership agreement.
- The liquidity of each partner's investment is low.

Limited Partnerships   A **limited partnership** is a modified form of a general partnership. The major difference between the two is that a limited partnership includes two classes of owners: general partners and limited partners. Similar to a general partnership, the general partners are liable for the debts and obligations of the partnership, but the limited partners are liable only up to the amount of their investment. The limited partners may not exercise any significant control over the organization without jeopardizing their limited liability status.[16] A limited partnership is usually formed to raise money or to spread out the risk of a venture without forming a corporation. Limited partnerships are common in real estate development, oil and gas exploration, and motion picture ventures.[17]

Corporations

A **corporation** is a separate legal entity organized under the authority of a state. Corporations are organized as either C corporations or subchapter S corporations. The following description pertains to C corporations, which are by far the most common and are what most people think of when they hear the word "corporation." Subchapter S corporations are explained later.

C Corporations   A **C corporation** is a separate legal entity that, in the eyes of the law, is separate from its owners. In most cases, the corporation shields its owners, who are called **shareholders**, from personal liability for the debts and obligations of the corporation. A corporation is governed by a board of directors, which is elected by the shareholders (explained in Chapter 6). In most instances, the board hires officers to oversee the day-to-day management of the organization. It is usually easier for a corporation to raise investment capital than a sole proprietorship or a partnership because the shareholders are not liable beyond their investment in the firm. It is also easier to allocate partial ownership interests in a corporation through the distribution of stock. Most C corporations have two classes of stock: common and preferred. **Preferred stock** is typically issued to conservative investors who have preferential rights over common stockholders in regard to dividends and to the assets of the corporation in the event of liquidation. **Common stock** is issued more broadly than preferred stock. The common stockholders have voting rights and elect the board of directors of the firm. The common stockholders are typically the last to get paid in the event of the liquidation of the corporation, that is, after the creditors and the preferred stockholders.[18]

Establishing a corporation is more complicated than a sole proprietorship or a partnership. A corporation is formed by filing **articles of incorporation** with the secretary of state's office in the state of incorporation. The articles of incorporation typically include the corporation's name, purpose, authorized number of stock shares, classes of stock, and other conditions of operation.[19] In most states, corporations must file papers annually, and state agencies impose annual fees. It is important that a corporation's owners fully comply with these regulations. If the owners of a corporation don't file their annual paperwork, neglect to pay their annual fees, or commit fraud, a court could ignore the fact that a corporation has been established, and the owners could be held personally liable for actions of the corporation. This chain of effects is referred to as "**piercing the corporate veil**."[20]

Some states are more hospitable than others in regard to the ease of incorporating, annual fees, and the nature of the laws governing corporations. Delaware is a popular state to register a corporation for several unique reasons. This issue is more fully described in the boxed feature titled "Savvy Entrepreneurial Firm."

A corporation is taxed as a separate legal entity. In fact, the "C" in the title "C corporation" comes from the fact that regular corporations are taxed under subchapter C of the Internal Revenue Code. A disadvantage of corporations is that they are subject to **double taxation**, which means that a corporation is taxed on its net income and, when the same income is distributed to shareholders in the form of dividends, is taxed again on shareholders' personal income tax returns. This complication is one of the reasons that entrepreneurial firms often retain their earnings rather than paying dividends to their shareholders. The firm can use the earnings to fuel future growth and at the same time avoid double taxation. The hope is that the shareholders will ultimately be rewarded by an appreciation in the value of the company's stock.

Another advantage of corporations is the ease of transferring stock. It is often difficult for a sole proprietor to sell a business and even more awkward for a partner to sell a partial interest in a general partnership. If a corporation is listed on a major stock exchange, such as the New York Stock Exchange or the NASDAQ, an owner can sell his or her shares at almost a moment's notice. This advantage of incorporating, however, does not extend to corporations that are not listed on a major stock exchange. As mentioned earlier in this book, there are approximately 2,800 companies listed on the New York Stock Exchange and 3,300 listed on the NASDAQ. These firms are **public corporations**. The stockholders of these 6,100 companies enjoy a **liquid market** for their stock, meaning that the stock can be bought and sold fairly easily through an organized marketplace. It is much more difficult to sell stock in closely held or private corporations. In a **closely held corporation**, the voting stock is held by a small number of individuals and is very thinly or infrequently traded.[21] A **private corporation** is one in which all the shares are held by a few shareholders, such as management or family members, and are not publicly traded.[22] The vast majority of the 1.3 million corporations in the United States are private corporations. The stock in both

Savvy entrepreneurial FIRM

For Many Firms, It Makes Sense to Incorporate in Delaware

www.state.de.us/corp

Have you ever wondered why so many corporations incorporate in Delaware? Although Delaware has a population of only 796,000 and encompasses a mere 1,954 square miles (Texas is 267,000 square miles), more than 500,000 business entities have made Delaware their legal residence. In fact, more than 50 percent of all publicly traded companies in the United States, including 58 percent of the Fortune 500, have chosen Delaware as their legal home.

Why is this the case? If a firm plans to be a corporation or a limited liability company, there are plenty of reasons for it to consider incorporating in Delaware. In general, Delaware has very modern and flexible corporate laws, and its chancery court has a reputation as one of the finest and fairest business courts in the nation. In addition, Delaware supports a state-of-the-art filing system that facilitates time-sensitive transactions. It is also inexpensive to incorporate in Delaware and can be done entirely online, without ever visiting the state. Once incorporated, a corporation or limited liability company (LLC) must retain a registered agent in Delaware to interface with the state on its behalf. There are many registered agents available that charge affordable fees.

There are other reasons companies are motivated to incorporate in Delaware. For example, Delaware law allows for a version of the LLC called a serial LLC. The major difference between a sole proprietorship or a partnership and an LLC is the limitation of liability that an LLC affords its owners. But say the owners of an LLC wanted to conduct more than one type of business but didn't want to create a separate corporation or LLC for each business, as is required in many states. The serial LLC allows different lines

of business to be treated separately from each other from a liability standpoint. So, for example, an LLC that owns several restaurants may insulate the LLC from liability for each individual restaurant if the operating agreement allows for it. This is an attractive benefit for a business that fits this profile.

Another reason that companies organize in Delaware is to shield their directors from personal liability for the actions of the firm. This is an issue of growing concern for many business organizations. A Delaware director shield law permits Delaware corporations to shield their directors in a more effective manner than most other states from personal liability in connection with their actions as board members.

While incorporating in Delaware may not be suitable for all firms, it is something that a savvy entrepreneurial firm should consider. The state of Delaware maintains an excellent Web site that explains the advantages of incorporating in Delaware. The site is available at *www.state.de.us/corp*.

Questions for Critical Thinking

1. Assume that several of your friends, who aren't business majors, have learned that many firms decide to incorporate in Delaware. They ask you to explain why this is the case. Go to the www.state.de.us/corp Web site to gain information to use to answer your friends' questions.

2. In your view, are there any ethical considerations associated with firms' decisions to incorporate in Delaware? If so, what are those issues, and how would you propose that firms deal with those ethical issues?

closely held and private corporations is fairly **illiquid**, meaning that it typically isn't easy to find a buyer for the stock.

A final advantage of organizing as a C corporation is the ability to share stock with employees as part of an employee incentive plan. Because it's easy to distribute stock in small amounts, many corporations, both public and private, distribute stock as part of their employee bonus or profit-sharing plans. Such incentive plans are intended to help firms attract, motivate, and retain high-quality employees.[23] **Stock options** are a special form of incentive compensation. These plans provide employees the option or right to buy a certain number of shares of their company's stock at a stated price over a certain period of time. The most compelling advantage of stock options is the potential rewards to participants when (and if) the stock price increases.[24] Many employees receive stock options at the time they are hired and then periodically receive additional options. As employees accumulate stock options, the link between their potential reward and their company's stock price becomes increasingly clear. This link provides a powerful inducement for employees to exert extra effort on behalf of their firm in hopes of positively affecting the stock price.[25]

To summarize, the advantages and disadvantages of a C corporation are as follows:

Advantages of a C Corporation
- Owners are liable only for the debts and obligations of the corporation up to the amount of their investment.
- Raising capital is easy.
- No restrictions exist on the number of shareholders, which differs from subchapter S corporations.
- Stock is liquid if traded on a major stock exchange.
- The ability to share stock with employees through stock option or other incentive plans can be a powerful form of employee motivation.

Disadvantages of a C Corporation
- Setting up and maintaining one is more difficult than for a sole proprietorship or a partnership.
- Business losses cannot be deducted against the shareholders' other sources of income.
- Income is subject to double taxation, meaning that it is taxed at the corporate and the shareholder levels.
- Small shareholders typically have little voice in the management of the firm.

Subchapter S Corporation   A **subchapter S corporation** combines the advantages of a partnership and a C corporation. It is similar to a partnership in that the profits and losses of the business are not subject to double taxation. The subchapter S corporation does not pay taxes; instead, the profits or losses of the business are passed through to the individual tax returns of the owners. It is also similar to a corporation in that the owners are not subject to personal liability for the behavior of the business. Because of these advantages, many entrepreneurial firms start as subchapter S corporations. There are strict standards that a business must meet to qualify for status as a subchapter S corporation:

- The business cannot be a subsidiary of another corporation.
- The shareholders must be U.S. citizens. Partnerships and C corporations may not own shares in a subchapter S corporation. Certain types of trusts and estates are eligible to own shares in a subchapter S corporation.
- It can have only one class of stock issued and outstanding (either preferred stock or common stock).
- It can have no more than 75 members. Husbands and wives count as one member, even if they own separate shares of stock.
- All shareholders must agree to have the corporation formed as a subchapter S corporation.

The primary disadvantages of a subchapter S corporation are restrictions in qualifying, expenses involved with setting up and maintaining the subchapter S status, and the fact that a subchapter S corporation is limited to 75 shareholders.[26] If a subchapter S corporation wants to include more than 75 shareholders, it must convert to a C corporation or a limited liability company.

Limited Liability Company

The **limited liability company (LLC)** is a form of business organization that is rapidly gaining popularity in the United States. The concept originated in Germany and was first introduced in the United States in the state of Wyoming in 1977. Along with the subchapter S corporation, it is a popular choice for start-up firms. As with partnerships and corporations, the profits of an LLC flow through to the tax returns of the owners and are not subject to double taxation. The main advantage of the LLC is that all partners enjoy limited liability. This differs from regular and limited partnerships, where at least one partner is liable for the debts of the partnership. The LLC combines the limited liability advantage of the corporation with the tax advantages of the partnership.[27] DreamWorks SKG, the movie studio started by Steven Spielberg, Jeffrey Katzenberg and David Geffen was an LLC until it went public in late 2004.

Some of the terminology used for an LLC differs from the other forms of business ownership. For example, the shareholders of an LLC are called "members," and instead of owning stock, the members have "interests." The LLC is more flexible than a subchapter S corporation in terms of number of owners and tax-related issues. An LLC must be a private business—it cannot be publicly traded. If at some point the members want to take the business public and be listed on one of the major stock exchanges, it must be converted to a C corporation.

The LLC is rather complex to set up and maintain, and in some states the rules governing the LLC vary. Members may elect to manage the LLC themselves or may designate one or more managers (who may or may not be members) to run the business on a day-to-day basis. The profits and losses of the business may be allocated to the members anyway they choose. For example, if two people owned an LLC, they could split the yearly profits 50-50, 75-25, 90-10, or any other way they chose.[28]

In summary, the advantages and disadvantages of an LLC are as follows:

Advantages of a Limited Liability Company
- Members are liable for the debts and obligations of the business only up to the amount of their investment.
- The number of shareholders is unlimited.
- The number of members, tax issues, and implementation is flexible.
- Because profits are taxed only at the shareholder level, there is no double taxation.

Disadvantages of a Limited Liability Company
- Setting up and maintaining one is more difficult and expensive.
- Tax accounting can be complicated.
- Some of the regulations governing LLCs vary by state.

The members of an LLC may run the business themselves, or they may call on outside managers to handle operations. These members chose to manage their business themselves and meet periodically to discuss the financial progress of their corporation.

The Legal Environment of the Internet

Most new businesses will utilize the Internet in their business operations. While not all businesses will sell products online, virtually all will have Web sites and will interact with customers, employees, and suppliers via the Internet. When the Internet was introduced in the early 1990s, many businesses approached it with an "anything goes" attitude, believing that it was alright to do almost anything online. As time goes on, however, the legal system is getting a better grip on the Internet, and more laws and regulations are being passed, and it is likely that additional laws and regulations will come into being with each passing year as the fascinating distribution channel known as the Internet evolves. Today, courts and jurisdictions around the world are taking control of what constitutes appropriate behavior online.[29] Today, it is important for entrepreneurs to be familiar with the Internet's legal environment.

The World Wide Web

There are three types of Web sites—shop window Web sites, contributed content Web sites, and full e-commerce Web sites—and each has its own set of legal issues to consider.[30]

Shop Window Web Sites

This type of Web site provides information about a company and its products but encourages very little interaction. Some authors call these sites "brochureware," meaning that the site is really nothing more than an electronic brochure.[31] A shop window Web Site is typically a first step for companies that may design a more sophisticated Web site later. The site provides people outside the company with an overview of the business and its products, history, management team, business partners, and financial information. Such a site also frequently provides directions to a company's headquarters location and contact information.

There are several important legal issues for shop window Web site owners to consider. First, all the content placed on the Web site, including pictures, graphs, text, images, narrative, and music, should be original unless specific permission has been obtained from the owners of the material to use it. Entrepreneurs should assume that anything they find on another Web site is copyrighted (copyrights are explained in Chapter 12) and can't be used without permission. Obtaining permission to use copyrighted material typically means getting a license or assignment of copyright from the rights holder. Sometimes it is hard to track down the owner of a picture or a piece of music. It is risky to use content online, however, without obtaining permission.

There are additional issues for the owners of shop window Web Sites to consider:

- A hyperlink takes a user from one Web site to another. It is usually highlighted on a Web page, and by clicking on the hyperlink, the user is automatically taken to a different Web page (or Web site). A deep link is a hyperlink that bypasses a Web site's home page and takes the user directly to an internal page. For example, instead of taking the user to the home page of a magazine, a deep link might take the user directly to an article from a previous issue of the magazine. Entrepreneurs should definitely avoid hyperlinking and deep linking to third-party Web sites unless they have permission from the holder of the rights to those sites.
- Pricing information should be frequently updated. Having misleading pricing information online could result in penalties levied against the firm. For example, sale prices should be removed from a Web site as soon as a sale is completed.
- Incorrect or misleading product descriptions can cause negative repercussions.
- Misleading comparative advertising, such as comparisons between products or services that are not intended for the same purpose, should be avoided.

Contributed Content Web Sites

Web sites that encourage visitors to interact are exposed to several additional forms of legal risks. The most common problem in this area arises when sites encourage visitors to interact by making discussion boards or chat rooms available. The owners of contributed content Web sites can be subject to civil or even criminal penalties unless reasonable measures are taken to control the material that appears on the Web site. Problem material includes libelous statements, infringements of copyright material, and obscene, threatening, or racially discriminatory material. To keep this material off a bulletin board or out of a chat room, entrepreneurs should monitor material before it appears on the Web site, regularly review what has been posted, remove any problematic material, and post a "notice and take down" procedure that removes inappropriate content as soon as it is posted.

These measures need to be addressed in a Web site's "terms and conditions" so that anyone viewing the Web site is aware of the steps taken to prevent problems from occurring. It is also a good idea to require a user to register before he or she can post a message on a bulletin board or participate in a chat room. Then, when problems occur, the user can be identified.[32]

Full E-Commerce Web Sites   Full e-commerce Web sites sell goods and services via the Web. Examples include Amazon.com, Expedia.com, and mvp.com. New businesses that plan to sell products or services via the Web should consult with an attorney to be sure they know all the current laws and regulations that apply. In addition, the sale of certain products and services is more heavily regulated than others. These products and services include wine and other alcoholic beverages, medicines (particularly prescription medicines), and financial services. Sites that permit betting are also heavily regulated, and users can place bets on the sites only if they live in certain areas.

An important caveat of selling online is to make sure to form a legally binding contact with the purchaser. To do this, many sites require their customers to scroll through a list of terms and conditions and click on an "I accept" button before a purchase can be completed. This topic is discussed in more detail later.

Trademarks and Domain Names

The emergence of the Internet has led to a variety of issues in trademark law and practice. Trademarks, which include any word, name, symbol, or device used to identify and distinguish one company's goods from another's, are discussed in Chapter 12. The domain name system used to register Internet addresses can easily lead to trademark infringement. In addition, the simple fact that the Internet is so easy to use and navigate has led businesses to become more sensitive to trademark infringement. For example, in the past, a consulting firm in Michigan operating under the name of Ivey Consulting may have never known that a similar firm in California operated under the same name. Now, it's easy for the firms to stumble across one another while surfing the Internet, which could result in a trademark infringement suit.

One of the thorniest issues related to trademarks and the Internet involves domain name disputes. A **domain name** is a company's Internet address (e.g., *www.intel.com*). Most companies want their domain name to be the same as their company's name. It is easy to register a domain name through an online registration services such as Network Solutions (*www.networksolutions.com*). The standard fee for registering and maintaining a domain name is $35 per year. On the Internet, no two domain names can be exactly the same, so frustration can arise when a company tries to register its domain name and the name is already taken. There are two reasons that a name may already be taken. First, a company may find that another company with the same name has already registered it. For example, if an entrepreneur started a company called Delta Semiconductor, it would find that the domain name *www.delta.com* is already taken by Delta Airlines. This scenario plays itself out every day and represents a challenge for new firms that have chosen fairly ordinary names. The firm can either select another domain name (such as *www.deltasemiconductor.com*) or try to acquire the name from its present owner. However, it is unlikely that Delta Airlines would give up *www.delta.com* for any price.

The second reason that a domain name may already be taken is that it might be in the hands of a cybersquatter. Until recently, some people—cybersquatters—registered the names of companies or individuals for the sole purpose of trying to resell the names (for a substantial profit) to those companies or individuals. For example, in the early years of the Internet, when many companies were still trying to figure out what the Internet was all about, one person alone registered over 250 domain names, including *www.deltaairlines.com* and *www.neiman-marcus.com.*[33] This practice is called **cybersquatting**, which is the act of registering a popular Internet address with the intent of reselling it to its rightful owner.[34] To stop this from happening, Congress passed the **Anticybersquatting Consumer Protection Act** in 1999. The act strengthened trademark laws to permit injured parties to sue for bad-faith registration of domain names. Under the law, a court can order the transfer of a domain name from a cybersquatter to its rightful owner. If actual damages are proved, the law permits an award of $1,000 to $100,000 per domain name.

Another form of domain name abuse is called **typosquatting**. Typosquatters register domain names that are nearly identical to the domain names used by legitimate organizations, except that they include a common spelling or typographical error. The intention of doing this is to catch people who make a common error when typing in a domain name and redirect them to another site.

Probably the most famous domain name dispute in the history of the Internet involved the actress Julia Roberts. In June 2000, an international arbitration panel ruled that an accused cybersquatter who registered the domain name *www.juliaroberts.com* had no legitimate interest in the name and registered it in bad faith. The panel awarded the name to Julia Roberts. In finding bad-faith intent, the arbitration panel cited evidence that the defendant had registered the names of several famous movie and sports figures and even tried to auction off the Julia Roberts domain name on eBay's Web site.

Electronic Contracts and Digital Signatures

learning **objective**

10. Explain the importance of the Electronic Signatures in Global and International Commerce Act.

As we mentioned earlier, it is important to form a legally binding contract with a purchaser for any major transaction when conducting business online. Whether contracts fulfilled online have the same legal standing as traditional paper contracts signed in ink was unclear when the Internet was first introduced in the early 1990s. This issue was resolved on October 1, 2000, when a new law, the **Electronic Signatures in Global and International Commerce Act**, went into effect. According to this act, electronic contracts and electronic signatures are now just as legal as traditional paper contracts signed in ink.[35] The passage of this act was considered a major victory for proponents of e-commerce and the Internet. Not only does the ability to consummate contracts online make buying and selling products via the Internet safer and more practical, it also provides an additional option for businesses looking for ways to improve efficiencies, reduce paperwork, and streamline their operations by using the Internet to conduct certain transactions rather than using the U.S. Postal Service, overnight delivery, or face-to-face meetings.

A "cyber," or electronic, contract is an agreement created and "signed" in electronic form. Signing occurs in two ways. First, as we said earlier, many Web sites require their customers to scroll through a list of terms and conditions and click on an "I accept" button before additional transactions, such as access to downloadable software, can occur. Second, an individual can write a contract on a computer and e-mail it to a customer or a business associate for review. If this person accepts the contract, he or she can e-mail the contract back with his or her electronic signature. Since it is obviously impossible to sign an electronic contract with an ink pen, people have used several different ways to attach signatures to electronic documents. One way is to type a signer's name into the signature area and then paste in a scanned version of the signer's signature. A more sophisticated approach is to use a **digital signature**. A digital signature is a computer-generated block of text that accurately identifies both the signer and the content, helping to ensure the authenticity and integrity of electronic documents. Both the sender and the receiver must have special software to create and verify a particular digital signature.

The use of digital signatures is being driven by the need to provide a higher level of confidence in executing contracts online. Most people are comfortable with traditional contracts because of the security and familiarity with paper documents and handwritten signatures. Digital signatures provide an extra degree of assurance that the parties executing the contract are who they say they are and that the actions of everyone involved are legitimate. Because the technology is still evolving, security issues regarding the use of digital signatures in electronic transmissions remain unsolved. More about how digital signatures work and the level of protection they provide appears in the boxed feature titled "Savvy Entrepreneurial Firm."

Savvy entrepreneurial FIRM

Making Use of Digital Signatures to Save Time and Expense

Suppose a job shop in Milwaukee contacted a semiconductor manufacturer on the West Coast and placed an urgent order for $200,000 worth of semiconductors. The two parties agreed on a price and executed a contract, and the semiconductors were shipped via air freight within four hours. Everything sounds good, but there is one interesting question: How did the contract get signed?

As the result of a law passed in 2000, electronic contracts and digital signatures are just as legal as traditional paper contracts signed in ink. So the contract may have been signed digitally. Here is how digital signatures work. Imagine that you own a consulting company and you want to send a digitally signed contract to a client named Pete via e-mail. After creating the contract, you enter your "private key"—a kind of password known only to you—into special software that produces a jumble of letters and symbols. This jumble of letters and symbols, which can be placed at the bottom of your e-mail or included as an attachment, is unique and constitutes your digital signature for the document. When Pete gets the e-mail, he enters your "public key"—a sort of nonsecret password that's available to anyone who wants to do business with you—into software that is compatible with the program you used to create the digital signature. The software then tells Pete whether it is you who sent the contract and whether anyone has tampered with it since it was sent.

There are two things that can potentially go wrong with this scenario, which is one of the reasons that it may take some time for the use of digital signatures to become more common. First, the private key that you used to create your digital signature has to remain private. If someone, such as a disgruntled employee, were to steal your private key, it could fall into the hands of someone who might impersonate you and cause problems. Second, Pete has to know that your public key, which you can send to him via e-mail, is authentic. If Pete doesn't know you, he can solve this problem by the use of a third party to verify your public key. There are a number of companies, called certification authorities, that provide this service for a small fee. The need to verify the public key, however, does add a level of complexity to the process.

The hope is that the use of electronic contracts and digital signatures, once the technology evolves and the use of these techniques becomes more widely adopted, will create a true digital advantage for many individuals and firms. The use of digital as opposed to traditional paper contracts represents another option for companies seeking ways to improve efficiencies, reduce paperwork, and streamline their operations.

Questions for Critical Thinking

1. Assume that you have just started an entrepreneurial venture. How comfortable would you be relying on electronic signatures to finalize contracts with your first customers? What actions could you take to reduce any anxiety you might have about accepting electronic signatures on contracts from customers?

2. Explain the concept of electronic signatures to three or four of your friends. What are their reactions to what you told them? How typical do you believe their reactions are?

3. Are there any special ethical challenges facing companies committed to accepting electronic signatures from suppliers and customers? If so, what are those challenges, and what recommendations can you offer firms to successfully cope with them?

1. Behaving in a professional manner and honoring all employment agreements are the two most important issues to consider when leaving an employer to launch an entrepreneurial venture.

2. A nondisclosure agreement is a promise made by an employee or another party (such as a supplier) not to disclose a company's trade secrets. A noncompete agreement prevents an individual from competing against a former employer for a specific period of time.

3. The criteria important for selecting an attorney for a new firm are shown in Table 8.2. Critical issues include selecting an attorney familiar with the start-up process, selecting an attorney who can assist you in raising money, and making certain that the attorney has a track record of completing his or her work on time.

4. It is important to ensure that a venture's founders agree on their relative interests in the venture and their commitment to its future. A founders' (or shareholders'

agreement) is a written document dealing with issues such as the split of equity between the founders of the firm, how individual founders will be compensated for the cash or the "sweat equity" they put into the firm, and how long the founders will have to stay with the firm for their shares to fully vest.

5. Suggestions for how new firms can avoid litigation include meeting all contractual obligations, avoiding undercapitalization, getting everything in writing, and promoting business ethics in the firm.

6. A code of ethics and ethics training programs are two techniques entrepreneurs use to promote high standards of business ethics in their ventures or firms. A code of ethics describes the general value system, moral principles, and specific ethical rules that govern a firm. An ethics training program provides employees with instructions for how to deal with ethical dilemmas when they occur.

7. The major differences between sole proprietorships, partnerships, corporations, and limited liability companies are shown in Table 8-4. These forms of

business organization differ in terms of number of owners allowed, cost of setting up and maintaining, personal liability of owners, continuity of business, methods of taxation, degree of management control, ease of raising capital, and ease of liquidating investments.

8. High-growth firms tend to organize as corporations or limited liability companies for two main reasons: to shield the owners from personal liability for the behavior of the firm and because organizing as a corporation or limited liability company makes it easier to raise capital.

9. A disadvantage of C corporations is that they are subject to double taxation. A C corporation is taxed on its net income, and when the same income is distributed to shareholders in the form of dividends, it is taxed again on the personal income tax returns of the shareholders.

10. According to the Electronic Signatures in Global and International Commerce Act, electronic contracts and electronic signatures are just as legal as traditional paper contracts signed in ink. The act became law on October 1, 2000.

KEY TERMS

Anticybersquatting Consumer Protection Act, 194

articles of incorporation, 188

buyback clause, 180

C corporation, 188

closely held corporation, 188

code of ethics, 182

common stock, 188

corporate opportunity doctrine, 177

corporation, 187

cybersquatting, 194

digital signature, 194

domain name, 193

double taxation, 188

Electronic Signatures in Global and International Commerce Act, 194

ethics training programs, 182

founders' agreement, 180

general partnership, 187

illiquid, 189

limited liability company, 190

limited partnership, 187

liquid market, 188

liquidity, 184

noncompete agreement, 178

nondisclosure agreement, 178

partnership agreement, 187

piercing the corporate veil, 188

preferred stock, 188

private corporation, 188

public corporations, 188

shareholders, 188

sole proprietorship, 184

stock options, 189

subchapter S corporation, 190

typosquatting, 194

REVIEW QUESTIONS

1. In general, do entrepreneurs tend to overestimate or underestimate their knowledge of the laws that pertain to starting a new firm? What does the answer to this question suggest that entrepreneurs do before they start a firm?

2. If an entrepreneur is quitting a traditional job to start a new firm, what are the two things he or she should keep in mind in order to leave his or her employer ethically?

3. What is the corporate opportunity doctrine? Why is it important for someone considering leaving a traditional

job to start a new firm to be mindful of the corporate opportunity doctrine during the last months of employment?

4. Describe the purpose of a nondisclosure agreement and the purpose of a noncompete agreement.

5. What are some of the more important criteria to consider when selecting an attorney for a new firm?

6. Describe several ways an entrepreneur can save on legal fees without compromising the value of a relationship with an attorney.

7. Describe what a founders' agreement is and why it's important for a team of entrepreneurs to have one in place when launching a venture.

8. Describe several ways entrepreneurial firms can avoid legal disputes.

9. Describe what is meant by the terms "code of ethics" and "ethics training programs." What is their purpose?

10. What are the advantages and disadvantages of organizing a new firm as a sole proprietorship? Is a sole proprietorship an appropriate form of ownership for an aggressive entrepreneurial firm? Why or why not?

11. Describe the differences between a general partnership and a limited partnership. Is a general partnership an appropriate form of ownership for two people pooling their resources to start a high-growth entrepreneurial firm?

12. What are the major advantages and disadvantages of a C corporation? How is a C corporation subject to double taxation?

13. What is the difference between preferred stock and common stock? Who gets paid first in the event of liquidation—the preferred stockholders or the common stockholders?

14. What is meant by the term "piercing the corporate veil"? What are the implications for the owners of a corporation if the corporate veil is pierced?

15. What are the differences between a public corporation, a closely held corporation, and a private corporation? Which type of corporation enjoys the highest level of liquidity for its stock?

16. What are stock options? Why would a corporation offer stock options to its employees?

17. What are the advantages and disadvantages of a limited liability company? Is a limited liability company an appropriate form of ownership for an aggressive entrepreneurial firm?

18. What are some of the legal issues that the owners of a shop window Web site should be concerned about?

19. What is meant by the term "cybersquatting"?

20. Describe the significance of the Electronic Signatures in Global and International Commerce Act. Was the passage of the act a step forward or a step backward for proponents of electronic commerce?

1. Janice Miller currently works for Green Mountain Coffee is Waterbury, Vermont. She has given Green Mountain Coffee her 30-day notice and plans to open a coffee restaurant of her own in a neighboring community after leaving her current job. She's excited about the next 30 days because she won't be starting any new projects at work, so she figures she can spend most of her time working on her new business idea, recruiting Green Mountain Coffee employees to work for her after she leaves, and thinking about how she can use Green Mountain Coffee's strategies in her new business. Does Janice have a good, ethical strategy for leaving her current job? If not, what should Janice be doing differently?

2. A good friend of yours, Tim Jensen, is starting a new firm. He asked you if you know any good attorneys, and you tell him that you used an attorney to draw up a will a couple of years ago and had good luck. Tim asked you for the attorney's name and phone number. Is Tim using a good strategy to select an attorney to help launch a new firm? If not, what would be a better strategy for selecting an attorney for Tim?

3. Jason, Martin, and Marie are working on an idea for a new company, which they hope to launch within three months. Marie is pressuring Jason and Martin to accompany her to see an attorney to draw up a founders' agreement for their firm. Both Jason and Martin think Marie is jumping the gun and don't see the need to spend money for a founders' agreement until the firm has been operating for a few weeks. If you were asked to weigh in on this disagreement, would you side with Marie or Jason and Martin? Explain your decision.

4. Nancy Wills is purchasing a business named Niagara Laser Optics near Buffalo, New York. The business has had several brushes with the law during the past several years, dealing with claims of false advertising and wrongful termination of employees. As a result, Nancy is very concerned about the ethical climate of the firm. What specific techniques could Nancy use to increase the emphasis placed on business ethics when she takes control of the firm?

5. Ted Peterson has saved money his entire life. He currently has $260,000 in savings, a $175,000 house that is free of debt, and over $20,000 in college savings funds for each of three kids. He just left a staff job with Ford Motor and plans to open a restaurant. He can't quite decide on the form of legal entity for his restaurant. He wants to shield his personal assets from the liabilities of the restaurant and also plans to bring on some investors to open a second restaurant if the first succeeds. Advise Ted on the form of business organization that might make the most sense for his new firm.

6. Karen and Jessica are general partners in a chain of women's clothing stores. The stores are called K&J Women's Shop and are located in Des Moines, Iowa.

Recently, Karen was at a school event for her daughter and was explaining her business to one of her daughter's teachers. The teacher told Karen, "I don't want to seem nosey, but is your business really organized as a general partnership?" Karen said, "Yes, why would you ask?" The teacher replied, "My father and uncle Ken owned a chain of clothing stores in Minnesota and almost lost everything, including their cars and houses, when a customer slipped on a patch of ice near the entryway to one of the stores several winters ago and sued dad and my uncle Ken. They settled the lawsuit out of court and immediately incorporated the business to shield their personal assets from the liabilities of their business." Karen thought, "Maybe I should see an attorney to see if Jessica and I should incorporate our business." Do you think Karen and Jessica need to see an attorney? If so, why?

7. Brian just formed a C corporation. The shareholders of the corporation will be he and his wife Carrie and his father Bob, who put $35,000 of cash into the business. Brian explained to his wife and dad that he organized the business as a C corporation because of the ease of transfer of ownership of the stock. He said that if any of the three of them wanted his or her money out of the corporation, that person could simply find a buyer for the stock, just like the shareholders of Microsoft do, and transfer the ownership. Does Brian have realistic expectations regarding the ease of getting out of his investment if he wants to? Why or why not?

8. Laura just took a job with Cisco Systems in San Jose, California. One of things that attracted her to Cisco was the stock option plan that Cisco offers its employees. Explain what is meant by a stock option plan and why a company such as Cisco Systems would offer stock options to its employees.

9. Meredith just launched an e-commerce Web site to sell music CDs. She has extensive descriptions of the many artists and bands featured on her Web site, including numerous hyperlinks and deep links to articles about the artists and bands in magazines and newspapers. You asked Meredith if she has permission from the magazines and newspapers she was linking to in her articles, and she said, "Are you kidding? I probably have links to over 100 different newspapers and magazines. In addition, why would I need permission? The newspapers and magazines I link to are probably glad to get the exposure." Is Meredith on solid ground regarding her reasoning about the hyperlinks? Explain your answer.

10. You just read an article about electronic contracts and digital signatures, and the author of the article briefly referred to the Electronic Signatures in Global and International Commerce Act passed in 2000. The author said, "This act is undoubtedly one of the most important pieces of legislation in the history of the Internet." Based on the information contained in this chapter, do you think the author is exaggerating? Why or why not?

you be the **VC**

Company: **Eclipse Aviation (www.eclipseaviation.com)**

Business idea: Build a jet airplane that is so small and inexpensive to operate that a new class of air limo services will emerge to make private jet travel accessible to middle-class individuals and companies.

Pitch: Private jet service is safe and convenient but is also very expensive. To remedy this problem, Eclipse Aviation, a start-up in Albuquerque, New Mexico, has designed and constructed a six-passenger jet that has been successfully flown and tested. Eclipse plans to sell the jet for about $850,000, which is about one-fourth the cost of the least expensive corporate jet on the market. And it's engineered to be very cheap to operate: less than $1 per mile, which is one-third to one-fifth what it costs to fly other small jets. Eclipse's first jet is dubbed the Eclipse 500. Eclipse hopes to sell the jet to individuals, corporations, and regional airlines or "limo services" that will use it to shuttle

individuals to and from municipal airports. As an added bonus, the Eclipse 500 will boast a safety feature no jetliner can match: a parachute big enough to float the plane gently down to the ground. The parachute is made by Ballistic Parachute Systems (www.brsparachutes.com), which is a company that develops and deploys parachute systems for small aircraft.

Q&A: Based on the material covered in this chapter, what questions would you ask the founders of this firm before making your funding decision? What answers would satisfy you?

Decision: If you had to make your decision on just the information provided in the pitch and the company's Web site, would you fund this firm? Why or why not?

Case 8.1

Zipcar: How Would You Organize the Company?
www.zipcar.com

Imagine the following scenario. You're a graduate student at the Massachusetts Institute of Technology (MIT) near Boston. You live in a graduate dorm and don't have a car because it's expensive to pay for a parking spot and you've grown accustomed to using public transportation. Once a month, however, you have to travel to a small town in western Massachusetts to work on a research project. It's a 90-mile round-trip. The first two times you went, you took the subway downtown to a rental car agency and rented a car. That was a hassle and added an hour and a half to your travel time.

Recently, you were telling a friend about your predicament, and she told you about Zipcar, a start-up company that offers its members affordable 24-hour access to private vehicles for short-term trips. It is not a car rental company because only members can reserve and use Zipcar vehicles. The idea of sharing rather than renting cars is a European concept that has recently moved to the United States. For MIT staff and graduate students, the membership dues are only $20 per year, and the $300 refundable security deposit has been waived. Zipcar has also negotiated special parking spaces around campus, including one space at your dorm. A member can reserve a car for as little as an hour, walk to a parking location (such as the place outside your dorm), unlock the car with a special card (called a Zipcard), drive it away, and return it to the same location by the agreed-on time. It costs $8.50 to $12.50 per hour, plus 18 cents per mile after 125 miles, to have access to a car, which includes gas and insurance. (Prices vary by location.) Zipcar's fleet includes Volkswagen Beetles, four-door Golfs, Jettas, and Passats; Honda Civics; Ford Focus wagons; and Toyota Priuses. Members are responsible for refueling with a special credit card when the car goes below a quarter tank; the bill goes directly to Zipcar.

Zipcar sounds pretty good, so you decided to learn more. You log on to Zipcar's Web site to see if you're eligible for membership. The site says that members need to be at least 21 years old, have a driver's license, and have a good driving record. You learn that you can apply online and that once your membership has been accepted, you can reserve a car when needed up to two months in advance. New members are subjected to a $60 60-day trial membership, which gives you two months of Zipcar driving privileges and $60 in driving credit. If you want to keep driving, you just pay as you go once your $60 is used up. You can also cancel your membership after 60 days with no further obligation.

After signing up and being approved for the trial membership, you start to wonder about Zipcar itself since you're taking a course in entrepreneurship. After doing a little research, you learn that Zipcar was founded near MIT in Cambridge, Massachusetts, a couple of years ago. The founder was Robin Chase, an MIT alumnus, who worked the past 20 years in the areas of finance and operations. Once Zipcar got off the ground in Boston, it expanded to Washington, D.C., New York City, and New Jersey. The company currently has about 5,000 members and 200 cars. In addition to loaning cars to individuals, Zipcar has formed alliances with several city agencies and local businesses. An example is Zipcar's partnership with the city of Greenbelt, Maryland, a suburb of Washington, D.C. Greenbelt uses Zipcar's services to round out its fleet of city vehicles. Zipcar won't release revenue figures, but a spokesperson recently told Fortune Small Business that the company is "operationally profitable." In addition, the spokesperson revealed that Zipcar plans to expand soon to Philadelphia and Denver.

One thing that you couldn't learn about Zipcar was its form of business organization. In your class on entrepreneurship, you just read a chapter about the legal aspects of starting a new business. What you read in that chapter caused you to wonder if Zipcar is a sole proprietorship, partnership, corporation, or limited liability company. You also wonder about the people who work for Zipcar. You noticed on Zipcar's Web site that its vice president of operations, Mark Hemingway, has an extensive background working for rental car companies. Reading about Mr. Hemingway's background made you wonder if he had trouble getting out of a noncompete agreement with a previous employer to help get Zipcar off the ground. You also wonder if Zipcar requires its employees to sign noncompete and nondisclosure agreements as a condition of their employment. That would only make sense. If Zipcar is successful, similar companies might sprout up in Boston and elsewhere and try to lure away some of Zipcar's key employees.

Finally, you wonder about Zipcar's name and whether its Internet domain name was still available when the company was founded.

Discussion Questions

1. What do you think is the most appropriate form of business ownership for Zipcar: a sole proprietorship, partnership, corporation, or limited liability company? Weigh the advantages and disadvantages of each form of business ownership for Zipcar as part of your answer.

2. If Zipcar started as a subchapter S corporation, do you think the company is still a subchapter S corporation today? As Zipcar continues to expand to additional cities, what would be the biggest limiting factor about remaining a subchapter S corporation rather than becoming a C corporation or a limited liability company?

3. If you had been advising the founder of Zipcar when the company started, what types of steps would you have suggested to avoid legal disputes and set high ethical standards for the firm?

4. If you were the chief information officer for Zipcar when the company started, what types of legal issues would you have had to deal with regarding the company's Web site?

Sources: Zipcar home page, www.zipcar.com (accessed February 10, 2003), and "4 Great Picks," Fortune Small Business, February, 2003.

Case 8.2

Business Ethics: Are Ethics Training Programs Helpful?

In light of the corporate scandals of the early 2000s, there is a growing awareness of the importance of business ethics. In general, a firm known for its high ethical standards will be more profitable than a company with a poor ethical reputation. Just think of the businesses with which you are familiar. Do you know a business that has a reputation for being fair and honest? If so, it's probably a busy and prosperous one. On the other hand, do you know of a business that you believe acts in its own best interests, taking advantage of customers when it can do so? Watch this business because it will encounter problems that may well lead to the firm's bankruptcy.

For business organizations, practicing good ethical behavior contributes positively to the bottom line because it builds trust in both customer and employee relations. In regard to customers, a reputation for good ethics reduces the cost of doing business. For example, if a firm with questionable ethics ships a truckload of 300 units of a product to a customer and the customer has to count the units to make sure that the number is correct (because the customer doesn't fully trust the shipper), that process adds to the order's cost. In contrast, if the supplier has a reputation for honesty and for getting orders right and the customer feels no need to count the units in the truck, the cost of counting can be avoided. The customer could then afford to pay a little more for the product or may become a more regular customer because of the trusting nature of the relationship. Similarly, when the owners or managers of a firm model strong ethical behavior to their employees and establish trusting relationships, employee misconduct drops. According to a survey completed by the Ethics Resource Center in Washington, D.C., only 25 percent of the respondents who said that their bosses "set a good example" of ethical behavior had witnessed misconduct within the past year in their companies. In contrast, 72 percent of the respondents who said that their bosses had not set a good example of ethical behavior had witnessed misconduct in their organization within the past year.

There are a number of tools entrepreneurs can use to reinforce high standards of ethical behavior in their organizations. Consider a code of ethics. In the United States, over 90 percent of large corporations have a code of ethics, and in Canada the percentage is nearly the same. It is not known how prevalent codes of ethics are in smaller entrepreneurial firms. The research on the effectiveness of codes of ethics is mixed, with some studies showing a strong relationship between the presence of codes of ethics and ethical behaviors in firms and other studies showing weak relationships. An important factor regarding whether a code of ethics is effective may be the extent to which it is emphasized by top management and carefully and continuously communicated to the firm's employees.

Firms also use ethics training programs to promote ethical behavior. Ethics training programs teach business ethics to help employees deal with ethical dilemmas. Most employees confront ethical dilemmas at some point during their careers. In fact, according to the Ethics Resource Center survey referred to previously, 13 percent of the respondents said that they had felt some pressure to compromise ethical standards in their jobs.

A number of companies provide ethics training programs for both large organizations and smaller entrepreneurial firms. Character Training International (CTI), a Seattle-based business ethics firm, offers a variety of ethics-related training services to companies, including on-site workshops, speeches, train-the-trainer curriculum, videos, and consulting services. A distinctive attribute of CTI is its focus on the moral and ethical roots of workplace behavior. In workshops, participants talk about the reasons behind ethical dilemmas and are provided practical, helpful information about how to prevent problems and how to deal appropriately with the ethical problems and temptations that do arise. The hope is that this training will significantly cut down on employee misconduct and fraud and will increase morale. A company with a slightly different approach is VisionPoint Productions, which produces videos that provide information to employees on specific ethics-related issues. One of VisionPoint's most recent training videos is "A.C.T. with Integrity: Real Situations for Discussion." The A.C.T. acronym stands for **A**nalyze the situation—**C**onsider the consequences—and **T**ake appropriate action. The video consists of a series of vignettes depicting ethics-related situations. Employees watch the vignettes in training sessions that are led by an experienced facilitator. After each vignette, the facilitator guides the participants through an evaluation of the issues and leads a discussion of the steps that could be taken to resolve each concern and preserve the organization's integrity. The vignettes cover the following topics:

- Document retention and destruction
- Use of intellectual property
- Confidential information
- Use of electronic/computer technology
- Conflict of interest
- Accepting and giving gifts
- Maintaining quality of products and services
- Providing accurate information
- Dealing with diversity and discrimination
- Gathering competitive information
- Comparing your organization to the competition
- Handling reports of violations

Most entrepreneurs, as is the case with most businesspeople, support initiatives to improve or strengthen their organization's business ethics. The question with which they struggle, however, is whether specific steps such as writing a code of ethics or investing in ethics training sessions are really helpful. It's a quandary that all entrepreneurs face as they try to make the best use of scarce resources, particularly in their venture's start-up days.

Discussion Questions

1. How important do you think it is for a new entrepreneurial firm to establish a high standard of ethical behavior from the beginning? How do high standards of ethical behavior help a firm avoid litigation? How do high standards of ethical behavior help a firm get and keep customers?

2. Do you believe that corporate codes of ethics are useful? What would be the determining factors in making a code of ethics highly effective in an entrepreneurial organization?

3. Do you believe that ethics training programs, such as the ones described in this case, can help employees prevent or deal with ethical dilemmas? What types of training programs do you think are the most helpful: programs that teach honesty and integrity or programs that deal with specific issues, such as copyright infringement and destroying documents? Explain your answers.

4. If you were an entrepreneur, how would you decide whether a particular set of videos or written material dealing with business ethics was worth the investment?

5. Choose several firms located in your local community. Visit with the entrepreneurs leading those firms and ask each person to describe his or her venture's ethical climate as well as how that climate was established and is maintained.

Sources: N. E. Bowie, "Companies Are Discovering the Value of Ethics," USA Today (magazine), January 1998; S. Leonard, "Walking the Talk," HR Magazine, October 2000, 256; M. S. Schwartz, "A Code of Ethics for Corporate Code of Ethics," Journal of Business Ethics 41 (2002): 27–43; Character Training Inc. home page, www.character-ethics.org (accessed February 11, 2003); and Vision Point Productions home page, www.vppi.com (accessed February 11, 2003).

writing a *business* plan

After studying this chapter, you should be ready to:

1. Explain the purpose of a business plan.

2. Discuss how a business plan can be a dual-use document.

3. Explain how the process of writing a business plan can be as important as the plan itself.

4. Identify the advantages and disadvantages of using software packages to assist in the preparation of a business plan.

5. Explain the difference between a summary business plan, a full business plan, and an operational business plan.

6. Explain why the executive summary may be the most important section of a business plan.

7. Describe a milestone and how milestones are used in business plans.

8. Explain the purpose of a "sources and uses of funds" statement.

9. Describe a liquidity event.

10. Detail the parts of an oral presentation of a business plan.

electronic arts: it all started with a business plan

With six seconds left in the final quarter, the Philadelphia Eagles field goal kicker, David Akers, is just about to attempt a 37-yard field goal. The Eagles are lined up against the New England Patriots in Super Bowl XXVIII. The Eagles are down by two points, and everyone is on his or her feet. If Akers makes it, the Eagles will win the Super Bowl. The ball is snapped, Akers gets the kick away, it sails over the outreached hands of the Patriots defensive players, and it splits the uprights. The Eagles win Super Bowl XXVIII.

But wait a minute. The New England Patriots didn't play the Philadelphia Eagles in Super Bowl XXVIII. They played the Carolina Panthers. So what's up with that? What's up with this description is that the game we are describing was played on a Sony PlayStation 2 in the family room of a 16-year-old boy in Ambler, Pennsylvania, rather than in an NFL stadium. The boy was one of the millions of people who purchased Madden NFL 2003, an electronic game so realistic that the boy coached the Eagles through an entire season worth of games to get his team to the Super Bowl. And don't think it was easy. During the season, he had to work around injuries, a three-game losing streak, and two last-second victories to make it to the Super Bowl.

Madden NFL 2003 is produced by Electronic Arts (EA), the world's largest producer of interactive electronic games. To reflect the changes in the NFL team rosters, this game changes annually. As a result, there's a good chance that the young

Pennsylvania man who won the Super Bowl playing Madden NFL 2003 will buy Madden NFL 2004, Madden NFL 2005, and so on.

EA sells a number of other popular games, including The Sims, Harry Potter, James Bond, and FIFA Soccer. In 2002 alone, EA had 16 games that sold over a million copies. The company had revenues of $1.7 billion and net income of over $101.5 million.[1] The company develops its games for PCs as well as for console systems such as Sony's PlayStation 2, Nintendo's GameCube, and Microsoft's Xbox.

Although EA is now a large, successful company, it is instructive to look back and see how it all came together. As it turns out, it all started with a business plan and the vision of one man, Trip Hawkins, to create a new type of electronic games company.

As an entrepreneur, Hawkins got his feet wet in his late teens as he created a company to market a tabletop football game he invented. The game, called Accu-Stat, was developed long before the days of the PC, and players used dice and charts of player characteristics and stats to draw up realistic strategies. Accu-Stat was the precursor to Madden NFL games. Reflecting on his first business, Hawkins remarked,

> Of course, I was 19 years old and had no idea what I was doing, so the business failed. But it was perhaps the most important experience of my work life because I discovered my love for creating games could combine with a passion for entrepreneurship, and that failure could be used to just add fuel to the furnace. For years, my best friends would say that the only reason I started Electronic Arts was so that someday I could make another football game.[2]

After this business failed in 1980, Hawkins went to work for Apple Computer, where he got excited about the emerging PC industry. Although he enjoyed his time at Apple, he was determined to start another business. But this time around, he was more deliberate and patient. It wasn't until 1982 that he decided to start a company to make electronic games, an idea accompanied by a full business plan.

Hawkins felt he needed a really "big idea" to differentiate his new company from the others in the computer games industry. He actually came up with three big ideas, each part of the original business plan that separated EA from similar software publishers at the time:

- EA introduced the concept of the "software artist." Unlike other software companies, EA hired software designers and film producers instead of programmers. Each game was treated like a Hollywood production, with writers, film animators, and musicians as part of the team. Creativity was not only encouraged but also demanded.
- EA distributed its products directly to retail stores. At the time EA was founded, software publishers sold their products through third-party distributors. EA felt that it could better feel the pulse of the market and monitor future trends by selling its products directly to its retailers.
- EA used its own proprietary tools and technology to produce its games through an organized and efficient process of cross-platform development.

Years later, Trip Hawkins observed that EA's original business plan was a "bit amazing" in how well it predicted the future of the company. He went on to say that what made EA a winning company from the start was "the combination of strategic vision with the raw ability to adapt from mistakes and adjust and stick with it."[3]

learning **objective**

1. Explain the purpose of a business plan.

learning **objective**

2. Discuss how a business plan can be a dual-use document.

This chapter discusses the importance of writing a business plan. Although some new ventures simply "wing it" and start doing business without the benefit of formal planning, it would be hard to find an expert who doesn't recommend preparing a business plan. A **business plan** is a written narrative, typically 25 to 35 pages long, that describes what a new business plans to accomplish and how it plans to accomplish it. For most new ventures, the business plan is a dual-purpose document used both inside and outside the firm. Inside the firm, the plan helps the company develop a "road map" to follow in executing its strategies and plans. Outside the firm, it introduces potential investors and other stakeholders with the business opportunity the firm is pursuing and how it plans to pursue it.

This chapter begins by discussing issues that entrepreneurs often grapple with when faced with the challenge of writing a business plan. Topics included in the first section of the chapter are reasons for writing a business plan, a description of who reads the business plan and what they're looking for, and guidelines to follow when preparing a written business plan. The second section of the chapter includes a complete outline of a business plan with a description of the material in each section of the plan. The third section of the chapter deals with strategies for how to present the business plan to potential investors.

The Business Plan

As illustrated in the basic model of the entrepreneurial process, shown in Chapter 1, the time to write a business plan is towards the end of the stage in the entrepreneurial process titled "Moving from an Idea to an Entrepreneurial Firm." It is a mistake to write a full business plan too early. The business plan must be substantive enough and have sufficient details about the merits of the new venture to convince the reader that the new business is exciting and should receive support.

At the outset, it is also important for an entrepreneur to recognize what a business plan is and what it isn't. It isn't a contract, an agreement, or a budget. Instead, it is a narrative description of a new business. Steve Jurvetson, the founder of Hotmail and now a prominent venture capitalist, captures this sentiment with the following words: "The business plan is not a contract in the way a budget is. It's a story. It's a story about an opportunity, about the migration path, and how [a business] is going to create and capture value."[4]

A large percentage of entrepreneurs do not write business plans for their new ventures. In fact, only 40 percent of the businesses that appeared in the 2002 Inc. 500 said that they had written a formal business plan before they launched their ventures.[5] These statistics should not deter an entrepreneur from writing a business plan, however. Consider that we do not know how many of the 2002 Inc. 500 firms that didn't write a business plan now wish they had. Many entrepreneurs say that the day-to-day pressures of getting a company up and running leave them little time for planning. If this is truly the case, it is unfortunate. There are clear advantages to writing a business plan, and these are illustrated throughout this chapter.

Why a Business Plan Is Important

A business plan is important for two major reasons. First, a business plan is an internal document that helps a new business flesh out its business model and solidify its goals. It should convince the reader that the business idea is viable and that the venture being created to exploit that idea has a bright future. When prepared carefully, the business plan acts as an important road map for the initial management team and the employees of the firm. In the opening case, Trip Hawkins didn't prepare a business plan for EA and then set it on a shelf. He used the plan to guide the company as he and his cofounders established the culture, structure, and the firm's early strategies.

The second reason a business plan is important is because it is a selling document for a company. It provides a mechanism for a young company to present itself to potential investors, suppliers, business partners, and key job candidates[6] by showing how all the pieces of a new venture fit together to create an organization capable of meeting its goals and objectives.[7]

Imagine that you have enough money to invest in one new business. You chat informally with several entrepreneurs at a conference for start-ups and decide that there are two new ventures that you would like to know more about. You contact the first entrepreneur and ask for a copy of his business plan. The entrepreneur hesitates a bit and says that he hasn't prepared a formal business plan but would love to get together with you to discuss his ideas. You contact the second entrepreneur and make the same request. This time, the entrepreneur says that she would be glad to forward you a copy of a 30-page business plan, along with a 15-slide PowerPoint presentation that provides an overview of the plan. Ten minutes later, the PowerPoint presentation is in your e-mail in-box with a note that the business plan will arrive by FedEx the next morning. You look through the slides, which are crisp and to the point, and do an excellent job of outlining the strengths of the business opportunity. The next day, the business plan arrives just as promised and is equally impressive.

The founders of a firm often meet for long hours to hammer out the specifics of their business plan. Writing a business plan is challenging, exciting, and essential. It is a blueprint not only for the present, but the future of the company.

Which entrepreneur has convinced you to invest in his or her business? All other things being equal, the answer is obvious—the second entrepreneur. The fact that the second entrepreneur has a business plan not only provides you with detailed information about the venture but also suggests that the entrepreneur has thought through each element of the business and is committed enough to the new venture to invest the time and energy necessary to prepare the plan. Consistent with this notion, a leading authority on business plans writes about the importance of having a business plan when trying to obtain bank financing:

> A business plan helps set you apart from the crowd. I've had a number of bankers tell me that while their banks don't require business plans, companies that submit plans immeasurably improve their chances of getting the funds they seek.
>
> Keep in mind that bankers are nervous, averse to risk. A written business plan carries an important message even before it is read: It says the company's executives are serious enough to do formal planning. That's an important message because bankers believe that those individuals who plan are better risks than those who don't, and more deserving of bank funds.[8]

Who Reads the Business Plan— And What Are They Looking For?

There are two primary audiences for a firm's business plan. Let's look at each of them.

A Firm's Employees   A clearly written business plan, which articulates the vision and future plans of a firm, is important for both the management team and the rank-and-file employees of a new venture. The management team sometimes argues that it's a waste of time to write a business plan because the marketplace changes so rapidly that any plan will become quickly outdated. While it's true that marketplaces can and often do change rapidly, the process of writing the plan may be as valuable as the plan itself. Writing the plan forces the management team to think through every aspect of its business and agree on its most important priorities and goals.[9] Just imagine the managers of a new firm sitting at a conference table hammering out the content of their business plan. In most instances, many heated discussions are likely to take place as the firm's founders reach agreement on the most important aspects of their operations.

A clearly written business plan also helps a firm's rank-and-file employees operate in sync and move forward in a consistent and purposeful manner. The existence of a business plan is particularly useful for the functional department heads of a young firm. For example, imagine that you are the newly hired vice president for management information systems for a rapidly growing start-up. The availability of a formal business plan that talks about all aspects of the business and the business's future strategies and goals can help you make sure that what you're doing is consistent with the overall plans and direction of the firm.

The confidentiality of a firm's business plan should be protected to avoid the possibility of the plan falling into the hands of a competitor. Many firms restrict the number of copies of their business plan that can be made. These companies assign specific copies to specific people and require that the plans be secured in locked file cabinets or desks when not in use. In addition, most companies stamp the front page of their business plans "Confidential—Do Not Reprint without Permission." While these measures may not prevent the intentional theft of a firm's business plan by a disgruntled employee, they can prevent the inadvertent loss of a copy of the plan. These measures are tightened considerably when a start-up is working on a product or service that is highly sensitive or proprietary. Companies that formulate their initial business plans in secret refer to themselves as operating in "**stealth mode**." For example, during the time that Dean Kamer was developing the Segway, the self-balancing two-wheeled human transporter, the project was code-named "Ginger." Great lengths were taken to keep secret what the company was doing until its patents were applied for and it was ready to unveil its product.

Investors and Other External Stakeholders   External stakeholders, such as investors, potential business partners, potential customers, and key employees who are being recruited to join a firm, are the second audience for a business plan. To appeal to this group, the business plan must be realistic and not reflective of overconfidence on the firm's part.[10] Overly optimistic statements or projections undermine a business plan's credibility, so it is foolish to include them. At the same time, the plan must clearly demonstrate that the business idea is viable and offers potential investors financial returns greater than lower-risk investment alternatives. The same is true for potential business partners, customers, and key recruits. Unless the new business can show that it has impressive potential, there is little reason to become involved as an investor.

A firm must validate the feasibility of its business idea, develop an effective business model, and have a good understanding of its competitive environment (as described in the earlier chapters of this book) prior to presenting its business plan to others. Sophisticated investors, potential business partners, and key recruits will base their assessment of the future prospects of a business on facts, not guesswork or platitudes. The most compelling facts a company can provide in its business plan are the results of its own feasibility analysis and the articulation of a distinctive and competitive business model. A business plan rings hollow if it is based strictly on an entrepreneur's predictions and estimates of a business's future prospects. The problems that can befall an overly optimistic business plan or a plan based on unsound economics are illustrated in the boxed feature titled "What Went Wrong?," which looks at the troubles experienced by the Women's United Soccer Association professional sports league.

In addition to the previously mentioned attributes, a business plan should disclose all resource limitations that the business must fill before it is ready to start earning revenues. For example, a firm may need to hire service people before it can honor the warranties for

what went **wrong?**

Women's Professional Soccer: Did a Flawed Business Plan Sink an Otherwise Good Idea?

www.wusa.com

After the U.S. women's soccer team's victory over the Chinese in the final game of the 1999 World Cup, there was a surge of interest in women's soccer. This interest culminated with the launching in 2000 of the Women's United Soccer Association (WUSA) league. From the outset, expectations were high, and some of the top female soccer players in the world agreed to participate. The financial portion of the league's business plan relied on meeting the following three objectives:

1. Finding eight sponsors who would provide $2.5 million each for exclusive sponsorship rights within certain categories, such as sports apparel, beverages, fast food, and automobiles

2. A 2.0 television rating (a rating point represents 1,084,000 households, or 1 percent of the nation's estimated 108.4 million television homes)

3. Average attendance of 6,500 per game at $12 per ticket

Regrettably, the financial portion of the league's business plan never coalesced. By the end of the 2002 season, only two sponsors, Hyundai and Johnson & Johnson, had signed on. The league's television rating was a measly 0.1. On September 15, 2003, the WUSA suspended operations because of financial trouble. Ironically, the league shut down just six days before the U.S. women's national soccer team launched its defense of its women's World Cup title.

What went wrong with the WUSA? Plenty—but as it turns out, the failure of the league may have had more to do with its business plan than with the potential for women's soccer as a spectator sport in the United States. First, the league was plagued by simple unsound economics. Start-up costs were far greater than expected, and large league and team staffs consumed large amounts of money. The teams were geographically dispersed (from Boston to San Diego), making travel expensive. In addition, the $2.5 million the league asked for in sponsorships may have been too high. Some observers believe that instead of trying to find eight

sponsors that would contribute $2.5 million each, the league should have gone after more sponsors at a lower cost. More sponsors would also have meant more companies promoting the league.

Second, the league failed to establish a brand identity and "buzz," or awareness of and a sense of anticipation about a product. Major League Baseball creates buzz in many ways. One popular way is by distributing bobblehead dolls of popular players or broadcasters during special promotional games. These figures quickly become collector's items. The WUSA never caught on to this type of promotional activity and therefore never got the public excited about women's professional soccer. This failing led to poor merchandise sales (such as T-shirts, soccer balls, and mugs) and a television audience that never materialized.

The lessons learned from the failure of the WUSA apply as much to business start-ups as to professional sports leagues. Many people still believe that there is enough interest in women's soccer to support a professional league. If a new league does emerge, however, it will require a revamped business plan.

Questions for Critical Thinking

1. Given what you read in this feature, what sources of information would you want to include in a second business plan that could be developed to support another effort to launch the WUSA?

2. Choose two or three new and seemingly successful firms in your local community. Schedule appointments with those firms' leaders. The purpose of your interview is to gain information from each entrepreneur about how he or she developed a business plan for his or her venture. Compared to the financial objectives for the WUSA, do the financial objectives for the ventures of those you interviewed seem more realistic?

Sources: "Beginning or the End?," Soccer America, October 6, 2003; and R. Taylor, "Yes, We Can Save Women's Pro Soccer," Brandweek, September 29, 2003, 22.

the products it sells. It is foolhardy for a new venture to try to downplay or hide its resource needs. One of the main reasons new ventures seek out investors is to obtain the capital needed to hire key personnel, further develop their products or services, lease office space, or fill some other gap in their operations. Investors understand this, and experienced investors are typically willing to help the firms they fund plug resource or competency gaps. Consider Don Valentine, the famous Silicon Valley venture capitalist. Valentine and his firm, Sequoia Venture Capital, funded many successful entrepreneurial firms during the

1980s and 1990s, including Cisco Systems and Yahoo! Reflecting on how his firm helped Cisco and Yahoo! plug their competency gaps, Valentine wrote,

> There's a great similarity between the two companies. When we encountered the Cisco start-up team, there were actually five employees. The thing that struck me was the cleverness of the people at Cisco—they had an appreciation of what they were really good at, and a profound recognition of what they knew nothing about. Our relationship was struck on the basis that Sequoia would provide management, a management process, and $2.5 million and Cisco would provide the technical side of things.
>
> Interestingly, we began Yahoo! on the same basis. We encountered two individuals (Jerry Yang and David Filo) whose greatest strength was the recognition of their weaknesses and their lack of experience. And we struck the same kind of arrangement. We would go out and develop the management team and the management process, and we would put up the start-up money. They would work at what they were interested in and very good at.[11]

A summary of who reads business plans and what they're looking for appears in Table 9.1.

Guidelines for Writing a Business Plan

There are several important guidelines that should influence the writing of a business plan. It is important to remember that a firm's business plan is typically the first aspect of a proposed venture that will be seen by an investor. If the plan is incomplete or looks sloppy, it is

learning **objective**

3. Explain how the process of writing a business plan can be as important as the plan itself.

Table 9.1 Who Reads a Business Plan, And What Are They Looking For?

Audience	What Are They Looking For?
Internal Audience	
Company founders and initial management team	This is the group that typically writes the plan. The process of writing a business plan forces the firm's initial management team to think through every aspect of the business and to reach a consensus regarding the most important priorities.
Rank-and-file employees	This group will be looking for a clear description of what the company plans to accomplish and how it plans to accomplish it. Information on these topics helps employees make sure that what they are doing is consistent with the company's objectives and intended direction.
Board of directors	For firms that have a board of directors, the business plan establishes a benchmark against which the top management team's performance can be measured.
External Audience	
Potential investors	For investors, the business plan provides evidence of the strength of the business opportunity, the quality of the firm's top management team, and other relevant information. Investors will also be looking for how they will realize their investment return, whether through an initial public offering, sale of the company, or management buyback.
Potential bankers	Bankers are interested in how and when money loaned to a start-up would be repaid and whether the start-up has collateral available to secure a loan. Bankers are also interested in how a company would survive potential setbacks.
Potential alliance partners and major customers	High-quality alliance partners and major customers are generally reluctant to enter into arrangements with unknown companies. A convincing business plan can help lessen their doubts.
Key recruits for jobs with the new firm	Key recruits will be looking primarily at the excitement of the business opportunity, the compensation scheme for key employees, and the future prospects of the firm.
Merger and acquisition candidates	Companies grow through acquisitions and engage in divestitures as a way of gaining liquidity. In either case, a potential merger or acquisition candidate will typically ask a company for a copy of its business plan to use as their first screening tool.

easy for an investor to infer that the venture itself is incomplete and sloppy.[12] It is important to be sensitive to the structure, content, and style of a business plan before sending it to an investor or anyone else who may be involved with the new firm.

Structure of the Business Plan

To make the best impression, a business plan should follow a conventional structure, such as the outline for the business plan shown in the next section. Although some entrepreneurs want to demonstrate creativity in everything they do, departing from the basic structure of the conventional business plan format is usually a mistake. Typically, investors are very busy people and want a plan where they can easily find critical information. If an investor has to hunt for something because it is in an unusual place or just isn't there, he or she might simply give up and move on to the next plan.

There are many software packages available that employ an interactive, menu-driven approach to assist in the writing of a business plan. Some of these programs are very helpful. However, entrepreneurs should avoid a boilerplate plan that looks as though it came from a "canned" source. The software package may be helpful in providing structure and saving time, but the information in the plan should still be tailored to the individual business. Some businesses hire consultants or outside advisers to write their business plans. While there is nothing wrong with getting advice or making sure that a plan looks as professional as possible, a consultant or outside adviser shouldn't be the primary author of the plan. Along with facts and figures, a business plan needs to project a sense of anticipation and excitement about the possibilities that surround a new venture, a task best accomplished by the creators of the business themselves.[13] Plus, savvy venture capitalists learn important things about entrepreneurs on the basis of their writing style, choice of words, and so forth.

Content of the Business Plan

The business plan should give clear and concise information on all the important aspects of the proposed venture. It must be long enough to provide sufficient information yet short enough to maintain reader interest. For most plans, 25 to 35 pages are sufficient. Supporting information, such as the résumés of the founding entrepreneurs, can appear in an appendix.

After a business plan is completed, it should be reviewed for spelling and grammar and to make sure that no critical information has been omitted. There are numerous stories about business plans sent to investors that left out important information, such as significant industry trends, how much money the company needed, or what the money was going to be used for. One investor even told the authors of this book that he once received a business plan that didn't include any contact information for the entrepreneur. Apparently, the entrepreneur was so focused on the content of the plan that he or she simply forgot to provide contact information on the business plan itself.[14]

Style or Format of the Business Plan

The appearance of the plan must be carefully thought out. It should look sharp but not give the impression that a lot of money was spent to produce it. The people who read business plans know that entrepreneurs have limited resources and expect them to act accordingly. A plastic spiral binder including a transparent cover sheet and a back sheet to support the plan is a good choice. A plan that is stapled together may look amateurish.

One of the most common questions that the writers of business plans ask is, How long and detailed should it be? The answer to this question depends on the type of business plan that is being written. There are three types of business plans, each of which has a different rule of thumb regarding length and level of detail. Presented in Figure 9.1, the three types of business plans are as follows:

- *Summary plan:* A **summary business plan** is 10 to 15 pages and works best for companies that are very early in their development and are not prepared to write a full plan. The authors of a summary business plan may be asking for funding to conduct the analysis needed to write a full plan (such as a feasibility analysis). Ironically, summary business plans are also used by very experienced entrepreneurs who may be

learning objective

4. Identify the advantages and disadvantages of using software packages to assist in the preparation of a business plan.

learning objective

5. Explain the difference between a summary business plan, a full business plan, and an operational business plan.

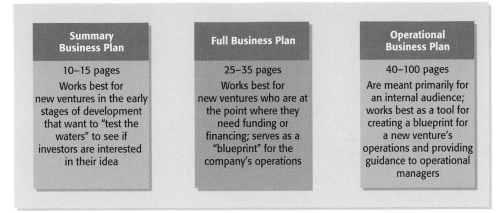

Figure 9.1

Types of Business Plans

Summary Business Plan

10–15 pages
Works best for new ventures in the early stages of development that want to "test the waters" to see if investors are interested in their idea

Full Business Plan

25–35 pages
Works best for new ventures who are at the point where they need funding or financing; serves as a "blueprint" for the company's operations

Operational Business Plan

40–100 pages
Are meant primarily for an internal audience; works best as a tool for creating a blueprint for a new venture's operations and providing guidance to operational managers

thinking about a new venture but don't want to take the time to write a full business plan. For example, if someone such as Meg Whitman, the chief executive officer (CEO) of eBay, was thinking about starting a new business, she might write a summary business plan and send it out to select investors to get feedback on her idea. Most investors know about Ms. Whitman's success at eBay and don't need detailed information.

- *Full business plan:* A **full business plan**, which is the assumed focus of our discussions to this point in this chapter, is typically 25 to 35 pages long. This type of plan spells out a company's operations and plans in much more detail than a summary business plan, and it is the format that is usually used to prepare a business plan for an investor. As we've mentioned, the readers of business plans are usually busy people, and a long, drawn-out plan simply will not be read. In fact, the sharper and more concise a full business plan is, the better. Detailed information, such as the résumés of the founders or pictures of product prototypes, can appear in an appendix.

- *Operational business plan:* Some established businesses will write an **operational business plan**, which is meant primarily for an internal audience. An operational business plan is a blueprint for a company's operations. Commonly running between 40 and 100 pages in length, these plans can obviously feature a great amount of detail. An effectively developed operational business plan can help a young company provide guidance to operational managers.

A cover letter should accompany a business plan sent to an investor or other stakeholders through the mail. The cover letter should briefly introduce the entrepreneur and clearly state why the business plan is being sent to the individual receiving it. As discussed in Chapter 10, if a new venture is looking for funding, it is a poor strategy to get a hold of a list of investors and blindly send the plan to everyone on the list. Instead, each person who receives a copy of the plan should be carefully selected on the basis that he or she is a viable candidate as an investor.

Outline of the Business Plan

A suggested outline of the full business plan appears in Table 9.2. A specific firm's business plan may vary, depending on the nature of the business and the personalities of the founding entrepreneurs. Most business plans do not include all the elements introduced in Table 9.2; we include them here for the purpose of completeness. Each entrepreneur must decide which specific elements to include in his or her business plan.

A business plan is intended to be a living document that can change if the situation warrants. As discussed throughout this book, new ventures must often bob and weave to keep in step with a changing environment. Many businesses update their business plans on an annual or semiannual basis to maintain the plan's effectiveness.

Table 9.2

Business Plan Outline

Cover Page
Table of Contents

I. **Executive Summary**
   A. The Opportunity
      • Problem to solve or need to be filled
   B. The Description of the Business
      • How the proposed business solves the problem or fills the need
   C. Competitive Advantage
      • Description of the business model
   D. The Target Market
   E. The Management Team
   F. Brief Summary of the Financial Projections
   G. Description of What the Business Needs
      • The amount of capital needed and what the capital will be used for, if the plan is going to a potential investor
   H. Exit Strategy for Investors (if the plan is going to investors)

II. **The Business**
   A. The Opportunity
      • Problem to solve or need to be filled
   B. The Description of the Business
      • How the proposed business solves the problem or fills the need
      • Brief company history or background
      • Company mission and objectives
   C. Competitive Advantage
      • Description of the business model
      • How the business will create a sustainable competitive advantage
   D. Current Status and Requirements
      • Description of where the business stands today
      • Description of what the business needs to move forward

III. **Management Team**
   A. Management Team
      • Management experience
      • Management ability
      • Technical expertise
   B. Board of Directors
      • Number of directors
      • Composition of the board
   C. Board of Advisers
      • Number of advisers
      • Composition of the advisory board
      • How the advisory board will be used
   D. Key Professional Service Providers
      • Law firm
      • Accounting firm
      • Business consultants

IV. **Company Structure, Intellectual Property, and Ownership**
   A. Organizational Structure
      • Organizational chart
      • Description of organizational structure
   B. Legal Structure
      • Legal form of organization
      • Ownership structure of the business
   C. Intellectual Property
      • Patents, trademarks, and copyrights applied for or approved

V. **Industry Analysis**
   A. Industry description
      • Industry trends
      • Industry size
      • Industry attractiveness (growing, mature, or in decline)
      • Profit potential

Table 9.2

(continued)

B. Target Market
  • Description of target market
C. Competitive position within target market
  • Competitor analysis

VI. Marketing Plan
  A. Product Feasibility and Strategy
    • Product strategy
    • Concept testing
    • Usability testing
  B. Pricing Strategy
  C. Channels of Distribution
  D. Promotions and Advertising

VII. Operations Plan
  A. Method of Production or Service Delivery
  B. Availability of Qualified Labor Pool
  C. Business Partnerships
    • Types of business partnerships
    • Purposes of business partnerships
  D. Quality Control
  E. Customer Support
    • Customer support strategies
    • Customer support obligations

VIII. Financial Plan
  A. Capital Requirements for the Next Three to Five Years
    • Sources and uses of funds
  B. Overview of Financial Projections
    • Explanation of how financial projections are prepared (assumption sheet)
  C. Income Statements
  D. Cash Flow Projections
  E. Balance Sheets
  F. Payback and Exit Strategy (if the business plan is sent to potential investors)

IX. Critical Risk Factors
  A. Management Risks
  B. Marketing Risks
  C. Operating Risks
  D. Financial Risks
  E. Intellectual Property Infringement
  F. Other Risks as Appropriate

X. Appendix
  A. Supporting Documents
    • Résumés of founders and key employees
    • Picture of product prototypes
    • Other documents as appropriate

Exploring Each Section of the Plan

Cover Page and Table of Contents The cover page should include the name of the company, its address, its phone number, the date, and contact information for the lead entrepreneur. Given today's technologies, the contact information should include a land-based phone number, an e-mail address, and a cell phone number. This information should be centered at the top of the page. Because the cover letter and the business plan could get separated, it is wise to include contact information in both places. The bottom of the page should include information alerting the reader to the confidential nature of the plan. If the company already has a distinctive trademark, it should be placed somewhere near the center of the page. A table of contents should follow the cover letter. It should list the sections and page numbers of the business plan and the appendices.

learning **objective**

6. Explain why the executive summary may be the most important section of a business plan.

Executive Summary   The **executive summary** is a short overview of the entire business plan; it provides a busy reader with everything that needs to be known about the new venture's distinctive nature.[15] In many instances, an investor will first ask for a copy of a firm's executive summary and will request a copy of the full business plan only if the executive summary is sufficiently convincing. The executive summary, then, is arguably the most important section of the business plan[16] in that if it fails to attract an investor's interest, he or she is unlikely to read the remainder of the plan. After reading the executive summary, an individual should have a relatively good understanding of what will be presented in greater detail throughout the plan. The most important point to remember when writing an executive summary is that it is not an introduction or preface to the business plan. Instead, it is meant to be a one- to two-page summary of the plan itself.

If the new venture is seeking financing or funding, the executive summary should state the amount of funds being requested. Some plans will state how much equity a business is willing to surrender for a certain amount of investment capital. In these instances, the executive summary will conclude with a statement such as "The firm is seeking $1 million in investment capital in exchange for a 15 percent ownership position." Other entrepreneurs are more leery about how much equity they are willing to surrender and leave their plans intentionally vague on this point.

Although the executive summary appears at the beginning of the business plan, it should be created after the plan is finished. Only then can an accurate overview of the plan be written.[17]

The Business   The most effective way to introduce the business is to describe the opportunity the entrepreneur has identified—that is, the problem to solve or the need to be filled—and then describe how the business plans to address the issue. This is the initial "hook" that captures the interest of the reader of a business plan. The description of the opportunity should be followed by a brief history of the company, along with the company's mission statement and objectives. An explanation of the company's competitive advantage and a brief description of the business model follow. The section should conclude with a summary of the firm's current status and a description of what it needs to move forward.

Using milestones is one particularly effective way of describing where a business stands today and what it needs for its future. A **milestone**, in a business plan context, is a noteworthy event in the past or future development of a business. A business could describe where it stands today by listing the date it was founded as its first significant milestone and then summarizing the company's history by referring to the major milestones that were achieved. The future of the business could be described in terms of projected milestones. The first projected milestone might be receiving the funding requested by the business plan. Additional projected milestones would then illustrate what could be accomplished with the funding in place and provide a time line for the future major events in the life of the firm.

learning **objective**

7. Describe a milestone and how milestones are used in business plans.

Management Team   As mentioned earlier, one of the most important things investors want to see when reviewing the viability of a new venture is the strength of its management team. If the team doesn't "pass muster," most investors won't read further. Primus Venture Partners, a venture-capital firm based in Cleveland, Ohio, is most interested in the following features when considering an investment: (1) proven management, (2) significant management ownership, (3) attractive market opportunity and economics, and (4) strong track record of success.[18] Note that the second attribute focuses on the amount of money that the management team has invested in the venture. The amount of money the management team has invested in a new venture is often called "**skin in the game**." Investors are wary of investing in a venture if the founders and the key members of the management team haven't put some of their own money (or "skin") into the venture. The management team of the venture should own a large enough equity stake to ensure that they are adequately motivated to weather the demands of building a successful firm.

The material in this section should include a brief summary of the qualifications of each key member of the management team, including his or her relevant employment and professional experiences, significant accomplishments, and educational background. Managers' résumés should appear in an appendix if they add useful information. If management team members have worked together before, that work-related experience should be emphasized. There is always a risk that people, regardless of how talented they are, won't be able to work together effectively. Management teams that have a track record of success are a lower risk to investors than a group of people who are new to one another.

The next portion of this section should include material on the board of directors if the firm has or plans to have one (in most cases it will). The composition of the board should be described. For example, if a firm plans to have five directors, the business plan should specify the sources (i.e., from inside the firm or from different places outside the firm) from which those directors would be drawn. A typical scenario for a new venture with five directors is to allocate two director slots to insiders (company founders and/or key management personnel), two director slots to outsiders (people who do not work for the firm), and one director slot for the investor. As we discussed in Chapter 6, many new ventures also have an advisory board.

This section should conclude by listing the professional service providers the firm works with—its law firm, its accounting firm, and any consulting firms. How these professionals have helped the firm achieve its initial objectives and milestones should be described.

Company Structure, Ownership, and Intellectual Property

This section should begin by describing the structure of the new venture, including the reporting relationships among the top management team members. A frequent source of tension in new ventures, particularly if two or more founders start out as "equals," is a failure to delineate areas of responsibility and authority.[19] To demonstrate that the founders have sorted out these issues, an organizational chart should be included. An **organizational chart** is a graphic representation of how authority and responsibility are distributed within a company.[20] A short narrative description should supply information on the most important reporting relationships shown in the chart.

The next part of this section should explain how the firm is legally structured in terms of whether it is a sole proprietorship, a partnership, a C corporation, a subchapter S corporation, a limited liability company, or some other form. This issue was discussed in detail in Chapter 8. The ownership structure of the business should also be revealed. If a founders' agreement exists, it should be included in an appendix.

The third portion of this section should discuss the intellectual property the firm owns, including patents, trademarks, and copyrights. This is an extremely important issue. Intellectual property forms the foundation for the valuation and competitive advantage of many entrepreneurial firms. Any significant patents, trademarks, and copyrights a firm has in its intellectual property pipeline should also be revealed unless the information is highly proprietary. If it is highly proprietary, the company should assert that it is operating in stealth mode with intellectual property issues. The importance of intellectual property is discussed in detail in Chapter 12.

Industry Analysis

This section should begin by discussing the major trends in the industry in which the firm intends to compete along with important characteristics of the industry, such as its size, attractiveness, and profit potential. For example, the health care industry in the United States is attractive to many investors because of the aging of the American population. Today, there are approximately 35 million people in the United States who are 65 years old or older. By about 2030, when the large demographic group known as the baby boomers reaches retirement age, that number will swell to 65 million to 75 million people.[21] This section should also discuss how the firm will diminish or sidestep the forces that suppress its industry's profitability. The firm's target market should be discussed next, along with an analysis of how the firm will compete in that market. To show how a firm's products or services stack up against the competition, the plan should include a competitor analysis (discussed in Chapter 4). A competitive analysis grid provides a visual way for an investor to quickly ascertain the major strengths and distinctive attributes of a new venture's product or service offerings compared to its competitors.

After reading the industry analysis, an investor should have a good grasp on the future prospects of the industry (or industries) in which the firm intends to compete along with an understanding of the target market the firm will pursue and how it will defend its position. One thing the business plan shouldn't include is a long-winded description of an industry, particularly if the plan will be sent to people who are already familiar with the industry. For example, a venture capitalist specializing in the electronic games industry doesn't need a lengthy description of the industry from an entrepreneur. Unnecessary content diminishes the value and appearance of a business plan.

It is important for a firm to think carefully about the industry in which it will compete and the target market it will pursue in developing its business plan. These points are illustrated in the boxed feature titled "Savvy Entrepreneurial Firm" on Red Bull, a company that makes energy drinks.

Marketing Plan   The marketing plan should immediately follow the industry analysis and should provide details about the new firm's products or services. This section of the business plan typically is carefully scrutinized. It is very important to investors, in particular, to be confident that a new venture has a product that people will buy and has a realistic plan for getting that product to market. As discussed in Chapter 5, the ability to get a product to market typically requires a network of business partners. These key partnerships should be discussed in this section. Information about the unique marketing issues facing new ventures is provided in Chapter 11.

This section should begin with a fuller description of the products the firm will sell than has been provided in previous sections of the plan. The results of the feasibility analysis should be reported, including the results of the concept tests and the usability

As baby boomers age, opportunities will grow for entrepreneurial firms in the healthcare industry. Look for entrepreneurial expansion in pharmaceutical, diagnostics, imaging, insurance, and other health-related businesses.

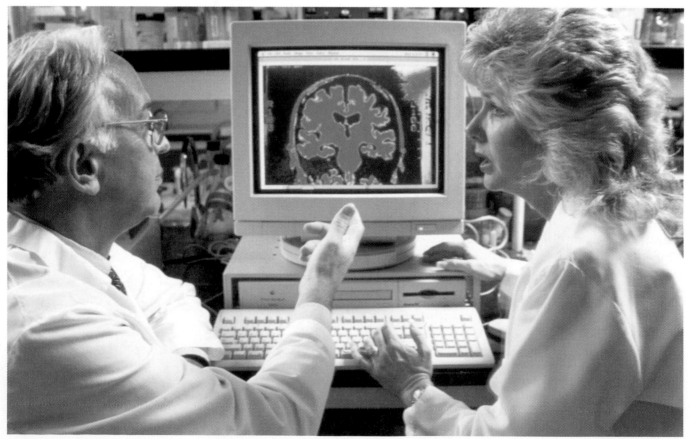

Savvy entrepreneurial FIRM

Red Bull: Showing the Value of a Tightly Focused Target Market

www.redbull.com

In 1982, Dietrich Mateschitz, an Austrian, was sitting in a hotel in Hong Kong when he learned about products called "tonic drinks," which athletes used to boost their energy. The drinks were popular in Asia at the time but were not marketed in Europe or the United States. The idea intrigued Mateschitz, and in 1984 he launched a company called Red Bull to market his version of the Asian tonic drinks. To get attention, he packaged the drink uniquely—Red Bull comes in a sleek, distinctively colored 8.3-ounce can with a red bull on the side. The drinks promised to provide athletes increased physical stamina, concentration, and vigilance to help them endure the rigors of their sports.

Red Bull quickly caught on in Austria and spread to neighboring countries. In 1992, Red Bull entered Hungary, which was the firm's first foreign market. The drink was introduced in the United States in 1997. Rather than setting out to capture the entire U.S. market, however, Red Bull's business plan concentrated on a much tighter target market. The company began its U.S. efforts by focusing on 16- to 29-year-olds involved in sports. The company then rolled out its campaign one region at a time, learning what worked best before going on to the next region. Today, Red Bull is sold in over 100 countries around the world. In total, customers now consume over a billion cans of Red Bull annually, making Red Bull the world's most popular energy drink.

There were a couple of other nifty aspects to Red Bull's U.S. business plan that set it apart from its competitors. One particularly successful tactic was to create buzz about the product before it even hit the market by offering free samples through sports clubs and other places in which athletes congregated. When the product finally hit the shelves, it sold quickly. The company also shopped for the hungriest distributors to keep its costs down. Finally, as demand grew, the company never took its eye off its target market: young athletes. Today, Red Bull still focuses on young athletes and sponsors many who are involved in extreme sports.

Red Bull's energy drinks are now making their way into the mainstream market, but the company's early success in the United States was due largely to its decision to focus on a clearly defined target market. By doing so—and by building excitement for the product before it was placed in stores, rolling out the product region by region, and learning as it went—Red Bull executed its U.S. business plan in an exemplary manner.

Questions for Critical Thinking

1. Go to Red Bull's Web site (www.redbull.com). What is your evaluation of the Web site in terms of its approach to appeal to young athletes? What features of the company's Web site do you believe target customers would find the most appealing. Why?

2. Gatorade competes against Red Bull. In your opinion, what would Red Bull's target market customers find more appealing about Red Bull compared to Gatorade? What does Red Bull do to outperform Gatorade in terms of the key characteristics appealing to Red Bull's target customers?

Sources: Arthur Andersen (2003); Red Bull home page, www. redbull.com (accessed June 2, 2004); Boston Consulting Group, Winning the New-Product War (Boston: Boston Consulting Group, 2002); and K. Hein, "A Bull's Market," Brandweek, May 28, 2001.

---

tests. A diagram or digital image of the product or the product prototype should be included if it can be done tastefully. An alternative is to include the diagram or image in an appendix to the plan. If the product is small or inexpensive enough—such as a type of nonperishable food—a sample of the product itself could be provided with the business plan. If the product is technologically sophisticated, it should be explained in everyday terms. Investors usually aren't scientists, so technical jargon and industry slang should be avoided. The plan should fully explain any request for funds to more fully develop a product or service. After the product has been described, the other elements of the firm's marketing mix, including pricing, channels of distribution, and promotions, should be addressed.[22] After reading this section of the plan, an investor should be confident that the firm's overall approach to its target market and its product strategy, pricing strategy, channels of distribution, and promotions strategy are in sync with one another and make sense.[23]

If a new venture wants to include more in its business plan than space allows or if the business plan is not a suitable format for providing certain information, the business plan can refer the reader to the company's Web site. However, it is vital that all technological aspects of the Web site work flawlessly throughout the time the business plan in begin distributed.

Operations Plan   This section of the plan deals with the day-to-day operations of the company. The section should begin by describing how the firm plans to manufacture its first product and how realistic the estimates are in this area.[24] The reader will want to know how much of the manufacturing the firm will do itself and how much will be contracted out to others. The location of the manufacturing facility should be specified, along with the availability of a qualified labor pool. Another important issue is how much inventory will need to be carried to meet customer needs. If the company is a service organization, similar information should be provided.

An overview of the manufacturing plan should be followed by a description of the network of suppliers, business partners, and service providers that will be necessary to build the product or produce the service the firm will sell. As described in Chapter 5, all firms are embedded in a network of partnerships that help bring its products and services to market. The major relationships should be described. Investors are suspicious about firms that try to do everything themselves.

A firm's quality control procedures should also be explained. It isn't necessary to go into detail, but the plan should indicate what monitoring or inspection processes will be built into the manufacturing process to ensure high quality. Customer support strategies should then be discussed. If a firm is obligated to provide after-sale support to its customers through a call center or other means, these obligations should be clearly described.

Any risks and regulations pertaining to the operations of the firm should be disclosed, such as nonroutine regulations regarding waste disposal and worker safety. This issue becomes important when a firm is producing waste products subject to Environmental Protection Agency regulations. A firm can incur substantial liability if its waste products are not disposed of appropriately.

An increasingly common feature of many business plans for start-ups is a reliance on outsourcing certain functions to third parties as a way of allowing the start-up to focus on its distinctive competencies. One of the most common areas that new firms outsource is human resource management, as illustrated in the boxed feature titled "Partnering for Success."

Financial Plan   The financial section of a business plan must demonstrate the financial viability of the business. A careful reader of the plan will scrutinize this section. The financial plan should begin with an explanation of the funding that will be needed by the business during the next three to five years along with an explanation of how the funds will be used. This information is called a **sources and uses of funds statement**.[25] It is also helpful to demonstrate where the money to fund the business has come from to date. Some business plans offer a time line of when money was infused into the business. The time line then typically shows the need for an additional infusion of capital (which is why the investor or banker is reading the plan) along with how the business will further progress if the additional capital is made available.

The next portion of this section includes financial projections, which are intended to further demonstrate the financial viability of the business. The financial projects should include three to five years of pro forma income statements, balance sheets, and statements of cash flows, as described in Chapter 7. It is crucial that an assumption sheet, which was also described in Chapter 7, precede the projections. Recall that the assumption sheet explains the basis for the numbers included in the pro forma financial statements.

It is important to remember that a business plan should be based on realistic projections. If it is not and the company gets funding or financing, there will most certainly be a day of reckoning. Investors and bankers hold entrepreneurs accountable for the numbers in their projections. If the projections don't pan out and it becomes obvious to the investors

learning **objective**

8. Explain the purpose of a "sources and uses of funds" statement.

Partnering for SUCCESS

Outsourcing Human Resource Management: An Increasingly Common Feature of the Business Plans of New Firms

As mentioned in Chapter 5, new ventures typically do not have the resources to perform all the tasks required to make their businesses work, so they rely on partners to perform key roles. An increasingly common role that new ventures are allowing partners to perform is the management of their human resources. Managers of start-ups are very busy and need to focus their energies on the core business issues facing their firms. Human resource management issues, such as screening job applicants, training, payroll, benefits administration, and regulatory compliance, are very time-consuming activities. In the minds of many start-up managers, spending time dealing with these issues makes no sense when there are professional human resource management firms that are experts at performing these tasks and that can do them at an affordable price.

Start-ups vary in terms of the amount of the human resource functions they outsource to others. Some firms outsource only administrative tasks, such as payroll processing and benefits administration. These firms partner with a payroll accounting firm such as Paychex or Ceridian. Paychex, in particular, focuses on small and medium-size businesses and currently processes the payrolls of more than 490,000 clients. In fact, its average client has just 14 employees, and a third have fewer than five. In addition to payroll, Paychex is capable of administrating its clients' benefits program, tax payment services, workers' compensation, and other routine human resource management functions.

Some start-ups outsource a broader range of their human resource management functions and partner with a company such as Automatic Data Processing or Administaff. These companies are called professional employer organizations (PEO) and act like an off-site human resource department for a small firm. Along with doing everything that Paychex does, PEOs can help a start-up with hiring, firing, training, regulatory compliance, and other more in-depth related issues. Outsourcing these tasks can save a busy company founder or management team untold hours of work and effort—hours that are best spent implementing the company's business plan.

One subtle yet significant thing that a business plan tells an investor is how the top management team of a start-up will spend their time. Well-placed partnering initiatives, such as those mentioned in this feature, signal an investor that a management team is committed to pouring 100 percent of its time and energy into the essential tasks that will make a new venture successful.

Questions for Critical Thinking

1. Go to the Web sites of various business publications (e.g., www.wsj.com or www.fortune.com) to study current outsourcing trends. What is your opinion of outsourcing? Given what you find during your search of business publications, develop two arguments—one supporting entrepreneurs use of outsourcing and one supporting the position that entrepreneurs shouldn't outsource activities required to run their ventures.

2. Assume that you intend to launch a venture to sell an organic fertilizer that you and your partner have developed. While developing the operations part of your firm's business plan, you and your partner started to discuss outsourcing as a way to control costs. For your proposed venture, what activities would you be willing to outsource, and what activities do you believe shouldn't be outsourced. Why?

or bankers that the numbers were too optimistic to begin with, the long-term credibility of the entrepreneurs involved will be damaged.

If the business plan is being sent to investors, the financial projections should be followed by a discussion of the rate of return that the investors can expect and how they will get their money back. A venture-capital firm will typically want to reclaim an investment in a fairly short period of time (three to five years), while a private investor, a business angel, or an institutional investor may have a longer-term investment horizon. Investors get their money back through a **liquidity event**, an occurrence that converts some or all of a company's stock into cash. The three most common liquidity events for a new venture are to go public, find a buyer, or merge with another company. For example, when a firm goes public, its stock starts trading on one of the major exchanges, such as the NASDAQ or the New York Stock Exchange. Once this happens, an investor can sell his or her stock through

learning **objective**

9. Describe a liquidity event.

the exchange—thereby converting the stock to cash. It is much harder for an investor to find a buyer for stock that isn't traded on a major exchange.

While it may seem odd to talk about selling a company at the time it is being founded, it is just good planning to have an **exit strategy** in mind. Commenting on this topic, Edwin A. Goodman, cofounder of Milestone Venture Partners in New York, said,

> From a venture and an astute entrepreneur's standpoint, you want to think about the endgame when you enter. An entrepreneur's emphasis should always be, "I have a good idea, here's the market and here's how I can address it and build a solid company." And as a secondary matter, [an entrepreneur] should say, "When we achieve those goals, we'll sell the company."[26]

Critical Risk Factors Although a variety of potential risks may exist (see the business plan outline in Table 9.2), a business should tailor this section to depict its truly critical risks. One of the most important things that a business plan should convey to its readers is a sense that the venture's management team is on the ball and understands the critical risks facing the business.

The critical risks a new business may face depend on its industry and its particular situation. For example, a business may be counting on the U.S. Patent and Trademark Office to grant a patent to protect its exclusive right to manufacture a product and to provide a barrier to entry for its competition. What if the patent isn't approved? Similarly, a business may be looking for an experienced chief financial officer to manage the growing financial complexities of its operations. A critical risk factor in this context would be the venture's inability to find a suitable candidate for this job on a timely basis. Most plans will include alternative courses of action.

Appendix Any material that does not easily fit into the body of a business plan should appear in an appendix—résumés of the top management team, photos or diagrams of product or product prototypes, certain financial data, and market research projections. The appendix should not be bulky and add significant length to the business plan. It should include only the additional information vital to the plan but not appropriate for the body of the plan itself.

Putting It All Together In evaluating and reviewing the completed business plan, the writers should put themselves in the reader's shoes to determine if the most important questions on the viability of their business venture have been answered. Table 9.3 lists the 10 most important questions a business plan should answer. It's a good checklist for any business plan writer.

Table 9.3

The 10 Most Important Questions a Business Plan Should Answer

1. Is the business just an idea, or is it an opportunity with real potential?
2. Does the firm have an exciting and sensible business model? Will other firms be able to copy its business model, or will the firm be able to defend its position through patents, copyrights, or some other means?
3. Is the product or service viable? Does it add significant value to the customer? Has a feasibility analysis been completed? If so, what are the results?
4. Is the industry in which the product or service will compete growing, stable, or declining?
5. Does the firm have a well-defined target market?
6. How will the firm's competitors react to its entrance into its markets?
7. Is the management team experienced, skilled, and up to the task of launching the new firm?
8. Is the firm organized in an appropriate manner? Are its strategy and business practices legal and ethical?
9. Are the financial projections realistic, and do they project a bright future for the firm? What rate of return can investors expect?
10. What are the critical risks surrounding the business, and does the management team have contingency plans in place if risks become actual problems?

Presenting the Business Plan to Investors

If the business plan successfully elicits the interest of a potential investor, the next step is to meet with the investor and present the plan in person. The investor will typically want to meet with the firm's founders. Because investors ultimately fund only a few ventures, the founders of a new firm should make as positive an impression on the investor as possible.

The first meeting with an investor is generally very short, about one hour.[27] The investor will typically ask the firm to make a 20- to 30-minute presentation using PowerPoint slides and use the rest of the time to ask questions. If the investor is impressed and wants to learn more about the venture, the firm will be asked back for a second meeting to meet with the investor and his or her partners. This meeting will typically last longer and will require a more thorough presentation.

The Oral Presentation of a Business Plan

When asked to meet with an investor, the founders of a new venture should prepare a set of PowerPoint slides that will fill the time slot allowed for the presentation portion of the meeting. The first rule in making an oral presentation is to follow instructions. If an investor tells an entrepreneur that he or she has one hour and that the hour will consist of a 30-minute presentation and a 30-minute question-and-answer period, the presentation shouldn't last more than 30 minutes. The presentation should be smooth and well rehearsed. The slides should be sharp and not cluttered with material.

learning **objective**

10. Detail the parts of an oral presentation of a business plan.

The entrepreneur should arrive at the appointment on time and be well prepared. If any audiovisual equipment is needed, the entrepreneur should be prepared to supply the equipment if the investor doesn't have it. These arrangements should be made before the meeting. The presentation should consist of plain talk and should avoid technical jargon. Start-up entrepreneurs may mistakenly spend too much time talking about the technology that will go into a new product or service and not enough time talking about the business itself. Another mistake entrepreneurs often make is not having the right material at their fingertips. For example, suppose that an entrepreneur has an exciting new product and has submitted a patent application to prevent others from producing the same product. If an investor asks, "When did you submit your patent application?," it makes a poor impression if the entrepreneur answers, "I can't remember the exact date, but I think it was in January or February of last year." Because the patent represents an essential part of the firm's ability to protect its competitive advantage, the entrepreneur should know or be able to locate within seconds the exact date the patent application was filed.

The most important issues to cover in the presentation and how to present them are as follows:

- *The company:* Offer a quick, one-slide overview of the company and its target market.
- *Opportunity (the problem to be solved or the need to be filled):* The heart of the presentation, it should be spread over two or three slides.
- *Solution:* Explain how the firm will solve the problem or how it will satisfy the need to be filled. This information should be spread over one or two slides.
- *The strength of the management team:* Briefly explain, in one or two slides, each manager's qualifications.
- *Intellectual property:* Explain, in one slide, the intellectual property the firm owns or will own pending approval.
- *Industry, target market, and competition:* In two or three slides, briefly review the industry in which the firm will compete, its target market, and its direct and indirect competitors. Explain specifically how the firm will compete against the established companies in its target market.
- *Financials:* Briefly discuss the financials. Stress when the firm will achieve profitability, how much capital it will take to get there, and when its cash flow will break even. This discussion should take two or three slides.
- *Offering, payback, and exit strategy:* In one slide, discuss the amount of money requested and the anticipated exit strategy.

This presentation format calls for the use of 10 to 15 slides. A common mistake entrepreneurs make is to prepare too many slides and then try to rush through them during a 30-minute presentation.

Questions and Feedback to Expect from Investors

Whether in the initial meeting or on subsequent occasions, an entrepreneur will be asked a host of questions by potential investors. The smart entrepreneur has a good idea of what to expect and is prepared for these queries. Because investors often come across as being very critical,[28] it is easy for an entrepreneur to get discouraged, particularly if the investor seems to be poking holes in every aspect of the business plan. It helps if the entrepreneur can develop a thick skin and remember that on most occasions the investor is simply doing his or her job. In fact, an investor who is able to identify weaknesses in a business plan does a favor for the entrepreneur. This is because the entrepreneur can take the investor's feedback to heart and use it to improve his or her product or service. Sometimes, a potential investor's feedback helps the entrepreneur learn how to prepare a more effective presentation. In both of these cases, the investor who seems particularly negative may benefit the entrepreneur.

In the first meeting, investors typically focus on whether a real opportunity exists and whether the management team has the experience and skills to pull off the venture. The investor will also try to sense whether the managers are highly confident in their own venture. The question-and-answer period is extremely important. Here investors are typically looking for how well an entrepreneur thinks on his or her feet and how knowledgeable he or she is about the business venture. Michael Rovner, a partner of Rob Adam's at AV Labs, put it this way: "We ask a lot of peripheral questions. We might not want answers—we just want to evaluate the entrepreneur's thought process."[29]

CHAPTER SUMMARY

1. A business plan is a written narrative that describes what a new business intends to accomplish and how it plans to achieve its goals.

2. For most ventures, the business plan is a dual-purpose document used both inside and outside the firm. Inside the firm, it helps the company develop a road map to follow in executing its strategies. Outside the firm, it acquaints potential investors and other stakeholders with the business opportunity the firm is pursuing and describes how the business will pursue that opportunity.

3. Writing a business plan can be as valuable as the plan itself. The work required to write a business plan forces the management team to think through every aspect of the business and to establish the most important priorities.

4. Many software packages can assist in the writing of a business plan. These packages provide structure and can save time. However, entrepreneurs should avoid using business plan software that produces boilerplate material. The information in the plan should always be tailored to the individual business.

5. A summary business plan is 10 to 15 pages and works best for companies in the early stages of development. These companies don't have the information needed for a full business plan but may put together a summary business plan to see if potential investors are interested in their idea. A full business plan, typically 25 to 35 pages, spells out a company's operations and plans in much more detail than a summary business plan and is the usual format for a business plan prepared for an investor. An operational business plan is usually prepared for an internal audience. It is 40 to 100 pages and provides a blueprint for a company's operations.

6. The executive summary is a quick overview of the entire business plan and provides a busy reader everything that needs to be known about the distinctive nature of the new venture. In many instances, an investor will ask for a copy of a firm's executive summary and will request a copy of the full business plan only when the executive summary is sufficiently convincing.

7. One particularly effective way of describing where a business stands today and what it needs to move forward is to use milestones. A milestone, in a business plan context, is a signpost of a noteworthy event in the past of the future development of a business.

8. The financial portion of a business plan should begin with an explanation of the funding that will be needed by the business during the next three to five years along with an

explanation of how the funds will be used. This information is called a sources and uses of funds statement.

9. Investors get their money back from investing in a firm through a liquidity event, which is an occurrence that converts some or all of a company's stock into cash. The three most common liquidity events for a new venture are to go public, find a buyer, or merge with another company.

10. When asked to meet with an investor, the managers of a new venture should prepare a set of PowerPoint slides that will fill the time slot allowed for the presentation portion of the meeting. The key topics to cover include the company, the opportunity, the strength of the management team, intellectual property (if there is any), industry analysis, financials, and offering, payback and the exit strategy.

KEY TERMS

business plan, 204

executive summary, 214

exit strategy, 220

full business plan, 211

liquidity event, 219

milestone, 214

operational business plan, 211

organizational chart, 215

skin in the game, 214

sources and uses of funds statement, 218

stealth mode, 207

summary business plan, 210

REVIEW QUESTIONS

1. What is a business plan? What are the advantages of preparing a business plan for a new venture? Explain your answer.

2. When is the appropriate time to write a business plan?

3. What are the two primary reasons for writing a business plan?

4. A business plan is often called a selling document for a new company. It what ways does a business plan provide a mechanism for a young company to present itself to potential investors, suppliers, business partners, and key job candidates?

5. It is often argued that the process of writing a business plan is as important as the plan itself, particularly for the top management team of a young firm. How is this so?

6. What are some of the ways to protect the confidentiality of a business plan?

7. What does a company mean when it says it is operating in stealth mode?

8. Why is it necessary for a business plan to be realistic? How will investors typically react if they think a business plan is based on unsubstantiated predictions and estimates rather than on careful thinking and facts? Explain your answer.

9. Why is it important for a business plan to be honest in regard to any gaps (or limitations) that the business has to fill before it is ready to begin earning revenues?

10. Who reads the business plan, and what are they looking for?

11. Why is it important for a business plan to follow a conventional structure rather than be highly innovative and creative?

12. Can business planning software packages be used effectively in preparing a business plan? What are the things to avoid when using such software packages?

13. What are the differences between a summary business plan, a full business plan, and an operational business plan?

14. What should be included on a business plan's cover page? Why is it important to include contact information on the first page of a business plan if the same information is included in the cover letter that accompanies the plan?

15. Many people argue that the executive summary is the most important section in a business plan. What is the basis of this argument? Do you think the executive summary is the most important section in a business plan, or do think this argument is overstated? Why?

16. Why is it important for a firm to describe the industry in which it intends to compete as part of its business plan? What are the most important topics to discuss in this section?

17. What is the purpose of a sources and uses of funds statement? Why is it important to include this statement in the financial section in a business plan? Explain your answer.

18. What is the purpose of an assumption sheet? Why is it important to include an assumption sheet in a business plan's financial section?

19. What is a liquidity event? Why are investors interested when a new venture thinks that a liquidity event will occur?

20. Why is it important for a business plan to address critical risk factors?

1. Brad Jones is the chief financial officer of an electronic games start-up venture located in San Diego. His firm has decided to apply for venture-capital funding and needs a business plan. Brad told Phil Bridge, the firm's CEO, that he could have the plan done in two weeks. Phil looked at Brad with surprise and said, "Wouldn't it be better if the entire management team of our firm worked on the plan together?" Brad replied, "The only reason we're writing the plan is to get funding. Getting a lot of people involved would just slow things down and be a waste of their time." Do you agree with Brad? Why or why not?

2. Christina Smith, who lives near Seattle, just left her job with Microsoft to start a business that will sell a new type of fax machine. She knows she'll need a feasibility analysis, a well-articulated business model, and a business plan to get funding, but she can't decide which project to tackle first. If Christina asked you for your advice, what would you tell her, and what rationale for your decision would you provide to Christina?

3. John Brunner is a biochemist at a major university. He is thinking about starting a business to commercialize some animal vaccines on which he has been working. John just registered for a biotech investment conference in San Francisco. A number of venture capitalists are on the program, and John hopes to talk to them about his ideas. John hasn't written a business plan and doesn't see the need to write one. When asked about this issue, he told a colleague, "I can sell my ideas without the hassle of writing a business plan. Besides, I'll have plenty of time to talk to investors at the conference. If they need additional information, I can always write something up when I get home." Explain to John why his approach to the development of a business plan is unwise.

4. Joan Barnes, who is launching a telecommunications start-up, just completed her business plan. She showed it to a close friend who read it and told Joan that she was somewhat surprised by some of the omissions in the plan. Joan's friend told her, "The plan is well written, but it doesn't say anything about the things you need to get your business up and running. The plan makes it sound like you have everything in place. You told me you need to hire a chief technology officer, you need to hire a patent attorney to file your patent applications, and you need to find an outside contractor to build your product." Joan replied, "There is no way that I'm going to tell a potential investor or business partner that I need all those things. I don't want them to think that I'm just starting. If I get the money I need, those things will fall into place very quickly." Do you agree with Joan? Do you think she's on the right track, or is she headed for trouble? Explain your answer.

5. Jared Watts, who lives in Topeka, Kansas, is starting a graphic design business and has just started to write his business plan. Jared was telling a couple of friends at lunch that he plans to write a plan like no one has ever seen before. He plans to skip the basic business plan format and write it in a comic book format to try to grab the attention of investors. Jared thinks the creativity of such a plan would really impress those thinking about investing in a graphic design business. Do you think Jared's idea will work? What are the advantages and disadvantages of Jared's approach?

6. SureTechRide is the name of an Internet Service Provider start-up that includes a founding team of five entrepreneurs. The founders spent the past three weeks writing a business plan that runs 77 pages. They aren't sure if they should go ahead and send it out or if they should try to revise it to make it shorter. The lead entrepreneur, Sally Davis, thinks they should go ahead and send it out, arguing, "The length of the plan will show investors that we really have a grip on things. They will appreciate our hard work." Do you agree with Sally? Should they go ahead and send out the plan, or should they revise it and try to make it shorter? Why?

7. Peter Ford, who lives in Fort Collins, Colorado, has read several books on how to raise money to fund a new venture. All of them say that investors focus on the strength of the top management team. Peter can't figure out why this is true. Recently, he wrote a letter to the editor of *Inc.* magazine and asked, "Why do investors put so much stock in the strength of the top management team of a start-up? If the start-up's product and marketing strategy isn't any good, what is the value of a strong top management team?" If you were the editor of *Inc.*, how would you reply to Peter's letter?

8. Recently, Jill, Diane, and Steven, the founders of a digital photography start-up, presented their business plan to a group of investors in hopes of obtaining funding. One of the investors asked the three, "How much of your personal money do you each have invested in the venture?" Is this an appropriate question? Why would an investor want to know how much of their personal money Jill, Diane, and Steven had invested in the start-up?

9. Tom Popper, who is launching a designer-clothing start-up, recently met with a consultant to talk about the process of writing a business plan. The consultant emphasized that the financial projections in the business plan should be based on a set of well-thought-out assumptions that can be clearly explained in the plan. If after the meeting Tom asked you why it is important to base the financial projections in a business plan on well-thought-out assumptions, what would you tell him?

10. Tracey Williams just got off the phone with an angel investor and is ecstatic because the investor asked her and

her management team to present their business plan next Thursday at 1:00 P.M. The investor said the meeting would last one hour and that 30 minutes would be devoted to the presentation of the business plan and that the remaining 30 minutes would be devoted to a question-and-answer session. Tracey wants to make the best of this opportunity and has turned to you for advice. How would you advise Tracey to prepare for this meeting?

you be the VC

Company: **HydroPoint** (**www.hydropoint.com**)

Business idea: Build a system that provides real-time weather data wirelessly to the controllers (which are electronic boxes) of irrigation systems to permit the systems to adjust their irrigation schedule according to the expected weather in the area.

Pitch: Have you ever seen a home owner, a golf course, or an office building watering its lawn during a rainstorm or shortly before or after it rained? Overwatering hurts the environment; it ruins lawns, wastes water, and can cause serious runoff problems. Using a patented system called WeatherTRAK, HydroPoint has developed a system that addresses this challenge. Every day, the WeatherTRAK data service transmits location-based weather data, wirelessly, to irrigation systems that are equipped with its controllers. Controllers are electronic boxes that regulate the timing and flow of water through an irrigation system. WeatherTRAK's controllers, which can be installed in new irrigation systems or retrofitted into existing ones, are suitable for both residential and commercial systems. On the basis of the weather forecast it receives, a WeatherTRAK controller automatically calculates the proper watering schedule for an irrigation system to which it is connected. The timing couldn't be better for this device. Many municipalities are struggling with maintaining a proper water supply and often impose watering restrictions during periods of drought. WeatherTRAK's system conserves water by reducing overwatering. The system also helps its customers save money by eliminating overwatering and keeping lawns and landscapes healthy.

Q&A: Based on the material covered in this chapter, what questions would you ask the founders of this firm before making your funding decision? What answers would satisfy you?

Decision: If you had to make your decision on just the information provided in the pitch and the company's Web site, would you fund this firm? Why or why not?

Case 9.1

Learning from Failure: Is Furniture.com's Business Plan More Convincing This Time Around?

www.furniture.com

Furniture.com was one of the biggest flameouts during the dot-com craze. The company was an online firm that promised to reinvent the furniture industry by featuring thousands of items on its Web site that could be purchased online and sent directly from the manufacturer to the consumer. According to the company's original business plan, this approach would vastly increase the selection of furniture available to consumers and save money by eliminating the furniture store.

As it turned out, the hype surrounding the business plan never panned out. Launched in June 1998, Furniture.com closed in November 2000. Curiously, however, the company, under new management and with a new business plan, has reemerged. In April 2002, the Furniture.com Web site went live again after 17 months in the dark. This turn of events has left many observers to wonder if Furniture.com's new business plan is more convincing than its previous one. Let's see what you think.

Furniture.com's original business plan was to take on the retail furniture industry, just as Amazon.com took on retail bookstores. The furniture industry seemed appealing. Home furnishings have high profit margins, and the high-flying U.S. economy, at the time Furniture.com was launched, produced seemingly endless streams of young families looking to buy the right couch or entertainment center for their new home. The business model also sounded good. By partnering directly with manufacturers,

Furniture.com could list literally thousands of items on its Web site and give picky consumers 500 sofas to choose from rather than the 50 they might see in visits to furniture stores. By buying direct, the company also promised to offer the lowest price available.

Unfortunately, there were several problems with this business plan that surfaced almost immediately after the company was launched. First, although margins in the furniture industry are high, selling furniture is a grueling business, fraught with manufacturing delays, high shipping costs, and intense competition. In addition, people typically like to see furniture before they buy it. While it sounds good to have 500 sofas to choose from, how many people will actually buy a sofa before they sit on it? In addition, the company was determined to get big fast. It poured millions into advertising to build its brand image and drive business to its Web site.

Order fulfillment became a nightmare. In many cases, manufacturers overpromised in terms of when products would be available, and shipping a large armoire from North Carolina (where many of them are made) to California (where many of them were bought) is more complicated than you might think. The company got many complaints about missing or late deliveries, and shipping costs were high. As losses mounted, the founders scrambled to arrange for new funding, but it was too little too late. All these factors converged to sink the company. Furniture.com filed for Chapter 11 bankruptcy court protection in November 2000 after burning through most of the $100 million it had raised from investors.

On April 15, 2002, Furniture.com resumed operations with a new management team and a different business plan. A group of former employees, led by Carl Prindle, who was a vice president of the original company, purchased the Furniture.com domain name and intellectual property for $1 million. This time, instead of taking on the furniture industry, Furniture.com has decided to partner with it. Instead of selling direct from the manufacturer, Furniture.com is partnering with brick-and-mortar furniture retailers in order to sell their inventories. Customers of the new site enter their ZIP codes and are shown only products that are available in their areas. Once an item is ordered, it is passed off to the local retailer, who handles the delivery and any returns. "That will ensure that we can get the product to

them and do it fairly quickly," new CEO Prindle said, noting that at the time of the firm's second launch, the intended average delivery time was 7 to 10 days. Furniture.com receives a commission for the furniture sold through its site.

The problem of trying out the new sofa has been solved too—sort of. Consumers will be able to try out the furniture they're interested in at the participating stores if they want to make the trip. There are other changes that differentiate the new Furniture.com from the old one. The company will spend very little on marketing. Instead, it will be featured on its partner's Web sites and through in-store promotions. It plans to grow slowly as it adds partners to its network. It will also feature a very modern and interactive Web site that will allow its customers to design a room online and that will provide access to an online furniture magazine.

Is Furniture.com's new business plan more convincing than its old one? The company is currently looking for more partners to expand the geographic reach of its Web site. "They're scaling methodically," says spokesman Don Goncalves. "They're looking forward to proving themselves."

Discussion Questions

1. Why do you think the original Furniture.com failed? Was its original business plan flawed, or did its managers simply do a poor job of executing the plan? Explain your answer.

2. What are the advantages of Furniture.com's new business plan compared to its original business plan? If you were an investor, would you be comfortable with the fact that a former vice president of the original company was now leading the revitalized company? Why or why not?

3. Does the new Furniture.com have a sensible and attractive business model? Why or why not?

4. Do you believe that the new Furniture.com will be successful? Make your answer as substantive and thoughtful as possible.

Sources: N. Wingfield, "Furniture.com Returns to Web in Deals with Established Stores," Wall Street Journal, April 15, 2002, B4; "Furniture.com: The Sequel," CIO Magazine, August 15, 2002.

Case 9.2

Helping Families Save for College: Does Upromise Have a Viable Business Plan?
www.upromise.com

While shopping for groceries, eating at a restaurant, or filling up your gas tank, you may have noticed an increasingly familiar logo. The logo is a small "U" wearing a graduation mortarboard followed by the name Upromise. Mention Upromise among your friends and relatives, and chances are that at least a few of them have opened a Upromise account.

Upromise is a for-profit start-up that was launched in 2001. The purpose of the company is to help families save for college. The idea is simple. Parents register free at the Upromise Web site, where they are asked for a credit card number. Friends

and relatives can sign up to help a family save too. Whenever the parent (or another party who is registered to contribute to an account) buys something from a Upromise partner, a small rebate is placed in the parent's account. The rebates range from one cent a gallon at Exxon to three percent of the purchase at Target. The cost of the purchase isn't affected. There are no receipts to keep track of or rebate forms to mail in. Upromise handles all the paperwork and maintains the parent's account. Once an account reaches a certain amount, Upromise urges the account holder to transfer the money into a state-run college savings account, called a 529 plan. A state-approved 529 plan provides tax advantages that Upromise isn't able to deliver.

To launch its venture, Upromise was able to attract venture-capital funding largely as the result of the strength and passion of its management team. Its founder, Michael Bronner, was the founder and longtime CEO of Digitas, a highly successful marketing firm. To strengthen the initial founding team, Bronner added George Bell, the former head of Internet portal Excite, as CEO. The company has both a board of directors and a board of advisers. Its board of directors includes Bill Bradley, a former U.S. senator and professional basketball player. Its board of advisers includes Kim Clark, dean of the Harvard Business School, and George Fisher, chairman of Eastman Kodak. Bronner and his team's passion for Upromise's service results primarily from the company's mission to help families save for college. "I wanted to make a difference," Bronner said after leaving Digitas in 2000 a wealthy man, "not run an operation." So far, the company has raised over $100 million in venture-capital funding.

Upromise appears to be a win-win proposition for everyone involved. Parents win by accumulating money for their children's education. The company estimates that a typical account will accumulate $12,000 to $20,000 over 15 years. While that amount won't pay for a four-year college education, it's a start. Upromise's partners, including McDonald's, Coca-Cola, Amazon.com, GAP, and over 150 other major corporations, win by gaining customer loyalty. The one question mark is whether Upromise's business plan is viable in the for-profit world. Its founders initially thought about establishing Upromise as a not-for-profit organization. They eventually decided, however, that the company would have the best chance of attracting top-quality talent and corporate partners as a for-profit entity.

The question mark surrounding Upromise's business plan is whether the company will be able to generate sufficient revenue to reach profitability and satisfy its investors. The company obtains its revenue from two sources. First, it receives a small fee for each Upromise transaction. For example, when a member buys $50 worth of merchandise at Target and Target places three percent of the purchase price, which amounts to $1.50 into the member's account, Upromise keeps a small percentage of the $1.50. Second, once a member's account reaches a certain level, Upromise encourages the member to transfer the money into a state-approved college 529 savings plan. Upromise has partnerships with firms such as Salomon Smith Barney and Fidelity that administer 529 plans. If a member signs up with one of one of those firms, Upromise receives a referral fee. The fear is that, over time, interest in Upromise may wane. The company currently has over four million members, but it's not known how many of its memberships are active. There is a possibility that members will tire of seeking out Upromise partners or that, as college admission prices increase, Upromise will play only a small role in helping them save for their children's college educations. Another problem is that overall awareness of state-approved college 529 savings plans is low. It's not known how many Upromise members will actually transfer funds to 529 plans, enabling Upromise to collect a referral fee.

It is clear that Upromise has the heart and spirit of a not-for-profit organization and has many proponents cheering it along. "Everyone wants this company to win," founder Michael Bronner said. Still, its investors will eventually want their money back through some type of liquidity event. For that to happen, the company will have to be not only profitable but also gaining momentum. The company can achieve those goals only if its business plan is fundamentally sound.

Discussion Questions

1. If you had the initial idea for Upromise, do you think you would have been able to write a convincing business plan? Based on the business plan outline provided in Table 9.2, what sections of Upromise's business plan do you think would have been the strongest? Which sections would have been the weakest?

2. If you had to prepare 12 to 15 PowerPoint slides to present Upromise's business plan, briefly describe how you would break down the presentation and the topic of information that you would include on each slide.

3. Has Upromise identified an attractive target market? If so, do you think its position within its target market is defensible? Was having a first-mover advantage important for Upromise? Why or why not?

4. Has Upromise done a good job of following the basic model of the entrepreneurial process shown at the beginning of this book? Justify your answer.

5. What type of liquidity event would most likely satisfy Upromise's investors?

Sources: Upromise home page, www.upromise.com (accessed May 18, 2004), and C. Adler, "A Killer Idea," Fortune Small Business, February 2003, 56–59.

getting *financing* or funding

After studying this chapter, you should be ready to:

1. Explain why most new ventures need to raise money at some point during their early life.

2. Identify the three sources of personal financing available to entrepreneurs.

3. Provide examples of how entrepreneurs bootstrap to raise money or cut costs.

4. Identify the three steps involved in properly preparing to raise debt or equity financing.

5. Explain the role of an elevator speech in attracting financing for a firm.

6. Discuss the difference between equity funding and debt financing.

7. Describe the difference between a business angel and a venture capitalist.

8. Explain why an initial public offering is an important milestone for a firm.

9. Discuss the SBA Guaranteed Loan Program.

10. Explain the advantages of leasing for an entrepreneurial firm.

cisco systems:
now for the rest of the story

Cisco Systems is the world's leading supplier of products that link computer systems to the Internet. Founded in 1984 and with 36,000 employees, the company currently has sales of $19 billion, no debt, and about $20 billion in cash and investments, and it dominates the market for routers and switches.[1] Cisco is also known for its aggressive acquisition strategy. Since 1993, it has acquired close to 80 companies to broaden its product lines and secure engineering talent.[2] All this effort has landed Cisco at the number 92 spot on the Fortune 500. As was the case for many companies, Cisco's performance declined during the burst of the Internet bubble. Today, however, the company is profitable and is well positioned for the future.

Sound impressive? It is. Cisco has come a long way since being launched. In fact, in 2000, Cisco was briefly the most valuable company in the world with a market capitalization of over $550 billion. But Cisco wasn't always so impressive, and Cisco's founders faced the same challenges as most entrepreneurs, particularly in the area of raising money.

If you remember from Chapter 2, Leonard Bosack and Sandra Lerner, who met in graduate school, fell in love, and got married, are Cisco's founders. After graduating, they took jobs managing computer networks at Stanford University. Bosack worked in the computer science department, while Lerner oversaw the computers at the graduate school of business. The two wanted to send electronic love letters to each other, but their computer networks were incompatible. So Len and Sandy figured out a way to connect the networks and, with the help of some colleagues, invented the router. A router is a black box consisting of a twist of cable and some agile software that enables computer networks to talk to one another. The router was the key to making Bosack and Lerner's computer systems compatible.[3]

After experimenting with their new invention, Bosack and Lerner realized that they were on to something.[4] Initially, the two tried to sell their product to existing computer companies, but none were interested, so they decided to start their own company. There were actually five founders, with colleagues Greg Setz, Bill Westfield, and Kirk Lougheed joining Lerner and Bosack to launch the venture.

As with the majority of entrepreneurial start-ups, Cisco had to grind it out at the beginning and work hard to find the funding it needed. To illustrate how difficult it was, here is how one author described the early days of Cisco Systems:

> At first, Lerner and Bosack set up shop in the house they shared with Bosack's parents in suburban Atherton, California, just up the road from Stanford. They bought a used mainframe and set it up in the garage. One bedroom served as the lab, another bedroom was turned into office space, and they used the living room to build and test. They hired friends, maxed out their credit cards, and took their initial orders over the nascent Internet.[5]

Despite these primitive beginnings, Bosack and Lerner persisted, and Cisco sold its first router in March 1986. There was no money for advertising or a sales staff, so the company developed its customer base strictly by word of mouth. Because of its product's strength, Cisco grew rapidly during its first two years. However, even though it was taking in $250,000 per month, the company was desperately short of cash. To help close the financial gap, Lerner went back to work for a while to bring in some money. By 1988, the founders knew that if Cisco were to grow and prosper, funding beyond what they themselves could provide would be required.

To raise funds, Lerner and Bosack started talking to venture capitalists. They were turned down time and time again. Finally, they met Don Valentine, the 77th investor they had approached. Valentine and his firm, Sequoia Capital, agreed to fund Cisco—but with some hefty strings attached. Later, reflecting on why so many venture capitalists turned down Bosack and Lerner and why Sequoia asked for so much, Valentine said,

> Ninety-nine percent of venture capitalists think of themselves as investing in great people. In this case, we looked right past Len and Sandy, and concentrated instead on the great potential market that existed for their product. They were good scientists and did a lot to set the tone for the company, but they had never managed a thing.[6]

In exchange for its $2.5 million investment, Sequoia received almost one-third of Cisco's stock, and Don Valentine became its chairman. Valentine was also granted the authority to recruit personnel and build the nascent firm's management structure. Lerner and Bosack assumed more technical roles. In 1988, Valentine hired John P. Morgridge, a seasoned manager, to serve as Cisco's first chief executive officer (CEO).

Under Morgridge's leadership, Cisco grew rapidly, and on February 16, 1990, the firm went public. Although the public offering made Bosack and Lerner rich, they clashed repeatedly with Morgridge and left the firm in 1995. Since then, Cisco has prospered, and the company is currently strong, profitable, and poised for future growth.

Of course, Cisco's story doesn't represent the experience of all new ventures. However, it does illustrate the types of challenges faced by many new firms. Start-ups often have difficulty raising money because they are unknown and untested. Founders must frequently use their own money and go to friends and family for help. If the firm is successful, it will typically outrun the capacity of its founders to scrape up enough money and will have to turn to investors or lenders to raise capital. This effort is often a grueling endeavor. As with Cisco's founders, many entrepreneurs hear the word "no" many times before they match up successfully with a banker or investor.

I n this chapter, we focus on the process of getting financing or funding. We start with a discussion of why firms raise capital, followed by a description of personal financing and the importance of personal funds, capital from friends and family, and bootstrapping in the early life of a firm. Then we'll turn to the different forms of equity, debt, and creative financing available to entrepreneurial firms, and we'll emphasize the importance of preparing to get these types of financing.

The Importance of Getting Financing or Funding

Few people deal with the process of raising investment capital until they need to raise capital for their own firm. Many entrepreneurs go about the task of raising capital haphazardly because they lack experience in this area and because they don't know much about their choices.[7] This shortfall may cause a business owner to place too much reliance on some sources of capital and not enough on others.[8] Entrepreneurs need to have as full an understanding of the alternatives that are available in regard to raising money as possible. And raising money is a balancing act. While a firm may need to raise money to survive, its founders usually don't want to deal with people who don't understand or care about their long-term goals.

The need to raise money catches some entrepreneurs off guard. Many entrepreneurs start their firms with the intention of funding all their needs internally. Commonly, though, entrepreneurs discover that operating without investment capital or borrowed money is more difficult than they anticipated. Because of this, it is important for entrepreneurs to understand the role of investment capital in the survival and subsequent success of a new firm.

Why Most New Ventures Need Funding

There are three reasons that most new firms need to raise money during their early life: cash flow challenges, capital investments, and lengthy product development cycles. These reasons are laid out in Figure 10.1. Let's look at each of them.

learning **objective**

1. Explain why most new ventures need to raise money at some point during their early life.

Cash Flow Challenges   As a firm grows, it requires an increasing amount of cash to service its customers. Often, equipment must be purchased and new employees hired and trained before the increased customer base generates additional income. The lag between spending to generate revenue and earning income from the firm's operations creates cash flow challenges, particularly for small firms and firms that are growing rapidly.

If a firm operates in the red, its negative real-time cash flow, usually computed monthly, is called its burn rate. A company's **burn rate** is the rate at which it is spending its capital until it reaches profitability. Although a negative cash flow is sometimes justified early in a firm's life—to build plant and equipment, train employees, and establish its brand—it can cause severe complications. A firm usually fails if it burns through all its capital before it becomes profitable. This is why inadequate financial resources is one of the primary reasons new firms fail.[9] A firm can simply run out of money even if it has good products and satisfied customers. This is what almost happened to Cisco Systems early in its life. Recall from the opening case that at one point Cisco was desperately short of cash even though it was bringing in $250,000 per month in revenue.

To prevent the firm from running out of money, most entrepreneurs need investment capital or a line of credit from a bank to cover cash flow shortfalls until their firms can

Figure 10.1

Three Reasons Start-Ups Need Funding

Cash Flow Challenges	Capital Investments	Lengthy Product Development Cycles
Inventory must be purchased, employees must be trained and paid, and advertising must be paid for before cash is generated from sales.	The cost of buying real estate, building facilities, and purchasing equipment typically exceeds a firm's ability to provide funds for these needs on its own.	Some products are under development for years before they generate earnings. The up-front costs often exceed a firm's ability to fund these activities on its own.

Being an entrepreneur in the biotech industry requires a lot of determination and patience. In the case of Scios, a biopharmaceutical company located in Freemont, CA, that "tortoise-like pace" paid off. Scios' Natrecor® has posted monumental sales and is a groundbreaking treatment for acute heart failure.

begin making money. It is usually difficult for a new firm to get a line of credit from a bank (for reasons discussed later). So new ventures often look for investment capital or try to arrange some type of creative financing.

Capital Investments   Firms often need to raise money early on to fund capital investments. While it may be possible for the firm's founders to fund its initial activities, it becomes increasingly difficult for them to do so when it comes to buying property, constructing buildings, purchasing equipment, or investing in other capital projects. Many firms are able to delay or avoid these types of expenditures by leasing space or co-opting the resources of alliance partners. However, at some point in its growth cycle, the firm's needs may become specialized enough that it makes sense to purchase capital assets rather than rent or lease them.

Lengthy Product Development Cycles   Firms need to raise money to pay the up-front costs of lengthy product development cycles. For example, it takes about two years and $4 million to develop an electronic game.[10] In the biotech industry, it often takes a decade or more to get a new medicine approved. For example, Scios, a biotech firm that was founded in 1982, got its first medicine approved in 2001, close to 20 years after its founding.[11] This tortoise-like pace of product development takes substantial up-front investment before the anticipated payoff is realized.

Although the biotech industry is an extreme example, lengthy product development cycles are present in many industries. Firms entering these industries require considerable capital up front to pay for the cost of developing products.

Sources of Personal Financing

learning **objective**

2. Identify the three sources of personal financing available to entrepreneurs.

Typically, the seed money that gets a company off the ground comes from the founders themselves[12]—from their personal savings, mortgages, retirement funds, and credit cards and by tapping into the cash value of life insurance. And all founders contribute **sweat equity** to their ventures, which represents the value of the time and effort that a founder puts into a new firm. Often, when assessing a firm, an investor will place some value on the founder's sweat equity along with any tangible assets that the founder may have put into the firm.[13]

Friends and family are the second source of funds for many new ventures. This form of contribution is often called "**love money**," which can consist of outright gifts, loans, or investments but often comes in the form of forgone or delayed compensation or reduced or free rent. For example, Cisco initially set up shop in the house that Lerner and Bosack shared with Bosack's parents. Similarly, Ted Waitt, the founder of Gateway Computer, got his start with a $10,000 loan from his grandmother. One potential hazard associated with accepting help from friends or family is that it can strain relationships if the new venture doesn't pan out.

Another source of seed money for a new venture is referred to as bootstrapping. **Bootstrapping** is the use of creativity, ingenuity, and any means possible to obtain resources other than borrowing money or raising capital from traditional sources.[14] (The term comes from the adage, "pull yourself up by your bootstraps.") Because it's hard for new firms to get financing or funding early on, many entrepreneurs end up bootstrapping out of necessity. There are many well-known examples of entrepreneurs who bootstrapped to get their start. Legend has it that Steve Jobs and partner Steve Wozniak sold a Volkswagen van and a Hewlett-Packard programmable calculator to raise $1,350, which was the initial seed capital for Apple Computer.

learning **objective**

3. Provide examples of how entrepreneurs bootstrap to raise money or cut costs.

There are many ways entrepreneurs bootstrap to raise money or cut costs. Some of the more common examples include the following:

- Minimizing personal expenses and putting all profits back into the business
- Avoiding unnecessary expenses, such as lavish office space or furniture
- Establishing partnerships and sharing expenses with partners
- Buying items cheaply but prudently through discount outlets or online auctions, such as eBay, rather than at full-price stores
- Leasing equipment rather than buying
- Sharing office space or employees with other businesses

Although many firms eventually turn to debt or equity financing, which we'll discuss next, the initial funds for a new venture usually come from the entrepreneurs, their friends and family, and bootstrapping. The boxed feature titled "Savvy Entrepreneurial Firm" explores bootstrapping and how it can save money for firms that move their processes online.

Preparing to Raise Debt or Equity Financing

Once a start-up's financial needs exceed what personal funds, friends and family, and bootstrapping can provide, debt and equity are the two most common sources of funds. The most important thing an entrepreneur must do at this point is determine precisely what the company needs and the most appropriate source of funds. A carefully planned approach to raising money increases a firm's chance of success and can save an entrepreneur considerable time.

The steps involved in properly preparing to raise debt or equity financing are shown in Figure 10.2. Each of these steps is discussed next.

Step 1: Determine precisely how much money the company needs
Constructing and analyzing documented cash flow statements and projections for needed capital expenditures are actions taken to complete this step. This information should already be in the business plan, as described in Chapter 9.

learning **objective**

4. Identify the three steps involved in properly preparing to raise debt or equity financing.

Figure 10.2

Preparation for Debt or Equity Financing

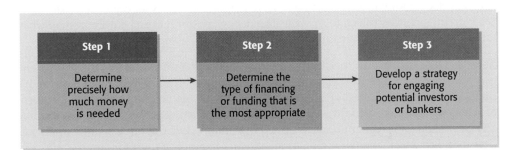

Step 1	Step 2	Step 3
Determine precisely how much money is needed	Determine the type of financing or funding that is the most appropriate	Develop a strategy for engaging potential investors or bankers

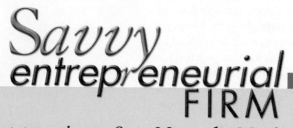

Savvy entrepreneurial FIRM

Bootstrapping to Save Money by Moving Processes Online

Delivering services via the Internet can reduce the amount of money a firm must spend on labor, raw materials, postage, building costs, and related expenses. Fortunately for companies wishing to conserve a limited amount of money, there are many opportunities to lower their costs by moving certain business processes online. Following are three examples of cost savings that are realized through delivering services digitally rather than through more traditional means.

Consumer Banking

Banking has traditionally been a labor-intensive industry. However, technology has continually pushed down the cost of banking, with the most dramatic drop made possible by the Internet. A recent study by Booz|Allen|Hamilton found that for banks, the cost per routine transaction, such as depositing a paycheck, varies according to the way that transaction is completed. For example,

In person (at the branch)	$3.00
Over the telephone	$1.50
Though an ATM	42 to 78 cents
Online via the Internet	6 to 12 cents

Dell Inc.

Each week, about 200,000 customers access Dell's Web site for troubleshooting tips, 90,000 download software options, and 50,000 check the status of an order request. Each of these visits saves Dell between $3 and $15, which is the estimated cost range of handling these types of inquires by phone. An added benefit is that because Dell's human resources are not overwhelmed by routine inquiries, the company can maintain technical support lines that are equipped to handle complex problems and provide exemplary customer service.

Cisco Systems

Cisco Systems sells hardware and software products that make the Internet work. Before the company revamped its Web site in 1996, customers would select products from an online catalog and fax their orders to Cisco. Because selecting Internet-related software and hardware products that are compatible with one another is a complicated process, about one-third of all faxed orders contained errors that delayed processing. Today, customers order online and an online "configurator" will alert them immediately if a configuration error has been made. This new procedure cuts the ordering process by days.

As is the case for many companies, Cisco has also found ways to eliminate a lot of additional costs via the Internet. For example, in the past, Cisco would send software purchases to its customers on CDs delivered overnight via FedEx. Today, software that is purchased online is simply downloaded. This one change alone, made possible by the Internet, saves Cisco over $500,000 per year in FedEx charges.

Questions for Critical Thinking

1. Think of the college or university you are attending or one you've attended previously. In what ways could the institution you are thinking about use the Internet to improve service to you while likely reducing its costs?

2. Assume that you and two of your close friends intend to open a restaurant in your local community. What actions could you take to bootstrap this operation, at least in the short term?

Sources: A. J. Slywotzky and D. J. Morrison, How Digital Is Your Business? (New York: Crown Business, 2000), and D. Bunnell, Making the Cisco Connection (New York: John Wiley & Sons, 2000).

Knowing exactly how much money to ask for is important for at least two reasons. First, a company doesn't want to get caught short, yet it doesn't want to pay for capital it doesn't need. Second, entrepreneurs talking to a potential lender or investor make a poor impression when they appear uncertain about the amount of money required to support their venture.

Step 2: Determine the most appropriate type of financing or funding   The two most common alternatives for raising money are equity and debt financing. **Equity financing** (or funding) means exchanging partial ownership in a firm, usually in the form of stock, for funding. Angel investors, private placement, venture capital, and initial public offering are the most common sources of equity funding (we will discuss all these sources later in the chapter). Equity funding is not a loan—the money that is received is not paid back. Instead, equity investors become partial owners of the firm. Some equity investors invest "for the long haul" and are content to receive a return on their investment through dividend payments on their stock. More commonly, equity investors have a three- to five-year investment horizon and expect to get their money back, along with a substantial capital gain, through the sale of their stock. The stock is typically sold following a liquidity event (described in Chapter 9).

Because of the risks involved, equity investors are very demanding and fund only a small percentage of the business plans they consider.[15] An equity investor considers the ideal candidate a firm that has a unique business opportunity, high growth potential, a clearly defined niche market, and proven management. Businesses that don't fit these criteria have a hard time getting equity funding. Many entrepreneurs are not familiar with the standards that equity investors apply and get discouraged when they are repeatedly turned down by venture capitalists and angel investors. Often, the reason they don't qualify for venture capital or angel investment isn't because their business proposal is poor but because they don't meet the exacting standards equity investors usually apply.[16]

Debt financing is getting a loan. The most common sources of debt financing are commercial banks and the Small Business Administration (SBA). The types of bank loans and SBA loans available to entrepreneurs will be discussed later in this chapter. In general, banks lend money that must be repaid with interest. Banks are not investors. As a result, bankers are interested in minimizing risk, properly collateralizing loans, and repayment as opposed to return on investment and capital gains. The ideal candidate for a bank loan is a firm with a strong cash flow, low leverage, audited financial statements, good management, and a healthy balance sheet. A careful review of these criteria demonstrates why it's difficult for start-ups to receive bank loans. Most start-ups are simply too early in their life cycle to have the set of characteristics bankers want.

Table 10.1 provides an overview of three common profiles of new ventures and the type of financing or funding that is appropriate for each profile. This table illustrates why most start-ups must rely on personal funds, friends and family, and bootstrapping at the outset and must wait until later to obtain equity or debt financing. Most new firms do not have the characteristics required by bankers or investors until they have proven their product or service idea and have achieved a certain measure of success in the marketplace.

Table 10.1

Matching a New Venture's Characteristics with the Appropriate Form of Financing or Funding

Characteristics of the New Venture	Appropriate Source of Financing or Funding
The business has high risk with an uncertain return: Weak cash flow High leverage Low to moderate growth Unproven management	Personal funds, friends, family, and other forms of bootstrapping
The business has low risk with a more predictable return: Strong cash flow Low leverage Audited financials Good management Healthy balance sheet	Debt financing
The business offers a high return: Unique business idea High growth Niche market Proven management	Equity

learning **objective**

5. Explain the role of an elevator speech in attracting financing for a firm.

Step 3: Developing a strategy for engaging potential investors or bankers

There are three steps to developing a strategy for engaging potential investors or bankers. First, the lead entrepreneurs in a new venture should prepare an **elevator speech**—a brief, carefully constructed statement that outlines the merits of a business opportunity. Why is it called an elevator speech? If an entrepreneur stepped into an elevator on the 25th floor of a building and found that by a stroke of luck a potential investor was in the same elevator, the entrepreneur would have the time it takes to get from the 25th floor to the ground floor to try to get the investor interested in his or her business opportunity. Most elevator speeches are 45 seconds to two minutes long.

There are many occasions when a carefully constructed elevator speech might come in handy. For example, many university-sponsored centers for entrepreneurship hold events that bring investors and entrepreneurs together. Often, these events include social hours and refreshment breaks designed specifically for the purpose of allowing entrepreneurs looking for funding to mingle with potential investors. An outline for a 60-second elevator speech is provided in Table 10.2.

The second step in developing a strategy for engaging potential investors or bankers is more deliberate and requires identifying and contacting the best prospects. First, the new venture should carefully assess the type of financing or funding it is likely to qualify for, as depicted in Table 10.1. Then, a list of potential bankers or investors should be compiled. If venture-capital funding is felt to be appropriate, for example, a little legwork can go a long way in pinpointing likely investors. A new venture should identify the venture funds that are investing money in the industry in which it intends to compete and target those firms first. To do this, look to the venture-capital firms' Web sites. These reveal the industries in which the firms have an interest. Sometimes, these sites also provide a list of the companies the firm has funded. For an example, access Sequoia Capital's Web site (*www.sequoia.com*), the venture fund that invested in Cisco Systems.

A cardinal rule of approaching a banker or an investor is to get a personal introduction. Bankers and investors receive many business plans, and most of them end up in a pile in their offices. To have your business plan noticed, find someone who knows the banker or the investor and ask for an introduction. This requirement is explained in blunt terms by Randall Stross, the author of *eBoys*, a book about the venture-capital industry. Stross spent two years observing the day-to-day activities at Benchmark Venture Capital, a prominent Silicon Valley venture-capital firm. According to Strauss,

> The business plan that comes in from a complete stranger, either without the blessing of someone the venture capital firm knows well or without professional recommendations that render an introduction superfluous, is all but certain not to make the cut. In fact, knowing that this is the case becomes a tacit requirement from the perspective of a venture guy: Anyone whom I don't know who approaches me directly with a business plan shows me they haven't passed Entrepreneurship 101.[17]

The third step in engaging potential investors or bankers is to be prepared to provide the investor or banker a completed business plan and make a presentation of the plan if requested. We looked at how to present a business plan in Chapter 9. The presen-

Table 10.2

Guidelines for Preparing an Elevator Speech

The elevator speech is a very brief description of your opportunity, product idea, qualifications, and market. Imagine that you step into an elevator in a tall building and a potential investor is already there; you have about 60 seconds to explain your business idea.	
Step 1: Describe the opportunity or problem that needs to be solved	20 seconds
Step 2: Describe how your product or service meets the opportunity or solves the problem	20 seconds
Step 3: Describe your qualifications	10 seconds
Step 4: Describe your market	10 seconds
Total	60 seconds

tation should be as polished as possible and should demonstrate why the new venture represents an attractive endeavor for the lender or investor. This point is emphasized by Irene Smith, founder of The Business Center, a provider of services to businesses including word processing and graphic design. Smith is also the author of *Diary of a Small Business*, in which she provides a candid assessment of her experiences as an entrepreneur. Commenting on the challenges involved with raising money, Smith said,

> I came to the conclusion that seeking outside financing, whether debt financing (borrowing money) or equity capital financing (sale of stock), is not a simple business problem. It is a marketing problem. Just as you must market your product or service to make it appealing to your potential customers, you must present your business to potential lenders or investors in a way that will make it an attractive investment for them. You must speak eloquently in a language to which they will respond—and that language is profit.[18]

Sources of Equity Funding

The primary disadvantage of equity funding is that the owners of the firm give up part of their ownership interest and may lose some control. This was certainly the case for the founders of Cisco Systems, who traded nearly one-third of Cisco's stock and essentially turned over control of the company to venture capitalist Don Valentine in exchange for $2.5 million in venture-capital funding. The primary advantage of equity funding is that because investors become partial owners of the firms in which they invest, they often try to help those firms by offering their expertise and assistance. In addition, unlike a loan, the money received from an equity investor doesn't have to be paid back. The investor receives a return on his or her investment through dividend payments and by selling the stock.

The three most common forms of equity funding are described next.

learning **objective**

6. Discuss the difference between equity funding and debt financing.

Business Angels

Business angels are individuals who invest their personal capital directly in start-ups. The prototypical business angel is about 50 years old, has high income and wealth, is well educated, has succeeded as an entrepreneur, and is interested in the start-up process.[19] These investors generally invest between $25,000 and $150,000 in a single company.[20] About 90 percent of angel investors are worth between $1 million and $10 million.[21] Mitch Kapor, the founder of Lotus Development, is a well-known business angel. Two of his most successful investments have been UUNet, the first Internet access provider, and RealNetworks, the Internet media company. Business angels initially funded many other familiar firms. For example, Apple Computer received its initial investment capital from Mike Markkula, who obtained his wealth as an executive with Intel. In 1977, Markkula invested $91,000 in Apple and personally guaranteed another $250,000 in credit lines. When Apple went public in 1980, his stock in the company was worth more than $150 million.[22]

The number of angel investors in the United States has increased dramatically over the past decade, partly because of the high returns that some report.[23] Nationwide, angels invest $20 billion to $30 billion annually into some 30,000 small companies. By comparison, venture capitalists invest about $22 billion per year in start-ups and growing companies. In exchange for their investment, angels expect a rather hefty annual return—usually in the neighborhood of 35 to 40 percent.[24] They also usually fill a seat on the board of directors of the firms in which they invest and provide varying levels of managerial input. An example of an organization working on behalf of business angels and providing the entrepreneurs it funds considerable assistance is SpencerTrask, as illustrated in the boxed feature titled "Partnering for Success."

Business angels are valuable because of their willingness to make relatively small investments. This gives access to equity funding to a start-up that needs just $50,000 rather than the $1 million minimum investment that most venture capitalists require. Many angels are also motivated by more than financial returns; they enjoy the process of

Partnering for SUCCESS

SpencerTrask: More Than Just an Investor

www.spencertrask.com

SpencerTrask is a private venture firm making investments on behalf of business angels and private investors. Rather than just investing money, the firm actively partners with the start-ups it supports and contributes to their success in a number of ways.

TechRx, which provides solutions for drugstores and pharmacy companies, is one of SpencerTrask's investments. A pressing problem pharmacies face is the labor-intensive paperwork involved in dispensing prescription medicines. Many pharmacists spend up to two-thirds of their time on administrative tasks rather than talking to patients and filling prescriptions. To solve this problem, TechRx has developed central processing solutions that relieve local pharmacists of much of this burden. A pharmacy using a central processing solution directs all of its call-in prescriptions to a call center that handles chores such as insurance approval. This process frees up local pharmacists to fill prescriptions and talk to patients and improves the efficiency of the entire process.

SpencerTrask invested $10 million in TechRx. At the same time, it activated what it calls its Value Creation Network to draw on the expertise of its investors to help TechRx build a successful business. It helped TechRx recruit senior-level people to strengthen its management team and expand sales and marketing. In addition, one of SpencerTrask's operating executives, Joe Porfeli, took a sabbatical to become chairman and CEO of TechRx for a

period of time. With a seasoned management team in place, TechRx cofounder Tim Burns had the freedom to spend his time building world-class products and services.

Today, TechRx is the leading provider of drug fulfillment solutions. The company processes over 1.2 billion prescriptions annually and dominates the market with leading pharmacy chain customers such as Kroger, CVS, Eckerd, and many others.

Questions for Critical Thinking

1. As a potential entrepreneur, do you see any potential disadvantages of Spencer Trask's services? If so, what are those possible disadvantages, and how would you cope with them?

2. Go to different business publications' Web sites (e.g., www.startupjournal.com, www.businessweek.com, or www.fortune.com). Search these Web sites for articles dealing with angel investors. At the time of your search, what are the major issues facing angel investors? What are the major issues facing those trying to gain support from angel investors? As a potential entrepreneur, how do you respond to the information you have obtained about angel investors?

Sources: SpencerTrask home page, www.spencertrask.com (accessed March 23, 2004), and TechRx home page, www.techrx.com (accessed March 23, 2004).

mentoring a new firm. Oron Strauss is a 1995 Dartmouth College graduate who received angel funding. Recalling an experience with his angel investor, Strauss said,

> About a year ago, when I was having a particularly bad week, I fired off a long, heartfelt e-mail message to my angel. I explained, in great detail, the difficulties I faced and my thoughts about them. His response was succinct: "All sounds normal. You're handling it well. Keep up the good work." My first reaction was disappointment over what struck me as a curt response. Then I realized that the angel had given me the best possible response. He understood that what I was going through was normal and that I would make it.[25]

Business angels are difficult to find. Most angels remain fairly anonymous and are matched up with entrepreneurs through referrals. To find a business angel investor, an entrepreneur should discretely work his or her network of acquaintances to see if anyone can make an appropriate introduction.

There are pockets of organized groups of angels, such as the Band of Angels. This is a group of 150 former and current high-tech executives and entrepreneurs who provide counsel and capital to start-up companies. Each month, the Band of Angels meets and considers three start-ups. The Band of Angels is located in the Silicon Valley, has been in business over eight years, and has invested close to $100 million in 148 early-stage start-ups.[26]

Venture Capital

Venture capital is money that is invested by venture-capital firms in start-ups and small businesses with exceptional growth potential.[27] There are about 650 venture-capital firms in the United States that provide funding to about 3,000 to 4,000 firms per year. In 2002, the venture-capital industry invested $21.2 billion. The peak year for venture-capital investing was 2000, when $106.6 billion was invested at the height of the e-commerce trend. The $21.2 billion invested in 2002 is almost identical to the amount invested in 1998, just prior to the dot.com craze.[28] In 2003, venture-capital investing totaled only $16.9 billion, meaning that the decline that started in 2001 continued through this year, although projections were that the decline would stop by late 2004 or early 2005.[29]

Venture-capital firms are limited partnerships of money managers who raise money in "funds" to invest in start-ups and growing firms. The funds, or pools of money, are raised from wealthy individuals, pension plans, university endowments, foreign investors, and similar sources. A typical fund is $75 million to $200 million and invests in 20 to 30 companies over a three- to five-year period.[30] The venture capitalists that manage the fund receive an annual management fee in addition to 20 to 25 percent of the profits earned by the fund. The percentage of the profits the venture capitalists get is called the **carry**. So if a venture-capital firm raised a $100 million fund and the fund grew to $500 million, a 20 percent carry means that the firm would get, after repaying the original $100 million, 20 percent of the $400 million in profits, or $80 million. The investors in the fund would get the remainder. Venture capitalists shoot for a 30 to 40 percent annual return on their investment or more and a total return over the life of the investment of 5 to 20 times the initial investment.[31]

Because of the venture-capital industry's lucrative nature and because in the past venture capitalists have funded high-profile successes such as Google, Cisco Systems, eBay, and Yahoo!, the industry receives a great deal of attention. But actually, venture capitalists fund very few new firms in comparison to business angels and relative to the number of firms needing funding. Remember, venture capitalists fund about 3,000 to 4,000 companies per year, compared to 30,000 funded by business angels. And only about half the investments that venture capitalists make each year are to new firms—the other investments are to existing firms that need additional funding.

learning **objective**

7. Describe the difference between a business angel and a venture capitalist.

The telecommunications industry is a potential "home run" for venture capitalists. Just think of how many people you see talking on a cell phone, how much you depend on your Internet connection, and the luxury of your cable or satellite TV so you can watch your favorite show or sporting event.

The investment preferences of venture capitalist are also fairly narrow. For example, in 2002, 20 percent of all venture-capital investments were in the software industry.[32] Telecommunications, networking, computers and peripherals, semiconductors, medical devices, and biotechnology are other industries attracting funding from venture capitalists. As mentioned earlier in this chapter, many entrepreneurs get discouraged when they are repeatedly rejected for venture-capital funding, even through they may have an excellent business plan. Venture capitalists are looking for the "home run" and so reject the majority of the proposals they consider.

Venture capitalists know that they are making risky investments and that some investments won't pan out. In fact, most venture firms anticipate that about 15 to 25 percent of their investments will be home runs, 25 to 35 percent will be winners, 25 to 35 percent will break even, and 15 to 25 percent will fail.[33] The home runs must be sensational to make up for the break-even firms and the failures.

Still, for the firms that qualify, venture capital is a viable alternative for equity funding. An advantage to obtaining this funding is that venture capitalists are extremely well connected in the business world and can offer a firm considerable assistance beyond funding. Firms that qualify typically obtain their money in stages that correspond to their own stage of development. Once a venture capitalist makes an investment in a firm, subsequent investments are made in **rounds** (or stages) and are referred to as **follow-on funding**. Table 10.3 shows the various stages in the venture-capital process, from the seed stage to buyout financing.

An important part of obtaining venture-capital funding is going through the **due diligence** process, which refers to the process of investigating the merits of a potential venture and verifying the key claims made in the business plan.

Firms that prove to be suitable for venture-capital funding should conduct their own due diligence of the venture capitalists with whom they are working to ensure that they are a good fit. An entrepreneur should ask the following questions and scrutinize the answers to them before accepting funding from a venture-capital firm:

- Do the venture capitalists have experience in our industry?
- Do they take a highly active or passive management role?
- Are the personalities on both sides of the table compatible?
- Does the firm have deep enough pockets or sufficient contacts within the venture-capital industry to provide follow-on rounds of financing?
- Is the firm negotiating in good faith in regard to the percentage of our firm they want in exchange for their investment?

Table 10.3

Stages (or Rounds) of Venture-Capital Funding

Stage or Round	Purpose of the Funding
Seed funding	Investment made very early in the life of a business to fund the development of a prototype and feasibility analysis.
Start-up funding	Investment made to firms exhibiting few if any commercial sales but in which product development and market research are reasonably complete. Management is in place, and the firm has completed its business model. Funding is needed to start production.
First-stage funding	Funding that occurs when the firm has started commercial production and sales but requires additional financing to ramp up its production capacity.
Second-stage funding	Funding that occurs when a firm is successfully selling a product but needs to expand both its production capacity and its markets.
Mezzanine financing	Investment made to a firm to provide for further expansion or to bridge its financing needs before a public offering of stock or before a buyout.
Buyout funding	Funding provided to help one company acquire another.

Along with traditional venture capital, there is also **corporate venture capital**. This type of capital is similar to traditional venture capital except that the money comes from corporations that invest in start-ups related to their areas of interest.

Initial Public Offering

Another source of equity funding is to sell stock to the public by staging an **initial public offering** (IPO). An IPO is the first sale of stock by a firm to the public. When a company goes public, its stock is typically traded on one of the major stock exchanges. Most entrepreneurial firms that go public trade on the NASDAQ, which is weighted heavily toward technology, biotech, and small-company stocks.[34] An IPO is an important milestone for a firm.[35] Typically, a firm is not able to go public until it has demonstrated that it is viable and has a bright future.

learning **objective**

8. Explain why an initial public offering is an important milestone for a firm.

Firms decide to go public for several reasons. First, it is a way to raise equity capital to fund current and future operations. Amazon.com, for example, went public in May 1977 and raised over $40 million by selling stock to the public. Second, an IPO raises a firm's public profile, making it easier to attract high-quality customers, alliance partners, and employees. Third, an IPO is a liquidity event that provides a mechanism for the company's stockholders, including its investors, to cash out their investments. Finally, by going public, a firm creates another form of currency that can be used to grow the company. It is not uncommon for one firm to buy another company by paying for it with stock rather than with cash.[36] The stock comes from "authorized but not yet issued stock," which in essence means that the firm issues new shares of stock to make the purchase. In fact, a large percentage of Cisco System's 70-plus acquisitions were paid for in this manner.

Although there are many advantages to going public, it is a complicated and expensive process. The first step in initiating a public offering is for a firm to hire an investment bank. An **investment bank** is an institution, such as Credit Suisse First Boston, that acts as an underwriter or agent for a firm issuing securities.[37] The investment bank acts as the firm's advocate and adviser and walks it through the process of going public. The most important issues the firm and its investment bank must agree on are the amount of capital needed by the firm, the type of stock to be issued, the price of the stock when it goes public (e.g., $12 per share), and the cost to the firm to issue the securities.

There are a number of hoops the investment bank must jump through to assure the Securities and Exchange Commission (SEC) that the offer is legitimate. During the time the SEC is investigating the potential offering, the investment bank issues a **preliminary prospectus** that describes the offering to the general public. The preliminary prospectus is also called the "red herring." After the SEC has approved the offering, the investment bank issues the **final prospectus**, which sets a date and issuing price for the offering.

In addition to getting the offering approved, the investment bank is responsible for drumming up support for the offering. As part of this process, the investment bank typically takes the firm's top management team wanting to go public on a **road show**, which is a whirlwind tour that consists of meetings in key cities where the firm presents its business plan to groups of investors.[38] If enough interest in the offering is created, the offering will take place on the date scheduled in the prospectus. If it isn't, the offering will be delayed or canceled.

Timing and luck play a role in whether a public offering is successful. For example, a total of 332 IPOs raised about $50 billion in 1999, the height of the Internet bubble. When the bubble burst in early 2001, the IPO marketplace all but dried up, particularly for technology and telecom stocks. In 2002, only eight technology and telecom deals went public, the fewest in recent memory.[39] The picture didn't improve in 2003, a year in which a total of only 68 IPOs (with a value of $15 billion) took place. The total of 68 deals in 2003 was the lowest since 1979.[40] However, 32 IPOs, with a total value of $7.2 billion, took place in the first quarter of 2004, a level of activity suggesting that the market for IPOs was improving. But, this uptick in activity could be misleading, in that the vitality of the IPO marketplace hinges largely on the state of the overall economy and the mood of the investing public. For example, interest rate increases in mid-2004 were expected to lead to a 5-10 percent reduction in the issuance of IPOs that took place in the first quarter of that year.[41] One thing a new venture must guard itself against is getting caught up in the euphoria of a rising stock market and rushing its IPO to catch the wave of a rising market. The problems that can result from this approach are illustrated in the boxed feature titled "What Went Wrong?"

what went **Wrong?**

Why Rushing an IPO Isn't Such a Good Idea

www.akamai.com

In the late 1990s and the early 2000s, the Internet bubble was at its height. The bubble was created by the public's enthusiasm over the Internet and the proclamation from many quarters that the Internet was going to "change everything," including how businesses would be funded and operate. The height of the bubble was July 1999 to February 2001—a time when money flowed into technology companies at a breathtaking rate. Venture capitalists invested about $80 billion in start-ups during this period, and the NASDAQ Composite Index rose by 74.4 percent. Investor euphoria was at an all-time high. At least two new terms—day trading and day trader—entered the vocabulary. Some people were so caught up in investing that they literally spent their entire days trading stocks. There was talk of soon reaching "Dow 30,000," an expectation that proved to be pure fantasy.

In the spring of 2001, the bubble burst. Investors and the public at large realized that the Internet wasn't going to change everything. Many investors took heavy losses. But it wasn't just investors who were hurt. Many start-ups would have been better off if the bubble had never happened. Why? In some cases, firms rushed their public offerings to catch the wave of the rising stock market, and when the bubble burst, their share prices fell faster than they had earlier risen. This chain of events caused tremendous heartache among the firms that were affected. Akamai Technologies was one of these firms. (Today, this firm's official name is Akamai.)

A team of entrepreneurs from the Massachusetts Institute of Technology launched Akamai Technologies in August 1998. The firm was established with the intention of finding a solution to the growing problem of congestion on the Internet. The company got off to a good start. In its first few months, it hired a seasoned CEO, attracted the attention of customers, and applied for patents on its core technologies. In October 1999, Akamai went public, just 14 months after it started. Its stock price, which debuted at $26 per share, quickly ran up to $345 per share. By early 2001, it had 1,300 employees and was managing 9,700 servers in 56 countries.

Then, in early 2001, the Internet bubble burst. Although Akamai was growing, it wasn't yet profitable and fell out of favor with investors. By the fall of 2001, its stock price had fallen to less than $4 per share. Its customers, suppliers, and employees were startled by this turn of events and became nervous about Akamai's ability to survive. Moreover, rumors circulated that the company was for sale.

What went wrong at Akamai? While part of its troubles may have been due to management blunders, the company was primarily a victim of the general loss of confidence in technology companies following the burst of the dot-com bubble. The fact that it went public so early contributed to its problems. The rapid increase in its stock price, followed by its rapid decline, drew attention to the company and frightened its stakeholders. In reality, in the midst of everything that was happening, the company was patiently executing its business model and following its plan. Nothing it did justified a stock price of $345 per share or a price of $4 per share. But it's hard for the public to believe that when a company's stock price is high it isn't doing something spectacular and that when its stock price is low it isn't in trouble. As a result, when Akamai's stock price sank to $4 per share, it lost the confidence of the people it needed the most to build its business. Right or wrong, people judged Akamai on the basis of its stock price rather than on the quality of its products and services.

The lesson to be learned from this case is that it's dangerous for a firm to rush its IPO, particularly if it is new and its true value is unknown. If Akamai had waited to launch its IPO until its business model was better understood and its customers, suppliers, and employees had a better sense of the firm's long-term potential, its stock price probably would not have suffered as severe gyrations as it did, even in a volatile market.

Questions for Critical Thinking

1. As a potential entrepreneur, what have you learned by reading this case in addition to the matter of the mistake of rushing to the IPO stage? List three or four lessons you are taking away from reading about the experiences of Akamai Technologies.

2. As the founders of Akamai Technologies or as the firm's seasoned CEO, what could you have said to customers, suppliers, and shareholders to alleviate their concerns as the price of the company's stock was rapidly sinking?

3. Go to Akamai's Web site (www.akamai.com). What is the price of a share of Akamai today? How has its business changed since going public in 1999? Using data from the Web site, evaluate the firm's current financial performance.

Source: D. Mills, Buy, Lie, and Sell High: How Investors Lost Out on Enron and the Internet Bubble *(Upper Saddle River, N.J.: Financial Times Prentice Hall, 2002).*

A variation of the IPO is a **private placement**, which is the direct sale of an issue of securities to a large institutional investor. When a private placement is initiated, there is no public offering, and no prospectus is prepared.

Sources of Debt Financing

Debt financing involves getting a loan or selling corporate bonds. Because it is virtually impossible for a new venture to sell corporate bonds, we'll focus on obtaining loans.

There are two common types of loans. The first is a single-purpose loan, in which a specific amount of money is borrowed that must be repaid in a fixed amount of time with interest. The second is a line of credit, in which a borrowing "cap" is established and the borrower can use the credit at his or her discretion. Lines of credit require periodic interest payments.

There are two major advantages to obtaining a loan as opposed to equity funding. The first is that none of the ownership of the firm is surrendered—a major advantage for most entrepreneurs. The second is that interest payments on a loan are tax deductible in contrast to dividend payments made to investors, which aren't.

There are two major disadvantages of getting a loan. The first is that it must be repaid, which may be difficult for a start-up that is focused on getting its company off the ground. Cash is typically "tight" during a new venture's first few months and sometimes for a year or more. The second is that lenders often impose strict conditions on loans and insist on ample collateral to fully protect their investment. Even if a start-up is incorporated, a lender may require that an entrepreneur's personal assets be collateralized as a condition of the loan.

The two most common sources of debt financing available to entrepreneurs are described next.

Commercial Banks

Historically, commercial banks have not been viewed as practical sources of financing for start-up firms.[42] This sentiment is not a knock against banks; it is just that banks are risk adverse, and financing start-ups is risky business. Instead of looking for businesses that are "home runs," which is what venture capitalists seek to do, banks look for customers who will reliably repay their loans. As shown in Table 10.1, banks are interested in firms that have a strong cash flow, low leverage, audited financials, good management, and a healthy balance sheet. Although many new ventures have good management, few have the other characteristics, at least initially. But banks are an important source of credit for small businesses later in their life cycles.

There are two reasons that banks have historically been reluctant to lend money to start-ups. First, as mentioned previously, banks are risk adverse. In addition, banks frequently have internal controls and regulatory restrictions prohibiting them from making high-risk loans. So when an entrepreneur approaches a banker with a request for a $500,000 loan and the only collateral the entrepreneur has to offer is the recognition of a problem that needs to be solved and a plan to solve it and perhaps some intellectual property, there is usually no practical way for the bank to help. Banks typically have standards that guide their lending, such as minimum debt-to-equity ratios, that work against start-up entrepreneurs.

The second reason banks have historically been reluctant to lend money to start-ups is that lending to small firms is not as profitable as lending to large firms, which have historically been the staple clients of commercial banks. If an entrepreneur approaches a banker with a request for a $50,000 loan, it may simply not be worth the banker's time to do the due diligence necessary to determine the entrepreneur's risk profile. Considerable time is required to digest a business plan and investigate the merits of a new firm. Research shows that a firm's size is an important factor in determining its access to debt capital.[43] The $50,000 loan may be seen as both high risk and marginally profitable (based on the amount of time it would take to do the due diligence involved), making it doubly uninviting for a commercial bank.[44]

Despite these historical precedents, some banks are starting to engage start-up entrepreneurs—although the jury is still out regarding how significant these lenders will become. When it comes to start-ups, some banks are rethinking their lending standards and are beginning to focus on cash flow and the strength of the management team rather than on collateral and the strength of the balance sheet. Actions taken by Bank of America and Wells Fargo, in particular, are encouraging.[45] This evolution in thinking has been brought about in part because banks are losing their staple clients—big corporations—to other sources of capital. Entrepreneurs should follow developments in this area closely.

SBA Guaranteed Loans

learning objective

9. Discuss the SBA Guaranteed Loan Program.

Approximately 50 percent of the 9,000 banks in the United States participate in the **SBA Guaranteed Loan Program**. While these loans typically aren't available to start-ups, they are an important source of funding for small businesses in general.

The most notable SBA program available to small businesses is the **7(A) Loan Guaranty Program**. This program accounts for 90 percent of the SBA's loan activity. The program operates through private-sector lenders that provide loans that are guaranteed by the SBA. The loans are for small businesses that are unable to secure financing on reasonable terms through normal lending channels. The SBA does not currently have funding for direct loans, nor does it provide grants or low-interest-rate loans for business start-ups or expansion.

Almost all small businesses are eligible to apply for an SBA guaranteed loan. The SBA can guarantee as much as 85 percent (debt to equity) on loans up to $150,000 and 75 percent on loans of over $150,000. In most cases, the maximum guarantee is $1 million. A guaranteed loan can be used for working capital to expand a new business or start a new one. It can also be used for real estate purchases, renovation, construction, or equipment purchases. To obtain an SBA guaranteed loan, an application must meet the requirements of both the SBA and the lender. An individual must typically pledge all of his or her assets to secure the loan.[46]

Creative Sources of Financing and Funding

Because financing and funding are difficult to obtain, particularly for start-ups, entrepreneurs often use creative ways to obtain financial resources. Even for firms that have financing or funding available, it is prudent to search for sources of capital that are less expensive than traditional ones. The following sections discuss three of the more common creative sources of financing and funding for entrepreneurial firms.

Leasing

learning objective

10. Explain the advantages of leasing for an entrepreneurial firm.

A **lease** is a written agreement in which the owner of a piece of property allows an individual or business to use the property for a specified period of time in exchange for payments. The major advantage of leasing is that it enables a company to acquire the use of assets with very little or no down payment. The two most common types of leases that new ventures enter into are leases for facilities and leases for equipment.[47] For example, many new business lease computers from Dell Inc. The advantage for the new business is that it can gain access to the computers it needs with very little money invested up front.

There are many different players in the leasing business. Some vendors, such as Dell, lease directly to businesses. As with banks, the vendors look for lease clients with good credit backgrounds and the ability to make the lease payments. There are also **venture-leasing firms** that act as brokers, bringing the parties involved in a lease together. These firms are acquainted with the producers of specialized equipment and match these producers with new ventures that are in need of the equipment. One of the responsibilities of these firms is conducting due diligence to make sure that the new ventures involved will be able to keep up with their lease payments.

Most leases involve a modest down payment and monthly payments during the duration of the lease. At the end of an equipment lease, the new venture typically has the option to stop using the equipment, purchase it at fair market value, or renew the lease. Lease deals that involve a substantial amount of money should be negotiated and entered into with the same amount of scrutiny as getting financing or funding. Leasing is almost always more expensive than paying cash for an item, so most entrepreneurs think of leasing as an alternative to equity or debt financing. While the down payment is typically lower, the primary disadvantage is that at the end of the lease, the lessee doesn't own the property or equipment.[48] Of course, this may be an advantage if a company is leasing equipment, such as computers or copy machines, that can rather quickly become technologically obsolete.

Government Grants

The Small Business Innovation Research (SBIR) and the Small Business Technology Transfer (SBTT) programs are two important sources of early-stage funding for technology firms. These programs provide cash grants to entrepreneurs who are working on projects in specific areas. The main difference between the SBIR and the SBTT programs is that the SBTT program requires the participation of researchers working at universities or other research institutions.

The **SBIR Program** is a competitive grant program that provides over $1 billion per year to small businesses for early-stage and development projects. Each year, 10 federal departments and agencies are required by the SBIR to reserve a portion of their research-and-development funds for awards to small businesses. The agencies that participate, along with the types of areas that are funded, are shown in Table 10.4. Guidelines for how to apply for the grants are provided on each agency's Web site, along with a description of the types of projects the agencies are interested in supporting. The SBIR is a three-phase program, meaning that firms that qualify have the potential to receive more than one grant to fund a particular proposal. These three phases, along with the amount of funding available for each phase, are as follows:

- **Phase I** is a six-month feasibility study in which the business must demonstrate the technical feasibility of the proposed innovation. Funding available for phase I research ranges from $75,000 to $100,000, depending on the agency involved.
- **Phase II** awards are made for up to $750,000 for as long as two years to successful phase I companies. The purpose of a phase II grant is to develop and test a prototype of phase I innovations. Funding available for phase II research ranges from $300,000 to $750,000, depending on the agency involved. Some agencies have **fast-track programs** where applicants can simultaneously submit phase I and phase II applications.
- **Phase III** is the period during which phase II innovations move from the research-and-development lab to the marketplace. No SBIR funds are involved. At this point, the business must find private funding or financing to commercialize the product or service. In some cases, such as with the Department of Defense, the government may be the primary customer for the product.

Historically, less than 15 percent of all phase I proposals are funded, and about 30 percent of all phase II proposals are funded. The payoff for successful proposals, however, is high. The money is essentially free. It is a grant, meaning that it doesn't have to be paid back and no equity in the firm is at stake. The real payoff is in phase III if the new venture can commercialize the research results.

The **SBTT Program** is a variation of the SBIR for collaborative research projects that involves small businesses and research organizations, such as universities or federal laboratories. More information about the SBTT program can be obtained from the SBA.

Table 10.4 Small Business Innovation Research: Three-Phase Program

Phase	Purpose of Phase	Duration	Funding Available (varies by agency)
Phase I	To demonstrate the proposed innovation's technical feasibility.	Up to six months	$75,000–$100,000
Phase II	Available to successful phase I companies. The purpose of a phase II grant is to develop and test a prototype of the innovation validated in phase I.*	Up to two years	$300,000–$750,000
Phase III	Period in which phase II innovations move from the research-and-development lab to the marketplace.	Open	No government funding involved. At this point, businesses must find private funding or financing to commercialize the product.

* Some agencies have a fast-track program where applicants can submit phase I and phase II applications simultaneously. Government agencies that participate in the program: Department of Agriculture, Department of Commerce, Department of Defense, Department of Education, Department of Energy, Environmental Protection Agency, Department of Health and Human Services, NASA, National Science Foundation, and Department of Transportation.

Strategic Partners

Strategic partners are another source of capital for new ventures.[49] Indeed, strategic partners often play a critical role in helping young firms fund their operations and round out their business models.

Biotechnology, for example, relies heavily on partners for financial support (we'll discuss an example of this in one of the chapter's closing cases). Biotech firms, which are typically fairly small, often partner with larger drug companies to conduct clinical trials and bring products to market. Most of these arrangements involve a licensing agreement. A typical agreement works like this. A biotech firm licenses a product that is under development to a pharmaceutical company in exchange for financial support during the development of the product and beyond. This type of arrangement gives the biotech firm money to operate while the drug is being developed. In fact, more than 50 percent of the money that funds biotech firms comes from alliance partners, so the formation of such alliances is a critical competency for a new biotech firm.[50]

Alliances also help firms round out their business models and conserve resources. For example, as we discussed in Chapter 5, Dell Inc. can focus on its core competency of assembling computers because it has assembled a network of partners that provides it critical support. Intel provides it chips, Microsoft provides it software, UPS provides it access to shipping, and so forth. While Dell is a familiar example, savvy new ventures work hard to find partners to perform functions that would be expensive and distracting for them to perform themselves.

Finally, many partnerships are formed to share the costs of product or service development, to gain access to a particular resource, or to facilitate speed to market.[51] In exchange for access to plant and equipment and established distribution channels, new ventures bring an entrepreneurial spirit and new ideas to these partnerships. These types of arrangements can help new ventures lessen the need for financing or funding.

CHAPTER SUMMARY

1. For three reasons—cash flow challenges, capital investment needs, and the reality of lengthy product development cycles—most new firms need to raise money at some point during the early part of their life.

2. Personal funds, friends and family, and bootstrapping are the three sources of personal financing available to entrepreneurs.

3. Entrepreneurs are often very creative in finding ways to bootstrap to raise money or cut costs. Examples of bootstrapping include minimizing personal expenses and putting all profits back into the business, establishing partnerships and sharing expenses with partners, and sharing office space and/or employees with other businesses.

4. The three steps involved in properly preparing to raise debt or equity financing are as follows: determine precisely how much money is needed, determine the type of financing or funding that is most appropriate, and develop a strategy for engaging potential investors or bankers.

5. An elevator speech is a brief, carefully constructed statement outlining a business opportunity's merits.

6. Equity funding involves exchanging partial ownership in a firm, which is usually in the form of stock, in exchange for funding. Debt financing is getting a loan.

7. Business angels are individuals who invest their personal capital directly in start-up ventures. These investors tend to be high-net-worth individuals who generally invest between $25,000 and $150,000 in a single company. Venture capital is money that is invested by venture-capital firms in start-ups and small businesses with exceptional growth potential. Typically, venture capitalists invest at least $1 million in a single company.

8. An initial public offering is an important milestone for a firm for four reasons: it is a way to raise equity capital, it raises a firm's public profile, it is a liquidity event, and it creates another form of currency (company stock) that can be used to grow the company.

9. The main SBA program available to small businesses is referred to as the 7(A) Loan Guaranty Program. This program operates through private-sector lenders providing loans that are guaranteed by the SBA. The loans are for small businesses that are unable to secure financing on reasonable terms through normal lending channels.

10. A lease is a written agreement in which the owner of a piece of property allows an individual or business to use the property for a specified period of time in exchange for payments. The major advantage of leasing is that it enables a company to acquire the use of assets with very little or no down payment.

bootstrapping, 233

burn rate, 231

business angels, 237

carry, 239

corporate venture capital, 241

debt financing, 235

due diligence, 240

elevator speech, 236

equity financing, 234

fast-track programs, 245

final prospectus, 241

follow-on funding, 240

initial public offering, 241

investment bank, 241

lease, 244

love money, 233

preliminary prospectus, 241

private placement, 243

road show, 241

rounds, 240

SBA Guaranteed Loan Program, 244

SBIR Program, 245

SBTT Program, 245

7(A) Loan Guaranty Program, 244

sweat equity, 232

venture capital, 239

venture-leasing firm, 244

1. What are the three most common reasons most new firms need to raise money in their early life?

2. What is meant by the term "burn rate"? What are the consequences of experiencing a negative burn rate for a prolonged period of time?

3. What is meant by the term "sweat equity"?

4. Define the term "love money." Provide two examples of forms of love money.

5. What is bootstrapping? Provide several examples of how entrepreneurs bootstrap to raise money or cut costs. In your judgment, how important is the art of bootstrapping for an entrepreneurial firm?

6. Describe the three steps involved in properly preparing to raise debt or equity financing.

7. Briefly describe the difference between equity funding and debt financing.

8. Describe the most common sources of equity funding.

9. Describe the most common sources of debt financing.

10. What is the purpose of an elevator speech? Why is the preparation of an elevator speech one of the first things an entrepreneur should do in the process of raising money?

11. Why is it so important to get a personal introduction before approaching a potential investor of banker?

12. Describe the three steps required to effectively engage potential investors or bankers.

13. Identify the three most common forms of equity funding.

14. Describe the nature of business angel funding. What types of people typically become business angels, and what is the unique role that business angels play in the process of funding entrepreneurial firms?

15. Describe what is meant by the term "venture capital." Where do venture-capital firms get their money? What types of firms do venture capitalists commonly want to fund? Why?

16. Describe the purpose of an initial public offering. Why is an initial public offering considered to be an important milestone for an entrepreneurial firm?

17. What is the purpose of the investment bank in the initial public offering process?

18. In general, why are commercial banks reluctant to loan money to start-ups?

19. Briefly describe the SBA's 7(A) Loan Guaranty Program. Do most start-up firms qualify for an SBA guaranteed loan? Why or why not?

20. What is a Small Business Innovation Research (SBIR) grant? Why would a firm want to apply for such as grant if it so qualified?

1. Pretend that you are either Leonard Bosack or Sandra Lerner; that the year is 1988; that your company, Cisco Systems, is four years old; and that you have reached the point where you need investment capital. Write a 60-second elevator speech to pitch Cisco Systems to investors.

2. Doug Malone is a computer programmer at Activision, a maker of electronic games. In a year or so, Doug plans to leave Activision to launch his own firm. A colleague of Doug's recently asked him, "Where do you plan to get the money to fund your new venture?" Doug replied, "I really don't think I'll need to raise any money. I have $35,000 in the bank, and think I can fund the start-up and growth of the firm myself." Do you think Doug is being realistic? If not, what steps will Doug have to take to properly fund his firm?

3. Tina Russell is in the early stages of launching a new firm and has been attending seminars to get information about funding. Several of the seminars have had business angels and venture capitalists on the program. Tina has casually spoken with several of these individuals but has only made small talk. A friend of Tina suggested that she develop an elevator speech to use when she runs into potential investors. If Tina asked you, "What in the world is an elevator speech, and why would I need one?," what would you tell her?

4. John Baker is in the midst of starting a computer hardware firm and thinks he has identified a real problem that his company will be able to solve. He has put together a management team and has invested $250,000 of his own money in the project. John feels that time is of the essence and has decided to try to obtain venture-capital funding. How should he go about it?

5. Cathy Mills has spent the past five years bootstrapping a very successful consumer software company. Her company now has strong cash flow and a healthy balance sheet, and she has put together an impressive management team. Cathy has decided to branch out into business software and needs $150,000 to start her new division. Given Cindy's situation, what type of funding or financing do you think she would be eligible for? Explain your answer.

6. Bill Ryan, who lives near Michigan State University, has just opened a chain of salad and soup restaurants. He needs capital to expand and fortunately is a casual acquaintance with several business angels, venture capitalists, and bankers. If Bill asked you which of his alternatives would be the most likely to offer him financing, what information would you need from Bill to provide him an informed opinion?

7. Patricia Rob is the CEO of a medical equipment company that is on the verge of going public. She recently decided to write an e-mail message to her entire workforce to explain the reasons the company was going public. If you were Patricia, what would you include in the message? Explain your answer.

8. Ed Sayers just returned from a meeting with his banker with a frustrated look on his face. He tosses his keys on the kitchen counter and tells his wife, "I just can't understand where my banker is coming from. I have a great idea for a new firm, but the bank isn't interested in helping me with a loan. Tomorrow, I'm going to visit a couple of other banks to see if I have better luck." Do you think Ed will have any better luck with the second and third banks he visits? Why or why not?

9. Pam Sherman, who lives near New Orleans, is in the process of setting up a manufacturing facility that will produce highly specialized equipment for the oil drilling industry. The high cost of equipment is an issue with which Pam is struggling. She has talked to several investors who have balked at funding the equipment. Pam has thought about leasing instead of buying but isn't quite sure if leasing is the way to go. If Pam asked you your advice, what would you tell her?

10. Alex Gondolas is in the early stages of developing a new laser optics technology that may be of interest to the U.S. Department of Defense. Alex recently attended a seminar for start-ups and was advised to apply for a Small Business Innovation Research grant to fund his project. Alex thought about applying for the grant but decided it was too much hassle and paperwork. If you were advising Alex, would you tell him to rethink his decision? Why or why not?

you be the VC

Company: Onebox (www.onebox.com)

Business idea: Provide individuals with a single location to retrieve their voice mail, e-mail, and fax messages.

Pitch: Most people have a regular phone number, cell phone number, and at least one e-mail address. For many, it can be quite a chore retrieving messages left at these different sites. Onebox makes it easy providing subscribers a single location, or "one box," from which all messages can be retrieved. The service, which runs from $9.95 to $14.95 per month, works like this. Subscribers are given a phone number for voice messages and faxes and a Web-based e-mail account. They can then automatically forward all of their e-mail, voice box, and even fax accounts to their Onebox account or have messages left directly at the Onebox address. The messages can then be retrieved via the Web from a PC or mobile phone. Voice messages are played back using a streaming audio program. E-mail messages retrieved from a mobile phone can be read to the user via Onebox's proprietary text-to-speech program.

Q&A: Based on the material covered in this chapter, what questions would you ask this firm's founders before making your funding decision? What answers would satisfy you?

Decision: If you had to make your decision on just the information provided in the pitch and on the company's Web site, would you fund this firm? Why or why not?

Google: A Portrait of One Start-Up's Funding Journey
www.google.com

Google is the most popular search engine on the Internet. Its main Web site, at www.google.com, conducts over 150 million searches a day. The company also licenses its technology to more than 100 companies, including America Online (AOL) and other leading portals. The firm's name is a play on words. The word "googol" refers to the number one followed by 100 zeros. As far as scientists know, there isn't a googol of anything in the universe—not stars, grains of sand, or particles of dust. Still, the name reflects the company's mission to organize the seemingly endless material on the World Wide Web. Somehow, "googol" became "Google," which is now one of the Internet's most commonly recognized names.

As a company, Google is universally admired. It is technologically savvy, treats its employees well, and is financially prudent. The firm is known for its democratic culture in which employees are encouraged to spend roughly 20 percent of their time working on any project they believe will best benefit the company. Founders Sergey Brin and Larry Page assert that their firm isn't a conventional place to work and that they never intend for it to become so.

Google is also a somewhat peculiar firm in an admirable sort of way. It was launched in the midst of the Internet bubble but never overextended itself, particularly regarding its finances. Unlike many of its Silicon Valley peers, it has moved with deliberation, hasn't rushed to an IPO, and has slowly built its business. In fact, the way Google has funded its operations is quite impressive. It hasn't been flashy, but it's been highly effective. In mid-2004, Google was planning its IPO launch for later that year. Analysts expected that the firm would raise at least $2.7 billion through what was anticipated to be the year's hottest IPO.[52]

Larry Page and Sergey Brin, two computer science graduate students at Stanford University, founded Google in 1998. The two met in 1995 and by 1996 started collaborating on a search engine technology. As with most students, Page and Brin didn't have much money and had to scrounge around campus to find the hardware they needed to work on their project. They realized they were on to something and started trying to license their search technology to major portals. They didn't have any luck, so they decided to try to make a go of it on their own as a stand-alone company.

To get Google off the ground, Page and Brin needed a little money to move out of Page's dorm room, which acted as Google's first data center, and pay off credit cards they had run up to buy equipment. So they put their PhDs on hold and started looking for an angel investor. They targeted Andy Bechtolsheim, a friend of a faculty member and one of the founders of Sun Microsystems. Bechtolsheim invested $100,000 after seeing a demo of Google's search technology. According to company lore, the $100,000 check that Bechtolsheim wrote was made out to Google Inc. instead of Page and Brin. This caused a small dilemma since there was no Google Inc. at the time. The check sat in Page's desk for a couple of weeks while the founders scrambled to set up a corpora-

tion. Page and Brin went to friends and family to raise more money. In total, they raised almost $1 million to get Google going.

On September 7, 1998, Google opened its doors in Menlo Park, California, in a small office attached to the garage of a friend. Google quickly outgrew its first facility and moved into more adequate surroundings. By early 1999, the company's search engine was processing 500,000 queries per day even though it was still being tested. Interest in Google was also growing, and articles about the company were starting to appear in magazines. People were initially somewhat perplexed by Google's plain Web site yet outstanding performance. On June 7, 1999, the company announced that it had secured $25 million in venture-capital funding from Sequoia Capital and Kleiner Perkins Caufield & Byers, two of the Silicon Valley's most prestigious venture-capital firms.

Google hired more people, but its surroundings didn't change much; the company stayed in modest facilities. Eventually, Google moved to its current headquarters in Mountain View, California, which is called the Googleplex, and the company has continued to grow. On June 26, 2000, Google and Yahoo! announced a partnership that solidified Google's reputation. In the months that followed, more partnership deals were announced, further propelling Google's standing. In early 2002, Google signed an agreement with AOL to provide Web search services to AOL users.

Google's revenue model also started to shift from licensing income for its search technology to paid listings. A paid listing delivers an advertiser's message alongside a search result. For example, if you type the words "computer games" into a search engine, you will see listings of computer games vendors to the side of the search results. Google's pact with AOL boosted its prominence in this market. According to Google CEO Eric Schmidt, "The AOL deal will put Google on the map for paid listings."

By carefully managing its resources, Google has avoided the need for additional funding beyond what it received from the venture capitalists in 1999. It recently announced plans to go public. Despite its success, it is still located in modest facilities, and its more than 10,000 servers are basically a collection of low-cost personal computers linked together and working in parallel. What once was just a couple of doctoral students working together on a research project is now a company with tremendous momentum. The momentum, however, has not been created by round and round of funding. In contrast, careful founders, able managers, and outstanding technology have created this momentum—a momentum desired by all founders of start-up ventures.

Discussion Questions

1. Draw a time line of Google's history in terms of raising money. Start the time line in 1998 (when the company was founded), extend it through the period covered by

the case, and search the Internet for recent information about Google's attempts to raise money or launch an IPO. Write a short critique of Google's performance in the area of raising money.

2. Look at Table 10.1 in this chapter. At the time Google raised venture-capital funding, to what extent did it resemble the ideal candidate for venture-capital funding as stipulated by the table?

3. Although this topic is not covered in detail in this case, to what extent do you think Google's strategic partners have helped it avoid the need to obtain additional funding or financing? What role has Google's strategic partners played in its overall success?

4. Make a list of the factors that you think have contributed to Google's success. Which of these factors can other new ventures practice?

Sources: Google home page, www.google.com/corporate/history.html (accessed July 19, 2004); "Page Revs Up Google's Engine," R&D Magazine, November 2002, 40–41; M. Mangalindan and J. Angwin, "Google Lands Pact with AOL, Strengthening IPO Prospects," Wall Street Journal, May 2, 2002, B5; C. Hymowitz, "Google Founders Face Wealth, Resentment and a Changed Culture," Wall Street Journal Online, www.wsj.com (accessed May 18, 2004); R. Sidel, "Google to Unveil Range for Its IPO Soon," Wall Street Journal Online, www.wsu.com (accessed July 19, 2004).

Case 10.2

Biogen Idec Inc.: How the Smart Use of Alliances Helped a Biotech Firm Avoid the Need for Additional Funding
www.biogen.com

Biogen, one of the two firms that merged in late 2003 to form Biogen Idec Inc., is one of the world's oldest biotechnology companies. Finding new ways to successfully treat diseases is the main thrust of biotechnology companies. A group of European and U.S. scientists founded Biogen in Geneva, Switzerland, in 1978. The scientists, two of whom later received Nobel Prizes for their work, were committed to harnessing the power of human genes to improve human health.

During the 1980s and early 1990s, Biogen developed a variety of products that it licensed to larger drug companies. Because of the time it takes to develop pharmaceutical products and get them approved, most biotech firms rely on larger drug companies to fund their operations in exchange for the rights to their products. If a product is successful, the biotech firm will also receive ongoing licensing income. These types of arrangements are necessary to keep biotech firms funded, certainly during the ventures' early years. In many instances, however, they force biotech firms to give up the lion's share of the income from the products they develop.

Among other treatments, Biogen focuses on the treatment of multiple sclerosis (MS), a progressive disease that attacks the central nervous system. MS, which has no known cure, afflicts one million people worldwide and almost 350,000 in the United States. In the early 1990s, Biogen started working on a drug called AVONEX, which slows the progression of physical disabilities resulting from MS. In 1994, the company received a positive response from the Food and Drug Administration (FDA) to its phase III trials of the product.

A positive response to phase III trials is a major milestone in developing a new drug. All drugs go through both preclinical and clinical trials before they are approved for human use. If the drug makes it through preclinical trials, it is subjected to three phases of clinical trials, which get progressively more demanding and expensive. A description of each phase is shown here:

Phases of Clinical Trials in the Approval Process of a New Drug (trials mandated by the FDA)

Phase	Description
I	20 to 80 volunteers used to determine safety of drug and dosage
II	100 to 300 patient volunteers used to look for usefulness and side effects
III	1,000 to 5,000 patient volunteers used to monitor adverse reactions to long-term use

These trials are very time consuming and expensive, and an experimental drug can be terminated at any stage in the process. In fact, only about one out of every 250 experimental drugs entering preclinical testing concludes successful phase III trials.

As a result of the large bets that biotech firms place on the drugs they are developing, it is easy to imagine how elated a firm is when one of its drugs receives a positive response to its phase III testing. John Palmer, the director of operations for Biogen, recalls his company's reaction when it opened the letter from the FDA with its evaluation of AVONEX's phase III testing:

> We opened the envelope with the phase III results and said, "Oh my God!" It was that promising. We knew we had something—an important drug to manufacturer and distribute.

As often happens in business, however, this opportunity presented a challenge. At the time Biogen got the FDA's letter regarding AVONEX, it was only a $140 million company with modest capabilities. The company found itself at a critical juncture. Would it continue to license its most promising products to large pharmaceutical companies in exchange for operating income, or would it become a real operating drug company itself?

Although positive phase III results do not mean that a drug is approved, Biogen moved forward under the assumption that final approval would be granted. At this point, the company felt that it had three options in regard to manufacturing and marketing AVONEX:

Option 1: Partner with a major drug company for its funding and supply chain capabilities

Option 2: Build a complete supply chain in-house

Option 3: Outsource some or all of the manufacturing and delivery activities

Option 1 was rejected because the company felt that the economic possibilities associated with AVONEX were simply too large to give most of the profits away to Merck, Pfizer, or one of the other large drug companies. Option 2 wasn't realistic simply because the company lacked the time and money. Even through Biogen went public in 1984, it was not strong enough to pursue additional debt or equity financing. The only remaining option was option 3, which involved a challenging combination of bootstrapping, partnering, and outsourcing to work around the time constraints and financial hurdles involved.

The rest of the story is a legend in the biotech industry. The first thing the company did was evaluate the four steps in a drug's production and distribution:

Step 1: Manufacturer the drug in bulk

Step 2: Formulation (AVONEX needed to be freeze-dried and warehoused in cold storage)

Step 3: Packaging and labeling

Step 4: Distribution to retailers, physicians, and patients

The company felt that it could manufacturer AVONEX in its existing facilities near Boston but that it would need to find partners to do the rest. This approach is what some scholars call building a network of companies to bring a product to market. Biogen placed itself at the center of the network and set out to find the best-qualified companies to assume responsibilities for steps 2 to 4 in the process. By using this approach, Biogen significantly decreased the capital it needed to bring AVONEX to market.

Biogen was successful in finding effective partners. Its rule of thumb was to find companies that excelled at what they were doing, that were big enough to offer flexibility and skills, yet that were small enough to consider Biogen an important customer. Putting together the AVONEX network of partner-ship was a demanding task. While Biogen outsourced steps 2 to 4, it didn't outsource the responsibility for managing them. The final approval for AVONEX was faxed to Biogen on May 17, 1996, at 11 A.M. and become Biogen's first fully owned product. The first shipments of the drug reached pharmacy shelves 35 hours later. No drug had ever reached pharmacy shelves in such a short time following FDA approval.

AVONEX became the U.S. market share leader within six months of launch for the treatment of MS and now accounts for more than half the company's $1 billion in annual revenues. The AVONEX story dispels the myth that companies need massive amounts of financing or funding to get things done. In Biogen's case, it was able to launch AVONEX with a little ingenuity and the smart use of alliances rather than large amounts of funding. This experience was part of the foundation for Biogen's continuing success, leading to its merger with IDEC Pharmaceuticals Company in late 2003. With first-quarter 2004 sales revenue of almost $550 million, Biogen Idec Inc. was committed to joining its complementary resources to find treatments for diseases. Strategic alliances remain an important aspect of how Biogen Idec Inc. develops, manufacturers, and markets its products.

Discussion Questions

1. Why do you think Biogen didn't try to issue new shares of stock or go to a large bank to try to get financing to fund the launch of AVONEX? What would have been the advantages and disadvantages of each of these approaches for Biogen? Explain your answer.

2. If Biogen had licensed AVONEX to a large drug company in exchange for operating incomes and ongoing licensing fees, do you think that Biogen would be a $1 billion company today? Why or why not?

3. Do you think Biogen was smart in the way it put together its partnership network? If so, explain your answer. Will it be more difficult for Biogen Idec Inc., which is a larger firm, to successfully form and use alliances?

4. Assume that you are an entrepreneur wanting to successfully launch a new venture. What can you learn from this case that might be helpful to you?

Sources: Biogen home page, www.biogen.com (accessed March 28, 2003, and May 18, 2004); D. Bovet and J. Martha, Value Nets: Breaking the Supply Chain to Unlock Hidden Profits (New York: John Wiley & Sons, 2000); and T. Abate, The Biotech Investor (New York: Times Books, 2003).

unique
marketing issues

OBJECTIVES

After studying this chapter, you should be ready to:

1. Explain the purpose of market segmentation.

2. Describe the importance of selecting a target market.

3. Explain why it's important for a start-up to establish a unique position in its target market.

4. Describe why it's important to position a company's products on benefits rather than features.

5. Illustrate the two major ways in which a company builds a brand.

6. Identify the four components of the marketing mix.

7. Explain the difference between a core product and an actual product.

8. Contrast cost-based pricing and value-based pricing.

9. Explain the differences between advertising and public relations.

10. Weigh the advantages and disadvantages of selling direct versus selling through intermediaries.

curves: how serving an underserved market led to success

In the early 1990s, most fitness centers in the United States targeted people between the ages of 20 and 30. They focused on fitness and sports and typically offered exercise equipment and classes such as aerobics. Amenities ranged from towel service and showers to massages, swimming pools, and child-care. Most centers sold annual or monthly memberships. Some of these memberships were expensive, running as high as $1,800 per year.

But Gary Heavin and his wife, Diane, had a different idea. They wanted to open a fitness center targeted to an underserved part of the market—overweight women who had never worked out before, women who were pressed for time, and women who were intimidated by conventional co-ed

gyms. In 1992, they opened the first Curves Fitness Center in Harlingen, Texas. From the outset, Curves was a different kind of fitness center. Heavin believed that many women 30 and older cared deeply about their health and appearance, but didn't want to join a fitness club full of people who were already fit. He also figured that if he made the center convenient and affordable, it would inspire middle-aged women to give fitness a try.[1]

Heavin's entrepreneurial idea was on target. Since the first Curves opened, the company has become one of the fastest growing franchise organizations in the United States. There are now over 8,500 Curves Fitness Centers in the United States, Canada, and 30 other countries. There is one Curves for every two McDonald's in the U.S.

The company's independently owned and operated franchises currently pull in about $750 million a year from almost four million members. Franchises are launched at a rate of about 200 per month.

What has made Curves and its founder so successful? First, by setting his sights on a clearly defined group of potential customers, Heavin has carved out a market for Curves that had never been served before. Curves captured the attention of women in its target market, and generated tremendous positive word-of-mouth. In fact, until recently, the company has spent almost nothing on advertising. Most of its new members come from referrals.

Secondly, Curves has tremendous emotional appeal to its target market. Simply by targeting unfit women who were 30 years of age and older, rather than women in their teens and 20s, Curves explicitly and implicitly told this group, "We know how you feel. We know it's not easy to go to a fitness center if you're a little embarrassed about how you look. You're important enough that we've created a company just for you. We care." By positioning itself in this way, Curves has become an advocate for women 30 and older, while other fitness companies compete for the younger, mostly fit market. "What Curves has done is broken through the perception that you have to be fit, coordinated and thin to go to a gym," says Bill Howland, director of research for the International Health, Racquet and Sports Association. "They've carved out a niche within the population that had never been served."[2]

The third reason Curves is successful is that its product works for its customers. Its approach to fitness is simple and fun and fits into the time and budgetary constraints of its core clientele. Its gyms are small and offer only one service: a tightly structured 30-minute workout on eight to 12 exercise machines. The machines are located in a circle, and a recorded voice tells you when to move to the next machine. Because the centers are small, help when needed is never far away. There are no showers, massages, or fruit drinks available. You walk in, work out, and walk out, all in just over half an hour. This approach gives busy women who form the target market the ability to participate without sacrificing a large portion of their day. It also allows them to shower and dress in the privacy of their own home.

The approach has kept costs down for both the members and the franchisees. Membership fees range from $29 to $49 per month, depending on the location. A Curves franchise costs $29,000, which is low by franchise standards. "A few years ago, this company called Curves started showing up on our lists," says Maria Anton, executive editor of *Entrepreneur* magazine, which recently ranked Curves the fastest-growing franchise in the world. "We said, 'Whoa, where did this company come from?'"

I n this chapter, we'll look at the marketing challenges confronting entrepreneurial firms. Marketing involves a range of issues, from promotions to selecting a target market, to managing distribution channels. Marketing is a broad subject, and there are many books dedicated to marketing and its subfields. This chapter zeros in on the marketing challenges that are most pressing for young entrepreneurial firms.

We begin this chapter by discussing how firms define and select their target markets. Curves got off to a good start by choosing its target market wisely. Next, we discuss two issues that are particularly important for new firms—selling benefits rather than features and establishing a brand. The chapter concludes by discussing the four key facets of marketing as they relate to young entrepreneurial firms. These four facets, commonly referred to as the "4Ps" of marketing, are product, price, promotion, and place (or distribution).

Selecting a Market and Establishing a Position

In order to succeed, a new firm must address this important question: Who are our customers, and how will we appeal to them? A well-managed start-up approaches this query by following a three-step process: segmenting the market, selecting or developing a niche within a target market, and establishing a unique position in the target market. In each of these steps, shown in Figure 11.1, the new firm must answer an important question that will help it pinpoint its market and determine how to attract customers in that market. Gary Heavin, the founder of Curves, addressed these issues when he crafted the initial

strategy for his company. When asked about the importance of having a clearly defined target market in the fitness industry, he said,

> There are so many fitness companies that it is dog-eat-dog in the general fitness industry. The only hope for the average small fitness provider is that they focus on something and do that better than anything else.[3]

As noted in Chapter 3, a firm's **target market** is the limited group of individuals or businesses that it goes after or tries to appeal to. It is important that a firm first choose its target market and position itself within its target market because virtually all its marketing decisions hinge on these critical initial choices. If other marketing decisions are made first, such as choosing an advertising campaign, there is a danger the firm will not send a clear message to the public. For example, it would have been foolish for Curves to have paid for ads that depicted men and women in their 20s working out when the company ultimately decided to target women in their 30s and older. By selecting its target market first, Curves was able to make sure that all its decisions were consistent with the needs of its target market customers.

Segmenting the Market

The first step in selecting a target market is to study the industry in which the firm intends to compete and determine the different potential target markets in that industry. This process is called **market segmentation** and is important because a new firm typically only has enough resources to target one market segment, at least initially. Markets can be segmented in a number of different ways, including product type, price point, and customers served.[4] For example, the computer industry can be segmented by product type (i.e., handheld computers, laptops, PCs, minicomputers, and mainframes) or customers served (i.e., individuals, businesses, schools, and government). A firm will typically select the segment that represents the best prospects for entry, as discussed in Chapter 3, and that is the most compatible with its own core competencies.

There are several important objectives a new firm should try to accomplish as part of its market segmentation process:[5]

- The process should identify one or more relatively homogeneous groups of prospective buyers within the industry the firm plans to enter in regard to their wants and needs. For Curves, women in their 30s and older who feel the most comfortable belonging to a fitness center strictly for women is such a segment.
- Differences within the segment the firm chooses should be small compared to differences across segments. For example, most women in their 30s and older who fit into the Curves segment of the fitness center market probably have fitness-related needs that are quite similar to one another but quite different from the segment of the fitness center market catering to young men who are into weightlifting.
- The segment should be distinct enough so that its members can be easily identified. Once identified, advertising and promotional campaigns can be established to appeal specifically to the target market.
- Finally, it should be possible to determine the size of the segment so that a firm knows how large its potential market is before it aggressively moves forward. Curves

has been so successful, in part, because its market segment is huge despite the fact that it was almost completely ignored before Curves was founded. A firm's growth can quickly plateau if its market segment is too small—even if the people in its segment are very satisfied with its product or service.

As mentioned previously, markets can be segmented a number of ways, including by product type, price point, and customers served. Sometimes a firm will segment its market on more than one dimension to drill down to a specific market niche that it thinks it is uniquely capable of serving. Curves segments its market first on customers serviced and second on price (it is less expensive to join than most fitness centers). Following the lead of Curves, there are now firms serving other previously underserved segments of the fitness market. An example is My Gym Children's Fitness Center, a franchise organization designed to help children aged three months to nine years develop physically, cognitively, and emotionally.

Selecting a Target Market

Once a firm has segmented the market, the next step is to select a target market, as Curves did. As discussed in Chapter 3, the market must be sufficiently attractive, and the firm must have the capabilities to serve it. Typically, a firm (especially a start-up venture) doesn't target an entire segment of a market because many market segments are too large to target successfully. Instead, most firms target a niche within the segment. For example, one segment of the computer industry is handheld computers (or personal digital assistants as they are sometimes called). Within this segment, there are several smaller niche markets that are targeted by different companies. A **niche market** is a place within a market segment that represents a narrower group of customers with similar interests. Two of the largest companies in the market for handheld computers, Research in Motion (RIM) and palmOne, serve different niches. Historically, RIM has served business users who want their handheld devices to have wireless connectivity so that they can send and receive e-mail and browse the Web while on the run. In contrast, palmOne has traditionally served the consumer part of the handheld computer market, which is more concerned with the ability to store and retrieve information, such as addresses and appointments, rather than send and receive e-mail or browse the Web.[6]

2. Describe the importance of selecting a target market.

learning **objective**

The niche market that Research in Motion (RIM) focuses on is the business professional. RIM's success is rooted in its ability to understand the needs of its customers in that target segment. A businessperson is constantly on the run—to and from meetings, conference calls, and the airport. RIM's product helps these individuals keep in touch with the home office and organize their contacts and calendars.

In most cases, the secret to appealing to a niche market is to understand the market and meet its customers' needs. By focusing on a clearly defined market, a firm can become an expert in that market and then be able to provide its customers with high levels of value and service. This advantage is one of the reasons why Philip Kotler, a world-renowned marketing expert, says that "there are riches in niches."[7]

Sometimes firms make the mistake of selecting a market and then rushing forward without fully understanding that market or its customers. Other times, firms try to appeal to multiple markets simultaneously and spread themselves too thin, not becoming an expert in any specific market. Firms that determine and then focus on a single niche have a better chance of becoming experts in that market and reaping the accompanying rewards.

The biggest challenge a new firm faces when selecting a target market is choosing a market that is attractive enough to be interesting but is different enough that the firm isn't just another face in the crowd. A firm's choice of target markets must also be in sync with its business model and the backgrounds and skills of its founders and other personnel. A firm must also continually monitor the attractiveness of its target market. Societal preferences change, and a firm's target market can lose its attractiveness through no fault of its own. It is important that a firm be aware of the changes in its target market and react before it's too late, as illustrated in the boxed feature titled "What Went Wrong?"

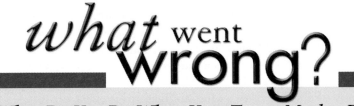

What Do You Do When Your Target Market Dries Up?

www.enesco.com

As society changes, people's preferences for products change too. Sometimes target markets dry up not because of anything a company did but because its customers' tastes change. When this happens, entrepreneurs need to know how to reposition the company so that it survives.

One firm, the Enesco Group, found itself in just this predicament. The company, which makes collectible figurines and other giftware, makes a line of figurines known as Precious Moments. The small figurines depict children and animals in cute poses. Enesco created more than 1,000 styles of these figurines, often "suspending" or "retiring" a figure to suggest scarcity. In 1996, the company's peak sales year, it sold about $206 million in Precious Moments merchandise. But by 2002, the line's sales had slipped to about $96 million.

What went wrong? According to new chief executive officer (CEO) Daniel DalleMolle, "It was obvious to me from the outside that collectibles are changing." While DalleMolle's wife collects thimbles and silver spoons, his 20-year-old daughter has no interest in collecting these items. DalleMolle concluded that his daughter's sentiment reflected a broader social trend.

To get the Precious Moments figurines back on track, DalleMolle decided that they needed to be repositioned in the marketplace. Up to that time, the figurines had sold for $24.99 to $300 through more than 30,000 gift shops. DalleMolle wondered if some consumers might want a taste of the concept without spending so much money. So he decided to start selling Precious Moments trinkets, such as the little objects that go on the top of gifts, for as little as $2.99 through mass merchandisers such as Wal-Mart. "It promotes the brand," DalleMolle says, which might interest people in looking for the higher-margin figurines in gift shops. He is also pushing additional ways to sell Precious Moments products, such as through so-called multilevel sales with at-home parties. According to DalleMolle, no matter how successful a firm's most popular product is, the firm should always be looking to develop the next generation of its offerings.

Questions for Critical Thinking

1. Choose a firm in your local community, such as an ethnic-food restaurant, selling to a niche market. Interview the firm's entrepreneur or manager to determine what he or she is doing to continuously study the needs of the firm's customers. How is the firm prepared to respond to possible changes in its customers' needs? Do you think these actions are sufficient to allow the firm to respond as necessary to changes in its customers' needs?

2. What risks does a product such as Precious Moments figurines face from large firms? In other words, how might Mattel and Hasbro threaten the survivability of the figurines? What could be done to prevent these risks from negatively affecting the Enesco Group's sales?

Source: J. Bailey, "What to Do When Your Hot Item Starts to Cool," Wall Street Journal, September 16, 2003, B10, © 2003 by Dow Jones & Co., Inc. Reproduced with permission.

learning **objective**

3. Explain why it's important for a start-up to establish a unique position in its target market.

Establishing a Unique Position

After selecting a target market, the firm's next step is to establish a "position" within it that differentiates it from its competitors. As we discussed in Chapter 4, position is concerned with how the firm is situated relative to competitors. In a sense, a position is the part of a market or of a segment of the market the firm is claiming as its own. A firm's market position can be understood by studying the features of its goods or services. For example, BMW's position (luxury) in the automobile market differs from Chevrolet's position (functional). Clearly, these products differ from each other in substantial ways. Even within the luxury automobile market, BMW's position (more sports-driving oriented) differs from that of Lexus (more luxury-features oriented). Likewise, Curves position in the fitness market differs from Gold Gym's position. The term "differentiation" was introduced in Chapter 3, where we emphasized that a firm's position in the marketplace determines how it is situated relative to its competitors. From a marketing perspective, this translates into the image of the way a firm wants to be perceived by its customers and answers the question, Why should someone in our target market buy our product or service instead of our competitors'?[8] Of course, once a firm positions itself in a certain way, it must be able to follow through with a product or service offering that lives up to the image it has created. However, no amount of positioning will help when customers have tried the firm's product or service and are dissatisfied with their experience.

A firm establishes a unique position in its customers' minds by consistently drawing attention to two or three of its product's attributes that define the essence of what the product is and what separates it from its competitors. (If more than two or three attributes are emphasized, it is easy for potential customers to get confused.[9]) For example, in its promotions, Curves highlights three attributes: it features a 30-minute workout, it offers its members lots of emotional support, and it is just for women. Plus, the women appearing in the firm's ads look just like the target market Curves serves. By choosing its emphasis carefully, Curves creates an image of itself in the minds of its potential customers. It hopes that this image is appealing to its target market and that its customers will be able to easily differentiate what it has to offer from what its competitors offer.

A firm's decision about how to position itself relative to its competitors starts with a product or service idea that is tested and refined through feasibility analysis and marketing research, as we discussed in earlier chapters. To underscore the importance of getting this process right, venture capitalists estimate that as many as 60 percent of business failures could be prevented through better prelaunch marketing research.[10]

Oakley, the sunglasses company, has done an excellent job of positioning itself and delivering on its promises. We discuss Oakley in the boxed feature titled "Savvy Entrepreneurial Firm."

Firms often develop a **tagline** to reinforce the position they have staked out in their market, or a phrase that is used consistently in a company's literature, advertisements, promotions, stationery, and even invoices and thus becomes associated with that company. An example is Nike's familiar tagline, "Just do it." The Nike tagline, which was introduced in 1988, implies that people don't need to be told they should exercise—they already know that. The challenge is to "Just do it." The beauty of this simple three-word expression is that it applies equally to a 21-year-old triathlete and a 65-year-old mall walker. This clever tagline, along with Nike's positioning strategy, helped it expand its product line beyond running shoes to athletic products for all age-groups.[11]

Table 11.1 is a short matching quiz that asks you to match several well-known companies with their taglines. A company has created a successful tagline if the message makes you think immediately of its products or services and the position it has established in its market.

Key Marketing Issues for New Ventures

Although there are many marketing issues with which new firms must grapple, both selling benefits rather than features and establishing a brand are critical to the early success of a new venture. A lack of attention to either of these issues can cripple a firm's marketing efforts by sending confusing messages to the firm's intended customers.

Savvy entrepreneurial FIRM

Oakley: Stamping a Strong Image in Customers' Minds

www.oakley.com

Although sunglasses had been around for a long time before Oakley came on the scene, the company has created a category and market position that are virtually its own and has achieved impressive growth. Oakley (named after its founder's dog) started as a company that sold handgrips and goggles for motorcycle racing. In the mid-1980s, the firm started selling sunglasses. Since that time, it has grown substantially, achieving a sales volume of over $520 million in 2003. Oakley is now a recognized leader in the sunglasses industry.

Much of Oakley's success can be attributed to its positioning. Rather than producing typical sunglasses, Oakley's glasses are innovative, state-of-the art products that are both high quality and visually appealing. Oakley also projects a brash counterculture persona, similar in sprit to the persona projected by Harley-Davidson. In its ads and promotions, Oakley says that its foundation is built on three fundamental precepts or attributes: find opportunity, solve with technology, wrap in art.

By adhering to these principles, Oakley has stamped an image of itself in the minds of its customers as a creative, technologically savvy, and independent (i.e., answering only to itself) company. This position resonates with a large customer base that wants to perceive itself as similarly "hip"—at least part of the time. Because of the position it commands, Oakley can charge a premium price for its glasses. Most of Oakley's sunglasses sell in the $65 to $375 range, depending on the style and features. Even the names of Oakley's sunglasses reinforce the company's brash image. For example, its metal-frame glasses include choices that are named Mars, X Metal XX, Penny, and Romeo and Juliet.

Oakley is currently branching into high-performance athletic shoes, watches, and apparel and is patterning its positioning strategy in these markets after its experience with sunglasses.

Questions for Critical Thinking

1. Do you think Oakley's attempt to position itself in athletic shoes, watches, and apparel in ways similar to how it is positioned in the sunglasses market will work? Why or why not?

2. Develop a list of attributes for Oakley's sunglasses that differs from the list you would develop to describe the attributes of sunglasses you could purchase in Wal-Mart and Target. What are the primary attributes of Oakley's sunglasses for which customers are willing to pay?

Sources: "Oakley Inc.," Standard & Poor's Stock Report, www. standardandpoors.com (accessed May 15, 2004), and Oakley 2003 10-K report.

Table 11.1

Match the Company to Its Tagline

Company	Tagline
WebMD	Learn Something New Every Day
Outback Steakhouse	Don't Wear It. Use It.
LeapFrog	The Way Car Buying Should Be
The Cheesecake Factory	Dramatically Improving People's Lives
Sun Microsystems	No Rules. Just Right.
Nokia	Your Trusted Guide to Gifting
Timberland	Be Great
CarMax	Something for Everyone
Power Bar	Making the Right Health Care Decisions
1-800-FLOWERS.com	Bring Some Home Today
Amgen	We Make the Net Work
Krispy Kreme Doughnuts	Connecting People

learning **objective**

4. Describe why it's important to position a company's products on benefits rather than features.

Selling Benefits Rather Than Features

Many entrepreneurs make the mistake of positioning their company's products or services on features rather than benefits. A positioning or marketing strategy that focuses on the features of a product, such as its technical merits, is usually much less effective than a campaign focusing on what the merits of the product can do.[12] Consider a cell phone manufacturer that claims, "Our cell phones are equipped with sufficient memory to store 100 phone numbers." The ability to store 100 phone numbers is a feature rather than a benefit. While features are nice, they typically don't entice someone to buy a product. A better way for the manufacturer to market the same cell phone would be to say, "Our cell phone lets you store up to 100 phone numbers, giving you the phone numbers of your family and your friends at your fingertips." This statement focuses on benefits. It tells a prospect how buying the product will enhance his or her life.

One of the most successful advertising campaigns ever launched by McDonald's contained ads that featured the jingle, "You deserve a break today—at McDonald's." McDonald's could have stressed the cleanliness of its stores or the speed of its service, both of which are features. Instead, it struck a chord with people by focusing on one of the biggest benefits of eating at McDonald's—not having to cook. Although not as obvious in today's society, not having to cook a meal at home was a major advantage when McDonald's starting using this tagline.

Entrepreneurs should tout a product or service's benefits before describing its features. Sometimes this is hard to do. For example, it is easy to see why an engineer who has just invented a new product wants to talk about that product's technical specifications. Similarly, it is natural for a company that has just developed an improved digital camera to want to point out all the bells and whistles that its camera has that other cameras don't. However, one of the most fundamental precepts of marketing is that "customers don't buy features, they buy benefits."[13] The first thing most customers want to know is how the product or service will help them accomplish their goals or improve their lives.

Establishing a Brand

learning **objective**

5. Illustrate the two major ways in which a company builds a brand.

A **brand** is the set of attributes—positive or negative—that people associate with a company. These attributes can be positive, such as trustworthy, innovative, dependable, or easy to deal with. Or they can be negative, such as cheap, unreliable, arrogant, or difficult to deal with. The customer loyalty a company creates through its brand is one of its most valuable assets. Lending support to this sentiment, Russell Hanlin, the CEO of Sunkist Growers, said, "An orange is an orange . . . is an orange. Unless . . . that orange happens to be a Sunkist, a name 80 percent of consumers know and trust."[14] By putting its name on an orange, Sunkist is making a promise to its customers that the orange will be wholesome and fresh. It is important that Sunkist not break this promise. Some companies monitor the integrity of their brands through a program of **brand management**, or protecting the image and value of an organization's brand in consumers' minds. This means that if Sunkist discovered that some of its oranges weren't fresh, it would take immediate steps to correct the problem.

Table 11.2 lists the different ways people think about the meaning of a brand. All the sentiments expressed in the table are similar, but they illustrate the multifaceted nature of a company's brand.

The difference between a company's brand and its positioning strategy is this: the brand is all about the attributes and promises that people associate with a company, and the position is all about the details. For example, the Curves brand suggests that the company is helpful, caring, and discreet and has the best interests of its members in mind. It backs up these claims through its positioning strategy, which is based on low prices, a quick yet effective 30-minute workout, convenient locations, and a cheerful staff that is always willing to lend support.

Start-ups must build a brand from scratch. One of the keys is to create a strong personality for the firm that appeals to the chosen target market.[15] Southwest Airlines, for example, has created a brand that denotes fun. This is a good fit for its target market: people traveling for pleasure rather than business. Similarly, Starbucks has created a brand that denotes warmth and hospitality, encouraging people to linger and buy additional products. A company ultimately wants its customers to strongly identify with it—to see themselves as "Southwest Airlines flyers" or "Starbucks coffee drinkers." People won't do this, however, unless they see a company as being different from competitors in ways that create value for them as customers.

Table 11.2

What's a Brand? Different Ways of
Thinking about the Meaning of a Brand

- A brand is a promise.
- A brand is a guarantee.
- A brand is a pledge.
- A brand is a reputation.
- A brand is an unwritten warrantee.
- A brand is an expectation of performance.
- A brand is a presentation of credentials.
- A brand is a mark of trust and reduced risk.
- A brand is a collection of memories.
- A brand is a handshake between a company and its customers.

Source: Adapted from D. Travis, *Emotional Branding: How Successful Brands Gain the Irrational Edge* (Roseville, Calif.: Prima Ventures, 2000).

So how does a new firm develop a brand? On a philosophical level, a firm must have meaning in its customers' lives.[16] It must create value—something for which customers are willing to pay. Imagine a father shopping for airline tickets so that he can take his three children to see their grandparents for Christmas. If Southwest Airlines can get his family to their destination for $75 per ticket cheaper than its competitors, Southwest has real meaning in the father's life. Similarly, if a teenage boy enjoys playing John Madden football with his friends and always wants the latest version of the game, Electronic Arts, the maker of the game, has real meaning in his life. Firms that create meaning in their customers' lives stand for something in terms of benefits, whether it is low prices, fun, quality, friendliness, dependability, or something else. This meaning creates a bond between a company and its customers.

iRobot produces the popular Roomba robotic vacuum cleaner. Although iRobot is enjoying much success as a smaller and newer company, it will eventually face the challenge of having to establish a strong brand image for its product if it is to continue growing. Expanding the business will be challenging because iRobot will be competing against bigger and more established corporations such as Electrolux and Dirt Devil.

On a more practical level, brands are built through a number of techniques, including advertising, public relations, sponsorships, support of social causes, and good performance. A firm's name, logo, Web site design, and even its letterhead are part of its brand. It's important for start-ups, particularly if they plan to sell to other businesses, to have a polished image immediately so that they have credibility when they approach their potential customers.

Most experts warn against placing an overreliance on advertising to build a firm's image. A more affordable approach is to rely on word of mouth, the media, and ingenuity to create positive buzz about a company. Creating **buzz** means creating awareness and a sense of anticipation about a company and its offerings.[17] This process can start during feasibility analysis, when a company shows its concept statement to prospective buyers or industry experts. Unless a company wants what it is doing to be kept secret (to preserve its proprietary technology or its first-mover advantage), it hopes that people start talking about it and its exciting new product or service. In addition, newspapers, magazines, and trade journals are always looking for stories about interesting companies. If a new company can get a favorable review of its products or services in a magazine or a trade journal, it lends a sense of legitimacy to a firm that would be hard to duplicate through advertisements.

Focusing too much on the features and benefits of their products is a common mistake entrepreneurs make when trying to gain attention from the media. Journalists are typically skeptical when entrepreneurs start talking about how great their products are relative to those of their competitors. What journalists usually prefer is a human interest story about why a firm was started or a story focused on something that's distinctly unique about the start-up.

Sometimes entrepreneurs go out on a limb and try innovative tactics to get their firm noticed. An example is what Zach Nelson, the founder of MyCIO.com (now called McAfee ASaP), did when his firm was first launched:

> One of the great things we did when we first launched MyCIO.com is that we draped our entire eleven-story building on Highway 101 with the MyCIO.com logo. It was the world's largest billboard. The City of San Jose wasn't very happy with us for doing it, but they let us keep it up for a month. Everyone that I called after we ran that giant billboard I received a return call back from.[18]

Tactics such as these are a little tricky, and the wisdom of them must be considered on a case-by-case basis. What Nelson was trying to do for MyCIO.com was to get people talking about his company and wondering what it was trying to do.

Ultimately, a strong brand can be a very powerful asset for a firm. Fifty-two percent of consumers say that a known and trusted brand is a reason to buy a product.[19] As a result, a brand allows a company to charge a price for its products that is consistent with its image. A successful brand can also increase the market value of a company by 50 to 75 percent.[20] This increased valuation can be very important to a firm if it is acquired, merges with another firm, or launches an initial public offering. **Brand equity** is the term that denotes the set of assets and liabilities that are linked to a brand and enable it to raise a firm's valuation.[21] Although the assets and liabilities on which a firm's brand equity will vary from context to context, it usually is grouped into the following five categories:

- Brand loyalty
- Name recognition
- Perceived quality (of a firm's products and services)
- Brand associations in addition to quality (e.g., good service)
- Other proprietary assets, such as patents, trademarks, and high-quality partnerships

One technique that companies use to strengthen their brands is to enter into a cobranding arrangement with other firms. **Cobranding** refers to a relationship between two or more firms where the firms' brands promote each other. An example of a cobranding arrangement between Starbucks and Barnes & Noble is provided in the boxed feature titled "Partnering for Success."

Partnering for SUCCESS

Cobranding: Partnering to Increase Brand Strength

www.starbucks.com
www.barnesandnoble.com

You're standing in line at Starbucks and notice a cardboard display on the counter with a large Barnes & Noble logo on it. Investigating further, you see that the display is filled with CDs featuring music typically played in Starbucks cafés. You think it's a little curious that Starbucks would let Barnes & Noble display its brand so prominently in its restaurant. You wonder what's up with this type of arrangement.

What you see is an example of cobranding, an increasingly popular way for firms to partner with one another and promote their brands. Think about it. As customers are paying for their coffee, they are presented with an opportunity to buy music from a well-known source. Starbucks and Barnes & Noble are trying to blend their brands in an attempt to merge audiences. Starbucks has the type of customers that Barnes & Noble wants to serve and vice versa. And the products don't compete with each other. By cobranding, the positive aspects of each company's brand and products rub off on the other.

Another example of cobranding is called component cobranding, by which one company will advertise that its products contain the components of another. The most famous example of this approach is the "Intel Inside" campaign. If a computer has Intel components inside, the positive image associated with Intel will rub off on the computer and help sell it. Intel wins too because the more computers that are sold, the more demand there is for Intel products.

Before a firm enters into a cobranding arrangement, it should consider the following three questions:

- Will the cobranding arrangement maintain or strengthen my brand image?
- Do I have adequate control over how my partner will display or use my brand?
- Are their tangible benefits associated with attaching my brand to my partner's brand? For example, will my partner's brand have a positive effect on my brand and actually increase my sales?

If the answer to each of these questions is yes, then a cobranding arrangement may be a very wise marketing approach.

Questions for Critical Thinking

1. In your opinion, what are some other cobranding arrangements Starbucks should consider. Why?

2. What advantages and disadvantages for a start-up firm do you believe are associated with a cobranding arrangement?

Source: S. Bedbury, A New Brand World (New York: Viking, 2002).

The Four Ps of Marketing for New Ventures

Once a company decides on its target market, establishes a position within that market, and establishes a brand, it is ready to begin planning the details of its marketing mix. A firm's **marketing mix** is the set of controllable, tactical marketing tools that it uses to produce the response it wants in the target market.[22] Most marketers organize their marketing mix into four categories: product, price, promotion, and place (or distribution). For an obvious reason, these categories are commonly referred to as the four Ps.

The way a firm sells and distributes its product dramatically affects a company's marketing program. This effect means that the first decision a firm has to make is its overall approach for selling its product or service. Even for similar firms, the marketing mix can vary significantly, depending on the way the firms do business. For example, a software firm can sell directly through its Web site or through retail stores, or it can license its product to another company to be sold under that company's brand name. A start-up that plans to sell directly to the public would set up its promotions program in a much different way than a firm planning to license its products to other firms. A firm's marketing program should be consistent with its business model and its overall business plan.

Let's look more closely at the four Ps. Again, these are broad topics for which entire books have been written. In this section, we focus on the aspects of the four Ps that are most relevant to new firms.

learning **objective**

6. Identify the four components of the marketing mix.

learning **objective**

7. Explain the difference between a core product and an actual product.

A firm's **product**, in the context of its marketing mix, is the good or service it offers to its target market. Technically, a product is something that takes on physical form, such as an MP3 player, an electronic game, or a laptop computer. A **service** is an activity or benefit that is intangible and does not take on a physical form, such as an airplane trip or advice from an attorney. But when discussing a firm's marketing mix, both goods and services are lumped together under the label "product."

Determining the product or products to be sold is central to the firm's entire marketing effort. As stressed throughout this book, the most important attribute of a product is that it adds value in the minds of its intended customers. It must project a clear reason for its target market to embrace it. Let's think about this by comparing vitamins with pain pills, as articulated by Henry W. Chesbrough, a professor at Harvard University:

> We all know that vitamins are good for us and that we should take them. Most of us, though, do not take vitamins on a regular basis, and whatever benefits vitamins provide do not seem to be greatly missed in the short term. People therefore pay relatively very little for vitamins. In contrast, people know when they need a pain killer. And they know they need it now, not later. They can also tell quite readily whether the reliever is working. People will be willing to pay a great deal more for a pain reliever than they pay for a vitamin. In this context, the pain reliever provides a much stronger value proposition than does a vitamin—because the need is felt more acutely, the benefit is greater and is perceived much more quickly.[23]

This example illustrates at least in part why investors prefer to fund firms that potentially have breakthrough products, such as a software firm that is working on a product to eliminate e-mail spam or a biotech firm that is working on a cure for a disease. These products are pain pills rather than vitamins because their benefits would be felt intensely and quickly. In contrast, a new restaurant start-up or a new retail store may be exciting, but these types of firms are more akin to a vitamin than a pain pill. The benefits of these businesses would not be felt as intensely.

As the firm prepares to sell its product, an important distinction should be made between the core product and the actual product. While the core product may be a CD that contains an antivirus software program, the actual product, which is what the customer buys, may have as many as five characteristics: a quality level, features, design, a brand name, and packaging.[24] For example, the Norton antivirus program is an actual product. Its name, features, warranty, ability to upgrade, packaging, and other attributes have all been carefully combined to deliver the benefits of the product: protecting computers and their contents against damage and protecting computer users against work interruption. When first introducing a product to the market, an entrepreneur needs to make sure that more than the core product is right. Attention also needs to be paid to the actual product—the features, design, packaging, and so on—that constitute the collection of benefits that the customer ultimately buys. Anyone who has ever tried to remove a product from a frustratingly rigid plastic container knows that the way a product is packaged is part of the product itself. The quality of the product should not be compromised by missteps in other areas.

The initial rollout is one of the most critical times in the marketing of a new product. All new firms face the challenge that they are unknown and that it takes a leap of faith for their first customers to buy their products. Some start-ups meet this challenge by using **reference accounts**. A **reference account** is an early user of a firm's product who is willing to give a testimonial regarding his or her experience with the product. For example, imagine the effect of a spokesperson for Dell Inc. saying that Dell used a new computer hardware firm's products and was pleased with their performance. A testimonial such as this would pave the way for the sales force of this new firm's hardware, and the new firm could use it to reduce fears that it was selling an untested and perhaps ineffective product.

To obtain reference accounts, new firms must often offer their goods or services to an initial group of customers for free or at a reduced price in exchange for their willingness to try the product and for their feedback. There is nothing improper about this process as long as everything is kept aboveboard and the entrepreneur is not indirectly "paying" someone to offer a positive endorsement. Still, many entrepreneurs are reluctant to give away products, even in exchange for a potential endorsement. But there are several advantages to getting a strong set of endorsements: credibility with peers, noncompany advocates who are willing to talk to the press, and quotes or examples to use in company brochures and advertisements.

Price

Price is the amount of money consumers pay to buy a product. It is the only element in the marketing mix that produces revenue; all other elements represent costs.[25] Price is an extremely important element of the marketing mix because it ultimately determines how much money a company can earn. The price a company charges for its products also sends a clear message to its target market. For example, Oakley positions its sunglasses as innovative, state-of-the art products that are both high quality and visually appealing. This position in the market suggests a premium price that Oakley charges. If Oakley tried to establish the position described previously and charged a low price for its products, it would send confusing signals to its customers. In addition, the lower price wouldn't generate the sales revenue Oakley requires to continuously differentiate its sunglasses from competitors' products in ways that create value for customers.

Most entrepreneurs use one of two methods to set the price for their products: cost-based pricing or value-based pricing.

learning **objective**

8. Contrast cost-based pricing and value-based pricing.

Cost-Based Pricing

In **cost-based pricing**, the list price is determined by adding a markup percentage to a product's cost. The markup percentage may be standard for the industry or may be arbitrarily determined by the entrepreneur. The advantage of this method is that it is straightforward, and it is relatively easy to justify the price of a good or service. The disadvantage is that it is not always easy to estimate what the costs of a product will be. Once a price is set, it is difficult to raise it, even if a company's costs increase in an unpredicted manner. In addition, cost-based pricing is based on what a company thinks it should receive rather than on what the market thinks a good or service is worth. It is becoming increasingly difficult for companies to dictate prices to their customers, given customers' ability to comparison shop on the Internet to find what they believe is the best bargain for them.

Value-Based Pricing

In **value-based pricing**, the list price is determined by estimating what consumers are willing to pay for a product and then backing off a bit to provide a cushion. What a customer is willing to pay is determined by his or her perceived value of the product and by the number of choices available in the marketplace. A firm influences its customers' perception of the value through positioning, branding, and the other elements of the marketing mix. Most experts recommend value-based pricing because it hinges on the perceived value of a product or service rather than cost-plus markup, which, as stated previously, is a formula that ignores the customer.[26] A gross margin (a company's net sales minus its costs of goods sold) of 60 to 80 percent is not uncommon in high-tech industries. An Intel chip that sells for $300 may cost $50 to $60 to produce. This type of markup reflects the perceived value of the chip. If Intel used a cost-based pricing method instead of a value-based approach, it would probably charge much less for its chips and earn less profit.

Most experts also warn entrepreneurs to resist the temptation to charge a low price for their products in the hopes of capturing market share. This approach can win a sale but generates little profit. In addition, most consumers make a **price-quality attribution** when looking at the price of a product or service. This means that consumers naturally assume that the higher-priced product is also the better-quality product.[27] If a firm charges a low price for its products, it sends a signal to its customers that the product is low quality regardless of whether it really is.

A company can't charge premium prices, however, without delivering on its positioning and branding promises and unless the circumstances are right. As explained in Chapter 4, some industries have very low barriers to entry and intense competition, making it difficult for a firm to charge high prices regardless of how differentiated its good or service is. To charge a premium price, one or more of the following circumstances must be present:

- Demand for the product is strong relative to supply
- Demand for the product is inelastic (people will buy at any price)
- The product is patent protected and has a clearly defined target market

- The product offers additional features that are valued (e.g., a strong warranty)
- A new technology is being introduced
- The product serves a compelling need (it is a pain pill rather than a vitamin)
- The product is positioned as a luxury product

The ability to charge a premium price is an issue that a firm should consider when developing its positioning and branding strategies.

In some instances, price is a strategic factor for a firm and is an important part of its business model and how it creates value for its customers. The SAS Institute, for example, uses pricing as a strategy. Located in Cary, North Carolina, the SAS Institute is one of the world's largest privately held software companies. It provides data warehousing and decision support software to target markets in business, government, and education. All its products are licensed, not sold. This approach is unique among software vendors. According to a company brochure,

> SAS Institute's pricing strategy is designed to foster Win/Win relationships with our customers that lead to building productive long-term partnerships. The strategy is to establish pricing consistent with the value received by SAS software customers, as they implement mission critical applications.[28]

SAS charges its customers a first-year licensing fee and an annual fee to renew the license. In contrast, most of its competitors sell their products outright, along with a yearly maintenance contract. According to SAS, the advantages of its pricing strategy, which never locks a customer into more than a one-year licensing agreement, are as follows:

- The cost of entry is low (it's typically cheaper to pay SAS its initial licensing fee than it is to buy software from one of SAS's competitors and enter into a maintenance contract)
- The return on investment is rapid
- The customer always has the most current release
- The customer always has the most current documentation
- Technical support is available
- All updates are provided during the license period

The SAS Institute's customers do business with it both because of the quality of its products and because of the nature of its pricing strategy. Their strategy works, as SAS renews 98 percent of its customers annually.

Promotion

Promotion refers to the activities the firm takes to communicate the merits of its product to its target market. Ultimately, the goal of these activities is to persuade people to buy the product. While there are a number of these activities, most start-ups have limited resources, meaning that they must carefully study promotion activities before choosing the one or ones they'll use. Let's look at the most common activities entrepreneurs use to promote their firms.

learning **objective**

9. Explain the differences between advertising and public relations.

Advertising   **Advertising** is making people aware of a product or service in hopes of persuading them to buy it. Advertising's major goals are to do the following:

- Raise customer awareness of a product
- Explain a product's comparative benefits
- Create associations between a product and a certain lifestyle

These goals can be accomplished through a number of media, including direct mail, magazines, newspapers, radio, television, and billboard advertising. However, advertising has some major weaknesses, including the following:

- Low credibility
- The possibility that a high percentage of the people who see the ad will not be interested
- Message clutter (meaning that after hearing or reading so many ads, people simply tune out)

- Relatively costly compared to other forms of promotions
- The perception that advertising is intrusive[29]

Because of these weaknesses, most start-ups do not advertise their products or services broadly. Instead, start-ups tend to use advertising for specific tasks, such as placing an ad in an industry trade journal just before an important trade show in an effort to raise awareness of the new product.

Most marketing experts are suspicious of the value of advertising, particularly for new firms. As suggested by his comments, Philip Kotler, one of the world's foremost marketing experts, is among those who question the value of advertising, at least as the sole form of promoting a company's products:

Ads primarily create product awareness, sometimes product knowledge, less often product preference, and more rarely, product purchase. That's why advertising cannot do the job alone. Sales promotion may be needed to trigger purchase. A salesperson might be needed to elaborate on the benefits and close the sale. What's worse, many ads are not particularly creative. Most are not memorable. Take auto ads. The typical one shows a new car racing 100 miles an hour around mountain bends. But we don't have mountains in Chicago [which is where Kotler lives]. And 60 miles an hour is the speed limit. And furthermore, I can't remember which car the ad featured. Conclusion: Most ads are a waste of the companies' money and my time.[30]

The steps involved in putting together an advertisement are shown in Figure 11.2. Typically, for start-up firms, advertisements are the most effective if they're part of a coordinated marketing campaign.[31] For example, a print ad might feature a product's benefits and direct the reader to a Web site for more information. The Web site might offer access to coupons or other incentives if the visitor fills out an information request form (which asks for his or her name, address, and phone number). The names collected from the information request form could then be used to make sales calls.

Entrepreneurs should be aware that a poorly crafted ad runs the risk of irritating the firm's target audience. In fact, in direct response to advertising, negative terms such as "junk mail," "spam," and "telemarketing" (which is not in itself a negative word, although many people associate it with being interrupted) have become part of standard language. The "mute" button on a television remote was designed primarily to silence ads. There are no easy ways for advertisers to meet these challenges, but they point out the importance of making sure that an advertisement is carefully crafted, that it is consistent with the brand image a firm wants to convey, and that it is geared to its target market.

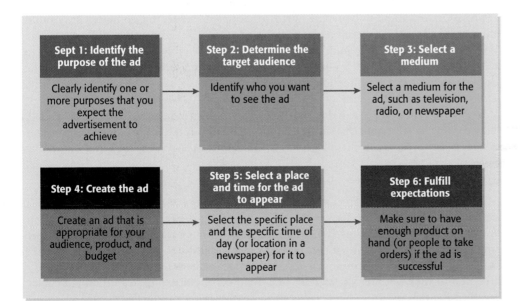

Figure 11.2

Steps Involved in Putting Together an Advertisement

Sept 1: Identify the purpose of the ad
Clearly identify one or more purposes that you expect the advertisement to achieve

Step 2: Determine the target audience
Identify who you want to see the ad

Step 3: Select a medium
Select a medium for the ad, such as television, radio, or newspaper

Step 4: Create the ad
Create an ad that is appropriate for your audience, product, and budget

Step 5: Select a place and time for the ad to appear
Select the specific place and the specific time of day (or location in a newspaper) for it to appear

Step 6: Fulfill expectations
Make sure to have enough product on hand (or people to take orders) if the ad is successful

Public Relations   One of the most cost-effective ways to increase the awareness of the products a company sells is through public relations. **Public relations** refer to efforts to establish and maintain a company's image with the public. The major difference between public relations and advertising is that public relations is not paid for—directly. The cost of public relations to a firm is the effort it makes to network with journalists and other people to try to interest them in saying or writing good things about the company and its products.

There are a number of techniques that fit the definition of public relations. These include the following:

- *Press releases:* A **press release** is an announcement made by a firm that is circulated to the press. Firms typically circulate press releases when something positive happens, such as the launch of a new product or the hiring of a new executive.
- *News conferences:* A **news conference** is the live dissemination of new information by a firm to invited media. A firm might call a news conference to announce a breakthrough new product or service innovation.
- *Media coverage:* In most cases, start-ups try to cultivate media coverage, as long as it is positive. **Media coverage** includes mention of a firm in either print media, such as newspapers or magazines, or broadcast media, such as radio or television.
- *Articles in the industry press and periodicals:* Firms particularly like to be placed on lists that draw attention to a positive aspect of their performance. For example, *Fortune* magazine publishes several lists a year, including the Small Business 100, the 100 Fastest-Growing Firms in America, and the 100 Best Companies to Work For. Firms work hard to get on these lists so that they can tout this distinction as a seal of approval from an unbiased source.
- *Civic, social, and community involvement:* Firms often try to create a positive image of their organizations by asking their employees to be involved in civic clubs and events, such as the Chamber of Commerce or the Rotary Club.

Many start-ups emphasize public relations over advertising primarily because it's cheaper and helps build the firm's credibility. In their book *The Fall of Advertising and the Rise of PR*, Al and Laura Ries argue that in launching a new product, it is better to start with public relations than advertising because people view advertising as the self-serving voice of a company that's anxious to make a sale. Advertising, according to the authors, is largely discounted. In contrast, public relations allows a firm to tell its story through a third party, such as a magazine or a newspaper. If a magazine along the lines of *Inc.* or *BusinessWeek* publishes a positive review of a new company's products, consumers are likely to believe that those products are at least worthy of a try. They think that because these magazines have no vested interest in the company, they have no reason to stretch the truth or lie about the usefulness or value of a company's products.[32]

There are many ways in which a start-up can enhance its chances of getting noticed by the press. One technique is to prepare a **press kit**, which is a folder that contains background information about the company and includes a list of its most recent accomplishments. The kit is normally distributed to journalists and made available online. Another technique is to be present at industry trade shows and other events. A **trade show** is an event at which the goods or services in a specific industry are exhibited and demonstrated. Members of the media often attend trade shows to get the latest industry news. For example, the largest trade show for the computer industry is COMDEX, which is held in Las Vegas every fall. Many companies wait until this show to announce their most exciting new products. They do this in part because they have a captive media audience that is eager to find interesting stories to write about.

Other Promotions-Related Activities   There are many other activities that help a firm promote and sell its products. Some firms, for example, give away free samples of their products. This technique is used by pharmaceutical companies that give physicians free samples to distribute to their patients as appropriate. Many food companies distribute free samples in grocery and discount stores. A similar technique is to offer free trials such as a three-month subscription to a magazine or a two-week membership to a fitness club to try to hook potential customers by exposing them directly to the product or service.

Another technique is event sponsorships. Many firms sponsor sporting events, enter floats in parades, or sponsor civic events, such as a concert series, to align their names with something of interest to their target markets. Whether these types of techniques are cost effective is usually unclear; it's difficult to determine how much a firm gains from sponsoring a Little League baseball team or a concert series.

A fairly new technique that has received quite a bit of attention is **viral marketing**, which facilitates and encourages people to pass along a marketing message about a particular product or service. The most well-known example of viral marketing is Hotmail. When Hotmail first started distributing free e-mail accounts, it put a tagline on every message sent out by Hotmail users that read "Get free e-mail with Hotmail." Within less than a year, the company had several millions users. Every e-mail message that passed through the Hotmail system was essentially an advertisement for Hotmail. The success of viral marketing depends on the pass-along rate from person to person. Very few companies have come close to matching Hotmail's success with viral marketing. However, the idea of designing a promotional campaign that encourages a firm's current customers to recommend its product or service to future customers is well worth considering.

Place (or Distribution)

Place, or distribution, encompasses all the activities that move a firm's product from its place of origin to the consumer. A **distribution channel** is the route a product takes from the place it is made to the customer who is the end user.

The first choice a firm has to make regarding distribution is whether to sell its products directly to consumers or through intermediaries (such as wholesalers and retailers). Within most industries, both choices are available, so the decision typically depends on how a firm believes its target market wants to buy its product. For example, it would make sense for a recording company that is targeting the teen market to produce digital recordings and sell the recordings directly over the Web. Most teens have access to a computer and know how to download music. In contrast, it wouldn't make nearly as much sense for a recording company targeting retirees to use the same distribution channel to sell its music offerings. A much smaller percentage of the retiree market has access to computers and knows how to download music from the Web. In this instance, it would make more sense to produce CDs and sell them through retail outlets where retirees shop.

Figure 11.3 shows the difference between selling direct and selling through an intermediary. Let's look at the strengths and weaknesses of each approach.

Selling Direct Many firms sell direct to customers. Being able to control the process of moving their products from their place of origin to the end user instead of relying on third parties is a major advantage of direct selling. Examples of companies that sell direct are Abercrombie & Fitch, which sells its clothing exclusively through company-owned stores, and Amway, Avon, and Mary Kay, which sell their products through home or office sales parties.

The disadvantage of selling direct is that a firm has more of its capital tied up in fixed assets because it must own or rent retail outlets or must field a sales force to sell its products. It must also find its own buyers rather than have distributors that are constantly looking for new outlets for the firm's products.

learning **objective**

10. Weigh the advantages and disadvantages of selling direct versus selling through intermediaries.

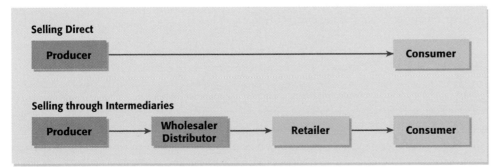

Figure 11.3

Selling Direct Versus Selling Through Intermediaries

The advent of the Internet has created new opportunities for firms to sell direct. Companies such as Amazon.com and Travelocity have built their entire business models around selling direct, and many firms that once sold their products exclusively through retail stores are now also selling directly online. The process of eliminating layers of middlemen, such as distributors and retailers, to sell directly to customers is called **disintermediation**. This is a tricky process, particularly if a firm wants to sell online and through its traditional distribution channels simultaneously. For example, if a firm has traditionally sold its products through electronics stores and is now offering the same products for sale online, the electronics stores may refuse to stock the products or may insist that they be sold online for the same price offered in the stores. This problem is referred to as channel conflict. **Channel conflict** occurs when two or more separate marketing channels (e.g., online sales and retail sales) are in conflict over their roles in selling a firm's products or services.

Selling through Intermediaries   Firms that sell through intermediaries typically pass off their products to wholesalers who place them in retail outlets to be sold. An advantage of this approach is that the firm does not need to own as much of the distribution channel. For example, if a company makes CD players and the players are sold through retail outlets such as Best Buy and Circuit City, the company avoids the cost of building and maintaining retail outlets. It can also rely on its wholesalers to manage its relationship with Best Buy and Circuit City and to find other retail outlets to sell its products.

The disadvantage of selling through intermediaries is that a firm loses control of its product. There is no guarantee that Best Buy and Circuit City will talk up the firm's product as much as the manufacturer would if it had its own stores. At times, it may also be more costly to sell through wholesalers than to sell direct. Just because a firm eliminates the middlemen in its supply chain by selling direct doesn't mean that it eliminates the functions they perform. Companies such as Abercrombie & Fitch that sell direct still have to get their products from the place they are produced to the customer.

Some firms enter into exclusive distribution arrangements with channel partners. **Exclusive distribution arrangements** give a retailer or other intermediary the exclusive rights to sell a company's products in a specific area for a specific period of time. The specific area is usually a county or a metropolitan area. The advantage to giving out an exclusive distribution agreement is to motivate a retailer or other intermediary to make a concerted effort to sell a firm's products without having to worry about direct competitors. For example, if Nokia granted Cingular the exclusive rights to sell a new type of cell phone, Cingular would be more motivated to advertise and push the phone than if many or all cell phone companies had access to the same phone.

One choice that entrepreneurs are confronted with when selling through intermediaries is how many channels to sell through. The more channels a firm sells through, the faster it can grow. But there are two problems associated with selling through multiple channels, particularly early in the life of a firm. First, a firm can lose control of how its products are being sold. For example, the more retailers through which Liz Claiborne sells its clothing, the more likely it is that one or more retailers will not display the clothes in the manner the company wants. Second, the more channels a firm sells through, the more opportunity there is for channel conflict. If a trendy store in a mall is selling Liz Claiborne clothes and a discount outlet at the edge of town starts selling the same clothes for half the price, do you think the store in the mall will be upset?

The four Ps represent the heart of a firm's marketing strategy. Early attention to each of the components of the four Ps—product, price, promotion, and place (or distribution)—can help a firm get its marketing efforts off to a good start.

CHAPTER SUMMARY

1. The first step in selecting a target market is to study the industry in which the firm intends to compete and determine the different potential target markets within that industry. This process is called market segmentation. Markets can be segmented in a number of ways, including product type, price point, and customers served.

2. A firm typically only has enough resources to target one market segment—at least initially. By focusing on a clearly defined target market, a firm can become an expert in the market and by doing so provide its customers high levels of value and service.

3. After a firm has selected its target market, the next step is to establish a "position" within it that differentiates it from its competitors. The term "position" was introduced in Chapter 4, where it was emphasized that a firm's position in the marketplace determines how it is situated relative to its competitors. From a marketing perspective, this translates into the image of the way a firm wants to be perceived by its customers. Importantly, position answers the question, Why should someone in our target market buy our good or service instead of our competitors?

4. Many entrepreneurs make the mistake of creating a strategy that focuses on the features of a product, such as its technical merits. This approach is usually less effective than a campaign focusing on the benefits of owning the product, such as convenience or being able to keep in better touch with family or friends.

5. A company's brand is the set of attributes people associate with it. On a philosophical level, a firm builds a brand by having meaning in its customers' lives. It must create value. On a more practical level, brands are built through advertising, public relations, sponsorships, supporting social causes, and good performance.

6. A firm's marketing mix is the set of controllable, tactical marketing tools that it uses to produce the response it wants in its target market. Most marketers organize their marketing mix around the four Ps: product, price, promotion, and place (or distribution).

7. The product itself is a firm's core product, such as the CD that contains an antivirus program. The actual product, which is what the customer buys, is more encompassing. It may have as many as five characteristics: a quality level, features, design, a brand name, and packaging.

8. In cost-based pricing, the list price is determined by adding a markup percentage to the product's cost. In value-based pricing, the list price is determined by estimating what consumers are willing to pay for a product and then backing off a bit to provide a cushion.

9. Advertising is making people aware of a good or service in hopes of persuading them to buy it. Public relations refers to efforts to establish and maintain a company's image with the public. The major difference between the two is that advertising is paid for, while public relations isn't—at least directly. The cost of public relations to a firm is the effort it makes to network with journalists and other people to try to interest them in saying and/or writing good things about the company.

10. The first choice a firm must make regarding distribution is whether to sell its products directly to consumers or through intermediaries (e.g., wholesalers and retailers). An advantage of selling direct is that it allows a firm to maintain control of its products rather than relying on third parties. The disadvantage is that it has more capital tied up in fixed assets because it must own (or rent) retail outlets or must field a sales force to sell its products. An advantage of selling through intermediaries is that a firm doesn't have to own much of its distribution channel (e.g., trucks and retail outlets). A disadvantage of this approach is that a firm loses total control of its product. There is no guarantee that the retailers it sells through will talk up and push its products as much as the manufacturer would if it had its own stores.

KEY TERMS

advertising, 266

brand, 260

brand equity, 262

brand management, 260

buzz, 262

channel conflict, 270

cobranding, 262

cost-based pricing, 265

disintermediation, 270

distribution channel, 269

exclusive distribution arrangements, 270

market segmentation, 255

marketing mix, 263

media coverage, 268

news conference, 268

niche market, 256

place, 269

press kit, 268

press release, 268

price, 265

price-quality attribution, 265

product, 264

promotion, 266

public relations, 268

reference account, 264

service, 264

tagline, 258

target market, 255

trade show, 268

value-based pricing, 265

viral marketing, 269

REVIEW QUESTIONS

1. What is a target market? Why is it important for a firm to choose its target market carefully?

2. Explain the importance of market segmentation. Describe several ways in which markets can be segmented.

3. Why is market segmentation the first step in the process of selecting a target market?

4. What is a niche market? Provide examples of niche markets in the food and beverage industries.

5. Describe what is meant by a firm's positioning strategy?

6. Describe how a firm decides to position itself relative to its competitors.

7. What is a tagline? What is your favorite tagline? Why?

8. Why is it important for firms to sell the benefits of its products rather than the features?

9. What is a brand? Provide an example of a brand that you buy frequently and describe the mental image that pops into your mind when you hear or see the brand's name.

10. What is the purpose of brand management?

11. What is the difference between a company's brand and its positioning strategy?

12. Why is it important for a company to have meaning in its customer's lives? What does this concept have to do with successfully establishing a brand?

13. What is buzz? Provide an example of a firm that has created effective buzz for its product.

14. Describe the difference between a core product and an actual product.

15. What is a reference account? How can having a reference account help a new firm?

16. Contrast cost-based pricing and value-based pricing.

17. What is meant by the phrase "price-quality attribution"? How does an understanding of this phrase help an entrepreneur know how to price his or her product?

18. Contrast the roles of advertising and public relations in promoting a firm and its products.

19. What is the purpose of a press release?

20. Contrast the advantages of selling direct versus the advantages of selling through an intermediary.

APPLICATION QUESTIONS

1. Reread the opening case. After reading the case, do you think that Curves was effective in establishing a market position? Why or why not?

2. Paul Bustamante is in the process of opening a music store in Tallahassee, Florida. After touring the store, a friend asked him, "Who's your target market?" Paul shrugged and said, "Kids who go to Florida State I guess, but I haven't given it much thought." What could Paul gain by thinking more carefully about his target market?

3. If you decided to start a small-business consulting service in Columbus, Ohio, how would you approach the following topics: market segmentation, selecting a target market, and developing a positioning strategy?

4. A friend of yours, Allison Velasco, is in the process of developing a new type of peanut butter. She is very excited because her peanut better is both fat free and tastes good. Allison showed you a list of 12 things that are unique about her peanut butter, and she said, "I can't wait to talk to potential customers about each of these unique properties of my peanut butter." You realize that Allison means well but that she's going to blow it if you don't teach her a little bit about how to set up a positioning strategy and how many attributes to talk about. If you decided to help Allison in this way, what would you tell her?

5. Assume that you just invented a new type of computer printer that can be easily folded up and carried like a laptop computer. You have decided to start a company to produce the computer. Decide on a name and a tagline for your new company.

6. Derek Smith just opened a new restaurant that focuses on healthy food, such as salads, soups, and smoothie drinks, made from natural ingredients. He named the restaurant Derek's Health Escape. The jingle that Derek wrote for his first ad is "Fiber, nutrition, vitamins, and low-fat, that's what Derek's Health Escape is all about." Do you like Derek's jingle? If so, explain why. If not, suggest an alternative and explain why your jingle is better than Derek's.

7. Make a list of things that Derek Smith could do to create buzz about Derek's Health Escape.

8. Tammy Ryan has developed a new type of nutritional bar. What are the different ways that Tammy can create interest in her product and legitimize it before she tries to sell it?

9. Jim has just developed a new computer program that will help computer networks recognize and eliminate e-mail spam. Jim doesn't know how to price his product. Describe to Jim the two most common methods of pricing and give him your recommendation for how to price his product.

10. Kelly Andrews has developed a new line of jewelry that has created some positive buzz among friends and some business stores in her local community. When asked by a reporter, "Where do you plan to sell your jewelry?," Kelly said, "Hopefully everywhere—jewelry stores, Target, Wal-Mart, gift shops, online, through catalogs, and a dozen other places." Write a critique of Kelly's approach.

you be the VC

Business idea: Produce a device that helps people track the progress of their exercise plan and display the results in a manner that helps them stay committed to their plan.

Pitch: Most people know that they need to exercise to stay healthy. However, simply buying a pair of running shoes or joining a health club is rarely the answer. People must be motivated to stay committed to an exercise plan. One thing that sports psychologists have found helps people stay committed is to keep track of their daily progress. It is also very motivating to people to graphically see the results of their exercise efforts and to be able to share their accomplishments with friends and family. SportBrain is the answer. It is a small device that clips to a person's belt and records how far the person walked or ran during a day. The product comes with a little cradle that plugs into a phone line. At the end of a day, the user drops the device into the cradle and sends the data to SportBrain for analysis. The data are then displayed on a Web site that shows the user

the distance he or she covered that day. The information is displayed in charts and graphs that are designed to help the user stay committed. For example, the user can see how his or her daily, weekly, or monthly results compare with his or her goals. A great deal of interesting information is also provided, such as how many steps were taken during a day, how many calories were burned, and so forth. The SportBrain hardware sells for around $140. The company will charge $8.25 to $14.95 per month for its online tracking service.

Q&A: Based on the material covered in this chapter, what questions would you ask the firm's founders before making your funding decision? What answers would satisfy you?

Decision: If you had to make your decision on just the information provided in the pitch and on the company's Web site, would you fund this firm? Why or why not?

Case 11.1

Nokia: How One Company Built Its Brand
www.nokia.com

Have you every watched someone choose a cell phone? After they've signed up for a plan, they are usually given the option of buying a Motorola, an Ericsson, or a Nokia product. How do they choose? Usually their decision boils down to what the different brand names mean to them. If the customer is 16 to 24 years old or is heavily influenced by someone in that age range, there's a good chance the choice is a Nokia. Why? Because one out of two people in this age range think Nokia cell phones are cool. Technically, Nokia uses the style term "fashion" to describe the cool dimension.

Nokia phones are considered cool by this age-group because of the company's unique branding strategy. Nokia is a Finnish company, and its efforts to build a unique brand for the company didn't begin until the early 1990s. Prior to that time, the company sold phones under a variety of names, including Mobira, RadioShack, and cellular operators' private labels. To lead the effort to build a more unifying brand, Nokia hired Anssi Vanjoki, a former 3M executive. To learn about branding, Anssi studied highly successful companies, such as Nike and Daimler-Benz (the forerunner com-

pany of DaimlerChrysler). These companies, he noted, built their brands into everything they did, including design, production, and distribution. This strategy was in contrast to conventional thinking, which placed advertising at the center of a firm's branding strategy. The notion that a company should build its brand into everything it does had a profound impact on Anssi's approach to building Nokia's branding strategy.

Anssi was concerned that cell phones were becoming commodities, with little technical differences among the competing companies' models. To differentiate Nokia from its competitors, Anssi decided to focus Nokia's brand on the human side of technology rather than on the technical features of cell phones that were being emphasized at the time. To emphasize the human side of technology, Anssi developed the slogan "Connecting People" to emphasize the difference between Nokia's strategy and that of its competitors.

To penetrate the U.S. market with its people-oriented branding strategy, Nokia developed a unique positioning strategy. In every one of its advertisements and market promotions, the firm included the message (though not necessarily in these exact words) "Only Nokia Human Technology enables you to get more out of life." In many cases, the ads included the tagline "We call this human technology." This tactic was designed to build trust with its target audience and to come across as empathetic, as though Nokia were saying that it understood what people wanted out of life and how it could help. Nokia clearly wanted to be known as the cell phone company that cares about people. This strategy left Nokia's competitors wondering what position they should take because Nokia took the best position for itself.

To support its position, Nokia injected a lot of personality into its products. Its phones are curvy and easy to hold. Most Nokia phones have a large display window that Nokia designers describe as "the eye into the soul of the product." To appeal to teens and young adults, the company designed faceplates with different colors and equipped the phones with different ring tones, making it possible for people to personalize their phones. The soft key touch pads also add to the feeling of friendliness. All these innovations lead to sales not only for first-time cell phone buyers but also for people who are replacing their phones. Nokia's current CEO, Jorma Ollila, says that Nokia research has found that one-half of cell phone users replace their phones because they are broken, lost, or need a new contract, while the other half upgrade because of technology, brand, or functionality. Anyone with a teenager knows that a cell phone doesn't have to be broken to fail the "cool" test.

There are three things in particular that Nokia has done over the years to make its branding and positioning strategies work. First, it has elevated the importance of branding to the highest levels within the consciousness of the firm. This standard was set early. In 1991, at the time its branding strategy was being formulated, Anssi Vanjoki wrote a memo that read,

> The brand is Nokia . . . [meaning that the company and its products would share the same name]. Brand management is a necessity in the class of technological leadership and low-cost manufacturing for us. It is an element of survival and prosperity in our business.

The second thing that Nokia has done is to continue studying its target market to determine the features and benefits its customers want. Ultimately, the company doesn't want to build cell phones that it thinks are cool—it wants to build cell phones

that its customers think are cool. Being able to print images to a Hewlett-Packard printer from one of Nokia's camera phones is a new feature attracting customers' attention. The importance of building "cool" cell phones was affirmed in a survey that Nokia conducted in the mid-1990s that suggested that cell phones had evolved over the years to become personal accessories. People want their cell phones to express their tastes and personalities just like their clothing and jewelry do.

Third, Nokia's branding and positioning strategies have recognized that a rational appeal to buy a firm's products must be balanced with an emotional appeal to be successful. Nokia has consistently tried to win the trust and confidence of customers, something that is paramount for the success of technology firms.

Today, Nokia is the number one maker of cell phones in the world. Although it is a large firm, it behaves in an entrepreneurial manner. Any firm can learn from Nokia's orientation and commitment to branding.

Discussion Questions

1. Does Nokia try to sell features or benefits? Provide evidence from the case to support your claim.

2. What are the fundamental attributes of Nokia's brand? What are the practical benefits associated with each attribute?

3. What are the emotional reasons someone might buy a Nokia cell phone? How important do you think these reasons are?

4. According to the chapter, a firm's positioning strategy addresses the question, Why should someone in our target market buy our good or service instead of our competitors'? Do you think Nokia's positioning strategy adequately answers this question? Why or why not?

Sources: "Printing from a Cell Phone, Wall Street Journal Online, www.wsj.com (accessed May 19, 2004); "Nokia Corp.," Standard & Poor's Stock Report, www.standardandpoors.com (accessed May 15, 2004); M. Haikio, Nokia: The Inside Story (London: Pearson Education, 2001); P. Tamporal and K. C. Lee, Hi-Tech Hi-Touch Branding (New York: John Wiley & Sons, 2001); and D. Steinbock, The Nokia Revolution (New York: American Management Association, 2001).

Case 11.2

eBags: The Four Ps of a Successful Online Retailer
www.ebags.com

In 1998, Jon Nordmark left an executive position at Samsonite and cofounded eBags, an online retailer of luggage, briefcases, backpacks, and other types of bags. Through frugal management and good customer service, eBags weathered the dot-com storm and is an Internet survivor. In fact, the company reported its first profitable quarter in 2003 and its third consecutive positive cash flow quarter. These numbers are quite a feat for an Internet retailer. At least 895 U.S. Internet companies have gone

under since January 2000, according to Webmergers.com, a site that tracks the performance of Internet companies.

Since the company was founded, a large percentage of its effort has been devoted to its marketing program. The four Ps—product, price, promotion, and place—are as important for Internet companies as brick-and-mortar retailers. In fact, a discussion of each of the Ps provides a sense of the attributes that have led to eBag's survival and success.

Product: In its four years, eBags has grown from a few hundred products to offer more than 8,000 products from 157 brands. It carries products from all the major brands, including Samsonite, Nike, American Tourister, and Timbuk2.

As with most Internet retailers, eBags takes advantage of the virtually unlimited space offered by the virtual world. A disadvantage that regular stores have in carrying luggage is that it takes up so much floor space. "Why is most luggage black? Because people [can't] afford the floor space to sell different colors," Bob Kagle, one of the venture capitalists who funded eBags, once observed. Echoing this theme, Bob Cobb, an eBags executive, said, "We've got one popular [bag] that comes in three colors. The number one color is red. People love the fact that they can see their luggage coming off the baggage carousel."

Price: Although it's not exactly known how eBags prices its products (pricing is usually a trade secret), it is aggressive in its pricing, one of the factors that lures shoppers to its Web site. Just recently, the company has become ever-more aggressive in this area by offering lowest-price guarantees and a completely free returns policy.

In all areas of its marketing mix, eBags tests its practices before they are implemented. For example, before it implemented its lowest-price guarantee, it conducted a test in which half the visitors to its Web site were offered the 110 percent price guarantee and the other half weren't. The test showed a 10 percent increase in the sales conversion rate (people who shopped and then made a purchase) for the visitors who were offered the guarantee as opposed to those that weren't.

Promotion: In regard to promotions, eBags has not done a lot of advertising. Instead, it has relied largely on public relations and word of mouth to drive traffic to its Web site. Interestingly, in an odd sort of way, the failure of so many Internet companies has drawn attention to the survivors. eBags is frequently mentioned in news articles about Internet survivors. The articles typically focus on what eBags has done right to survive.

In addition, eBags has a clean, easy-to-navigate Web site to make shopping at eBags a satisfying experience. It also continues to improve the navigation of its site to make products easy to find. For example, eBags recently upgraded its Web site to make it more intuitive to a shopper's particular interests. If a shopper conducts a search for backpacks, he or she will be prompted to choose a brand, price, color, or size, after which the site will display extensive details on products within the chosen category. The company also uses its Web site to help its customers shop for special occasions. For example, in the fall of 2003, eBags launched a back-to-school center that displayed top 10 lists of products in particular categories, such as school backpacks for young children and for college students. The top 10 lists present each product with customer ratings as well as detailed descriptions.

In late 2002, eBags launched a catalog to complement its Web site. The catalog is attractive and provides eBags another means of placing its products in front of potential customers.

Place (or distribution): One of the keys to eBag's success is its distribution strategy. Normally, offering the number of products that eBags does would cost a fortune in warehousing. It would also require eBags to assume the risk of trying to anticipate consumer demand. To keep its costs down and to avoid this risk, eBags uses a simple yet innovative strategy to manage its inventory: it has none. Instead, eBags employs a strategy called drop shipping. With drop shipping, eBags and other online merchants maintain little or no inventory. Instead, they rely on manufacturers and wholesalers to ship products directly to consumers. Profit margins on drop-shipped items tend to be lower because the retailer shares the profits of the sale with the manufacturer or distributor. But for eBags, drop shipping has been a great deal.

Here's how it works. eBags takes an order that is then electronically transmitted to the appropriate shipper, such as Samsonite. Samsonite then packages and ships the item, usually in a day or so. The product is shipped in a box with eBag's logo and name, and the buyer never knows the difference. The practice turned eBags—instantly and with little risk—into a "category killer" almost overnight. A category killer is a firm that concentrates on one product and offers such a wide selection that it becomes difficult for firms that offer only a small selection of the product to compete. An example is Home Depot in the hardware industry. eBags sees itself as a category killer in the bags industry. "Its probably one of the most important reasons why we survived," Mr. Cobb said.

Discussion Questions

1. In what way does eBag's add value in the minds of its target customers?

2. What is the difference between eBag's core product and its actual product? Describe its actual product and your assessment of whether the actual product provides an attractive or an unattractive mix of characteristics.

3. Visit eBag's Web site at www.ebags.com. Visit all areas of the site, including the area labeled "About eBags." Make a list of all the things that eBags is doing or that other people are doing for it to promote its Web site. Which of these items do you think has been the most important to eBag's success. Why?

4. What are the fundamental attributes of the positioning strategy of eBags and its brand? Do you think its positioning and branding strategies are working? Why or why not?

Sources: D. Fuscaldo, "How Can Online Retailers Carry So Many Products? eSecret is 'Drop Shipping,'" Wall Street Journal, April 28, 2003, R7; "eBags Lifts Conversion Rates with Free Returns, Price Guarantees," Internet Retailer, July 15, 2003, and "eBag-Ging Profits on a Dime," Rocky Mountain News, November 23, 2002.

the importance of *intellectual* property

After studying this chapter, you should be ready to:

1. Define the term "intellectual property" and describe its importance.

2. Discuss the four major forms of intellectual property: patents, trademarks, copyrights, and trade secrets.

3. Specify the rules of thumb for determining whether a particular piece of intellectual property is worth the time and expense of protecting.

4. Describe the six-step process for obtaining a patent.

5. Identify the four types of trademarks.

6. Identify the types of material that are eligible for copyright protection.

7. Discuss the legal environment that facilitates trade secret protection.

8. Identify the most common types of trade secret disputes.

9. Identify some of the physical measures that firms take to protect their trade secrets.

10. Explain the two primary reasons for conducting an intellectual property audit.

switchboard inc.: the key role of intellectual property in its early success

If you're planning a trip, moving to a new community, looking for a business, or simply interested in finding the phone number of an old friend, Switchboard has you covered. Founded in 1995, Switchboard is an Internet-based company that provides online directory services. For free, a user can go to its Web site and search an online directory of over 106 million people, 13 million businesses, and 4 million e-mail addresses. In addition, the site offers access to maps, driving directions, online "yellow pages," and city guides for major U.S. cities. Essentially, Switchboard connects people—consumers with businesses, businesses with businesses, and so forth.

When it was launched in 1996, Switchboard was an Internet pioneer. It was the first site to

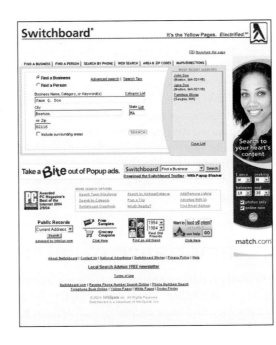

offer free access to telephone numbers and addresses nationwide. Soon after the successful debut of its "white pages," Switchboard added to its Web site an easy-to-use "yellow pages" directory. This service enabled the company to start generating income by selling traditional bricks-and-mortar businesses advertising space online. Switchboard knew from the start that if it were successful, competitors would try to imitate its services. Because of this, the company has aggressively used intellectual property laws to protect the unique aspects of its business. For example, Switchboard has several patents, including one protecting its Web site's ability to display search results quickly and in a well-organized manner. This patent prevents any other Web site from managing its search functions exactly as Switchboard does. To maintain exclusive rights to the names of its services and the designs of its logos, the company has a number of trademarks. For example, "Switchboard," "MapsOnUs," "My Corner," "Nearbuy," and "Deals Nearbuy" are all registered trademarks of Switchboard Inc. This means that no other company can use these names. Finally, the company protects its written material with copyrights and owns a number of Internet domain names that describe its services.

In addition, all of Switchboard's employees have signed nondisclosure and assignment of invention agreements. Company employees cannot legally divulge trade secrets, and any invention that an employee makes on the job belongs to Switchboard. The company is also careful when working with vendors and business partners. These compa-nies are also required to sign nondisclosure agreements before they get to any of Switchboard's behind-the-scenes activities.

For Switchboard, the combination of patents, trade-marks, copyrights, and trade secrets it uses to protect its intellectual property is critical to its success. There are now over 40 major Web sites offering online directory services. Each of these sites competes with Switchboard in one or more areas. Several of these sites are owned by heavy-weights such as Yahoo!, America Online, and Verizon. However, because of Switchboard's diligence in the area of intellectual property protection, none of its competitors can match what Switchboard has done in several key areas. Switchboard sees these unique areas as being a vital part of its ability to remain competitive in the future.

Like Switchboard, many entrepreneurial firms have valuable intellectual property. In fact, virtually all businesses, including start-ups, have knowledge, information, and ideas that are critical to their success. For at least three reasons, it is important for businesses to recognize what intellectual property is and how to protect it. First, the intel-lectual property of a business often represents its most valuable asset. Think of the value of the eBay trademark, the Nike "swoosh" logo, or the Microsoft Windows operating system. All of these are examples of intellectual property, and because of intellectual property laws, they are the exclusive properties of the firms that own them. Second, it is important to understand what intellectual property is and how to protect it to avoid unintentional viola-tions of intellectual property laws. For example, imagine the hardship facing an entrepre-neurial start-up if it selected a name for its business, heavily advertised that name, and was later forced to change the name because it was infringing on a trademark. Finally, intellec-tual property can be licensed or sold, providing valuable licensing income.

This chapter begins by defining intellectual property and exploring when intellectual property protection is warranted. There are costs involved with legally protecting intellec-tual property, and the costs sometimes outweigh the benefits. Next, we discuss the four key types of intellectual property. The chapter ends with a discussion of the importance of con-ducting an intellectual property audit, which is a proactive tool an entrepreneurial firm can use to catalog the intellectual property it owns and determine how its intellectual property should be protected.

The Importance of Intellectual Property

learning **objective**

1. Define the term "intellectual property" and describe its importance.

Intellectual property is any product of human intellect that is intangible but has value in the marketplace. It is called "intellectual" property because it is the product of human imagina-tion, creativity, and inventiveness.[1] Traditionally, businesses have thought of their physical assets, such as land, buildings, and equipment, as their most important assets. Increasingly, however, a company's intellectual assets are the most valuable. As illustrated in the Switchboard Inc. example, intellectual property consists of intangible assets such as an inven-tion, a business's logo, and a company's Internet domain name. All these assets can provide a business with a competitive advantage in the marketplace, and the loss of such assets can be just as costly (if not more so) to a business as the loss of physical property or equipment.

Consider eToys, a high-profile dot-com that failed in March 2001. Before it shut down, the company spent millions of dollars building its brand and familiarizing shoppers with the eToys name and distinctive logo. In the spring of 2001, KB Toys, a traditional bricks-and-mortar toy store, bought eToys assets (trademarks, logos, software, and so forth) in a bankruptcy sale for $14 million. While eToys didn't have a lot of physical assets that KB Toys

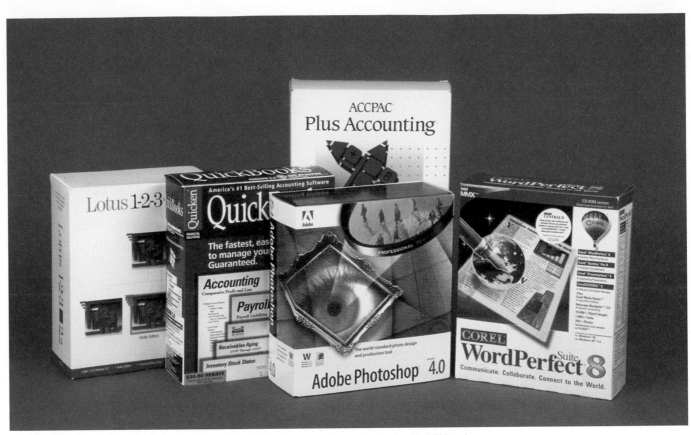

If you purchase the latest version of Adobe Photoshop, the $130 or so you pay is not for the CD-ROM and disks themselves. The value you are paying for is in the access you now have to the intellectual property contained on the disk.

needed, what KB was really after was the eToys name, its logo, its Web site design, and access to its customer list—in other words, its intellectual property. KB had learned through focus groups that the eToys name and logo were more popular than its own, even though KB has been in business for years and operates more than 1,300 stores in all 50 states. KB is now using eToy's intellectual property to make its own operations more competitive.[2] In fact, KB used this intellectual property to establish KBtoys.com. To enhance service, customers can return or exchange items purchased from KBtoys.com in any of the KB toys stores.[3]

In terms of the value attributed to intellectual property, the KB Toys story is not unusual. Microsoft, for example, paid $425 million for a small company called WebTV, primarily to acquire the company's strong patent portfolio.[4] Not all firms, however, are as intellectual property savvy as Microsoft and KB Toys. In fact, common mistakes that entrepreneurial firms make are not properly identifying all their intellectual property, not fully recognizing the value of their intellectual property, not using their intellectual property as part of their overall plan of success, and not taking sufficient steps to protect it.[5] These challenges are represented in Figure 12.1. It can be difficult, however, to determine what qualifies as intellectual property and whether it should be legally protected. Every facet of a company's operations probably owns intellectual property that should be protected. To illustrate this point, Table 12.1 provides examples of the intellectual property that typically reside with the departments of midsize entrepreneurial firms.

Determining What Intellectual Property to Legally Protect

There are two primary rules of thumb for determining whether intellectual property protection should be pursued for a particular intellectual asset. First, a firm should determine whether the intellectual property in question is directly related to its competitive advantage. For example, Amazon.com has a business method patent on its "one-click" ordering

Figure 12.1

Common Mistakes Firms Make in Regard to Intellectual Property

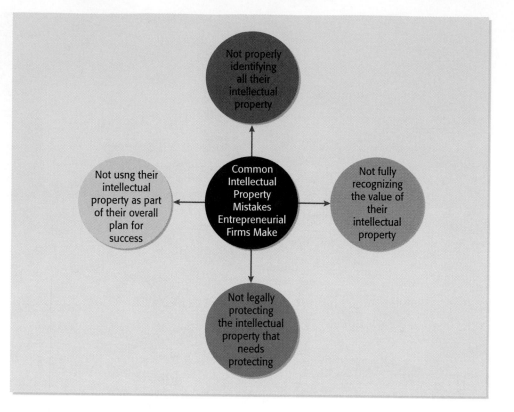

Table 12.1

Examples of the Intellectual Property That Typically Resides with the Departments of a Midsized Entrepreneurial Firm

Department	Forms of Intellectual Property Typically Present	Usual Methods of Protection
Marketing	Names, slogans, logos, jingles, advertisements, brochures, pamphlets, ad copy under development, customer lists, prospect lists, and similar items	Trademark, copyright, and trade secret
Management	Recruiting brochures, employee handbooks, forms and checklists used by recruiters in qualifying and hiring candidates, written training materials, and company newsletter	Copyright and trade secret
Finance	Contractual forms, PowerPoint slides describing the company's financial performance, written methodologies explaining how the company handles its finances, and employee pay records	Copyright and trade secret
Management information systems	Web site design, Internet domain names, company-specific training manuals for computer equipment and software, original computer code, e-mail lists	Copyright, trade secret, and Internet domain name registry
Research and development	New and useful inventions and business processes, improvements to existing inventions and processes, and laboratory notes documenting invention discovery dates and charting the progress on various projects	Patents and trade secrets

system, which is a nice feature of its Web site and is arguably directly related to its competitive advantage. (This particular patent is evaluated in greater detail in Case 12.1 in this chapter). Similarly, when Yahoo! launched a Web site specifically designed for children and named it Yahooligans, it would have been foolish for the company not to trademark the Yahooligans name. In contrast, if a business develops a product or business method or produces printed material that isn't directly related to its competitive advantage, intellectual property protection may not be warranted.

The second primary criterion for determining whether intellectual property protection should be pursued is to determine whether an item has value in the marketplace. A common mistake that young companies make is to invent a product, spend a considerable amount of money to patent it, and find that it has no market. As discussed in Chapter 3, business ideas should be properly tested before a considerable amount of money is spent developing and legally protecting them. Owning the exclusive right to something no one wants is of little value. Similarly, if a company develops a logo for a special event, it is probably a waste of money to register it with the U.S. Patent and Trademark Office if there is a good chance the logo will not be used again.

On other occasions, obtaining intellectual property protection is crucial because if a firm creates a hot product, it will invariably be imitated unless intellectual property laws prevent it. The boxed feature titled "Savvy Entrepreneurial Firm" provides an illustration of an instance in which a firm not only was diligent in protecting its intellectual property but also went to court to defend it.

Savvy entrepreneurial FIRM

Protecting Intellectual Property: Sometimes Even Beanie Babies Must Have Their Day in Court

www.ty.com

Savvy firms are always on the lookout for people who infringe on their intellectual property and take legal action when necessary. In 1997, this scenario played out at Ty, Inc., the maker of Beanie Babies.

Ty started selling Beanie Babies in 1993. The Beanie Babies, which are cute little stuffed animals, became immensely popular. They are copyrighted as "soft sculptures" under federal copyright laws. Ty limited the production of each individual Beanie Baby, thus creating a collectible market for them. Collectors valued some Beanie Babies that originally sold for $5 for as much as $2,000. One Beanie Baby produced by Ty was named Squealer the Pig.

In the mid-1990s, a competitor of Ty, GMA Accessories, came out with a competing line of its own small stuffed animals. One of GMA's animals that looked identical to Ty's Squealer the Pig was named Preston the Pig. Ty sued GMA for copyright infringement. GMA resisted, so the case went to court.

In court, GMA claimed that Preston the Pig was created independently of Ty's Squealer the Pig, so it wasn't in violation of copyright law. The Copyright Act forbids copying unless an independent creation results in an identical work. After examining the evidence, including samples and photographs of Ty's Squealer the Pig and GMA's Preston the

Pig, the court ruled that GMA had engaged in copyright infringement. The court pointed out that GMA had access to Ty's Beanie Babies as soon as they were available for sale. Because Ty's Squealer and GMA's Preston looked nearly identical, the court ruled that Preston couldn't have been produced independently. In making its argument, the court stated that the public could be misled into believing that it was buying Beanie Babies rather than the GMA knockoffs and that Ty would suffer irreparable harm if GMA were allowed to continue selling Preston the Pig. GMA appealed, and the court of appeals upheld the lower court's ruling.

In this case, the copyright law did exactly what it is designed to do: protect Ty from copyright infringement.

Questions for Critical Thinking
1. Assuming that the courts had ruled in GMA's favor, what could GMA then do to outperform Ty in the selling of stuffed animals?

2. Go to the Ty Web site (www.ty.com). After examining the firm's products, decide how you as an entrepreneur could develop a product that could compete with Beanie Babies that doesn't infringe on Ty's intellectual property.

Source: H. R. Cheeseman, Contemporary Business and E-Commerce Law *(Upper Saddle River, N.J.: Prentice Hall, 2003).*

learning **objective**

2. Discuss the four major forms of intellectual property: patents, trademarks, copyrights, and trade secrets.

The Four Key Forms of Intellectual Property

Patents, trademarks, copyrights, and trade secrets are the four key forms of intellectual property. We discuss each form of intellectual property protection in the following sections. Intellectual property laws exist to encourage creativity and innovation by granting individuals who risk their time and money in creative endeavors exclusive rights to the fruits of their labors for a period of time. Intellectual property laws also help individuals make well-informed choices. For example, when a consumer sees an In-N-Out Burger restaurant, she knows exactly what to expect because only In-N-Out Burger is permitted to use the In-N-Out Burger trademark for hamburgers, fries, and related products.

One special note about intellectual property laws is that it is up to the entrepreneur to take advantage of them and to safeguard his or her intellectual property once it is legally protected. While police forces and fire departments are available to quickly respond if an entrepreneur's buildings or other physical assets are threatened, there are no intellectual property police forces or fire departments in existence. The courts prosecute individuals and companies that break intellectual property laws. However, it is up to the individual entrepreneur to understand intellectual property laws, safeguard intellectual property assets, and initiate litigation if his or her intellectual property rights are violated. As we explained in "Savvy Entrepreneurial Firm," Ty became aware of what it believed was an infringement of its intellectual property and acted to protect it.

learning **objective**

3. Specify the rules of thumb for determining whether a particular piece of intellectual property is worth the time and expense of protecting.

Patents

A **patent** is a grant from the federal government conferring the rights to exclude others from making, selling, or using an invention for the term of the patent.[6] The owner of the patent is granted a legal monopoly for a limited amount of time. However, a patent does not give its owner the right to make, use, or sell the invention; it gives the owner only the right to exclude others from doing so. This is a confusing issue for many firms. If a company is granted a patent for an item, it is natural to assume that it could start making and selling the item immediately. But it cannot. A patent owner can legally make or sell the patented invention only if no other patents are infringed on by doing so.[7] For example, if an inventor obtained a patent on a computer chip and the chip needed technology patented earlier by Intel to work, the inventor would need to obtain permission from Intel to make and sell the chip. Intel may refuse permission or ask for a licensing fee for the use of its patented technology. While this system may seem odd, it is really the only way the system could work. Many inventions are improvements on existing inventions, and the system allows the improvements to be patented, but only with the permission of the original inventors, who usually benefit by obtaining licensing income in exchange for their consent.[8]

Patent protection has deep roots in U.S. history and is the only form of intellectual property right expressly mentioned in the original articles of the U.S. Constitution. The first patent was granted in 1790 for a process of making potash, an ingredient in fertilizer. The patent was signed by George Washington and was issued to a Vermont inventor named Samuel Hopkins. Patents are important because they grant inventors temporary, exclusive rights to market their inventions. This right gives inventors and their financial backers the opportunity to recoup their costs and earn a profit in exchange for the risks and costs they incur during the invention process. If it weren't for patent laws, inventors would have little incentive to invest time and money in new inventions. "No one would develop a drug if you didn't have a patent," Dr. William Haseltine, the chief executive officer (CEO) of Human Genome Sciences, a biotech firm, once said.[9]

Since the first patent was granted in 1790, the U.S. Patent and Trademark Office has granted over six million patents. There is increasing interest in patents, as shown in Table 12.2, as advances in technology spawn new inventions. The U.S. Patent and Trademark Office, the sole entity responsible for granting patents, is strained. It was expected that in 2003, an average of 27.7 months would lapse between the date of first filing to receive a U.S. patent.[10]

Table 12.2

Growth in Patent Applications
in the United States

	2001	2002	2003
Applications received	345,732	356,493	366,493
Patents issued	183,972	184,378	187,017
Average time for approval	24.7 months (actual)	26.1 months (target)	27.7 months (target)

Source: Budget of the United States Government, fiscal year 2005.

The Three Types of Patents

There are three types of patents: utility patents, design patents, and plant patents. Because they are typically of the greatest interest to entrepreneurs, we focus here on utility and design patents.

Utility patents are the most common type of patent and cover what we generally think of as new inventions. Patents in this category may be granted to anyone who "invents or discovers any new and useful process, machine, manufacture, or composition of matter, or any new and useful improvement thereof."[11] There are three basic requirements for utility patents: the invention must be useful, it must be novel in relation to prior arts in the field, and it must not be obvious to a person of ordinary skill in the field. The term of a utility patent is 20 years from the date of the initial application. After 20 years, the patent expires, and the invention falls into the public domain, where others can use it. Consider the pharmaceutical industry. Assume that a drug produced by Pfizer is prescribed for you and that, when seeking to fill the prescription, your pharmacist tells you there is no generic equivalent available. The lack of a generic equivalent typically means that a patent owned by Pfizer protects the drug and that the 20-year term of the patent has not expired. If the pharmacist tells you there is a generic version of the drug available, that typically means that the 20-year patent has expired and that other companies are now making a drug chemically identical to Pfizer's. The price of the generic version of the drug is generally lower because the manufacturer of the generic version of the drug is not trying to recover the costs Pfizer (in this case) incurred to develop the drug in question.

A utility patent cannot be obtained for an "idea" or a "suggestion" for a new product or process. A complete description of the invention for which a utility patent is sought is required, including drawings and technical details. In addition, a patent will not be issued if the invention has been described in any printed publication anywhere in the world or was in public use or offered for sale anywhere in the United States for more than one year prior to the time an application for a U.S. patent is filed. The latter recommendation is particularly important to remember. Sometimes entrepreneurs are forced to pay patent attorneys extremely high fees because the firm invents a product, sells it for 11½ months, and then realizes that the product can never be patented unless the company finds a patent attorney willing to work feverishly to put together the filing in two weeks to meet the "one year after first use" deadline.

Recently, utility patent law has added business method patents, which have been of particular interest to Internet firms. A **business method patent** is a patent that protects an invention that is or facilitates a method of doing business. Patents for these purposes were not allowed until 1998, when a federal circuit court issued an opinion allowing a patent for a business method, holding that business methods, mathematical algorithms, and software are patentable as long as they produce useful, tangible, and concrete results. This ruling opened a Pandora's box and has caused many firms to scramble to try to patent their business methods. Since 1998, the most notable business methods patents that have been awarded have been Amazon.com's one-click ordering system, Priceline.com's "name-your-price" business model and Netflix's method for allowing customers to set up a rental list of movies they want mailed to them. (We further examine Amazon.com's one-click ordering system in Case 12.1 in this chapter.)

Design patents are the second most common type of patent and cover the invention of new, original, and ornamental designs for manufactured products.[12] A design

Table 12.3

Summary of the Three Forms
of Patent Protection, the Types
of Inventions the Patents Cover,
and the Duration of the Patents

Type of Patent	Types of Inventions Covered	Duration
Utility	New or useful process, machine, manufacture, or composition of material or any new and useful improvement thereof	20 years from the date of the original application
Design	Invention of new, original, and ornamental designs for manufactured products	14 years from the date the patent is granted
Plant	Any new varieties of plants that can be reproduced asexually	20 years from the date of the original application

patent is good for 14 years from the grant date. While a utility patent protects the way an invention is used and works, a design patent protects the way it looks. As a result, if an entrepreneur invented a new version of the computer mouse, it would be prudent to apply for a utility patent to cover the way the mouse works and for a design patent to protect the way the mouse looks. Although all computer mice perform essentially the same function, they can be ornamentally designed in an infinite number of ways. As long as each new design is considered by the U.S. Patent and Trademark Office to be novel and nonobvious, it is eligible for design patent protection. This is not a trivial issue in that product design is increasingly becoming an important source of competitive advantage.

Plant patents protect new varieties of plants that can be reproduced asexually. Such plants are reproduced by grafting or crossbreeding rather than by planting seeds. The new variety can be different from previous plants in its resistance to disease or drought or in its scent, appearance, color, or productivity. Thus, a new color for a rose or a new type of hybrid vegetable would be eligible for plant patent protection. The term for plant patent protection is 20 years from the date of the original application.

Table 12.3 provides a summary of the three forms of patent protection, the types of inventions the patents cover, and the duration of the patents.

Who Can Apply for a Patent?

Only the inventor of a product can apply for a patent. If two or more people make an invention jointly, they must apply for the patent together. Someone who simply heard about the design of a product or is trying to patent something that is in the public domain may not apply for a patent.

There are notable exceptions to these rules. First, if an invention is made during the course of the inventor's employment, the employer typically is assigned the right to apply for the patent through an **assignment of invention agreement** signed by the employee as part of the employment agreement. A second exception is that the rights to apply for an invention can be sold. This option can be an important source of revenue for entrepreneurial firms. If a firm has an invention that it doesn't want to pursue on its own, the rights to apply for a patent on the invention can be sold to another party.

The Process of Obtaining a Patent

Obtaining a patent is a six-step process, as illustrated in Figure 12.2.

learning **objective**

4. Describe the six-step process for obtaining a patent.

Step 1. Make sure the invention is practical: As mentioned earlier, there are two rules of thumb for making the decision to patent. Intellectual property that is worth protecting typically is directly related to the competitive advantage of the firm seeking the protection or has independent value in the marketplace.

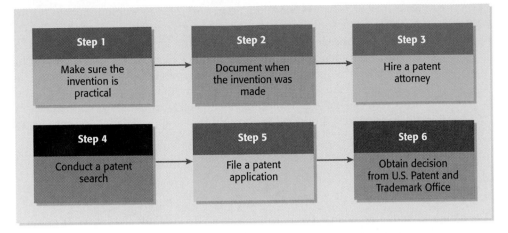

Figure 12.2

The Process of Obtaining a Patent

Step 1	Step 2	Step 3
Make sure the invention is practical	Document when the invention was made	Hire a patent attorney

Step 4	Step 5	Step 6
Conduct a patent search	File a patent application	Obtain decision from U.S. Patent and Trademark Office

Step 2. Document when the invention was made: Put together a set of documents clearly stating when the invention was first thought of, dates on which experiments were conducted in perfecting it, and the date it was first used and found to operate satisfactorily. Inventors should get in the habit of filling out an "invention logbook" on a daily basis to record their activities. An **invention logbook** documents the dates and activities related to the development of a particular invention. As soon as an inventor has an idea for an invention, he or she should write down a complete description of the invention, make sketches of it, and describe in detail how it works. The inventor should then sign and date the documents and indicate that he or she is the inventor. If possible, a notary or another party without a financial interest in the invention should witness the inventor's signature. This step is important because if two inventors independently develop essentially the same invention, the right to apply for the patent belongs to the person who came up with it first.

Step 3. Hire a patent attorney: It is highly recommended that an inventor work with a patent attorney. Even though there are "patent-it-yourself" books and Web sites on the market, it is generally naive for an entrepreneur to think that the patent process can be successfully navigated without expert help. As an indication of the difficulty of writing a patent application, the U.S. Patent and Trademark Office requires all attorneys and agents to pass a tough exam before they can interact with the agency on behalf of a client. A total of 80 percent of all candidates fail each time the exam is administered.[13] It typically takes a good patent attorney 30 to 60 days to prepare a patent application.

Step 4. Conduct a patent search: To be patentable, an invention must be novel and different enough from what already exists. A patent attorney typically spends several hours searching the U.S. Patent and Trademark Office's database (which is available online at *www.uspto.gov*) to study similar patents. After the search is completed and the patents that are similar to the invention in question have been carefully studied, the patent attorney renders an opinion regarding the probability of obtaining a patent on the new invention.

Step 5. File a patent application: The fifth step, if the inventor decides to proceed, is to file a patent application with the U.S. Patent and Trademark Office. Unlike copyright and trademark applications, which can be prepared and filed easily by their owners, patent applications are highly technical and almost always require expert assistance. Approximately 80 percent of inventors retain patent attorneys or agents to prepare and file their patent applications.[14] Hiring a patent attorney to complete and file a patent application costs from $5,000 upward, depending on the complexity of the application.

Step 6. Obtain a decision from the U.S. Patent and Trademark Office: When the U.S. Patent and Trademark Office receives a patent application, it is given a serial number, assigned to an examiner, and then waits to be examined. The patent examiner investigates the application and issues a written report ("Office Action") to the applicant's patent attorney, often asking for modifications to the application. Most of the interactions that applicants have with the U.S. Patent and Trademark Office are by mail. Occasionally, an inventor and his or her lawyer will meet face to face with a patent examiner to discuss the invention and the written report. There is room to negotiate with the patent office to try to make an invention patentable. Eventually, a yes or no decision will be rendered. A rejected application can be appealed, but appeals are rare and expensive.

Trademarks

A **trademark** is any word, name, symbol, or device used to identify the source or origin of products or services and to distinguish those products or services from others. All businesses want to be recognized by their potential clientele and use their names, logos, and other distinguishing features to enhance their visibility. Trademarks also provide consumers with useful information. For example, consumers know what to expect when they see a GAP store in a mall. Think of how confusing it would be if any retail store could use the name GAP.

As is the case with patents, trademarks have a rich history. Archaeologists have found evidence that as far back as 3,500 years ago, potters made distinctive marks on their articles of pottery to distinguish their work from others. But consider a more modern example. The original name that Jerry Yang and David Filo, the cofounders of Yahoo!, selected for their Internet directory service was "Jerry's Guide to the World Wide Web." Not too catchy, is it? The name was later changed to Yahoo!, which caught on with early adopters of the Internet and now is one of the most recognizable trademarks in America.

If Jerry and David did not reconsider their company name, which was "Jerry's Guide to the World Wide Web," what would have been the fate of Yahoo!? Today, Yahoo! is a leading global Internet company that entertains millions daily.

The Four Types of Trademarks

There are four types of trademarks: trademarks, service marks, collective marks, and certification marks (see Table 12.4). Trademarks and service marks are of the greatest interest to entrepreneurs.

Trademarks, as described previously, include any word, name, symbol, or device used to identify and distinguish one company's products from another's. Trademarks are used in the advertising and promotion of tangible products, such as Quicken for software, Gateway for computers, and Electronic Arts for electronic games.

Service marks are similar to ordinary trademarks, but they are used to identify the services or intangible activities of a business rather than a business's physical product. Service marks include Princeton Review for test prep services, eBay for online auctions, and Kinko's for photocopying.

Collective marks are trademarks or service marks used by the members of a cooperative, association, or other collective group, including marks indicating membership in a union or similar organization. The American Bar Association and The International Franchise Association are examples of collective marks.

Finally, **certification marks** are marks, words, names, symbols, or devices used by a person other than its owner to certify a particular quality about a product or service. The most familiar certification mark is the UL mark, which certifies that a product meets the safety standards established by Underwriters Laboratories. Other examples are the Good Housekeeping Seal of Approval, Stilton Cheese (a product from the Stilton region in England), and Carneros Wines (from grapes grown in the Napa Valley of northern California).

learning **objective**

5. Identify the four types of trademarks.

Table 12.4

Summary of the Four Forms of Trademark Protection, the Type of Marks the Trademarks Cover, and the Duration of the Trademarks

Type of Trademark	Type of Marks Covered	Duration
Trademark	Any word, name, symbol, or device used to identify and distinguish one company's goods from another	Renewable every 10 years, as long as the mark remains in use
	Examples: *Broadview, E*trade, Gateway, Oracle, Sun Microsystems*	
Service mark	Similar to trademarks; are used to identify the services or intangible activities of a business, rather than a businesses physical products	Renewable every 10 years, as long as the mark remains in use
	Examples: *Ameritrade, Amazon.com. eBay, Starbucks, Yahoo!*	
Collective mark	Trademarks or service marks used by the members of a cooperative, association, or other collective group	Renewable every 10 years, as long as the mark remains in use
	Examples: *Information Technology Industry Council, International Franchise Association, Rotary International*	
Certification mark	Marks, words, names, symbols, or devices used by a person other than its owner to certify a particular quality about a good or service	Renewable every 10 years, as long as the mark remains in use
	Examples: *Canadian Standards Association, Florida Oranges, ISO 9000, Underwriters Laboratories*	

What Is Protected Under Trademark Law?

Trademark law protects the following items:

- *Words:* All combinations of words are eligible for trademark registration, including single words, short phrases, and slogans. Oracle, Walt Disney Pictures, and Just Do It are examples of words and phrases that have been registered as trademarks.
- *Numbers and letters:* Numbers and letters are eligible for registration. Examples include 3M, CNN, and AT&T. Alphanumeric marks are also registerable, such as 1-800-FLOWERS.
- *Designs or logos:* A mark consisting solely of a design, such as the Golden Gate Bridge for Cisco Systems or the Nike swoosh logo, may be eligible for registration. The mark must be distinctive rather than generic. As a result, no one can claim exclusive rights to the image of the Golden Gate Bridge, but Cisco Systems can trademark its unique depiction of the bridge. Composite marks consist of a word or words in conjunction with a design. An example is the trademark for Zephyrhill's bottled water, which includes the Zephyrhill's name below a picture of mountain scenery and water.
- *Sounds:* Distinctive sounds can be trademarked, although this form of trademark protection is rare. The most recognizable examples are the MGM's lion's roar, the familiar four-tone sound that accompanies "Intel Inside" commercials, and the Yahoo! yodel.
- *Fragrances:* A fragrance of a product may be registerable as long as the product is not known for the fragrance or the fragrance does not enhance the use of the product. As a result, the fragrance of a perfume or room deodorizer is not eligible for trademark protection, while stationery treated with a special fragrance in most cases would be.
- *Shapes:* The shape of a product, as long as it has no impact on the product's function, can be trademarked. The unique shape of the monitor on Apple's iMac computer is protectable. The Coca-Cola Company has trademarked its famous curved bottle. The shape of the bottle has no effect on the quality of the bottle or the beverage it holds; therefore, the shape is not functional.
- *Colors:* A trademark may be obtained for a color as long as the color is not functional. For example, Sound Safety Products sells foam earplugs that are bright yellow. The color of the earplugs has no bearing on the functionality.
- *Trade dress:* The manner is which a product is "dressed up" to appeal to customers is protectable. This category includes the overall packaging, design, and configuration of a product. As a result, the overall look of a business is protected as its trade dress. In a famous case, *Two Pesos, Inc., v. Taco Cabana International Inc.*, the U.S. Supreme Court protected the overall design, colors, and configuration of a chain of Mexican restaurants from a competitor using a similar decor.

Trademark protection is very broad and provides many opportunities for businesses to differentiate themselves from one another. The key for young entrepreneurial firms is to trademark their products and services in ways that draw positive attention to them in a compelling manner.

Exclusions from Trademark Protection

There are notable exclusions from trademark protection that are set forth in the U.S. Trademark Act:

- *Immoral or scandalous matter:* A company cannot trademark immoral or scandalous matter, including profane words.
- *Deceptive matter:* Marks that are deceptive cannot be registered. For example, a food company couldn't register the name "Fresh Florida Oranges" if the oranges weren't from Florida.
- *Descriptive marks:* Marks that are merely descriptive of a product or service cannot be trademarked. For example, an entrepreneur couldn't design a new type of golf ball and try to obtain trademark protection on the words "golf ball." The words "golf ball" describe a type of product rather than a brand of product, such as Top-Flite or Maxfli.

This issue is a real concern for the manufacturers of very popular products. Recently, Xerox was in danger of losing trademark protection for the Xerox name because of the common use of the word "Xerox" as a verb (e.g., "I am going to Xerox this").

- *Surnames:* A trademark consisting primarily of a surname, such as Anderson or Smith, is typically not protectable. An exception is a surname combined with other wording that is intended to trademark a distinct product, such as William's Fresh Fish or Smith's Computer Emporium.

The Process of Obtaining a Trademark

As illustrated in Figure 12.3, selecting and registering a trademark is a three-step process. Once a trademark has been used in interstate commerce, it can be registered with the U.S. Patent and Trademark Office for a renewable term of 10 years and can theoretically remain registered forever as long as the trademark stays in use.

Technically, a trademark does not need to be registered to receive protection and to prevent other companies from using confusingly similar marks. Once a mark is used in commerce, such as in an advertisement, it is protected. There are several distinct advantages, however, in registering a trademark with the U.S. Patent and Trademark Office: registered marks are allowed nationwide priority for use of the mark, registered marks may use the trademark registration symbol (®), and registered marks carry with them the right to block the importation of infringing goods into the United States. The right to use the trademark registration symbol is particularly important. Attaching the trademark symbol to a product (e.g., My Yahoo!®) provides notice of a trademark owner's registration. This posting allows an owner to recover damages in an infringement action and helps reduce an offender's claim that it didn't know that a particular name or logo was trademarked.

There are three steps in selecting and registering a trademark:

Step 1. Select an appropriate mark: There are several rules of thumb to help business owners and entrepreneurs select appropriate trademarks. First, a mark, whether it is a name, logo, design, or fragrance, should display creativity and strength. Marks that are inherently distinctive, such as the McDonald's Golden Arches; made-up words, such as Exxon and Kodak; and words that evoke particular images, such as Double Delight Ice Cream, are strong trademarks. Second, words that create a favorable impression about a product or service are helpful. A name such as Safe and Secure Childcare for a day care center positively resonates with parents.

Step 2. Perform a trademark search: Once a trademark has been selected, a trademark search should be conducted to determine if the trademark is available. If someone else has already established rights to the proposed mark, it cannot be used. There are several ways to conduct a trademark search, from self-help searches to hiring a firm specializing in trademark clearance checks. The search should include both federal and state searches in any states in which business will be conducted. If the trademark will be used overseas, the search should also include the countries where the trademark will be used.

Although it is not necessary to hire an attorney to conduct a trademark search, it is probably a good idea to do so. An attorney-assisted search can usually be conducted for around $1,000.[15] If a mark is going to be used for only a limited time or a business owner does not believe that the value of the mark justifies the $1,000 search fee, self-searches can be conducted. A simple-to-use

Figure 12.3

The Process of Obtaining a Trademark

Step 1

Select an appropriate mark

Step 2

Perform a trademark search

Step 3

Create rights in the trademark

search engine is available at the U.S. Patent and Trademark Office's Web site (*www.uspto.org*). Using this Web site, a person can check the agency's database of 2.7 million registered, abandoned, canceled, and expired marks and pending applications. Adopting a trademark without conducting a trademark search is risky. If a mark is challenged as an infringement, a company may have to destroy all its goods that bear the mark (including products, business cards, stationary, signs, and so on) and then select a new mark. The cost of refamiliarizing customers with an existing product under a new name or logo could be substantial.

Step 3. Create rights in the trademark: The final step in establishing a trademark is to create rights in the mark. In the United States, if the trademark is inherently distinctive (think of Starbucks, Microsoft, or Dell), the first person to use the mark becomes its owner. If the mark is descriptive, such as Twin Cities Consulting or Northern Michigan Apples, using the mark merely begins the process of developing a secondary meaning necessary to create full trademark protection.

There are two ways that the U.S. Patent and Trademark Office can offer further protection for firms concerned about maintaining the exclusive rights to their trademarks. First, a person can file an **intent-to-use trademark application**. This is an application based on the applicant's intention to use a trademark. Once this application is filed, the owner obtains the benefits of registration. The benefits are lost, however, if the owner does not use the mark in business within six months of registration. Further protection can be obtained by filing a formal application for a trademark. The application must include a drawing of the trademark and a filing fee (ranging from $380 to $760, depending on the size of the firm applying for the trademark). After a trademark application is filed, an examining attorney at the U.S. Patent and Trademark Office determines if the trademark can be registered.

Copyrights

A **copyright** is a form of intellectual property protection that grants to the owner of a work of authorship the legal right to determine how the work is used and to obtain the economic benefits from the work.[16] The work must be in a tangible form, such as a book, operating manual, magazine article, musical score, computer software program, or architectural drawing. If something is not in a tangible form, such as a speech that has never been recorded or saved on a computer disk, copyright law does not protect it.

Businesses typically possess a treasure trove of copyrightable material, as illustrated earlier in Table 12.1. A work does not have to have artistic merit to be eligible for copyright protection. As a result, things such as operating manuals, advertising brochures, and training videos qualify for protection. The 1976 Copyright Act governs copyright law in the United States. Under the law, an original work is protected automatically from the time it is created and put into a tangible form whether it is published or not. The first copyright in the United States was granted on May 31, 1790, to a Philadelphia educator named John Barry for a spelling book.

What Is Protected by a Copyright?

learning **objective**

6. Identify the types of material that are eligible for copyright protection.

Copyright laws protect "original works of authorship" that are fixed in a tangible form of expression. The primary categories of material that can be copyrighted follow:

- *Literary works:* Anything written down is a literary work, including books, poetry, reference works, speeches, advertising copy, employee manuals, games, and computer programs. Characters found in literary works are protectable if they possess a high degree of distinctiveness. A character that looks and acts like Garfield the cartoon cat would infringe on the copyright that protects Garfield.
- *Musical compositions:* A musical composition, including any accompanying words, that is in a fixed form (e.g., a musical score, a cassette tape, a CD, or an MP3 file) is protectable. The owner of the copyright is usually the composer and possibly a

lyricist. **Derivative works**, which are works that are new renditions of something that is already copyrighted, are also copyrightable. As a result of this provision, a musician who performs a unique rendition of a song written and copyrighted by Aerosmith or by Metallica can obtain a copyright on his or her effort. Of course, Aerosmith or Metallica would have to consent to the infringement on its copyright of the original song before the new song could be used commercially, which is a common way that composers earn extra income.

- *Dramatic works:* A dramatic work is a theatrical performance, such as a play, comedy routine, newscast, movie, or television show. An entire dramatic work can be protected under a single copyright. As a result, a dramatic work such as a television show doesn't need a separate copyright for the video and audio portions of the show.
- *Pantomimes and choreographic works:* A pantomime is a performance that uses gestures and facial expressions rather than words to communicate a situation. Choreography is the arrangement of dance movements. Copyright laws in these areas protect ballets, dance movements, and mime works.
- *Pictorial, graphic, and sculptural works:* This is a broad category that includes photographs, prints, art reproductions, cartoons, maps, globes, jewelry, fabrics, games, technical drawings, diagrams, posters, toys, sculptures, and charts.

Other categories of items covered by copyright law include motion pictures and other audiovisual works, sound recordings, and architectural works.

As can be seen, copyright law provides broad protection for authors and the creators of other types of copyrightable work. The most common mistake entrepreneurs make in this area is not thinking broadly enough about what they should copyright.

Exclusions from Copyright Protection

There are exclusions from copyright protection. The main exclusion is that copyright laws cannot protect ideas. For example, an entrepreneur may have the idea to open a soccer-themed restaurant. The idea itself is not eligible for copyright protection. However, if the entrepreneur writes down specifically what his or her soccer-themed restaurant will look like and how it would operate, that description is copyrightable. The legal principle describing this concept is called the **idea–expression dichotomy**. An idea is not copyrightable, but the specific expression of an idea is.

Other exclusions from copyright protection include facts (e.g., population statistics), titles (e.g., *Introduction to Entrepreneurship*), and lists of ingredients (e.g., recipes).

How to Obtain a Copyright

As mentioned, copyright law protects any work of authorship the moment it assumes a tangible form. Technically, it is not necessary to provide a copyright notice or register work with the U.S. Copyright Office to be protected by copyright legislation. The following steps can be taken, however, to enhance the protection offered by the copyright statutes.

First, copyright protection can be enhanced for anything written by attaching the copyright notice, or "**copyright bug**" as it is sometimes called. The bug—the letter "c" inside a circle—typically appears in the following form: © [first year of publication] [author or copyright owner]. Thus, the notice at the bottom of a magazine ad for Dell Inc.'s computers in 2005 would read © 2005 Dell Inc. By placing this notice at the bottom of a document, an author (or company) can prevent someone from copying the work without permission and claiming that they did not know that the work was copyrighted. Substitutes for the copyright bug include the word "Copyright" and the abbreviation "Copr."

Second, further protection can be obtained by registering a work with the U.S. Copyright Office. Filing a simple form and depositing one or two samples of the work with the U.S. Copyright Office completes the registration process. The need to supply a sample depends on the nature of the item involved. Obviously, one could not supply one or two samples of an original painting. The current cost of obtaining a copyright is $30 per item. Although the $30 fee seems modest, in many cases it is impractical for a prolific author to register everything he or she creates. In all cases, however, it is recommended that the copyright bug be attached to copyrightable work and that registration be contemplated on a case-by-case basis. A copyright can be registered at any time, but filing promptly is recommended and makes it easier to sue for copyright infringement.

Copyrights last a long time. According to current law, any work created on or after January 1, 1978, is protected for the life of the author plus 70 years. For works made for hire, the duration of the copyright is 95 years from publication or 120 years from creation, whichever is shorter. For works created before 1978, the duration times vary, depending on when the work was created. After a copyright expires, the work goes into the public domain, meaning it becomes available for anyone's use.

Copyright Infringement

Copyright infringement is a growing problem in the United States and abroad, with estimates of the costs to owners as more than $20 billion per year. For example, less than a week after the film was released in the United States, bootleg video discs of the original Harry Potter movie were reported to be for sale in at least two Asian countries.[17] **Copyright infringement** occurs when one work derives from another or is an exact copy or shows substantial similarity to the original work. To prove infringement, a copyright owner is required to show that the alleged infringer had prior access to the copyrighted work and that the work is substantially similar to his or her own.

There are many ways to prevent infringement. For example, a technique frequently used to guard against the illegal copying of software code is to embed and hide in the code useless information, such as the birth dates and addresses of the authors. It's hard for an infringer to spot useless information if he or she is simply cutting and pasting large amounts of code from one program to another. If software code is illegally copied and an infringement suit is filed, it is difficult for the accused party to explain why the (supposedly original) code included the birth dates and addresses of its accusers.

The rampant illegal downloading and sharing of music files—copyright infringement—is a major challenge the music industry is trying to overcome. Hackers are always looking for the next way to skirt the law.

Current law permits limited infringement of copyrighted material. Consider **fair use**, which is the limited use of copyrighted material for purposes such as criticism, comment, news reporting, teaching, or scholarship. This provision is what allows textbook authors to repeat quotes from magazine articles (as long as the original source is cited), movie critics to show clips from movies, and teachers to distribute portions of newspaper articles. The pretense of the law is that the benefit to the public from such uses outweighs any harm to the copyright owner. Other situations in which copyrighted material may be used to a limited degree without fear of infringement include parody, reproduction by libraries, and making a single backup copy of a computer program for personal use.

One of the most famous copyright infringement cases involved Napster, the company that was launched by then 18-year-old Shawn Fanning and his partner, Sean Parker, in 1999. Napster, which quickly became one of the hottest sites on the Internet, made it possible for its users to swap MP3-format music files fairly easily using the company's software. The Napster case is highlighted in the boxed feature titled "What Went Wrong?"

Copyrights and the Internet

Every day, vast quantities of material are posted on the Internet and can be downloaded or copied by anyone with a computer. Because the information is stored somewhere on a computer or Internet server, it is in a tangible form and probably qualifies for copyright protection. As a result, anyone who downloads material from the Internet and uses it for personal purposes should be cautious and realize that copyright laws are just as applicable for material on the Internet as they are for material purchased from a bookstore or borrowed from a library. Because the Internet is still fairly new, the courts have been busy sorting out Internet-related copyright issues.

Copyright laws, particularly as they apply to the Internet, are sometimes difficult to follow, and it is easy for people to dismiss as contrary to common sense. For example, say that a golf instructor in Phoenix posted a set of "golf tips" on his Web site for his students to use as they prepare for their lessons. Because the notes are on a Web site, anyone can download the notes and use them. As a result, suppose that another golf instructor, in Houston, ran across the golf tips, downloaded them, and decided to distribute them to his students. Under existing law, the second golf instructor probably violated the intellectual property rights of the first. Arguably, he should have gotten permission from the first golf instructor before using the notes even if the Web site didn't include any information about how to contact the first instructor. To many people, this scenario doesn't make sense. The first golf instructor put his notes on a public Web site, didn't include any information about how to obtain permission to use them, and didn't even include information about how he could be contacted. In addition, he made no attempt to protect the notes, such as posting them on a password-protected Web page. Still, intellectual property rights apply, and the second instructor runs the risk of a copyright infringement suit.

There are a number of techniques available for entrepreneurs and Webmasters to prevent unauthorized material from being copied from a Web site. Password protecting the portion of a site containing sensitive or proprietary information is a common first step. In addition, there are a number of technical protection tools available on the market that limit access to or the use of online information, including selected use of encryption, digital watermarking (hidden copyright messages), and digital fingerprinting (hidden serial numbers or a set of characteristics that tend to distinguish an object from other similar objects).

Trade Secrets

Most companies, including start-ups, have a wealth of information that is critical to their success but does not qualify for patent, trademark, or copyright protection. Some of this information is confidential and needs to be kept secret to help a firm maintain its competitive advantage. An example is a company's customer list. A company may have been

learning **objective**

7. Discuss the legal environment that facilitates trade secret protection.

what went **wrong?**

Why the Courts Pulled the Plug on Napster

In May 1999, Shawn Fanning and Sean Parker, two college students, cofounded Napster and instantly created one of the Internet's hottest sites. Using Napster software, Internet users could access digitally compressed MP3-format music files stored on other users' computers that were connected to the Internet. Although Napster didn't actually provide a library of songs itself, it made a search engine available to users that listed the names and computer locations of songs on its users' computers, making possible peer-to-peer swapping of music files, including those that were copyrighted, for free. At its peak, Napster had over 50 million users who were sharing over three billion songs each month.

So what went wrong? For some time, the recording industry had been concerned about the swapping of copyrighted music online. However, prior to Napster, it was confined primarily to amateur Web sites. Napster was much more professional and moved the science of swapping music to a new level. As Napster's user base continued to grow, the industry started to take notice. It was clear that people were acquiring millions of songs every day, and the recording industry wasn't being paid anything for its products.

To put a halt to this, most of the world's biggest record labels, led by the Recording Industry Association of America, sued Napster in December 1999. The heavy metal band Metallica and rapper Dr. Dre joined the lawsuit. Metallica went as far as to submit a list of 300,000 users who had downloaded their music through Napster and demanded that they be revoked of their Napster privileges. Napster defended its position, arguing that it wasn't doing anything illegal. In fact, it argued not only that its Web site was perfectly legal but also that is was doing the recording industry a favor by promoting artists and encouraging sales. It also argued that sharing music was legal for consumers who weren't doing it to make a profit. After all, the argument went, who hasn't borrowed a cassette tape or other recording from a friend or family member and copied it for his or her own use? Napster alleged that it was simply facilitating this sharing process on a broader level.

On February 12, 2001, a day Napster loyalists dubbed "the day the music died," the federal court of appeals issued an almost total victory for the record companies. Although the court did not hold that Napster was an actual copyright infringer, the court did find Napster liable for contributory copyright infringement in violation of federal copyright law. The courts stated that Napster "knowingly encourages and assists in the infringement of copyrights" by others. When Napster tried to argue that it did not know of its users' infringing conduct, the court cited a document written by Napster cofounder Sean Parker that mentioned "the need to remain ignorant of users' real names and IP addresses since they are exchanging pirated music."

Although there is nothing inherently illegal about a creating a software program that allows for the swapping of files over the Internet, the bulk of files transferred through Napster were songs protected under the U.S. Copyright Act. As an active participant in helping its users gain access to this material, the courts had no choice but to rule against Napster. From Napster's point of view, it was never able to work around this complication. Napster obeyed the court and shut down its file-swapping service after the ruling. Later, it announced that it planned to launch a legal music download service with backing from Bertelsmann, a German music company. Regrettably, there was simply too much bad blood between Napster and the major record labels for the new service to come together. Eventually, Napster liquidated.

Ironically, Roxio, a company best known for its software that allows users to create their own compact discs, paid $5 million in November 2002 to buy the Napster name and trademark and is now launching a legal music download site under the Napster name. Roxio was quick to point out, however, that the service won't be based on the famous file-swapping technology championed by the original Napster. In 2004, in its new incarnation under Roxio, Napster launched a paid download service in the United Kingdom. This service, which formed legal publishing deals with various companies including EMI Group PLC and Vivendi Universal's Universal Music Group, quickly grew to over 700,000 titles. Initial subscriptions cost $9.95 per month.

Questions for Critical Thinking

1. You may know of individuals who used Napster's services before the court ruled against the firm. In your opinion, were these individuals engaging in unlawful actions? Justify your position.

2. Wippit is an online music service company. Go to the firm's Web site (www.wippit.com). How does this "legal" service differ from Napster's original business model? Do you think Wippit will be successful? Why or why not?

Sources: "Napster Opens U.K. Site," Wall Street Journal Online, *www.wsj.com (accessed May 21, 2004); H. R. Cheeseman,* Contemporary Business and E-Commerce Law *(Upper Saddle River, N.J.: Prentice Hall, 2003); A. Mathews and D. Clark, "Roxio to Buy Pressplay and Revive Napster Name,"* Wall Street Journal, May 19, 2003, B4; and A&M Records v. Napster, Inc., 239 F.3d 1004 (9th Cir. 2001).

extremely diligent over time tracking the preferences and buying habits of its customers, helping it fine-tune its marketing message and target past customers for future business. If this list fell into the hands of one or more of the company's competitors, its value would be largely lost, and it would no longer provide the firm a competitive advantage over its competitors.

A **trade secret** is any formula, pattern, physical device, idea, process, or other information that provides the owner of the information with a competitive advantage in the marketplace. Trade secrets include marketing plans, product formulas, financial forecasts, employee rosters, logs of sales calls, and laboratory notebooks. The medium in which information is stored typically has no impact on whether it can be protected as a trade secret. As a result, written documents, computer files, audiotapes, videotapes, financial statements, and even an employee's memory of various items can be protected from unauthorized disclosure.

Unlike patents, trademarks, and copyrights, there is no single government agency that regulates trade secret laws. Instead, trade secrets are governed by a patchwork of various state laws. The federal **Economic Espionage Act**, passed in 1996, does criminalize the theft of trade secrets. The **Uniform Trade Secrets Act**, which was drafted in 1979 by a special commission, attempted to set nationwide standards for trade secret legislation. Although the majority of states have adopted the act, most revised it, resulting in a wide disparity among states in regard to trade secret legislation and enforcement.

What Qualifies for Trade Secret Protection?

Not all information qualifies for trade secret protection. In general, information that is known to the public or that competitors can discover through legal means doesn't qualify for trade secret protection. If a company passes out brochures at a trade show that are available to anyone in attendance, nothing that is in the brochure can typically qualify as a trade secret. Similarly, if a secret is disclosed by mistake, it typically loses its trade secret status. For example, if an employee of a company is talking on a cell phone in a public place and is overheard by a competitor, anything the employee says is generally exempt from trade secret protection. Simply stated, the general philosophy of trade secret legislation is that the law will not protect a trade secret unless its owner protects it first.

Companies can maintain protection for their trade secrets if they take reasonable steps to keep the information confidential. In assessing whether reasonable steps have been taken, courts typically examine how broadly the information is known inside and outside the firm, the value of the information, the extent of measures taken to protect the secrecy of the information, the effort expended in developing the information, and the ease with which other companies could develop the information. On the basis of these criteria, the strongest case for trade secret protection is information that is characterized by the following:

- Is not known outside the company
- Is known only inside the company on a "need to know" basis
- Is safeguarded by stringent efforts to keep the information confidential
- Is valuable and provides the company a compelling competitive advantage
- Was developed at great cost, time, and effort
- Cannot be easily duplicated, reverse engineered, or discovered

Trade Secret Disputes

Trade secret disputes arise most frequently when an employee leaves a firm to join a competitor and is accused of taking confidential information with him or her. For example, a marketing executive for one firm may take a job with a competitor and create a marketing plan for his new employer that is nearly identical to the plan he was working on at his previous job. The original employer could argue that the marketing plan on which the departed employee was working when he left his job was a company trade secret and that the employee essentially stole the plan and took it to his new job. A more flagrant example would be the outright theft of information by one company or individual from another.

learning **objective**

8. Identify the most common types of trade secret disputes.

A company damaged by trade secret theft can initiate a civil action for damages in court. The action should be taken as soon after the discovery of the theft as possible. The defendant, if he or she denies the allegation, will typically argue that the information in question was independently developed (meaning no theft took place), was obtained by proper means (such as with the permission of the owner), is common knowledge (meaning it is not subject to trade secret protection), or was innocently received (such as through a casual conversation at a business meeting). Memorization is not a defense. As a result, an employee of one firm can't say that "all I took from my old job to my new one was what's in my head" and claim that just because the information he or she conveyed wasn't in written form, it's not subject to trade secret protection. If the courts rule in favor of the firm that feels its trade secret has been stolen, the firm can stop the offender from using the trade secret and obtain substantial financial damages.

Trade Secret Protection Methods

Aggressive protection of trade secrets is necessary to prevent intentional or unintentional disclosure. In addition, one of the key factors in determining whether something constitutes a trade secret is the extent of the efforts to keep it secret. Companies protect trade secrets through physical measures and written agreements.

learning **objective**

9. Identify some of the physical measures that firms take to protect their trade secrets.

Physical Measures   There are a number of physical measures firms use to protect trade secrets, from providing employees access to file cabinets that lock to much more elaborate measures. The level of protection depends on the nature of the trade secret. For example, although a retail store may consider its inventory control procedures to be a trade secret, it may not consider this information vital and may take appropriate yet not extreme measures to protect the information. In contrast, a biotech firm may be on the cusp of discovering a cure for a disease and may take extreme measures to protect the confidentiality of the work being conducted in its laboratories.

The following are examples of commonly used physical measures for protecting trade secrets:

- *Restricting access:* Many companies restrict physical access to confidential material only to the employees who have a "need to know." For example, access to a company's customer list may be restricted to key personnel in the marketing department.
- *Labeling documents:* Sensitive documents should be stamped or labeled "confidential," "proprietary," "restricted," or "secret." If possible, these documents should be secured when not in use. Such labeling should be restricted to particularly sensitive documents. If everything is labeled "confidential," there is a risk that employees will soon lose their ability to distinguish between slightly and highly confidential material.
- *Password protecting confidential computer files:* Providing employees with clearance to view confidential information by using secure passwords can restrict information on a company's computer network, Web site, or intranet. Companies can also write protect documents to ensure that employees can read but do not modify certain documents.
- *Maintaining logbooks for visitors:* Visitors can be denied access to confidential information by asking them to sign in when they arrive at a company facility and to wear name badges that identify them as visitors and requiring that a visitor always be accompanied by a company employee.
- *Maintain logbooks for access to sensitive material:* Many companies maintain logbooks for sensitive material and make their employees "check out" and "check in" the material.
- *Maintaining adequate overall security measures:* Commonsense measures are also helpful. Shredders should be provided to destroy documents as appropriate. Employees who have access to confidential material should have desks and cabinets that can be locked and secured. Alarms, security systems, and security personnel should be used to protect a firm's premises.

Some of these measures may seem extreme. However, unfortunately we live in a world that is not perfect, and companies need to safeguard their information against both inadvertent disclosure and outright theft. Steps such as shredding documents may seem like overkill at first glance but may be very important in ultimately protecting trade secrets. Believe it or not, there have been a number of cases in which companies have caught competitors literally going through the trash bins behind their buildings looking for confidential information.

Written Agreements   It is important for a company's employees to know that it is their duty to keep trade secrets and other forms of confidential information secret. For the best protection, a firm should ask its employees to sign nondisclosure and noncompete agreements, as discussed in Chapter 6.

Intellectual property is important enough that firms have started strictly for the purpose of helping match firms with intellectual property to sell or license with firms that need intellectual property to implement their business models. An example of a firm that was started for this purpose is Yet2.com, as illustrated in the boxed feature titled "Partnering for Success."

Partnering forSUCCESS

Yet2.com: Creating a Path between Owners of Intellectual Property and Those Who Could Benefit from Its Use

www.Yet2.com

Not long ago, Ben DuPont was still working for the company that bears his family name. His last job at DuPont & Co., the Fortune 500 chemical firm, was to find new sources of revenue for the company's apparel and fiber products. The toughest challenge was finding buyers. He would take products and technologies DuPont & Co. was interested in licensing, shop them around at other companies, and hope that somebody would bite. "After six months of doing this, you get to thinking there's got to be a better way," DuPont said.

The frustrations Ben DuPont felt when trying to find buyers for DuPont & Co.'s excess products and technologies gave birth to a business idea that quickly became Yet2.com. Yet2.com is an Internet-based company that provides a marketplace for the sale and/or licensing of intellectual property and provides a way for future business partners to find each other. The toolbar at the top of the company's Web site has headings labeled "Find a Technology" and "List a Technology." Here, firms such as DuPont & Co. can list proprietary technologies, in an anonymous manner, that they are willing to license or sell. Potential buyers or licensees can study the site, and if they spot something of interest, Yet2.com acts as a matchmaker, bringing licensor and licensee together. The reverse process also takes place. Firms can anonymously post their needs, and if a company has a licensable technology that can satisfy them, Yet2.com brings those parties together.

An early success story for Yet2.com involved a small, entrepreneurial start-up named ChromeaDex and the giant drug company Bayer. ChromeaDex's CEO, Frank Jaksch, was browsing Yet2.com's listing of technologies for license or sale one day and came across a technology his company desperately needed (which was anonymously listed by Bayer) but didn't have the resources to develop itself. Yet2.com helped ChromeaDex contact Bayer, and the two firms now have a vibrant business partnership.

For his part, Ben DuPont is thrilled with the early successes of Yet2.com, pointing out that the site creates a revenue source for companies looking to make money from their intellectual property and provides a convenient way for firms needing intellectual property to make their specific desires known. Yet2.com's revenues come from sponsorship income and from listing fees. By creating a way for business partners to find each other, this entrepreneurial firm has created a promising business for itself.

Questions for Critical Thinking

1. Yet2.com's "marketplace mission" is posted on its Web site (www.yet2.com). Go to the Web site, read the mission, and then evaluate the mission. Do you think this mission is reasonable as a driving force for this firm's operations? Why or why not?

2. Study Yet2.com's Web site a second time to better understand how the firm's business model works. What intellectual property do you think Yet2.com owns? What should Yet2.com do to protect its intellectual property?

Sources: A. A. Prado, "Linking Intellectual Property Buyers, Sellers," Investor's Business Daily, November 9, 2001; Yet2.com home page, www.Yet2.com (accessed May 23, 2004); and "Dealflow," Red Herring, April 1, 2001.

Conducting an Intellectual Property Audit

learning **objective**

10. Explain the two primary reasons for conducting an intellectual property audit.

The first step a firm should take to protect its intellectual property is to complete an intellectual property audit. This is recommended for firms regardless of size, from start-ups to mature companies. An **intellectual property audit** is conducted to determine the intellectual property a company owns.

The following sections describe the reasons for conducting an intellectual property audit and the basic steps in the audit process. Some firms hire attorneys to conduct the audit, while others conduct the audit on their own. Once an audit is completed, a company can determine the appropriate measures it needs to take to protect the intellectual property that it owns and that is worth the effort and expense of protecting.

Why Conduct an Intellectual Property Audit?

There are two primary reasons for conducting an intellectual property audit. First, it is prudent for a company to periodically determine whether its intellectual property is being properly protected. As illustrated in Table 12.5, intellectual property resides in every department in a firm, and it is common for firms to simply overlook intellectual property that is eligible for protection.

Table 12.5

Types of Questions to Ask When Conducting an Intellectual Property Audit

Patents	Copyrights
• Are products under development that require patent protection?	• Is there a policy in place regarding what material needs the copyright bug and when the bug is to be put in place?
• Are current patent maintenance fees up to date?	
• Do we have any business methods that should be patented?	• Is there a policy in place regarding when copyrightable material should be registered?
• Do we own any patents that are no longer consistent with our business plan, that could be sold or licensed?	• Is proper documentation in place to protect the company's rights to use the material it creates or pays to have created?
• Do our scientists properly document key discovery dates?	• Are we in compliance with the copyright license agreements we have entered into?

Trademarks	Trade Secrets
• Are we using any names or slogans that require trademark protection?	• Are internal security arrangements adequate to protect the firm's intellectual property?
• Do we intend to expand the use of trademarks in other countries?	• Are employees that do not have a "need to know" routinely provided access to important trade secrets?
• Do we need additional trademarks to cover new products and services?	
• Is anyone infringing on our trademarks?	• Is there a policy in place to govern the use of nondisclosure and noncompete agreements?
	• Are company trade secrets leaking out to competitors?

The second reason for a company to conduct an intellectual property audit is to remain prepared to justify its value in the event of a merger or acquisition. Larger companies purchase many small, entrepreneurial firms primarily because the larger company wants the small firm's intellectual property. The smaller firm should be ready to justify its valuation when a larger company comes calling.

The Process of Conducting an Intellectual Property Audit

The first step in conducting an intellectual property audit is to develop an inventory of a firm's existing intellectual property. The inventory should include the firm's present registrations of patents, trademarks, and copyrights. Also included should be any agreements or licenses allowing the company to use someone else's intellectual property rights or allowing someone else to use the focal company's intellectual property.

The second step is to identify works in progress to ensure that they are being documented in a systematic, orderly manner. This is particularly important in research and development. As mentioned earlier, if two inventors independently develop essentially the same invention, the right to apply for the patent belongs to the person who invented the product first. Properly dated and witnessed invention logbooks and other documents help prove the date an invention was made.

The third step of the audit is to specify the firm's key trade secrets and describe how they are being protected. Putting this information in writing helps minimize the chance that if a trade secret is lost, someone can claim that it wasn't really a trade secret because the owner took no specific steps to protect it.

CHAPTER SUMMARY

1. Intellectual property is any product of human intellect that is intangible but has value in the marketplace. It is called intellectual property because it is the product of human imagination, creativity, and inventiveness.

2. Patents, trademarks, copyrights, and trade secrets are the major forms of intellectual property. A common mistake companies make is not thinking broadly enough when identifying their intellectual property assets. Almost all companies, regardless of size or age, have intellectual property worth protecting. But to protect this property, firms must first identify it.

3. There are two rules of thumb for determining whether intellectual property is worth the time and expense of protecting. First, a firm should determine whether the intellectual property in question is directly related to its current competitive advantage or could facilitate the development of future competitive advantages. Second, it's important to know whether the intellectual property has independent value in the marketplace.

4. Obtaining a patent is a painstaking, five-step process that usually requires the help of a patent attorney. A patent can be sold or licensed, which is a common strategy for entrepreneurial firms.

5. Trademarks, service marks, collective marks, and certification marks are the four types of trademarks. Trademark law is far reaching, helping businesses be creative in drawing attention to their products and services. Examples of marks that can be protected include words, numbers and letters, designs and logos, sounds, fragrances, shapes, and colors. Immoral or scandalous matter, deceptive matter, descriptive marks, and surnames are ineligible for trademark protection.

6. Copyright law protects original works of authorship that are fixed in a tangible form of expression. This is a broad definition and means that almost anything a company produces that can be written down, recorded, or videotaped or that takes a tangible form itself (such as a sculpture) is eligible for copyright protection. Examples of copyrightable material include literary works, musical compositions, dramatic works, and pictorial, graphic, and sculptural works.

7. Unlike patents, trademarks, and copyrights, there is not a single government agency that regulates trade secret laws. Instead, trade secrets are governed by a patchwork of various state laws. The federal Economic Espionage Act does criminalize the theft of trade secrets.

8. Trade secret disputes arise most frequently when an employee leaves a firm to join a competitor and is accused of taking confidential information with him or her. Firms protect their trade secrets through both physical measures and written agreements.

9. There are a number of physical measures that firms use to protect trade secrets. These include restricting access, labeling documents, password protecting computer files, maintaining logbooks for visitors, and maintaining adequate overall security measures.

10. There are two primary reasons for conducting an intellectual property audit. First, it is prudent for a company to periodically assess the intellectual property it owns to determine whether it is being properly protected. Second, a firm should conduct a periodic intellectual property audit to remain prepared to justify its value in the event of a merger or acquisition.

KEY TERMS

assignment of invention agreement, 284

business method patent, 283

certification marks, 287

collective marks, 287

copyright, 290

copyright bug, 291

copyright infringement, 292

derivative works, 291

design patents, 283

Economic Espionage Act, 295

fair use, 293

idea–expression dichotomy, 291

intellectual property, 278

intellectual property audit, 298

intent-to-use trademark application, 290

invention logbook, 285

patent, 282

plant patents, 284

service marks, 287

trademark, 286

trade secret, 295

Uniform Trade Secrets Act, 295

utility patents, 283

REVIEW QUESTIONS

1. What distinguishes intellectual property from other types of property, such as land, buildings, and inventory? Provide several examples of intellectual property and describe their importance to a firm.

2. What are the two primary rules for determining whether intellectual property protection should be pursued for a particular intellectual asset?

3. Who is responsible for finding out if one firm is infringing on the intellectual property rights of another? What happens once a case of infringement is discovered?

4. What are the major differences between utility patents and design patents? Provide an example of each.

5. What is a business method patent? Provide an example of a business method patent and explain how having a business method patent can provide a firm a competitive advantage in the marketplace.

6. Provide an example of a design patent. Explain how having a design patent can provide a firm a competitive advantage in the marketplace.

7. Describe the purpose of an assignment of invention agreement. Is it a good idea for firms to ask their employees to sign assignment of invention agreements?

8. What are the six steps in applying for a patent? Make your answer as thorough as possible.

9. What is a trademark? Provide several examples of trademarks and describe how they help a firm establish a competitive advantage in the marketplace.

10. What are the three steps involved in selecting and registering a trademark?

11. What is meant by the term "trade dress"?

12. What is a copyright?

13. In the context of copyright law, what is meant by the term "derivative work"? Provide an example of when this concept is important for the creators of copyrightable material.

14. If an entrepreneur has an idea for a themed restaurant based on television game shows (such as Jeopardy, Who Wants to Be a Millionaire, or Hollywood Squares), is the idea itself eligible for copyright protection? Why or why not?

15. What is a copyright bug? Where would one expect to find the bug, and how is it used?

16. What is meant by the phrase "copyright infringement"? Would you characterize copyright infringement as a minor or as a major problem in the United States and abroad? Explain.

17. What is a trade secret? Provide an example of a trade secret and describe how it helps a firm establish a competitive advantage in the marketplace.

18. What information does not qualify for trade secret protection? Make your answer as thorough as possible.

19. What types of physical measures do firms take to protect their trade secrets?

20. What are the two primary purposes of conducting an intellectual property audit? What risks does a company run if it doesn't periodically conduct an intellectual property audit?

1. Amy Rozinski owns a small optics firm named Northland Optics. About 11 months ago, the company invented a new product that has sold extremely well to consumers in a localized area. Amy has decided to wait a year to see how the product does and will then apply for a patent if the product appears to have a good future. Is this a good strategy? Why or why not?

2. Pete Aguilar just invented a new computer mouse that helps relieve the stress that people sometimes feel in their hand after using a computer all day. A friend told Pete to apply for a design patent in order to protect the functionality of his device. Is Pete's friend right?

3. Pam Tarver just opened an information technology consulting company and has thought for a long time about what to name it. She finally settled on the fictitious name Infoxx. Infoxx is not a word; it is just a bunch of letters that Pam thought looked good together and her customers would remember. Is Pam's made-up word trademarkable?

4. Rick Sanford lives in a small community in northern Minnesota. He is planning to open the only fried chicken restaurant in his area and would like to trademark the words "fried chicken." Because of his special circumstances, can he do this?

5. Helen Downey just finished writing a book about Yahoo!, including how the company was started and how it helped pioneer the rapid growth of the Internet. In the book, Helen doesn't reveal anything new about that company and in many cases simply retells stories about the early days of Yahoo! that others have told. Still, Helen wrote the book, which took considerable research and work on her part. Can Helen copyright her book?

6. Mary Morrison is the CEO of a small computer company but makes her living going around the country making motivational speeches at conventions and corporate events. Although her standard speech isn't written down or hasn't been recorded, Mary has it committed to memory, which makes it easy for her as she travels from event to event. Is Mary's speech copyrightable?

7. Maggie Simpson has always admired her Grandmother Thompson's cooking and has considered putting together a cookbook titled *Grandma Thompson's Favorite Recipes*. Some of Grandma's recipes are truly original, and before she writes the book, Maggie would like to copyright several of the most original ones. Can she do this?

8. Jack Young is the CEO of a small graphic design company in Orlando, Florida. Several months ago, he spent an entire day searching the Web site of Dolphin Graphics, a larger graphics design firm in Miami. From its Web site, Jack was able to put together a list of Dolphin's major customers and is using the list to prospect new customers for his firm. After discovering what Jack is doing, Dolphin has threatened to sue Jack if he doesn't stop using its customer list, which it claims is a trade secret. Is Jack infringing on Dolphin's trade secrets?

9. After working for Prime Optics for five years, Sarah Simic went to work for Tech Optical, one of Prime's major competitors. A year later, Tech came out with a new product that made a big splash in the marketplace. Prime Optics sued Sarah, complaining that when Sarah worked at Prime, she was part of a team that developed a nearly identical product that Prime planned to roll out later that year. Sarah said that she lived up to her nondisclosure agreement with Prime and didn't take any documents from Prime to Tech. The only thing that she told her new colleagues at Tech, Sarah said, were the things she remembered about the project she was working on at Prime. Is Sarah in the clear? Why or why not?

10. Two years ago, Mike Carini opened a restaurant called Mike's Italian. To his horror, Mike just found out that several disgruntled customers have launched a Web site with the Internet address *www.avoidmikesitalian.com*. The site contains testimonials of people who have eaten at Mike's and have not been satisfied. Is there anything that Mike can do to shut down the Web site?

you be the VC

Company: **PRINTDreams**
(*www.printdreams.com*)

Business idea: Establish a global de facto standard for mobile pocket printers based on PrintDreams RMPT (Random Movement Printing Technology).

Pitch: Although PDA, cell phones, and laptop computers are handy to use while on the go, these devices are usually not attached to a printer—particularly when a person is away from his or her office. To solve this problem, PrintDreams has developed a technology that makes mobile printers a reality. This is how the technology works. The PrintBrush, which is the product's name, is about the size of a cell phone. Text and pictures can be loaded onto the PrintBrush from a personal digital assistant (PDA) or other mobile device using Bluetooth wireless networking. Then the PrintBrush is swept by hand across any type of paper (the paper is not in the printer) regardless of its size, shape, or thickness. The PrintBrush prints the text and images as it goes. PRINTDreams will produce its own printer and will license the patented PMPT

technology to other manufacturers. A demonstration of how the product works is provided on its Web site. To envision how the product works without visiting the Web site, try this. Pretend that you have downloaded a document to your PrintBrush. Take your cell phone, place it on the left side of a sheet of paper, and slowly move the phone from left to right across the paper. If your cell phone were a PrintBrush, it would have printed out the material you downloaded on the paper as it moved across it.

Q&A: Based on the material covered in this chapter, what questions would you ask the firm's founders before making your funding decision? What answers would satisfy you?

Decision: If you had to make your decision on just the information provided in the pitch and the company's Web site, would you fund this firm? Why or why not?

Case 12.1

Amazon's "One-Click" Ordering System: A Pioneer Business Method Patent
www.amazon.com

Amazon.com debuted in July 1995 and almost instantly became one of the most popular sites on the Internet. Jeff Bezos, Amazon's colorful CEO, launched the site to make "book buying fun." The company has experienced tremendous growth since 1995 and is the largest retailer on the Internet. Along with books, it now sells music, DVDs, videos, electronics, software, and a variety of other items. It reported its first-ever quarterly profit in early 2002. Analysts expected the firm's 2004 net income to reach $430 million.

Since its inception, Amazon has been at the forefront of many Internet innovations. It has consistently been one of the most heavily visited and widely written about sites on the

Internet. In September 1997, shortly before the onset of the busy Christmas season, Amazon launched a "one-click" ordering system to make it more convenient for customers to order from its site. The system allowed customers to make repeat purchases with one click of the mouse rather than having to fill out credit card and billing information for each shopping trip. To use the feature, customers must have previously registered their names, addresses, and credit card information with the company.

Although the one-click system was an innovative new tool for Amazon to differentiate itself from its competitors, it was a business method rather than a product or process and didn't neatly fit into any of the three forms of patent protection (i.e., utility patent, design patent, or plant patent). Although business methods were technically patentable, they were rarely successful, based on the U.S. Patent and Trademark Office's notion that business methods were ideas rather than products or processes. Since the one-click system was a business method, no patent application was filed when it was first introduced. However, in July 1998, when a federal court upheld a patent for a method of calculating the net asset value of mutual funds, the idea that business methods were not successfully patentable changed. The court ruled that patent laws were intended to protect any method as long as it produced a useful, concrete, and tangible result. Amazon's patent lawyers rolled up their sleeves and went to work.

In September 1999, Amazon was awarded a patent (U.S. Patent No. 5,960,411) on its "one-click" ordering system. Immediately, there were outcries from critics, claiming that by awarding a single firm a patent on what was fast becoming an industry standard, the U.S. Patent and Trademark Office would slow the growth of the Internet. Criticism was also leveled at Amazon and Jeff Bezos personally for moving so quickly to patent a business method that clearly could help all firms build effective presences on the Internet. One company called BountyQuest went so far as to offer a cash reward for anyone who could find evidence of a prior art (or prior business method) that would invalidate Amazon's patent.

The arguments reached fever pitch in October 1999, when Amazon filed suit against Barnesandnoble.com alleging patent infringement. For several months, Barnesandnoble.com had been using a checkout system called "Express Lane," which was similar to Amazon's one-click system. Amazon accused Barnesandnoble.com of illegally copying its patented checkout system and demanded that it cease and desist immediately. In its suit, Amazon argued that "the one-click feature is one of Amazon.com's signature strategies for differentiating itself from the competition and building loyalty among its customers." A spokesman for Barnesandnoble.com shot back, saying, "We believe the allegations to be completely without merit, and we will vigorously defend our position."

Just two months later, in December 1999, a federal judge ordered Barnesandnoble.com to stop using the one-click feature of its Express Lane ordering system, agreeing with Amazon's complaint. Earlier, Jeff Bezos, defending the suit, said, "We spent thousands of hours to develop our 1-Click process, and the reason we have a patent system in this country is to encourage people to take these kinds of risks and make these kinds of investments for our customers." The judge issuing the preliminary injunction apparently agreed with this logic and wrote that Amazon would face "irreparable harm" if it did not have exclusive use of the one-click feature during the holidays, when as many as 10 million people were expected to shop online for the first time.

The litigation between Amazon and Barnesandnoble.com has not been fully resolved. Similar suits, levied by other companies against their rivals, have followed. For example, shortly after Amazon filed suit against Barnesandnoble.com,

Priceline.com sued Microsoft's Expedia.com for violation of one of its business method patents. The criticism of Amazon was rekindled when the company announced in February 2000 that it had obtained a business method patent covering its affiliate program that lets other merchants establish sites within Amazon's Web site. The intensity of the criticism caused even Jeff Bezos, Amazon's CEO, to rethink his position on patent regulations. In an open letter on the Amazon.com Web site, he proposed that business method patents should last three to five years instead of 17 years as stipulated by current law. Bezos also suggested allowing outsiders to comment on proposed software patents before they are issued and offered to fund a software repository that patent examiners could use to determine if an idea is novel, which is the standard that innovations must meet to be awarded patent protection. Critics have argued that software patents often reward trivial innovations and that patent examiners do not do a good job of looking for similar existing software.

As an interesting epilogue to this case, the U.S. Patent and Trademark Office was not happy with Bezos's suggestions, although it appeared that Bezos was trying to help the agency find a way to cool the criticism of its policies and behaviors. A spokeswoman for the agency said that it would not support Bezos's proposed changes. "The system works for this technology in the same way it works for all technologies," the spokeswoman said.

Discussion Questions

1. Do you think that business method patents are a legitimate form of patent protection? If you were the CEO of an entrepreneurial firm that developed a unique and innovative business method, what criteria would you use to decide whether to patent it?

2. What is your impression of Amazon.com's patent policy? Do you believe that Amazon.com has the potential to slow the development of the Internet by aggressively trying to patent many of its business processes, such as the one-click ordering system and its affiliate program?

3. For a company like Amazon.com, how important of a factor is its intellectual property in enabling it to maintain a sustainable competitive advantage? Make your answer as thoughtful and substantive as possible.

4. Why do you think that the U.S. Patent and Trademark Office is resistant to modifying patent laws for software and Internet business processes? Do you think the agency is correct in its position? Why or why not?

Sources: "Amazon.com," Standard & Poor's Stock Report, www.standardandpoors.com (accessed May 22, 2004); S. Thurm, "Amazon.com Chief Executive Urges Shorter Duration for Internet Patents," Wall Street Journal, March 10, 2000, B3; S. Hansell, "Amazon Wins Court Ruling in Patent Case," New York Times, December 3, 1999; and L. Kaufman, "Barnesandnoble.com Faces Suit by Amazon over Patent," New York Times, October 23, 1999, C1.

A Classic Trademark Dispute: Harley-Davidson Versus The Hog Farm
www.harley-davidson.com
www.the-hog-farm.com

If you live near Buffalo, New York, and own a motorcycle that needs to be fixed, you're in luck. Just down the road, in West Seneca, New York, you can get the repairs you need at The Hog Farm, a motorcycle shop owned by Ron Grottanelli. Mr. Grottanelli, who likes to be called "Grott," opened The Hog Farm in 1969. From the beginning, the business serviced all makes and models of motorcycles and even built "custom bikes." The custom bikes, according to Grott, have always been particularly special, particularly in the early days. They had fancy paint, long front ends, and lots of chrome and were affectionately called "hogs."

As time passed, The Hog Farm grew, becoming a place for motorcycle enthusiasts to gather and enjoy one another's company. To facilitate this, The Hog Farm starting hosting a series of yearly events, including flea markets and celebrations over holiday weekends. To brand its events, the company started using the word "hog" more and more often. For example, it began hosting a "Hog Holiday" in July and a "Hog Labor Day Holiday" in September. It also started attaching the word "hog" to many of its products. For example, the company sells an engine degreaser called "Hog Wash."

Of course, from the early days of its existence, one of the brands of motorcycles that The Hog Farm worked on the most was Harley-Davidson. Grott remembers the bleakest days in Harley-Davidson's history, during the late 1960s and the early 1970s, when it looked as though the company might go under. During this period, Grott helped keep his customers fired up about motorcycles and feels like he helped keep the Harley-Davidson flame alive. Harley-Davidson recovered, reestablishing itself as a premier motorcycle manufacturer. In fact, Harleys have since become so popular that customers often wait over a year just for the privilege to buy one.

As motorcycles continued to gain popularity in the United States, everything was looking good for Grott and his business until a series of events took place that landed him and The Hog Farm in court opposite, of all companies, Harley-Davidson. In the 1980s, Harley started taking control of the word "hog," including registering it as a trademark in 1987. Following the registration, Harley started scouring the country looking for shops and companies that used the word "hog" when referring to motorcycles. To Harley-Davidson, a hog was a Harley, and no one else was entitled to use that name when referring to a motorcycle. When Harley finally caught up with The Hog Farm, it asked that it change its name and quit using the word "hog" when referring to motorcycles or related products.

Rather than giving in, however, Grott decided to fight, and a classic trademark dispute took shape. "You certainly have a memory lapse," Grott wrote to the company when it started demanding that he stop using the word "hog." "In the 50s,

60s, and 70s, you wanted no association [with the word "hog"]," he wrote. "You cringed whenever Harleys were included in discussions about motorcycles called hogs by the people that rode them; they were a means of escape from the square world." Harley didn't back down, and the case came to a head in federal district court near Buffalo. The courtroom was quite a scene and on opening day was packed with bikers supporting Grott. To try to diffuse the image of a big corporation trying to squash the little guy, a Harley attorney, in an interview outside the courtroom, said, "Harley-Davidson is not trying to hurt these people. All they are trying to do is protect their trademark." The trial, which went on for several days, basically boiled down to Harley's assertion that, by virtue of its trademark, it has exclusive rights to the word "hog" in reference to motorcycles. Grott argued that Harley's assertion was unreasonable because the word "hog" had been used to refer to motorcycles long before Harley trademarked it in 1987.

In announcing its decision, the court reviewed the trial and related the following facts. First, the court found that several periodicals and books have used the term "hog" to refer to motorcycles. The earliest source was a 1935 issue of *Popular Mechanics* that used the term "Hog Heaven" in the caption of a picture of some large motorcycles. Similarly, in 1965, a *Newsweek* article noted that the motorcycle gang Hell's Angels used the word "hog" to refer to big motorcycles. Further, the court pointed out that several American dictionaries and slang dictionaries defined the word "hog" as a form of large motorcycle.

In addition, the court found that throughout the 1970s and 1980s, many motorcycle enthusiasts began using the word "hog" when referring to Harley-Davidson motorcycles. Initially, Harley attempted to distance itself from any association of that word with its products. It was not until 1981 that Harley-Davidson began to use the word "hog" in its promotions and advertisements. The court found that Harley-Davidson itself recognized that the word "hog" referred in a generic sense to large motorcycles before it trademarked the word in 1987. The court therefore concluded that Harley-Davidson couldn't prevent Grott and The Hog Farm from using the word "hog" in connection with motorcycles. In essence, the court ruled that Harley-Davidson couldn't appropriate a term that was already in the public domain and turn it into its own private property.

So, The Hog Farm lives to see another day, and the Hog Holidays sponsored by Grott and his company continue without a name change. However, Grott remains irritated with the Harley-Davidson company and the actions it took against his firm. His anger and disappointment are suggested by the following comment, which recently appeared on his firm's Web site: "The Hog Farm celebrates 100 years of the Harley-Davidson motorcycle we love, and the company we hate!"

This case provides an important lesson in trademark law, particularly as it pertains to the protection of generic names from becoming the exclusive property of a single company.

Discussion Questions

1. Do you agree or disagree with the court's decision? Why or why not?

2. To what extent do you believe that The Hog Farm would have been harmed if it had lost the decision? If you were Ron Grottanelli and the decision had gone against you, how would you have rebranded your company?

3. What can other companies as well as entrepreneurs that are interested in trademark law learn from the case of Harley-Davidson versus The Hog Farm?

4. List several examples of names that are currently controlled by companies that you think are becoming "generic" enough that their trademark protection may be in jeopardy. What can a company do to prevent this from happening?

Sources: M. Beebe, "Hog Farm Trial Less Than Easy Ride," Buffalo News, October 27, 1996, B1, and R. Grottanelli, "History of the Hog Farm," www.the-hog-farm.com (accessed January 28, 2002 and July 21, 2004).

thirteen

preparing for and *evaluating* the challenges of growth

After studying this chapter, you should be ready to:

1. Explain the term "sustained growth."

2. Describe the potential downsides to firm growth.

3. Discuss the six most common reasons firms pursue growth.

4. Explain the advantages of having a scalable business model.

5. Describe the basic idea behind benchmarking and how benchmarking can be used to help a firm execute a successful growth strategy.

6. Describe the managerial capacity problem and how it inhibits firm growth.

7. Discuss the day-to-day challenges of growing a firm.

8. Identify the three myths that surround firm growth.

9. Identify the most prevalent growth-related firm attributes.

10. Describe the importance of having a commitment to growth.

starbucks: preparing for growth carefully

In 1982, Howard Schultz was vice president of U.S. operations for Hammarplast, a Swedish company that made kitchen equipment. One of his accounts was a small coffee retailer in Seattle named Starbucks. Schultz took particular notice of Starbucks because it consistently placed curiously large orders for a manual coffeemaker—a simple device that resembled a plastic cone set on a thermos. (Most retailers preferred to sell electric percolators, which brewed coffee faster and in larger quantities.) As the orders from Starbucks continued, Schultz grew more intrigued. One day he said to his wife, Sheri, "I'm going to see this company. I want to know what's going on out there."[1]

So Schultz flew to Seattle and arranged a tour of the Starbucks operations. In his book *Pour Your Heart into It*, Schultz remembered that when he first walked through the door of the original Starbucks store, he felt as if he had entered a temple for the worship of coffee. Behind a worn wooden counter stood bins containing coffees from all over the world. Along another wall was an assortment of coffee-making accessories, including a display of Hammarplast coffeemakers. An employee showed Schultz how the Hammarplast machine was used to make Starbucks coffee and said that the company recommended manual brewing because "part of the enjoyment is the ritual." Schultz began asking questions and was

307

fascinated by the Starbucks approach to selling and marketing coffee. Shortly thereafter, he joined Starbucks as director of marketing and retail operations.

A year later, Schultz took a trip to Italy that transformed his vision for Starbucks. He was struck by the centrality of coffee bars to Italian life and wondered if Starbucks could accomplish the same thing in the United States. He pictured Starbucks as a company that would become a daily part of its customers' lives—a safe and comfortable place to relax and enjoy a sense of community.[2] Schultz couldn't sell his vision to the owners of Starbucks, causing him to leave the company and start his own coffee bar, named Il Giornale, which means "daily" in Italian. In 1987, Schultz learned that the owners of Starbucks were willing to sell the company, so he raised $4 million and bought out his former colleagues. In late 1987, Howard Schultz became the chief executive officer (CEO) and major shareholder of Starbucks.

Since Schultz took the reins of Starbucks and implemented his vision for the firm, the company has experienced incredible growth. When Schultz took over, Starbucks had 17 stores in the Seattle area. Today, it has close to 7,800 locations on four continents and is opening an average of three new stores a day. Schultz and his team have increased the annual sales of Starbucks from $500 million to $4 billion. For years, Starbucks has experienced an annualized growth rate of more than 40 percent. At the same time, the company has remained financially prudent. It has almost no long-term debt, has steady earnings growth, and is financially solid.[3]

How did Schultz do it? Three ingredients of the success of Starbucks are particularly instructive regarding how to establish an entrepreneurial venture and manage a successful growth strategy. Each ingredient reflects a well-planned, conscientious, meticulously scripted approach to firm growth.

First, from the very beginning, Schultz focused on hiring and retaining high-quality employees and managers. Early on, for example, Schultz hired Howard Behar, an experienced manager, to head the company's retail operations and Orin Smith as the company's chief financial officer. Smith was a particularly key hire. With a Harvard MBA and 13 years of consulting experience at Deloitte & Touche, he brought discipline to the Starbucks operations without inhibiting its entrepreneurial spirit.

Schultz also developed a deep appreciation for the role that his *baristas*, or coffee brewers, played in creating an inviting environment for Starbucks customers. Schultz's appreciation for his employees showed: he spent money on employee benefits and training that could have been spent on advertising. In 1988, Starbucks become one of the first companies to extend full health benefits to part-time employees; in 1991, it became the first privately owned U.S. firm to offer a stock option program (called "bean" stock). Reflecting on his philosophy of managing and rewarding employees, Schultz wrote in his memoirs,

> We can be extremely profitable and competitive, with a highly regarded brand, and also be respected for treating our people well. In the end, it's not only possible to do both, but you can't really do one without the other.[4]

Treating employees well has paid off for Starbucks. After the company began offering part-time employees health benefits, the employee turnover rate dropped from as much as 175 percent per year to less than 65 percent. And it was the Starbucks employees in southern California who originally crafted the Frappuccino blended brand of bottled coffee, which has been enormously successful.

The second thing Schultz has done particularly well is to remain true to the core values and strengths of Starbucks despite its rapid growth. The simple formula of providing customers high-quality, freshly brewed coffee in a comfortable, secure, and inviting atmosphere is as important as ever and has enabled the company to build a strong brand and move forward with a consistent commitment to providing its customers a quality experience. For example, Starbucks has had many opportunities to sell its coffee through venues such as McDonald's, but the company has consistently rejected these opportunities. Because of its commitment to high quality, it does not want to risk cheapening its brand. In some instances, the company has licensed its coffee to vendors in airports and office buildings and specialty retailers such as Barnes & Noble. These exceptions are tightly controlled, however, to maintain the quality of the Starbucks experience. This philosophy has kept the Starbucks brand strong and has given the company a loyal customer base while enabling it to sell through venues that command high margins.

Finally, Starbucks has used multiple strategies to achieve growth. Its primary method has been geographic expansion. Starbucks does not franchise. Instead, over 90 percent of Starbucks outlets are company-owned stores, with the remaining 10 percent run by licensees. Its first international outlet was opened in Tokyo, Japan, in 1992, and the company currently has around 1,200 international locations. In most cases, Starbucks has entered international markets by partnering with local companies that know the local communities, issues, and culture. Schultz credits this approach as a key factor in making the international expansion of Starbucks both feasible and practical.[5] Aggressive geographic expansion, both domestically and internationally, is expected to continue.

In terms of products, the items the company sells through its retail stores have grown over the years, helping to increase same-store sales. Its coffee shops sell rich-brewed coffees, Italian-style espresso beverages, cold blended beverages, a variety of pastries and confections, coffee-related accessories and equipment, and other beverage items, such as tea, juice, and soda. The company has also experimented with novel ways to increase sales. For example, the company recently introduced the "Starbucks Card," which looks like a prepaid phone card and permits customers to prepay from $10 to $100 for Starbucks items. The card allows a customer to shop on the Starbucks Web site without using a credit card or to swiftly pay for items at a Starbucks store without worrying about cash. The cards also make nice gifts.

A third way Starbucks has spurred its growth is through what it calls its specialty operations. These operations seek to develop the Starbucks brand outside the company-owned retail stores through a number of channels, including business alliances, grocery channel licensing, warehouse club accounts, and other initiatives. An example is the North American Coffee Partnership, which is a 50-50 joint venture between Starbucks and Pepsi. The joint venture was launched in 1994 to develop and distribute ready-to-drink coffee-based products, such as Frappuccino and Starbucks Doubleshot. By the end of 2000, the joint venture was distrib-

uting bottled Frappuccino to approximately 250,000 supermarkets, convenience stores, and drugstores throughout the United States and Canada. Similarly, in 1996, Starbucks and Dryers launched a joint venture to develop and distribute Starbucks premium ice cream. By the end of 2000, the joint venture was distributing a variety of ice cream and specialty products to over 21,000 supermarkets throughout the United States. Starbucks also has a licensing agreement with Kraft, Inc. Through this agreement, Kraft produces and distributes Starbucks whole-bean and ground coffees to over 19,000 grocery and warehouse club accounts.

The biggest issue facing Starbucks today is whether its values will remain intact as it continues to expand. Reflecting on this challenge, which most successful entrepreneurial firms face at some point in their life cycle, Howard Schultz remarked,

> There is no doubt in my mind that Starbucks can realize its financial goals. A more fragile issue is whether our values and guiding principles will remain intact as we continue to expand. I for one would consider it a failure if we reached the $2 billion-plus level at the expense of our unique connection with our people.[6]

What Schultz is clearly worried about is that if Starbucks loses its unique connection with its people (its customers, employees, and business partners) as the result of its growth, it risks losing much more. It risks losing the charm, uniqueness, and commitment to quality that have been the cornerstones of its success.

The Starbucks case is unique in that the company has achieved remarkable sustained growth in a well-executed manner. Most new ventures and established entrepreneurial firms struggle with planning for and achieving sustained growth. **Sustained growth** is defined as growth in both revenues and profits over an extended period of time. According to a recent study by Bain & Company, an international consulting firm, only one in seven companies generates sustained, profitable growth.[7] The figures are even lower for rapid-growth firms such as Starbucks. According to the National Commission on Entrepreneurship, a rapid-growth firm is a firm that grows its employment by at least 15 percent per year. A study by the commission found that only 4.7 percent of businesses that existed in 1991 grew their employment by at least 15 percent per year or at least doubled their employment over the five years from 1992 to 1997.[8] In this chapter, we will consider a **rapid-growth firm** one that maintains a growth rate of at least 20 percent per year for five consecutive years.

Despite these numbers, most firms try to grow and see it as an important part of their ability to remain successful. This sentiment was expressed by Hewlett-Packard (HP) cofounder David Packard. Packard wrote that while HP was being built, he and cofounder Bill Hewlett had "speculated many times about the optimum size of a company." The pair "did not believe that growth was important for its own sake" but eventually concluded that "continuous growth was essential" for the company to remain competitive.[9] When HP published a formal list of its objectives in 1996, one of the seven objectives was growth.[10] For HP, acquiring Compaq Computer Corporation contributed to the firm's continuing commitment to growth. Growth is important for other reasons, as will be explained

learning **objective**

1. Explain the term "sustained growth."

thoroughly later in this chapter. For example, it is often necessary for firms to grow to have sufficient promotional opportunities available to retain high-performing employees. Similarly, when a firm's customers grow, it is often necessary for the firm itself to grow to maintain sufficient scale to meet its customers' needs.

In Chapter 14, we'll discuss growth strategies. However, we also devote attention to describing how firms prepare for growth as well as the important dynamics of the growth process. We begin this chapter with a general overview and discuss benchmarking as a technique for learning the tactics of successful growth firms. In the second section, we discuss the challenges of growth, including the managerial capacity problem, the day-to-day challenges of growing a firm, and the importance of developing and maintaining professional business practices. Finally, we look at the attributes of successful growth firms. Although growth is difficult to achieve, firms with specific attributes increase their chances of achieving and sustaining profitable growth.

Preparing for Growth

Most entrepreneurial firms want to grow. Especially in the short run, growth in sales revenue is an important indicator of an entrepreneurial venture's potential to survive today and be successful in the future. Growth is exciting and fast paced and for most businesses is an indication of success. In a recent study at the University of Minnesota, a group of executives and MBAs identified sales growth as the single most important indicator of business success.[11] Many entrepreneurial firms have grown quickly and have produced impressive results for their employees and owners: consider Starbucks, Amgen, Intuit, Microsoft, and GAP, among others.

Growth, however, is a double-edged sword. It can threaten the stability of a firm's operations in every area, from human resources to finance, if it is not managed properly. Finding the right growth strategy is tricky. Just months after Amazon.com announced that it intended to become "a place where you can buy anything for anyone" (denoting an aggressive growth strategy), the company laid off 15 percent of its workforce and started eliminating product lines under the slogan "Get the Crap Out."

The first Gap store was founded in 1969 in San Francisco. Today, Gap owns Gap Body, Gap Maternity, Gap Kids, Baby Gap, Banana Republic, and Old Navy, which together make up 3,000 stores with more than 150,000 employees in the United States, United Kingdom, Canada, France, Japan, and Germany.

In addition, whether growth increases the value of a firm is unclear. There is an emerging consensus that growth for its own sake or growth to satisfy the ego of the CEO or managers does not create value. Booz-Allen & Hamilton studied 1,828 publicly traded firms. The researchers found no short-term relationship and only a moderate long-term relationship (10 years or more) between revenue growth and shareholder value creation.[12] The owners and managers of entrepreneurial firms need a full understanding of the dynamics and the nature of the growth process. In this context, entrepreneurs must remember that growth is a possible means to profitability—it is not an end objective itself.

Reasons for Firm Growth

Firms pursue growth deliberately. That is not to say, however, that firms can always choose the pace of their growth. A firm's **pace of growth** is the rate at which it is growing on an annual basis. Sometimes firms are forced into a high-growth mode sooner than they would like. For example, when a firm develops a product or service that meets such a pervasive need that orders roll in very quickly, it must adjust quickly or risk faltering. In other instances, a firm experiences unexpected competition and must grow bigger to maintain its market share.

This section examines the six primary reasons firms try to grow to increase their profitability and valuation, as depicted in Figure 13.1.

Capturing Economies of Scale

Economies of scale occur when increasing production lowers the average cost of each unit produced. This phenomenon occurs for two reasons. First, if a company can get a discount by buying component parts in bulk, it can lower its variable costs per unit as it grows larger. **Variable costs** are the costs a company incurs as it makes sales. Second, by increasing production, a company can spread its fixed costs over a greater number of units. **Fixed costs** are costs that a company incurs whether it sells something or not. For example, it may cost a company $10,000 per month to air-condition its factory. The air-conditioning cost is fixed; cooling the factory will cost the same whether the company produces 10 or 10,000 units per month.

A related reason firms grow is to make use of unused labor capacity or other resources. For example, a firm may need exactly 2.5 salespeople to fully cover its trade area. Because a firm usually doesn't hire 2.5 salespeople (two full-time and one part-time person), it may hire three salespeople and expand its trade area.[13]

Executing a Scalable Business Model

Some companies have an incentive to grow because they have a scalable business model. A **scalable business model** is one in which increased revenues cost less to deliver than current revenues, so profit margins increase as sales go up. This is typically found in companies that have large up-front costs but have products or services with small per-unit variable costs. The classic example of a scalable business model is computer software. Developing software is very expensive, but delivering a copy of a software program to a consumer is relatively inexpensive. It may cost a software company such as Microsoft $10 million to develop a software program, but the per-unit cost of producing and selling the program is small from that point forward, so the profit margin increases as more and more copies are sold. This is why selling downloadable products over the Internet continues to create excitement. It may cost a publisher $1 million to produce a book and pay for an advertising campaign to promote it. If the customer can

learning **objective**

3. Discuss the six most common reasons firms pursue growth.

learning **objective**

4. Explain the advantages of having a scalable business model.

Figure 13.1

Appropriate Reasons for Firm Growth

- Economies of scale
- Executing a scalable business model
- Market leadership
- Influence, power, and survivability
- Need to accommodate the growth of key customers
- Ability to attract and retain talented employees

then download the book, the publisher's cost of goods sold falls to almost zero. Costs involved with printing, shipping, warehousing, and retailing the book are avoided by selling over the Internet.

The catch to having a scalable business model that actually works is having sufficient demand for the product to continually drive revenues up. Many of the Internet companies that purportedly had scalable business models never were able to generate enough interest in their products to make the scalability portion of the formula work. In some cases, the up-front costs were also just too high. For example, a firm that is launched to produce computer games that will be sold online has a business model that is theoretically very scalable. The business plan will say that the costs associated with developing the games will be covered by sales that involve low variable costs and that margins will increase as more and more copies of the games are sold. This works, however, only if consumers buy the games.

An example of an Internet-based scalable business model that has worked is MapQuest, as illustrated in the boxed feature titled "Savvy Entrepreneurial Firm."

Market Leadership   **Market leadership** occurs when a firm is the number one or the number two firm in an industry or niche market in terms of sales volume. Many firms work hard to achieve market leadership, to realize economies of scale in production, and to be recognized as the brand leader. Being the market leader also permits a firm to use slogans such as "Number 1 Software Producer in America" in its promotions, helping a firm win customers and attract talented employees as well as business partners.

A recent study affirmed the importance of market leadership to achieving growth. In each of the industries included in the study, the market leader grew faster than the industry growth rate. For example, in the athletic shoe industry, Nike's 27 percent yearly growth rate outpaced the industry growth of 6 percent per year for the period 1987–1997. A similar pattern was observed for Coco-Cola, Mattel, and Harley-Davidson in their respective industries.[14]

Influence, Power, and Survivability   Larger businesses usually have more influence and power than smaller firms in regard to setting standards for an industry, getting a "foot in the door" with major customers and suppliers, and garnering prestige. In addition, larger businesses can typically make a mistake yet survive easier than smaller firms. Commenting on this issue, Jack Welch, GE's former CEO, one said, "Size gives us another big advantage; our reach and resources enable us to go to bat more frequently, to take more swings, to experiment more, and unlike a small company, we can miss on occasion and get to swing again."[15]

A firm's capacity for growth affects its survival in additional ways. For example, a firm that stays small and relies on the efforts and motivation of its founder or a small group of people is vulnerable to the loss of their skills or interest in the firm. Once a firm grows, however, and has a larger staff and more products and services to offer, it usually gains momentum and is no longer as reliant on the efforts or motivation of a small number of founders or employees.

Need to Accommodate the Growth of Key Customers   Sometimes firms are compelled to grow to accommodate the growth of a key customer. For example, if Intel has a major account with an electronics firm buying a large number of its semiconductor chips and the electronics firm is growing at a rate of 20 percent per year, Intel may have to add capacity each year to accommodate the growth of its customer or else risk losing some or all of its business.

Ability to Attract and Retain Talented Employees   The final reason that firms grow is to attract and retain high-quality personnel. It is natural for talented employees to want to work for a firm that can offer opportunities for promotion, higher salaries, and increased levels of responsibility. Growth is a firm's primary mechanism to generate promotional opportunities for employees, while failing to retain key employees can be very damaging to a firm's growth efforts. High turnover is expensive, and in knowledge-based industries in particular, such as biotechnology and film production, a company's number one asset is the combined talent, training, and experience of its employees. In less knowledge-intensive settings, turnover may not be as critical, but it is still costly. Based on estimates from Merck & Company, Hewlett-Packard, and *Fortune* magazine, the average cost of turnover is 1.5 times the employee's salary.[16]

Savvy entrepreneurial FIRM

Moving Online to Achieve Rapid Scalability through the Power of Digitization

www.mapquest.com

In the mid-1960s, R. R. Donnelley & Sons, a communications company, started publishing road maps to give away in gas stations. Advertisers that ran ads in the margins of the maps paid for them. MapQuest was the name of the division of R. R. Donnelley & Sons that was responsible for producing the maps.

MapQuest grew and by the 1970s had become a leading supplier of custom maps to travel, textbook, and directory publishers. Throughout the early 1990s, MapQuest formed partnerships with several leading information-publishing companies and developed a number of electronic applications for maps. In February 1996, it launched a Web site, offering the first consumer-focused interactive mapping site on the Internet. The Web site instantly caught the attention of Web users and has been one of the heaviest trafficked Web sites on the Internet almost from its inception.

MapQuest is an extraordinary example of a company with a product that perfectly lends itself to scalability through digitization. Maps, driving directions, and yellow pages, which are the company's staple products, can easily be displayed in a digital format. And because MapQuest is a well-known brand and its service is popular, it is able to drive substantial traffic to its Web site. These factors combine to make the scalability of its business model possible. Once the company's fixed costs are covered—the costs associated with creating maps and the hardware and personnel necessary to support its Web site—the per-user variable cost of providing its online service is very low. This means that MapQuest can increase traffic to its site and command increased advertising revenue while incurring little added cost to service the additional users.

The results of MapQuest's efforts have been impressive. It is currently the number one mapping site on the Internet and serves up more than 300 million maps and more than 40 million sets of driving directions every month. To increase its numbers even further, the company is now moving beyond the PC and is offering its services through additional digital platforms, such as wireless handheld devices, including Palm Pilots. Explaining the rationale for expanding MapQuest's offerings to wireless devices, Jim Riesenback, an America Online (AOL) spokesman (MapQuest is a member of the AOL family of brands), remarked on the m-Travel.com Web site:

People want MapQuest maps and directions to be available no matter where they are. Expanding

MapQuest's leading Internet brand across multiple platforms not only meets our customers' needs but also maintains our leading position in location-based services.

MapQuest appears to be well positioned for explosive growth on wireless platforms. A recent survey by Jupiter Communications found that people who own wireless devices such as Palm Pilots request directions and traffic updates more than any other local application.

MapQuest's success can be attributed to three basic factors. First, its product is perfectly suited for digitization since maps, driving directions, and other printed material can be easily converted to a digital format. Second, the quality and convenience of its product are attractive to users, making scalability possible. Finally, the company has been able to maintain a leadership position in its industry by launching a top-notch Web site when the Internet was young, and remaining current by aggressively moving its offering onto emerging wireless platforms contributes to the firm's ability to maintain its leadership position.

Questions for Critical Thinking

1. An increasing number of automobiles are being sold with GPS (Global Positioning System) navigational systems. Are GPS systems a threat to MapQuest's success? If so, what can MapQuest do to reduce the seriousness of such a competitive threat?

2. Visit with three or four of your friends who have used MapQuest's service. How satisfied are your friends as MapQuest customers? What suggestions do your friends have regarding how MapQuest could improve its service?

3. Go to MapQuest's Web site (www.mapquest.com). Read about the partnerships MapQuest has formed with other firms. With what other types of firms do you think MapQuest might partner in the future to increase its revenue and profits?

Sources: MapQuest home page, www.mapquest.com (accessed May 25, 2004), and m-Travel home page, www.m-travel.com (accessed May 25, 2004).

learning **objective**

5. Describe the basic idea behind benchmarking and how benchmarking can be used to help a firm execute a successful growth strategy.

Benchmarking Against Successful Growth Firms

By **benchmarking**, a firm improves the quality of an activity by identifying and copying the methods of other firms that are successful in that activity. Firm growth provides an excellent opportunity for benchmarking. For example, if a small agricultural products firm in the Midwest decided to start exporting to Europe, it would be wise to identify other agricultural products firms in the Midwest that export to Europe so that it could study their methods and experiences. Usually, if the firm that a company is trying to "benchmark against" doesn't see it as a competitor, it will be helpful and supportive of the benchmarking effort. There are many well-known examples of firms that have successfully "benchmarked" against one another. For example, Ford Motor Company fashioned its Internet-based enterprise FordDirect.com along the lines of Dell's highly successful built-to-order concept.

Along with the insight into the best practices of the firms they benchmark against, there are additional advantages of benchmarking to a firm:

- Facilitating the setting of goals
- Motivating staff by showing what is possible
- Providing an early warning of competitive disadvantages

Each of these advantages is hard to capture in the absence of a formal benchmarking effort. The steps in a well-managed benchmarking program are shown in Table 13.1.

Challenges of Growth

Although growth has many advantages for the entrepreneurial firm, including broader access to markets, an enhancement in a firm's reputation, and the opportunity to work with larger and more experienced channel partners, growth is a challenging and rigorous process. Firm growth typically involves raising additional capital, recruiting new employees, learning how to supervise a larger organization, and accepting more risk.

The challenges impose an emotional toll on entrepreneurs and managers as well. A PricewaterhouseCoopers *Trendsetter Barometer* surveyed CEOs of America's fastest-growing firms. Thirty-two percent of those interviewed said that their own inability to manage or reorganize their business could be an impediment to growth over the next 12 months. In the press release announcing the results of the survey, a PricewaterhouseCoopers spokesman speculated on the reasons for this finding:

> Consider how much more complex management has become. In addition to running day-to-day operations and planning for the future, CEOs of growing companies must navigate their way through the challenges of strategic alliances, outsourcing, joint ventures, mergers and acquisitions, the worker shortage, and the Federal Reserve Board's next move, just to name a few.[17]

This type of sentiment should not discourage entrepreneurs but should alert them to the challenges involved. Let's look more closely at these challenges.

Table 13.1

Steps in a Benchmarking Program

Step	1	Form a benchmarking planning and review team
Step	2	Identify the specific function or business activity to be benchmarked
Step	3	Identify exemplary firms in the area to be benchmarked against
Step	4	Contact one or more of these firms and ask to study their methods
Step	5	Study the methods of the firm that you are benchmarking against
Step	6	Analyze your own methods (if you have any) in this particular area
Step	7	Compare the methods of the benchmark firm against your own
Step	8	If the benchmark firm outperforms your performance in this area, determine the reason for the differences
Step	9	Implement plans to bridge the gap between your methods and the benchmark firm's methods
Step	10	Follow up and review

Managerial Capacity

learning **objective**

6. Describe the managerial capacity problem and how it inhibits firm growth.

In her thoughtful book *The Theory of the Growth of the Firm*, Edith T. Penrose argues that firms are collections of productive resources that are organized in an administrative framework.[18] As an administrative framework, the primary purpose of a firm is to package its resources together with resources acquired outside the firm for the production of products and services at a profit. As a firm goes about its routine activities, the management team becomes better acquainted with the firm's resources and its markets. This knowledge leads to the expansion of a firm's **productive opportunity set**, which is the set of opportunities the firm feels it's capable of pursuing. The opportunities might include the introduction of new products, geographic expansion, licensing products to other firms, exporting, and so on. The pursuit of these new opportunities causes a firm to grow.

Penrose points out, however, that there is a problem with the execution of this simple logic. The firm's administrative framework consists of two kinds of services that are important to a firm's growth—entrepreneurial services and managerial services. **Entrepreneurial services** generate new market, product, and service ideas, while **managerial services** administer the routine functions of the firm and facilitate the profitable execution of new opportunities. However, the introduction of new product and service ideas requires substantial managerial services (or managerial "capacity") to be properly implemented and supervised. This is a complex problem because if a firm has insufficient managerial services to properly implement its entrepreneurial ideas, it can't simply quickly hire new managers to remedy the shortfall. It is expensive to hire new employees, and it takes time for new managers to be socialized into the firm's culture, acquire firm-specific skills and knowledge, and establish trusting relationships with other members of their firms.[19] When a firm's managerial resources are insufficient to take advantage of its new product and services opportunities, the subsequent bottleneck is referred to as the **managerial capacity problem**. James Vincent, CEO of Biogen, an entrepreneurial biotech firm, has argued convincingly in interviews that this capacity issue is his firm's number one growth constraint.[20]

As a firm grows, it is faced with the dual challenges of adverse selection and moral hazard. **Adverse selection** means that as the number of employees a firm needs increases, it becomes increasingly difficult for it to find the right employees, place them in appropriate positions, and provide adequate supervision.[21] The faster a firm grows, the less time managers have to evaluate the suitability of job candidates and the higher the chances are that an unsuitable candidate will be chosen. **Moral hazard** means that as a firm grows and adds personnel, the new hires typically do not have the same ownership incentives as the original founders, so the new hires may not be as motivated as the founders to put in long hours or may even try to avoid hard work. To make sure the new hires are doing what they were hired to do, the firm will typically hire monitors (i.e., managers) to supervise the employees. This practice creates a hierarchy that is costly and isolates the top management team from its rank-and-file employees.

Ideally, the entrepreneurial services of a firm (i.e., the identification of new opportunities) should push the managerial services of a new firm to their limit, which is the maximum rate at which a firm can theoretically grow. The results of a study of 400 small and medium-size firms in the United Kingdom reported that growth was an important objective of the majority of the firms in the sample but that the typical growth-inducing strategies, such as product innovation, product extensions, and geographic expansion, had not produced impressive results. These findings caused the researchers to conclude that the lack of growth in the firms in their sample was attributed to both external and internal factors, including motivational issues. Commenting on their results, the researchers wrote,

> The limitations on small and medium sized enterprises' ability to achieve sustained growth operates at many levels including the pool of talent at management's disposal; the rate at which new management resources can be added and integrated; and the speed with which proven managerial experience can be shared. To this must be added the *self-imposed limits on growth as reflected in managerial aspirations and objectives.*[22] (emphasis added)

Figure 13.2

Basic Model of Firm Growth

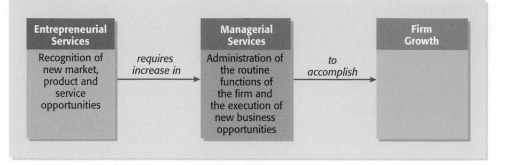

The basic model of firm growth articulated by Penrose is shown in Figure 13.2, while Figure 13.3 shows the essence of the growth-limiting managerial capacity problem.[23] Figure 13.3 indicates that the ability to increase managerial services is not friction free. It is constrained or limited by (1) the time required to socialize new managers, (2) how motivated entrepreneurs and/or managers are to grow their firms, (3) adverse selection, and (4) moral hazard.

The reality of the managerial capacity problem is one of the main reasons that entrepreneurs and managers worry so much about growth. Growth is a generally positive thing, but it is easy for a firm to overshoot its capacity to manage growth.

Safety First is an example of a company that mismanaged its growth. This firm makes the once-familiar "Baby on Board" car window signs. In the mid-1990s, the company had a six-year annual return on equity of over 100 percent, and sales had nearly tripled in just two years. During the same period, the company's stock price increased from $12 to $32.75 per share.[24] But by 1997, the company had lost more than $30 million in three years, and its stock price had fallen to under $6 per share. What happened? According to the company's 10-K report, its product offerings had proliferated to an unmanageable quantity, including products outside the company's core competency. In a few short years, the company had expanded from a handful of successful products to a product line of over 650 items covering a wide array of safety-related products. Inventories and expenses mounted, and the company nearly collapsed under the weight and stress of its own growth.

Typical Challenges of Growing a Firm

Along with the overarching challenges imposed by the managerial capacity problem, there are a number of day-to-day challenges involved with growing a firm, discussed in the following sections. As you'll see, these challenges indicate that no firm operates in a competi-

Figure 13.3

The Impact of Managerial Capacity

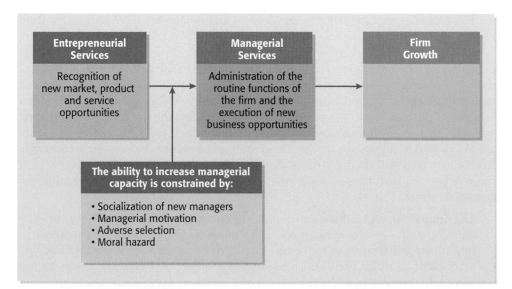

Source: Based on material in E. T. Penrose, *The Theory of the Growth of the Firm* (Oxford: Basil Blackwell, 1959).

tive vacuum. By this we mean that the actions one firm takes to grow will cause reactions from competitors. In turn, the firm trying to grow will respond to its competitors' responses, generating what is called a series of action–reaction competitive moves. Entrepreneurs must recognize that the efforts they take to grow their firms will be recognized and that responses to those actions by competitors will be forthcoming.

Cash Flow Management   As discussed in Chapters 7 and 9, as a firm grows, it requires an increasing amount of cash to service its customers. In addition, a firm must carefully manage its cash on hand to make sure it maintains sufficient liquidity to meet its payroll and cover its other short-term obligations. Growth usually increases rather than decreases the challenges involved with cash flow management because an increase in sales means that more cash will be flowing into and out of the firm.

Price Stability   If firm growth comes at the expense of a competitor's market share, a price war can result. For example, if an entrepreneur opens a video store near a Blockbuster that begins to erode Blockbuster's market share, Blockbuster will probably fight back by lowering prices. Because a price war (especially a longer-term one) typically helps no one but the customer, any growth strategy should consider competitors' responses and their effect on price stability.

Quality Control   Firm growth is typically accomplished by an increase in firm activity. This means that a firm must handle more service requests and paperwork and contend with more customers, stakeholders, and vendors. If a firm does not properly increase its resources to manage growth, then product or service quality may decline.

Capital Constraints   Capital constraints are an ever-present problem for growing firms. Several of the strategies for firm growth discussed in Chapter 14, including strategic alliances and licensing, are attractive because they help meet this challenge.

All these challenges are equally important and, if ignored, can cause a growth-oriented firm to not only stumble but also fail. The boxed feature titled "What Went Wrong?" tells the incredible story of the rapid raise and fall of one growth firm. The story is a vivid reminder of the challenges involved with growing a firm, even when a firm achieves impressive early success.

Developing and Maintaining Professional Business Practices

Many firms grow quickly and do not take the time to develop formal management systems or procedures. Although this approach may work for a while, it is rarely if ever sustainable. In fact, the four basic functions of management—planning, leading, organizing, and controlling—may be more important in growth firms than in any other type of organization. Sustainable growth is difficult and challenging and takes a lot of savvy to pull off, and growth-oriented firms are typically strapped for resources and can ill afford management miscues that waste limited or constrained financial capital.

Some firms recognize too late that they need to professionalize their business practices and stumble badly under the weight of rapid growth. Oracle, which develops information management software, almost made this mistake. Commenting on his firm's experience, Ray Lane, Oracle's former chief operating officer, said,

> We were at a billion dollars in revenue, and you cannot run a billion dollar company the way we were doing it. We had to make sure the business was run using professional business practices. This place is basically under control now, we understand our business pipeline, and we have a professional relationship with our customers, instead of the "*run-and-shoot*" offense we had in the 1980s.[25]

The need for an organization *to* grow must be tempered by the need to maintain control *of* growth. The trick is to find the right balance between the ability to move quickly and seize market opportunities and the need for a well-managed growth plan and professional business practices.

what went **wrong?**

LA Gear: How Managing Growth Poorly Can Cost a Firm Its Business

www.lagear.com

For LA Gear, the late 1980s were golden. The company was launched in 1979 to manufacture sweatshirts and jeans. In the early 1980s, however, it was so impressed by Reebok's success with aerobics shoes that it, too, started selling shoes—with a distinctive, "hip" Los Angeles style. Its initial products were enormous hits. First it produced a line of "Valley Girl" sneakers for teen girls and young women. The shoes were made of denim or patent leather and were adorned with feminine fringes. Then, in the mid-1980s, the company created children's shoes and walking shoes with small lights in the heels that blinked when the walker's soles hit the ground. The shoes, dubbed L.A. Lights, flew off the shelves, and it seemed as though LA Gear couldn't miss. In fact, the company's sales increased from $11 million in 1985 to $820 million in 1990.

This early success with customers caught the attention of investors, causing LA Gear to become the quintessential hot stock. After going public in 1986, the stock's split-adjusted price of $3 a share in 1987 soared to $50 a share within two years. But just as quickly as LA Gear heated up, it turned cold. The company filed for Chapter 11 bankruptcy protection in January 1998. What went wrong? Three things, all related to the hazards of rapid growth, sealed the company's fate.

First, instead of focusing its efforts on marketing research and product quality, rapid growth was LA Gear's first priority. When Robert Greenberg, one of the company's cofounders, saw an opportunity for LA Gear to expand, he took it regardless of whether convincing marketing research was available. Later, after being forced from the company in the early 1990s, Greenberg admitted, "I love to build. That's why I get in trouble; building too much." Second, in its thirst for growth, LA Gear quickly moved beyond producing shoes for teen girls and young women and rolled out a full line of sneakers to appeal to a broad spectrum of customers—including high-performance shoes for serious athletes. At the same time, the company branched into athletic clothing and accessories. Without doing anything to change its brand, which most people still associated with teenagers and young girls, LA Gear was now trying to be all things to all people. Quality started to suffer. In fact, in a particularly embarrassing moment for the company, one of the company's high-performance athletic shoes, worn by a Marquette University basketball player, lost its sole during a nationally televised game.

Finally, LA Gear found that a company that lives by the notion of "cool" can also die by the notion of "cool." As a result of failing to change its image before it branched out, the company produced shoes that just didn't sell. Most people still saw LA Gear as a company that was good at making feminine-looking shoes for young girls regardless of how many markets it entered. As a result, by 1991, LA Gear had 12 million shoes in its warehouses that nobody wanted and only $1.5 million in cash. Although the company tried various strategies through the early and mid-1990s to survive, it never fully recovered. Today, LA Gear is a relatively minor player in athletic products. However, it continues to try to provide what it calls "the ultimate Los Angeles gear" for customers and the games they want to play. In 2004, LA Gear signed Luke Walton (son of the famous Bill Walton) to wear the firm's basketball shoes. This was a Los Angeles–specific decision in that Luke Walton is from the area and played his rookie season in 2004 with the Los Angeles Lakers.

This case illustrates the many hazards of growth. Even though LA Gear, in retrospect, suffered from some obvious miscues, even under the best of circumstances rapid growth has to be managed carefully and prudently to be successful.

Questions for Critical Thinking

1. Using materials in this chapter, develop a list of actions LA Gear could have taken to better manage its growth during the 1980s and 1990s.

2. Do you think that the issues of moral hazard and adverse selection could have contributed to LA Gear's problems as described in this feature? If so, how?

3. Talk to some of your friends who are involved with sports. See if they are familiar with LA Gear and its products. If they are, how satisfied are they with the firm's products? If they aren't, ask if there is anything the firm could do to entice them to try its products.

Sources: LA Gear home page, www.lagear.com (accessed May 24, 2004); W. Joyce, N. Nohria, and B. Roberson, What Really Works (New York: HarperBusiness, 2003); and D. Darlin, "Getting beyond a Market Niche," Forbes, November 22, 1993, 106.

Myths About Growth

There are several common myths about firm growth that have the potential to confuse or misdirect entrepreneurs and managers. Let's look at the three most pervasive myths.

learning **objective**

8. Identify the three myths that surround firm growth.

Myth 1: Growth companies are predominantly technology and health care companies

Because so much attention has been paid to how quickly some well-known technology and health care companies have grown, such as Cisco Systems and Amgen, it is easy to get the idea that growth companies are predominantly technology and health care companies. While technology and health care companies are represented in any list of rapid-growth firms, they do not necessarily dominate. For example, the 2003 *Fortune* list of the 100 fastest-growing publicly traded small firms in America included just 22 health care firms and nine technology companies. Industries such as energy (eight firms), financial services (17 firms) and retail (nine firms) were also well represented on the list.

Myth 2: Rapid-growth firms emerge only in rapid-growth industries

Another common belief is that rapid-growth firms emerge primarily in rapid-growth industries. Of course, rapid-growth firms do exist in rapid-growth markets, but there are many examples of firms in fairly ordinary industries that have maintained impressive growth rates. For example, Momentum Marketing Services, a 1995 start-up, was ranked number 399 on *Inc.* magazine's list of the 500 fastest-growing private companies in America in 2003. Momentum is in the advertising and marketing industry, which is a relatively low-growth industry. The company grew 450 percent from 1998 to 2003. Its secret is that it develops innovative promotional campaigns. For example, Momentum was hired by GE Financial Services to help it introduce its Web site. Instead of running ordinary ads, the company dropped 5,000 wallets in office lobbies, elevators, and train stations in 10 cities. Anyone who picked up a wallet and opened it was invited to visit GE Financial Service's Web site to see if he or she had won a prize. (The company even discreetly filmed people's behavior when they noticed the wallets on the floor; several news programs aired the footage.)[26]

Nucor is an innovative steel company that has grown quickly through the use of sophisticated technology in its operations. Company operations are currently earning $11.38 billion in sales annually.

For most firms such as Momentum Marketing Services, rapid growth is dependent more on the ability to be creative and establish a leadership position within a chosen target market than on the ability to ride the wave of a rapidly growing market. In fact, rapidly growing markets are not always healthy markets for long-term participation in that they often burn out relatively quickly as capacity catches up with demand and consumers move on to the next fad or new technology.[27]

Myth 3: To grow quickly, you must have a first-mover advantage. As discussed in Chapter 3, a first-mover advantage is not always advantageous. Several firms have pioneered industries and grown quickly, such as Yahoo! in the Internet search engine industry and Cisco Systems in routers, but many firms have grown quickly by entering an industry later on. FedEx in overnight delivery, Nucor in steel, and Southwest Airlines in air travel are examples of non–first-mover firms that have been exceptionally successful. More specifically, while these companies were not first in their industries, they have sustained impressive growth rates.[28]

Attributes of Successful Growth Firms

learning **objective**

9. Identify the most prevalent growth-related firm attributes.

Many firms cannot effectively manage the complexities and demands associated with the growth process, in part because entrepreneurs and their advisers are not fully aware of the attributes of successful growth firms. Let's look at the systematic differences that tend to exist between growth firms and firms that are unable to achieve and sustain growth. These attributes—summarized in Table 13.2—also offer a solution, at least in part, to the challenges of growth described previously.

Growth-Related Firm Attributes

The presence of certain firm attributes, or qualities, facilitates the growth process. The attributes are discussed in the following sections.

Growth-Oriented Vision A **growth-oriented vision**, whether it is articulated through a vision statement, a mission statement, a values statement, or some other means, helps a firm crystallize the importance of growth for its stakeholders and ensures that its major decisions are made with growth in mind.[29]

Table 13.2

Growth-Related Firm Attributes

Attribute	Description
Growth-oriented vision	A growth-oriented vision and/or mission statement clearly communicates to relevant stakeholders the importance of growth to an organization.
Commitment to growth	A drive and commitment to achieve growth is frequently mentioned as a necessary precursor for successful growth.
Business growth planning	Planning helps a firm organize for growth and address the relevant managerial and strategic issues necessary to maintain growth.
Participation in business alliances	Business alliances help firms share costs, increase speed to market, gain economies of scale, and gain access to essential resources, knowledge, and foreign markets.
Geographic location that facilitates knowledge absorption	A firm located in a geographic area that is in close proximity to important external sources of knowledge will have better access to the knowledge and will be able to substitute a portion of the externally derived knowledge for more expensive internally generated knowledge.

It is not uncommon for a firm to formally articulate its vision for growth. A recent study by two Deloitte consultants reported that nearly 60 percent of the rapid-growth firms they are acquainted with have put their growth vision in writing. In contrast, only 15 percent of the slow-growth firms they are familiar with had done the same.[30] Vondafone, the innovative European telecommunications giant, is a company with a growth-oriented vision: it aims to be the world's leading wireless telecommunications and information provider. The company hopes to realize its vision through its growth objectives, which are laid out in its vision statement as follows:

Vondafone has a three pronged growth strategy to achieve its vision:

- Accelerated customer growth
- Geographic expansion
- New services for all our customers[31]

The importance of documenting a growth-oriented vision is supported by a broad-based global study by A. T. Kearney. Of the companies surveyed, 83 percent of the firms that are growing have a growth vision that is well defined and well communicated. In addition, more than half the growth firms said that articulating a growth vision was the turning point that drove them toward newfound growth.[32] Combining these findings with those reported by the Deloitte consultants allows us to highlight the importance of establishing a growth vision.

Commitment to Growth
The more vague concept of "**commitment to growth**" deals with the extent to which a firm is committed to pursuing growth. For growth to take place on a continual basis, it must be a deliberate choice made by the firm's owners/entrepreneurs and managers.[33] A recent *Trendsetter Barometer* survey of 402 fast-growth firms by PricewaterhouseCoopers confirmed this: the number one quality that the participants in the survey identified as facilitating growth was "depth of management commitment" to firm growth.[34] Thomas L. Doorley III, founder of Braxton Associates, an international consulting firm, has emphasized the importance of both a growth-oriented vision and a commitment to growth. Drawing on the experiences of his consulting practice, Doorley wrote, "We find that companies that grow actually take time to write down something that hammers out the growth theme in their vision, mission, or values statement." He describes one chief operating officer who wrote this growth mission who said, "We want to take advantage of our key assets—our brands, technologies, people, and alliances—to lead our key competitors in profitable market share growth." This mission is effective, says Doorley, "because it is high-level, yet tactical—any person can understand it."[35]

learning **objective**

10. Describe the importance of having a commitment to growth.

Business Growth Planning
Business growth planning is the process of setting growth-related goals and objectives, then mapping out a plan to achieve those goals and objectives.[36] The literature on planning suggests that firms that plan in a conscientious, thorough manner increase their chances of reaching their growth objectives.[37]

Participation in Business Partnerships
As emphasized in the "Partnering for Success" features throughout this book, participation in business partnerships also spurs growth. These relationships include joint ventures, networks, consortia, strategic alliances, trade associations, and interlocking directorates. In the case of joint ventures, networks, and strategic alliances, the consensus view is that participation in these types of business alliances accelerates a firm's growth by providing it access to a portion of its partner's resources, managerial talent, and intellectual capacities.[38] This chapter's "Partnering for Success" feature provides an example of how two firms, Amazon.com and Toysrus.com, have benefited by gaining access to each other's resources and expertise. It also provides a vivid illustration of how some firms address the managerial capacity problem we discussed earlier. By cooperating rather than competing, Toysrus.com and Amazon.com are able to minimize the resources they need to sell toys online.

Partnering for SUCCESS

Amazon.com and Toysrus.com Decide to Cooperate Rather Than Compete

www.amazon.com
www.toysrus.com

Rather than slugging it out for customers in the online marketplace for toys, Amazon.com and Toysrus.com formed an alliance that allows both companies to do what they do best. In August 2000, the two online retailers announced the formation of a 10-year strategic alliance to create a cobranded online toy and video game store. Prior to the agreement, both companies featured separate online toy stores.

The alliance is structured so that the companies share responsibility. Toysrus.com is in charge of identifying, purchasing, owning, and managing the inventory of toys. Amazon.com handles Web site development, order fulfillment, customer service, and housing the inventory in its U.S. distribution centers. When the agreement was announced, the then CEO of Toys "R" Us, John Eyler, explained the rationale for the partnership in an article in *E-Commerce Times*: "The strength of the Toys 'R' Us brand and our merchandising experience, combined with Amazon's unbeatable Internet savvy, will create an online presence second to none."

The Amazon.com–Toysrus.com partnership illustrates why firms partner with one another to grow. By partnering, each company is able to piggyback on its partner's expertise and conserve resources. Toys "R" Us's expertise is buying and selling toys, and Amazon.com's expertise is managing a Web site and customer service. The partnership enables the seamless selling of toys and video games over the Internet by allowing both companies to focus on their areas of expertise. Amazon.com doesn't have to hire employees to identify and purchase toys, and Toysrus.com doesn't have to hire a staff to develop and maintain an e-commerce Web site. Each company is able to tap into its partner's resources, thereby reducing the effect of the managerial capacity problem by lessening the resources they need to sell toys online.

Questions for Critical Thinking

1. As noted in this feature, the partnership between Amazon.com and Toys "R" Us deals with the managerial capacity problem. However, in your view, does this approach to each firm's managerial services have the potential to damage each partner's ability to deal with the entrepreneurial services challenge? Prepare as substantive answer to this question as possible.

2. This feature suggests that Toys "R" Us is committed to growth. Write what you believe the firm's growth vision might be that caused it to partner with Amazon.com.

Source: N. Macaluso, "Amazon, Toys 'R' Us Ink E-Commerce Pact," E-Commerce Times (accessed August 23, 2002).

Geographic Location That Facilitates Knowledge Absorption Locating in a geographic area that facilitates the absorption of knowledge from external sources, as described in Chapter 3, is typically to a firm's advantage. By being physically located near similar firms, a company can gain access to these firms' specialized suppliers, scientific knowledge, and technological expertise.[39]

CHAPTER SUMMARY

1. Sustained growth is defined as growth in both revenues and profits over an extended period of time.

2. Although most firms endeavor to grow, there are potential downsides to growth. Growth is a two-edge sword that can threaten the stability of a firm's operations in every area, from human resources to finance, if it is not managed properly.

3. Growth is not a random or chance event. It is something firms pursue deliberately. The six most common reasons that firms grow in an effort to increase their profitability and valuation are as follows: to capture economies of scale; to execute a scalable business model; to achieve market leadership; to maintain influence, power, and survivability; to accommodate the growth of key customers; and to maintain an ability to attract and retain talented employees.

4. A scalable business model is one in which increased revenues cost less to deliver than current revenues. As a result, profit margins increase as sales go up.

5. The basic idea behind benchmarking is that a firm can improve the quality of an activity by identifying and copying the methods of other firms that have been successful in that area. Firm growth is an excellent opportunity for benchmarking.

6. The managerial capacity problem suggests that firm growth is limited by the managerial capacity (i.e., personnel, expertise, and intellectual resources) that firms have available to implement new business ideas. The basic idea is that it does a firm little good to have exciting ideas about growth when it lacks the managerial capacity to implement its ideas.

7. The day-to-day challenges of managing growth include cash flow management, price stability, quality control, and capital constraints.

8. The three most pervasive myths about firm growth are that growth companies are predominantly technology companies, that rapid-growth firms emerge only in rapid-growth industries, and that to grow quickly, the firm must have a first-mover advantage.

9. The firm attributes that are most commonly related to firm growth include a growth-oriented vision, a commitment to growth, participation in business alliances, business growth planning, and a geographic location that facilitates the absorption of knowledge from external sources.

10. The variable commitment to growth deals with the extent to which a firm is committed to pursuing growth as a deliberate, ongoing strategy. The idea is that for growth to take place on a continual basis, it must be a deliberate choice made by the owners/managers of the firm.

adverse selection, 315

benchmarking, 314

business growth planning, 321

commitment to growth, 321

economies of scale, 311

entrepreneurial services, 315

fixed costs, 311

growth-oriented vision, 320

managerial capacity problem, 315

managerial services, 315

market leadership, 312

moral hazard, 315

pace of growth, 311

productive opportunity set, 315

rapid-growth firm, 309

scalable business model, 311

sustained growth, 309

variable costs, 311

1. What is sustained growth? Why is it important?

2. Are most firms rapid-growth firms? Explain your answer.

3. What are the potential downsides to firm growth?

4. Provide an example that describes why a firm might be forced to grow faster than it prefers.

5. Describe economies of scale as a means of firm growth.

6. Define the phrase "scalable business model." Provide an example of an industry that lends itself to scalable business models.

7. List three reasons firms work hard to achieve market leadership.

8. How does a firm's growth rate affect its ability to attract and retain talented employees?

9. Describe the basic idea behind benchmarking and how benchmarking can help a firm achieve its growth objectives.

10. Give a brief overview of the managerial capacity problem.

11. What are the differences between a firm's entrepreneurial services and its managerial services? How are these two services linked in regard to a firm's growth efforts?

12. Explain what is meant by adverse selection and moral hazard. What roles do these concepts play in facilitating or hindering a firm's growth efforts?

13. Explain why cash flow management, price stability, and quality control are important issues for a firm that is entering a period of rapid growth.

14. Why is it important for growth firms to develop and maintain professional business practices? Make your answer as substantive and thoughtful as possible.

15. In what industries do rapid-growth firms emerge? Explain your answer.

16. Why is it important for a firm to have a growth-oriented vision?

17. Why is it important for a firm to engage in business growth planning?

18. How does participation in business alliances facilitate firm growth?

19. How does participation in business alliances help a firm solve the managerial capacity problem?

20. Why is it to a firm's advantage to locate in a geographic area that is populated by similar firms?

APPLICATION QUESTIONS

1. Pete Martin just purchased a copy of *Inc.* magazine's annual issue that ranks the top 500 fastest-growing privately owned companies in America. Pete was amazed by some of the stories in the article and is more encouraged than ever to start his own art restoration firm. As is the case for many entrepreneurs leading many of the Inc. 500 firms, Pete believes his firm can grow 1,000 percent or more per year. He is ready to cash out his savings and get started. Is Pete starting a business with realistic expectations? If not, what should his expectations be?

2. Twelve months ago, Brittany Nelson launched a chain of stores that sell accessories for wireless communications devices. Her first store was in Memphis, and she in now expanding into northern Mississippi and western Tennessee. Brittany's company has grown quickly from one store to five, and she hopes to add 10 to 20 stores per year during the next five years. Recently, a friend told Brittany that maybe she should slow down a bit because a company can grow "too fast." Brittany brushed the suggestion aside, simply noting that things were going fine and that growth was "no problem." Do you think Brittany should think again about her friend's advice? What are the pitfalls of growing too quickly?

3. Brian Ward is a computer software engineer. He has an idea for a software product that he thinks could constitute the initial product for a new business. Brian recently read that software companies can grow quickly because software lends itself to a "scalable business model." Brian doesn't quite know what a scalable business model is and has asked you for an explanation. He would also like to know if there are any potential hazards in launching a business that is founded on a scalable business model. What would you tell him?

4. Three years ago, Chris Dees launched a medical products company that specializes in providing products for people with diabetes. His company is number one in its industry. Recently, a couple of competitors have entered the picture, and Chris is wondering if it is worth the fight to remain number one. In terms of firm growth, what advantages are there to being the market leader?

5. Troy Milton owns a successful consumer products firm in Oakland, California. The firm has a number of talented employees who have contributed significantly to the success of the company. The company has stalled in terms of growth. Curiously, Troy doesn't seem to be concerned, and a couple of his top employees have even observed that Troy seems to be enjoying the slower pace. In terms of his ability to retain his most talented employees, what risks does Troy run by letting his firm stall in terms of growth?

6. Ian Khalid lives in Gainesville, Florida, and has owned a fiber-optics company for five years. Although the company is profitable, he is worried about it because it isn't growing. Ian has heard about the concept of benchmarking and has asked you if benchmarking could play a role in helping him identify ways to grow his firm. What would you tell him? What types of firms should Ian attempt to benchmark against?

7. Doug Rypien owns a small electronics firm in central Illinois. He is thinking about trying to grow the firm outside its immediate trade area. He is even thinking about approaching some customers in Chicago, believing that he has a good chance of making some sales. What are some of the day-to-day challenges that Doug will probably experience if he tries to grow his company? Given the nature of Doug's business, which of the challenges do you think will be the most demanding?

8. Kevin Owens is thinking about starting a natural foods company in Springfield, Missouri, and hopes to grow the company fairly quickly throughout the Midwest. He just talked to a business consultant, however, who told him to forget it. The consultant said, "The only types of companies that grow quickly are technology companies." Do you agree with Kevin's consultant? Why or why not?

9. Meredith Colella is a food products engineer who has developed an innovative approach for the packaging of meat. Her approach will extend the shelf life of most meat products by about 30 percent. Meredith is getting ready to try to sell the idea to investors. What could Meredith tell the investors that would give them confidence that she is prepared to cope with the challenges of rapid growth?

10. Claudia Jones is the owner of a graphic design firm in Baton Rouge, Louisiana. She wants to grow her firm and has been told that it is a good idea to write down her "vision for growth" and share the vision with her employees. Claudia wonders if it's really worth her time to write out a formal vision for growth—she would rather just talk to her employees about growth in broad terms. Do you think it's worth Claudia's time to write out a formal vision for growth? Why or why not?

you be the VC

Business idea: Make cell phones more fun.

Pitch: Millions of cell phones are equipped with games, but the games are limited in number and aren't very challenging, so users tend to forget about them. Founded in 1999 and located in Stockholm, Sweden, Synergenix Interactive plans to change that through its Mophun ("more fun"—get it?) software. Once cell phone manufacturers install Mophun gaming technology into their phones and game developers create games using Mophun software, the fun can begin. All users will have to do is turn on their phones, go into the games menu, download a game, and play. Costs for downloading games will range from $2 to

$5 (which is how Synergenix will make most of its money), depending on the game, and are paid through your phone bill. Choices will range from old arcade-style games such as Asteriods to modern action games such as Street Fighter.

Q&A: Based on the material covered in this chapter, what questions would you ask the firm's founders before making your funding decision? What answers would satisfy you?

Decision: If you had to make your decision on just the information provided in the pitch and the company's Web site, would you fund this firm? Why or why not?

Case 13.1

Tellme Networks: Positioning Itself for Rapid Growth
www.tellme.com

Here's a transcript of a phone call you might make to Domino's pizza.

Domino's: Thanks for calling Domino's Pizza. May I have your phone number please?

You: Sure. My number is 487-2012.

Domino's: Thanks. Do you still live at 601 Pine Street?

You: Yes.

Domino's: May I have your order please?

You: I'd like a large sausage and mushroom pizza.

Domino's: Will that be carryout or delivery?

You: Delivery.

Domino's: Would you like any breadsticks or Coke products to go with the pizza?

You: Yes, thanks for reminding me. I'd like a two-liter bottle of Diet Coke.

Domino's: Anything else?

You: Nope.

Domino's: Thanks for your order. The total is $18.55. It will be delivered in about 40 minutes.

This sounds like an ordinary pizza order, right? It's not. This order involves only one human: you.

Tellme Networks is a start-up that is at the cutting edge of an emerging industry called voice commerce, or v-commerce, which is a new generation of computer-assisted phone services. John LaMacchia and Mike McCue launched Tellme in 1999. LaMacchia, who has a PhD in physics, is the former CEO of Cincinnati Bell and spent many years with AT&T. McCue, who founded his first company in 1989, is the former vice president for technology at Netscape. Tellme's service is set apart from pervious generations of computer-assisted phone services by the natural conversation that takes place between the caller and the computer.

Want to see for yourself? Make a quick call to Tellme at 1-800-555-Tell. The voices sound pleasant and conversational and offer access to all sorts of information. Try interrupting the speaker (don't worry about manners, it's a computer!) by saying "sports" or "traffic" and see what happens. After you've called a couple of times, Tellme even remembers what kind of information you're after. The purpose of the technology isn't to trick the caller into thinking that a human is on the other end of the line but rather to get away from the tedium of systems that ask you to "press 1 for accounting, press 2 for marketing, press 3 for shipping." The computer-enabled service can also connect a caller with one of hundreds of choices in seconds. This type of functionality isn't possible with human operators.

V-commerce mimics the functionality of the Internet, but instead of setting up a Web site to interact directly with customers, a company can set up a "phone site." The phone site can be used for a number of purposes, including taking orders, checking the status of a pending order, handling an exchange, or telling a person what movies are playing.

With a customer's permission, Tellme sites can also help customers drum up business via the Tellme Notifier. My Jiffy Lube Reminder is an example of the Tellme Notifier, which Jiffy Lube uses to voice alert its customers when it's time for an oil change. Jiffy Lube asks its customers for contact information and specifically asks permission to enroll them in the My Jiffy Lube Reminder program. An added benefit to Jiffy Lube is that many consumers give their cell phone numbers as their phone contact and often receive their notices when they are in their cars. This allows a customer to quickly verify that they need an oil change by checking the odometer. Tellme also makes money by hosting applications, reselling network capacity purchased through AT&T, and listing a company on its main directory.

So far, the company has landed some impressive accounts. Tellme systems currently sell movie tickets for Fandango, handle stock trades for E*Trade, direct Merrill Lynch clients to financial advisers, and dole out directory assistance numbers for AT&T. If you call to check on an Amazon.com order, it's Tellme that you're talking to. Tellme charges its customers 10 to 20 cents per call, which is a huge savings over the $5 to $10 per call that corporations spend for live operators. Tellme systems currently handle about a million calls per day—up from a million per week just a year ago.

There are substantial barriers to entry for participating in the v-commerce industry, including expensive equipment and ever-changing technology, so it's unlikely that corporations such as Domino's and E*Trade will develop their own v-commerce capabilities rather than outsource to a company such as Tellme.

Tellme hopes to scale its business model quickly as it adds more accounts, users, and functionality. The company is one of the best-funded new ventures of the early 2000s, with over a quarter billion dollars invested from prominent venture-capital firms such as Kleiner, Perkins, Caufield, & Byers and Benchmark Capital. Commenting on the firm's future in a *Red Herring* article published in late 2000, Kevin Harvey, a partner of Benchmark Capital, said, "Tellme offers a rare combination of massive market opportunities. Just as the Internet revolutionized the PC, Tellme will revolutionize the phone."

Discussion Questions

1. Why do you think Tellme is one of the best-funded new companies of the early 2000s? In your judgment, what is it about Tellme that has attracted the attention of prominent venture capitalists? If you were a venture capitalist, would you be interested in funding Tellme? Why or why not?

2. Provide an example of a company that has a business model that isn't scalable. In what ways is the company limited in its growth potential because its business isn't scalable?

3. If you were advising Tellme about the day-to-day challenges associated with rapid growth, which challenge do you think will be the most demanding for the company to deal with? Why?

4. Call 1-800-555-Tell. What do you think? Does the company's technology live up to its hype? Do you think the company will be successful? Why or why not?

Sources: Tellme home page, www.tellme.com (accessed March 1, 2004); S. Silverman, "Tellme Announces New Funding and Focus," Red Herring, October 4, 2000; and J. Easton, Going Wireless (New York: HarperCollins, 2002).

Case 13.2

Movie Gallery: Sustaining Growth by Focusing on Rural and Secondary Markets
www.moviegallery.com

Movie Gallery is the leading video rental store in rural and secondary markets. Rather than competing head on against industry leaders Blockbuster and Hollywood Video, Movie Gallery sticks to smaller towns the leaders have failed to serve. The company owns and operates over 2,000 retail stores that are located in all 50 states and seven Canadian provinces. The firm's quarterly sales revenue exceeded $200 million for the first time at the end of 2004's first quarter. Communities with populations between 3,000 and 20,000 that are suburban areas of larger towns are Movie Gallery's target markets. Only about a third of the company's stores compete directly with the larger chain movie rental stores.

Movie Gallery is headquartered 1,049 miles from Wall Street and 2,210 miles from Hollywood in Dothan, Alabama. The company started in 1985 through an unusual set of cir-cumstances. Cofounder Joe Malugen, who remains Movie Gallery's CEO, was a successful attorney who always wanted to start his own business. A client of his was in the video business but wanted to get out and talked Malugen into buying the business. Malugen and his partner, Harrison Parrish, took the original store, located in Dothan, and started replicating it across southern Alabama and the Florida panhandle. By 1994, the company had grown to 73 stores with annual revenues of $12 million.

To raise capital for additional expansion, Movie Gallery went public in late 1994. Since that time, the company has grown at an average annual rate of 16.3 percent. During that same period, the video rental industry grew at a rate of 6.1 percent per year. The industry is expected to continue to grow, primarily as the result of DVD rentals and sales. Currently, 90 percent of all households with televisions own a VCR or DVD player. Households that own a DVD player reached 41.7 million by mid-2003 and are projected to grow to 90.4 million by the end of 2010, according to Centris and Adams Media, two media research firms.

From late 1996 through 1998, the company slowed its pace of growth and devoted the majority of its time and energy toward completing system development, building its infrastructure, improving its balance sheet, and solidifying its strategy of penetrating rural and secondary markets. Because it had grown through a strategy of small acquisitions, it also spent time shaping and instilling a corporate culture. In 1999, the company revved up its growth strategy again and announced plans to build over 100 new stores per year and completing the 88-store acquisition of Blowout Entertainment. According to the Video Store Dealers Association, there are over 27,000 video rental stores in America. The three largest chains account for 8,600 stores, or 32 percent of the total. Independent operators, small chains, and other rental outlets own the remaining 18,400 stores. Believing that the industry will continue to consolidate into regional and national chains, Movie Gallery plans to fuel its growth through acquisitions and new construction in rural and secondary markets. While the large chains are continuing to grow, there is evidence that many independent operators are suffering and losing market share. The combination of increased product offerings, economies of scale, and access to capital is increasingly favoring large chains over independent operators in the video rental industry.

Movie Gallery believes that its focus on rural and secondary markets provides it several key advantages. It costs less to operate stores in smaller markets, largely as the result of avoiding head-to-head competition with Blockbuster and Hollywood Video. The company's principal competitors in its markets are single outlets that have a limited selection of videos, limited access to capital, and modest advertising budgets. Movie Gallery believes that it is the premier video rental store in most of its markets.

In addition, the markets in which Movie Gallery competes delay competition from new technologies and business formats. For example, video on demand, which will inevitably erode video rental sales, will probably be offered first in cities and make its way to smaller communities later. Similarly, the multitheater movie complexes, which in some cases offer up to 24 theaters in one location, do not provide an alternative to movie rentals in most of the smaller markets in which Movie Gallery competes because these multiplexes are not built in smaller communities.

Movie Gallery also plans to grow by increasing same-store sales, which is a common metric in retail industries. DVD and game rentals provide particularly promising growth opportunities. The movie studios are also becoming increasingly dependent on video rental stores as channels through which to earn revenue. The order of distribution of movies is currently (1) movie theaters, (2) hotels and airlines, (3) video rental stores, (4) pay-per-view, and (5) all other channels. According to industry sources, the video rental industry is the single largest source of revenue for movie studios. The increasing import role of video rental income is giving companies like Movie Gallery increasing clout in the movie industry, permitting Movie Gallery and its competitors the clout to shape revenue-sharing agreements with the studios that are more advantageous to video store companies than those in the past.

Its historical success suggests that Movie Gallery will continue to grow, increasing its influence in its carefully chosen niche markets while doing so. The company's ultimate goal, stated on its Web site, is to "be the dominant entertainment source for video and video game rental and sale in rural and secondary markets in the United States."

Discussion Questions

1. Why do you think Movie Gallery has been able to sustain its growth? What, if anything, will eventually slow its growth?

2. If at some point Movie Gallery decided to enter metropolitan markets, which of the day-to-day challenges to growth mentioned in this chapter do you think would be the most demanding. Why?

3. What steps has Movie Gallery taken to lessen the impact of the managerial capacity problem?

4. Are you optimistic or pessimistic about the future growth prospects of Movie Gallery? Explain your answer.

Sources: Movie Gallery home page, www.moviegallery.com (accessed May 24, 2004); Movie Gallery 2001 10-K (filed with the Securities and Exchange Commission); and E. Ochs, "Sweet Home Video, Alabama," Video Store, July 29, 2001.

fourteen

strategies
for *firm growth*

OBJECTIVES

After studying this chapter, you should be ready to:

1. Explain the difference between internal and external growth strategies.

2. Identify the keys to effective new product development.

3. Explain the common reasons new products fail.

4. Discuss a market penetration strategy.

5. Explain the term "international new venture."

6. Explain the objectives a company can achieve by acquiring another business.

7. Identify a promising acquisition candidate's characteristics.

8. Explain the term "licensing" and how licensing can be used as a growth strategy.

9. Explain the term "strategic alliance" and describe the difference between technological alliances and marketing alliances.

10. Explain the term "joint venture" and describe the difference between a scale joint venture and a link joint venture.

ask jeeves: using multiple paths to achieve firm growth

If you are a sailor in the U.S. Navy and want to get married in a Navy chapel, all you have to do is "Ask the Chief." Until recently, you would have had to make several phone calls to make the arrangements. Today, the Navy has simplified the process. A sailor can simply log on to the Navy Web site and access a search engine called "Ask the Chief." Ask the Chief allows sailors to ask questions in plain English and provides fast, easy access to relevant information. Ask the Chief is a service the U.S. Navy has purchased from Ask Jeeves, Inc., a rapidly growing Internet search technology company. The service is attractive to the Navy because it not only helps sailors get answers to their questions but also helps the Navy better understand the types of questions that sailors

have. For example, if the question "How do I get married in a Navy chapel?" is asked thousands of times in the early spring but is seldom asked in the fall and winter, that type of information is important to know. It might prompt the Navy to put a special link on its Web site or run special ads in Navy periodicals during the early spring, providing sailors instructions for how to reserve a Navy chapel.

Ask Jeeves was founded in 1996 and has a playful side to its serious business. The company is named after Jeeves, the butler in P. G. Wodehouse (1881–1975) novels who was the classic "gentleman's gentleman," and served his charge's every need. The Ask Jeeves version of Jeeves the butler is the most famous face on the Internet and serves as a trusted guide for its online users. The central mission of Ask Jeeves is to humanize the online experience, making powerful Internet search services available to its customers as it does so. The firm seeks to deliver the most differentiated search on the Web to its users.

To achieve its goals, Ask Jeeves is divided into two divisions: Web Properties and Jeeves Solutions. Web Properties consists of a portfolio of Web sites. The flagship site, AskJeeves.com, is the 14th most visited Web site in the United States, is the 18th most visited Web site in the world, and has 30 million unique users worldwide.[1] As with the Navy's site, AskJeeves.com allows users to ask questions in simple English. Following the success of Ask Jeeves, the company launched a site named Ask Jeeves for Kids. It is a child-friendly version of Ask Jeeves that enables children to get answers to frequently asked questions about a variety of topics, from soccer to homework. Along with developing new Web sites, the Web Properties division of Ask Jeeves has also grown through acquisition and international expansion. In 2001, the company acquired Teoma Technologies to obtain its advance search technologies. Since then, Teoma.com has been launched as a stand-alone search engine. In March 2004, Ask Jeeves acquired Interactive Search Holdings to increase its total share of the market for queries on the Web.[2] Ask Jeeves has gone international through a series of joint ventures with foreign partners. Its efforts in this area have paid off. Ask Jeeves UK, Ask Jeeves

Japan, and Ask Jeeves en Español are all major sites in their respective markets.

Ask Jeeves makes money through its Web Properties division by selling online advertising and by licensing its search technology to other users. It has gone from no sales in 1996 to sales of $74.1 million in 2002 to sales of $107 million in 2003. One unique capability that the company has to offer is that it can deliver an advertiser's message the moment a user asks a question and is most prone to buy. For example, when a user types in the question "What should I buy my mom for mother's day?," Ask Jeeves can deliver on the spot an ad from an online flower or gift company on the results page. If someone clicks through and makes a purchase, Ask Jeeves earns a commission. As Ask Jeeves adds sites and the sites become more popular and valuable to advertisers, its corporatewide revenues will increase.

Ask Jeeves's second division is Jeeves Solutions. Jeeves Solutions sells a product called JeevesOne, which is a customized search engine. The search engine sits behind a company's firewall and provides a format similar to the one purchased by the U.S. Navy. Its main strengths are in providing a company's customers an intuitive question-and-answer format to retrieve information and in providing a company a way to "listen in" on the needs of its customers. As the result of these capabilities, the U.S. Navy, SunTrust Bank, Travelocity, VISA, DaimlerChrysler, and Nike are among the corporate clients currently using JeevesOne.

A sk Jeeves is a typical young entrepreneurial firm. It is using various methods to leverage its technology core competency to successfully grow. Since 1996, it has grown through internal product development, acquisition, and licensing. Ask Jeeves is using joint ventures to expand into foreign markets as another means of growth. While this may seem like an aggressive mix of growth strategies to implement in a short period of time, it is not uncommon. Even start-ups typically use a variety of strategies to grow. As evidence of this, a survey by PricewaterhouseCoopers found that in a recent three-year period, more than half of America's fastest-growing companies have participated in multiple partnerships with outsiders in an effort to increase innovation and boost sales.[3] At the same time, another survey by the same firm found that 33 percent of fast-growth firms have already acquired at least one other business and that 41 percent plan to acquire another firm in the near term.[4] In addition, more than 60,000 business partnerships were formed in the 1990s. About half of these were strategic alliances, while the other half were joint ventures.[5]

This chapter discusses the most common strategies firms use to grow. The growth strategies are divided into internal strategies for growth and external strategies for growth, as shown in Figure 14.1.

learning **objective**

1. Explain the difference between internal and external growth strategies.

Internal Growth Strategies

Internal growth strategies rely on efforts generated within the firm itself, such as new product development, other product-related strategies, and international expansion. Many businesses, such as Starbucks and Kinko's, have grown through internal growth strategies. The distinctive attribute of internally generated growth is that a business relies on its own competencies, exper-

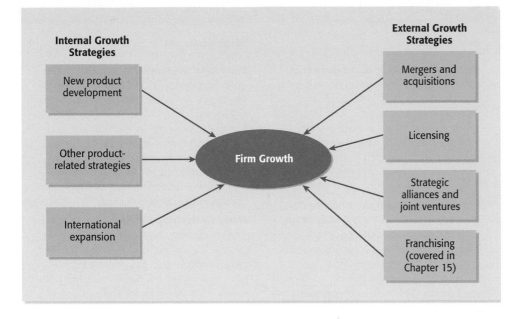

Figure 14.1

Internal and External Growth Strategies

tise, business practices, and employees. Internally generated growth is often called **organic growth** because it does not rely on outside intervention. There are limits to internal growth. As a company matures, it becomes more difficult to sustain its growth strictly through internal means. This is the challenge facing a company such as Starbucks. Even though it is still opening new restaurants and is developing new products, it is increasingly relying on partnerships with companies such as Dryers, which produces a Starbucks-branded ice cream, and Pepsi, which distributes Starbucks ready-to-drink coffee products, to fuel its growth. Table 14.1 lists the distinct advantages and disadvantages to internal growth strategies.

New Product Development

New product development involves the creation and sale of new products (or services) as a means of increasing firm revenues. In many fast-paced industries, new product development is a competitive necessity. For example, the average product life cycle in the computer software industry is 14 to 16 months. Because of this, to remain competitive, software companies must always have new products in their pipelines. For some companies, continually developing new products is the essence of their existence. The official vision of 3M, for example, is to be "the most innovative enterprise in the world."[6]

Although the development of new products can result in substantial rewards, it is a high-risk strategy. According to a recent Boston Consulting Group report, only 20 percent of new product launches with a budget of over $25 million succeed, and 90 percent of all product launches attract less than one percent market share.[7] The key is developing innovative new products that aren't simply "me-too" products entering already crowded markets. A recent PricewaterhouseCoopers survey reported that the chief executive officers (CEOs) of America's fastest-growing companies say that innovation, more than any other attribute, gives them a distinct advantage over their toughest competitors. The innovative firms in the survey expect to be rewarded with 30 percent faster revenue growth than their peers.[8]

When the development of new products is properly executed, there is tremendous upside potential. There are many biotech and pharmaceutical companies, for example, that not only have developed products that improve the quality of life for their customers but also provide reliable revenue streams. In most cases, the products are patented, meaning that no one else can make them, at least until the patents expire. Successful new products can also provide sufficient cash flow to fund a company's operations and provide resources to support the development of still additional new products. For example, Amgen, which is by far the biggest and most profitable biotech company, has two stellar pharmaceutical products, Epogen and Neupogen. Epogen is used for the treatment of anemia associated with chronic renal failure in dialysis patients, and Neupogen helps prevent infection in cancer patients undergoing certain types of chemotherapy. These products have provided the

learning **objective**

2. Identify the keys to effective new product development.

Table 14.1

Advantages and Disadvantages
of Internal Growth Strategies

Advantages	Disadvantages
Incremental, even-paced growth. A firm that grows at an even pace can continually adjust to changing environmental conditions to fine-tune its strategies over time. In contrast, a firm that doubles its size overnight through a merger or acquisition is making a much larger commitment at a single point in time.	***Slow form of growth.*** In some industries, an incremental, even-paced approach toward growth does not permit a firm to achieve competitive economies of scale fast enough. In addition, in some industries, it may not be possible for a firm to develop sufficient resources to remain competitive. A high level of merger and acquisition activity typically characterizes these industries.
Provides maximum control. Internal growth strategies allow a firm to maintain control over the quality of its products and services during the growth process. In contrast, firms that grow through collaborative forms of growth, such as alliances or joint ventures, must share the oversight function with their business partners.	***Need to develop new resources.*** Some internal growth strategies, such as new product development, require a firm to be innovative and develop new resources. While internal innovation has many positive attributes, it is typically a slow, expensive, and risky strategy.
Preserves organizational culture. Firms emphasizing internal growth strategies are not required to blend their organizational culture with another organization. As a result, the firm can grow under the auspices of a clearly understood, unified corporate culture.	***Investment in a failed internal effort can be difficult to recoup.*** Internal growth strategies, such as new product development, run the risk that a new product or service idea may not sell. As a result, the development cost may be difficult to recoup.
Encourages internal entrepreneurship. Firms that grow via internal growth strategies are looking for new ideas from within the business rather than from outside stakeholders or acquisition targets. This approach encourages a climate of internal entrepreneurship and innovation.	***Adds to industry capacity.*** Some internal growth strategies add to industry capacity, and this can ultimately help force industry profitability down. For example, a restaurant chain that grows through geographic expansion may ultimately force industry profitability down by continuing to open new restaurants in an already crowded market.
Allows firms to promote from within. Firms emphasizing internal growth strategies have the advantage of being able to promote within their own organizations. The availability of promotional opportunities within a firm provides a powerful tool for employee motivation.	

company sufficient revenue to cover its overhead, fund new product development, and generate profits for an extended period of time.

The keys to effective new product and service development, which are consistent with the material on opportunity recognition and feasibility analysis in Chapters 2 and 3, follow:

- *Find a need and fill it:* Most successful new products fill a need that is presently unfilled. "Saturated" markets should be avoided. For example, in the United States as well as most developed countries, consumers have a more-than-adequate selection of appliances, tires, credit cards, and long-distance telephone plans. These are crowded markets with low profit margins. The challenge for entrepreneurs is to find unfilled needs in attractive markets and then find a way to fill those needs.
- *Develop products that add value:* In addition to finding a need and filling it, the most successful products are those that "add value" for customers in some meaningful way.

- *Get quality right and pricing right:* Every product represents a balance between quality and pricing. If the quality of a product and its price are not compatible, the product may fail and have little chance for recovery. In slightly different words, customers are willing to pay higher prices for higher-quality products and are willing to accept lower quality when they pay lower prices.
- *Focus on a specific target market:* Every new product should have a specific target market in mind, as discussed in Chapter 11. This degree of specificity gives the product's manufacturer the opportunity to conduct a focused promotional campaign and select the appropriate distributors. The notion that "it's a good product, so somebody will by it" is a naive way to do business and often contributes to a firm's failure.
- *Conduct ongoing feasibility analysis:* Once a product is launched, the feasibility analysis and marketing research should not end. The response the product receives should be tested in focus groups and surveys, and incremental adjustments should be made when appropriate.

There is also a common set of reasons that new products fail. These include inadequate feasibility analysis, overestimation of market potential, bad timing (i.e., introducing the product at the wrong time), inadequate advertising and promotion, and poor service.

learning **objective**

3. Explain the common reasons new products fail.

One thing firms must guard against is testing the feasibility of a new product offering at the time it is introduced and then failing to retest the idea periodically to ensure that it continues to fill a need. If a firm's business environment changes, it may need to change its product offerings quickly to remain relevant. A breakdown in this process can result in business failure, as illustrated in the boxed feature titled "What Went Wrong?"

Other Product-Related Strategies

Along with developing new products, firms grow by improving existing products or services, increasing the market penetration of an existing product or service, or pursuing a product extension strategy.

Improving an Existing Product or Service

Often, a business can increase its revenue by **improving an existing product or service**—enhancing quality, making it larger or smaller, making it more convenient to use, improving its durability, or making it more up to date. Improving an item means increasing its value and price potential. Consider a business that uses a new technology to switch from processing film from two days to one hour. By increasing the convenience of its service, the business will most likely increase its film processing revenue potential. Similarly, software firms routinely increase revenues by coming out with "updated" versions of an existing software product.

A mistake many businesses make is not remaining vigilant enough regarding opportunities to improve existing products and services. It is typically much less expensive for a firm to modify an existing product or service and extend its life than to develop a new product or service from scratch.

Increasing the Market Penetration of an Existing Product or Service

A **market penetration strategy** seeks to increase the sales of a product or service through greater marketing efforts or through increased production capacity and efficiency. An increase in a product's market share is typically accomplished by increasing advertising expenditures, offering sales promotions, lowering the price, or increasing the size of the sales force. Consider Skechers, a shoe company that targets preteens, teenagers, and young adults. In January 2002, the company signed pop singer Britney Spears to an 18-month exclusive contract. As the result of an aggressive advertising campaign featuring Spears in its overseas markets, the company's international sales doubled.[9] Another example is the Starbucks Card described in Chapter 13. By making it more convenient for its customers to purchase its products, Starbucks is hoping to increase revenues and profits. The ultimate objective of a market penetration strategy is to increase net income along with total revenues. If an initiative costs more than the additional net income it generates, then the strategy would obviously be ineffective.

learning **objective**

4. Discuss a market penetration strategy.

what went **wrong?**

StorageNetworks: How One Firm Failed Because It Didn't Adjust to the Loss of Interest in Its Product Idea

Investors once thought that the idea championed by StorageNetworks was golden. Instead of buying expensive computer equipment to store their data, corporations could buy storage only as needed from StorageNetworks, which would keep the data readily accessible in giant "storage farms." The concept turned data storage into something akin to water or electricity. A customer would pay for storage only as it was used. The goal of StorageNetworks was to be the pacesetter in this seemingly promising industry.

At its peak, StorageNetworks, which was founded in late 1998, was worth $14 billion in market value. Today, that value has disappeared. In mid-2003, the company slashed its workforce and exited the data storage business, hoping to be acquired. When no suitors emerged, it decided to liquidate. What went wrong? There were two fundamental flaws in the "on demand" product offering of StorageNetworks. These flaws caused a steady loss of interest in the company and its product. Regrettably, StorageNetworks didn't react fast enough to change its product offering to survive.

The first flaw in the product offering of StorageNetworks was that its client companies became increasingly nervous about losing direct control over their data. (For example, consider whether you, as an entrepreneur, would want your financial and personal data stored by another company at an "off-site" location.) As a result, many of its customers eventually found new technologies enabling them to store their data in-house more efficiently. Second, many customers of StorageNetworks were large firms, such as Ford Motor

Company. While this sounds good, these firms eventually realized that because of their size, they could broker better deals with hardware vendors than StorageNetworks could. It was ultimately cheaper for a company such as Ford to build its own off-site storage than to purchase the services of StorageNetworks.

The StorageNetworks story is a reminder that firms must continually monitor the feasibility of their product offerings to remain competitive. If a company's product offerings lose favor among its core clientele, it must adjust quickly or else risk the fate that StorageNetworks experienced.

Questions for Critical Thinking

1. As we noted previously, finding a customer need and taking actions to fill that need is one of the keys to effective product development. In your opinion, did the product offering of StorageNetworks fill a need of corporate clients? Provide as much justification for your answer as possible.

2. Products sometimes fail because they are introduced at a time when the market isn't particularly receptive to them. High-quality, expensive items introduced just as an economy enters a recession may be an example of this issue. Do you think that the timing of the entry had anything to do with the failure of the product StorageNetworks offered? Why or why not?

Source: C. Forelle, "Storage-Farm Flop Points to Flaws in New Vogue," Wall Street Journal, August 28, 2003, B1.

Increased marked penetration can also occur through increased capacity or efficiency, which permits a firm to have a greater volume of product or service to sell. In a manufacturing context, an increase in product capacity can occur by expanding plant and equipment or by outsourcing a portion of the production process to another company. **Outsourcing** is work that is done for a company by people other than the company's full-time employees. For example, a firm that previously manufactured and packaged its product may outsource the packaging function to another company and as a result free up factory space to increase production of the basic product.

Extending Product Lines   A **product line extension strategy** involves making additional versions of a product so that it will appeal to different clientele. For example, a company may take a low-end product, make another version of it that is a little better, and then make another version of it that represents the top of the line. This is a strategy that allows a firm to take one product and extend it into several products without incurring significant additional development expense. Computer manufacturers provide a good example of how to execute a product line extension strategy. Each manufacturer sells several versions of its desktop and laptop computers. The different versions of the same computer typically represent good, better, and best alternatives based on processor speed, memory capacity, monitor size, graphic capabilities, and other features.

Firms also pursue product extension strategies as a way of leveraging their core competencies into related areas. For example, Abercrombie & Fitch has taken the expertise it developed through its Abercrombie stores and has used it to launch Hollister, a growing chain of retail stores that sell California "lifestyle" apparel and accessories. A book on the history of Oracle, a computer database software company, provides a particularly interesting example of the potential payoff of a product extension strategy. The example demonstrates that product extension strategies can take time and patience to pay off but can lead to breakthrough growth strategies:

> As Ellison (Oracle's CEO) recognized that he had sold a database to almost every one of the biggest companies in the world, he knew he would need new products to sell. That is how he came up with the idea of applications. Oracle applications would sit on top of and use Oracle databases to perform functions such as inventory management, personnel record keeping, and sales tracking. The proof of his thinking took almost seven years, but by 1995, the company generated nearly $300 million in license revenues from application products and an additional $400 million in applications-related services.[10]

Another firm that has done a good job of executing a product extension strategy is Outback Steakhouse, as illustrated in the boxed feature titled "Savvy Entrepreneurial Firm."

Geographic Expansion **Geographic expansion** is another internal growth strategy. Many entrepreneurial businesses grow by simply expanding from their original location to additional geographic sites. This type of expansion is most common in retail settings. For example, a small business that has a successful retail store in one location may expand by opening a second location in a nearby community. GAP, Kohl's, and Kinko's are examples of firms that have grown through geographic expansion. Of course, McDonald's is the classic example of incredibly successful growth through geographic expansion. The keys to successful geographic expansion follow:

- *Perform successfully in the initial location:* Additional locations can learn from the initial location's success.
- *Establish the legitimacy of the business concept in the expansion locations:* For example, a particular type of fitness center may be well accepted in its original location because it has been there a long time and has a loyal clientele. However, potential clientele in a neighboring community may be totally unacquainted with its unique products and services. A common mistake that firms make when they expand from one community to another is to assume that if something works in one community, it will automatically work in another.
- *Don't isolate the expansion location:* Sometimes the employees in an expansion location feel isolated and that they are not receiving adequate training and oversight from the headquarters location. It is a mistake to believe that an expansion location can excel without the same amount of attention and nurturing that it took to build the business in the original location.

International Expansion

International expansions is another common form of growth for entrepreneurial firms. Approximately 95 percent of the world's population and two-thirds of its total purchasing power are located outside the United States. As a result, in recent years, small businesses and entrepreneurial firms have become increasingly active in foreign markets. According to the Small Business Administration, 95.7 percent of U.S. exporters have fewer than 500 employees.[11] In addition, a growing number of the new firms that are launched in the United States are international new ventures. **International new ventures** are businesses that, from inception, seek to derive significant competitive advantage by using their

learning **objective**

5. Explain the term "international new venture."

Savvy entrepreneurial FIRM

Outback Steakhouse: Making a Product Extension Strategy Work

www.outback.com

Sometimes entrepreneurs are hard to understand. If you had started a restaurant chain in the cholesterol-conscious 1980s, what would you have put on the menu? Chicken? Fish? Pasta? Salads? Apparently, none of these ideas appealed to Chris Sullivan and Robert Bashman, the founders of Outback. Of all things, they started a steakhouse.

In fairness to Sullivan and Bashman, they actually had a sensible business idea. Despite the fat consciousness of the 1980s, they noticed that steakhouses were still doing well. What they needed was an attractive niche, so they positioned their first steakhouse, which opened in Tampa, Florida, in 1988, between the "high end" steakhouses that charged $25 for a steak and the "low end" steakhouses that charged $6.99 for a steak and salad. Along with offering an attractive price for a good meal, they did a lot of other things right. They created a unique atmosphere for their restaurant chain based on an Australian theme. As a way of keeping their employees "fresh," their restaurants are open only for the evening meal. They also made Outback Steakhouses fun. The restroom doors, for example, are labeled "Blokes" and "Aussies" instead of men and women. Menu items include "Shrimp on the Barbie" and "Bloomin' Onion." While at times these unusual names create confusion, they also help create a lighthearted atmosphere that is perfect for casual dining.

The number of Outback steakhouses has grown rapidly. Today, the firm operates in all 50 states in the United States as well as in 21 other countries. The company, however, hasn't relied exclusively on its steakhouses to fuel its overall growth. Over time, the founders have built on their experience of filling a "midrange niche" by developing a

family of restaurant chains to grow revenues and profits. The Outback Steakhouse family of restaurants includes Carrabba's Italian Grill, Roy's, Fleming's Prime Steakhouse and Wine Bar, Lee Roy Selmon's, and its newest restaurant, Bonefish Grill. In looking for new restaurant ideas, the company tries to identify concepts that fill a niche and possess broad appeal. All their restaurants also offer a good value and as is the case with Outback Steakhouse, are fun, lighthearted, and creative.

Outback Steakhouse has created a savvy new product development strategy that builds on what the company does best: run restaurants. The strategy has also consistently placed Outback's restaurant chains in the midprice range of attractive dining categories, proving to be a very profitable position.

Questions for Critical Thinking

1. Go to Outback Steakhouse's Web site (www.outback.com). Find information describing this firm's product extension strategy. For example, what foods are offered in the Outback restaurants. Why? What risks does the firm encounter while using a product extension strategy?

2. Conduct a survey of your friends who have eaten at Outback Steakhouse. What competitive threats do your friends see for this firm? In light of those threats, what do you think Outback should do to successfully deal with them? Could outsourcing be of any value to this firm in terms of controlling its costs and increasing its profitability? Why or why not?

Source: Outback 2001 Annual Report, www.outback.com (accessed April 2, 2004).

resources to sell products or services in multiple countries.[12] From the time they are started, these firms, which are sometimes called "global start-ups," view the world as their marketplace rather than confining themselves to a single country. Amazon.com, for example, was an international firm from its inception and now generates 34 percent of its sales from overseas markets.[13]

Although there is vast potential associated with selling overseas, it is a fairly complex form of firm growth. Let's look at the most important issues that entrepreneurial firms should consider in pursuing growth via international expansion.

Assessing a Firm's Suitability for Growth Through International Markets

Table 14.2 provides a review of the issues that should be considered, including management/organizational issues, product and distribution issues, and financial and risk man-

Management/Organizational Issues

Depth of management commitment. A firm's first consideration is to test the depth of its management commitment to entering international markets. Although a firm can "test the waters" by exporting with minimal risk, other forms of internationalization involve a far more significant commitment. A properly funded and executed international strategy requires top management support.

Depth of international experience. A firm should also assess its depth of experience in international markets. Many entrepreneurial firms have no experience in this area. As a result, to be successful, an inexperienced entrepreneurial firm may have to hire an export management company to familiarize itself with export documentation and other subtleties of the export process. Many entrepreneurial firms err by believing that selling overseas is not that much different than selling at home. It is.

Interference with other firm initiatives. Learning how to sell in foreign markets can consume a great deal of entrepreneurs' or managers' time. Overseas travel is often required, and selling to buyers who speak a different language and live in a different time zone can be a painstaking process. A firm should weigh the advantages of involvement in international markets against the time commitment involved and the potential interference with other firm initiatives.

Product and Distribution Issues

Product issues. A firm must first determine if its products or services are suitable for overseas markets. Many pertinent questions need to be answered to make this determination. For example, are a firm's products subject to national health or product safety regulations? Do the products require local service, supplies, or spare parts distribution capability? Will the products need to be redesigned to meet the specifications of customers in foreign markets? Are the products desirable to foreign customers? All these questions must have suitable answers before entering a foreign market is advisable. A firm can't simply "assume" that its products are salable in foreign countries.

Distribution issues. How will the product be transported from the United States to a foreign country? Is the transportation reliable and affordable? Can the product be exported from the United States, or will it have to be manufactured in the country of sale?

Financial and Risk Management Issues

Financing export operations. Can the foreign initiative be funded from internal operations, or will additional funding be needed? How will foreign customers pay the firm? How will the firm collect bad debts in a foreign country? These questions must obtain appropriate answers before initiating overseas sales.

Foreign currency risk. How will fluctuations in exchange rates be managed? If the entrepreneurial firm is located in America and it sells to a buyer in Japan, will the American firm be paid in U.S. dollars or in Japanese yen?

---

agement issues. If these issues can be addressed successfully, growth through international markets may be an excellent choice for an entrepreneurial firm. The major impediment in this area is not fully appreciating the challenges involved.

Foreign Market Entry Strategies   While the majority of entrepreneurial firms first enter foreign markets as exporters, firms also use licensing, joint ventures, franchising, turnkey projects, and wholly owned subsidiaries to start international expansion.[14] These strategies, along with their primary advantages and disadvantages, are explained in Table 14.3.

CNET Networks is a media company that reports technology news through Web sites, print media, and radio. Its flagship Web site is CNET.com, and its most recognizable print publication is *Computer Shopper* magazine. CNET is an example of an entrepreneurial firm using multiple methods to increase its revenues in foreign markets. For example, the company currently has a Web presence in more than 20 countries, including wholly owned

Foreign Market Entry Strategy	Primary Advantage	Primary Disadvantage
Exporting. Exporting is the process of producing a product at home and shipping it to a foreign market. Most entrepreneurial firms begin their international involvement as exporters.	Relatively inexpensive way for a firm to become involved in foreign markets.	High transportation costs can make exporting uneconomical, particularly for bulky products.
Licensing. A licensing agreement is an arrangement whereby a firm with the proprietary rights to a product grants permission to another firm to manufacture that product for specified royalties or other payments. Proprietary services and processes can also be licensed.	The licensee puts up most of the capital needed to establish the overseas operation.	A firm in effect "teaches" a foreign company how to produce its proprietary product. Eventually, the foreign company will probably break away and start producing a variation of the product on its own.
Joint ventures. A joint venture involves the establishment of a firm that is jointly owned by two or more otherwise independent firms. Fuji-Xerox, for example, is a joint venture between an American and a Japanese firm.	Gain access to the foreign partner's knowledge of local customs and market preferences.	A firm loses partial control of its business operations.
Franchising. A franchise is an agreement between a franchisor (the parent company that has a proprietary product, service, or business method) and a franchisee (an individual or firm that is willing to pay the franchisor a fee for the right to sell its product, service, and/or business method). U.S. firms can sell franchises in foreign markets.	The franchisee puts up the majority of capital needed to operate in the foreign market.	Quality control.
Turnkey projects. In a turnkey project, a contractor from one country builds a facility in another country, trains the personnel that will operate the facility, and *turns* over the *keys* to the project when it is completed and ready to operate.	Ability to generate revenue.	It is usually a one-time activity, and the relationships that are established in a foreign market may not be valuable to facilitate future projects.
Wholly owned subsidiary. A firm that establishes a wholly owned subsidiary in a foreign country has typically made the decision to manufacture in the foreign country and establish a permanent presence.	Provides a firm total control over its foreign operations.	The cost of setting up and maintaining a manufacturing facility and permanent presence in a foreign country can be high.

operations in Australia, France, Germany, Singapore, and the United Kingdom. It also has a number of joint ventures and licensees around the world. CNET broadcasts on 910 AM in the San Francisco Bay Area and worldwide at its Web site (*www.cnetradio.com*).

Selling Overseas   Many entrepreneurial firms first start selling overseas by responding to an unsolicited inquiry from a foreign buyer. It is important to handle the inquiry appropriately and to observe proper protocols when trying to serve the needs of customers in foreign markets. Following are several rules of thumb for selling products in foreign markets:

- Answer requests promptly and clearly. Do not ignore a request just because it lacks grammatical clarity and elegance. Individuals using a nonnative language to contact a business located outside their home nation often are inexperienced with a second language.

- Replies to foreign inquires, other than e-mail or fax, should be communicated through some form of airmail or overnight delivery. Ground delivery is slow in some areas of the world.
- A file should be set up to retain copies of all foreign inquiries. Even if an inquiry does not lead to an immediate sale, the names of firms that have made inquiries will be valuable for future prospecting.
- Keep promises. The biggest complaint from foreign buyers about U.S. businesses is failure to ship on time (or as promised). The first order is the most important. It sets the tone for the ongoing relationship.
- All correspondence should be personally signed. Form letters are offensive in some cultures.
- Be polite, courteous, friendly, and respectful. This is simple common sense, but politeness is particularly important in some Asian cultures. In addition, avoid the use of business slang that is indigenous to the United States, meaning that the slang terms lack meaning in many other cultures.
- For a personal meeting, always make sure to send an individual who is equal in rank to the person with whom he or she will be meeting. In some cultures, it would be seen as inappropriate for a salesperson from a U.S. company to meet with the vice president or president of a foreign firm.

External Growth Strategies

External growth strategies rely on establishing relationships with third parties, such as mergers, acquisitions, strategic alliances, joint ventures, licensing, and franchising. Each of these items is discussed in the following sections, with the exception of franchising, which is discussed separately in Chapter 15.

Intel has created many partnerships with the strength of its Pentium brand. It has numerous alliances and joint ventures with computer manufacturers worldwide.

An emphasis on external growth strategies results in a more fast-paced, collaborative approach toward growth than the slower-paced internal strategies, such as new product development and expanding to foreign markets. External growth strategies level the playing field between smaller firms and larger companies.[15] For example, Pixar, the small animation studio that produced the animated hits *Monsters, Inc.* and *Finding Nemo*, previously had a number of key strategic alliances with Disney. By partnering with Disney, Pixar effectively co-opted a portion of Disney's management savvy, technical expertise, and access to distribution channels. During the time of its relationship with Disney, Pixar looked bigger and was able to compete more effectively with larger organizations. The relationship with Disney helped Pixar grow and enhance its ability to effectively compete in the marketplace. Similarly, by acquiring other companies, relatively young firms such as Pixar can gain access to patents and proprietary techniques that take larger firms years to develop on their own.

There are distinct advantages and disadvantages of emphasizing external growth strategies, shown in Table 14.4.

Mergers and Acquisitions

Many entrepreneurial firms grow through mergers and acquisitions. A **merger** is the pooling of interests to combine two or more firms into one. An **acquisition** is the outright purchase of one firm by another. In an acquisition, the surviving firm is called the **acquirer**, and the firm that is acquired is called the **target**. This section focuses on acquisitions rather than mergers because entrepreneurial firms are more commonly involved with acquisitions than mergers. In most cases, the entrepreneurial firm is the target, meaning that it is the firm being acquired, but not always. There are many examples of entrepreneurial firms that have grown through acquiring other firms.

Acquiring another business can fulfill several of a company's needs, such as expanding its product line, gaining access to distribution channels, achieving competitive economies of scale, or expanding the company's geographic reach. In most cases, a firm acquires a competitor or a company that has a product line or distinctive competency that it needs. Apogent Technologies is an example of an entrepreneurial firm acquiring other companies to obtain new products. Apogent makes laboratory and medical products, ranging from microscope slides to orthodontic appliances. Nearly half its annual sales growth is generated by acquisitions. Most of Apogent's acquisition targets are small firms that have attractive laboratory or medical products. Once an acquisition is made, Apogent boosts the sales of the acquired firm's products by assimilating them into its robust distribution network.

Although it can be advantageous, the decision to grow the entrepreneurial firm through acquisitions should be approached with caution.[16] Many firms have found that the process of assimilating another company into their current operation is not easy. Primarily for this reason, 65 to 70 percent of acquisitions fail to deliver anticipated results.[17] The most important issues to consider when pursuing an acquisition strategy follow.

Finding an Appropriate Acquisition Candidate   If a firm decides to grow through acquisition, it is extremely important for it to exercise extreme care in finding acquisition candidates. Many acquisitions fail not because the companies involved lack resolve but because they were a poor match to begin with. There are typically two steps involved in finding an appropriate target firm. The first step is to survey the marketplace and make a "short list" of promising candidates. The second is to carefully screen each candidate to determine its suitability for acquisition. The key areas to focus on in accomplishing these steps are as follows:

- The target firm's openness to the idea of being acquired and its ability to obtain key third-party consent. The third parties from whom consent may be required include bankers, creditors, suppliers, employees, and key customers.
- The strength of the target firm's management team, its industry, and its physical proximity to the acquiring firm's headquarters.
- The perceived compatibility of the target company's top management team and its corporate culture with the acquiring firm's top management team and corporate culture.
- The past and projected financial performance of the target firm.

learning objective

6. Explain the objectives a company can achieve by acquiring another business.

learning objective

7. Identify a promising acquisition candidate's characteristics.

Table 14.4 Advantages and Disadvantages of Growth Emphasizing External Growth Strategies

Advantages	Disadvantages
Reducing competition. If a firm acquires a competitor, it reduces its competition. This step often helps a firm establish price stability by eliminating the possibility of getting in a price war with at least one competitor. By turning potential competitors into partners, alliances and franchises can also reduce the amount of competition the firm experiences.	**Incompatibility of top management.** The top managers of the firms involved in an acquisition, an alliance, a licensing agreement, or a franchise organization may clash, making the implementation of the initiative difficult.
Getting access to proprietary products or services. Acquisitions or alliances are often motivated by a desire on the part of one firm to gain legitimate access to the proprietary property of another.	**Clash of corporate cultures.** Because external forms of growth require the combined effort of two or more firms, corporate cultures often clash, resulting in frustration and subpar performance.
Gaining access to new products and markets. Growth through acquisition, alliances, or franchising is a quick way for a firm to gain access to new products and markets. Licensing can also provide a firm an initial entry in a market.	**Operational problems.** Another problem that firms encounter when they acquire or collaborate with another firm is that their equipment and business processes may not be fully compatible.
Access to technical expertise. Sometimes, businesses acquire or partner with other businesses to gain access to technical expertise. In franchise organizations, franchisors often receive useful tips and suggestions from their franchisees.	**Increased business complexity.** Although the vast majority of acquisitions and alliances involve companies that are in the same or closely related industries, some enterpreneurial firms acquire or partner with firms in unrelated industries. This approach vastly increases the complexity of the combined business. The firm acquiring a brand or partnership with another company to gain access to its brand may subsequently fail to further develop its own brand and trademarks. This failure can lead to an increased dependency on acquired or partnered brands, reducing the firm's ability to establish and maintain a unique identity in the marketplace.
Access to an established brand name. A growing company that has good products or services may acquire or partner with an older, more established company to gain access to its trademark and name recognition.	**Loss of organizational flexibility.** Acquiring or establishing a partnership with one firm may foreclose the possibility of acquiring or establishing a partnership with another firm.
Economies of scale. The combination of two or more previously separate firms, whether through acquisition, partnering, or franchising, often leads to greater economies of scale for the combined firms.	**Antitrust implications.** Acquisitions and alliances are subject to antitrust review. In addition, some countries have strict antitrust laws prohibiting certain business relationships between firms.
Diversification of business risk. One of the principal driving forces behind all forms of collaboration or shared ownership is to diversify business risk.	

- The likelihood that the target firm will retain its key employees and customers if it is acquired.
- The identification of any legal complications that could impede the purchase of the target firm and the extent to which it has protected its intellectual property through patents, trademarks, and copyrights.
- The extent to which the acquiring firm understands the business and industry of the target firm.

The screening should be as comprehensive as possible to provide the acquiring firm sufficient data to determine realistic offering prices for the firms under consideration. A common mistake among acquiring firms is to pay too much for the businesses they purchase. Firms can avoid this mistake by basing their bids on hard data rather than on guesses or intuition. A recent PricewaterhouseCoopers report characterized the ingredients of a successful acquisition as follows:

> The companies that win the most [through acquisitions] know what they're looking to acquire, understand why the target company is of value to them, and have a plan that lays out the benchmarks necessary to capture value.[18]

Steps Involved in an Acquisition Completing an acquisition is a nine-step process, as illustrated in Figure 14.2:

Figure 14.2

The Process of Completing the
Acquisition of Another Firm

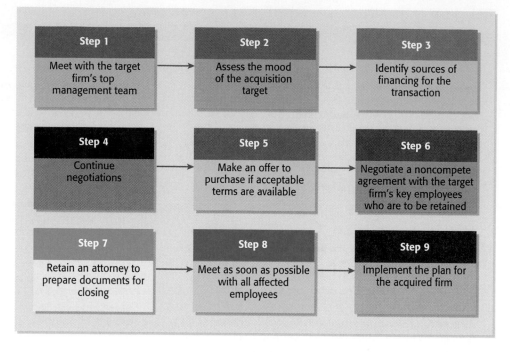

Step 1. Meet with the top management team of the acquisition target: The acquiring firm should have legal representation at this point to help structure the initial negotiations and help settle any legal issues. The acquiring firm should also have a good idea of what it thinks the acquisition target is worth.

Step 2. Assess the mood of the acquisition target: If the target is in a "hurry to sell," it works to the acquiring firm's advantage. If the target starts to get cold feet, the negotiations may become more difficult.

Step 3. Identify sources of financing for the transaction: The acquiring firm should be financially prepared to complete the transaction if the terms are favorable.

Step 4. Continue negotiations: If a purchase is imminent, obtain all necessary shareholder and third-party consents and approvals.

Step 5. Make an offer to purchase if acceptable terms are available: Both parties should have the offer reviewed by attorneys and certified public accountants who represent their interests. Determine how payment will be structured.

Step 6. Negotiate a noncompete agreement with the target firm's key employees who are to be retained after the acquisition: This agreement, as explained in Chapter 6, limits the rights of the key employees of the acquired firm to start the same type of business in the acquiring firm's trade area for a specific amount of time.

Step 7. Retain an attorney to prepare the documents for closing: Complete the transaction.

Step 8. Meet as soon as possible with all affected employees: A meeting should be held as soon as possible with the employees of both the acquiring firm and the target firm. Articulate a vision for the combined firm and ease employee anxiety where possible.

Step 9. Implement the plan for the acquired firm: In some cases, the acquired firm is immediately assimilated into the operations of the acquiring firm. In other cases, the acquired firm is allowed to operate in a relatively autonomous manner.

Other Issues There are several other issues to consider when pursuing a strategy of growth through acquisition. The first involves common misperceptions that exist pertaining to the advantages of growth through acquisition. The three primary myths associated with acquisitions are identified and discussed in Table 14.5.

Myth 1: Diversification significantly reduces the risk of business failure.

Some firms acquire other firms in an effort to "balance" their portfolios and reduce their overall exposure to risk. Although a diversified line of products and services can help a firm manage its risk, this fact alone is an insufficient reason to grow through acquisition. Many managers find that it is difficult to provide adequate oversight for a firm that is "outside" of their area of expertise and become frustrated when they try to keep pace with the changes that are taking place in multiple locations.

Myth 2: Failing business that can be "turned around" represent the best acquisition opportunities.

While a failing business may be able to be bought for a song, it may take substantial resources and time to restore the business to health. Typically, buying a strong business and making it stronger is a more realistic approach.

Myth 3: Past performance is a guarantee of future performance.

Just because an acquisition target has performed well in the past is no guarantee that it will perform well in the future.

Licensing

Licensing is the granting of permission by one company to another company to use a specific form of its intellectual property under clearly defined conditions. Virtually any intellectual property a company owns that is protected by a patent, trademark, or copyright can be licensed to a third party. Licensing can be a very effective way of earning income, particularly for intellectual property–rich firms, such as software and biotech companies. For example, in a recent year, Qualcomm, the company that supplies the technology that makes cell phones work, obtained one-third of its $2.7 billion revenues through licensing income. Similarly, during the same period, Siebel Systems, a company that makes software that helps firms track the behavior of their customers, earned roughly 40 percent of its $2 billion in revenue through licensing income.

The terms of a license are spelled out through a **licensing agreement**, which is a formal contract between a licensor and a licensee. The **licensor** is the company that owns the intellectual property. The **licensee** is the company purchasing the right to use it. A license can be exclusive, nonexclusive, for a specific purpose, and for a specific geographic area.[19] In almost all cases, the licensee pays the licensor an initial payment plus an ongoing royalty for the right to use the intellectual property. There is no set formula for determining the amount of the initial payment or the royalties—these are issues that are part of the process of negotiating a licensing agreement.[20] Entrepreneurial firms often press for a relatively large initial payment as a way of generating immediate cash to fund their operations.

Along with generating income, another distinct advantage of licensing for entrepreneurial firms is that it spreads the risk and cost of developing new technologies. For example, Ask Jeeves, as described in this chapter's opening case, develops superior Internet search technologies. It would be expensive and risky for Ask Jeeves to invest in new search technologies simply to enhance its own search engines. Instead, Ask Jeeves spreads the risk and cost of its efforts by immediately licensing the new technology to third parties along with using it for its own purposes. The key for a firm such as Ask Jeeves is to find companies willing to license its technology that are not direct competitors and that won't erode its own market share. An ever-present danger in licensing (and its most compelling disadvantage) is that a licensor may inadvertently create a competitor that quits licensing its products and starts selling something just dissimilar enough that it does not infringe on the licensing agreement.

There are two principal types of licensing: technology licensing and merchandise and character licensing.

Technology Licensing   **Technology licensing** is the licensing of proprietary technology that the licensor typically controls by virtue of a utility patent. This type of licensing agreement typically involves one of two scenarios. First, as described in the Ask Jeeves

learning **objective**

8. Explain the term "licensing" and how licensing can be used as a growth strategy.

example, firms develop technologies to enhance their own products and then find non-competitors to license the technology to spread out the costs and risks involved. Second, companies that are tightly focused on developing new products pass on their new products through licensing agreements to companies that are more marketing oriented and that have the resources to bring the products to market. Qualcomm is a perfect example of technology licensing. It invents and designs chips and software for cell phones. It then licenses the chips and software to larger, more marketing-oriented companies, such as Ericson, Motorola, and Nokia, that produce the cell phones and bring them to market.

Striking a licensing agreement with a large firm can involve tough negotiations. An entrepreneur should carefully investigate potential licensees to make sure they have a track record of paying licensing fees on time and are easy to work with. To obtain this information, it is appropriate to ask a potential licensee for references. It is also important that an entrepreneur not give away too much in regard to the nature of his or her proprietary technology in an initial meeting with a potential licensee. This challenge means finding the right balance of piquing a potential licensee's interest without revealing too much. Nondisclosure agreements, described in Chapter 6, should be used in discussing proprietary technologies with a potential licensee.

Merchandise and Character Licensing   **Merchandise and character licensing** is the licensing of a recognized trademark or brand that the licensor typically controls through a registered trademark or copyright. For example, Harley-Davidson licenses its trademark to multiple companies that place the Harley trademark on T-shirts, jackets, collectibles, gift items, jewelry, watches, bike accessories, and so on. By doing this, Harley not only generates licensing income but also promotes the sale of Harley-Davidson motorcycles. Similarly, entrepreneurial firms such as Yahoo!, eBay, and Starbucks license their trademarks not only to earn licensing income but also to promote their products or services to a host of current and potential customers.

The key to merchandise and character licensing is to resist the temptation to license a trademark too widely and to restrict licensing to product categories that have relevance and that appeal to a company's customers. If a company licenses its trademark too broadly, it can lose control of the quality of the products with which its trademark is identified. This outcome can diminish the strength of a company's brand. For example, consumers expect a certain level of quality when they purchase a Starbucks-branded product. If Starbucks started licensing its trademark indiscriminately, it would inevitably end up on products that disappoint consumers and result in a gradual loss of confidence in the Starbucks brand. To avoid this from happening, companies should restrict their licensing to product categories that have relevance and appeal to their customers and that reflect the quality image the

Startups with strong brands have the opportunity to extend the value of their trademark by licensing it or entering into partnerships. Starbucks, for example, has partnered with Dreyers to create a line of Starbucks ice cream, which includes flavors such as Java Chip, White Chocolate Latte, and Classic Coffee.

company is trying to convey. For example, a company such as Liz Claiborne might license its trademark to a watch manufacturer that is interested in producing a line of "Liz Claiborne" men's and women's watches. Liz Claiborne would want to make sure that the watches bearing its trademark were fashionable, were of similar quality as its clothing, and were appealing to its clientele. Liz Claiborne can enforce these standards through the terms of its licensing agreements.

Strategic Alliances and Joint Ventures

The increase in the popularity of strategic alliances and joint ventures has been driven largely by a growing awareness that firms can't "go it alone" and succeed. As with all forms of firm growth, strategic alliances and joint ventures have advantages and disadvantages. We present these points in Table 14.6.

Strategic Alliances   A **strategic alliance** is a partnership between two or more firms developed to achieve a specific goal. According to a recent survey, over three-fourths of technology businesses are active in strategic alliances, with the typical participant involved in an average of seven alliances. Of those involved, 92 percent said that alliances are important to their growth, including 63 percent that rated alliances as critically or very important.[21] Alliances tend to be informal and do not involve the creation of a new entity (such as in a joint venture). An example of a firm that has made alliances a central portion of its growth strategy is 1-800-FLOWERS, as illustrated in the boxed feature titled "Partnering for Success."

learning **objective**

9. Explain the term "strategic alliance" and describe the difference between technological alliances and marketing alliances.

Table 14.6   Advantages and Disadvantages of Participating in Strategic Alliances and Joint Ventures

Advantages	Disadvantages
Gain access to a particular resource. Firms engage in strategic alliances and joint ventures to gain access to a particular resource, such as capital, employees with specialized skills, or modern production facilities.	**Loss of proprietary information.** Proprietary information can be lost to a partner who is already a competitor or will eventually become one. This is a common worry.
Economies of scale. In many industries, high fixed costs require firms to find partners to expand production volume as a means of developing economies of scale.	**Management complexities.** Because strategic alliances and joint ventures require the combined effort of two or more firms, they are often difficult to manage. Frustrations and costly delays often occur.
Risk and cost sharing. Strategic alliances and joint ventures allow two or more firms to share the risk and cost of a particular business endeavor.	**Financial and organizational risks.** The failure rate for strategic alliances and joint ventures is high.
Gain access to a foreign market. Partnering with a local company is often the only practical way to gain access to a foreign market.	**Risk becoming dependent on a partner.** A power imbalance arises if one partner becomes overly dependent on the other. This situation increases the potential for opportunism on the part of the stronger partner. Opportunistic behavior takes advantage of a partner.
Learning. Strategic alliances and joint ventures often provide the participants the opportunity to "learn" from their partners.	**Partial loss of decision autonomy.** Joint planning and decision making may result in a loss of decision autonomy.
Speed to market. Firms with complementary skills, such as one firm being technologically strong and another having strong market access, partner to increase speed to market in hopes of capturing first-mover advantages.	**Partners' cultures may clash.** The corporate cultures of alliance partners may clash, making the implementation and management of the alliance difficult.
Neutralizing or blocking competitors. Through strategic alliances and joint ventures, firms can gain competencies and market power that can be used to neutralize or block the moves of a competitor.	**Loss of organizational flexibility.** Establishing a partnership with one firm may foreclose the possibility of establishing a partnership with another firm.

Source: Adapted from B. R. Barringer and J. S. Harrison, "Walking a Tightrope: Creating Value Through Interorganizational Relationships," *Journal of Management* 26, no. 3 (2002): 367–403.

1-800-Flowers.com: 40,000 Partners and Growing

www.1800flowers.com

1-800-Flowers.com sells fresh flowers and gifts for adults and children primarily through its toll-free number and the Internet. As is the case for many companies, it has a number of key partnerships. In the case of 1-800-FLOWERS, it promotes its products through strategic relationships with leading Web sites. The company's relationships include, among others, those it has established with America Online, Yahoo!, Microsoft, and American Greetings.

Although this collection of relationships sounds impressive, it might not be the firm's most important category of partnerships. The company also has an extensive affiliate program that has grown to approximately 40,000 Web sites operated by third parties. An affiliate program is a way for online merchants to get more exposure by offering a commission to Web sites that are willing to feature ads for their products. In the case of 1-800-FLOWERS, this is how it works. If you have a Web site, you can become part of the 1-800-FLOWERS affiliate program. 1-800-FLOWERS will provide you banner ads and other forms of advertising to place on your site. Each time a visitor from your site clicks through to the 1-800-FLOWERS site and makes a purchase, you earn a commission. If a customer from your site clicks through to 1-800-FLOWERS and doesn't buy anything right away but purchases something within 10 days, you are still credited for the sale. The company's affiliates include such Web sites as Looksmart.com, Upromise.com, Ebates.com, iWon.com, BizRate.com, and SchoolPop.com.

Well-managed affiliate programs, such as the one featured by 1-800-FLOWERS, are organized in a way that builds trust and ensures that affiliates get paid. For example, LinkShare tracks all 1-800-FLOWERS purchases made via an affiliate and then pays the affiliates at the end of each month. Commissions are paid on a sliding scale, depending on the amount purchased. 1-800-FLOWERS pays a commission of 6 percent for monthly sales under $1,000 and up to 8 percent for monthly sales over $12,500. The most attractive aspect of affiliate programs is that they are true win-win situations for all parties involved. 1-800-FLOWERS vastly increases its exposure by placing ads on 40,000 Web sites, and each time a purchase is made through one of those sites, the owner earns a commission.

1-800-FLOWERS "qualifies" its affiliates before they are admitted to the program. The qualifying step, which is commonly adopted by firms using affiliates, is included to ensure that the company doesn't partner with an affiliate that tarnishes its image or brand. In general, 1-800-FLOWERS is looking for affiliate Web sites characterized by the following:

- Are aesthetically pleasing
- Do not display content that may be deemed pornographic or offensive
- Are fully up and functional
- Are not personal home pages or personal Web sites

Through its affiliate program, 1-800-FLOWERS has literally created partnerships with the owners of over 40,000 Web sites. Worldwide, Forrester Research predicts that affiliate programs will represent 20 percent, or $53 billion, of e-commerce sales by 2005, compared with an estimated $10.5 billion in 2001.

Questions for Critical Thinking

1. All parties to a strategic alliance, such as those 1-800 FLOWERS has formed with various companies, must possess desirable attributes or skills. What does 1-800 FLOWERS "bring to the table" that is attractive to its partners? Prepare as comprehensive a list as possible to answer this question.

2. Ask several of your friends who have used the 1-800 FLOWERS service to describe their experiences. As customers, were they satisfied? If so, why? If not, what aspects of the firm's service disappointed your friends as customers, and what could 1-800 FLOWERS do to avoid those problems in the future?

Sources: 1-800-FLOWERS 2001 10-K filing, and 1-800-Flowers homepage, www.1800flowers.com (accessed April 12, 2004).

Technological alliances and marketing alliances are two of the most common forms of alliances.[22] **Technological alliances** feature cooperation in research and development, engineering, and manufacturing. Research-and-development alliances often bring together entrepreneurial firms with specific technical skills and larger, more mature firms with experience in development and marketing. By pooling their complementary assets, these firms can typically produce a product and bring it to market faster and cheaper than either firm could alone.[23] Pfizer's blockbuster drug Celebrex, for example, was created via a technological alliance. Celebrex is a prescription arthritis medicine. **Marketing alliances** typically match a company with a distribution system with a company that has a product to sell in order to increase sales of a product or service. For example, an American food company may initiate an alliance with Nestlé (a Swiss food company) to gain access to Nestlé's distribution channels in Europe. The strategic logic of this type of alliance for both partners is simple. By finding more outlets for its products, the partner that is supplying the product can increase economies of scale and reduce per-unit cost. The partner that supplies the distribution channel benefits by adding products to its product line, increasing its attractiveness to those wanting to purchase a wide array of products from a single supplier.

Both technological and marketing alliances allow firms to focus on their specific area of expertise and partner with others to fill their expertise gaps. This approach is particularly attractive to entrepreneurial firms, which often don't have the financial resources or time to develop all the competencies they need to bring final products to market quickly. Michael Dell describes the early years of Dell Inc.:

> As a small start-up, we didn't have the money to build the components [used to make up a PC] ourselves. But we also asked, "Why should we want to?" Unlike many of our competitors, we actually had an option: to buy components from the specialists, leveraging the investments they had already made and allowing us to focus on what we did best—designing and delivering solutions and systems directly to customers. In forging these early alliances with suppliers, we created exactly the right strategy for a fast-growing company.[24]

Joint Ventures   A **joint venture** is an entity created when two or more firms pool a portion of their resources to create a separate, jointly owned organization.[25] An example is Beverage Partners Worldwide, which is a joint venture between Coca-Cola and Nestlé. The joint venture markets ready-to-drink chilled teas and coffees, including Nestea, Nestea Cool, and Belte.

A common reason to form a joint venture is to gain access to a foreign market.[26] In these cases, the joint venture typically consists of the firm trying to reach a foreign market and one or more local partners. In 1999, Ask Jeeves formed Ask Jeeves International, a separate division of the company assigned to forming joint ventures with foreign companies to deliver country-specific versions of its Web site. When asked to describe what Ask Jeeves was looking for in a joint venture partner, Rob Wrubel, the company's CEO at the time, said, "We [focus] on forming joint ventures with strategic partners that provide access to mass audiences, powerful knowledge of a country's customers, and a keen understanding of the rapidly developing Internet marketplace."[27]

To date, Ask Jeeves has entered into joint venture arrangements with local partners to provide its search engine technology to the United Kingdom, Japan, and the worldwide Spanish-speaking market. Through these joint ventures, Ask Jeeves has gained access to local markets, knowledge of local customers, media exposure, and increased sales.

Joint ventures created for reasons other than foreign market entry are typically described as either scale or link joint ventures.[28] In a **scale joint venture**, the partners collaborate at a single point in the value chain to gain economies of scale in production or distribution. This type of joint venture can be a good vehicle for developing new products or services. For example, Pfizer, Microsoft, and IBM are partners in a joint venture that is developing software and services to handle administrative chores for physicians' offices.[29] In a **link joint venture**, the position of the parties is not symmetrical, and the objectives of the partners may diverge. For example, many of the joint ventures between American and Canadian food companies provide the American partner with access to Canadian markets and distribution channels and the Canadian partner with the opportunity to add to its product line.

Joint ventures formed by entrepreneurial firms are typically established to increase speed to market and capitalize on opportunities for innovation and learning. Microsoft, for example, had formed 20 joint ventures by 2000, primarily for these purposes. Among all joint ventures, those among competitors have the highest risk of failure because outside the joint venture, the partners' products and geographic markets often overlap.[30] This makes it difficult for the partners to define the boundaries of the joint venture and often leads to disagreements and discord.

A hybrid form of joint venture that has become popular among large high-tech firms is to take small equity stakes in promising young companies. In these instances, the large companies act in the role of corporate venture capitalists, as explained in Chapter 10. Intel officially established a venture-capital program in the early 1990s. Investing in private companies, this program's seeks to help start-up ventures grow from their initial stages to a

learning **objective**

10. Explain the term "joint venture" and describe the difference between a scale joint venture and a link joint venture.

point of either issuing an initial public offering or being acquired. As of July 2004, Intel had over 220 active investments fitting this profile.[31] The division of Intel's venture-capital program into three different funds to support different technological thrusts shows the sophistication of Intel's efforts as a corporate venture capitalist. Firms typically make investments of this nature in companies with the potential to be either suppliers or customers in the future. The equity stake provides the large company a "say" in the development of the smaller firm. On occasion, the larger firm that has a small equity stake will acquire the smaller firm. These transactions are called **spin-ins**. The opposite of a spin-in is a **spin-out**, which occurs when a larger company divests itself of one of its smaller divisions. Microsoft, for example, spun off Expedia, its Web travel site, in November 1999.

CHAPTER SUMMARY

1. Internal growth strategies rely on efforts generated within the firm itself, such as new product development, other product related strategies, international expansion, and Internet-driven strategies. External growth strategies rely on establishing relationships with third parties, such as mergers, licensing, strategic alliances, joint ventures, and franchising.

2. The keys to effective new product development are as follows: find a need and fill it, develop products that add value, get quality right and pricing right, focus on a specific target market, and conduct an ongoing feasibility analysis.

3. The reasons that new products fail include an inadequate feasibility analysis, overestimation of market potential, bad timing (i.e., introducing a product at the wrong time), inadequate advertising and promotion, and poor service.

4. A market penetration strategy seeks to increase the sales of a product or service through greater marketing efforts or through increased production capacity and efficiency.

5. International new ventures are businesses that, from inception, seek to derive significant competitive advantage from the use of resources and the sale of outputs in multiple countries.

6. Acquiring another business can fulfill several of a company's needs, such as expanding its product line, gaining access to distribution channels, achieving competitive economies of scale, or expanding the company's geographic reach.

7. A promising acquisition candidate has the following characteristics: operates in a growing industry, has proprietary products and/or processes, has a well-defined and established market position, has a good reputation, is involved in very little if any litigation, is open to the idea of being acquired by another firm, is positioned to readily obtain key third-party consent to an acquisition, and is located in a geographic area that is easily accessible from the acquiring firm's headquarters location.

8. Licensing is the granting of permission by one company to another company to use a specific form of its intellectual property under clearly defined conditions. Virtually any intellectual property a company owns can be licensed to a third party. Licensing can be a very effective way of earning income, particularly for intellectual property rich firms, such as software and biotech companies.

9. A strategic alliance is a partnership between two or more firms that is developed to achieve a specific objective or goal. Technological alliances involve cooperating in areas such as research and development, engineering, and manufacturing. Marketing alliances typically match one firm with a partner's distribution system that is attractive to the company trying to increase sales of its products or services.

10. A joint venture is an entity that is created when two or more firms pool a portion of their resources to create a separate, jointly owned organization. In a scale joint venture, the partners collaborate at a single point in the value chain to gain economies of scale in production or distribution by combining their expertise. In a link joint venture, the position of the parties is not symmetrical, and the objectives of the partners may diverge.

KEY TERMS

acquirer, 340
acquisition, 340
external growth strategies, 339
geographic expansion, 335
improving an existing product or service, 333
internal growth strategies, 330
international new ventures, 335
joint venture, 347
licensee, 343
licensing, 343
licensing agreement, 343
licensor, 343
link joint venture, 347
market penetration strategy, 333

marketing alliances, 346

merchandise and character
   licensing, 344

merger, 340

new product
   development, 331

organic growth, 331

outsourcing, 334

product line extension
   strategy, 334

scale joint venture, 347

spin-ins, 348

spin-outs, 348

strategic alliance, 345

target, 340

technological alliances, 346

technology licensing, 343

REVIEW QUESTIONS

1. Describe the difference between an internal and an external growth strategy. Provide examples of each strategy and how each one contributes to firm growth.

2. Under what circumstances is new product development a competitive necessity?

3. Describe some of the common reasons new products fail.

4. What is a market penetration strategy? Provide an example of a market penetration strategy and describe how effectively using it might increase a firm's sales.

5. What is a product line extension strategy? Provide an example of a product line extension strategy and describe how its effective use might increase a firm's sales.

6. What is a geographic expansion strategy, and what are the keys to implementing a successful geographic expansion strategy for an entrepreneurial firm? Make your answer as complete as possible.

7. What is an international new venture? Explain why it might be to the benefit of an entrepreneurial start-up to position itself as an international new venture from the outset.

8. What are the six foreign market entry strategies? Briefly describe each strategy.

9. What are several rules of thumb to follow for selling products overseas?

10. Describe the difference between a merger and an acquisition. In what ways can acquisitions help firms fill their needs?

11. What are the characteristics of a promising acquisition candidate?

12. What are the nine steps involved in completing an acquisition?

13. What does the term "licensing" mean? How can licensing be used to increase a firm's revenues?

14. Describe the purpose of a licensing agreement. In a licensing agreement, which party is the licensor, and which is the licensee?

15. Describe the difference between technology licensing and merchandise and character licensing. Provides examples of both types of licensing and how they can increase a firm's sales.

16. Over the past several years, why have strategic alliances and joint ventures become increasingly prevalent growth strategies? Make your answer as thoughtful and as thorough as possible.

17. Describe the difference between technological alliances and market alliances. Provide examples of both types of alliances and how they can increase a firm's sales.

18. What is a joint venture?

19. How does a joint venture differ from a strategic alliance?

20. Describe the difference between a scale joint venture and a link joint venture. Provide examples of both types of joint venture and how their effective use can increase a firm's sales.

APPLICATION QUESTIONS

1. Ann Beaty owns a database software firm in Portland, Oregon. She currently has three products that are sold through office supply stores in the Northwest. Ann is frustrated because she hasn't increased her revenues during the past three years. Provide Ann some suggestions for growth strategies she might pursue.

2. Taylor Jenkins has developed a new type of athletic shoe. He hopes to sell his product in retailers such as Foot Locker. Before he approaches Foot Locker, however, he wants to make sure that his product has the best chance of being successful. What criteria or rules of thumb can Taylor use to make sure that his product has "all the right stuff" before he takes it to Foot Locker?

3. Karen Paulsen has developed a new piece of computer hardware that she is convinced is a sure hit. She can't imagine that the product could fail. She just remembered that you are taking a course in entrepreneurship, however, and calls you on your cell phone. Her question is, "Is there a common set of reasons that cause products to fail? If there is, I'd like to know them so I can make sure to avoid them before I pitch my new product to anyone." What would you tell her?

4. Chad Caldwell manufacturers cookware that is sold to restaurants for their kitchens. He isn't really interested in developing new products but has been wondering lately about the options he has for increasing his sales. What

advice would you give Chad if he asked you if there are any "product-related strategies short of developing new products" that he could utilize to increase his sales?

5. Jim Morrissey owns a small tool-and-die shop that makes parts for the automobile industry. Lately, he has been wondering about exporting but has no idea whether exporting is a good idea for his firm. Provide Jim a list of factors to consider in assessing his firm's suitability for growth through international markets.

6. Donna Hawkins owns a small print shop in Sunnyvale, California. She is determined to grow her overall operation. She has decided to grow by acquiring other print shops and related businesses. She would like to start the process by broadly surveying the market to develop a "short list" of promising acquisition candidates. Help Donna make a checklist of the characteristics to evaluate in screening acquisition candidates.

7. Brian Brunner is an entrepreneur who has invented several devices that are used in the telecommunications industry. He has patented the devices, which he manufacturers in a job shop in St. Louis. Brian sells the devices directly to AT&T and Sprint. Last week, Brian got a certified letter in the mail from Motorola, indicating that firm's interest in licensing the technology that is represented in one of his devices. Brian doesn't know anything about licensing and has turned to you for help.

What would you tell Brian about licensing, and how would you suggest that he respond to Motorola's letter?

8. Imagine that you are the CEO of Burton Snowboards, a company that makes snowboards and related equipment. A clothing company has approached you about licensing your company's name in order to start selling a line of Burton Snowboard–labeled winter clothing, including sweaters, jackets, mittens, socks, and boots. What issues should you consider to evaluate this request?

9. Entrepreneur Mary Phillips is a software engineer and owns a small software company in Murfreesboro, Tennessee. A software firm in Cincinnati that would like to enter into a strategic alliance with her to share the research-and-development expense of producing a new software product, has approached her. Mary has asked you if this type of arrangement is common and if strategic alliances are a legitimate vehicle through which to achieve firm growth. What would you tell her?

10. Peter Cook owns an e-commerce Web site that sells camping and boating supplies. He spends a lot of time on the Internet and sees the phrase "affiliate program" periodically but has never really figured out what an affiliate program is all about. Explain to Peter what an affiliate program is and how he could set up an affiliate program to drive traffic to his Web site.

you be the VC

Company: NatureMaker (www.naturemaker.com)

Business Idea: Create handcrafted low-maintenance steel trees that are used in building lobbies and other enclosed areas to create a pleasant ambience.

Pitch: Many building owners use trees, shrubs, plants, and other vegetation to create a pleasant atmosphere in their lobbies, atriums, and other public areas. The owners often want a particular kind of tree or plant to fit the desired mood. Trees, in particular, can very effectively add to an atmosphere. For example, a hotel near Disney World may want a collection of palm trees to enhance the decor in its lobby and to place around its swimming pool. Traditionally, building owners have used real trees. The problem with real trees is that they are difficult to keep healthy and maintain, particularly if they are indoors. NatureMaker solves this problem by producing low-maintenance steel trees. The trees are created in NatureMaker's award-winning public studio under the direction of internationally renowned ecologist/sculptor Bennett Abrams. The trees feature proprietary, fire-retardant naturalistic bark that bonds permanently to the steel structure and looks remarkably real.

The company has produced a variety of steel trees, from seven-story redwoods to exotic sculpted banyans and palms. Each tree is individually crafted and is a testament to Mr. Abrams's sensitivity to nature and dedication to detail. The welders, sculptors, painters, scenic artists, and engineers who build the trees reflect Mr. Abrams's passion and energy in creating world-class, original arboreal art. Because of the flexibility that NatureMaker enjoys in "building" rather than growing its trees, it can create trees that function as educational tools, architectural ornaments, and sources of entertainment, along with trees that are strictly made to add to a building's decor. The firm's Web site offers pictures of many of the trees it has developed for customers.

Q&A: Based on the material covered in this chapter, what questions would you ask the firm's founders before making your funding decision? What answers would satisfy you?

Decision: If you had to make your decision on just the information provided in the pitch and the company's Web site, would you fund this firm? Why or why not?

Freeplay Energy: Poised for Growth by Creating Self-Sufficient Energy Products
www.freeplay.net

Have you ever had your cell phone battery go dead just when you needed it the most? What if you could reach around the back of the phone when that happens, turn a crank for 30 seconds, and generate enough juice for five more minutes of talk time? If you could buy a device to attach to your cell phone that could do that, would you? If your answer is yes, put a little money aside. Freeplay Energy, a British electronics company, has already developed a half-pound, hand-cranked generator for Motorola cell phones and is working on devices for other manufacturers' phones.

Freeplay has an interesting start-up story. In 1991, British inventor Trevor Baylis saw a television program about AIDS in Africa. A comment was made during the show that advice on how to prevent the spread of AIDS could be disseminated to people by radio, if only radios and in particular batteries weren't so expensive. In a flash of inspiration, Trevor wondered why radios couldn't be powered the same way as clocks by winding them up to produce energy. Trevor built a prototype of his idea that he called a "Clockwork Radio." The idea showed promise, and enough backing was generated to carry out the necessary scientific and market research to make the Clockwork Radio a reality.

While Trevor was completing his work, the Clockwork Radio concept was featured in a British television documentary in 1994 that was viewed by Chris Staines, another British inventor. Staines and his business partner, Rory Stear, immediately realized that the potential for self-sufficient electronics could go much further than radio. The partners decided to take Trevor's idea to the next level. Their next step was to obtain a grant from the British government to commercialize the idea, and the self-sufficient energy industry and Freeplay Energy Group (the company started to commercialize the idea) were born.

After perfecting the Clockwork Radio, Freeplay starting producing hand-cranked radios that were distributed by AIDS relief agencies in Africa. (A complete description of how hand-cranked radios work is provided on the Freeplay Web site.) The benefits of the radios were immediately recognized, and Freeplay garnered the attention and support of a number of humanitarian agencies, including the Red Cross, CARE, the European Union, and the United Nations. Over 150,000 Freeplay radios were eventually produced and distributed in at least 40 developing countries. It is estimated that these self-sufficient windup radios have benefited in excess of three million people directly and over 30 million people indirectly by providing them with a vehicle for information and education despite a lack of electricity and batteries in their communities.

To further investigate the possible applications of its Clockwork Radio technology, Freeplay quickly evolved into a commercial company focusing on designing and producing useful self-sufficient energy products. The company knew that it could apply its technology to almost any small electrical device, including flashlights, cell phones, laptop computers, and various types of radios. It also knew that users often get caught trying to use these types of devices when their batteries are low and no source of electricity is readily available. The company has branched out some and now produces self-sufficient energy via solar panels, rechargeable batteries, and its patented windup capabilities.

To spur its growth, Freeplay has developed key partnerships with several manufacturers, including Coleman, Motorola, Burton McCall, and Li & Fung Limited. These partnerships were formed to develop and distribute windup electronics products. Coleman is an American company that sells camping and outdoor recreational equipment. Through joint development efforts with the company, Freeplay has developed a range of Coleman-branded audio and illumination products that incorporate Freeplay's unique technology. In partnership with Motorola, Freeplay has developed a self-sufficient energy cell phone, as described earlier. Freeplay considers this alliance to be particularly important because Motorola's world-class brand and global distribution network allows Freeplay to showcase its self-sufficient energy technology to literally millions of potential cell phone customers around the world. Burton McCall is a major distributor in the United Kingdom and is partnering with Freeplay to distribute Freeplay-branded products throughout that nation. Finally, Li & Fung Limited is a Hong Kong–based outsource manufacturing firm that manufactures Freeplay-branded and cobranded products.

The most compelling aspect of Freeplay's offerings is that they cross almost all socioeconomic groups in terms of their appeal. The products are valuable in areas where consumers are not able to afford batteries or electricity. As described previously, Freeplay's products are typically distributed by relief agencies in these areas. The firm's products are also valuable to middle-class and affluent consumers who are constantly on the go. Commenting on the attractiveness of Freeplay-equipped cell phones, Gary Brandt, a Motorola spokesperson, remarked,

> The FreeCharge product [which is Motorola's name for its Freeplay cell phone attachment] will provide our customers with extended usage of their mobile phones. We understand that our consumer's lifestyles are more mobile today than ever before and, at Motorola, we are bringing products to market, such as the FreeCharge, that make their lives easier and their mobile phone experiences more reliable.

As it looks to the future, Freeplay is guided by a firm commitment to broaden its product offerings and "make energy available to everybody all of the time." The company's growth strategy is to maintain its leadership in creating and developing self-sufficient energy products by establishing its own products in the market and by forming strategic alliances with major partners.

Discussion Questions

1. Do you think Freeplay has a highly attractive business idea, an idea that is average in its potential, or an idea that will wane in its attractiveness as time goes on? Explain your answer.

2. What growth strategies is Freeplay currently utilizing? What, if any, additional growth strategies do you think the company should pursue?

3. What are the advantages and disadvantages of a growth strategy that relies heavily on establishing strategic alliances and joint ventures with larger firms? Which potential disadvantages of strategic alliances should Freeplay guard itself against as it continues to seek alliances with larger firms?

4. Is Freeplay a good acquisition candidate for a large electronics firm such as Philips, Motorola, or Sony? Why or why not?

Sources: Freeplay home page, www.freeplay.net (accessed October 4, 2003); Motorola home page, www.Motorola.com (accessed October 4, 2003); and Coleman home page, www.coleman.com (accessed October 4, 2003).

Case 14.2

SportsLine.com: Creating Novel Ways to Spur Corporate Growth
www.cbs.sportsline.com

If you're among the 100 million sports fans in America, you've probably heard of SportsLine.com. SportsLine.com is the leading provider of Internet sports content, e-commerce, contests, and fantasy leagues. It is the official Web site of the NFL, the PGA Tour, and the NCAA championships. SportsLine.com is also a major online partner of CBS and America Online (AOL).

SportsLine.com was founded in 1994. The company, which appeals to the same clientele as rival ESPN, has the stated goal to be "the number one global sports Internet company." To reach this goal, SportsLine.com has divided its revenue streams into two categories: (1) advertising and marketing services and (2) subscriptions and premium products. An analysis of these categories provides a picture of the road map that SportsLine.com is following to meet its growth and profitability objectives.

Advertising and Marketing Services

The advertising and marketing services category includes revenue from online ad sales, sponsorships, and e-commerce initiatives. Through its in-house staff, freelance sports journalists, and media partners, SportsLine.com provides up-to-date sports news and information for all major professional and college sports 24 hours a day, seven days a week, including previews, game summaries, audio and video clips, and color photographs. This information is distributed through the following Web sites, which SportsLine.com produces with a group that it envisions as a core group of strategic partners, such as the following:

- CBS.SportsLine.com
- NFL.com (and other league Web sites)
- Golfweb@pgatour.com
- MVP.com
- Vegasinsider.com

In most cases, SportsLine.com is responsible for the technical development, production, and maintenance of the Web sites it creates for third parties as well as customer service, merchandise sales, and other forms of support. In exchange for its services, SportsLine.com generally is entitled to receive a percentage of the sponsorships, advertising, and other revenues generated from the sites. In addition to these relationships, SportsLine.com is the exclusive provider of sports information to CBS and AOL. It also provides sports gaming information and features electronic odds on all major sports events through its Vegasinsider.com Web site.

Users of SportsLine.com's U.S.-targeted Web sites are predominantly male, 76 percent are between the ages of 25 and 54, 86 percent have attended college, and 43 percent have an annual incomes greater than $75,000. Because of these favorable demographics, SportsLine.com has actually grown its online advertising revenues during the past couple of years (on a year-over-year comparable basis) despite the general decline in online advertising revenues being experienced by many companies. The company also believes that there are a lot of sports fans who work in factories and other jobs where they don't use computers during the day and as a result do not spend a lot of their free time online. As these people eventually become regular Internet users, SportsLine.com feels that its user base will grow substantially.

Subscription and Premium Products

The subscription and premium products category includes fantasy products for professional sports leagues. These fantasy products allow participants to form their own teams by assembling a group of athletes from a sport and following their performance on a daily or weekly basis. These fantasy teams can then perform in competitions administered by SportsLine.com for merchandise or cash prizes. The teams can also compete in leagues administered by users on the company's Web site. During 2003, more than 100,000 paid fantasy leagues representing about 1.1 million teams, were formed in the company's fee-based baseball, football, basketball and hockey fantasy games. SportsLine.com also syndicates fantasy sports services on the Web. Its current clients in this area include NFL.com, AOL, and CNNSI.com.

In addition to separating its revenue streams into two distinct divisions, SportsLine.com has made additional key decisions that have impacted its growth potential. In early 2001, the company sold 6.9 million shares of common stock to CBS, giving the broadcaster a 32 percent stake in SportsLine.com. This initiative has broadened SportsLine.com's range of initiatives with CBS and, it is hoped, will provide CBS with added incentive to make its relationship with SportsLine.com more profitable than ever. The company has also continued to deepen its relationship with both AOL and the NFL. Both of these affiliations provide SportsLine.com with multiple alternatives to generate advertising and e-commerce revenues.

SportsLine.com has also engaged in a number of strategic acquisitions to broaden its portfolio of offerings and to speed up its pace of entry into key markets. In 1998, SportsLine.com acquired a company called GolfWeb to get itself into the golf business. Another acquisition was DBC sports, which provided SportsLine.com with access to competencies in the area of sports oddsmaking and analysis. This acquisition made SportsLine.com's Vegasinsider.com Web site and sports oddsmaking service possible. SportsLine.com's premier fantasy product, Commissioner.com, was also acquired via acquisition. SportsLine.com gained control of Commissioner.com, the number one fantasy product on the Internet, when it acquired

Daedalus Corporation. Looking forward, SportsLine.com is currently evaluating key acquisition targets in foreign markets, where it doesn't have the resources to go into a country, hire a staff, and cover sports as well as people who already have an established business in the country.

As SportsLine.com continues to grow, it hopes to see its strong brand and the scalability inherent in its business model show positive results. In mid-2004, the firm was projecting that it would be profitable during the last half of its 2004 fiscal year. The key drivers of SportsLine.com's efforts to grow and operate profitably will continue to be advertising and sponsorship income, along with strong performances on the part of its fantasy products and related offerings.

Discussion Questions

1. Evaluate SportsLine.com's strategies for growth. Do you think the company has done a good job generating positive avenues towards growth, or do you think there is more the company should be doing?

2. Name SportsLine.com's major strategic alliances. How important do you think these strategic alliances are to the company? How much do you think SportsLine.com would be hurt if it lost its alliances with CBS, AOL, or the NFL?

3. Do you think SportsLine.com's fantasy league products are sustainable, or do you think they are a fad that will eventually wane in terms of their popularity? How much of its future do you think the company should bet on these products?

4. What steps is SportsLine.com taking to position itself favorably against its largest rival, ESPN?

franchising

After studying this chapter, you should be ready to:

1. Explain what franchising is and how it differs from other forms of business ownership.

2. Describe the differences between a product and trademark franchise and a business format franchise.

3. Explain the differences among an individual franchise agreement, an area franchise agreement, and a master franchise agreement.

4. Describe the advantages of setting up a franchise system as a means of firm growth.

5. Identify the rules of thumb for determining when franchising is an appropriate form of growth for a particular business.

6. Discuss the factors to consider in determining whether owning a franchising is a good fit for a particular person.

7. Identify the costs associated with buying a franchise.

8. Discuss the advantages and disadvantages of buying a franchise.

9. Identify the common mistakes franchise buyers make.

10. Describe the purpose of the Uniform Franchise Offering Circular.

cartridge world: franchising for firm growth

There is one frustration that most computer printer owners have in common: the replacement cost of ink cartridges. When a cartridge runs out, it can often cost $30 or more to buy a replacement cartridge. That price seems steep to most students and other people—especially those that do a lot of printing!

If this scenario describes you, help is on the way. Cartridge World, a franchise organization that specializes in refilling empty cartridges, has opened 50 outlets in the United States. An indicator of how rapidly Cartridge World is growing is the fact that it is currently selling new franchises at the rate of five per week.

The idea behind Cartridge World is to offer an affordable alternative to buying expensive

printer replacement cartridges. A consumer can bring an empty ink cartridge to a Cartridge World store, wait while the cartridge is professionally refilled, and leave with a full cartridge at about half the price of a new one purchased from other sources.

Cartridge World was launched in Australia in 1988. To spur its growth, it started selling franchises in 1997. Since then, it has sold 360 franchises in Australia and Europe, and 50 in the United States. While the idea of refilling ink cartridges rather than buying new ones isn't new, Cartridge World is the first company to set up retail stores that offer ink cartridge refills while you wait. The bet is that consumers will make a habit of getting their existing cartridges refilled, rather than buying new ones, if the process is simple and convenient. To make the process convenient, Cartridge World wants to open stores at an aggressive pace. "We want to be the McDonald's of ink and toner," says Burt Yarkin, chief executive of Cartridge World North America, based in Emeryville, California. "We're going right into people's neighborhoods and becoming part of their daily lives."[1]

Cartridge World is using franchising as its growth strategy, primarily to co-opt the resources of its franchisees to quickly grow its business. The cost of a Cartridge World franchise is between $100,000 and $155,000, depending on the location. These figures, which include a one time franchise fee of $25,000 to $35,000 and the capital needed to start up the business, show the beauty of franchising for a company like Cartridge World. If Cartridge World sells 500 franchises in the United States in the next 10 years (which is probably a conservative estimate), the company will collect $12.5 million to $17.5 million in franchise fees, and its franchisees will invest between $25 million and $47.5 million for land and equipment to open their stores. This is money the company would have had to raise through other means if it had decided to expand via company-owned stores rather than franchise outlets.

With a focus on even more growth, Cartridge World offers a range of products including new ink and laser cartridges, specialty papers for quality photographic prints, copier toners, fax supplies, printers and cash register ribbons in addition to its core service of cartridge refilling. The idea behind adding products is to become a true one-stop-shop for printer supplies. To make sure that Cartridge World customers are properly guided in their purchase decisions, the company offers an intensive two-week training program for new franchisees. A new franchisee is acquainted with every aspect of operating a Cartridge World store, and is provided a detailed business operations manual and computer software. Additional training and technical advice is provided on an ongoing basis.

As with Cartridge World, many retail and service organizations find franchising an attractive method to facilitate firm growth. Some industries, such as restaurants, hotels, and automobile service, are dominated by franchise organizations. In other industries, franchising is less common, although franchise systems have recently popped up in industries as diverse as Internet Service Providers, furniture restoration, cellular services, and senior care.

There are some instances in which franchising is not appropriate. For example, new technologies are typically not introduced through franchise systems, particularly if the technology is kept secret or is complex. Why? Because franchising, by its very nature, involves the sharing of knowledge between a franchisor and its franchisees, and this, in large franchise organizations, can involve thousands of people. The inventors of new technologies typically involve as few people as possible in the process of rolling out their new products or services because they want to keep their trade secrets secret. They typically reserve their new technologies for their own use or license them to a relatively small number of companies, with strict confidentiality agreements in place.[2]

Still, franchising is a common method of business expansion and is growing in popularity. In 1950, fewer than 100 franchisors existed in the United States. Today, there are roughly 1,200 franchise systems in the United States, collectively accounting for about one-third of all retail sales.[3] The number of franchise systems grows by about 200 per year.[4] You can even go to a Web site (*www.franchising.com*) to examine the array of franchises available for potential entrepreneurs to consider. This Web site groups franchising opportunities by type (e.g., automotive, rental services, and so forth). This categorization highlights the breadth of franchising opportunities now available for consideration.

Unfortunately, not all the news about franchising is positive. Because many franchise systems operate in competitive industries and grow quickly, the failure rate is relatively high. It is estimated that three-quarters of all franchise systems fail within 12 years of their founding.[5] Plus, despite its proliferation, franchising is a relatively poorly understood form of business ownership and growth. While most students and entrepreneurs generally know what franchising is and what it entails, there are many subtle aspects to franchising that can be learned only through experience or careful study.

We begin this chapter, which is dedicated to franchising as an important potential path to entrepreneurship, with a description of franchising and when it is appropriate to use franchising. We then explore setting up a franchise system from the franchisor's per-

Smoothie franchises such as Planet Smoothie and Smoothie King are examples of business format franchises. Smoothie King has certainly used this approach to its advantage. It operates more than 340 locations in 34 states and opens new stores on a weekly basis in the U.S.

spective and buying a franchise from the franchisee's point of view. Next, we look at the legal aspects of franchising. We close this chapter by considering a few additional topics related to franchising.

What Is Franchising, and How Does It Work?

Franchising is a form of business organization in which a firm that already has a successful product or service (**franchisor**) licenses its trademark and method of doing businesses to other businesses (**franchisees**) in exchange for an initial franchise fee and an ongoing royalty.[6] Some franchisors are established firms, while others are first-time enterprises being launched by entrepreneurs. This section explores the origins of franchising and how franchising works.

learning **objective**

1. Explain what franchising is and how it differs from other forms of business ownership.

What Is Franchising?

The word "franchise" comes from an old dialect of French and means privilege or freedom. Franchising has a long history. In the Middle Ages, kings and lords granted franchises to specific individuals or groups to hunt on their land or to conduct certain forms of commerce. In the 1840s, breweries in Germany granted franchises to certain taverns to be the exclusive distributors of their beer for the region. Shortly after the U.S. Civil War, the Singer Sewing Machine Company began granting distribution franchises for its sewing machines and pioneered the use of written franchise agreements. Many of the most familiar franchises in the United States, including Kentucky Fried Chicken (1952), McDonald's (1955), Burger King (1955), Midas Muffler (1956), and H&R Block (1958), started in the post–World War II era of the 1940s and 1950s.

The franchise organization Comfort Keepers demonstrates how franchises are started. A year before the company was founded, Kristina Clum, a registered nurse, noticed that her parents were having trouble with ordinary daily chores. She wanted someone to come into their home to help them but was unable to find anyone. So Kristina and her husband Jerry founded a business dedicated to helping seniors cope with everyday nonmedical tasks, such as meal preparation, light housekeeping, grocery shopping, laundry, and errands. The first Comfort Keepers office was opened in Springfield, Ohio, in March 1998, and the second was opened in Dayton a year later.

Comfort Keepers is a timely idea that addresses a need for a particular target market. As we've discussed in earlier chapters, having a solid business idea is critical to achieving firm growth. In mid-2003, there were 35.9 million people in the United States over the age of 65. This figure accounted for 12 percent of the U.S. population in 2003. However, these figures are projected to increase to 86.7 million people over the age of 65 (representing 21 percent of the U.S. population) by the year 2050.[7] The services offered by Comfort Keepers may provide some seniors the option of staying in their homes as opposed to entering more costly assisted living centers.[8] In August 1999, the company began franchising and by 2004 had over 400 franchise outlets. At a total franchise investment cost of between $40,000 and $65,000, Comfort Keepers claimed that it was one of the least expensive franchises available to investors/entrepreneurs.[9]

The Comfort Keepers concept lends itself to franchising because the company has a good trademark and a good business method. And because the nature of the business keeps the cost of starting a Comfort Keepers franchise relatively low, as we noted previously, there is a substantial pool of people available to purchase the franchise. For Comfort Keepers and its franchisees, franchising is a win-win proposition. Comfort Keepers wins because it is able to use its franchisees' money to quickly grow its business and strengthen its brand. The franchisees win because they are able to start a business in a growing industry relatively inexpensively and benefit by adopting the Comfort Keepers trademark and method of doing business.

Another example of a sound franchise system is Batteries Plus, as illustrated in the boxed feature titled "Savvy Entrepreneurial Firm."

How Does Franchising Work?

There is nothing magical about franchising. It is a form of business growth that allows a business to get its products or services to market through the efforts of business partners or "franchisees." As described previously, a franchise is an agreement between a franchisor (the parent company, such as Comfort Keepers and Batteries Plus) and a franchisee (an individual or firm that is willing to pay the franchisor a fee for the right to sell its product, service, and/or business method).[10] Subway, for example, is a very successful franchise system. The franchisor (Subway, Inc.) provides the rights to individual businesspersons (the local franchisees) to use the Subway trademark and business methods. The franchisees, in turn, pay Subway a franchise fee and an ongoing royalty for these privileges and agree to operate their Subway restaurants according to Subway, Inc.'s standards.

learning **objective**

2. Describe the differences between a product and trademark franchise and a business format franchise.

There are two distinctly different types of franchise systems: the product and trademark franchise and the business format franchise. A **product and trademark franchise** is an arrangement under which the franchisor grants to the franchisee the right to buy its products and use its trade name. This approach typically connects a single manufacturer with a network of dealers or distributors. For example, General Motors has established a network of dealers that sell GM cars and use the GM trademark in their advertising and promotions. Similarly, British Petroleum (BP) has established a network of franchisee-owned gasoline stations to distribute BP gasoline. Product and trademark franchisees are typically permitted to operate in a fairly autonomous manner. The parent company, such as GM or BP, is generally concerned more with maintaining the integrity of its products than with monitoring the day-to-day activities of its dealers or station owners. Other examples of product and trademark franchise systems include agricultural machinery dealers, soft-drink bottlers, and beer distributorships. Rather than obtaining a royalty or franchise fee, the product and trademark franchisor obtains the majority of its income from selling its products to its dealers or distributors at a markup.

The second type of franchise, the **business format franchise**, is by far the more popular approach to franchising and is more commonly used by entrepreneurial firms. In a business format franchise, the franchisor provides a formula for doing business to the franchisee along with training, advertising, and other forms of assistance. Fast-food restau-

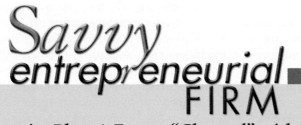

Batteries Plus: A Future "Charged" with Possibilities

www.batteriesplus.com

Savvy entrepreneurial firms recognize the difference between products that people think are *nice* to have and products that people *must* have. Typically, building a business around products that people must have—those that people rely on—is the better bet for firms wanting to consistently earn profits.

Consider batteries. Although most batteries are minor items in terms of their size and cost, they can cause havoc when they run down. Remember when you desperately needed a flashlight, and the batteries were dead or you were in the middle of an important cell phone call, and the battery ran out? Most people describe these occasions as a real hassle. And finding the right replacement battery for some items can be an even greater hassle.

Batteries Plus is a chain of batteries-only stores that are designed to help people solve these problems. The first store was opened in 1988 in Hartland, Wisconsin, and the company now has more than 225 with new locations opening weekly. The stores are typically in a freestanding building and have a bright and pleasant decor. The company's slogan, "1000's of Batteries for 1000's of Items," is an accurate description of what the business sells. In addition to selling batteries for common items such as flashlights, watches, cameras, and computers, the company sells batteries for unusual items such as larynx batteries for electronic voice boxes, batteries for glow-in-the dark fishing bobbers, and backup batteries for ATM machines. In fact, Batteries Plus has over 12,000 SKUs (stock-keeping units). This number of SKUs shows the breadth and depth of its product lines. The company also offers reconditioning and rebuilding

services for old batteries. Each Batteries Plus store has a "Tech Center," where trained technicians use state-of-the-art equipment to rebuild battery packs for items such as surveying equipment, scientific instruments, and laptop computers.

Batteries Plus believes that its future is bright. The market for batteries in the United States alone is $20 billion annually, and that figure is expected to increase 6.4 percent per year through the middle of this decade. The company also believes that as our society becomes more portable, consumers will increasingly rely on batteries for technological items such as laptops, cell phones, personal organizers, and pagers. With its dual emphasis on selling new batteries and rebuilding old ones, the company is prepared for a future that is "charged" with possibilities.

Questions for Critical Thinking

1. As a potential entrepreneur, would you be interested in considering Batteries Plus as a franchise operation? Why or why not? To answer this question, you might want to go to the firm's Web site (www.batteriesplus.com) to obtain additional information that could inform your decision.

2. If you were a franchisee for Batteries Plus, what risks would you face in your efforts to profitably operate your franchise?

Sources: "A Charged Up Business: Batteries Plus Offers Opportunity to Cash In on Today's Battery-Powered Society," Franchise Opportunities Guide, fall–winter 2001; Batteries Plus home page, www.batteriesplus.com (accessed May 26, 2004).

---

rants, convenience stores, Internet Service Providers, and consulting services are well-known examples of business format franchisees. While a business format franchise provides a franchisee a formula for conducting business, it can also be very rigid and demanding. For example, fast-food restaurants such as McDonald's and Wendy's teach their franchisees every detail of how to run their restaurants, from how many seconds to cook french fries to the exact words their employees should use when they greet customers (such as, "Will this be dining in, or carry out?"). Business format franchisors obtain the majority of their revenues from their franchisees in the form of royalties and franchise fees.

For both product and trademark franchises and business format franchises, the franchisor–franchisee relationship takes one of three forms of a franchise agreement. The most common type of franchise arrangement is an **individual franchise agreement**. This type of agreement involves the sale of a single franchise for a specific location. For example, an individual may purchase a CD Warehouse franchise to be constructed and operated at 901 West 10th Street in Boulder, Colorado. An **area franchise agreement** allows a franchisee to own and operate a specific number of outlets in a particular geographic area. For

learning **objective**

3. Explain the differences among an individual franchise agreement, an area franchise agreement, and a master franchise agreement.

example, a franchisee may purchase the rights to open six CD Warehouse franchises within the city limits of Jacksonville, Florida. Finally, a **master franchise agreement** is similar to an area franchise agreement, with one major difference. A master franchisee, in addition to having the right to open and operate a specific number of locations in a particular area, also has the right to offer and sell the franchise to other people in its area. For example, Fourth R is a franchise organization that provides computer training for businesses and adults. The company sells master franchise agreements that provide a master franchisee the right to open a certain number of Fourth R outlets in a defined geographic area. After its own outlets have been opened, the master franchisee can then sell the rights to open additional Fourth R locations in the same area to other individuals. The people who buy franchises from master franchisees are typically called **subfranchisees**.

An individual who owns and operates more than one outlet of the same franchisor, whether through an area or a master franchise agreement, is referred to as a **multiple-unit franchisee**. Multiple-unit franchisees are common in both small and large franchise chains, and this source of growth far outpaces the units added by new franchisees in most franchise organizations.[11] For the franchisee, there are advantages and disadvantages to multiple-unit franchising. By owning more than one unit, a multiple-unit franchisee can capture economies of scale and reduce its administrative overhead per unit of sale. The disadvantages of multiple-unit franchising are that the franchisor takes more risk and makes a deeper commitment to a single franchisor. In general, franchisors encourage multiple-unit franchising. By selling an additional franchise to an existing franchisee, a franchisor can grow its business without adding to the total number of franchisees with whom it must maintain a relationship to conduct its business.

Establishing a Franchise System

Establishing a franchise system should be approached carefully and deliberately. While the process is a familiar one to a company such as McDonald's, which as of March 2004 had established a total of 18,149 franchised restaurants (representing 62 percent of its total sales volume),[12] franchising is quite an unfamiliar process to new businesses, such as Cartridge World and Comfort Keepers. Franchising is a complicated business endeavor, and an entrepreneur must look closely at all of its aspects before deciding to franchise. It can often involve the managerially demanding tasks of training, supporting, supervising, and nurturing franchisees.

An entrepreneur should also be aware that over the years a number of fraudulent franchise organizations have come and gone and left financially ruined franchisees in their wake. Because of this, franchising is a fairly heavily regulated form of business expansion. Even with this regulation, though, caution is in order for those pursuing franchising as a business opportunity.

Despite the challenges, franchising is a popular form of expansion. It is particularly attractive to new firms in retailing and services because it helps firms grow quickly and alleviates the challenge of raising substantial amounts of money. There is some anecdotal evidence, however, that many companies are hasty in putting together their franchise programs and as a result do a poorer job than they could were they to take their time.[13] Although franchising is often touted as an easy way to rapidly expand a business, an effective franchise system needs to be as consciously initiated, managed, and supported as any other form of business expansion.[14]

Now let's look more closely at the issues to consider when putting together a franchise system.

When to Franchise

Retail firms grow when two things happen: first, when the attractiveness of a firm's products or services become well known, whether it is a new restaurant or an Internet consulting company, and, second, when a firm has the financial capability to build the outlets needed to satisfy its demand. In order for a company to grow, it has at least two options. One alternative is to build company-owned outlets. However, this choice presents a company with the challenge of raising the money to fund its expansion. As discussed in Chapter 10, this is typically done through debt, investment capital, or earnings, none of which is easy to achieve for a start-up venture.

Franchising is another growth alternative available to firms. Franchising is perhaps especially attractive to young firms in that the majority of the money needed for expansion comes from the franchisees. Franchising is appropriate when a firm has a strong or potentially strong trademark, a well-designed business method, and a desire to grow. A franchise system will ultimately fail if the franchisee's brand doesn't add value for customers and its business method is flawed or poorly developed.

In some instances, franchising is simply not appropriate. For example, franchising works for Burger King but would not work for Wal-Mart. While Burger King has a large number of franchise outlets, each individual outlet is relatively small and has a limited menu, and policies and procedures can be written to cover almost any contingency. In contrast, although Wal-Mart is similar to Burger King in that it too has a strong trademark and thousands of outlets, Wal-Mart stores are much larger, more expensive to build, and more complex to run than Burger King restaurants. It would be nearly impossible for Wal-Mart to find an adequate number of qualified people who would have the financial capital and expertise to open Wal-Mart stores of their own.

Steps to Franchising a Business

Setting up a franchise system is a nine-step process, as illustrated in Figure 15.1. The first step in developing a system that will remain successful is to set it up carefully and conscientiously.

Step 1. Develop a franchise business plan: The business plan should follow the format of a conventional business plan as we discussed in Chapter 9, and should fully describe the rationale for franchising the business and should act as a blueprint for rolling out the franchise operation.

Step 2. Get professional advice: Before going further, a potential franchisor should seek advice from a qualified franchise attorney, consultant, or certified public accountant. If the business is not realistically franchisable, then a qualified professional can save a potential franchisor a lot of time, money, and frustration by urging that the process be stopped. If the business is franchisable, then it is advisable to get professional advice to help direct the entire process.

Step 3. Conduct an intellectual property audit: As discussed in Chapter 12, this step is necessary to determine the intellectual property a company owns and to ensure that the property is properly registered and protected. All original written, audio, and visual material, including operating manuals, training videos,

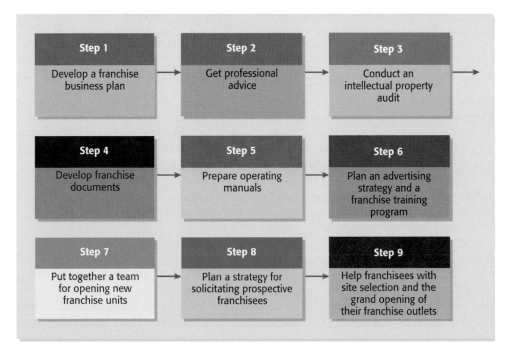

Figure 15.1

Nine Steps in Setting Up a Franchise System

advertising brochures, audiotapes, and similar matter, should be afforded copyright protection. If a firm has a unique business method, it should consider obtaining a business method patent. These protective measures are vital because once a company starts franchising, its trademarks and business methods will be disseminated, making them more visible to customers and competitors. In addition, a franchisor should make sure that its trademark is not infringing on the trademark of any other firm.

Step 4. Develop franchise documents: The documents necessary to franchise a business are discussed later in this chapter. At the beginning, however, a prospective franchisor should prepare the Uniform Franchise Offering Circular (this circular is explained in detail later in this chapter) and the Franchise Agreement. A franchise attorney can provide specific information regarding the content and format of these documents.

Step 5. Prepare operating manuals: Businesses that are suitable for franchising typically have a polished business system that can be fairly easily taught to qualified franchisees. The franchisor should prepare manuals that document all aspects of its business system.

Step 6. Plan an advertising strategy and a franchise training program: Prospective franchisees will want to see an advertising strategy and a franchisee-training program in place. The scope of each program should match the speed at which the franchisor wants to grow its business.

Step 7. Put together a team for opening new franchise units: A team should be developed and prepared to help new franchisees open their franchise units. The team should be well trained and equipped to provide the franchisee a broad range of training and guidance.

Step 8. Plan a strategy for soliciting prospective franchisees: There are many channels available to franchisors to solicit and attract potential franchisees. Franchise trade fairs, newspaper ads, franchise publications, and Internet advertising are examples of these channels.

Step 9. Help franchisees with site selection and the grand opening of their franchise outlet: Location is very important to most businesses, so a franchisor should be heavily involved in the site selection of its franchisees outlets. The franchisor should also help the franchisee with the grand opening of his or her franchise outlet.

Along with these specific steps, it is also important for a franchisor to remember that the quality of relationships that it maintains with its franchisees often defines the ultimate success of the franchise system. It is to the franchisor's advantage to follow through on all promises and to establish an exemplary reputation. This is an ongoing commitment that a franchisor should make to its franchisees.

Selecting and Developing Effective Franchisees

The franchisor's ability to select and develop effective franchisees strongly influences the degree to which a franchise system is successful. For most systems, the ideal franchisee is someone who has good ideas and suggestions but is willing to work within the franchise system's rules. Bold, aggressive entrepreneurs typically do not make good franchisees. Franchisees must be team players to properly fit within the context of a successful franchise system.

Once franchisees are selected, it is important that franchisors work to develop their franchisees' potential. Table 15.1 contains a list of the qualities that franchisors look for in prospective franchisees and the steps that franchisors can take to develop their franchisees' potential.

Advantages and Disadvantages of Establishing a Franchise System

learning **objective**

4. Describe the advantages of setting up a franchise system as a means of firm growth.

There are two primary advantages to franchising. First, early in the life of an organization, capital is typically scarce, and rapid growth is needed to achieve brand recognition and economies of scale. Franchising helps an organization grow quickly because franchisees

Table 15.1

Selecting and Developing Effective Franchisees

Qualities to Look for in Prospective Franchisees

- Good work ethic
- Ability to follow instructions
- Ability to operate with minimal supervision
- Team oriented
- Experience in the industry in which the franchise competes
- Adequate financial resources and a good credit history
- Ability to make suggestions without becoming confrontational or upset if the suggestion is not adopted
- Represents the franchisor in a positive manner

Ways Franchsiors Can Develop the Potential of Their Franchisees

- Provide mentoring that supersedes routine training
- Keep operating manuals up to date
- Keep product, services, and business systems up to date
- Solicit input from franchisees to reinforce their importance in the larger system
- Encourage franchisees to develop a franchise association
- Maintain the franchise system's integrity

provide the majority of the capital.[15] For example, if Comfort Keepers were growing via company-owned outlets rather than franchising, it would probably have only a handful of outlets rather than the more than 400 it has today. Many franchisors even admit that they would have rather grown through company-owned stores but that the capital requirements needed to grow their firms dictated franchising. This sentiment is affirmed by an executive at Hardee's who wrote the following about the growth of this fast-food chain:

> Hardee's would have preferred not to have franchised a single location. We prefer company-owned location. But due to the heavy capital investment required, we could only expand company-owned locations to a certain degree—from there we had to stop. Each operation represents an investment in excess of $100,000; therefore, we entered the franchise business.[16]

Second, a management concept called **agency theory**, which we discussed in Chapter 13, argues that for organizations with multiple units (such as restaurant chains), it is more effective for the units to be run by franchisees than by managers, who run company-owned stores. The theory is that managers, because they are usually paid a salary, may not be as committed to the success of their individual units as franchisees, who are in effect the owners of the units they manage.[17]

The primary disadvantage of franchising is that an organization allows others to profit from its trademark and business method. For example, each time Cartridge World sells a franchise, it gets a $22,750 franchise fee and an ongoing royalty, which is usually four to five percent of gross sales. However, if Cartridge World had opened a store itself in the same location, it would be getting 100 percent of the gross sales and net profits from the location. This is the main reason some organizations that are perfectly suitable for franchising grow through company-owned stores rather than franchising. An example is Darden Restaurants Inc., the parent company of Red Lobster, Olive Garden, Bahama Breeze, and Smokey Bones BBQ. With over 1,300 locations, this firm is the world's largest publicly held casual dining restaurant chain.[18] All of Darden's units are company owned. Starbucks and Jamba Juice are additional examples of companies that are suitable for franchising but have no franchise outlets. A more complete list of the advantages and disadvantages of franchising as a means of business expansion is provided in Table 15.2.

Table 15.2 Advantages and Disadvantages of Franchising as a Method of Business Expansion

Advantages	Disadvantages
Rapid, low-cost market expansion. Because franchisees provide most of the cost of expansion, the franchisor can expand the size of its business fairly rapidly.	***Profit sharing.*** By selling franchises instead of operating company-owned stores, franchisors share the profits derived from their proprietary products or services with their franchisees. For example, before being acquired by FedEx, Kinko's did not sell franchises, allowing it to retain all its profits.
Income from franchise fees and royalties. By collecting franchise fees, the franchisor gets a fairly quick return on the proprietary nature of its products/services and business system. The franchisor also receives ongoing royalties from its franchisees without incurring substantial risk.	***Loss of control.*** It is typically more difficult for a franchisor to control its franchisees than it is for a company to control its employees. Franchisees, despite the rules governing the franchise system, still often view themselves as independent businesspeople.
Franchisee motivation. Because franchisees put their personal capital at risk, they are highly motivated to make their franchise outlets successful. In contrast, the managers of company-owned outlets typically do not have their own capital at risk. As a result, these managers may not be prone to work as hard as franchisees or be as attentive to cost savings.	***Friction with franchisees.*** A common complaint of franchisors is dealing with the friction that often develops between franchisors and franchisees. Friction can develop over issues such as the payment of fees, hours of operation, caveats in the franchise agreement, and surprise inspections.
Access to ideas and suggestions. Franchisees represent a source of intellectual capital and often make suggestions to their franchisors. By incorporating these ideas into their systems, franchisors can in effect leverage the ideas and suggestions of their individual franchisees.	***Managing growth.*** Franchisors that are in growing industries and have a strong trademark often grow quickly. While this might seem like an advantage, rapid growth can be difficult to manage. A franchisor provides each of its franchisees a number of services, such as site selection and employee training. If a franchise system is growing rapidly, the franchisor will have to continually add personnel to its own staff to properly support its growing number of franchisees.
Cost savings. Franchisees share many of the franchisor's expenses, such as the cost of regional and national advertising.	***Differences in required business skills.*** The business skills that made a franchisor successful in his or her original business are typically not the same skills needed to manage a franchise system. For example, Sam Jones may be a very effective owner/manager of a seafood restaurant. That does not necessarily mean, however, that he will be an effective manager of a franchise system if he decided to franchise his seafood restaurant concept.
Increased buying power. Franchisees provide franchisors increased buying power by enlarging the size of their business systems, allowing them to purchase larger quantities of products and services when buying those items.	***Legal expenses.*** Many states have unique laws pertaining to franchising. As a result, if a franchisor sells franchises in multiple states, legal expenses can be high to properly interpret and comply with each state's laws. Unfortunately, from the franchisor's point of view, some of the toughest laws are in the most populated states.

learning **objective**

5. Identify the rules of thumb for determining when franchising is an appropriate form of growth for a particular business.

When a company decides to investigate franchising as a means of facilitating growth, it should ensure that it and its product or service meet several criteria. Businesses that vary from these heuristics are less likely to make effective franchise systems. Before deciding to franchise, a firm should consider the following:

- *The uniqueness of its product or service:* The business's product or service should be unique along some dimension that customers value. Businesses with a unique product or service typically have the best potential to expand.
- *The consistent profitability of the firm:* The business should be consistently profitable, and the future profitability of the business should be fairly easy to predict. When developing a franchise system, a company should have several prototype outlets up and running to test and ensure the viability of the business concept. Remember, a franchisee is supposed to be buying a method of doing business that is "proven"—at least to a certain extent. Franchisors who learn how to run their businesses through the trial and error of their franchisees have typically franchised their businesses prematurely (especially from the franchisees' point of view).

- *The firm's year-round profitability:* The business should be profitable year-round, not only during specific seasons. For example, a lawn and garden care franchise in North Dakota should be set up to provide the franchisee supplemental products and services to sell during off-peak seasons. Otherwise, owning the franchise may not be an attractive substitute for a full-time job.
- *The degree of refinement of the firm's business systems:* The systems and procedures for operating the business should be polished and the procedures documented in written form. The systems and procedures should also be fairly easy to teach to qualified candidates.
- *The clarity of the business proposition:* The business proposition should be crystal clear so that the prospective franchisee fully understands the business proposition to which he or she is committing. The relationship between the franchisor and the franchisee should be completely open, and communication between them should be candid.

After determining that its firm satisfies these criteria, a company should step back and review all the alternatives for business expansion. No single form of business expansion is the best under all circumstances. For any business, the best form of expansion is the one that increases the likelihood the firm will reach its objectives.

In some instances, the ability to establish creative partnerships forms the basis for a franchise organization, as illustrated in the boxed feature titled "Partnering for Success."

KnowledgePoints Launches a Successful Franchise System Through Creative Partnership Arrangements

www.knowledgepoints.org
In 1979, W. Barry Fowler founded Sylvan Learning Centers to provide a tutoring service to help kids improve their reading and math skills. Since then, Sylvan has grown to over 900 centers and has helped more than one million students improve their academic performance.

In 1985, Mr. Fowler sold his interest in Sylvan but stayed on for a few years as an executive. In the mid-1990s, an acquaintance told Mr. Fowler that her daughter had been diagnosed with a reading problem but that the family couldn't afford the $45-an-hour tutoring charged by Sylvan and similar centers. That dilemma inspired Mr. Fowler to find a way to provide high-quality tutoring to kids in need at a more affordable price. After experimenting with various business models, Mr. Fowler founded KnowledgePoints to address the problem. Here's how it works.

KnowledgePoints is a for-profit tutoring service that partners with nonprofits to deliver its services. KnowledgePoints provides the tutors and its partners, including churches, schools, parks departments, YMCAs, and occasionally for-profit places such as health clubs, with the facilities for the tutoring. The tutoring costs $25 to $30 an hour—which is well below the cost of Sylvan and similar centers. By partnering with nonprofits, KnowledgePoints is able to significantly lower its facility

and personnel costs, and the company passes those savings on to customers.

KnowledgePoints is a franchise organization, although its does not sell individual franchises. Instead, it sells geographic territories of 400,000 people for $50,000 and up. This approach allows a franchisee to work with multiple sites and provides for uniform quality of tutoring across a geographic area.

Through its creative approach to partnering, KnowledgePoints is able to fulfill its mission of providing tutoring to children who wouldn't be able to afford it otherwise.

Questions for Critical Thinking

1. As a potential entrepreneur, would you be interested in obtaining a KnowledgePoints geographic territory? Why or why not?

2. What is your reaction to the firm's apparent mixing of for-profit entrepreneurship with a social objective? Is this a reasonable course of action for a firm to take? Can entrepreneurs be socially responsible while seeking to generate profits through their firm's operations?

Sources: P. Thomas, "Creative Partnerships Unlock a New Market," Wall Street Journal, June 24, 2003, B9, and KnowledgePoints home page, www.knowledgepoints.com (accessed November 16, 2003).

Buying a Franchise

Now let's look at franchising from the franchisee's perspective. Purchasing a franchise is an important business decision involving a substantial financial commitment. Potential franchise owners should strive to be as well informed as possible before purchasing a franchise and should be well aware that it is often legally and financially difficult to exit a franchise relationship. Indeed, an individual franchise opportunity should be meticulously scrutinized. Close scrutiny of a potential franchise opportunity includes activities such as meeting with the franchisor and reading the Uniform Franchise Offering Circular, soliciting legal and financial advice, and talking to former franchisees who have dropped out of the system one is considering. In particularly heavily franchised industries, such as fast food and automobile repair, a prospective franchisee may have 20 or more franchisors from which to make a selection. It is well worth a franchisee's time to carefully select the franchisor that best meets his or her individual needs.[19]

Is Franchising Right for You?

learning objective

6. Discuss the factors to consider in determining whether owning a franchising is a good fit for a particular person.

Purchasing a franchise should be weighed against the alternatives of buying an existing business or launching an entrepreneurial venture from scratch. Answering the following questions will help determine whether franchising is a good fit for people thinking about starting their own business:

- Are you willing to take orders? Franchisors are typically very particular about how their outlets operate. For example, McDonald's and other successful fast-food chains are very strict in terms of their restaurants' appearance and how the units' food is prepared. Franchising is typically not a good fit for people who like to experiment with their own ideas or are independently minded.
- Are you willing to be part of a franchise "system" rather than an independent businessperson? For example, as a franchisee you may be required to pay into an advertising fund that covers the costs of advertising aimed at regional or national markets rather than the market for your individual outlet. Will it bother you to have someone use your money to develop ads that benefit the "system" rather than only your outlet or store? Are you willing to lose creative control over how your business is promoted?
- How will you react if you make a suggestion to your franchisor and your suggestion is rejected? How will you feel if you are told that your suggestion might work for you but can be put in place only if it works in all parts of the system?
- What are you looking for in a business? How hard do you want to work?
- How willing are you to put your money at risk? How will you feel if your business is operating at a net loss but you still have to pay royalties on your gross income?

None of these questions is meant to suggest that franchising is not an attractive method of business ownership. It is important, however, that a potential franchisee be fully aware of the subtleties involved with franchising before purchasing a franchise outlet.

The Cost of a Franchise

learning objective

7. Identify the costs associated with buying a franchise.

The initial cost of a business format franchise varies, depending on the franchise fee, the capital needed to start the business, and the strength of the franchisor. The average initial investment for about 8 of every 10 franchise units operating in the United States is less than $250,000 (excluding the cost of real estate).[20] Capital costs vary. For example, McDonald's typically provides the land and buildings for each franchisee's unit. In contrast, other organizations require their franchisees to purchase the land, buildings, and equipment needed to run their franchise outlets. Table 15.3 shows the total costs of buying into several franchise organizations. As you can see, the total initial cost ranges from a low of $36,000 for a Curves International franchise to more than $2.8 million for a Burger King franchise.

Also shown in Table 15.3 is a breakdown of the number of company-owned units and the number of franchise units maintained by each organization. Company-owned units are managed and operated by company personnel, and there is no franchisee involved. Franchise organizations vary in their philosophies regarding company-owned versus franchised units. As we noted earlier in this chapter, some companies (e.g., Subway) are strictly

Table 15.3 Initial Costs to the Franchisee of a Sample of Franchise Organizations

Franchise Organization	Year Founded	Company-Owned Units	Franchised Units	Franchise Fee	Capital Requirements	Total Initial Cost to the Franchisee
Burger King	1954	746	7,500	$40,000	$300,000+	$340,000+
CD Warehouse	1992	64	239	$20,000	$132,000–$169,000	$152,000–$189,000
Comfort Keepers	1998	3	158	$13,750	$18,900–$37,900	$32,650–$51,650
General Nutrition Centers	1935	2,842	1,718	$35,000	$132,681–$182,031	$167,681–$217,031
Image Art Etc.	1999	0	30	$22,750	$50,000–$60,000	$72,750–$82,750
Smoothie King	1973	1	261	$25,000	$40,000–$50,000	$65,000–$75,000
Subway	1965	0	14,700	$10,000	$63,400–$174,700	$73,400–$184,700
WSI Internet	1995	0	700+	$34,700	$35,000–$50,000	$69,700–$84,700

Source: The Franchise Handbook, spring 2002.

franchisors and have no company-owned units. Other companies, such as General Nutrition Centers, maintain large numbers of both company-owned and franchised units.

When evaluating the cost of a franchise, prospective franchisees should consider all the costs involved. Franchisors are required by law to disclose all their costs in a document called the Uniform Franchise Offering Circular and send it to the franchisee. (We'll talk about this document in more detail later in this chapter.) To avoid making a hasty judgment, a franchisee may not purchase a franchise for 10 days from the time the circular is received. The following costs are typically associated with buying a business format franchise:[21]

- *Initial franchise fee:* The initial franchise fee varies, depending on the franchisor, as shown in Table 15.3.
- *Capital requirements:* These costs vary, depending on the franchisor, but may include the cost of buying real estate, the cost of constructing a building, the purchase of initial inventory, and the cost of obtaining a business license. Some franchisors also require a new franchisee to pay a "grand opening" fee for its assistance in opening the business.
- *Continuing royalty payment:* In the majority of cases, a franchisee pays a royalty based on a percentage of weekly or monthly gross income. Note that since the fee is typically assessed on gross income rather than net income, a franchisee may have to pay a monthly royalty even if the business is losing money. Royalty fees are usually around five percent of gross income.[22]
- *Advertising fees:* Franchisees are often required to pay into a national or regional advertising fund, even if the advertisements are directed at goals other than promoting the franchisor's product or service. (For example, advertising could focus on the franchisor's attempt at attracting new franchisees.) Advertising fees are typically less than three percent of gross income.
- *Other fees:* Other fees may be charged for various activities, including training additional staff, providing management expertise when needed, providing computer assistance, or providing a host of other items or support services.

The most important question a prospective franchisee should consider is whether the fees and royalties charged by a franchisor are consistent with the franchise's value or worth. If they are, then the pricing structure may be fair and equitable. If they are not, then the terms should be renegotiated or the prospective franchisee should look elsewhere.

Finding a Franchise

There are thousands of franchise opportunities available to prospective franchisees. The most critical step in the early stages of investigating franchise opportunities is to determine the type of franchise that is the best fit. For example, it is typically unrealistic for someone who is not a mechanic to consider buying a muffler repair franchise. A franchisor teaches a franchisee a business system, not a trade. Before buying a franchise, a potential franchisee should imagine him- or herself operating the prospective franchise or, better yet, should spend a period of time working in one of the franchisor's outlets. After working in a print shop for a week, for example, someone who thought she might enjoy running a print shop might find out that she hates it. This type of experience could help someone avoid making a mistake that is costly both to him or her as a franchisee and to the franchisor.

There are many periodicals, Web sites, and associations that provide information about franchise opportunities. Every Thursday, for example, ads for franchise opportunities appear in special sections of the *Wall Street Journal* and *USA Today*. Periodicals featuring franchise opportunities include *Inc., Entrepreneur* (especially the January issues), *Nation's Business*, and franchise-specific magazines such as *The Franchise Handbook* and *Franchise Opportunities Guide*. Prospective franchisees should also consider attending franchise opportunity shows that are held periodically in major U.S. cities and the International Franchise Exposition, which is held annually in Washington, D.C. The Small Business Administration is another good source of franchise information.

Because of the risks involved in franchising, the selection of a franchisor should be a careful, deliberate process. One of the smartest moves a potential franchise owner could make is to talk to current franchisees and inquire whether they are making money and whether they are satisfied with their franchisor. Table 15.4 contains a list of sample questions to ask a franchisor and some of its current franchisees before investing.

Advantages and Disadvantages of Buying a Franchise

There are two primary advantages to buying a franchise over other forms of business ownership. First, franchising provides an entrepreneur the ability to own a business using a tested and refined business method. This attribute lessens the probability of business fail-

learning **objective**

8. Discuss the advantages and disadvantages of buying a franchise.

Table 15.4

Questions to Ask before Buying a Franchise

Questions to Ask a Franchisor

- What is the background of the company and its performance record?
- What is the company's current financial status?
- What are the names, addresses, and phone numbers of existing franchisees in my trade area?
- Describe how you train and mentor your franchisees.
- If at some point I decide to exit the franchise relationship, how does the exit process work?
- In what ways do you work with a franchisee that is struggling?

Questions to Ask Current Franchisees

- How much does your franchise gross per year? How much does it net? Are the procedures followed to make royalty payments to the franchisee burdensome?
- Are the financial projections of revenues, expenses, and profits that the franchisor provided me accurate in your judgment?
- Does the franchisor give you enough assistance in operating your business?
- How many hours, on average, do you work?
- How often do you get a vacation?
- Have you been caught off guard by any unexpected costs or expectations?
- Does your franchisor provide you ongoing training and support?
- If you had to do it all over again, would you purchase a franchise in this system? Why or why not?

ure. In addition, the trademark that comes with the franchise often provides instant legitimacy for a business.[23] For example, a woman opening a new Curves fitness center would likely attract more customers than a woman opening a new independently owned fitness center because many women who are a part of the target market of Curves have already heard of the firm and have a positive impression of it. Second, when an individual purchases a franchise, the franchisor typically provides training, technical expertise, and other forms of support. For example, many franchise organizations provide their franchisees periodic training both at their headquarters location and in their individual franchise outlets.

The main disadvantage of buying a franchise is the cost involved. As mentioned earlier, the franchisee must pay an initial franchise fee. He or she must also pay the franchisor an ongoing royalty as well as pay into a variety of funds, depending on the franchise organization. Thus, franchisees have both immediate (i.e., the initial franchise fee) and long-term (i.e., continuing royalty payments) costs. By opening an independent business, an entrepreneur can keep 100 percent of the profits if it is successful.

Table 15.5 contains a list of the advantages and disadvantages of buying a franchise.

Table 15.5   Advantages and Disadvantages of Buying a Franchise

Advantages	Disadvantages
A proven product or service within an established market. The most compelling advantage of buying a franchise is that the franchise represents a proven product or service within an established market.	***Cost of the franchise.*** The initial cost of purchasing and setting up a franchise operation can be quite high, as illustrated in Table 15.3.
An established trademark or business system. The purchase of a franchise with an established trademark provides franchisees with considerable market power. For example, the purchaser of a McDonald's franchise has a trademark with proven market power.	***Restrictions on creativity.*** Many franchise systems are very rigid and leave little opportunity for individual franchisees to exercise their creativity. This is an often-cited frustration of franchisees.
Franchisor's training, technical expertise, and managerial experience. Another important attribute of franchising is the training, technical expertise, and managerial experience that the franchisor provides the franchisee.	***Duration and nature of the commitment.*** For a variety of reasons, many franchise agreements are difficult to exit. In addition, virtually every franchise agreement contains a noncompete clause. These clauses vary in terms of severity, but a typical clause prevents a former franchisee from competing with the franchisor for a period of two years or more.
An established marketing network. Franchisees that buy into a powerful franchise system are part of a system that has tremendous buying power and substantial advertising power and marketing prowess.	***Risk of fraud, misunderstandings, or lack of franchisor commitment.*** Along with the many encouraging stories of franchise success, there are also many stories of individuals who purchase a franchise only to be disappointed by the franchisor's broken promises.
Franchisor ongoing support. One of the most attractive advantages of purchasing a franchise rather than owning a store outright is the notion that the franchisor provides the franchisee ongoing support in terms of training, product updates, management assistance, and advertising. A popular slogan in franchising is that people buy franchises to "be in business for themselves but not by themselves."	***Problems of termination or transfer.*** Some franchise agreements are very difficult and expensive to terminate or transfer. Often, a franchisee cannot terminate his or her franchise agreement without paying the franchisor substantial monetary damages.
Availability of financing. Some franchisors offer financing to their franchisees, although these cases are the exception rather than the rule. This information is available in section 10 of the UFOC.	***Poor performance on the part of other franchisees.*** If some of the franchisees in a franchise system start performing poorly and make an ineffective impression on the public, that can affect the reputation and eventually the sales of a well-run franchise in the same system.
Potential for business growth. If a franchisee is successful in its original location, the franchisee is often provided the opportunity to buy additional franchises from the same franchisor. For many franchisees, this prospect offers a powerful incentive to work hard to be as successful as possible.	***Potential for failure.*** Some franchise systems simply fail to reach their objectives. When this happens, franchisees' wealth can be negatively affected. Indeed, when a franchise system fails, it commonly brings its franchisees down with it.

Steps in Purchasing a Franchise

Purchasing a franchise system is a seven-step process, as illustrated in Figure 15.2. The first rule of buying a franchise is to avoid making a hasty decision. Again, owning a franchise is typically costly and labor intensive, and the purchase of a franchise should be a careful, deliberate decision. Once the decision to purchase a franchise has been nearly made, however, the following steps should be taken. If at any time prior to signing the franchise agreement the prospective franchisee has second thoughts, the process should be stopped until the prospective franchisee's concerns are adequately addressed.

Step 1. Visit several of the franchisor's outlets: Prior to meeting with the franchisor, the prospective franchisee should visit several of the franchisor's outlets and visit with their owners and employees. During the visits, the prospective franchisee should continually ask herself, "Is this the type of business I would enjoy owning and operating or managing?"

Step 2. Retain a franchise attorney: A prospective franchisee should have an attorney that represents his or her interests, not the franchisor's. The attorney should prepare the prospective franchisee for meeting with the franchisor and should review all franchise documents before they are signed. If the franchisor tries to discourage the prospective franchisee from retaining an attorney, this is a red flag.

Step 3. Meet with the franchisor and check the franchisor's references: The prospective franchisee should meet with the franchisor, preferably at the franchisor's headquarters. During the meeting, the prospective franchisee should compare what she observed firsthand in the franchised outlets with what the franchisor is saying. Additional references should also be checked. The Uniform Franchise Offering Circular is a good source for references. In section 20 of this document, there is a list of all the franchisees that have dropped out of the system in the past three years along with their contact information. Several of these should be called. Although it may seem to be overkill, the mantra for prospective franchisees is to check, double-check, and triple-check a franchisor's references.

Step 4. Review all franchise documents with the attorney: The franchise attorney should review all the franchise documents, including the Uniform Franchise Offering Circular and the franchise agreement.

Figure 15.2

Seven Steps in Purchasing a Franchise

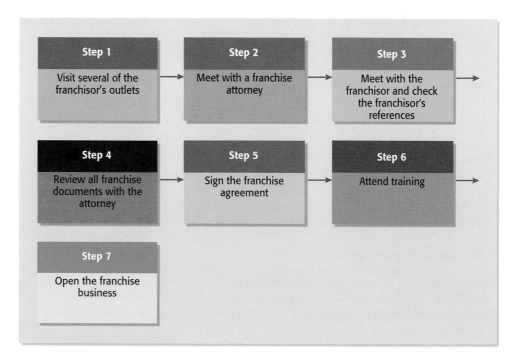

Step 5. Sign the franchise agreement: If everything is a go at this point, the franchise agreement can be signed. The franchise agreement is the document in which the provisions of the franchisor–franchisee relationship are outlined. We discuss this agreement in greater detail later in this chapter.

Step 6. Attend training: Almost all franchise organizations provide their franchisees training. For example, Cartridge World, as mentioned in this chapter's opening feature, requires each of its new franchisees to attend a two week training program at its corporate headquarters.

Step 7. Open the franchise business: For many franchises, particularly restaurants, the first two to three weeks after it opens may be its busiest period, as prospective customers "try it out." This is why many franchise organizations send experienced personnel to help the franchisee open his or her business as smoothly as possible. One goal of a franchisee is generating positive word of mouth about his or her business right from the start.

Watch Out! Common Misconceptions About Franchising

learning **objective**

9. Identify the common mistakes franchise buyers make.

Despite the abundance of advice available to them, many franchisees make false assumptions about franchising. Part of the explanation for this is that franchising has an attractive lure. It is easy to become enthralled with the promise of franchising and not spend an adequate amount of time examining the potential pitfalls. The following is a list of misconceptions that franchisees often have about franchising.

- *Franchising is a safe investment:* Franchising, in and of itself, is no safer an investment than any other form of business ownership.

- *A strong industry ensures franchise success:* While it is generally important to operate in a growing industry, the strength of an industry does not make up for a poor product, a poor business system, poor management, or inappropriate advertising. There are many firms that fail in growing industries just as there are firms that succeed in unattractive ones.

- *A franchise is a "proven" business system:* A franchisor sells a franchisee the right to use a system. Whether the system is proven or not is subject to the test of time. Obviously, companies such as Subway and McDonald's have systems that are polished and that have worked well over time. Most prospective franchisees, however, cannot afford a McDonald's or a Subway unit and will be considering a lesser-known franchise. All too frequently, companies start selling franchises before their systems are anywhere close to being proven.

- *There is no need to hire a franchise attorney or an accountant:* Professional advice is almost always needed to guide a prospective franchisee through the franchise purchase process. A prospective franchisee should never give in to the temptation to save money by relying solely on the franchisor's advice.

- *The best systems grow rapidly, and it is best to be a part of a rapid-growth system:* While some franchise systems grow rapidly because they have a good trademark and a polished business system, other franchise systems grow quickly because their major emphasis is on selling franchises. While it is to a franchisee's benefit to be part of a system that has a solid trademark and business system—as that trademark and system will attract more customers—some franchise systems grow so quickly that they outrun their ability to provide their franchisees adequate support.

- *I can operate my franchise outlet for less than the franchisor predicts:* The operation of a franchise outlet usually costs just as much as the franchisor predicts.

- *The franchisor is a nice person—he'll help me out if I need it:* Although it may be human nature to rely on the goodwill of others, don't expect anything from your franchisor that isn't spelled out in the franchise agreement.

Legal Aspects of the Franchise Relationship

According to the Federal Trade Commission, a franchise exists any time that the sale of a business involves (1) the sale of goods or services that bear a trademark, (2) retention of significant control or assistance by the holder of the trademark on the operation of the business, and (3) royalty payments by the purchaser of the business to the owner of the trademark for the right to use the trademark in the business.

The legal and regulatory environment surrounding franchising is based on the premise that the public interest is served if prospective franchisees are as informed as possible regarding the characteristics of a particular franchisor. The offer and sale of a franchise is regulated at both the state and the federal level.

Federal Rules and Regulations

Except for the automobile and petroleum industries, federal laws do not directly address the franchisor–franchisee relationship. Instead, franchise disputes are matters of contract law and are litigated at the state level. During the 1990s, Congress considered several proposals for federal legislation to govern franchise relationships, but none became law.

However, the offer and sale of a franchise is regulated at the federal level. According to Federal Trade Commission (FTC) Rule 436, franchisors must furnish potential franchisees with written disclosures that provide information about the franchisor, the franchised business, and the franchise relationship. The disclosures must be supplied at least 10 business days before a franchise agreement can be signed or the franchisee pays the franchisor any money.[24] In most cases, the disclosures are made through a lengthy document referred to as the **Uniform Franchise Offering Circular** (UFOC), which is accepted in all 50 states and parts of Canada. The UFOC contains 23 categories of information that give a prospective franchisee a broad base of information about the background and financial health of the franchisor. A summary of the information contained in the UFOC is provided in Table 15.6. A prospective franchisee should fully understand all the information contained in the UFOC before a franchise agreement is signed.

The UFOC requires the franchisor to attach a copy of the franchise agreement and any other related contractual documents to the circular. The **franchise agreement**, or contract, is the document that consummates the sale of a franchise. While franchise agreements vary,

learning **objective**

10. Describe the purpose of the Uniform Franchise Offering Circular.

The fitness industry represents one of the most rapidly growing areas of franchising because it caters to all ages and demographics. Consider Town Sports International (TSI). TSI operates in New York, Washington, Boston and Philadelphia. Founded in 1974, today TSI has more than 350,000 memberships and is the largest network of health clubs in the northeastern United States. TSI also has locations in Switzerland.

Table 15.6 Information Contained in the Uniform Franchise Offering Circular (UFOC) Along with Explanations of Their Meanings

Section and Item	Explanation
1. The franchisor, its predecessors, and affiliates 2. Business experience of the franchisor 3. Litigation experience of the franchisor 4. Bankruptcy on the part of the franchisor	These items provide information about the franchisor's operating history, business affiliations, and past litigation and bankruptcy experience, if any. It is not uncommon for a large company to have experienced some litigation. It would be a red flag, however, if a disproportionate percentage of the litigation involved suits with current or former franchisees.
5. Initial franchise fee 6. Other fees 7. Initial investment	These items specify the fees that the franchisee is subject to along with the franchisees initial investment, which can be quite substantial. The "other fees" section should be carefully studied to avoid any surprises.
8. Restrictions on sources of products and services 9. Franchisee's obligations	These items stipulate the franchisee's obligations, along with restrictions pertaining to where the franchisee is permitted to purchase its supplies and services. Some franchise agreements require the franchisee to purchase its supplies from the franchisor.
10. Financing available 11. Franchisor's obligations	These items spell out the franchisor's obligations, along with a description of the financing (if any) that the franchisor offers to the franchisee. The franchisor's obligations typically include providing assistance in opening the franchise's unit, ongoing training, and advertising.
12. Territory 13. Trademarks 14. Patents, copyrights, and proprietary information	These items describe the territorial rights granted the franchisee (if any) and the franchisor's right to grant other franchises and open company-owned outlets. In addition, item 13 and 14 specify the principal trademarks, patents, and copyrights and other proprietary information owned by the franchisor and the extent to which these items can be used by the franchisee.
15. Obligation to participate in the actual operation of the franchise business	This section addresses the franchisee's obligation to participate personally in the operation of the franchise. Franchisors typically do not want absentee franchisees.
16. Restrictions on what the franchisee may sell 17. Renewal, termination, transfer, and dispute resolution	These sections deal with what the franchisee may sell and how the franchisor resolves disputes with its franchisees. Item 17 also contains important information about the manner in which franchisees can renew, terminate, and/or transfer their franchise.
18. Public figures	This section lists public figures affiliated with the franchise through advertising and other means.
19. Earnings claim	If a franchisor makes an earnings claim in connection with an offer of a franchise, then certain past and projected earnings information must be provided.
20. List of outlets	This section is quite exhaustive and contains (1) the number of franchises sold by the franchisor, (2) the number of company-owned outlets, (3) the names of all franchisees and the addresses and telephone numbers of all their outlets (within certain limitations), (4) an estimate of the number of franchises to be sold in the next year, and (5) a list of all franchisees (covering the past three years) who have dropped out of the system, including their last known home addresses and telephone numbers.
21. Financial Statements	This section contains the franchisor's previous two years of independently audited financial statements.

22. Contracts
23. Receipt
    Attachments:
    Franchise Agreement (or contract)
    Equipment Lease
    Lease for Premises
    Loan Agreement
	These last two sections contain copies of the documents that franchisees have to sign.
	These are the common exhibits attached to the UFOC.

each agreement typically contains two sections: the purchase agreement and the franchise or license agreement. The purchase agreement typically spells out the price, the services to be provided by the franchisor to the franchisee, and the "franchise package," which refers to all the items the franchisee has been told to expect. The franchise or license agreement typically stipulates the rights granted to the franchisee (including the right to use the franchisor's trademark), the obligations and duties of the franchisor, the obligations and duties of the franchisee, trade restrictions, rights and limitations regarding the transfer or termination of the franchise agreement, and who is responsible for attorney fees if disputes arise.

The federal government does not require franchisors to register with the Federal Trade Commission (FTC). The offer of a franchise for sale does not imply that the FTC has examined the franchisor and has determined that the information contained in the franchisor's UFOC is accurate. The franchisor is responsible to voluntarily comply with the law, and it is the responsibility of prospective franchisees to exercise due diligence in investigating franchise opportunities. Although most franchisor–franchisee relationships are conducted in an entirely ethical manner, it is a mistake to assume that a franchisor has a fiduciary obligation to its franchisees. What this means is that if a franchisor had a **fiduciary obligation** to its franchisees, it would always act in their best interest, or be on the franchisees' "side." Commenting on this issue, Robert Purvin, an experienced franchise attorney, wrote,

> While the conventional wisdom talks about the proactive relationship of the franchisor to its franchisees, virtually every court case decided in the U.S. has ruled that a franchisor has no fiduciary obligation to its franchisees. Instead, U.S. courts have agreed with franchisors that franchise agreements are "arms length" business transactions.[25]

This quote suggests that a potential franchisee should not rely solely on the goodwill of a franchisor when negotiating a franchise agreement. A potential franchisee should have a lawyer who is fully acquainted with franchise law and should closely scrutinize all franchise-related legal documents.

State Rules and Regulations

In addition to the FTC disclosure requirements, 17 states have laws providing additional protection to potential franchisees. California, Florida, Hawaii, Illinois, Indiana, Maryland, Michigan, Minnesota, New York, North Dakota, Rhode Island, South Dakota, Texas, Utah, Virginia, Washington, and Wisconsin are the states in which these laws have been established. In most of these states, a franchisor is required to file its UFOC with a designated state agency, making the UFOC public record. In these states, a designated agency typically reviews the UFOC for compliance with law. In most of these 17 states, a franchisor can be prevented from selling a franchise if the state agency in charge is not satisfied that the UFOC is complete, understandable, and fully compliance with FTC Rule 436.

By requiring franchisors to file their UFOC's with a state agency, these states provide franchise purchasers important legal protection, including the right to sue a franchisor for violation of state disclosure requirements (if the franchise purchaser feels that full disclosure in the offering circular was not made). For example, if Joshua Clark purchased a franchise in one of the states fitting the profile described previously and six months later discovered that the franchisor did not disclose an issue required by the UFOC (and, as a result, felt that he had been damaged), Clark could seek relief by suing the franchisor in state court. All 17 states providing additional measures of protection for franchisees also regulate some aspect of the termination process.[26] Although the provisions vary by state, they typically restrict a franchisor from terminating the franchise before the expiration of the franchise agreement, unless the franchisor has "good cause" for its action.

More About Franchising

There are a number of additional issues pertaining to the franchisor–franchisee relationship. Four important topics, for both franchisors and franchisees, are franchise associations, franchise ethics, international franchising, and the future of franchising as a method of business ownership and growth.

Franchise Associations

Many franchise systems have organized **franchise associations** (or franchise advisory councils) to represent the franchisees' collective interests and to provide a forum for franchisees to communicate with one another. Examples include the Econo Lodge Franchise Association, which claims to be the oldest industry franchise association in the United States,[27] and the North American Association of Subway Franchisees. Most franchise associations maintain a cooperative relationship with their franchisor and deal with routine issues of mutual interest to their members. There are franchise associations, however, that have developed fairly contentious relationships with their franchisors. These associations and their franchisors typically disagree over some key issue. For example, a common complaint among the franchisees of large restaurant chains is that franchisors expand by adding new units that are in close proximity to their existing units. The argument is that the new units, which benefit the franchisor, hurt the existing franchisees by cannibalizing a portion of their sales. In cases such as this, the franchise association is used as a tool to gain leverage with the franchisee.

There are also several prominent national franchise associations, each of which has a specific mission. The American Association of Franchisees and Dealers and the American Franchise Association represent the rights of franchisees. Lobbying for legislation that protects and benefits franchisees is one of the primary activities in which both of these associations are engaged. The International Franchise Association represents the rights of both franchisors and franchisees and has a similar although more balanced mission. Finally, the National Franchise Council represents the rights and interests of large franchisors.

Franchise Ethics

The majority of franchisors and franchisees are highly ethical individuals who are interested only in making a fair return on their investment. In fact, according to a recent FTC report, instances of problems between franchisors and their franchisees tend to be isolated occurrences rather than prevalent practices.[28] There are certain features of franchising, however, that make it subject to ethical abuse. An understanding of these features can help franchisors and franchisees guard against making ethical mistakes. These features are the following:

- *The get-rich-quick mentality:* Some franchisors see franchising as a get-rich-quick scheme and become interested more in selling franchises than in using franchising as a legitimate means of distributing their product or service. These franchisors have a tendency to either oversell the potential of their franchise or overpromise the support they will offer to their franchisees.

- *The false assumption that buying a franchise is a guarantee of business success:* Buying a franchise, as is the case with all other business investments, involves risk. Any statement to the contrary is typically misleading or unethical. A franchisor must steer clear of claims that it has the "key" to business success, and a franchisee needs to be wary of all such claims.

- *Conflicts of interest between franchisors and their franchisees:* The structure of the franchise relationship can create conflicts of interest between franchisors and their franchisees. For example, franchisees benefit from the profits of a unit, while franchisors benefit from increased revenues (recall that a franchisor's royalty is typically paid on a percentage of gross profits rather than net profits). This anomaly in the franchise arrangement can motivate franchisors to take steps that boost revenues for the entire system but hurt profits for individual franchisees. For example, a franchisor might insist that a franchisee sell a product that has high revenue but low net income. Similarly, a franchisor might sell several franchises in a given geographic area to maximize the revenue potential of the area regardless of the effect on each individual franchisee's net income. These actions can at times be ethically questionable and can often lead to contentious conflicts of interests in franchise systems.

Despite the protection of law and the advocacy of franchise associations, individual franchisors and franchisees must practice due diligence in their relationships. "Buyer beware" is a good motto for franchisors selecting franchisees and prospective franchisees selecting franchisors. Entering into a franchise relationship is a major step for both parties and should be treated accordingly. The metaphor used frequently to describe the franchisor–franchisee relationship is marriage. Similar to marriage, the franchisor–franchisee relationship is typically close, long term, and painful to terminate. Each side of the franchise partnership should scrutinize the past ethical behavior of the other before a franchise agreement is executed.

International Franchising

International opportunities for franchising are becoming more prevalent as the markets for certain franchised products in the United States have become saturated.[29] For example, heavily franchised companies, such as McDonald's, Kentucky Fried Chicken, and Curves, are experiencing much of their growth in international markets. The trend toward globalization in many industries is also hastening the trend toward international franchising. Regional initiatives, such as the North American Free Trade Agreement, are making it increasingly attractive for U.S. firms to offer franchises for sale in foreign countries. Many new franchise organizations have made international expansion part of their initial business plans. An example is WSI Internet, which is a U.S. company that was founded in 1995 and now has franchise outlets in more than 80 countries.

Foreign firms are also taking advantage of the trend toward globalization and are offering franchises in the United States and other countries. For example, Bass Hotels and Resorts, which operates Holiday Inn, Holiday Inn Express, and Staybridge Suites, is a British franchisor with over 2,700 hotels in 90 countries. Similarly, Informatics is a Singapore-based franchisor that operates several franchise chains, including CAL (computer-assisted learning for young people) and Cambridge Child Development Centers. A U.S. citizen who is thinking about buying a franchise domestically or abroad may be confronted with the choice of buying from an American company or a foreign company regardless of the location in the world. For U.S. citizens, these are some of the steps to take before buying a franchise in a foreign country:

- *Consider the value of the franchisor's name in the foreign country:* There are very few franchise systems whose names are known worldwide. Beyond a select few—McDonald's, Coca-Cola, and Budweiser come to mind—the majority of trademarks well known to Americans may be known to only a small percentage of the population of a foreign country. When considering the purchase of a U.S.-based franchise in a foreign country, carefully evaluate the value of the trademark in that country.
- *Get a good lawyer:* Many of the legal protections afforded to prospective franchisees in the United States are unavailable in foreign countries, highlighting the need for the purchaser of a franchise in a foreign country to obtain excellent legal advice. All the hazards involved with purchasing a domestic franchise are magnified when purchasing a franchise in a foreign country.
- *Determine whether the product or service is salable in a foreign country:* Just because a product or service is desirable to Americans is no guarantee of success in a foreign culture. Before buying a franchise in a foreign country, determine if sufficient marketing research has been conducted to ensure that the product or service will have a sufficient market in the foreign country.
- *Uncover whether the franchisor has experience in international markets:* It is typically not a good idea to be a franchisor's "test case" to see if the franchisor wants to operate in foreign markets. Be leery of franchisors with aggressive expansion plans but little international experience.
- *Find out how much training and support you will receive from the franchisor:* If your franchise unit will be in a foreign country and the franchisor remains headquartered in the United States, make sure you fully understand the amount of training and support you can expect. Will the franchisor have an area representative in your country? If not, do you have to make an international phone call each time you want to talk to your franchisor? Will your franchisor be willing to travel to the foreign country to offer you training and support? Who pays for the international travel of the franchisor's training staff? Who is responsible for advertising in the foreign country, the franchisor or the franchisee?
- *Evaluate currency restrictions:* Evaluate any restrictions that the foreign country places on the convertibility of its currency into U.S. dollars.

what went **wrong?**

Watch Out: Plenty Can Go Wrong in Opening Franchise Outlets Overseas

Although the Internet, satellite television, and Hollywood movies have increased the demand for American products abroad, franchisors should take care not to rush into opening franchise outlets overseas. Because many of the easiest countries into which U.S. firms can export their products and services, such as Canada and England, are already saturated with U.S. franchised outlets, this leaves only more difficult foreign markets. Differences in language and the customs associated with a nation's culture are examples of factors making franchising very challenging in these more difficult foreign markets. Indeed, plenty can go wrong because of the complexities of operating overseas.

Sometimes, franchisors run into unique challenges in foreign markets, and sometimes they simply make mistakes. Both types of complications typically result from a lack of familiarity with the foreign markets the companies are trying to enter. Here are some examples of mistakes U.S. franchisors have made when trying to enter foreign markets:

- Burger King didn't register its trademark in Australia before another restaurant group did. If you walk through the Sydney Airport, you'll pass hamburger stands called Burger King and Hungry Jack's. Burger King is a local company—U.S. Burger King sandwiches are sold at Hungry Jack's.

- A donut concept failed in Brazil because people felt the hole meant they were being shortchanged.

- In Malaysia, a company put up a hotel, but no one would go inside because the door was on the wrong side of the building, violating the residents' religious norms.

The challenges that franchisors confront in foreign markets can also lead to mistakes if they're not careful. For example, TCBY's slogan, "None of the guilt, all of the pleasure," isn't used in Japan because the Japanese culture does not have the same interpretation of the word "guilt" as America. Similarly, Marriott International abruptly broke off negotiations to build a 350-room hotel in an unnamed foreign city when it discovered that its overseas investors

planned to sell interests in the hotel, just like a condo. Marriott quickly realized that if the deal had gone through, they might have ended up doing business with 350 individuals rather than a single franchisee.

Fortunately, there is plenty of help for franchise organizations that want to initiate international franchising. Many of the consultants listed on the International Franchise Association's Web site have international experience. In addition, help is available from the U.S. Small Business Administration, more than 100 Export Assistance Offices located across the United States, and through the U.S. government's export portal at *www.export.gov*.

Questions for Critical Thinking

1. In this feature, we considered a number of things that can go wrong when trying to pursue what appear to be franchising opportunities in some foreign markets. Using insights you've drawn from this chapter as well as your study of the book's first 14 chapters, prepare a list of reasons firms or entrepreneurs might be willing to accept the risks of establishing a franchise unit in a challenging foreign market. In slightly different words, what are the potential advantages of franchising in challenging international markets?

2. The examples of franchising mistakes made by Burger King and Marriott International, as described in this feature, may surprise you. Why is it that large organizations such as Burger King and Marriott International sometimes err when pursuing apparent franchising opportunities in difficult or challenging foreign markets? Prepare a list of factors you believe could cause large, long-lived organizations to make these types of mistakes.

Sources: J. Bennett, "Some Franchises Don't Translate Well Overseas," Wall Street Journal, www.startupjournal.com (accessed October 28, 2003), and J. Bennett, "Why U.S. Franchises Face Problems Abroad," Wall Street Journal, www.startupjournal.com (accessed October 28, 2003).

To avoid some of the potential problems alluded to here, U.S. franchisors typically structure their expansion into a foreign country through the following:

- *Direct franchising arrangement:* Under a direct franchise arrangement, the U.S. franchisor grants the rights to an individual or a company (the developer) to develop multiple franchised businesses within a country or territory. For example, if Midas Muffler decided to sell franchises for the first time in Spain, Midas may grant the rights to a Spanish company to develop multiple Midas franchises there.

- *Master franchise agreement:* Under a master franchise arrangement, the U.S. firm grants the right to an individual or company (the master franchisee) to develop one or more franchise businesses and to license others to develop one or more franchise businesses within the country or territory.
- *Other agreements:* Combinations of other arrangements are also employed by franchisors expanding to foreign markets. Examples include joint venture arrangements, direct-sales arrangements, or straight franchising agreements.

Even when a company adheres to these safeguards, there is plenty that can go wrong when opening franchise outlets overseas. This topic is addressed in the boxed feature titled "What Went Wrong?"

The Future of Franchising

The future of franchising appears bright. Franchise organizations represent a large and growing segment of the retail and service sectors of U.S. businesses and are in some cases replacing more traditional forms of small business ownership.[30] According to the International Franchise Association (IFA), franchising represents about $1 trillion in annual retail sales in the United States and involves 320,000 franchised outlets in 75 industries. In addition, the IFA estimates that franchising employs more than eight million people, that a new franchise outlet opens somewhere in the United States every eight minutes, and that approximately one out of every 12 retail business establishments is a franchised business.[31] More and more college graduates are choosing careers in industries that are heavily dominated by franchising. The availability of digital business tools, which increase the effectiveness of franchise organizations in a variety of ways, is also making franchising more desirable. As franchising continues to become a more pervasive form of business, regulators and franchise associations are likely to intervene in ways that strengthen the viability of the franchise concept.

CHAPTER SUMMARY

1. A franchise is an agreement between a franchisor (the parent company, such as McDonald's), and a franchisee (an individual or firm that is willing to pay the franchisor a fee for the right to sell its product or service).

2. There are two distinctly different types of franchise systems: the product trademark franchise and the business format franchise. A product trademark franchise is an arrangement under which the franchisor grants to the franchisee the right to buy its products and use its trade name. Automobile dealerships and soft-drink distributorships are examples of product trademark franchises. In a business format franchise, the franchisor provides a formula for doing business to the franchisee along with training, advertising, and other forms of assistance. Curves, Comfort Keepers, and Cartridge World are examples of this type of franchise system.

3. An individual franchise agreement involves the sale of a single franchise for a specific location. An area franchise agreement allows a franchisee to own and operate a specific number of outlets in a particular geographic area. A master franchise agreement is similar to an area franchise agreement with one major exception. In addition to having the right to operate a specific number of locations in a particular area, the franchisee also has the right to offer and sell the franchise to other people in the area.

4. The advantages of setting up a franchise system include rapid, low-cost market expansion; income from franchise fees and royalties; franchisee motivation; access to ideas and suggestions; cost savings; and increased buying power. The disadvantages of setting up a franchise system include sharing profits with franchisees, loss of control, friction with franchisees, managing growth, differences in required business skills, and legal expenses.

5. The rules of thumb for determining whether franchising is a good choice for growing a business are as follows: the product or service the business sells should be unique; the business should be consistently profitable; the business should be profitable year-round, not only during a specific season; the business system and procedures should be polished; and the business proposition should be clear so that the prospective franchisee fully understand the relationship to which he or she is committing.

6. Preparing answers to the following questions helps the entrepreneur determine if franchising is a good fit for him or her as a way to launch a venture. Are you willing to take orders? Are you willing to be part of a franchise system? How will you react if you make a suggestion to your franchisor and your suggestion is rejected? What are you looking for in a business? How willing are you to put your money at risk?

7. The following costs are typically associated with buying a business format franchise: initial franchise fee, capital requirements (such as land, buildings, and equipment), continuing royalty payment, advertising fee, and other fees (depending on the franchise system).

8. The advantages of buying a franchise include a proven product or service within an established market; an established trademark or business system; franchisor's training, technical expertise, and managerial experience; an established marketing network; franchisor ongoing support; availability of financing; and potential for business growth. The disadvantages of buying a franchise include cost of the franchise; restrictions on creativity; duration and nature of commitment; risk of fraud, misunderstanding, or lack of franchisor commitment; problems of termination or transfer; and the possibility of poor performance on the part of other franchisees.

9. The common mistakes made by franchise buyers include believing that franchising is a completely safe investment, believing that a great industry ensures franchise success, putting too much faith in the idea that a franchise is a "proven" business system, believing that there is no need to hire a franchise attorney or accountant, being overly optimistic about how fast the franchise outlet will grow, believing that "I can operate my franchise outlet for less than the franchisor predicts," and believing that just because the franchisor is a nice person, he or she will always be there to help out when needed.

10. The Uniform Franchise Offering Circular (UFOC) is a document with 23 categories of information. This document provides a prospective franchisee a broad base of information about a franchisor's background and financial health. The UFOC must be provided by the franchisor to a prospective franchisee at least 10 business days before a franchise contract can be signed or the franchisee pays the franchisor any money.

KEY TERMS

agency theory, 363

area franchise agreement, 359

business format franchise, 358

fiduciary obligation, 374

franchise agreement, 372

franchise associations, 375

franchisees, 357

franchising, 357

franchisor, 357

individual franchise agreement, 359

master franchise agreement, 360

multiple-unit franchising, 360

product and trademark franchise, 358

subfranchisees, 360

Uniform Franchisor Offering Circular, 372

REVIEW QUESTIONS

1. What is franchising, and how does it differ from other forms of business ownership?

2. Describe the differences between a product and trademark franchise and a business format franchise. Provide an example of both types of franchise arrangements.

3. What is the difference between an individual franchise agreement, an area franchise agreement, and a master franchise agreement?

4. What are the nine basic steps in setting up a franchise system?

5. What are the advantages and disadvantages of establishing a franchise system?

6. What are the rules of thumb for determining whether franchising is a good choice for a particular business? Provide an example of a business that wouldn't be suitable for franchising.

7. What are some of the issues an entrepreneur should consider when trying to answer the question, "Is franchising a good choice for me?"

8. What are the costs involved in purchasing a business unit franchise? Are these costs similar across franchise systems, or do they vary widely?

9. Explain why it's to the franchisor's advantage to receive its royalty payment on the gross income rather than net income of its franchise outlets.

10. Describe some of the resources available to prospective franchisees to identify franchise opportunities.

11. What are the principal advantages and disadvantages of buying a franchise?

12. What are the seven steps involved in purchasing a franchise?

13. What are some of the common misconceptions franchisees often have about franchising?

14. What is the purpose of the Uniform Franchise Offering Circular (UFOC)? Are there any regulations regarding when the UFOC must be provided to a prospective franchisee? If so, what are they?

15. What is the purpose of a franchise agreement? Identify the two sections of the franchise agreement and describe the purpose of each section.

16. What is a franchise association? If you were the owner of a Subway franchise, would you welcome or discourage the creation of a franchise association by the franchisees in your system? Why?

17. What are some of the aspects of franchising that make it subject to ethical abuses?

18. For U.S. citizens, what are the main issues that should be considered before buying a franchise in a foreign country?

19. What are the main reasons that many U.S. franchise systems are expanding into global markets? Do you think this expansion will continue to gain momentum or will decline over time? Explain your answer.

20. Does franchising have a bright or a dim future in the United States? Make your answer as substantive and thoughtful as possible.

APPLICATION QUESTIONS

1. Several executives from Coca-Cola have decided to leave their jobs to launch a new chain of a Dairy Queen type of restaurant called Thirst Burst Etc. They want to grow quickly. Would franchising be a good choice for them? Why or why not?

2. Bill Watts has decided to buy a sub shop franchise called Deluxe Subs. He lives in Cedar Falls, Iowa, and will be the first Deluxe Subs franchisee in the state. Along with buying a Deluxe Subs franchise, Bill would also like to purchase the rights to offer and sell Deluxe Subs franchises to other people in the Cedar Falls area. What type of franchise agreement should Bill negotiate with Deluxe Subs? For Bill, what are the advantages and disadvantages of this type of arrangement?

3. Sarah Gandy works for a computer consulting firm in Salt Lake City. For some time, she has been thinking about either starting her own computer consulting company or buying a computer consulting franchise. She knows that you have been taking a course in entrepreneurship and asks you to tell her a little bit about what a franchise costs and how to identify a good franchise system. What would you tell her?

4. Helen Partridge owns a very successful chain of Web site development businesses. She currently has 21 offices spread across Illinois, Indiana, and Ohio. She is thinking about franchising her business as a means of expanding beyond the Midwest. Helen has always believed in getting professional advice before making a major decision. Who should Helen talk to, and what types of questions should she ask before making the decision to franchise her business?

5. Jason Carpenski is a serial entrepreneur. Although he is only 35, he has already started three businesses. Jason loves launching businesses because he likes being his own boss and enjoys the independence an entrepreneurial career offers him. Recently, Jason sold his latest business, a communications equipment start-up, and is looking for a new opportunity. He just attended a franchise fair and is extremely interested in buying a printing and copying franchise. Do you think Jason is a good candidate to buy a franchise in an established franchise system? Why or why not?

6. Joan Wagner has worked for Walgreen's for several years as a photo processor. She just inherited a nice sum of money and has decided to purchase a Cartridge World franchise. Before she signs the franchise agreement, however, she wants to make sure that she fully understands the advantages and disadvantages of buying a franchise. What would you tell Joan if she asked you for this information?

7. Suppose you ran into an old friend who is just about to buy into a handheld computer accessories retail franchise. He tells you that he is excited about the opportunity because the system he is about to buy into (1) is in an industry that virtually guarantees its success, (2) has a "proven" business system, and (3) is operated by people who are so honest that he can skip the expense of hiring a franchise attorney to review the documents he has to sign. If your friend asked you, "Be honest with me now—, am I being naive, or does this sound like a great opportunity?," what would you tell him? Why?

8. Suppose you saw an ad in your local newspaper for a franchise opportunity that caught your attention. You called the phone number listed in the ad and liked what you heard. As a result, you scheduled a time to meet with a representative of the franchise organization at a nearby Panera Bread restaurant. After learning more about the opportunity, you tell the representative that you're really interested and would like more information. If the opportunity is legitimate and the organization you are dealing with complies with the law, what should you expect from this point forward?

9. If you own a franchise in a franchise system that turns out to be hard to deal with, how can starting a franchise association help you and your fellow franchisees deal with this issue?

10. Suppose you are an American citizen living in England. You just lost your job with a telecommunications firm that merged with a French company. You would like to stay in England and are thinking about buying a franchise in an American cell phone retail company that is expanding to Europe. What are some of the issues you should evaluate before buying an outlet in an American franchise system that is selling franchises in England?

Company: **1-800-GOT-JUNK?**
(www.1800gotjunk.com)

Business idea: At one point or another, most people have something around their house that they want to get rid of but can't haul away themselves, such as a broken appliance, a worn-out couch, or simply accumulated "stuff." These items often become irritants. Most people would gladly pay a little money to get rid of their unwanted junk.

Pitch: 1-800-JUNK is a national franchisor that sets up local franchises to remove junk from people's homes. By calling 1-800-JUNK, the customer schedules a time for the junk removal. A clean, shiny truck arrives on time at the customer's home, manned by a friendly, uniformed crew. A price quote will be made to the customer before the junk is loaded and hauled away. 1-800-JUNK has been featured in several periodicals, including *Fast Company, USA Today,* and the *Wall Street Journal.*

Q&A: Based on the material covered in this chapter, what questions would you ask the firm's founders before making your funding decision? What answers would satisfy you?

Decision: If you had to make your decision on just the information provided in the pitch and the company's Web site, would you fund this firm? Why or why not?

Case 15.1

LifeStyle Technologies: Equipping Homes for Technology through Franchising
www.lifestech.com

Imagine this: You're building a new home. Before you put up the drywall, you want to make sure it is wired for a variety of home technologies. You're planning to have a security system, landscape lighting, surround sound, Internet access, and an intercom. You would also like to connect at least three computers to the same laser-jet printer. The first computer will be in your office, the second will be in the family room, and the third will be in your daughter's bedroom. You ask your builder to set up the wiring. He shrugs and says that he'll have to line up separate subcontractors to wire each system. He also says that you'll need to get busy picking out the systems you want so they can be installed before the house is finished. You're willing to do it but dread running all over town pricing different systems.

If you think this all sounds like a hassle, LifeStyle Technologies would be the first to agree. LifeStyle, through its franchises and company-owned stores, works with real estate developers and home builders to design and install technology-related wiring for new homes and to provide home owners "one-stop" shopping for their home technology needs. The company, which is headquartered in Charlotte, North Carolina, was founded in 2000. It is headed by a management team with over 40 years of experience in the low-voltage wiring, home security, and satellite industries.

The idea behind LifeStyle Technologies is that an increasing number of people want technology-related products in their homes but run into a variety of problems when they try to buy and install them. For starters, most homes, even new ones, are not built with the installation of items such as computer networks, sophisticated security systems, surround sound, and intercom systems in mind, so when faced with the prospect of knocking out drywall to install cables and wires, many home owners simply pass. In addition, many people simply don't know what to buy. In many communities, there is no "one-stop" center featuring a variety of home technologies that can be integrated into a seamless system. Moreover, residential developers and builders often face the same set of challenges confronting home owners in terms of seamless home technology systems. Commonly, developers and builders would like to offer more technology-related options to their buyers, but it's difficult to design integrated systems, and it's a hassle to deal with multiple subcontractors.

LifeStyle Technologies was designed to solve these problems. The company has the expertise, business methods, and proprietary software needed to help home owners wire and equip their homes to accommodate a variety of integrated technology products. Each of the company's outlets contains a 2,000-square-foot showroom and areas set aside for customers to consult with LifeStyle Technologies consultants. A typical franchise will sell to three main sets of buyers:

- *New construction:* Builders and developers
- *Retrofitting existing homes:* Architects, remodeling contractors, designers, and home owners
- *Commercial operations:* Real estate agents, designers, architects, and business owners

To help its franchisees generate leads, the company has established partnerships with a number of well-known builders. The builders offer LifeStyle's wiring services and products as part of the packages they sell to home buyers and in return are able to lower their costs through the efficiencies gained by working with only one supplier. A sample of the builders on board includes Toll Brothers, McDonald York, and Parker Lancaster Homes.

The company has a growing list of franchise outlets. The first were launched in technology-savvy communities such as Atlanta, Dallas, and Raleigh, North Carolina, to test the LifeStyle Technologies concept. It costs between $154,000 and $195,500 to launch a LifeStyle Technologies franchise, which includes a $40,000 initial franchise fee. The company believes that the demographics of the marketplace are moving in its favor and that the market for what some people call "smart homes" is just taking off. The Raleigh location, for example, has been operating since January 2001, and it reached profitability after only seven months. Raleigh is considered an attractive market because it is growing and is located within the Research Triangle of North Carolina. The company hopes to base the majority of its franchise outlets, which numbered 15 as of mid-2004, in rapidly growing metropolitan areas.

For its franchisees, LifeStyle offers training and ongoing support in business operations, proprietary software, sales and quoting, and technical areas. Franchisees are able to use the company's name and marks, which are rapidly becoming recognized in the home-building industry for quality and customer service. A variety of benefits are offered to franchisees, including advertising/marketing programs, the ability to purchase products in bulk, location selection and setup, and periodic franchise meetings. In addition, by joining the LifeStyle Technology family, a franchise owner can tap into the network of national relationships the company has established for sales leads and other purposes.

LifeStyle Technologies is plowing new ground for franchising as a means of business growth and ownership. It is a technologically intense company that has developed a business method for helping home owners with real needs. Additional companies may follow suit and move franchising beyond its traditional areas, such as restaurants, automobile repair shops, and convenience stores, and into areas that are more technologically advanced and that appeal to a new category of potential franchise owners.

Discussion Questions

1. Do you think that LifeStyle Technologies has a business concept that lends itself to franchising, or do you think franchising is inappropriate for this company? Justify your answer.

2. If you were a prospective franchisee, what would impress you about LifeStyle Technologies? Would you have any reservations? If so, what would they be?

3. If LifeStyle's business model catches on and it is able to add franchises rapidly, do you think that competitors will quickly arise and offer a similar set of products and services? If this happens, what competitive advantage will LifeStyle have over its competitors? Explain your answer.

4. Along with wiring and equipping homes to accommodate technological devices, what other technologically intense activities or industries might lend themselves to franchising?

Sources: "LifeStyle Technologies Franchise Sold to SGD Holdings," The Business Journal *(Raleigh–Durham, N.C.), December 21, 2002; and LifeStyle Technologies home page, www.lifestech.com (accessed April 10, 2004).*

Case 15.2

IFX International: Helping Franchisees Better Communicate with Their Franchisors and with Each Other
www.ifxonline.com

Suppose you own a smoothie franchise, it's seven o'clock at night, and you're having trouble with a new piece of equipment. You can't call the home office because it is closed for the evening. You're panicking a bit because you expect a rush of business around 9:30, when the high school basketball game is over. You really need the new piece of equipment working before the crowds show up.

If your franchisor has set up an intranet system through IFX International, you may be in luck. An intranet is a private, password-protected Web site that is accessible only to authorized users, such as the franchisees of a franchise system. IFX is a company that designs and hosts intranet systems for franchise organizations. Intranets are affectionately referred to as "lifelines" because they instantly connect a user with a treasure trove of

information. For example, the smoothie franchisee could log on to his company's intranet to have instant access to the owner's manual for the equipment with which he is experiencing a problem. The site may also have a direct link to the equipment's manufacturer. If neither of these options works, the franchisee could enter the intranet's chat room and post a message, such as "Urgent—I need help fixing the new smoothie machine in the next two hours. If you've had trouble with the cooling unit, please let me know if you've figured out how to fix it." It's anyone's bet, but another franchisee may check the chat room, remember how he or she solved the problem, and return the message.

IFX was founded in 1996 with the vision of developing Web-based technologies to help franchisors better communicate with their franchisees. It is a privately held company whose founder has 18 years of franchise management experience, five years of intranet/extranet development-hosting experience, and over 100 franchise clients. Its client list includes Baskin-Robbins, Ben & Jerry's, General Nutrition Centers, Two Men and a Truck, and U.S. Lawns. The company is led by Daniel Martin, whose lengthy career in franchising includes a stint as the franchise area developer for Creative Croissants in southern California. Since its launch, IFX has quickly emerged as the leading application provider for franchisor–franchisee communication systems.

Although the company sells a variety of products, its most widely adopted offering is the intranet system. Intranets are attractive to firms of all sizes because they don't require a lot of capital to establish. IFX charges a franchisor a $9,700 flat fee to create a complete intranet system and hosts the system for a modest monthly fee. All a franchisee needs to make use of the intranet is a PC and a standard Internet connection. The primary purpose of an intranet is to provide a secure environment in which a company can disseminate information and provide communication services to the people it does business with. With IFX's systems, all information and communications exchanged within the intranet is absolutely private and self-contained and is available only to authorized participants.

The beauty of an intranet system is the broad array of information and other services that it can bring to the fingertips of qualified users, 24 hours a day, seven days a week, simply by logging on to the Web site. For example, a typical intranet system set up by IFX includes several features. Think about how useful the following features would be to the franchisees of a major franchise system:

- *Online manuals:* All the company's manuals can be placed online, making revisions easy. The system can also alert franchisees when important revisions have been made to their manuals.

- *Online news:* A news section can provide franchises with valuable tips, news and information, and links to news stories and articles about the company.

- *Q&A:* A question-and-answer module can provide franchisees with the ability to direct questions to specific departments or individuals within the organization. This module can be designed to allow franchisors the option to permit selected viewing by other users, providing valuable information to other members of the franchise network.

- *Enhanced e-mail:* The mail module allows a franchisor to issue electronic messages to individual franchisees or selected groups of franchisees at the touch of a button. Some systems enhance security by requiring both the sender and the recipient to enter a special password to view the message. Another security measure is the ability to tag a message "Urgent," "For Your Eyes Only," and/or "Acknowledgement Required."

- *Chat rooms or discussion groups:* Most intranets have a chat room or forum where members of the organization can discuss issues and help one another solve problems. In addition, many intranets have group discussion forums that focus on specific issues. For example, a franchisor such as Ben & Jerry's could schedule an online discussion for its franchisees at 2:00 P.M. Eastern Standard Time on June 6 to discuss customer service issues.

- *Operational issues:* Most intranets also facilitate routine operational issues, such as permitting franchisees to order supplies, pay monthly royalties, post job openings, and view training courses online. In turn, a broad array of useful information is often available to franchisees that can be uploaded and used in a local franchise unit. For example, many franchisors place marketing material, such as camera-ready flyers, point-of-sale brochures, and newspaper ads, on their intranet sites to be uploaded and used by the franchisees.

In addition to these benefits, a secure intranet system can save a franchisor thousands of dollars a year in printing, mailing, shipping, travel, long-distance telephone, and fax costs. Imagine the cost savings for a company such as Subway, which at the end of 2003 had 15,784 franchises in the United States, 1,803 in Canada, and 1,651 in other countries. If an intranet can save Subway $200 per year in printing and mailing costs for each of its franchised outlets, that amounts to a savings of well over $3 million annually.

In the increasingly competitive world of franchising, it behooves all firms to look for ways to increase their effectiveness and reduce costs. Corporate intranet systems, such as those provided by IFX International, help franchisors and their franchisees better communicate, cut expenses, and provide higher levels of customer service to their clientele.

Discussion Questions

1. If you were a franchisor, what capabilities would you include in your corporate intranet? How would you involve your franchisees in designing and implementing the intranet system?

2. What do you think is the driving force behind the gradual widespread use of intranet systems in the franchising industry? How do you think intranet systems will evolve in the coming years? What are the risks that franchisors face if they decide to not invest in intranet systems? Explain your answer.

3. Pick a well-known franchise organization. Explain how a franchise owner in that organization would use a corporate intranet on a daily basis.

4. Other than communicating with one another through intranet systems, in what other ways could the franchisees of a franchise organization help each other, especially when the franchisor's offices are closed?

Source: IFX International home page, www.ifxonline.com (accessed April 10, 2004).

Case 1   Hotmail: Delivering E-Mail to the World

Oliver A. Hugo and Elizabeth Garnsey, case writer
Judge Institute of Management Studies, University of Cambridge

Introduction

"Don't tell anyone! This isn't what we're supposed to be working on," Ray Tomlinson warned a colleague when he despatched one of the first e-mail messages ever sent in 1971.[1] He was employed at the time by Bolt, Beranek & Newman, a firm developing parts of the Pentagon-financed ARPANET infrastructure that later evolved into the Internet.

The immediate popularity of Tomlinson's 'SNDMSG' programme soon laid his fears to rest. Larry Roberts, director of DARPA (Defense Advanced Research Projects Agency) and in charge of running the ARPANET (Advanced Research Projects Agency Network) project, soon became an enthusiastic user. Roberts "jumped onto the system and began doing all his communication by electronic mail. That, in turn, forced researchers dependent on Roberts for their funding to get online, and the system quickly went from being a convenience to becoming an essential tool."[2]

At the height of the cold war ARPANET had been conceived as a distributed network that would be able to withstand nuclear attacks by eliminating vulnerable centralised or decentralised servers. The distributed network architecture (schematically outlined in Figure 1 below), conceived by Paul Baran at RAND Corporation, implied that a single piece of data could take multiple routes to reach its destination. Even if large parts of the network were destroyed, non-affected areas would still be able to transport information.

Although the early Internet infrastructure was not designed with the primary objective of providing interpersonal e-mail communication, the 'SNDMSG' command was an immediate and unanticipated success among ARRANET researchers and a harbinger of the commercial potential of this technology. Len Kleinrock a key figure in ARPANET's history, reflected during the Internet boom that even early on ". . . some of us began to see, this is bigger than what we created. That was the first glimpse."[3]

The early 1980s witnessed the establishment of the 'Simple Message Transfer Protocol' (SMTP) which, together with the 'Transmission Control Protocol' and the 'Internet Protocol' (the now familiar TCP and IP standards) laid the grounds for a steady growth of e-mail adoption. By 1990, about 15 million e-mailboxes existed world-wide, 13 million of which were located in the United States (see Figure 2). Throughout these years, e-mail usage remained the province of university academics and government officials. Even the emerging private online networks, like Delphi, Quantum Computer Services (the predecessor of AOL) and 'The Well' did not provide gateways that allowed full-scale user interaction with the Internet. It was not until 1992, when the U.S. Senate relaxed limitations on the commercial usage of the National Science Foundation (NSF) infrastructure, which carried much of the Internet traffic, that business activity

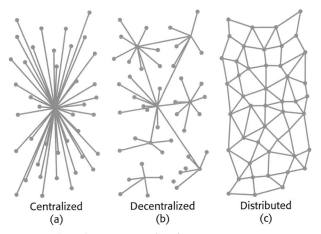

Centralized (a)   Decentralized (b)   Distributed (c)

Figure 1: *Three distinctive network architectures*
(Source: Paul Baran (1964): "On Distributed Communications: I. Introduction to Distributed Communications Network," RAND Corporation, Research Memorandum (RM-3420-PR) Santa Monica, CA.) Copyright RAND 1964. Reprinted with permission.

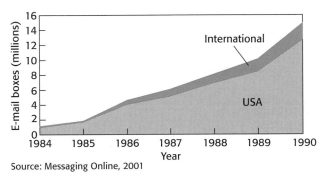

Source: Messaging Online, 2001

Figure 2: *Millions of e-mailboxes worldwide 1984–1990*

This case was written by Oliver A. Hugo and Elizabeth Garnsey, Judge Institute of Management Studies, University of Cambridge. It is intended to be used as the basis for class discussion rather than to illustrate either effective or ineffective handling of a management situation.

The case was compiled from published sources and the authors would like to thank Jack Smith, co-founder of Hotmail, and Eric Arnum, former editor of Messaging Online, for their support in developing this case study.

began to accelerate. The complete privatisation of the NSF network in 1994 further opened the new medium to commercial activity.

The 'electronic messaging industry' that arose from these governmental-military-academic origins can be characterised as the group of firms that jointly enabled a new form of interpersonal and text-based communication. Closely related user needs included directory services, manageability, security and privacy of communications (Figure 3 below).

The Formation of Hotmail

The Hotmail electronic messaging service was the brainchild of two young engineers: Sabeer Bhatia and Jack Smith. In the early 1990's, they worked at Apple Computer, later joining a Silicon Valley start-up called Firepower Systems. Originally from Bangalore, India, Sabeer Bhatia was greatly impressed by IT entrepreneurs who had become legendary, including Steve Jobs of Apple and Scott McNealy of SUN. Although he had originally intended to return to Bangalore after completing his studies at Stanford University, Bhatia was inspired by the 'Silicon Valley Dream' and became determined to start his own firm. Because of the U.S. recession in the early 1990s this plan had to be suspended when he graduated.

In 1995, the recession had subsided and the media spotlight on successful Silicon Valley start-ups like Netscape and Yahoo rekindled Bhatia's desire to create his own firm. He reminded his friend Jack Smith daily that they were surrounded by people who were making millions from their start-up companies: "Jack! What are we

doing here, wasting our lives?"[4] Bhatia's persuasive efforts succeeded and Jack Smith agreed to start a new firm with him. They were still regular employees when they began to prepare their new venture.

Their first business idea revolved around a product they termed 'JavaSoft,' a database that built on Sun's new Java technology and that could be used for storing personal information over the Internet. Bhatia and Smith presented their idea to many venture capitalists but without success. To most investors, the business proposal seemed double deficient: the JavaSoft idea appeared to lack distinctiveness while the founders lacked business experience. Overall, Bhatia and Smith's JavaSoft plan was rejected in 20 attempts to obtain finance.

Determined to succeed, the entrepreneurs revised their business plans after each discussion with an investor. Afraid that their corporate e-mail might be monitored since they were still in regular employment, they exchanged new versions of the plan through their private AOL e-mail accounts which they could log into from work. However, their employer suddenly set up a new firewall which prevented accessing AOL from the office. Still reluctant to transmit the business plan via the corporate network, the budding entrepreneurs were forced to swap the plan on diskettes, a practice which they found cumbersome and frustrating.

Jack Smith's creative solution to their problem of sending and receiving private e-mail at work became the basis for their revolutionary Hotmail service. He pointed out that they could both view web sites from work. "Why don't we simply have our e-mails displayed on a web page?"[5] He realised that they could easily adapt the JavaSoft database to store and display e-mail messages as HTML documents via regular Internet browsers. This would circumvent corporate firewalls and make content tracking by employers more difficult since the messages would reside on a server external to the company. Also, the reprogramming of JavaSoft—originally conceived as a database for storing personal information over the Internet—would be relatively straightforward.

At first, the entrepreneurs considered developing Hotmail in parallel to JavaSoft, using it to showcase their main product's possibilities. But they soon came to focus exclusively on Hotmail, proposing to provide the service at no cost to the user and funding it through revenue from advertisers. Successful Internet start-ups before them, notably Netscape and Yahoo, had been able to offer a free service. Yahoo's growth suggested it was possible to generate revenue through banner ads.

The founders had to continue their search for funding but Bhatia and Smith were concerned about disclosing the Hotmail concept to an unethical investor. Like many of the best ideas, this one seemed obvious once articulated and would be easy to appropriate. They had to

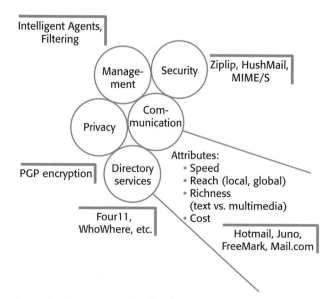

Figure 3: *Consumer needs in the electronic messaging industry*

implement their business concept before anyone else could and this required taking care to whom they showed the idea. To find a trustworthy investor, the entrepreneurs continued to approach investors with the JavaSoft plan, using it to test VCs based on their reactions. Only if the VC had gained their respect during this 'mock discussion' would the founders actually disclose the sensitive Hotmail messaging idea.

The idea for free e-mail via the web—Hotmail—soon caught the interest of the venture capital firm Draper Fisher Jurvetson from whom they received $300K in funding. After organising an additional $100K loan, Sabeer Bhatia and Jack Smith founded Hotmail in the first months of 1996. Bhatia demonstrated remarkable negotiation skills. The experience of earlier rejections did not prevent him from adopting a tough stance during these talks:

> " 'He's the most interesting negotiator I've ever met,' Jurvetson says. Tim Draper made the perfectly reasonable offer of retaining 30 percent ownership on a $1 million valuation. Sabeer held out for double that valuation—their cut, 15 percent. The negotiations got nowhere, so Sabeer shrugged and stood up and walked out the door. His only other available option was a $100,000 family-and-friends round that Jack Smith had arranged as a backup—not nearly enough money. 'If we'd gone that route, Hotmail wouldn't exist today,' says Jack. Draper and Jurvetson relented; they called back two days later to accept their 15 percent."[6]

Draper Fisher Jurvetson were already acquainted with the concept of 'Internet companies' as they had previously invested in the start-up Four11, a directory services firm that registered e-mail addresses for Internet users. At a party organised by the VC for its portfolio companies, Hotmail's founders were introduced to Mike Santullo, the CEO of Four11.

Santullo told them that Four11 had been founded in 1994 by himself and Larry Drebes as a database tailored "to help people find people." By the end of 1996, the firm had formed partnerships with Yahoo, Intel, Netscape, Microsoft, NYNEX, Infoseek, USWEST and WebTV, among others. Its services included an extensive e-mail register, a complete US telephone directory as well as government and celebrity listings. Industry sources lauded the service. PC Meter ranked it as the number one directory for customer reach in 1997 and PC Magazine had described it as the most comprehensive 'people finder' on the Internet. Discussing their business ventures, the founders of Hotmail and Four11 soon realised that they could forge a strategic alliance: Hotmail could register its users in Four11's directory.

Encouraged by their common investor, Hotmail and Four11 decided to set up the strategic relationship, hoped to benefit all parties. The proposition seemed simple: (1) Four11 would increase the numbers of addresses in its database, (2) Hotmail would offer an additional service to its users, and (3) the VC would benefit indirectly through increasing activity of its investee firms.

In June 1996, a serious problem suddenly raised its head. Less than six months after start-up and only one month prior planned service launch set for an Independence Day launch on 4th July, Hotmail had unexpectedly burned through the available venture funding and was out of cash. Up to that point, competitors in the web-based free e-mail category had not yet emerged, so Bhatia and Smith were still hoping to reap an advantage by launching Hotmail in July before anyone else provided a similar service.

The founders were reluctant to raise additional funds before launch, fearing undue dilution of their equity stakes. Recognising that their bargaining position would be improved with a functioning service, they persuaded their fifteen (in part freelance) employees to forego their salary checks and to continue to work for stock options only. Their persuasive efforts succeeded despite the alternatives open to employees in Silicon Valley, where both salary and stock options came with almost every job. As a result, Hotmail operated without additional cash for several weeks, on the basis of employees' willingness to support the venture.

The acute lack of cash also prevented the extensive investment into marketing that many believed necessary to launch a new Internet-based service. However, a suggestion by their VC, Draper Fisher Jurvetson, helped Hotmail to overcome this problem. The idea was to simply add "PS Get your own free Hotmail at www.hotmail.com" to the bottom of every outgoing message, effectively turning every despatched e-mail into a piece of free advertising. This approach subsequently came to be known as 'viral marketing.'

Bhatia and Smith were at first sceptical. They knew that the Internet community—historically steeped in a culture of publicly funded resources and freeware—remained highly averse to advertising. 'Spammers' (firms that abused the medium by circulating advertising material) were subject to Internet attacks. The following example and comment were symptomatic.

> "In April 1994 a Phoenix law firm posted an advertisement to 6,000 Usenet (Internet) news groups. The presence of an ad on the Internet provoked a firestorm of protest from over 30,000 Internet users who flooded the lawyers' mailboxes with hate-mail, conducted terrorist-type acts against the lawyers, and eventually led the Internet service provider to

cut off the law firm's access. (...) Why is advertising on the Internet controversial? A key reason is that it does not fit with the existing Internet culture. In some ways it is subversive to that existing culture, and bringing commercialization to the Internet can be seen as a colonization of one culture by another."[7]

The venture capitalist recalls "It was very contentious at the time. Would users balk at having this automatic addition to the content of their private messages?"[8]

In the end, Hotmail's venture capitalists were able to convince the entrepreneurs that the viral marketing technique should be given a try. According to Draper: "When we first suggested it, they were taking the purist point of view, saying, 'We can't do that—it's spamming! (...) But by the end of the conversation, it dawned on them that it wasn't much different from running a banner ad."[9] Also, they tempered the ad by clearly separating it from the main message via a line and removing the prefix "PS" from the text.

Far from causing outrage among users, 'viral marketing' produced spectacular subscriber base growth for Hotmail from the day of its launch. The implied personal endorsement by the sender appeared to be valued and the website address made it very easy for new users to take up the offer. Hotmail's founders and employees excitedly tracked user base growth in real time using modified pagers. In the first hour 100 users signed on, 200 in the second, 250 in the third. By September, Hotmail boasted a total of 100,000 subscribers, by January 1997 1,000,000, and this number rose to 8,000,000 by October of that year. No means of communication had ever spread so fast. The firm's record growth had begun.

Having demonstrated its viability and rapid subscriber base growth, Hotmail was able to raise additional rounds of venture capital funding on the basis of an increased valuation. By August 1996, the firm was valued at $7 million, by October at around $20 million, up from $2 million in January of the same year. By June 1997, Hotmail had raised a total of $5.6 million in venture capital finance and operated with 35 employees.

Another impact of rapid growth related to the directory firm Four11, the partner firm that was an early witness of Hotmail's expansion. According to Sabeer Bhatia, Hotmail had sent "more subscribers to Four11's directory in three or four months than they had amassed in two years."[10] Now aware of the tremendous opportunity free e-mail seemed to represent, Four11 began to develop its own free e-mail capability internally—termed RocketMail—thus entering into head-to-head competition with Hotmail (see Figure 4).

There were different views on this controversial decision. The common investor, Draper Fisher Jurvetson, argued that Hotmail's rapid growth had begun to affect

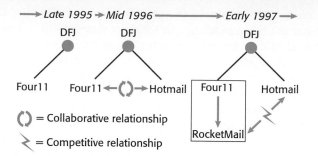

Figure 4: *The evolution of the 'triad' relationship between Draper Fisher Jurvetson (VC), Four11 (directory services firm), and Hotmail (free e-mail firm).*

Four11's relative position in their portfolio. The VC believed that the firm's "growth was so strong that the power in the relationship shifted toward Hotmail, and Four11 realized they had to develop their own e-mail service."[11] For Four11's CEO, on the other hand, the decision reflected a logical step given the nature of consumer needs in online communication: "We focused on Internet directories at the beginning, but we decided that we needed to expand our model to include different online communications services—one of which was Web-based e-mail."[12]

In response to the new competitive relation between two of their portfolio firms, Draper Fisher Jurvetson reorganised internally. Hotmail was looked after by Steve Jurvetson and Four11 by Tim Draper. The VC partners agreed to erect a "Chinese Wall" between them by not discussing issues pertaining to these rival firms, thus avoiding legal problems that could arise from a conflict of interests. This internal reorganisation was not easy to uphold in practice, however. Steve Jurvetson recalls: "It was frustrating because we're used to working as a team, and suddenly 100 percent of my focus had to be on Hotmail (...) I can remember standing outside a Four11 meeting, looking through the glass doors and wondering what they were talking about."[13]

A negative consequence of the firm's extremely fast user base growth was server overload. By December 1996, Hotmail's service levels became increasingly spotty as the subscriber base spurted towards the 1 million mark. The firm's unexpected popularity by now taxed the servers far beyond their capacity and the founders needed to react to keep the service operational.

Hotmail could try to solve this problem in a number of ways. For a start, it could simply ration the service and thus limit the amount of usage their servers had to support. However, the founders were reluctant to accept the reduction of their growth rate which this would entail. As Jack Smith recalls: "We never considered rationing (although we joked about it, because we were 'here to provide free e-mail to everyone,' and become the largest e-mail provider in the world."[14]

A second option would be to increase capacity by adding new servers. However this turned out to be more difficult than originally envisaged because a simple purchase and installation of new servers would not solve the problem. Jack Smith explained.

". . . why didn't we simply add more servers to address the capacity issue? We did that to some extent, but ultimately architecture defines scalability. Especially in an e-mail system where there's messaging involved, and there is no data storage overlap between users, scalability is complex."[15]

Thus the question became how could Hotmail acquire a more scalable e-mail technology? Due to the immaturity of messaging software at the time, such a technology could not be purchased on the open market:

"These were the early days of Internet architecture . . . In those days the right solution couldn't be had at any price. We were the fastest growing e-mail provider, and about the largest . . . Any vendor solution (of any type) we tried melted down under our loads . . . Today solutions are available that would have made things easier."[16]

Jack Smith was now left with only one solution: to develop a new, more scalable technology internally and implement it while minimising interruption to the firm's one million current users. The co-founder pointed out: "This is tantamount to replacing the engine of the car while driving it down the highway at 75 miles per hour."[17] He explained to us:

"I architected the scaleable solution myself, and drew no input from outside (who else had the battle scars?). . . . my solution was a bit unorthodox at the time, and I received no real buy-in from the Hotmail engineers either. I forced the redesign to occur by doing the implementation of it with a couple engineers in parallel to the rest of the Hotmail engineering initiatives."[18]

By early March 1997, the new technology had been successfully installed and it offered a degree of scalability vastly higher than conventional e-mail products. The rapid growth of Hotmail's user base could continue and signup rates grew to higher levels than ever before.

Hotmail's revenues did not expand as easily as its user base. It achieved about $4 million in its first full year of operation, rising to an expected $20 million by the end of 1998. At the end of 1997 Bhatia stated that the service could be profitable, but is choosing to reinvest proceeds into expansion. Much uncertainty still surrounded the notion of advertising on the Internet while advertisers remained unsure as to how consumers would react to the new medium. To further grow its revenue base, Hotmail replaced its five person sales team in March 1997 with Softbank Interactive Marketing (a professional new media advertising reseller) and allowed third party content providers to distribute news and other content to members who agreed to receive it. Bhatia insisted that instead of Hotmail paying content providers, the content providers should pay Hotmail for access to the growing membership base.

Microsoft and Yahoo Enter the Scene

When it launched Microsoft Network in 1995, Microsoft had decided not to offer free e-mail, viewing the concept as unproven and risky. According to a spokesperson at the time, "we don't think it's a clear-cut win yet, so at the launch of the Microsoft Network there won't be sponsored e-mail."[19] However, the rapid growth of Hotmail and competing services (RocketMail, Juno) convinced Microsoft to reassess this opportunity and consider integrating free e-mail into its Internet presence. So strong did this perception become that Bill Gates reportedly "told a meeting of MSN employees that there were three things wrong with them, and screwing up plans to build an e-mail system was number one."[20] But Microsoft was not alone in making such plans: Yahoo was also giving thought to enhancing its directory with free e-mail functionality. It did not take long before these two firms contacted Four11 and Hotmail.

When Microsoft and Yahoo approached Hotmail and Four11/RocketMail for what initially were reseller discussions, their common venture capitalist, Draper Fisher Jurvetson, interpreted this as an opportunity to exit from the engagement and pushed the discussion on a different trajectory. "Yahoo wanted a free-mail service for its Web directory, and Microsoft wanted a free-mail capability for its online service. The venture backers of Four11 and Hotmail . . . , however, wanted to sell the whole works."[21]

The process of negotiation that culminated in the sale of Hotmail to Microsoft and RocketMail to Yahoo was complex. In September 1997, Draper Fisher Jurvetson's bargaining position was enviable: it held significant stakes in two rapidly growing free e-mail providers that together accounted for 64% of all web-mail boxes known to exist. To counter this bargaining position, Microsoft emphasized its determination to enter the free e-mail business on its own, should a deal fail to transpire.

An observer portrayed the situation:

"At one point, apparently, Microsoft was thinking of buying Four11, and DFJ was weighing its own options. 'One of our thoughts was to merge the two companies,' Mr. Draper says. 'It was a bit of a chess game. (...)' Mr. Jurvetson says the role of the VC in instances like these is extremely delicate. 'The last thing we wanted was for the two companies to compete with each other, to get acquired, and to weaken each other in the process,' he explains, 'The worst case would have been for Microsoft to play the two off against each other.' "[22]

In October 1997, not Microsoft but Yahoo acquired Four11 for approximately $93 million. After this sale, the VC concentrated on divesting Hotmail. "The Four11 deal both freed up Mr. Draper to work with Hotmail and gave him experience that undoubtedly helped the negotiations with Microsoft."[23]

According to Shirish Nadkarni, director of product planning for Microsoft Network and Microsoft's main negotiator, "Hotmail had demonstrated that it was capable of easily handling vast amounts of e-mail without significant problems, and should be capable of handling even more."[24]

A record valuation was achieved in a multi-stage negotiation process in which Microsoft initially offered about $100 million for Hotmail. The sale probably also benefited from Sabeer Bhatia's excellent negotiation skills which had been proven on several prior occasions. About two months later, in December 1997, Hotmail was then sold to Microsoft in a record transaction amounting to approximately $395 million.

After this acquisition was announced in the media it exerted a powerful effect on the emerging Internet industry. First, it provided the VC and Internet start-up community with a new precedent for 'comparable transactions.' According to Hotmail's founder: "Once Microsoft bought us, valuations [of Internet firms] went through the roof in 1998 and 1999. Everyone started using that as a benchmark."[25] As a result, more financial resources were released to Internet firms generally and messaging ventures in particular.

Moreover, Hotmail's rapid growth and sale to Microsoft raised awareness of 'viral marketing.' Other Internet firms tried to imitate the widely publicised technique and consultancies emerged that offered 'viral marketing services.' A senior analyst from Jupiter Communications observed that "the reason why these companies are coming to market (...) is that everybody is trying to find a way to systematically harness the power of viral marketing."[26] Ultimately even traditional marketers, for instance Procter & Gamble, employed it in the launch of conventional products such as shampoo.

Lastly, after the endorsement of free e-mail implied by Microsoft's and Yahoo's acquisition of Hotmail and Four11 respectively, free e-mail came to be perceived as indispensable for online firms. But soon even traditional companies like American Express began to offer web-mail to their customers, while others like United Airlines, began to adopt a web-based solution to messaging for their internal communication needs.

After Microsoft's much-publicised acquisition of Hotmail, the firm continued to innovate and add new services. Hotmail integrated more tightly with the extensive Microsoft Network and continued to grow at a rapid pace. By the end of 2000, the firm had accumulated around 86 million active mailboxes and reached an estimated $100 million in annual revenue. By May 2001, over 100 million users had signed up from all over the world. According to Microsoft, on a typical day more new accounts are opened on Hotmail than babies born in the world.

Hotmail will take its place among the pioneers in business history, an entrepreneurial venture that opened Internet e-mail to the multitudes.

Questions

1. How did Hotmail come to develop its unique business idea? What light does this throw on the process of detecting an opportunity for a new business?

2. What resource constraints were faced by Hotmail and how did the entrepreneurs overcome them? What key resources were created and why?

3. What led to the adoption of viral marketing? Were there any dangers associated with this decision? If so, could anything have been done to reduce these?

4. How was Hotmail supported and constrained by the network in which it was embedded?

5. More specifically, comment on the advantages and disadvantages of strategic partnerships in the light of Hotmail's experience with Four11.

6. What was the role of the venture capitalist in this case? Were there any asymmetries in the relationship with Hotmail?

Appendix

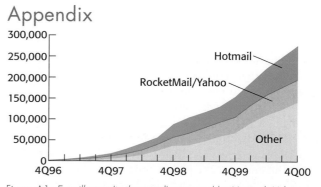

Figure A1: *E-mailboxes (in thousand) managed by Hotmail, Yahoo and other web-mail providers*
(*Source: Messaging Online 2001; Reproduced by permission*)

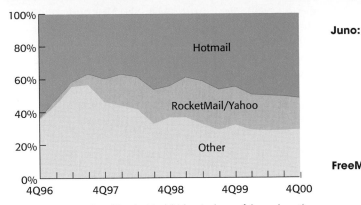

Figure A2: *Hotmail and RocketMail/Yahoo's share of the web-mail market (in %)*
(Source: Messaging Online 2001; Reproduced by permission)

COMPETITORS

Juno: Founded in 1995 and launched its service in April 1996. A dial-up based free e-mail service backed by New York investment bank DE Shaw & Company and led by Charles Ardai, a former employee of this bank. Juno invested up to $20 million in its launch phase and was guaranteed support of up to $100 million from DE Shaw for further investment following its launch.

FreeMark: A dial-up service founded in 1994, but that only went live in April 1996 after a major change in its business idea. The firm was shut down at the end of 1996 having acquired approximately 50,00 subscribers.

2%   2%
2%   2%
3%   2%
3%   1%
4%   1%
5%   1%
7%   15%
19%   31%

▨ Hotmail	▨ NetEase
▨ RocketMail/Yahoo	▨ Netscape WebMail
▨ Excite Inbox	▨ Lycos Mail
▨ Lycos Mail &MailCity	▨ iVillage
▨ Sina.com SinaMail	▨ Rediff.com RediffMail
▨ NBCi	■ Kimo Mail
▨ USA.Net Net@ddress	▢ Juno Online
▨ UOLmail	▨ Other

Figure A3: *Market shares of firms in the web-mail service market (year 2000).*
(Source: Messaging Online 2001; Reproduced by permission)

ESTIMATED FINANCIALS*

	1996	1997	1998	1999	2000
Sales	<$1M	$4M	$20M	na	$100M
Mailboxes	1M	8M	na	na	86M
Employees	30	60	144	na	na

(*All figures are end-of-year estimates)

Bibliography

[EMMS 1998] Electronic Mail & Messaging Systems (1998). "Microsoft Buys Hotmail, Improving Its Industry Position Against cc:Mail," 12.1.1998.

Baran, P (1964). "On Distributed Communications: I. Introduction to Distributed Communications Network," *RAND Corporation* Research Memorandum (RM-3420-PR), August 1964.

Besser, H (1994). "A clash of cultures on the Internet," *San Francisco Chronicle* (http://www.gseis.ucla.edu/~howard/Papers/sf-chron.html (accessed 18.3.2001))

Bronson, G (1995). "Message as medium—Free e-mail service will carry ads," *Interactive Age*, 8.5 1995.

Bronson, P (1998). "HotMale," *Wired*, 6.12, December 1998.

Bronson, P (2000). *The Nudist on the Late Shift*. Vintage: London.

Cavender, S (1998). "Legends," *Forbes ASAP*, 5.10.1998, pp. 126–127.

Gimein, M (1998). "Ten VCs Who Matter," *The Industry Standard*, 5.10.1998.

Harbrecht, D (2000). "Hotmail's Creator Is Starting Up Again, and Again, and . . . ," *Business Week Online*, 14.9.2000.

Hatlestad, L (1999). "Free Mail Explosion," *Red Herring Magazine*, 1.6.1999.

Hugo, O A and E W Garnsey (2001). "The Emergence of Electronic Messaging and the Growth of Four Entrepreneurial Entrants," *Proceedings of the 9th High-Technology Small Firms Conference*, Manchester (31.5.2001).

Jurvetson, S and T Draper (1999). "Viral Marketing," online at www.drapervc.com. (Note: An edited version of this paper was later published in *Business 2.0*)

Messaging Online (2001). "Mailbox Report Presentation," by Eric Arnum, Editor of Messaging Online (*provided in personal communication with Oliver Hugo*).

Parker, P (2000). "A Start-Up Story: How and Why Favemail Shifted Its Strategy," *ChannelSeven*, 26.7.2000.

PR Newswire (1997). "Hotmail is Now the Cyber Home to More Than Two Million Users," *PR Newswire*, 27.2.1997.

Segaller, S (1999). *Nerds 2.0.1*. TV Books: New York.

Smith, J (2001). *Personal Communication with Oliver Hugo*. 29.10.2001

Wilson, D L (1998). "Microsoft Buys HotMail Corp," *San Jose Mercury News*, 2.1.1998.

Case 2 Collège Coach

Carl Hedberg, case writer
Arthur M. Blank Center for Entrepreneurship Babson College

Michael London and Stephen Kramer sat in front of the television at Stephen's apartment in Brookline, Massachusetts, which served as the corporate offices of College Coach, the college admissions advisory service they had started up seven months earlier. Feedback from their pilot retail classes and from a corporate workshop had been encouraging. The partners had identified three distinct business models: retail classes for students, corporate workshops, and high school guidance consulting. They now needed to consider which models to pursue, and related to that strategic plan was a decision on the type of facility they would require to run their operations. The partners had recently secured the services of a public relations firm, and Michael slipped one of the products of that relationship into the VCR. They smiled as a well-known local network news reporter began:

> In the locker room and on the field of play, coaches are there to make sure every player lives up to his or her potential. So how about a hired gun to help make sure your teenager gets his or her best shot at the college admissions game? . . . Michael London and Stephen Kramer fancy themselves the Knute Rockney and Vince Lombardi of the college-bound crowd . . .

Friends and Partners

Stephen and Michael met as freshmen at Babson College in Wellesley, Massachusetts. Back in high school, Michael had become intrigued by the intricacies of applying to college, and he found Stephen to be an effective and interested brainstormer on the idea of starting a business to help students through the process. In their second year they created Waterboys, an on-campus water cooler sales and delivery service. This venture proved successful and the partners were voted runners-up for the school's annual business initiative award.

After college Michael joined the Marketing Development Program at Digital Equipment Corporation, and attended the evening MBA program at Boston University. He later worked as a Senior Consultant at Harte-Hanks Direct Marketing in Philadelphia, but continued to research the college admissions advisory opportunity. In fact, in the years following his undergraduate education, he had served as an independent consultant to over 100 college-bound students.

Stephen initially worked at Arthur D. Little, where he assisted clients in developing strategic plans, creating market entry strategies, and improving operations. After graduating from the Harvard Business School, he joined Fidelity Ventures in Boston. He kept in touch with Michael and they continued to develop a plan for their college advisory business. Stephen commented:

> At Fidelity I was in charge of starting up and running their for-profit education [venture capital] practice. We looked at companies that were providing service in the education space: tutorial in nature, preparation in nature, software, and long distance learning businesses. Michael and I had a lot of interesting conversations about the various business models that I was being exposed to, and we applied this to what we were thinking about within our opportunity.

By the spring of 1998 they were meeting every weekend, either in Boston or in the Philadelphia area, to work on their business plan. As their commitment to the opportunity increased, interest in their jobs began to wane. Fall is a critical time for seniors preparing to apply to colleges, and the pair realized that if they wanted to offer pilot classes by that time, they would have to devote their full energies to College Coach. They gave their employers their notices, and by July they had become partners in the field of college admissions advising.

The Demand for College Advisory Services

Applying to college had become a demanding and stressful process that included transcripts, SAT scores, essays, short answer questions, interviews and the securing of letters of recommendation. Competition to attend the best schools was evidenced by the fact that in 1998 the University of Pennsylvania rejected 300 high school valedictorians, Stanford turned away 10,000 straight-A students with high SATs, and Berkeley rejected 5,000 applicants with similar achievements.

In 1995, 62% of the 1.7 million high school seniors in the U.S. applied to college. This percentage tended to be higher in states with large white-collar populations. In Massachusetts, for example, 71% of the 49,681 public school graduates and nearly 100% of the 10,281 private

This case was prepared by Carl Hedberg under the direction of Professor William Bygrave. © Copyright Babson College, 1999. All rights reserved.

school graduates continued on to college. Nationally, 3% had used the services of independent educational consultants in 1995, which was up from 1% in 1991. The average expense for these services was between $1,000 and $1,500. It was expected that college advisory services would eventually achieve a market demand on par with the 375,000 students that currently enroll each year in SAT test preparation classes.

The overall population of college-bound students was expected to rise dramatically over the next 10-20 years for two reasons:

- The ever-widening disparity between high school and college graduate pay scales was forcing more and more families to conclude that college was no longer an option but a requirement, and
- The "baby boom echo," as it had been called, was expected to increase high school populations by twenty percent over the next 10–20 years.

The market was being served primarily by earnest, well-meaning parents, overworked high-school counselors, and independent advisors (usually former high school counselors or former college admissions officers), who typically worked out of their home. Parents were often ineffective not only because of their lack of expertise but because this task fell at a time when parent-child relationships could be somewhat strained. The average high school counselor in the U.S. was responsible for over 300 students, and in addition to college advising, their tasks included dealing with issues such as drugs, general discipline and teenage pregnancy. As a result, guidance counselors spent little time with the majority of the student body, and with regard to college advising, tended to work with the most talented students and with students with special needs. The best were exciting to work with, and the challenged students often had active parents who advocated on their behalf. Effective independent counselors were hard to locate and the best could cost thousands of dollars.

College testing prep centers like Kaplan and Princeton Review had certainly been watching the growing demand for college admission advising, and Kaplan's website [www.1.kaplan.com] offered a range of helpful advice and services on the subject. Until recently, however, the college advisory market had attracted no growth-oriented corporate entrants. In February of 1997, Carlos Watson left a lucrative position with McKinsey & Co. and founded Achieva, a venture-backed company based in Palo Alto, California. Achieva charges fees ranging from a few hundred dollars to as much as $3,000 for full-service college admissions counseling that includes test preparation and tutoring. Significant start-up capital enabled the company to open eight centers in the first year, with twenty-two more West Coast centers planned for 1999. By the year 2002 Watson expected to have gone public

and opened 250 Achieva centers across the U.S. On the opposite coast, Stephen Kramer and Michael London had plans of their own.

College Coach

The partners had completed the business plan by early summer of 1998, and had left their jobs without having any commitment other than to spend their own money to get the operations up and running, and to build a successful college advisory business. College Coach would assist families in determining an appropriate mix of target schools for each student. Developing compelling applications and interview strategies for those choices would be the cornerstone of the business, but they also planned to assist parents and students in the difficult task of applying for and securing financial aid.

Michael and Stephen immediately set out to raise the $500,000 they would need to fund the first eighteen months of operations. They contacted family members, who initially provided the requisite hand-wringing admonishments about the opportunity costs of leaving two great jobs and about how little actual experience Michael and Stephen had in the education field.

The founders broadened their search for capital. Stephen was adept at dealing with investor issues and Michael could sell the model in his sleep. In less than two months they closed on $575,000 from seven investors that included family friends, personal friends and colleagues. Five investors held straight equity and two held debt with warrants. These were relatively inexpensive start-up funds, and preserved a good portion of the equity for the substantial venture capital infusion they were planning to seek early in 2001. This second round would help them achieve their five-year goal of operating in 17 markets with yearly revenues of $15 million.

Raising funds was a critical component in being able to hold trial classes in the fall, but developing a compelling, professional curriculum for College Coach was their number one priority. The partners conducted surveys with students, parents, guidance counselors and others to determine the relative importance of each of the key elements of the college admissions process. They contracted with experts in the field of designing curriculum, and partnered them with content experts such as essay writers, leading admissions officers and college financial aid officers. As with the surveys, parent and student input was crucial to insure that the College Coach program would resonate with the target audience. The project, along with copyrighting expenses, cost just under $30,000. The result was an elaborate 1,000-page manual that included group exercises, games, and role-playing interviews (See Exhibit 1 for a College Coach promotional piece that provides an overview of the course offerings). The partners were very satisfied with the curriculum, but

---

The College Coach Workshop

College Selection—College Coach knows the right questions to ask students and parents to create a personalized college list. Once the list is complete, College Coach uses its knowledge about the admissions process and past applicants to determine a student's likelihood of getting into each school. College Coach maintains a near-flawless record at predicting admission outcomes.

Student Marketing—College Coach lets students understand what it is like to be an admissions officer. Using this intelligence as a weapon, each student works with College Coach to discover what makes him/her special and to sell that "special something" to colleges-gaining an admissions edge.

Organization—Students have a lot to think about and College Coach has a proven way of assisting students to get their hands around all of it. Should I do early decision? How many schools should I apply to? Is on-line easier? What do schools think of the common application? Do I really have to write so many essays? Can I read my recommendations? Does the school need to receive my application by the 15th or does it just have to be postmarked by that day? College Coach gives students control over the college admissions process by arming them with organizational tools and answering any college questions that arise.

Essay Writing— Essay specialists work with students to complete their main essay. Unlike their English teacher or tutor, College Coach goes far beyond structure and grammar. Utilizing its proprietary essay writing techniques and individualized marketing themes, College Coach ensures students create memorable, powerful, award-winning essays that gain college acceptances. Students say that College Coach is the best cure for writer's block.

Interviewing—There is only one way for your student to become a strong interviewer—practice, practice, practice. Students sharpen their interviewing skills by preparing with real college admissions interviewers from the nation's top universities. Dressed for success, students are interviewed and critiqued by a series of admissions officers of differing styles. Students graduate College Coach with confidence and improved interview techniques that will never be forgotten.

Recommendations— Colleges expect students to receive strong teacher recommendations. Students fail to realize they can influence a teacher's recommendation with coaching. College Coach helps students maximize their chances of impressing admissions officers with standout letters of recommendation.

Paying for College—Financial Aid Experts teach parents how the financial aid process works and how it can benefit any family, regardless of income. Designed specifically for the parents of College Coach students, this session explains all the options available to finance their child's education. Parents leave with greater knowledge and in many cases more money for the future.

---

they also understood that even the best program would fail unless it was properly presented to the students.

Staffing

The College Coach plan emphasized that the partners would manage the business, and the classes would be executed—based on the curriculum—by people who had an ability to teach. This would be part-time work paying between $15 and $20 per hour. For the trial classes the previous fall, they had worked hard to secure individuals with impressive, relevant backgrounds. Michael indicated that he and Stephen were surprised by the results:

> We had a director of admissions. We also had an essay writer with an undergrad from Tufts and a Masters and a PhD from Brandeis, who had taught five years of freshman English at Brandeis. We found that credentials did not make them great at what we do. I think the students were somewhat more forgiving than we were; they may have had mediocre teachers in high school. But we need great

teachers. Those are the people the students are going to talk about when they go home.

The partners turned to the schools of education at Harvard and Boston College, where they found an interested pool of graduate students who had some high school classroom experience. They also invited potential candidates to present a piece of the College Coach curriculum and be critiqued by an educator from Harvard. This exercise revealed that the best teachers were motivational types who have taught high school English, and who have some experience in college admissions. Stephen and Michael were satisfied that they could successfully staff their classes. It was evident, however, that turnover would be high, and that, as they expanded operations, access to teaching colleges would be an important site-selection criteria.

Full-time personnel at the corporate level would be minimal. Stephen and Michael would serve respectively as Chief Operating Officer and Chief Marketing Officer. A third key individual was the Director of Education, for which they chose a former superintendent of the Needham (Massachusetts) public school system. His task was primarily to help forge relationships with area high schools. In addition, an operations manager would be brought on to support the activities of the College Coach offices. In-bound calls during peak direct marketing periods would be handled either by an in-house telemarketing group or by contracting with an independent telemarketing firm.

For specific projects, the partners planned to hire temporary workers or utilize student interns from area colleges. For example, during the spring of 1999, four Babson College students were working on a variety of tasks, including setting up a prospect/client database, and researching the competition, benefit-friendly corporations, and on-line college application services. In addition, at the end of the semester two of the students were planning to collaborate on the design and implementation of a College Coach PR event at a local high school.

The fund-raising agreement stipulated that the investors had the right to elect an individual to join the founders on a three-person Board of Directors. This person had not been chosen as yet. A Board of Advisors was also planned. The partners hoped to attract respected professionals from leading universities and the business community who could offer their expertise in such functional areas as business scaling, corporate benefits, and retail consumer marketing.

Retail Classes

In selling their retail program, the partners found that many of the students they were targeting lead busy lives with sporting commitments, extra-curricular activities at school, and other private lessons like music and SAT preparation. College Coach students could expect to spend 14 hours in class and in addition be assigned a few hours of homework. So, while the company was virtually alone in offering this type of classroom advisory instruction, they were competing heavily for the student's available time.

Initially parents had expressed concern as to whether group instruction would adequately satisfy the needs of a range of students. This did not appear to be a problem since the curriculum presented the material clearly enough to enable everyone to achieve at their own level. In fact, Michael felt that in many ways group instruction was a more valuable experience than a one-on-one session:

> It was interesting in our first class because in a classroom setting someone with a 900 SAT and a C-Average can say to a bright kid, 'Your essay doesn't make sense; it's confusing. You are trying to use big words and it doesn't mean anything.' They are less threatened than in a normal class. People who may not be great students feel very comfortable voicing

their opinions in a classroom like ours because it's not real school.

In the fall they provided two classes for 15 students who paid $500 each. In the spring they expected to have a second round of pilot classes with 50 students paying a more realistic fee of $700. These clients were mostly juniors hoping to get an early jump on the process by visiting potential schools during their spring break. This would end the pilot sessions. By the following year their goal was to scale the business to support a target enrollment of 250, with an average class size of 15 students.

Despite some challenges with the teaching staff, overall the partners were pleased with how their test classes had been received. They had some early-decision application successes and deferrals, but the real test of the College Coach program would come after April 1st when the colleges released their regular decisions.

Throughout the fall of 1998, most of the focus had been on building an effective program for classroom instruction. At the same time, the partners had been investigating and developing what they felt were two other equally viable markets—high schools and "benefit friendly" corporations.

High School Consulting

One direct result of the heightened competition for spots at top schools was that high school administrators were under increasing pressure to provide their students with adequate college guidance. This pressure was certainly felt in average school systems with low admissions ratios to good schools, but it was most acute at public schools in affluent communities and in private schools. The difference was that private schools, with tuitions often exceeding $15,000 a year, were less inclined to acknowledge their weakness in this area by seeking or accepting assistance from an outside organization.

Since College Coach was an outside contractor and not part of the union, selling to schools frequently involved quite a bit of political wrangling. Guidance counselors were often defensive, and school committees tended to have a wide range of opinions on almost any issue. The best approach was to first sell the superintendent on the idea from a value-cost-benefit perspective, and then have that person move it down the chain of command to the principal and finally to the guidance counselors. The partners felt that having the various school officials on board would go a long way in tempering possible objections from the school committees and union groups.

Their Director of Education proved to be an effective prospector, and their program had been presented to a number of school systems in the Boston area. By February of 1999, however, the partners had become a bit disappointed with the inability of this "hired gun" to close sales. So far they had secured just one deal, but Stephen and Michael were optimistic about signing up a few local high schools by the end of the spring semester.

Stephen and Michael adopted a consultative approach with schools since no two administrations seemed to be dealing with their guidance challenges in the same way. Some expressed interest in having College Coach provide one-day student workshops. Others were considering summer training programs for their guidance counselors, and one school involved in an administrative turnover was looking at the possibility of transferring the entire college advising function to College Coach. The partners were confident that they had the flexibility to service these potential accounts, each of which would represent a unique allocation of administrative and teaching resources.

Corporations

Michael and Stephen discovered that selling to corporations involved a difficult process similar to that of selling to school systems; they needed to target senior management and have them advocate the idea down the line. Early on Stephen had decided to approach Fidelity, where he had contacts in all levels of the company. He contacted the director of the company's Work-Life department, but soon realized that this individual was "more of an executer than a buyer." It became clear that the decision to adopt a discretionary benefit such as College Coach would have to come from the senior staff.

In the late fall, Stephen managed to get a referral to the president and COO of American International Group (AIG), the largest insurance company in the world, with 17,000 employees in the U.S. In the five minutes they were given to present their program, the partners successfully generated enough interest to be referred to the vice president of human resources. He happened to have a child in high school, as did the next in line, the director of worldwide training. These two championed the project within AIG and in December, College Coach presented a lunchtime workshop on Wall Street that was videoconferenced to 30 AIG centers around the world.

The partners were also retained to provide one-on-one counseling to every interested AIG employee, either in New York City or over the phone. Financially the project just broke even, but they felt it had been a huge success in terms of understanding the corporate market. Stephen commented on the experience:

> AIG looks for benefits that permeate all levels of the organization, and the group we presented to was very diverse. We had VP kids and kids of the people who load the trucks all night. Management saw 150 families get involved in one benefit, and this was

one of their primary success indicators. They also perceived that somehow we relieved stress and increased productivity because these employees were not spending time on the Internet looking at colleges. College Coach helped them through the process in a much more time-efficient way.

AIG expressed an interest in having College Coach return each year, and provided a referral to another multinational company based in New York. The partners began to develop a strategy for selling their services to a number of firms in Manhattan. Their plan was to organize a tight schedule of classes that would maximize their time spent on this annual visit to New York City. Although this past workshop had been held during the busy season for college advisory work, the goal was to concentrate corporate sessions in the summer months. They were also looking into the possibility of increasing sales by partnering with a well-established company that provided benefits to corporations, such as Cerridian and Workplace Connections.

Marketing

The two primary marketing objectives of the College Coach plan were to create name/brand recognition and to sell their admissions advisory services. At present the industry had no organized competition, and it was likely that many consumers were unaware of the availability of professional advisory classes. Therefore, in this and in subsequent markets that they entered, a large percentage of their promotional budget would be allocated to public relations efforts such as event sponsorship, media interviews, and speaking engagements. Following the second year of operations, the mix would include radio and newspaper advertising, with an ongoing emphasis on direct marketing.

Direct mail was viewed as the most cost-effective means of acquiring new clients. To reach potential retail customers, the partners planned to purchase lists from companies such as American Student Lists. A mailing in late 1998 to local upscale families with high school seniors generated enough interest to fill the pilot classes, but Stephen and Michael felt that the lists were not comprehensive enough. Their current database contained referrals and prospects pulled in from advertising and promotions, but eventually they hoped to increase the quality and depth of the lists by developing relationships with local high schools and community groups.

The company's promotional materials emphasized that the College Coach program worked well because each of the challenges of the application process were broken out and dealt with individually. They asserted that this strategy lowered stress and maximized the student's ability to pinpoint their relative strengths and weaknesses. In terms of addressing the competition, College Coach pointed out that private counselors were limited by their own bias and personal experience, and that guidance counselors simply had too many students to work with to be effective. Michael thought that a campaign dealing specifically with the failings of school guidance departments would be particularly successful, but he was hesitant to jeopardize the high school relationships they were trying to build.

Facility Strategies

The fall retail classes had been well received, and e-mails of praise were arriving from AIG participants. The curriculum had worked well, and it was now time to move operations out of Stephen's apartment. In the Boston area, general office space ranged from $15 to $25 a square foot in outlying towns, and from $25 to $40 downtown and in certain hot-market suburbs. Their business plan called for a leased 2,500 square foot facility in a densely populated town with high drive-by visibility. At an estimated cost of $80,000, the build-out was to include two classrooms with state-of-the-art technology, breakout rooms for one-on-one sessions, and a resource library store. Monthly lease expense for the first center was estimated at $5,000, which would include corporate office space. As operations grew, high volume towns more than twenty miles from the center would be served by satellites located in college/high school classrooms, synagogues, churches and community centers. These teaching centers would be operated only in the peak activity months each fall, and often charged as little as $25 a night for the space.

This "center-based" strategy had been modeled on what Kaplan had done with their educational centers. Building brand equity was a key element of the College Coach plan, and it was felt that having storefronts with high-impact signage would be an effective way to achieve an established and credible image.

The opposite end of the branding/location strategy spectrum was represented by Kaplan competitor Princeton Review. From a central office in New Jersey, this company had successfully built their brand equity almost entirely through advertising. Princeton Review avoided expensive storefront locations and conducted their classes in community centers close to their target markets. Both models had worked in building large businesses with tremendous brand equity, and advisors to College Coach seemed split as to which would be the most appropriate course to follow. Michael commented,

> Marketing people think we need to have a high-profile location to build the brand. Operations/finance people would say, "What do you need [a center] for? Spend the real estate money on ads and hold classes at area community space." Do we do

first-floor retail with signage and draw them in, or do we attract customers with aggressive advertising? There is a trade-off.

Preparing for Growth

The news piece concluded with a Newton (Massachusetts) student commenting on his high school's guidance program;

> "I don't think I've ever received a bad comment from my guidance counselor, and that's not bad, but you want to get some constructive criticism." The reporter then continued; "Jake Cohen is waiting to hear from eight schools he applied to from UMass to Princeton, but with the help of College Coaches, Cohen says he's got the confidence, that whatever happens, he's given it his best shot . . . "

The partners felt that with continued publicity of that kind they could expect to grow quickly throughout the Boston area. Reflecting on their first few months in business, they agreed that three discoveries had been particularly encouraging.

1. Stephen and Michael's skill sets complemented each other and they worked well together as partners.
2. They were able to execute a successful program using a curriculum that they were at least 80% satisfied with.
3. Corporations and high schools would buy, and these represented two additional markets.

The decision as to what type of facility to create was closely linked to promotional activities. Investing in a high-profile retail site with full-service teaching facilities was in part a marketing strategy to gain exposure and credibility. On the other hand, they could rent simple offices, steer clients to classes at community centers, and allocate the lease and build-out savings to further bolster their marketing campaign.

Given their limited resources, the partners determined that it would be difficult to pursue more than two of the three business models they had been developing. In making their choice, they needed to consider which models would work best together.

A recent call from the Kaplan Educational Centers indicated that word was spreading about College Coach activities. Stephen and Michael knew from their research that Kaplan was owned by The Washington Post, was well-capitalized, and had in the past acquired a number of smaller businesses in their industry. The partners were intrigued by Kaplan's interest and met with the corporate director of pre-college programs and his regional vice president. Although no offers were made, it was clear that the Kaplan people were impressed and would continue to monitor the progress of College Coach.

Preparation Questions

The partners were finding it difficult to service all three business models they had identified. If they chose to pursue two markets, which would be most complementary? What are the advantages and disadvantages of each business model? Consider lead generation potential, public relations opportunities, and account servicing logistics. What type of location should they choose, and how will their choice affect their marketing strategy? If the partners feel that there is a real possibility that a large potential partner such as Kaplan will continue to show interest, should this have an impact on their location and marketing decisions?

Case 3 Jack Sprat's Restaurant

Dan D'Heilly and Mark Helman, case writers
Arthur M. Blank Center for Enterpreneurship Babson College

In November of 1995, Chris Harami, nascent entrepreneur, and soon-to-be founder of Jack Sprat's Restaurants, pondered his year-old business plan. The plan was a work-in-process, but he hoped to open the first Jack Sprat's Restaurant during the summer of 1996. Chris wondered how to best ensure success.

During the course of his research, he had discovered that many restaurateurs used consultants to launch new restaurant concepts.* People in the industry agreed that using a consultant was usually a good idea. However, hiring a consultant was expensive, and the seed money was coming from his father—a financially secure (but very conservative and not rich) physician. He had retainer bids from consultants of between $50,000 and $150,000, and they all proposed rewriting the business plan as the first order of business. The consultant that Chris selected was Arlene Spiegel. She was enthusiastic about the concept and submitted the low bid.

Chris had written a professional-quality business plan in graduate school, then wrote and rewrote the plan for Jack Sprat's, so the value he saw in hiring a consultant was centered on building a successful team, and less on the business plan rewrite. Chris believed that Jack Sprat's could someday be a hot IPO and he wanted Arlene on the team to make sure it would happen, but his father did not understand the need. Was his father trying to micromanage the venture, or was this a role Chris wanted him to play? And did Chris really need a consultant to overhaul his plan, or was he just avoiding the leap into action. It was clear that they needed to conserve their scarce resources for the road ahead, but this might actually be a very conservative move.

Chris Harami

A connoisseur of fine cuisine and a cooking enthusiast, Chris had contemplated owning a restaurant from an early age. Now, at age 28, he was ready to move. His role models were his aunt and uncle who had been in the restaurant business since the 1960s. He liked the lifestyle:

*In the restaurant industry, new operations are usually designed around a single theme (e.g., American west steakhouse, home-cooking, ethnic). The theme is combined with the type of restaurant (e.g., fine dining, casual, fast food) and referred to as the "concept."

It was very social, almost like being in show business—they were celebrities. They were always talking to customers and they received a lot of recognition in the community. For years, my parents talked about opening a restaurant, but they never got into the details. It was always a distant, foggy dream.

Chris was overweight as a youth, and he consciously worked to control his weight as an adult. He was prone to the "yo-yo" weight-loss syndrome. He would diet and lose weight, then go off the diet and regain his original size. Chris was determined to lose weight, so he exercised regularly and vigorously. Unfortunately, his exercise program only offered a partial solution to his weight-loss problem. He felt and looked better, but didn't drop much weight.

Chris worked part-time in several restaurants while attending Pace University in New York City (Exhibit 1). He fell in love with the business and decided that he would someday open his own restaurant. Chris graduated with a business degree in 1990 and lived at home following college.

Things changed suddenly at the Harami's household when a stress test on his father revealed severe coronary blockage. His father, a physician, needed open-heart surgery. Afterwards, Dr. Harami was put on a diet low in fats, sodium, and cholesterol, and high in fiber. In support of this new lifestyle, the whole family changed the way they ate. Chris' exercise routine combined with his new diet reduced his waist size from 38 to 33. He was sold on the benefits of a healthy diet.

MBA: Crepe du Jour, s'il vous plait

In 1992, Chris enrolled in the Babson Graduate School of Business to "obtain the knowledge necessary to become a successful entrepreneur." One of his classes was New Venture Creation, a course where students formed teams to write business plans. In that class, his five-person team created a business plan for a chain of French quick-service restaurants (QSR) they called "Crepe du Jour." In the course of creating the business plan, Chris learned a great deal about success and failure in the restaurant business. Chris graduated in May 1994 with the intention of starting a chain of Crepe du Jour QSRs with his French team-member, Michael Tapiro.

As they continued to develop their plan, a negative trend became unmistakable: Their idea was not being

This case was prepared by Dan D'Heilly and Mark Helman under the direction of Professor William Bygrave. © Copyright Babson College, 1996. All rights reserved.

Exhibit 1

CHRISTOPHER C. HARAMI

Experience:

Fall 1994   NEW ENGLAND BOOK COMPONENTS   HINGHAM, MA
Marketing Consultant
- Perform market research study to determine size and value of market.
- Forecast finanncial and marketing impact of eleven key industry segments.
- Assist management in defining key success factors and strategic focus.

1993   FLIGHT LTD.   KRASNODAR, RUSSIA
Trade Consultant
- Provided framework for Flight Ltd. to become an international trading entity, and supplier of goods to government level buyers.
- Developed strategic business plan to export Russian products to the West.
- Initiated contact and assisted in negotiating first successful import contracts between Flight Ltd., and Greek international trading firm.

1991–1992   CSM TRADING   WAYNE, NJ
Owner/ Manager
- Founded and managed an import/export company which specialized in high end consumer products.
- Imported high quality woolen goods from Australia, and New Zealand.

1990–1991   LIBBYS CORPORATION   PATERSON, NJ
Restaurant Manager
- Managed restaurant with annual sales of over $1 million.
- Led team of 15 employees.

1990   PIZZA AND MORE   WAYNE, NJ
Restaurant Manager
- Managed full service Italian restaurant.
- Managed in-house computer system.

1989   BENNIGANS   WAYNE, NJ
Server
- Waited tables and insured quality presentation of meal.

1986-87   THE ROOST   SAN JOSE, CA
Cook
- Cooked fast food meals for college students in campus foodservice facility.

Education:

1992–1994   BABSON GRADUATE SCHOOL OF BUSINESS,   WELLESLEY, MA
Master of Business Administration degree, May 1994. Concentrations in International Marketing, Entrepreneurship.
Fall 1993, NORWEGIAN SCHOOL OF MANAGEMENT, OSLO, NORWAY
Exchange program, concentrations in Euromanagement, Energy-management European business technique.

1987–1990   PACE UNIVERSITY   NEW YORK, NY
Bachelor of Business Administration, June, 1990. Concentration in International Marketing.

---

well-received by industry analysts. The standard reaction to their idea was, "Crepes?!" They did additional research on the history of French restaurants in America and the idea lost momentum as they found a trail of failed French restaurants with precious few success stories. For example, the Magic Pan, a crepe restaurant chain similar to their concept, had failed in the mid-1980s. By the end of summer, they decided to defer to the wisdom of the experts. Michael trekked back to France, and Chris reinvigorated his job search.

Russian (Career) Roulette

In spite of his desire to start a restaurant empire, Chris kept his resume current and almost took a position with Deloitte & Touche in Russia. He had spent the summer working in Krasnowdar while in graduate school. He loved the adventure, and the feeling that he was making a difference in the world.

Babson College belonged to a consortium of graduate schools and consulting firms called the MBA Enterprise Corporation, a nonprofit placement organization assisting businesses grow in the former Soviet Union and in other developing countries. It was through this agency that Chris received an offer from Deloitte & Touche following graduation. This position required an 18-month commitment beginning in February 1995. He was torn between this chance to work abroad for a top consulting company, and his desire to pursue his entrepreneurial dream.

Jack Sprat's: High-Potential Opportunity or Wishful Thinking?

In the fall of 1994, Chris found himself talking with a friend, John Farmian, about working out and eating healthy. During the course of the conversation, John commented that it would be great to have a restaurant that served healthy *and* tasty fast-food. Chris knew immediately that this was an idea worth exploring, "It was so obvious. There was nothing at all filling that niche in the restaurant industry." With a new start-up vision in focus, and the preliminary research going well, he turned down the consulting opportunity in Russia.

Chris and John decided to become partners. They were friends and fellow Babson alumni, and both felt they could get access to family money with a well-designed business plan. John had the additional motivation of wanting to stay in the United States. He was a Turkish national in Boston on a student visa—their restaurant would sponsor his green card. Soon they were at work on a business plan for a low-fat/fat-free, gourmet-quality QSR.

With the basic concept in place, they began to think of names for their new venture. While laying in bed one evening, Chris happened to remember the words to "Jack Sprat," the Mother Goose nursery rhyme—eureka!

Jack Sprat could eat no fat, his wife could eat no lean;
And between the two of them, they licked the platter clean.

Although Chris and John developed the idea together, John was a somewhat reluctant partner. From the beginning, Chris led the investigation and contributed most of the ideas. Within six months, the partnership was finished. Chris told John that he would have a job waiting for him at Jack Sprat's if it ever came together.

Little by little, it seemed John's enthusiasm was fading. It was hard to get him to sit down and talk about the business. We talked to a few architects together, but it was really over pretty quickly. After a while, I realized that I was the one with the entrepreneurial fever. After that, I recruited other friends and classmates, but no one was ready to commit.

On the Road Benchmarking Fat-Free America

Chris' research quickly uncovered a large and expanding low-fat/fat-free products segment in the prepared goods market (i.e., the low-fat/fat-free products segment in the supermarket). Food service was one of the largest business segments in the nation, with sales of just under $300 billion, in 1994. Of that, the fast food market was nearly $100 billion, which represented 33 percent of the total "eat away from home" food sales. In addition, they found that the American fat-free and lite packaged goods market was $24.8 billion in 1993, and it was estimated that it would reach to $29.5 billion in 1994. Projections called for steady growth at about 5 percent per year into the near future.

He also found some low-fat/fat-free restaurants in California and Florida, but they were more reminiscent of the counterculture health food movement of days past than the concept Chris was developing:

In February 1995, Chris went to Los Angeles, California, to see a couple of successful low-fat/fat-free restaurants. First, he visited Sprouts, a small, full-service restaurant, with about 60 seats and a take-out counter. Chris said, "The food was marginal and the portions were skimpy. Why have small portions when it's low-fat/fat-free food?" Chris visited another Californian restaurant called Juicers. It was started in 1989 by a professional bicyclist who was frustrated by the lack of healthy food in restaurants. His smoothies (blended drinks made with fruit and yogurt) were popular among friends, so he opened a QSR. By 1995, he had 30 to 40 restaurants in the Los Angeles area.

Chris also traveled to Boca Raton, Florida, to visit a local restaurant chain called Healthy Way. This was another successful low-fat/fat-free restaurant that did not impress him. "I was even less impressed (but perhaps more excited) about Healthy Way because it was so simple. It was very cheaply put together, yet it was very successful." The success of these restaurants led Chris to believe that he had discovered a gap in the market. "Each of the restaurants had major flaws, so I thought, 'If these places are successful, I'll have a real winner when I do it right.'"

The only restaurants even similar to our idea seemed like something left over from the seventies. You know the type, granola restaurants with bean sprout-avocado sandwiches, and wheat juice cocktails. Our idea was not anything like those, in fact, the only similarity was that both emphasized healthy eating.

Another Restaurant Chain? Yes!

In March 1995, Chris attended The Northeast Food-service Exhibition at the World Trade Center in downtown Boston. Many vendors were selling quality low-fat/fat-free products: sauces, precooked entrees, desserts, and so on. These vendors told Chris there was phenomenal demand for low-fat/fat-free packaged products. When asked if they thought there was a need for a lowfat/fat-free restaurant chain, they responded with a resounding "Yes."

Chris also contacted the Boston branch of the Small Business Administration in April 1995. There Chris met Maximilian Charm, an SBA consultant who had a chain of Burger King franchises. As a successful QSR owner, Max was enthusiastic about the potential of Chris' idea. He told Chris that the reason most restaurants failed was not because of an inherent flaw in the restaurant business, but rather because their owners did not plan thoroughly enough before launching the business (this was especially true for the mom-and-pop operations). Max argued that restaurateurs who have done the research and put together a quality business plan usually succeed. He urged Chris to return when the business plan was complete, because there was a good chance that he could arrange for an SBA-guaranteed loan.

The largest annual food trade show in the world was the National Restaurant Show. In May 1995, it was held at Chicago's McCormack Place and vendors at the show met Chris' plan with enthusiasm. One vendor, Skinny Cow Inc., a provider of private-labeled low-fat/fat-free cheese for companies like Alpine Lace and Healthy Choice, was particularly helpful. They referred Chris to a consultant with experience in QSR chain start-ups, and an interest in lowfat/fat-free foods, Arlene Spiegel. Following the Chicago show, Chris was convinced that this was a great business opportunity. Now he asked, "How are we going to do it?"

Jack Sprat's Business Plan

From the beginning, Chris' plan called for creating a national chain of restaurants; he wanted it to be a high-potential venture. The chain would have two basic types of restaurants: stand-alone and hosted QSRs. The key differences between the two types of restaurants were 1. size, 2. location, 3. menu selection, and 4. customer base—both would be quick service restaurants.

Stand-alone restaurants would be larger with more menu variety, and they would be situated in high traffic locations. They would use typical QSR locations such as busy urban street corners, strip malls, and shopping com-

plexes. Stand-alones had to pull customers into the store "off of the street." By contrast, hosts would supply customer-traffic for hosted stores.

Hosted stores would have fewer menu items and be smaller than stand-alone restaurants. They would also be located within larger institutions such as in the lobby of a hotel. The goal was to have these scaled-down, "express" versions in each city that had Jack Sprat's stand-alone operations. The origin of the hosted location idea was Chris' aunt and uncle, the restaurant owners. They had been approached about opening hosted locations in local healthcare establishments and Chris speculated that he could find hosts in health-conscious organizations (e.g., hospitals, gyms, schools).

Chris planned to have the first two restaurants operational in 1996, a stand-alone and a host location. This would be followed by a quick expansion once the prototypes proved the concept. The restaurants would not need to pay back the investment to prove the concept, simply generating positive cash flow would demonstrate attractiveness (Exhibits 2 and 3). He was told that if the first locations succeed, financing will not be a problem for the rest:

> You have to pay your dues before outside money shows up. But if you bring a successful new concept to the market, investment money will come knocking on your door.

Anticipating rapid growth, Chris planned to outsource some operational departments once the company began to grow. He thought that food preparation in particular, could be macromanaged with maximum tradeoff satisfaction. Given the right criteria, an outside vendor could maintain high quality standards while reducing management complexity:

> I wanted to create something like a virtual franchise. Many aspects of the business could be outsourced to stay in control, while allowing us to expand rapidly. I wanted to make everything basically idiot-proof. A lot of people thought there would have to be a chef on-site. No. Not at all. Of course, an executive chef would be on staff or retainer to create the recipes, but he would not be there each day preparing food. The trend was for almost everything to come pre-made. A foodservice supplier would use our recipes to make our food. Our staff would just heat it up. Prior to that, when we are just beginning, we would make food in-house, then hourly staff would work for just a few dollars an hour to assemble meals. No chef would be on site (and on the payroll) each day. This is one reason why efficiently planned operations were so critical.

Sources of Funds		Uses of Funds	
Seed Money	$35,000	Equipment	$115,000
Startup Funding (Loans/Equity)	450,000	Furniture and Fixtures	80,000
SBA Guaranteed Loan	75,000	Leasehold Improvements	45,000
		Construction	50,000
		Working Capital	35,000
		Pre-opening Expenses (Training)	5,000
		Consulting Expenses	25,000
		Opening Inventory—Supplies	10,000
		Architect—Engineering Services	15,000
		Management Salary—Pre-Opening	15,000
		Legal Fees	10,000
		Signage	8,000
		Marketing Expenses	15,000
		Lease and Utility Deposits	7,000
		Location Consulting	5,000
		Brokerage Fees	5,000
		Accounting Fees	5,000
		Graphics	10,000
		Development Expenses	35,000
		Contingency	65,000
Total	560,000	Total	560,000

Chris knew that location is a key consideration for a foodservice business. Boston had a relatively health-conscious, trendy, and educated population; perfect for the Jack Sprat's concept. He noted that many successful chains had started here—Boston Market, Pizzeria Uno, and Au Bon Pain, to name a few. Also, Chris found it easier and cheaper than trying to get started in New York City. Real estate in New York City was twice as expensive as Boston.

To reach his target customer, he wanted to locate Jack Sprat's in prime business districts, with a strong concentration of professionals and higher income wage earners. Sites would be preliminarily selected using the following general guidelines, then additional demographic and psychographic criteria for the typical customer in the area would be applied:

- Heavy lunch and dinner traffic.
- Dense target consumer-base close to the site.
- Close proximity to main shopping areas and travel routes.
- Heavy foot or road traffic.
- Positioning on the "going home" side of traffic, so consumers can stop by on their way home from work conveniently.
- Availability of a suitable 1,500 to 3,000 square foot location.

Chris was also considering locating near existing restaurants that catered to the same target consumer as Jack Sprat's. This way he would get the benefit of the demographic research conducted by a large chain for no cost at all:

This is exactly what Burger King does. If you notice, Burger King is nearly always located very near McDonald's. McDonald's does the research and Burger King just follows them right to a new location.

In April 1995, a place in Boston, on Newbury Street, went up for sale. The customer in that area of Boston seemed to fit with Chris's concept. But the price was extremely high at about $225,000 for essentially buying some used physical equipment from the previous restaurant and the lease agreement. Two factors dampened Chris's enthusiasm for this site: 1. He thought it might be too trendy, where passersby would perhaps be more tempted by the boutique restaurants of the area, and 2. Back Bay is a historic district, strictly limiting the dynamics of businesses there. Renovations, innovative designs, fancy signs, and so on were all subject to guidelines set by local committees—they might not let Chris implement his business plan.

Chris contacted several real estate brokers to inquire about potential sites. He was told that before he signed a contract for a site, he should have his business plan complete, and all the financing ready. This would prevent him from wasting money on a location for months before he

Exhibit 3: *Estimated Monthly Pro Forma Income Statement, May 31, 1997 to May 31, 1998*

	May	Jun	Jul	Aug	Sept	Oct	Nov	Dec	Jan	Feb	Mar	Apr	Total
TOTAL REVENUES	75,431	70,200	67,669	61,425	70,200	71,550	63,788	58,556	56,194	51,975	63,788	65,138	775,914
CGS—FOOD	18,858	17,550	16,917	15,356	17,550	17,888	15,947	14,639	14,049	12,994	15,947	16,285	193,979
GROSS PROFIT	56,573	52,650	50,752	46,069	52,650	53,663	47,841	43,917	42,146	38,981	47,841	48,854	581,936
GEN. AND ADM. EXP	5,000	5,000	5,000	5,000	5,000	5,000	5,000	5,000	5,000	5,000	5,000	5,000	60,000
RENT	6,000	6,000	6,000	6,000	6,000	6,000	6,000	6,000	6,000	6,000	6,000	6,000	72,000
MANAGEMENT EXP.	5,666	5,666	5,666	5,666	5,666	5,666	5,666	5,666	5,666	5,666	5,666	5,666	67,992
EMPLOYEE WAGES	16,595	15,444	14,887	13,514	15,444	15,741	14,033	12,882	12,363	11,435	14,033	14,330	170,701
WAGE RELATED	4,000	4,000	4,000	4,000	4,000	4,000	4,000	4,000	4,000	4,000	4,000	4,000	48,000
DEPREC EXP.	3,268	3,268	3,268	3,268	3,268	3,268	3,268	3,268	3,268	3,268	3,268	3,268	39,216
AMORT EXP.	833	833	833	833	833	833	833	833	833	833	833	833	9,996
INSURANCE EXP.	500	500	500	500	500	500	500	500	500	500	500	500	6,000
MARKETING EXP.	—	1,000	1,000	1,000	2,000	1,000	1,000	500	500	500	1,000	1,000	10,000
ACCTG./LEGAL	—											15,000	15,000
RE. TAXES	800	800	800	800	800	800	800	800	800	800	800	800	9,600
NET PROFIT	13,911	10,139	8,798	5,488	9,139	10,855	6,741	4,968	3,216	979	6,741	(7,544)	73,431
INTEREST EXP.	625	617	609	601	592	584	576	567	559	550	541	532	6,953
PRE-TAX PROFIT	13,286	9,522	8,189	4,887	8,547	10,271	6,165	4,401	2,657	429	6,200	(8,076)	66,478
CURRENT INC. TAX	3,720	2,666	2,293	1,368	2,393	2,876	1,726	1,232	744	120	1,736	(2,261)	18,614
PROFIT AFTER TAX	9,566	6,856	5,896	3,518	6,154	7,395	4,439	3,169	1,913	309	4,464	(5,814)	47,864
DIVIDENDS	—	—	—	—	—	—	—	—	—	—	—	—	—
ADJ. TO RET. EARN	9,566	6,856	5,896	3,518	6,154	7,395	4,439	3,169	1,913	309	4,464	(5,814)	47,864

was ready to begin building. They also told him that locations for his type of QSR concept were not that hard to find. Chris decided to stop location shopping until the business plan was done.

Expansion Strategy

Short-Term Goals

Chris' immediate goal was to develop a base of operations, from which further growth could be established. Funding for the construction and operation of the first Jack Sprat's facility would come partially from his family and the rest from outside sources. During its initial period of operation (3 to 6 months), Chris had plans, subject to obtaining further financing and the success of the original location, to begin construction of additional facilities. Chris wanted to have additional Jack Sprat's open within a year of launching the initial location.

He did not know exactly how fast he would be able to grow, but he knew that similar chains had grown very quickly after their initial rollout. For example, Boston Market had expanded to 21 sites in its first two years of existence, and Bertucci's had grown to 20 sites in its first six years.

Long-Term Growth

To capitalize on what he felt would be tremendous market demand, and Jack Sprat's position as first-to-market with this concept, Chris established an aggressive expansion plan. Funding for the expansion would be derived from long-term bank debt, a second round of (nonfamily) equity, and Jack Sprat's cash flow (see Exhibits 2 and 3).

During the initial phase, store locations would be clustered in Boston for marketing efficiencies. As media purchases spread awareness of the concept into neighboring towns, other cities in New England would be targeted. Next, Jack Sprat's would be located throughout the Northeast, and finally to more distant areas. Chris was confident that Jack Sprat's would be operating nationally by the year 2005. He felt that demand was great enough to support hundreds, and maybe thousands of locations.

Chris felt that there were many options for rapid growth: company-owned and operated locations, strategic partnerships, franchising, and selling or licensing the concept. Chris did not think that the method of expansion needed to be established immediately, as long as the issues involved with remote ownership and management were considered in the business design. The current problem was getting the business plan finished in such a way that this expansion would be relatively easy when the time arrived.

Financing the Vision

Shortly after developing Jack Sprat's first business plan summary and deciding not to pursue the Russian opportunity, Chris contacted entrepreneurship professor Bill Bygrave for advice. In addition to advice, Bygrave put Chris in touch with potential angel investors. A group of local doctors had called him with a similar restaurant idea. They often recommended low-fat, no cholesterol diets, but it was hard for their patients to find healthy food in restaurants. Over the phone, the doctors liked Chris and his idea, so they set up a formal meeting. Chris put together a presentation to sell the concept, but the meeting faltered for reasons unrelated to the idea: The doctors had expected Chris to be older and more experienced. A dialog continued for a couple of months, but ultimately, the doctors weren't interested.

Thinking back to his entrepreneurial finance class, Chris looked for ways to get free consulting. He tried to make a deal with the dean of a culinary university, Johnson and Wales. Chris proposed an internship project where Johnson and Wales students would get experience in leading-edge restaurant development work. They would help develop recipes, a menu, and the restaurant layout. The dean indicated that the school did not endorse projects, but that he would be willing to do it himself for standard consulting fees. Several other culinary institutions responded in the same way—once there was an established business, they welcomed internship opportunities, but they were not interested in supporting startups.

It was time to find out what resources Chris' family were going to contribute. First, he presented the idea to the family's restaurant experts: his aunt and uncle. They liked it, in fact, they had been approached about similar ideas a couple of times. One was a consortium of local hospitals who wanted a low-fat/fat-free menu for heart patients. Another was a critical care facility that wanted to host a low-fat/fat-free restaurant. They were not interested in either venture at the time, but it provided evidence of a demand for this type of restaurant. They encouraged Chris to move forward and recommended the investment to Chris' father, Dr. Harami, but they did not offer financial support due to a recent expansion of their own restaurant that ran into seven figures.

Dr. Harami knew a great deal about nutrition, but when Chris told him about Jack Sprat's, he didn't understand, "If you want to be in foodservice, why don't you just open a hamburger joint?" From this initial discussion in the fall of 1994, until the family meeting in the summer of 1995, Chris actively sought to assuage his father's concerns and gain his support for the venture.

Finally, Dr. Harami, Mrs. Harami, and their three sons gathered for a meeting to decide if this would be a good use of the family money. Out of this meeting came a few key decisions. First, they decided to invest $250,000. Second, they would all serve on the board of directors. Third, Chris' younger brothers, Steve, age 26, and Matt, age 24, would actively participate in the planning and management of Jack Sprat's Restaurants. Steve had an MBA from Rutgers University and restaurant experience and Matt was eager to learn. Finally, Dr. Harami would determine when the time was right to make the investment. This was an open-ended commitment: Dr. Harami could decide that the timing was never right. He was concerned that Chris did not have enough practical experience to pull this off. Chris filed the incorporation papers on August 17, 1995.

Wanted: QSR Training Program

The day after the family meeting, Chris saw an ad in a local paper announcing the planned opening of a new Chicago Jake's restaurant. Chicago Jake's was a national chain of quick service restaurants. Chris thought that he would get good experience helping an established chain open a new location and learn many things he would need to know for his own business. He also remembered his father's concerns about practical experience, and called to ask for a job at the new store.

Chris told the store manager that he wanted to learn the business so that he could open his own QSR chain. The store manager was nonplused, but wanted to hire him anyway, "I need people who can speak English for the grand opening, but I can't hire an MBA who wants to open his own restaurant." So he had Chris interview with his boss, the regional manager, who agreed to hire him if he would commit to staying 90 days. The regional manager agreed to provide on-the-job training in how to open and run a new fast-food restaurant. He would be a floater, involved with all aspects of the business.

He was initially assigned to two stores that were already open. First, Chris worked in a low-income area store, then he worked in a high-income area store. The differences between the two were fascinating, "These stores were laid-out and operated in completely different ways, and I got to learn both operations."

Next, he went to the new store a week before the grand opening. Chris helped install equipment and organize the launch. Once open, he helped troubleshoot and run it; Chris learned all aspects of managing the new restaurant. "I saw the good, the bad, and yes, the ugly. It was a great experience." Chris stayed more than two months—until a new manager decided that it was time for him to go.

Wanted—QSR Guru

By this point, Chris was convinced that Jack Sprat's was a winner. Research supported it, industry insiders embraced it, and he had the support of his family, but he was still worried about his lack of experience. If anything, the two months with Chicago Jake's served to underscore how much he didn't know:

There were so many things which the layman would never think of. To create a single dish, you need about 20 ingredients. Then to actually cook it, put it together, hold it properly, and serve it perfectly, there's a lot of different equipment that you need. It requires an efficient step-by-step process, and, as a layman, you don't know these things. These days it's a science, and I worry about being able to do it right the first time, because with my limited funding I cannot afford to make many mistakes.

We had a great idea and we'd done our homework, but none of us had ever built a restaurant chain from scratch. That made me nervous because we were betting the farm on this venture. I wanted as much probability of success as I could possibly get. I wanted a guru, somebody who knew all the ins and outs, had the network, knew the suppliers, and could help me bring this concept to reality.

Chris wanted to hire a consultant, he felt that having a well-respected consultant help him execute his plan would offer a much greater probability of success, but his father did not. Chris' aunt and uncle had not used one, and their restaurant was a success, so Dr. Harami couldn't see why his business-degreed son needed a consultant. To compound matters, Dr. Harami asked around, and he did not know of anyone who had used a restaurant consultant.

Undeterred, Chris requested a list of restaurant consultants from the National Restaurant Association. He was pleased to find Skinny Cow's referral, Arlene Spiegel, on this list. He contacted consultants based in Boston and New York City, where the first restaurants would be located. Most of the consultants sent "impressive, but distant proposals." They did not seem to be enthusiastic about the "lean gourmet" concept. Also, they were all very expensive, ranging from $50,000 to $150,000 for a business plan rewrite.

All the firms had similar qualifications and experience. Chris checked their references, and all came back with high praise. After meeting with numerous consultants, Chris chose Arlene Spiegel's company, Market Discoveries, Inc. He gave six reasons for choosing her: 1. Good interpersonal chemistry. 2. A high level of involvement in health food issues. 3. Her enthusiasm for the Jack Sprat's concept. 4. The unsolicited referral from Skinny Cow. 5. An excellent resume and references (he called them all). 6. A negotiated price (she agreed to sign-on for $25,000).

Arlene Spiegel, Food Consultant

Arlene Spiegel was recognized as one of the nation's leading foodservice specialists. She had won awards for achievements in foodservice, food and menu development, and food and beverage merchandising for many major fast-food companies including McDonald's, Burger King, and KFC. She also developed and re-engineered the in-house dining services for Chase Manhattan Bank, Marriott, and Holiday Inn, as well as developing branded concepts for Coca-Cola, Chock Full O' Nuts, and others. In addition, her expertise included facilities planning, brand development, procurement, staffing, training, and promotion. For her many achievements, she was named the "Foodservice Woman of the Year" in 1982, and in 1987 she received the prestigious Pacesetter Award for her innovations in foodservice marketing.

Arlene recently joined forces with four other foodservice professionals to form the IBM Foodservice Consulting Consortium. This group, sponsored by IBM, offered consulting services to IBM's restaurant clients. IBM was the largest vendor of restaurant POS systems. In addition to restaurants, Arlene had done a lot of work for hospitals and the medical community.

Decision Point

On the one hand, Chris thought his father was ready to move forward. But on the other hand, Dr. Harami didn't want to spend precious resources to have a consultant rewrite Chris' "MBA-informed business plan." His father insinuated that the desire to hire a consultant might be a sign that Chris didn't have enough confidence in the Jack Sprat's concept. Chris was left with a tough decision; he wanted to hire Arlene, but if he insisted, Dr. Harami might get cold feet and decide that the timing was not yet right for funding the venture.

Chris felt that the window of opportunity for Jack Sprat's was open now, and he didn't want to risk another delay.

Discussion Points

1. Should Chris insist on hiring Arlene Spiegel?

2. Evaluate Jack Sprat's Restaurant as a high-potential venture.

3. Evaluate Chris' progress to date.

4. What advice would you give Dr. Harami?

Case 4   AllAdvantage.com: An Internet Infomediary

Brent D. Beal, case writer
Louisiana State University

> You're bigger than life, just stay bigger than life,
> Venture Capital Firm to Jim Jorgensen, Founder and CEO
> of AllAdvantage.com, February 2000

It was Monday, July 3, 2000, and Jim Jorgensen, founder and CEO of AllAdvantage.com, had a lot on his mind. AllAdvantage had just announced that its upcoming initial public offering (IPO), scheduled for mid-July, would be delayed indefinitely due to "unfavorable market conditions." Although withdrawing its bid to go public was a disappointment, Jorgensen believed it was only a temporary setback. The last 18 months had been exhilarating. AllAdvantage had gone from an idea to a 700-employee firm flush with more than $130 million in venture capital. Jorgensen believed the company was on the cusp of establishing itself as an Internet infomediary—a trusted third party that would bring buyers and sellers together in cyberspace and profit from its role as matchmaker.

Despite its successes, the last 6 months had been difficult for the company. The NASDAQ stock index, which had peaked at 5048.62 on March 10, 2000, was now hovering around 3000, and there had been a decisive shift in investor expectations. Many new Internet start-ups—companies from which AllAdvantage derived a significant portion of its revenue—were shutting down or being forced into bankruptcy. As a result, AllAdvantage was having difficulty selling its ad inventory. Jorgensen understood that the business climate in which the company had been founded, and in which it had prospered, had changed. AllAdvantage had pursued a "growth-at-any-cost" strategy in response to the demands of venture capitalists and the perceived expectations of the capital market. Now, Jorgensen realized, the only way for AllAdvantage to survive was to demonstrate that its business model created significant value—value that would soon lead to profitability. The rules of the game had changed, and unless AllAdvantage adapted it would face the same fate as other prominent dot-coms that had ceased to exist.

Jorgensen glanced at the clock on the wall in his office: It was nearly noon. In less than 24 hours, he would meet with AllAdvantage's top executives. Although the company had been gradually moving away from its growth-at-any-cost strategy, which had propelled it to promi-

nence during the Internet boom, there was a growing sense among the top management team that the pace of change would have to quicken. There were sharp differences of opinion, however, about what changes were needed and how the firm should go about moving toward profitability. Jorgensen knew that changing the firm's strategy would require coordinated and enthusiastic support from the company's leadership and that he, as founder and CEO, needed to present a coherent plan around which consensus could be built. He needed to decide what direction AllAdvantage would take, and time was running out. Jorgensen stood up abruptly and walked out of his office. "Maybe a walk around the parking lot will do me some good," he thought.

The Company

AllAdvantage was founded by Jim Jorgensen and three Stanford graduate students (Carl Anderson, Johannes Pohle, and Oliver Brock) and launched from Jorgensen's garden shed on March 30, 1999. The idea for AllAdvantage emerged from a discussion about privacy on the Internet. It seemed to company founders that there needed to be a way for individuals to come together and sell their aggregated attention and demographic data to advertisers while maintaining their individual privacy. The "aha," according to Jorgensen, was the idea to develop a downloadable software program that members could install on their personal computers; this program would be used for viewing advertisements. By the end of 1999, AllAdvantage had thrust itself front and center onto the Internet scene. *The Wall Street Journal, The Washington Post, Fortune, Business Week, Business 2.0,* and other high-profile business publications were writing about the company; venture capital firms had injected more than $130 million into the venture; and a small army of experienced executives had joined the AllAdvantage management team.

AllAdvantage wanted to be the leading Internet infomediary. On one side of the infomediary equation were Internet companies that desperately wanted to connect with customers interested in their products and services. On the other side of this equation were customers in search of products and services but wary of divulging personal information to potential advertisers out of a desire to protect their privacy and to avoid being deluged by irrelevant (an annoying) sales pitches. AllAdvantage, with its proprietary ViewBar, promised to create value for both marketers and customers by playing matchmaker:

This case is based on interviews, publicly available news releases, and business-press commentary; the people and events described in the case are real. I thank Jim Jorgensen and Alex Gourevitch at AllAdvantage for their time and hospitality. I also thank Dennis Hallack for some valuable research assistance in the early stages of preparing the case. Copyright © 2002 by the Case Research Journal *and Brent D. Beal.*

Marketers would be able to target their sales pitches to interested customers, and customers would be able to simultaneously protect their privacy and enjoy filtered advertising tailored to their personal preferences and tastes. In the abstract, the infomediary business model was easy to understand. As explained in an article in the *Financial Times*,

> The company's business model is breathtakingly simple. It sells Internet advertising, but instead of spending money on content to attract users to view a Web page, it generates advertising inventory using an entirely different mechanism. Users download a piece of software called the ViewBar, which sits on their screen and pumps out a nonstop succession of advertisements.

Jorgensen realized that AllAdvantage would have to find a way to overcome the classic "chicken-and-egg" problem inherent in its business model: AllAdvantage could not sell advertising until it had an audience of potential customers for advertisers to target, but without advertising revenue, it would be impossible to attract an audience. The same dilemma is present in television, radio, and print advertising—that is, magazines cannot sell advertising without a subscription base, but they cannot build a subscription base without advertising dollars to pay for content with which to attract readers.

Jorgensen's unique solution to this problem is what distinguished AllAdvantage. Unlike its infomediary counterparts in the physical world, AllAdvantage would not develop any content of its own. AllAdvantage would deliver advertising to subscribers via a small software program, the ViewBar, that would occupy a small 1-inch strip at the bottom (or top) of a computer user's monitor. The ViewBar would piggyback on the Internet itself: The Internet would be the content. Unlike television, radio or print media, AllAdvantage would not have to worry about content; it would just sell advertising. To motivate Internet users to join the AllAdvantage community and download the ViewBar, AllAdvantage promised to pay 50 cents per hour for time spent surfing the Internet with the ViewBar, up to 40 hours a month. Directly compensating individuals for viewing advertising, although impractical in the case of traditional media, was, Jorgensen believed, not only possible in cyberspace, but it was imperative. Consumers' time was valuable, and they had a right to be compensated for their attention. In addition to monetary compensation, Jorgensen believed that AllAdvantage members would value AllAdvantage's ability to deliver customized or targeted advertising tailored to members' specific tastes and predilections without requiring members to surrender personal information directly to individual companies or marketers.

To generate immediate interest and accelerate the growth of a community of AllAdvantage members, Jorgensen went one step further than simply compensating AllAdvantage members for surfing the Internet with the ViewBar. AllAdvantage encouraged members to tout the company to friends, family, and acquaintances by creating a multilevel compensation structure. In addition to the 50 cents per hour each member received for time spent surfing with the ViewBar displayed, each member also collected 10 cents per hour for the time each direct referral spent surfing and 5 cents per hour for referrals of referrals, down 4 levels. The multilevel marketing approach dramatically increased the earning potential for individuals willing to persuade their friends and acquaintances to join the AllAdvantage community. It created a viral marketing context in which "friends spammed[1] friends."

Although AllAdvantage's practice of directly compensating Internet users for viewing ads was criticized by some as being fundamentally unsound, the business model was similar in many respects to the prize giveaways conducted by radio stations. The profit potential, contrary to the views of some observers, was substantial. Each member cost AllAdvantage a maximum of 80 cents per hour (50 cents per hour to each surfing member plus an additional 30 cents per hour to referrers). During an hour of surfing, AllAdvantage could display approximately 200 banner ads or one-fifth of a CPM.[2] The going rates for CPMs were between $10 (for random or run-of-the-network ads) and $60 (for highly targeted ads). Even at the low end of this range ($10/CPM), AllAdvantage would make 2 1/2 times the cost of member payments in ad revenue.

AllAdvantage's viral marketing approach produced impressive results: Over 250,000 individuals signed up during the first 10 days. In September 1999, AllAdvantage served more than 1 billion ad impressions to its rapidly expanding membership. In November, AllAdvantage served 4 billion ad impressions. By the start of 2000, the company had grown to nearly 600 employees and had begun preparing for a lucrative initial public offering (IPO). By July 2000, just 16 months after signing up its first member, total membership surpassed 7 million. According to Jim Jorgensen, Asset Management/Alloy Ventures, the first venture capital firm to invest in AllAdvantage, kept telling them, "[You're] bigger than life, just stay bigger than life." There was a period in early 2000 when there was such palpable enthusiasm and sense of manifest destiny on the part of employees that some observers compared it to a young Apple in the early 1980s.

Achievements

As Jorgensen walked, he could not help but reflect on all the things the company had done right over the last 18 months. AllAdvantage was now the recognized leader in the emerging pay-to-surf industry. AllAdvantage had no serious competition, although more than 40 copycat firms had emerged in the wake of the company's success. AllAdvantage was the only pay-to-surf company that had received significant venture capital financing. They were the only company that had achieved sufficient scale to support their own global sales force. Jorgensen reflected on the different challenges the company had faced— everything from software development to problems with member spam to international expansion. Each of these challenges had shaped the company in important ways.

Software

In March 1999, when the AllAdvantage founders had decided to launch their new venture, the technology they planned to utilize to execute their business plan existed only on paper. They had not developed the communication software that AllAdvantage members would need to download and install on their personal computers—software that would allow AllAdvantage to broadcast a constant stream of ads to member desktops while simultaneously tracking member movements and online preferences. The initial pitch to potential AllAdvantage members was something to this effect: "Sign up now. In a few months, we'll have the software ready for you to download, and you can start earning money."

A beta version of the software was subsequently released in June 1999. In July 1999, the ViewBar was formally released to AllAdvantage members. A Mac version of the ViewBar was introduced in beta in November 1999 and formally released to all members in April 2000. A new version of the PC ViewBar was released in February 2000 and included several features designed to make the ViewBar more than just a mechanism for delivering advertising. For example, the new ViewBar released in February 2000 included quick links designed to allow AllAdvantage members to hop directly from the ViewBar to sponsors' Web sites. It also included direct access to search engines.

Jorgensen believed that ViewBar technology was one of the most important assets that AllAdvantage possessed. It allowed AllAdvantage to track member movement on the Internet and to use that information to target its advertising. With typical Internet banner advertising, the advertiser had no control over when, how long, or how frequently someone would see a particular ad. The ViewBar overcame these limitations. Jorgensen was convinced that this capability gave AllAdvantage a competitive edge over other online advertising intermediaries.

Financing

AllAdvantage had successfully raised an impressive sum of money from private investors. In April 1999, just 2 months after opening its virtual doors, AllAdvantage announced first-round funding of $2 million from Alloy Ventures. In September of that same year, the company raised an additional $31 million from a group of investors led by Walden Media and Information Technology Fund, Times Mirror TMCT Ventures, Partech International, J&W Seligman's New Technology Funds, and, again, Alloy Ventures. In early February 2000, the company announced that it had secured $100 million in additional equity financing from a group of investors led by SOFT-BANK Capital Partners. SOFTBANK invested $70 million; other investors included Putnam Investments and T. Rowe Price.

Executive Talent

AllAdvantage had no problem hiring experienced executives. For example, in August 1999, AllAdvantage announced that David Backman-Robertson, former CNN Interactive vice president, would assume the title of vice president of sales at AllAdvantage.com. In September 1999, AllAdvantage.com announced that Rich LeFurgy, cofounder and current chair of the Internet Advertising Bureau, would join its board of directors. These and other appointments demonstrated that AllAdvantage could successfully attract experienced management.

International Expansion

By the end of 1999, AllAdvantage membership had grown to nearly 4 million. A significant percentage of those members lived outside the United States, the United Kingdom, and Canada. To leverage its growing international membership, AllAdvantage had moved rapidly to expand its service to as many foreign countries as possible. AllAdvantage launched in the United Kingdom in August 1999 and by October had signed up more than 50,000 U.K. members. In March 2000, AllAdvantage announced that it had released localized versions of its software, the ViewBar, to members in France, Germany, Japan, the United Kingdom, and Australia/New Zealand. By the end of March, AllAdvantage had local offices in the United States, London, Paris, Hamburg, Tokyo, and Sydney. By July 2000, AllAdvantage offered paid Web surfing in 20 countries.

Fighting Spam

It became apparent almost immediately that AllAdvantage's marketing strategy had an undesired side effect: It induced members to send unsolicited e-mail or spam. Although spam did not directly affect AllAdvantage operations, it was not a trivial issue. The multilevel marketing strategy employed by the company created significant incentive for members to build referral downlines. An AllAdvantage member, for example, could send an e-mail to thousands of addresses gleaned from the Internet or other sources with an eye-catching message like "Make Money Fast" and generate a significant number of referrals. Spam generated by AllAdvantage members had the potential to alienate key members of the Internet community, including newsgroup moderators, network administrators, Web-based e-mail providers, and others. In the long run, the negative publicity and ill will generated by AllAdvantage spam had the potential to undermine the company's legitimacy and hamper its ability to do business on the Internet.

In August 1999, AllAdvantage hired Ray Everett-Church as chief privacy officer and vice president. Church was the cofounder of Coalition Against Unsolicited Commercial E-Mail or CAUCE. AllAdvantage also canceled the accounts of members caught sending spam and routinely posted warnings against such activity with lists of canceled account numbers on their Internet site. These actions convinced the Internet community that AllAdvantage was not just another bulk e-mail pyramid scheme and that its antispam stance was more than just self-serving posturing. This was particularly important for AllAdvantage because its business depended on gaining the trust of its members—members who were asked to give AllAdvantage personal information with the understanding the AllAdvantage would not divulge that information to individual advertisers.

Problems

Jim Jorgensen knew that the company's recent achievements did not mean much now. What mattered was what the company did in the future. It seemed that just a few months ago, AllAdvantage had seemed invincible. Where had things gone wrong? "Not all of this is our fault," Jim thought. "Things happened that we couldn't have predicted."

AllAdvantage, like other dot-coms, was being advised by its venture capitalists, by its investment bankers, and even by its own board members to burn cash like rocket fuel. What mattered was growth—what mattered was staying "larger than life." AllAdvantage was being advised that the equity markets would finance their losses if they stayed larger than life. As Jorgensen explained,

> The bankers were a significant influence. When you're running a business, the business needs to be profitable in order to be sustainable. When you have bankers, venture capitalists, telling you, "just grab market share, just grab market share," it makes a difference. The bankers and venture capitalist suspended the profitability constraint—they were telling us we didn't need to be profitable until 2003.

As long as equity markets were willing to finance the company's losses, it made perfect sense to keep the throttle wide open. AllAdvantage was selling advertising to other dot-coms—other companies that needed to show growth at almost any cost. In April 2000, however, the situation changed dramatically. Equity markets, particularly the NASDAQ, experienced a significant correction, and investor sentiment shifted dramatically. The market was not interested in just growth anymore: It wanted profits. Again, as explained by Jorgensen,

> We were out on the edge with dot-com money—and it was flyer money. Our clients were the first to get hurt when things turned. Things shuttered a little in April—advertising didn't drop but it didn't go up—that was when the NASDAQ went south. But in May advertising dropped and just got worse from there.

Despite the shift in market sentiment, Jorgensen believed in the business model. He was certain that AllAdvantage had the potential to generate significant economic value because the cost of retaining the attention of its growing membership was significantly less than the advertising revenue that could be realized from selling access to its members (Appendix, Exhibit 1). During the first quarter of 2000, however, AllAdvantage posted an operating loss of $66 million on revenues of just $9.1 million (Appendix, Exhibit 2 through Exhibit 4). The company had paid out $32.7 million directly to members during this same time period. What had gone wrong? Why had projected profits failed to materialize? There were a number of reasons.

Declining Advertising Rates

An opinion article in *InfoWorld* in 1999 began with this assertion: "Online advertising is dead." This was, of course, an overstatement designed to attract attention, but nonetheless it served to highlight the fact that Internet advertising, particularly banner advertising, was becoming increasingly difficult to defend as an effective advertising method. Click-through rates (the percentage of banner ads that viewers click), which averaged more than 2 percent in 1997, have steadily declined to less than .5 percent. CPM rates (cost per thousand impressions) have been on a downward trend for the past several years, and a recent report from AdRelevance suggests that this trend might continue into the foreseeable future. In July 2000, rate card CPMs for full banner advertising (468 by 60 pixels) averaged approximately $30, down nearly 10 percent from an average of nearly $33 6 months earlier. The most common rate card price was $25. It was unusual for firms to sell advertising for full rate card price, however. The average discount during the first 6 months of 2000 was 33 percent.

AllAdvantage responded to falling CPM rates by shifting its advertising sales from intermediaries such as 24/7 and DoubleClick to direct sales. This had the immediate benefit of cutting out third-party commissions on ad sales, which often ran as high as one-third of ad revenue, but it forced AllAdvantage to increase it employee count to nearly 600, 220 of which were involved in direct sales.

It also required AllAdvantage to open local offices in London, Paris, Tokyo, and Sydney as well as throughout the United States.

Difficulty of Delivering Targeted Advertising

The rate card price for highly targeted banner advertising was substantially more than for run-of-site (or untargeted) ads. In July 2000, highly targeted ad space was selling for as much as $100 per thousand impressions or 4 times the average CPM rate.

AllAdvantage had emphasized the potential of targeted advertising. Because the ViewBar was a two-way communication device and could access information displayed in members' browsers, AllAdvantage could track the sties that members visited and the keywords that members typed into search engines. Information about member browsing habits, if exploited properly by AllAdvantage, would allow it to carefully target advertising to those members most likely to respond. AllAdvantage would then be able to charge a substantial premium for its advertising space.

Unfortunately, as of July 2000 AllAdvantage had not been very successful in exploiting the potential of targeted ads. Jorgensen explained:

> Not many companies sell it, so not many companies want it. It is a chicken-and-egg problem. Also, we have had a tough time with integration. DoubleClick's system (DART) serves ads, but it isn't set up to handle targeted ads. We had to build our ViewBar so that it acts like a Web page so that it requests ads from DoubleClick. We have a lot of information about members in our computers, but we can't get that information into the stream. We can't get that information into the communication that goes on between the ViewBar and DoubleClick. Only 2 to 3 percent of our ads are targeted. Most are just run of the Web, and we get a CPM of maybe $7 for that type of advertising.

Poor Demographics

Some critics had honed in on the problem of self-selection, given the fact that AllAdvantage could only target members that had volunteered (by registering) to view the ads. As observed in an article in *InfoWorld Daily News*, "People who earn money surfing do so as a lark or are students or do not have much income, and so [they] want the money rather than the personalized advertising. Such surfers are not likely to spend money with online advertisers because they simply do not have the money to spare." AllAdvantage tried to counter this assertion by releasing zip code membership information. The top three zip codes with the most AllAdvantage members

were 90210 (Beverly Hills, CA), 24060 (Blacksburg, VA), and 94086 (Sunnyvale, CA—Silicon Valley). Despite this zip code information, the perception that AllAdvantage members might not represent an ideal demographic group may have had an adverse impact on its CPM rates.

Another factor may also have been the incentive structure created by the firm's multilevel marketing approach. The maximum amount that an individual member could earn for personal surfing was around $10, depending on the specific hour limit in place in the country in which the member resided and the month in which the member surfed. It is reasonable to suspect that this amount may represent inadequate compensation for surrendering a significant portion of one's desktop screen to a constant stream of advertising. The real money was in referrals. For example, Ron Streeter, a freelance graphic artist from Syracuse and an AllAdvantage member, earned $2,044 in November 1999; all but $12.50 was a result of indirect surfing or time his referrals and the referrals of his referrals spent online.

AllAdvantage only rewarded individuals for the time their referrals spent online up to the time they themselves spent online. In other words, if Ron Streeter had only surfed for 10 hours in November, he would have only received credit for the time his referrals surfed up to a maximum of 10 hours, and his check would have been reduced by about 60 percent. In other words, Mr. Streeter received around $80 an hour for surfing. This incentive structure locked people into surfing: They had to surf in order to benefit from the surfing time of referrals. Despite the best efforts of AllAdvantage to enhance the utility of the ViewBar or deliver personalized advertising to AllAdvantage members, for many members the primary benefit was purely financial. For these individuals, the constant stream of advertising was simply an inconvenience, and they were unlikely to pay much attention to the ads. This suspicion is confirmed by members like Mike Jones, a freshman at the University of Virginia, who stated the following: "We do it just for the check. I've never heard of anyone who had bought anything from the ads."

In contrast, the ideal AllAdvantage member would be an individual who values the utility of the ViewBar and the opportunity to view targeted advertising that would allow the user to more efficiently locate needed items or services. Unfortunately, the incentive structure developed by AllAdvantage, although successful in turning the company into a marketing machine, probably did not attract the most desirable group of individuals from an advertisers point of view. This may also have contributed to the company's inability to charge premium CPM rates.

Fraud

Another factor contributing to AllAdvantage's losses may have been the fact that advertisers could not be sure that individuals were paying attention to their ads. Of course this same concern plagues almost every other advertising medium, from television (viewers may opt to run to the bathroom rather than view commercials), to radio (listeners may switch channels), and to print media (readers may simply ignore the ads). In AllAdvantage's case, some members simply blocked out the ad window with masking tape.

Another concern was fraudulent surfing or "cheating." The ViewBar only records active surfing time—the software detects keyboard use and mouse movement and does not credit time spent connected to the Internet but not actively viewing Web content. Enterprising hackers, however, have written and popularized several programs that mimic active surfing. Many of these programs are available for free on the Internet, including one called "FakeSurf." College dormitories are full of flashing monitors animated by fake surfing programs that allow students to literally make money while they sleep. Phillip Greenspun, a researcher at MIT who teaches a class on advanced Web programming, has asserted that any of his students could build a near-perfect surfing spoofer. Officials at pay-to-surf companies have insisted that they can detect fake surfing.

By far the most serious cases of fraudulent behavior by AllAdvantage members were attempts to artificially generate referrals and referral surfing time. For example, clever hackers attempted to write software that would directly interface with AllAdvantage's member database. They then attempted to register thousands of referrals and simulate surfing time for each of these referrals. AllAdvantage hired a Ph.D. from Cambridge to head a Community Protection Group; at its peak, more than 20 full-time employees were part of this group. AllAdvantage also received some valuable tips from other AllAdvantage members. As Jim Jorgensen explained, "I'm sure we lost $100,000 or $200,000—I don't know how much. We got the problem solved, but it was a distraction."

AllAdvantage delayed member payments for May, June, and July 2000, citing fraudulent surfing as the primary cause. Many members were advised that their checks would be substantially reduced once referral commissions from fraudulent surfing were subtracted.

Difficulty of Keeping Up with Membership Growth

Within 5 months of the firm's launch, AllAdvantage was signing up new members at a rate of 10,000 to 20,000 a day. More than 2 million members registered in the first 120 days. Each new member who surfs 20 hours in a given month increases AllAdvantage's potential ad inventory by 4,000 ad impressions. In September 1999, AllAdvantage served more than 1 billion ad impressions; in November, the company served more than 4 billion impressions. "As far as our advertising inventory, we sold it all, but at what price? There is a limit to the number of advertisers that want to reach our members."

Decisions

Jorgensen knew that AllAdvantage must convince its backers that its business model created real economic value. Now that AllAdvantage had withdrawn its IPO bid, its investors would be particularly concerned about any future operating losses. Jorgensen was painfully aware that the balance sheet was a mess (Appendix, Exhibits 2–4). Since its founding in March 1999, AllAdvantage had lost $102.7 million. From inception through March 31, 2000, AllAdvantage had paid out nearly $50 million in member payments, but only taken in slightly more than $14 million in advertising revenue. If its investors were to be expected to back the company until it could go public, AllAdvantage would have to explain why these past operating results were not indicative of future financial performance. Jorgensen would have to chart a clear path to profitably and convince AllAdvantage investors that patience was in their best financial interest. Clearly, AllAdvantage would have to embrace significant change.

Despite the challenges that lay ahead, Jorgensen was confident that the AllAdvantage business model had a great deal of potential. Although the company had its critics, its business model was similar in several respects to prize giveaways by radio stations or advertising firms that used drawings or raffles as incentive to encourage individuals to fill out information cards or listen to customized sales pitches. The basic idea of rewarding an audience for its time and attention was not new—it was a business model that had been proven effective in a number of different business settings. The only difference was that AllAdvantage had the capability to monitor individual behavior and offer rewards directly to each individual in the audience rather than give away prizes to a lucky few. When the costs and profit potential were broken down by member and hour, AllAdvantage's potential was obvious:

200 banner ads (one-fifth CPM)	$2.00 ($10 per CPM, one-fifth CPM)
1 hour of surfing (by member)	− .80 ($.50 to individual + $.30 to up line)
Total Profit (per member, per hour)	$1.20 (150% gross profit)

AllAdvantage could display approximately 200 ads (one-fifth of a CPM) per hour to each member. At a CPM rate of $10 (substantially below the going rate for targeted banner ads), the firm would realize a gross profit of 150 percent. Even at a CPM rate of $5, AllAdvantage would enjoy a 25 percent gross margin. Jorgensen was confident that once the company worked through some of its growing pains (and the unusual or one-time expenses associated with such rapid growth), it would be in a position to earn a substantial return on investment. Jorgensen saw three broad approaches to the company's future.

Tactical Responses

AllAdvantage had set out to be an Internet infomediary; its pay-to-surf program was a means to that end. The program had turned AllAdvantage into a marketing machine—it was signing up around 20,000 new members a day—and had propelled the company to prominence. Unfortunately, AllAdvantage's pay-to-surf approach had also produced a severe imbalance between member payments and advertising revenues. It contributed to this imbalance in at least two ways: (1) It obligated AllAdvantage to pay members regardless of whether or not the company was able to sell its advertising inventory and (2) it produced an incentive structure that attracted individuals who were unlikely to respond to advertisers' sales pitches, thereby making it difficult for AllAdvantage to demand high CPM rates.

Jorgensen knew that if he and his team of top executives intended to argue that the current imbalance between member payments and advertising revenue could be rectified, they would need to answer some difficult questions regarding the company's ability to sell its advertising inventory and the CPM rates that the company would likely be able to charge. The biggest uncertainty in this equation was AllAdvantage's ability to sell targeted rather than run-of-the-network advertising. Jorgensen understood that AllAdvantage's inability to sell targeted advertising, as it had initially planned, had resulted in realized CPM rates substantially below what the company had projected.

In addition to targeted advertising, AllAdvantage might also consider tying member payments to advertising revenues. Other pay-to-surf companies, Like Value-Pay.com. were offering to pay members a fixed percentage of advertising revenues and were, therefore, assured a positive gross margin; that is, if advertising revenue were less than expected, member payments would be reduced accordingly. Or AllAdvantage might elect to follow the lead of companies like IWon.com, FreeLotto.com, MyPoints.com, or WebMillion.com and compensate viewers with something other than cash—perhaps points that could redeemed for various prizes, entries in prize drawings, or coupons.

Jorgensen understood that AllAdvantage would have to take into account how its members might react to such changes. For example, in early June 2000, AllAdvantage had "infuriated" its members by reducing the number of maximum hours it paid for watching ads. AllAdvantage had consistently emphasized since its founding that it was working toward a maximum of 40 hours of paid monthly surfing for its members. When the ViewBar was initially released, the maximum was set at 15 hours, but was sub-

sequently raised to 25 hours. The announcement by AllAdvantage that maximum surfing hours would be reduced signaled to members that the promise of 40 hours of surfing would probably never materialize. The lower surfing maximum translated into significant monthly earning reductions for members with substantial referral income; in many cases, monthly earnings were reduced by 30 percent to 40 percent.

AllAdvantage downplayed the changes. In an e-mail to members, CEO Jim Jorgensen characterized the changes as a "global rebalancing." AllAdvantage set the payout currency; the direct surfing compensation rate (53 cents in the United States); the primary, direct, and indirect surfing compensation rates (53 cents, 10 cents, and 5 cents, respectively, in the United States); the maximum payable hours per month (15 in the United States); and the minimum payout threshold ($30 in the United States) for members in all the international markets in which the company operated. The company pushed back its payment schedule from 30 days to 45 days. The net result of these changes, according to AllAdvantage's legal filings, was to reduce what would have been an average payment of $6.49 per user per month to $4.54—a reduction in expected member payments of just over 30 percent.

Although these changes had raised the irc of some of its members, AllAdvantage did not expect member growth to slow considerably. Jorgensen understood, however, that there were limits to how much the company could reduce member payments and maintain its current growth rate. If AllAdvantage were to adopt a compensation policy that did not contain a multilevel component, for example, members would no longer have any incentive to sign up friends and acquaintances, and member referrals would decline significantly.

How much emphasis should AllAdvantage place on growing its member base? How important was its member community to its long-range strategic objectives? Was it important that AllAdvantage keep paying its members? If so, how much? Should AllAdvantage continue paying cash? Should it continue paying members for the surfing time of referrals? Jorgensen was also aware that there were a growing number of AllAdvantage executives that felt that the pay-to-surf approach was now more of a liability than an advantage. As Alex Gourevitch, the company's PR director, explained, "The lights were so powerful, the fragrance so strong, it was making our users lose sight of the usefulness of the ViewBar. It was making everyone miss what we were really about. We set out to be an infomediary." Alex and other executives wanted to focus on the utility and convenience of the ViewBar rather than the company's pay-to-surf marketing approach. This certainly seemed reasonable, given the company's current situation. Jorgensen understood that these questions and issues would have to be addressed.

Strategic Moves

AllAdvantage had actively set out to build a community of AllAdvantage members, but was this really essential to its stated objective of being an Internet infomediary? Jorgensen thought about some of the new programs AllAdvantage had introduced in recent months. There was the AdVantage Network, for example. AllAdvantage intended to sell and deliver targeted advertising to Internet users' persistent desktop objects (PDOs) on behalf of other companies that had built online communities centered around the delivery of advertising through software similar to the AllAdvantage ViewBar. In many cases, these companies were more than happy to outsource the sale of advertising and content delivery to companies in a better position to perform these functions. As Jorgensen explained:

> We started the AdVantage Network; we started working with companies like Spinway, FreeI, Conducent, and Radiate. There are others; we started selling ads for them. At first, we were just solving a reach problem. We were trying to serve the advertising community, and we needed to be able to offer access to other communities, to more communities than just our own members.

Jorgensen believed that the AllAdvantage AdVantage Network might result in some potentially profitable opportunities for the company. AllAdvantage was aware of these opportunities when they decided to launch the network. Again, as Jorgensen explained:

> We also thought that once we got our nose in the tent, we could sell them our technology; we had the ViewBar, and we had some experience handling permanent desktop objects. We had that capability, and we thought that that might be something that we could do. We might be able to license them our technology or reach some other arrangement.

The AdVantage Network allowed AllAdvantage to access members of other ready-made communities. It gave AllAdvantage the chance to leverage its investment in its ViewBar technology and to more fully utilize its sales force and thereby realize some economies of scale.

There were other opportunities in addition to the AdVantage Network. For example, in March 2000, AllAdvantage announced that it had partnered with NetCreations, Inc., a leading provider of opt-in e-mail marketing services. NetCreations and AllAdvantage agreed to build e-mail lists that would allow AllAdvantage members to receive ads and information tailored to their personal profiles. In May 2000, the firm announced that it had partnered with myCIO.com (a Network Associates, Inc., business) to provide antivirus software and software updates to AllAdvantage members. In July, it signed an agreement with San Francisco-based Providian Financial Corp., the nation's sixth largest card issuer, to promote Providian's Internet Aria Visa. Also in July, AllAdvantage entered into an arrangement with RioPort, Inc., a leading Internet music service provider, to offer its members a special discount on the popular RioPort Audio Manager jukebox software. These arrangements were not dependent on the capabilities of the ViewBar or, necessarily, on AllAdvantage maintaining its own community of members.

Jorgensen wondered if AllAdvantage should put more effort into establishing similar types of marketing arrangements with other firms. Should it focus on licensing its technology to other firms with read-made communities? Should it focus on providing services to these other firms?

Exit Strategies

Although Jorgensen believed in AllAdvantage, he understood that unless he and his top managers could convince investors that the AllAdvantage business model created economic value, the company would be forced to exit the industry. Although the company had nearly $85 million in the bank, its investors would not stand idly by while AllAdvantage burned through its cash. Unless its investors believed that money invested in AllAdvantage would generate a substantial return, they would not be willing to risk their capital.

Jorgensen thought about potential buyers for the firm. What exactly did AllAdvantage have to offer? What kinds of firms might be interested?

If the decision were made to exit the industry and a suitable buyer could not be found, then the firm would have to consider simply closing its doors, returning unused capital to its investors, and selling off its assets. Jorgensen wondered what course of action would best serve the interests of the firm? Of employees? Of investors?

Jorgensen wondered if he should bring up the possibility of exit. Should they discuss it? Should selling the firm or shutting down be considered viable strategic options? Is ceasing operations an outcome that business managers should choose or is it something that creditors or investors force on a company? Jorgensen could not help but feel that it was inappropriate to raise the subject with his top executives: It might signal a lack of confidence on his part in their ability to run the company.

Jorgensen paused just outside the company's front door. He glanced at his watch; he had been outside nearly an hour. Regardless of how things turned out, he thought, the last 18 months had been a wild ride. Jorgensen headed to his office to sketch out comments for tomorrow's board meeting. He would probably be here all night.

Appendix

Exhibit 1: *AllAdvantage.com Ad Rates*

Product	468 H 60 Banner[a]	120 H 60 Tile
Behavioral Targeting[b]	na	na
Web Page Targeting	$50	$40
Site Targeting	$50	$40
Keywords	$35	$20
Channel Targeting		
Retail/Auction	$30	$15
Auto	$40	$20
Careers	$40	$20
Entertainment	$30	$15
Finance	$40	$20
Health and Beauty	$35	$20
Higher Education	$35	$20
News	$30	$15
Sports	$25	$12
Technology	$50	$25
Travel	$60	$30
Subchannels	$60	$30
Run-of-Channels	$20	$12
Desktop Billboards[b]	na	na
Run-of-Web	$10	$6
Blitz	$150,000	$100,000
AllPlay! Sponsorship[b]	na	na
QuickLinks Sponsorship[b]	na	na
Filters	Add $5 per	Add $3 per

[a]Prices are per CPM or thousand impressions, except for Blitz, which is per campaign.
[b]Rates negotiated on an individual basis between client and AllAdvantage.

Exhibit 2: *Consolidated Statement of Operations and Consolidated Balance Sheet**

	Period from inception (March 24, 1999) to September 10, 1999	Three Months Ended December 31, 1999	Period from inception (March 24, 1999) to December 31, 1999	Three Months Ended December 31, 1999
Revenues	235	5,016	5,251	9,100
Costs and Expenses:				
Direct Member Costs	2,192	14,949	17,141	32,744
Sales and Marketing	1,580	10,022	11,602	26,927
General and Administrative	3,302	5,042	8,344	6,016
Product Development	1,267	1,644	2,911	6,106
Depreciation and Amortization	78	270	348	580
Stock-Based Compensation	244	1,303	1,547	2,788
Total Costs and Expenses	8,663	33,230	41,893	75,161
Loss from Operations	(8,428)	(28,214)	(36,642)	(66,061)
Interest Expense	(570)	(257)	(827)	(536)
Interest Income	10	350	360	959
Net Loss	(8,988)	(28,121)	(37,109)	(65,638)
Net Loss per Share:	(1.27)	(3.52)	(5.04)	(8.20)

	December 31, 1999	March 31, 2000
Consolidated Balance Sheet Data		
Cash, Cash Equivalents and Restricted Cash	30,019	87,345
Total Assets	39,871	104,497

*Figures in 000s.

Exhibit 3: *Balance Sheet**

	December 31, 1999	March 31, 2000	Pro Forma Stockholders' Equity at March 31, 2000
		(Unaudited)	
Assets			
Current Assets			
Cash and Cash Equivalents	20,019	85,345	
Restricted Cash	10,000	2,000	
Accounts Receivable, Net of Allowance of $235 and $672 at			
December 31, 1999, and March 31, 2000, Respectively	4,523	7,641	
Prepaid Expenses and Other Assets	624	1,470	
Deferred Offering Costs	—	675	
Total Current Assets	35,166	97,131	
Property and Equipment, Net	4,705	7,366	
Total Assets	39,871	104,497	
Liabilities and Stockholder's Equity			
Current Liabilities			
Accounts Payable	1,753	5,456	
Accrued Member Payables	12,239	30,759	
Other Accrued Liabilities	5,362	12,626	
Customer Advance	19,830	19,601	
Deferred Revenue	75	2,278	
Current Portion of Capital Lease Obligations	383	440	
Total Current Liabilities	39,642	71,160	
Capital Lease Obligations, Net of Current Portion	254	212	
Total Stockholders' Equity	(25)	33.125	33.125
Total Liabilities and Stockholders' Equity	39,871	104,497	

*Figures in 000s.

Exhibit 4: *Cash Flow Statement**

	Period from Inception (March 24, 1999) to December 31, 1999	Three Months Ended March 31, 2000
		(Unaudited)
Operating Activities		
Net Loss	(37,109)	(65,638)
Selected Changes in Assets and Liabilities		
Accounts Receivable	(4,523)	(3,118)
Accounts Payable and Other Accrued Liabilities	7,115	10,967
Accrued Member Payables	12,239	18,520
Net Cash Used in Operating Activities	(9,914)	(26,844)
Financing Activities		
Net Cash Provided by Financing Activities	34,223	95,294
Net Increase in Cash and Cash Equivalents	20,019	65,326
Cash and Cash Equivalents at Beginning of Period		20,019
Cash and Cash Equivalents at End of Period	20,019	85,345

*Figures in 000s.

References

Chidi, G. A., "Pay-to-Surf," *InfoWorld Daily News*, July 21, 2000.

"Cash from Your Desktop Adverts," *Financial Times*, London, Edition 1, June 1, 1999, 15.

Jackson, T., "Sweeping Costs Aside," *Financial Times*, London, Edition 1, September 5, 2000, 15.

Foster, E., "Viral Marketing Goes One Step Too Far—To a Place Where Friends Spam Friends," *InfoWorld*, February 7, 2000, 93.

Gimein, M., "The Dumbest Dot-Com, " *Fortune.com*, June 19, 2000.

"Dot-Coms Lost Millions by Giving Money Away for Surfing the Internet," *The Plain Dealer*, August 7, 2000, C:6.

Vickers, M., "Dot-Com Business Models from Mars," *BusinessWeek Online*, September 4, 2000.

Cha, A. E., and L. Walker, "A Pyramid Marketing Ploy Clicks," *The Washington Post*, Final Edition, December 8, 1999, A:1.

Batstone, D., "Ad It Up," *Business 2.0*, February 1, 2000.

Jorgensen, J., cofounder and CEO of AllAdvantage.com, *Personal Interview*, December 12, 2000.

"Alladvantage.com Unveils Multilingual ViewBar Communications Software," *Company Press Release*, April 25, 2000.

"Alladvantage.com Appoints Distinguished Internet Privacy Advocate Ray Everett-Church Chief Privacy Officer," *Business Wire*, August 31, 1999.

"Alladvantage.com Scores $31 Million and Strategic Allies with Plan to Bring Next-Level Internet to Advertisers," *Business Wire*, September 8, 1999.

"Alladvantage.com Appoints David Martin Vice President of Business Intelligence," *Company Press Release*, February 8, 2000.

"Alladvantage.com Names Tobin Trevarthen Vice President, Business Development," *Business Wire*, May 23, 2000.

"Advantages for the Advantaged," *Dow Jones News Service*, November 14, 1999.

Bonello, D., "Alladvantage.com Rolls Out First U.K. Surfer Payments to Its Members," *New Media Age*, October 28, 1999, 9.

"Alladvantage.com Introduces Localized Payment Policy," *Company Press Release*, June 1, 2000.

Jackson, T., "Boldness Bar None," *Financial Times*, London, Edition 1, July 4, 2000, 14.

Balint, K., "Surf for Cash," *The San Diego Union-Tribune*, August 27, 2000, H:1.

Tweney, D., "Online Advertising: A $3 Billion Industry Limping on Its Last Legs," *InfoWorld*, October 4, 1999.

"The Science (or Art?) of Online Media Planning," *AdRelevance* (www.adrelevance.com), 2000.

"Online Advertising Rate Card Prices and Ad Dimensions," *AdRelevance* (www.adrelevance.com), 2000.

Cha, A. E., and L. Walker, "Online Firms Pay Surfers to Click Away," *Newsbytes*, December 8, 1999.

Metinko, C., "Hayward, California-Based Internet Habits Tracker Delays IPO Plan," *Contra Costa Times*, July 9, 2000.

Kirby, C., "Pay-to-Surf Not Paying Off for Web Sites," *The San Francisco Chronicle*, Final Edition, July 12, 2000, C:1.

Bridis, T., "Alladvantage.com Upsets Its Paid Ad-Watchers," *The Wall Street Journal*, June 5, 2000, B:8.

Gourevitch, A., director of public relations at AllAdvantage.com, *Personal Interview*, December 12, 2000.

"NetCreations, Alladvantage.com Team Up to Build 100% Opt-In E-Mail lists," *Business Wire*, March 13, 2000.

"Alladvantage.com Teams with MyCIO.com to Automatically Deploy Antivirus Software Updates," *Company Press Release*, May 25, 2000.

"Providian Signs Deal with Infomediary," *Card Fax*, July 13, 2000, 2.

"Infomediary at Work," *Business Wire*, July 28, 2000.

Case 5 Jon Hirschtick's New Venture

Dan D'Heilly and Tricia Jackel, case writers

Arthur M. Blank Center for Entrepreneurship Babson College

August, 1994, 12 months after John Hirschtick left a great job to found a new venture in the software industry, SolidWorks, the deal was looking good. The seed capital discussions had shifted into high gear as soon as Michael Payne joined the SolidWorks team. After working on the deal for nine months, Axel Bichara, the Atlas Venture vice president originating the project, finally got a syndicate excited about it: Atlas Venture, North Bridge Venture Capital Partners, and Burr, Egan, Deleage & Co. presented an offer sheet to SolidWorks two weeks after Michael was on-board.

This process was particularly interesting because Jon and Axel had worked together for most of the past eight years. They met at MIT in 1986 and cofounded Premise, Inc., a Computer Aided Design (CAD) software company, in 1987. After Premise was bought by Computervision, they joined that team as managers. Now, they sat on opposite sides of the table for Axel's first deal as the lead venture capitalist.

Jon and the other founders thought the valuation and terms were fair, but the post-money* equity issue was unresolved. They had to decide how much money to raise. Did they want enough capital to support SolidWorks until it achieved a positive cash flow, or should they take less money and attempt to increase the entrepreneurial team's post-money equity?

If they took less money now, they could raise funds later, when SolidWorks might have a higher valuation. But they would be gambling on the success of the development team and the investment climate. If their product was in beta testing with high customer acceptance, raising more money would probably be fast and fun, but if they hit any development snags, the process could take a lot of time and yield a poor result.

Jon Hirschtick: 1962–1987

Jon grew up in Chicago in an entrepreneurial family. He fondly remembers helping with his father's part-time business by traveling to stamp collectors' shows across the Midwest. In high school, he was self-employed as a magician.

*Post-money valuation: the value of a company's equity after additional money is invested.

The entrepreneurial impulse continued during his undergraduate years. Jon recalls the Blackjack team he played with at MIT:

> We raised money to get started. At the same time, we developed a probabilistic system for winning at Blackjack. The results were amazing! We tripled our money in the first six months, doubled it during the next six months, and doubled it again in the next six months. We produced a 900 percent annualized return. I learned a useful lesson: you really can know more than the next guy, and make money by applying that knowledge. We tackled Blackjack because people thought it was unbeatable; we studied it, and we won. The same principle applies to entrepreneurship. Opportunities often exist where popular opinion holds that they don't.

Jon's introduction to CAD came from a college internship with Computervision during the summer of 1981. Computervision was one of the most successful start-up companies to emerge during the 1970s. By the early 1980s, it dominated the CAD market.

After earning a master's degree in mechanical engineering (M.E.) at MIT, John managed the MIT CAD laboratory. He supervised student employees, coordinated research projects, and conducted tours for visitors.

Axel Bichara: 1963–1987

Axel was born in Berlin and attended a French high school. In 1986, while studying at the Technical University of Berlin for a master's degree in mechanical engineering, he won a scholarship to MIT. Axel had worked in a CAD research lab in Germany, so he selected the CAD laboratory for his work-study assignment at MIT.

Early CAD Software

CAD software traces its roots to 1969 when computers were first used by engineers to automate the production of drawings. CAD was used by architects, engineers, designers, and other planners to create various types of drawings and blueprints. Any company that designed and manufactured products (e.g., Ford, Sony, Black & Decker) was a prospective CAD software customer.

This case was written by Dan D'Heilly and Tricia Jaekle under the direction of Professor William Bygrave. Funding provided by the Ewing Marion Kauffman Foundation and the Frederic C. Hamilton Chair for Free Enterprise Studies. © Copyright Babson College, 1995. All rights reserved.

An Entrepreneurship Class: January 1987

Visitors to the MIT CAD lab often complained about problems that Jon knew he could solve. He enrolled in an entrepreneurship class to write a business plan for a CAD startup company, Premise, Inc. Jon described the decision to quit his job and start a company.

> I once heard Mitch Kapor* use a game show metaphor to describe the entrepreneurial impulse. He said, "Part of the entrepreneurial instinct is to push the button before you know the answer and hope it will come to you before the buzzer." That's what happened for us: we didn't know how to start a company, or how to fund it, but Premise got rolling, and we came up with answers before we ran out of time.

Jon and Axel were surprised and delighted to find each other in the entrepreneurship class. They had worked together for the past month on a project at the CAD lab, and they decided to become partners in the first class session. Axel recalled:

> It was coincidence that we enrolled in the same class, but it was clear that we should work together. Jon had had the idea for a couple of months, and we started work on the product and the business plan immediately.

Axel took the master's exam at MIT in October 1987, and at Technical University of Berlin in July 1988. He was still a student at both universities when he and Jon started Premise. Axel graduated with highest honors from both institutions.

Premise, Inc.: 1987–1991

Premise went from concept to business plan to venture capitalist-backed startup in less than six months. As Axel remembered:

> The class deadline for the business plan was May 14. On June 1, we had our first meeting with venture capitalists, and by June 22, we had a handshake deal with Harvard Management Company for $1.5m. We actually received an advance that week. It was much easier than it should have been, but the story's 100 percent true.

*Mitchell Kapor founded Lotus Development Corporation.

In the first quarter of 1989, Premise raised its second round of capital. Harvard Management and Kleiner Perkins Caufield & Byers combined to finance the product launch. The product shipped in May to very positive industry reviews, but sales were slow. Premise's software didn't solve a large mass-market problem. As Jon later recalled:

> I've seen successful companies get started without talent, time, or money—but I've never seen a successful company without a market. Premise targeted a small market. I had a professor who said it all, "The only necessary and sufficient condition for a business is customers."

By the end of 1990, the partners had decided that the best way to harvest Premise was an industry buyout. They hired a Minneapolis investment banking firm to find a buyer. Wessels, Arnold & Henderson was considered one of the elite investment banking firms serving the CAD industry. Premise attracted top-level service providers because of the prestige of its venture capitalist partners. Jon explained:

> Several bankers wanted to do the deal, and a big reason was because they wanted to work with our venture capitalists. We had top venture capitalists, and that opened all kinds of doors. This is often under-appreciated. I believe in shopping for venture capital partners.

Wessels, Arnold & Henderson were as good as their reputation. As Axel recalled:

> We sold Premise to Computervision on 7 March 1991. Computervision bought us for our proprietary technology and engineering team. It was a good deal for both companies.

Computervision: 1991–1993

As part of the purchase agreement, Jon and Axel joined the management team at Computervision. They managed the integration of Premise's development team and product line for one year before Axel left to study business in Europe. Jon stayed on after Axel's departure.

Revenues for the Premise team's products grew 200 percent between 1991 and 1993, and perhaps as important as direct revenue, their technology was incorporated into some of Computervision's high-end products. In January 1993, Jon was promoted to director of product definition for another CAD product. He stayed in this position for eight months. After two years at Computervision, he was ready for new horizons. He resigned effective August 23, 1993. (See Exhibit 1 for excerpts from his letter of resignation.)

This is my explanation for wanting to leave CV . . . The other day you asked me whether I was leaving because I was unhappy, or whether I really want to start another company. I strongly believe that it is because I really want to work on another entrepreneurial venture.* I want to try to build another company that achieves business value . . .

I am interested in leaving CV to pursue another entrepreneurial opportunity because I seek to:

1. Be a part of business strategy decisions. I want to attend board meetings and create business plans, as I did at Premise.
2. Select, recruit, lead, and motivate a team of outstanding people. I believe that one of my strengths is the ability to select great people and form strong teams.
3. Represent a company with customers, press, investors, and analysts. I enjoy the challenge of selling and presenting to these groups.
4. Work on multidisciplinary problems: market analysis, strategy, product, funding, distribution, and marketing. I am good at cross-functional problem-solving and deal-making.
5. Work in a fast-moving environment. I like to be in a place where decisions can be made quickly, and individuals (not just me) are empowered to use their own judgment.
6. Work in a customer-driven and market-driven organization. I find technology and computer architecture interesting only as they directly relate to winning business. I want to focus on building products customers want to buy.
7. Have significantly equity-based incentives. I thrive on calculated risks with large potential rewards.
8. Be recognized for having built business success. I measure "business success" by sales, profitability, and company valuation; I want to directly impact business success. Recognition will follow. I admit that this ego-need plays a part in my decision.

Summary

I've decided I want to work on an entrepreneurial venture . . . This is more a function of what I do best than any problems at CV . . . I don't have any delusions about an entrepreneurial company being any easier. I know first-hand that start-up companies have at least as many obstacles as large established companies—but they are the obstacles I want.

*Underlines in original

After a holiday in the Caribbean, Jon purchased new computer equipment, called business friends and associates, and began working on a business plan. He didn't have a clear product idea, but his market research suggested that the time was ripe for a new CAD startup.

CAD Software Market in the 1990s

By the 1990s, the hottest CAD software performed a function called solid modeling. Solid modeling produced three-dimensional computer objects that resembled the products being built in almost every detail. It was primarily used for designing manufacturing tools and parts. Solid modeling was SolidWorks' focus. The key benefits driving the boom in solid modeling were:

1. Relatively inexpensive CAD prototypes could be accurate enough to replace costly (labor, materials, tooling, etc.) physical prototypes.
2. The elimination of physical prototype dramatically improved time-to-market.
3. More prototypes could be created and tested, so product quality was improved.

However, not all CAD software could manage solid modeling well enough to effectively replace physical prototypes.

Most vendors offered CAD software based on computer technology from the 1970s and 1980s. IBM, Computervision, Intergraph, and other traditional market leaders were losing market share because solid modeling required software architecture that worked poorly on older systems.

As one of the industry's newest competitors, Parametric Technology Corp. (PTC) was setting new benchmarks for state-of-the-art solid modeling software. (It was an eight-year-old company in 1994.) CAD was a mature and fragmented industry with many competitors, but PTC thrived because other companies tried to make older technology perform solid modeling functions.

Worldwide mechanical CAD software revenues were projected at $1.8 billion for 1995, with IBM expected to lead the category with sales of $388 million. PTC was growing over 50 percent annually and had the second highest sales, with $305 million in projected revenue. Industry analysts predicted 3 percent to 5 percent revenue growth per year, with annual unit volume projected to grow at 15 percent. The downward pressure on prices was squeezing margins, so many stock analysts thought that the market was becoming unattractive. However, PTC traded at a P/E between 21 and 40 in 1994.

Axel After Computervision: 1992–1994

After five years in the United States, Axel decided to attend an MBA program in Europe. From his experiences at Premise and Computervision, he had become intrigued with the art and science of business management and he was ready for a geographic change.

INSEAD was his choice. Located in Fontainebleau, an hour south of Paris, INSEAD was considered one of the top three business schools in Europe. The application process included two alumni interviews, and one of Axel's interviewers was Christopher Spray, the founder of Atlas Venture's Boston office. Atlas Venture was a venture capital firm with offices in Europe and the United States. It had $250 million under management in 1994.

Since Axel had a three-month break before INSEAD started, Chris asked him to consult on a couple of Atlas Venture's projects. Axel found he enjoyed evaluating business proposals "from the other side of the table." He graduated in June 1993 and joined the Boston office of Atlas Venture as a vice president with responsibility for developing high-tech deals.

Axel reflected on the relationship between business school training and venture capital practice.

> I was qualified to become a venture capitalist because of my technical and entrepreneurial background; business school just rounded out my skills. You do not need a bunch of MBA courses to be a successful venture capitalist. Take finance, for example, I learned everything I needed from the core course. People without entrepreneurial experience who want to be venture capitalists should take as many entrepreneurship courses as possible.

Jon Founds SolidWorks: 1993–1994

Jon's business plan focused on CAD opportunities. He explained,

> I knew that this big market was going through major changes, with more changes to come. From an entrepreneur's perspective, I saw the right conditions for giving birth to a new busi-

ness. I also knew I had the technical skills, industry credibility, and vision needed to make it happen. This was a pretty rare situation.

SolidWorks' product vision evolved slowly from Jon's personal research and from discussions with friends. He was careful to avoid using research that Computervision might claim as proprietary. He was concerned about legal issues, because he would be designing software similar to what Computervision was trying to produce. Axel explained:

> Both Computervision and SolidWorks wanted to produce a quality solid modeling product. Solid modeling technology was still too difficult to learn and use. Only PTC's solid modeling software really worked well enough. The rest made nice drawings but could not replace physical prototypes for testing purposes.

There were only 50,000 licensed solid modeling terminals in the United States, and most of them belonged to PTC, but there were over 500,000 CAD terminals. There were two main reasons PTC did not have a larger market: (1) its products required very powerful computers, and (2) it took up to nine months of daily use to become proficient with PTC software. SolidWorks' goal was to create solid modeling software that was easier to learn, and modeled real-world parts on less specialized hardware (see Figure 1).

This vision was not unique in the industry. Many CAD companies were developing solid modeling software, and the low-end market was wide open. SolidWorks' major advantage was its ability to use recent advances in software architecture and new hardware platforms—it wasn't tied to antique technology. Attracting talented developers was the top priority in this leading-edge strategy.

Figure 1: *Competitive Positioning Grid*

	Computer Aided Drafting & Add-ons	Production Solid Modeling
Low-end		
Windows	Autodesk	SolidWorks
~$5K per station	Bentley	
VAR Channel	CADKEY	
High-end		
UNIX	Applicon	PTC
~$20K per station	CADAM	
Direct Sales		

Teambuilding

Jon's wife, Melissa, enthusiastically supported his decision to resign from Computervision. Jon explained:

> Some spouses couldn't deal with a husband who quits a secure job to start a new company. Melissa never gave me a hard time about being an entrepreneur.

Jon described his priorities in October 1993 when he decided to launch SolidWorks:

> I knew I needed three things: good people, a good business plan, and a good proof-of-concept.* I needed a talented team that could set new industry benchmarks, but there was no way I could get those people without a persuasive prototype demonstration.
>
> The venture capitalists wanted a solid business plan, but that wouldn't be enough. They wanted a strong team. I needed fundable people who were also CAD masters. Venture capitalists couldn't understand most complex technologies well enough to be confident a high-tech business plan was really sound, so they looked at the team and placed their bets largely on that basis. If the proof-of-concept attracted the team then the team and the business plan would attract the money. I needed a team that could create the vision and make venture capitalists believe it was real.

Jon worked on finding the team and developing the proof-of-concept concurrently; but the proof-of-concept was his first priority. He worked on it daily. In his search for cofounders, Jon talked to dozens of people; he even posted a notice on the Internet, but "none of those guys worked out."

Recruiting posed another dilemma—how to get people to work full-time without pay, while the company retained the right to their output? He resolved this problem by creating consulting agreements that gave SolidWorks ownership of employees' work and made salaries payable at the time of funding. As it turned out, this arrangement only lasted nine months. Jon described his approach to recruiting.

> I always paid for the meal when I talked with someone about SolidWorks. I wanted them to feel confident about it, and that meant that I had

*"Proof-of-concept" is a term that refers to a computer program designed to illustrate a proposed project. Also referred to as a "prototype," it is used for demonstration purposes and it is limited but functional in ideal circumstances.

to act with confidence. The deal I offered was: no salary, buy your own computer, work out of your house, and we're going to build a great company. I'd done it before, so people signed on.

Axel described Jon's management style as, "visionary, he's a talented motivator, and a strong leader."

Robert Zuffante: CAD Engineer/Consultant

A major development in 1993 was the addition of super-star consultant Bob Zuffante as manager of proof-of-concept development. Jon needed time to write the business plan and recruit his team. He had been working on the prototype for over a month when Bob took over development. Jon recalled the situation.

> I hadn't seen him since we were students together at MIT, but when I thought about the skills I needed, my mental rolodex came up with his name. I always thought about working with him again. We talked in late November, and about a month later, he began work on the prototype.

Bob knew Jon and Axel from MIT where he earned a master's degree in mechanical engineering. He had worked in the CAD industry for over ten years and had managed a successful consulting business. His arrival at SolidWorks allowed Jon to focus on other pressing issues.

Scott Harris: CAD Marketer

Scott Harris worked at Computervision for eleven years, where he managed development and marketing activities. Most notably, Scott was the founder and manager of Computervision's product design and definition group. He also managed the eleven-person solid modeling development group, and acted as technical liaison between Computer vision's customers and R&D engineers.

Scott was let go by Computervision during a large-scale lay-off. He was skeptical when Jon first told him about the SolidWorks vision, but he became a believer after seeing a proof-of-concept demonstration. Scott stopped looking for a job and started working full-time for SolidWorks almost immediately. Scott was impressed, "The prototype was the embodiment of a lot of the things I was thinking about. This was the way solid modeling should perform."

Scott started with SolidWorks about six weeks after Bob signed on. He became involved in the marketing sections of the business plan and in the product definition process. He ran focus groups, conducted demonstrations for potential customers, and analyzed the purchasing process. He kept the development team focused on customer needs—how did customers really use CAD software, and what did they need that current products lacked?

The Business Plan

When Bob came on in January, Jon turned to the business plan with a passion. The plan went through a number of versions as Jon and his advisors wrestled with key issues such as positioning, competitive strategy, and functionality. By the end of March, the plan was polished enough for Jon to show it to venture capitalists. Axel recalled:

> Jon and I decided that the business plan was ready to show in April, so I scheduled a presentation at Atlas. Jon gave the presentation to Barry [Barry Fidelman, Atlas general partner] and myself—market, team, and concept. Overall, Barry was encouraging, but not excited. He thought Jon's story was not crisp enough; he was looking for money to take on some very large companies; and the CAD market was not that attractive. It was a rocky start.

Initial Financing Attempts

In addition to negotiating with Atlas Venture, Jon met with other venture capital firms and rewrote the business plan several times. Axel described the rationale behind this process.

> If you talk to too many people and you do not make a good impression, it will be much harder to get funding, because the word on the street will be, "this deal will not fly." Meet with 4 or 5 venture capitalists at most, then revise the plan if you are not getting the right response. After each major revision, show it again to the lead venture partner.

While there were promising discussions with several venture capitalists, Atlas did not want to be the sole investor, and SolidWorks did not win support from other venture capitalists during the spring or summer.

Jon was contacted by an established CAD software company in May 1994. It wanted to acquire SolidWorks—essentially the development team and the prototype. The proposal was attractive, it included signing bonuses and stock. Scott recalled his excitement.

> This was a big shot in the arm. It meant that other industry insiders respected our vision and talent enough to put up their money and take the risk. This was like a cold bucket of Gatorade on a hot day.

Jon stopped seeking venture capital for about a month while he considered the buyout offer. If the offer was a boost to morale, the way the team rejected it was even more meaningful. Jon talked to each person (several other programmers had joined during the spring), and they were unanimous in wanting to continue towards their original goal. Affirming their commitment reinvigorated the team.

Turning Point: Michael Payne, CAD Company Founder

The most significant advance that summer began with a due diligence meeting set up by Atlas Venture. Atlas wanted the SolidWorks team to meet its agent, Michael Payne, who had recently resigned from PTC. Michael had cofounded PTC, the number one company in CAD software. He was one of the most influential people in the industry.

Michael had grown up in London. He earned his bachelor's degree in electrical engineering from Southampton University and his master's degree in solid-state physics from the University of London. He came to the United States and worked many years for RCA designing computer chips. Michael continued his education at Pace University, where he earned an MBA. His senior CAD development experience began in the 1970s when he ran the CAD/CAM design lab at Prime Computer. He was subsequently recruited by Sam Geisberg, the visionary behind PTC. Michael recalled their first meeting in 1986, Sam had some kind of crazy prototype, and I said, "Hey, we can do something with that. This is what we should be working on."

PTC was founded in 1986 with Michael as vice president of development, and within five years the company had created a new set of CAD industry benchmarks. For FY 1993, PTC sales were $163 million, it earned a pretax profit margin over 40 percent, and reached a market capitalization* of $1.9 billion. Michael's reputation as a development manager was outstanding. Remarkably, PTC had never missed a new product release date, and it released products every six months. This was considered a near-impossible feat in software development. He left PTC in April 1994 during a management dispute, about two months before the due diligence meeting with SolidWorks.

Jon had never met Michael, but knew by reputation that he was a tough character. The SolidWorks team was worried about two possibilities: that Michael would say they were on the wrong track, or that he might take their ideas back to PTC. Jon recalled the meeting.

---

*Market capitalization is the value of the company established by the selling price of the stock times the number of shares outstanding.

Bob and I were on one side of the table and Michael and Axel on the other. I decided to gamble on a dramatic entrance. Before we told him anything about SolidWorks, I asked Michael to show his cards. I asked him to tell us what he thought were the greatest opportunities in the CAD market. Michael mentioned many of the things we were targeting. I couldn't imagine a better way to start the meeting.

We presented our plan and prototype. Michael asked us a lot of tough, confrontational questions. Afterwards, he told Atlas Venture, "These guys have a chance." Coming from him, that was high praise.

The due diligence meeting was also the beginning of a dialogue between Michael and Jon about joining SolidWorks. Over the next couple of months, Michael decided to join the team. Jon described the synergy between them.

You almost couldn't ask for two people with more different styles, but we got along well because we were united in our philosophy and vision. We found that our stylistic differences were assets; they crated more options for solving problems.

Michael talked about his motivation for joining the SolidWorks team.

I couldn't go work for a big company because I didn't have any patience for petty politics. A start-up was my only option. The larger the company, the more focused it would be on internal issues rather than on making a product that customers would buy. Customers don't care about technique, they care about the benefits of the technology.

Jon focused on CAD features that I knew customers wanted, and he had a prototype demonstrating that he could do it. It was also quicker and easier than what was on the market. Being able to develop it was another matter. They still had to build it. Implementation, that's where I would be useful. I told them, "Give me whatever title you want; I just want to run development."

Team Adjustments

Michael's arrival created an imbalance in the SolidWorks team, and it took time to sort it out. In fact, Michael didn't join the team until the last week in August. Jon described his thoughts about team cohesion.

When I decided to start SolidWorks, I had three goals:

1) work with great people,
2) realize the vision of a new generation of software, and
3) make a lot of money.

We didn't go looking for Michael Payne, but when he came along it was an easy decision. It can be hard to bring in strong players, but if those are your three goals, the decision falls out of the analysis rather naturally.

Bob and I had to give up the reins in some areas so Michael could come on board. We weren't looking for a top development manager because we thought we already had two. The change took some getting used to, but it was clearly the right thing to do.

Jon focused on team building, and Michael became the development manager. There were still big talent gaps, especially in sales and finance, but those positions could be filled when they were closer to the product launch. Michael was satisfied, "We didn't have a vast team, but you don't start out with a vast team, and we had a terrific nucleus."

September 1994

Atlas arranged for Jon to talk with venture firms interested in joining the investment syndicate. The team met with Jon Flint of Burr, Egan, Deleage & Co. and Rich D'Amore of North Bridge Venture Capital Partners. After completing their due diligence investigations, both firms joined the syndicate. Jon Hirschtick recalled the situation.

I was pleased that Jon Flint and Rich D'Amore decided to invest. I had met Jon many years earlier and thought very well of him. Rich also impressed me as a very knowledgeable investor. Both had excellent reputations and I looked forward to having them join our board.

An offer sheet was presented to SolidWorks two weeks after Michael officially joined the SolidWorks management team. Now the team had to decide how much money they really wanted. Michael's last venture, PTC, only needed one round of capital, and our team wanted to go for one round, too. SolidWorks' monthly cash burn rate was projected to average about $250,000 and they planned to launch the product in a year, so they needed $3 million for development. Sales and marketing would also need money; they decided that $1 million should be enough to take them through the product launch to generating positive cash flow. To that total, they added a

Exhibit 2 *Pro Forma*

	1994	1995	1996	1997	1998
Revenue	$ —	$ 175,000	$ 3,010,000	$8,225,000	$17,115,000
Cost of Sales	$ —	$ 31,500	$ 541,800	$1,480,500	$ 3,080,700
Sales & Marketing	$ 71,919	$ 765,920	$ 1,930,000	$3,030,000	$ 5,822,500
R&D	$ 605,544	$ 1,126,208	$ 1,350,000	$1,500,000	$ 2,050,000
G&A	$ 185,954	$ 445,175	$ 650,000	$ 800,000	$ 1,050,000
Total Expenses	$ 863,417	$ 2,368,803	$ 4,471,800	$6,810,500	$12,003,200
Operating Income	$(863,417)	$(2,193,803)	$(1,461,800)	$1,414,500	$ 5,111,800
Margin Analysis					
Cost of Sales		18.0%	18.0%	18.0%	18.0%
Gross Profit		82.0%	82.0%	82.0%	82.0%
Sales & Marketing		437.7%	64.1%	36.8%	34.0%
R&D		643.5%	44.9%	18.2%	12.0%
G&A		254.4%	21.6%	9.7%	6.1%
Operating Income		−1253.6%	−48.6%	17.2%	29.9%

$500,000 safety margin. SolidWorks asked Atlas to put together an offer sheet based on raising $4.5 million.

SolidWorks received the offer sheet during the first week of September. It gave a $2.5 million pre-money valuation with a 15 percent post-money stock option pool.* For SolidWorks' business plan proforma, see Exhibit 2). These terms were fairly typical for a first round deal, but the SolidWorks team didn't like what happened to their post-money equity when they ran the numbers.

*The pool of company stock reserved for rewarding employees in the future.

Questions

1. Why has this deal attracted venture capital?

2. Can the founders optimize their personal financial returns and simultaneously ensure that SolidWorks has sufficient capital to optimize its chance of succeeding? What factors should the founders consider?

3. How can the syndicate optimize its potential return? What factors should it consider?

4. After you have answered questions #2 and #3, structure a deal that will serve the best interests of the founders, the company, and the venture capital firms.

Case 6 Meg Whitman—The Driving Force Behind eBay

A. Neela Radhika, case writer
ICMR Center for Management Research

> "People say eBay has a bullet-proof business model. But it's Whitman who keeps it dodging bullets."
>
> From an article published in www.allperson.com, in August 2000.[1]

At the Helm of Success

In October 2002, Fortune Magazine ranked Meg Whitman (Whitman), CEO of online auction major eBay, as the world's third most powerful women in business, after Carly Fiorina and Oprah Winfrey. According to Fortune, Whitman 'ruled the Internet,' and under her leadership, eBay's revenues and profits doubled every year. Reportedly, eBay's stock grew by 30% during 2001, even as the technology sector across the world experienced a severe downturn.

Such recognition was nothing new for Whitman; she received many accolades for her contribution to eBay and for her managerial abilities. Whitman was ranked number one on the Worth Magazine's list of the Best CEOs in 2002. Since 2000, she had been continuously named as one of the 25 most powerful business managers in the world by BusinessWeek magazine. eBay also won many awards under her leadership (Refer to Exhibit 1 for a list of awards received by Whitman and eBay).

Reportedly, Whitman was an old-fashioned, low-key manager, who did not possess the 'star-quality' of Carly Fiorina, CEO of Hewlett-Packard, or the electric energy and charisma of Jeff Bezos, the founder of Amazon.com. But still, Whitman had succeeded where many had failed. While many dotcom businesses crashed in the late 1990s and early 2000s, Whitman steered eBay towards success. According to analysts, eBay was the only Internet company that had registered continuous growth and profits since its inception in 1995.

Industry observers felt that Whitman's trust in eBay's business model and her business acumen were the major reasons for the company's growing revenues. Revenues increased from $4 million in early 1998 (when she joined eBay) to $1 billion by late 2002 (See Exhibit 2 for eBay's Income Statement). This was attributed to her strong belief in eBay's business model and its customers. In fact, such was her belief in this model that in September 2000, at the depths of the dot-com depression, she set a target of earning $3 billion in revenues by 2005. Commenting on this in early 2003, Whitman said, "I think people thought we were nuts because we set that in the middle of

2000 when we did $425 million in revenues. Now it seems very reasonable and we are absolutely standing by it."

Background Note

eBay

In September 1995, Pierre Omidyar (Omidyar), a software programmer in his early 20s, founded eBay as Auction Web (the site's domain name was ebay.com). The idea reportedly originated from the difficulty that Omidyar's fiancee faced when trying to collect Pez dispensers[2] from the San Francisco Bay area. Auction Web enabled people to trade through auctions on the Internet.

Omidyar aimed at leveraging the vast potential of the Internet by developing an online marketplace that allowed person-to-person trading in the auction format. He created a simple business model which allowed buyers and sellers to decide the value of items and connect with others, for a small commission for every item placed and sold on the site.[3] Using this model, Auction Web soon became one of the leading online sites in the world.

Omidyar wanted the power of the market to stay with individuals and not with companies. He felt that it was important to let users take responsibility for building the eBay community. Omidyar encouraged users to communicate directly with him through e-mail so that he could incorporate their suggestions and fix the problems they faced on the site. This type of customer focus reportedly gave users a sense of ownership and participation.

In 1996, Omidyar introduced the Feedback Forum, a sort of credit reporting system, to eliminate the problems caused by anonymity and the physical distance between buyers and sellers, viz, fraud and cheating. Under this system, buyers and sellers were encouraged to rate each transaction positive, negative or neutral, thus offering their perception of the credibility of the buyer or seller. These ratings helped users determine whether a buyer or seller was trustworthy. Commenting on this, Peter Kollock, sociology professor, University of California, Los Angeles (UCLA) said, "As high tech as eBay is, the closest analogue to what they have created is the original small-town market. It is a market that relies on identity and reputation for risk management."[4]

Apart from this in 1996, Omidyar also introduced online bulletin boards for users, which allowed them to guide fellow users or new users. This considerably reduced customer support costs of Auction Web and also increased the loyalty of users towards eBay. In 1996, Omidyar appointed Jimmy Griffith (Griffith), who had been voluntarily helping new users and existing users through their auction processes, as the first customer

Exhibit 1

Awards Received By Whitman

Award Received	Awarding Institution	Date
BusinessWeek Top 25 Managers—Meg Whitman	Business Week	January 2002
Worth Magazine Top 50 CEOs—9th Place	Worth Magazine	May 2000
Top 50 Most Powerful Women in American Business	Fortune	October 1999
Mirabella's The 25 Smartest Women	Mirabella	October 1999
The New Establishment—The 50 Most Powerful Leaders in the Information Age	Vanity Fair	October 1999
e.biz 25—The Most Influential People in Electronic Business	Business Week	September 1999
Ernst & Young's Entrepreneur of the Year Award	Ernst & Young	July 1999
The e-Gang 12 mavericks who are rewriting the rules of the Web	Forbes	July 1999
Ernst & Young's Entrepreneur of the Year Award	Ernst & Young	June 1999
E-Retailer of the Year Award	E-Retailer	May 1999
Women to Watch	New Woman Magazine	May 1999
Worth Magazine Top 50 CEOs	Worth Magazine	May 1999
Editor's Choice award	PC Magazine	Mar 1999
Top 25 Female Professionals	San Jose Business Journal	Feb 1999
Entrepreneurs of the Year	Business Week	January 1999

Source: www.ebay.com

Major Awards Received by eBay

Award Received	Awarding Institution	Date
Business 2.0 Top 100 Fastest Growing Technology Companies	Business 2.0	October 2002
Fortune Magazine Top 100 Fastest Growing Companies.	Fortune Magazine	September 2002
Web's 50 Best Sites	PC World	July 2002
Fast 500 ranked eBay the #1 fastest growing company	Deloitte & Touche	November 2001
World Class Awards 2000	PC World	July 2000
22nd Annual Entrepreneurial Company of the Year	Harvard Business School	May 2000
Forbes Favorite Auction Site	Forbes	December 1999
CIO 100 Award	CIO Magazine	August 1999
Business 2.0 Top 100—eBay rated #14	Business 2.0 Magazine	August 1999
Business Week Info Tech 100	Business Week	July 1999
E-Retailer of the Year Award	E-Retailer	May 1999
Brand Week/Ad Week 'Top Marketer of the Year' Award	Brand Week/Ad Week	May 1999
The Webby Awards—Top E-Commerce Site	The Webby Awards	March 1999
Top of the Net '98	Yahoo!! Internet Life	January 1999
Winner of Hot IPO	Bloomberg Personal Magazine	October 1998
A must-see Web destination	Wall Street Journal	September 1998

Source: www.ebay.com

support representative of Auction Web. Griffith established eBay East, which soon became the main customer-support center of eBay. In 1996, Jeff Skoll (Skoll) joined the business as eBay's President. In the same year, Auction Web changed its name to eBay and was incorporated under the new name.

Omidyar believed that as long as the business model worked, the community of users would grow by itself. Hence, Omidyar and Skoll devoted most of their time strengthening the site technically to support the increasing user base. Omidyar's trust in the business model and the users was well placed—by 1997, the user base was

Particulars	1997	1998	1999	2000	2001	(in $million) 2002
Net revenues	41.370	86.129	224.724	431.424	748.821	1,214.100
Cost of net revenues	8.404	16.094	57.588	95.453	134.816	213.876
Gross profits	32.966	70.035	167.136	335.971	614.005	1,000.224
Operating expenses: Sales and marketing	15.618	35.976	96.239	166.767	253.474	349.650
Product development	0.831	4.640	24.847	55.863	75.288	104.636
General and administrative	6.534	15.849	43.919	73.027	105.784	171.785
Payroll expense on employee stock options	—	—	2.337	2.442	4.015
Amortization of acquired intangible assets		0.805	1.145	1.433	36.591	15.941
Merger related costs		—	4.359	1.550	—	—
Total operating expenses	22.983	57.270	170.509	300.977	473.579	646.027
Income (loss) from operations	9.983	12.765	(3.373)	34.994	140.426	354.197
Interest and other income (expense), net	(1.951)	(0.703)	21.412	46.025	46.276	49.209
Impairment of certain equity investments		—	—	—	(16.245)	(3.781)
Income before income taxes	8.032	12.062	18.039	81.019	170.457	399.625
Provision for income taxes	(0.971)	(4.789)	(8.472)	(32.725)	(80.009)	(145.946)
Net Income	7.061	7.273	9.567	48.294	90.448	253.679

Source: www.ebay.com

doubling every three months. In fact, it was increasing much too quickly for the management to handle efficiently. By mid-1997, Auction Web became one of the most visited sites on the Internet, with more than 150,000 users (in mid-1996 it had only 5,000 users).

With this meteoric increase in users, came the need for investment to support the company's rapid growth. In June 1997, Omidyar and Skoll approached Benchmark Capital (Benchmark), a leading venture capital firm in the US, for investment. Benchmark invested $4.5 million in eBay and obtained a 22% stake in the company.

As the company was growing too fast (at a 70% compounded monthly growth rate), the founders felt the need for an efficient manager. They wanted someone who could make the right strategic decisions and had the ability to build the infrastructure, which would enable eBay to sustain meteoric growth in user base as well as revenues/profits. Benchmark delegated the responsibility of finding such a manager to David Beirne (Beirne), one of the well-known headhunters in Silicon Valley. Soon, Beirne zeroed in on Whitman.

Meg Whitman

Born in August 1956, Margaret C. Whitman, popularly known as Meg Whitman, was the youngest child of a Wall Street executive. Whitman, who grew up in Long Island, New York, was a studious and clever student. An exceptionally academically oriented person, she graduated in Economics from Princeton University.

She had *The Wall Street Journal* delivered to her dormitory at Princeton University, which was unusual during the disco era of the 1970s. Dick Boyce, partner, Texas Pacific Group (an equity investment firm) and Whitman's classmate at Princeton, said, "Myself and other classmates thought she was strange because she got *The Wall Street Journal* in her room. She always had a very strong orientation toward business. She was very ambitious."[5] Whitman's inclination for business took her to Harvard University, where she received her Masters in Business Administration.

She began her career in 1979 as a brand manager at Procter & Gamble (P&G), where she learnt her marketing basics and gained first hand training in brand management. In 1982 she left P&G to become a Vice President at Bain & Co., leading consultancy firm. After nearly eight years at Bain and Co., she shifted to a number of different companies and continued to climb the corporate ladder.

Whitman worked as a senior vice president at Walt Disney's Consumer Products division between 1989 and 1992. During this period, she opened the first Disney stores in Japan. This experience helped her learn the basics of running a business efficiently. In 1993, Whitman joined StrideRite, a major shoemaker, as its President and was instrumental in the revival of the Ked's brand during her tenure there.

In 1995, she left StrideRite to join Florists' Transworld Delivery (FTD), as its President and went on to become its CEO. Whitman was credited for turning around FTD, which was incurring losses at the time of her joining.

However, she did not remain at FTD after the company returned to profitability. In early 1997, she shifted to Hasbro, a leading toy maker to head the global operations of Playskool and Mr. Potato Head brands.[6]

In November 1997, when Beirne called Whitman, she rejected the job of CEO of eBay as she had never heard of the company before. At that period in time, she was looking forward to a more challenging and bright future at Hasbro. She reportedly did not want to risk her future prospects at, in her own words 'an obscure, no-name Internet company' with less than three dozen employees and revenues of $4 million. Moreover, taking up a job at eBay meant shifting her family from Boston to California, which seemed ridiculous as her family was well settled in Boston. Her husband was the head of the Neurosurgery Department at the Massachusetts General Hospital and her two sons were quite happy with their school.

Beirne's persistence in making her accept the eBay offer finally paid off when she agreed to fly to California to meet eBay's founders and investors. It took only two meetings for Omidyar, Skoll and the representatives of Benchmark, to convince her of eBay's potential. What clinched the deal was the fact that eBay provided people with an opportunity which they did not find before on the Internet and that it helped build an entirely new community. Commenting on what made her accept the proposal, Whitman said, "Two things. One is that this website had created a functionality for people that did not exist before the Internet. And then Pierre Omidyar, eBay's founder, said that people had met their best friends on eBay, had traveled with other eBay users. That people had connected over a shared area of interest. I said, This is huge."[7]

And finally in March 1998, she joined eBay.[8] Reportedly, Whitman's decision to join eBay was based on her instincts. In her words, "There's no substitute in the land-based world for eBay. I just had an overwhelming instinct that this thing was going to be huge."[9] Right from the time of her entry, she had to play many different roles at eBay: management consultant, marketer, financial analyst, strategist, leader, and customer.

Whitman—An Exceptional Manager

Whitman found eBay akin to a 'den of geeks' who were handpicked by Omidyar. She knew that she was brought into the company to build the eBay 'brand' and to bring some professionalism into the company, which was soon to be listed on the stock exchange. Her first job was to prepare eBay for its first IPO.

However, before she made any changes at eBay, she focused on gaining a comprehensive understanding of eBay's business model. Whitman said, "I came in and I said Pierre has created something incredibly important here that is growing very rapidly and has clearly struck the consumer nerve. My objective is to find out as much as I possibly can about what he has created and what is wonderful about what he has created."[10] She soon understood that it was the customers, whom she referred to as the eBay community, who made the business model so powerful. Hence, she initially focused on making eBay even more acceptable to customers and investors.

To prepare eBay for the IPO, Whitman changed the appearance of eBay's home page by replacing its grey and white colors with bright primary colors. A bizarre looking apple, chosen as eBay's Mascot, also appeared on the site. Whitman also created separate age-restricted sites for firearm and pornography auctions, thus ensuring that they would not cause inconvenience to other customers.

All efforts to improve eBay appeared to have been wasted, when the stock market fell in mid-1998, when the company was preparing for its IPO (due in September 1998). Many Internet startups dropped their IPO plans when the market was crashed, but Whitman decided to go ahead. She and her team of executives traveled across the US to convince brokerage firms of eBay's potential. Finally, on September 24, 1998, eBay went public. On the very first day of trading, share price shot up to $18.8 from the IPO price of $6 per share. Reportedly, the success of eBay's IPO revived the entire market for Internet IPOs during that period.

To build eBay into a leading auction site worldwide, Whitman had to develop an outstanding, experienced and enthusiastic team of senior executives and employees. She began building such a team immediately after she joined eBay.

Whitman filled many key senior positions with efficient and experienced personnel from marketing and business consulting domains. Reportedly, the new executives were reminded time and again about the difference between other businesses and eBay. Whitman ensured that all the marketing and consultancy people she brought were first educated about the Internet and eBay mission and objectives before they began applying their knowledge to their work. Whitman said, "Everyone that I brought into the company from the old economy had to get educated about the Web and what was special about eBay, and then begin to bring lessons learned from the old economy and how they would relate to the new economy."[11] Whitman also employed thousands of employees through the late 1990s to offer customer support and technical support to the site.

According to analysts, her ability to attract the right people to the company helped eBay a lot. And her decision to hire highly experienced executives to run an Internet company (unlike other Internet companies, which chose youngsters during that period) proved right later on. Equipped with experience, conventional thinking and professionalism, these executives prevented eBay from taking the path of other Internet companies that disappeared without a trace when the dotcom bubble burst.

However, with growing riches came the scrutiny of the media. In no time, eBay attracted considerable criticism from the media for selling firearms. During that period, reports of auction frauds were rampant in the media and many articles warned customers of escalating instances of fraud at eBay. Though eBay's founders insisted that the fraud percentage at eBay was negligible (27 reported cased out of millions of auctions on the site), Whitman understood the possible impact of such reports. She realized the fact that the Feedback Forum was not enough to earn the trust of customers. Hence, she decided to take some action in this area.

In January 1999, she announced a comprehensive trust and safety program. Under this program she set up a Trust & Safety department and employed hundreds of executives across the world to ensure the safety of transactions on eBay. As part of this program, eBay offered buyers free insurance for items that cost up to $200. It also offered sellers a chance to pay $5 and have their identity verified by Equifax, a credit-rating agency. Under this program, eBay promised to take severe action against sellers and buyers resorting to fraud. eBay also developed and implemented advanced software to help identify fraud. Whitman also banned the sale of firearms on eBay and transferred pinup calendars and risqué postcards to age restricted sites.

These changes reflected a major shift in eBay's policy—for the first time, the company made top-down decisions instead of relying on customers' suggestions. Analysts felt that although Whitman had regard for customers' contribution in building eBay, she was also prepared to take timely action on her own when the need arose. Whitman continued to take such strategic decisions regarding eBay's future whenever required.

When she joined eBay, Whitman had no technical knowledge about online sites. But she quickly learned the importance of technology for eBay. When in mid-1999, eBay's site crashed for 22 hours and remained unstable for the next few weeks. Whitman realized that the IT department of eBay was unable to support the phenomenal growth in traffic and was stretched to breaking point. Constant crashing of eBay's website was taking a heavy toll on the company: customers expressed anger and dissatisfaction and the company's stock price plummeted. Whitman observed, "Without technology, we do not have a company, It was very clear that I had to step in and provide the leadership to get us through this."[12]

Whitman appointed Maynard Webb (Webb), a former CIO at Gateway Inc. (San Diego), to head eBay's IT department. eBay invested more than $200 million in strengthening its technology division. By 2000, Webb had built one of the most powerful e-commerce systems in the world for eBay. The company's technology problems were brought under control and the average crash time was reduced to only a few seconds per month. By now, Whitman also had transformed herself into a technically astute CEO with a clear understanding of technology related issues.

Reportedly, Whitman was a hands-on CEO in her initial years at eBay. As the number of employees was less, she had to do many things personally. In Whitman's own words, "When I came to eBay there really was not a marketing group, so I actually wrote the first marketing plan. I tried to help the company figure out who their first set of customers was and utilized the 20 people that were at the company, but it was very hands-on at first. We were in a small space—600 square feet—so there were a tremendous amount of hands-on projects that I did." In mid-1999, when eBay's site crashed quite frequently, Whitman literally lived at the office. According to eBay sources, she attended all technical meetings and spent many nights helping the technical staff solve problems with the Sun Microsystems computers and the Oracle database software by constantly interacting with experts from these two companies.

Whitman believed that once data was available, it was easier to take strategic decisions and have things under control. She therefore turned eBay into a business data reservoir by filling most of the senior management positions with ex-consultants. Jeff Jordan, who was brought into head eBay's US business, formerly worked for the Boston Consulting Group. Similarly, Matt Bannick, head of international operations, and Gary Briggs, Vice President of eBay's consumer marketing division, were formerly employed at McKinsey & Company.

Whitman attached great importance to metrics, which even led to a popular saying at eBay, "If it moves, measure it."[13] According to Whitman, "If you can not measure it, you cannot control it. Being metrics-driven is an important part of scaling to be a very large company. In the early days you could feel it, you could touch it. Now that is more difficult, so it has to be measured."[14] Whitman believed that measurement and statistics provided early warnings and thus helped the company anticipate and deal with problems.

Led by her focus on metrics, Whitman created a new rank of employees at eBay called Category Managers. These managers closely studied the changing trends in eBay's 23 major categories and over 35,000 subcategories. They measured the growth/decline in sales and worked towards promoting their respective categories. As the category managers had only indirect control over products in their category, they used marketing and merchandizing techniques—enhancing the look and presentation of the product on the site and providing simple tips and tools to buyers and sellers—to make better deals.

As category managers measured and analyzed everything on the site, it became easy for eBay to find out instantly which product was selling well on the site. Accordingly, decisions regarding the product category to be promoted were taken. For example, when a senior category manager for fashion noticed in 2002 that sales of women's shoes were growing, eBay introduced a separate category for women's shoes within two months to cash in on the trend.

Whitman adopted a conservative approach to the company's finances. According to Bob Quinn, a senior executive at eBay, Whitman managed costs very closely. He said that she always demanded a clear line of return on every investment made. Commenting on this, Whitman said, "The financial discipline of the bottom line really matters, having a return-based investment philosophy—I am spending a dollar on something so what am I going to get back for that?"[15]

A few analysts called Whitman a 'management stodgy' and a 'slow-footed CEO' because even during the dotcom boom, she avoided risk and focused on financial fundamentals. However, the performance of eBay silenced her critics. Appreciating her managerial abilities, Tim Bajarin, President, Creative Strategies (Campbell), said, "Truly a visionary, but more importantly she is an exceptional manager. Vision is one thing, and there is a lot of that in the Silicon Valley. Execution is another. She is remarkable at actually getting things done."[16]

Whitman perceived herself as a 'Level 5 Manager'—a reference to Jim Collin's description of levels of manager in his book, 'Good to Great'. According to Jim Collins, Level 5 managers are humble, uncharismatic and highly determined people who give credit to their subordinates.

Whitman & Customer Focus

The eBay community was always Whitman's first priority as she credited it with the company's success. Commenting on the community's role, she said, "We provide the marketplace, but it is the users who build the company. They bring the product to the site, they merchandise the product and they distribute it once sold."[17]

The lessons she learned from her experience at leading consumer companies such as P&G and Hasbro also made her focus strongly on consumers. Reportedly, the first lesson Whitman jotted down in a journal she maintained while she worked as a brand manager at P&G was "It is all about the customer." According to eBay sources, Whitman referred to that journal occasionally before taking decisions regarding branding and marketing. Her devotion to customer service was evident in the fact that she employed hundreds of customer support executives. These executives were available 24 hours a day to help eBay customers with their queries and dealings and to listen to customer complaints and suggestions.

In 1999, Whitman launched the 'Voice of the Customer' program. As part of the program, a dozen loyal eBay customers were invited to the company headquarters every year. The customers and eBay staff discussed the company's strengths as well as shortcomings. eBay executives made a note of the suggestions made by this group and worked towards their implementation. As a result of this program, problems associated with new features and policies declined considerably.

eBay also held teleconferences at least twice a week to allow users to vote on the performance or effectiveness of every new feature or policy. Such initiatives reportedly evoked a feeling of ownership and loyalty in the community towards eBay, which in turn resulted in increased revenues and profits for the company.

Whitman knew that frequent site crashes could alienate even loyal customers. She therefore invested in advanced technology systems that reduced the number of crashes and improved service. In addition, she ensured prompt response to customer e-mails. As satisfied customers referred the site to other people, the benefits were manifold (more than half of eBay's customers came through referrals by existing customers). Whitman called this phenomenon as 'a small-town feel on a global scale' (since in small towns, 'word-of-mouth publicity' worked better than other modes of advertising or marketing).

Whitman constantly devised new techniques to tap the eBay community's expertise. For example, before eBay restructured its collectibles categories in 2001 (to make the search for these products easier), it mailed over 1.2 million customers to find out their opinion on the proposed structure. Over 10,000 customers responded and many of their suggestions were implemented by the company. As the strong focus on customers flowed right from the top (Whitman), analysts felt that eBay's growth was but natural.

eBay also offered guidance and training to customers by sponsoring seminars at various locations across the US. The company called this program 'eBay University' as company executives taught interested customers how to navigate the site and effectively sell/buy products. eBay University also offered loads of hints and tips on doing business on eBay—courtesy eBay insiders. Reportedly, the customers generally doubled their selling activity after attending training classes held by eBay. Many small merchants made a fortune on eBay by selling their merchandise on the site. Though they continued to offer their merchandise in the real world, they used eBay because they discovered that it was a very profitable distribution channel.

Whitman made eBay a transparent marketplace by providing customers a 24-hour access to every new trend, regulation and sale. This enabled eBay sellers and buyers to make informed decisions. Whitman encouraged eBay employees to work like civil servants rather than as corporate managers to gain the support and loyalty of the community. She consistently strove to deliver superior customer service. Once, when a customer protested against a new policy that routed bidders (who were losing an auction) to similar auctions, Whitman and Omidyar personally met the customer. They took note of his complaints and modified the policy within two days. In another instance, when a few impatient eBay bidders suggested that the auctions be speeded up, Whitman launched a 'Buy It Now' feature (in January 1999).[18]

Many times Whitman stepped into the shoes of customers (by buying and selling on eBay) to gain first hand experience of the company's services. She also urged other employees to sell on eBay so that they could detect and solve customer problems. Whitman ensured that she was easily available to the customers at all times; her e-mail, 'meg@ebay.com,' was very popular with eBay users. Reportedly, she received hundreds of mails everyday, many of which she personally responded to.

Whitman credited the community for the introduction of many successful business categories on eBay. She said, "At Hasbro, we used to spend a lot of time trying to pick the next hot toy – the next Cabbage Patch Kid, or the next Pokemon. At eBay, we do not worry about that. Our army of users figures out what is hot before we even know."[19]

Commenting on the role of eBay's customers in expanding the business, Whitman said, "The R&D lab here is our community of users and it is an undirected R&D lab; they figure out how to best use this platform. The organic nature of this business is really quite stunning. We did not sit in a room five years ago and say let us have our users get into the used car business—they did it on their own. When you think of where we have come from which was really almost 100% collectibles to 25 major categories, the diversification of the platform is remarkable and it happened organically—once we saw it happening we did some things to help it but it is largely driven by the community of users."[20]

By early 2003, the eBay community was playing many roles: product-development team, sales and marketing team and supply management team. Commenting on the involvement of the customers in the business, Whitman said, "It is far better to have an army of a million than a command-and-control system."[21]

Analysts felt that Whitman's success lay in the creation of a huge base of passionate, loyal and evangelistic customers who refused to do business anywhere other than on eBay.

Whitman—The Strategist

Though Whitman credited the community for eBay's success and growth, she soon realized that like a government in a democracy, eBay could not leave every decision to its customers. The responsibility of taking the crucial strategic decisions necessary for expanding eBay's reach and business was entirely her own.

By mid-1999, Whitman was working hard towards making eBay a global online marketplace. Her expansion plan focused on the following areas: targeting high priced items and big sellers, making acquisitions that complemented eBay's business, increasing the product categories and range of items available, and expanding into international markets.

In line with the above, she acquired Butterfield & Butterfield (B&B), a San Francisco-based 134 year old auction house, in exchange for eBay stock worth $260 million. Whitman expected the B&B acquisition to accelerate eBay's entry into the premium segment and thus help the company increase its earnings. Since the average B&B auction closed at $1,400, eBay's expected commission on auction would be $400, which was substantially higher than the commission eBay received on its own auctions. The average eBay auction closed at $47, yielding a commission of only $3.

eBay also acquired Kruse International, an automobile auction company, which was expected to provide it with a steady supply of high priced goods and an efficient group of appraisers. Whitman also increased the company's focus on fixed price retailing (i.e. no-bid sales) since goods could be sold faster in this type of format than the auction format. As a part of this, in 1999, eBay acquired half.com, an online retailing outfit that sold used items such as books and CDs at fixed prices.

Whitman made strategic investments in various other businesses in the early 2000s. In 2000, eBay invested $22 million in Tradeout.com, a New York-based business-to-business (B-to-B) start-up. In 2001, Whitman bought iBazar, which had online auction sites in eight European countries, to strengthen eBay's presence in Europe. In mid-2002, eBay bought PayPal, an online-payment service, to cut down on back-end processing costs (eBay's credit card payment division was losing money).

In the early 21st century, Whitman focused on attracting high-priced and brand name products from leading companies. She persuaded leading companies to sell their excess inventory on eBay by giving them special privileges. For example, for a $499 monthly fee, instead of the $10 monthly fee normally charged by eBay, big companies could use their own logo on the site to distinguish themselves from other sellers. Whitman also introduced a PowerSeller program, which provided additional customer support to big merchants.

As a result of these initiatives, many major companies (such as Sun Microsystems) began selling products worth millions on eBay. As the economy weakened in the early 21st century, more and more such companies tried to dispose of their inventories through eBay, much to the latter's delight. Some such companies were IBM, Sears Roebuck and Walt Disney.

Whitman also entered into strategic agreements with leading media companies such as AOL Time Warner and Disney. Under these agreements, media companies encouraged their customers to shop at eBay. Reportedly, as a mutual benefit strategy, AOL Time Warner also encouraged its customers to use the website by running television advertisements, which mentioned how easy it was to find any item/perfect gift on eBay.

In the early 2000s, Whitman also focused on expanding the portfolio of merchandise sold through eBay. She wanted eBay to conduct more regional auctions so that people could trade big items such as cars and boats that could not be shipped easily. By 2002, eBay had nearly 20 major categories and over 18,000 subcategories. Some of the major categories included cars, antiques, fine art, real estate and computers. The computer category was one of the major categories that attracted leading companies. Major sellers in eBay's computer and electronic categories included IBM, Dell, Palm and Sun Microsystems. The major products in these categories were computers, routers, servers, digital cameras, hubs and laptops.

Whitman's knowledge of business and marketing helped her drive growth at eBay. When eBay launched a special category for automobiles called eBay Motors, Whitman realized that many buyers would be reluctant to purchase such products online. To address this concern, eBay offered assurance programs that included free limited warranty on used cars and other fee-based services to ensure the proper working of the automobile. Reportedly, by end of fiscal 2002, eBay Motors evolved into the largest car dealer in the US, earning more than $1 billion in revenues from the sale of used cars and car parts.

During the early 21st century, Whitman continued to expand eBay internationally. By 2002, eBay established local sites in 53 cities in the US and five other countries (Canada, Japan, Australia, Germany and the UK).

According to eBay sources, Whitman was determined to globalize the business. Analysts observed that though Whitman seemed to focus on communities, she also quietly and rapidly set about to restructure eBay to ensure its future growth and profitability and thus please investors and the stock market. Many analysts felt that Whitman's strategies were suitable for a company which had gone public. They were of the opinion that it was but natural for such a company to try to attract people with deeper pockets.

The positive stock price movements that occurred every time Whitman made a strategic announcement showed that eBay's investors supported her decisions. By the end of fiscal 2002, eBay had successfully completed its transition from a plain auction website into the world's largest consumer-commerce site.

Whitman—Leading eBay

In the early 21st century, Whitman emerged as one of the most popular leaders in dotcom world on account of eBay's phenomenal success. Commenting on her journey from a novice to a leader in the dotcom world, Whitman said, "In the beginning, I was certainly not an entrepreneur who came up with the idea, but I think I was fairly entrepreneurial in trying to figure out how to bring that idea to life and build a backbone for the company that could take it to the next level."[22]

Reportedly, Whitman's optimism was largely responsible for the positive environment at eBay. According to sources at eBay, she developed a work culture of fun, trust and openness and kept the entire organization focused on the company's key objectives and priorities.

According to Whitman's associates, her ability to stay focused on her goals and her positive frame of mind distinguished her from most of her counterparts. Commenting on Whitman's optimism, Steve Westly, eBay's Vice President (Marketing & Business Development), said, "She is relentlessly optimistic. She stands out, with a combination of drive and executive maturity."[23] Her willingness to trust her instincts also helped her steer eBay successfully. According to Whitman, she made about 20 decisions a day, and reportedly quite a few of those decisions were based on intuition! Since the Internet business was a dynamic one that demanded timely and quick actions, Whitman's decision making style paid rich dividends. Commenting on this, Whitman said, "In this space, the price of inaction is higher than the price of making a mistake."[24]

Whitman shared a cordial and friendly relationship with all her employees. She dressed casually and worked from a cabin (which was only slightly bigger than the other cabins) like many of her employees. Reportedly, she had the talent to persuade others to deliver what she wanted. Commenting on this, Scott McNealy, CEO, Sun Microsystems, who had an opportunity to work with Whitman while fixing eBay's site crash problems, said, "She has an amazing velvet-glove touch. Instead of making me angry, she made me want to do just about anything we could to solve her problem. And that is what we did."[25]

Whitman demanded the ability to decide quickly and act fast from her executives. According to company sources, she set an example for her executive team by taking prompt decisions. Matt Freivald (Freivald), President and CEO, NetMind Technologies, said that Whitman bought NetMind technology[26] within weeks after a two-minute briefing on the product. He said, "How many other CEOs in this space are so quick to see and act on a new vision? Not many, I think. This is one of the reasons that eBay is able to stay ahead of their competition."[27]

Similarly, in 1999, when Whitman realized that advanced credit-card processing capabilities provided amazon.com a competitive advantage, she quickly acquired BillPoint, an online system, which allowed customers to pay via e-mail. In the same manner, in 2001, when Whitman noticed that the fixed-price sales of half.com were increasing she began promoting fixed-price sales on eBay, with the objective of making eBay the biggest retailer on the Internet.

However, despite her friendly demeanor, Whitman did not spare executives who did not deliver on promises or were slow. When a newly hired technology chief failed to fix problems fast during site crashes, she fired him immediately. According to Rajiv Dutta, CFO, eBay, said, "She will completely chew them (unsuccessful executives) out."[28]

Analysts remarked that though Whitman did not invent eBay, she transformed it from a start-up to a powerhouse. They attributed this transformation to Whitman's focus on eBay's core competencies. According to an analyst, "People tend to get very, very enamored of other areas the company could participate in. She has made sure the company continues to maintain its focus on core competencies."[29]

When amazon.com set up its own auction website in March 2002, many analysts speculated that Whitman might dispense with eBay's person-to-person format and turn the site into a retailing site to expand its business. However, Whitman had no intention of turning eBay into a retailing site like amazon.com. She said, "We are going to stick with our personal trading community, a community that grows out of commerce. It is what our customers want."[30] Even when eBay invested $22 million in TradeOut.com (in 2000), a B-to-B auction startup, she did not involve eBay in B-to-B trading. According to Whitman, the investment was only strategic in nature and that eBay would remain focused on its person-to-person auction business.

Michael Useem, Director, Wharton Center for Leadership and Change Management, praised Whitman's leadership abilities, saying, "Meg Whitman is the top of the heap. Here is a pioneer who has built a company into a fully developed form. When the history of this particular era is written, she will be in that history."[31]

Criticism of Whitman

Despite Whitman's focus on eBay's community, she received criticism from the community on account of her focus on high priced products and big companies. Many of eBay's old customers complained that doing business on eBay had become an unhappy experience in the early 21st century and that eBay was ignoring small customers for bigger ones. An old customer said that eBay was ignoring her in favor of bigger clients and was not even responding to her mails. She said, "I feel like I am in a co-dependent relationship. I write to them, I get no response. I e-mail them, nothing. I am being abused."[32]

Some of eBay's old customers also criticized eBay's practice of creating distinct categories for companies like Disney on its site. For example, eBay allocated a special subcategory for Disney products (under the Disneyana category). Commenting on this, David Steiner, an eBay trader and president of AuctionBytes.com, an online watchdog site, said, "The general consensus of veteran sellers is that they have forsaken the people who built them in favor of corporate sellers."[33]

eBay sellers feared that the presence of major companies (with popular brands) on the site might severely damage their prospects. The buyers would, in all probability, choose to buy branded products from known companies rather than from unknown sellers. They accused Whitman of defeating one of the major purposes of eBay—creating trusting relationships between people across the world. Customers also expressed displeasure at eBay's increase in fees in January 2001—the second fee hike in 13 months—and said that eBay was taking undue advantage of its growing popularity and reach.[34]

A few analysts also criticized some of Whitman's strategic decisions. In 2002, eBay pulled out of Japan because of Yahoo!'s dominance in the market. Whitman was criticized for backing out of a potential market without putting up much of a fight. Analysts also termed the acquisition of B&B a strategic blunder. They felt that synergies from the integration of B&B into eBay were few and elusive. As eBay could not reap any benefits from B&B, it sold B&B in 2002 for a negligible price.

The delay in acquiring PayPal proved to be another costly mistake. Analysts claimed that Whitman tried hard to force the BillPoint System on eBay customers and that it took her a long time to accept defeat and opt for PayPal. Analysts felt that this was one of Whitman's costliest mistakes, as eBay had to pay a much higher price for PayPal than it might have had to, if PayPal had been acquired a year earlier.

In October 2002, Whitman got embroiled in a major controversy. That year, the congressional investigators appointed by the US House Financial Services Committee[35] to investigate the practice of "spinning"[36] in investment banking firms revealed their findings. According to them, Goldman Sachs and Co, a New York-based investment services firm, could have practiced 'spinning,' as it offered the top executives of its top clients chance to buy into the IPOs arranged by it.

The investigators said that Whitman, as CEO of eBay, a top client of Goldman Sachs, had taken part in more than a 100 IPOs (since 1996) arranged by Goldman Sachs and earned nearly $1.8 million in profits by quickly selling those shares.[37] Whitman denied such accusations and said that she had done nothing wrong and had not helped

Goldman Sachs in any manner to win additional business from eBay. Sources at Goldman Sachs also supported Whitman by saying that Whitman had not participated in any IPO arranged by Goldman Sachs after she had joined Goldman Sachs as director (in mid-2002).

Though the market did not react strongly to the news, analysts said that the news definitely brought Whitman under the microscope as eBay had been using Goldman Sachs services since 1996 (eBay's first IPO in 1998 was also arranged by Goldman Sachs). Reportedly, eBay paid more than $8 million in fees to Goldman Sachs since 1996. The fact that Whitman was serving on the Goldman Sachs board added to criticism against her. Thereafter, in December 2002, Whitman quit the board of Goldman Sachs saying that she wanted to avoid the controversy and criticism that the position attracted.

Whitman agreed that she had made a few mistakes during her tenure at eBay. According to her, one of her major mistakes was delaying the recruitment of key senior executives, especially Webb, whom she brought in finally when the site crashing problem reached alarming proportions.

However, Whitman treated these strategic blunders or mistakes as learning experiences. She said that though mistakes had been committed, they were corrected in time before much damage was done.

Problems Facing Whitman

Many customers remained loyal to eBay despite the above problems since it allowed them to get the highest prices for their auctions. However, the increasing number of customers registering with other auction sites was a worrying trend for eBay. Analysts felt that if this trend picked up momentum, eBay might soon become just one of the many choices for customers. They observed by alienating the customers, Whitman was placing eBay at risk.

Industry observers felt that instead of focusing on expanding eBay's operations through acquisitions and new categories, Whitman should first focus on creating a value for the eBay brand among customers. According to Philip Anderson, Associate Professor (Internet Strategy), Tuck School of Business (Dartmouth), eBay should position itself as a company that delivered perfect transactions rather than as a company that offered an exhaustive range of goods for sale (its current positioning).

Whitman would have to overcome many hurdles to achieve her revenue goal of $3 billion by 2005. Reportedly in mid-2002, the number of listings on eBay in the US was on the decline. Many categories such as travel, real estate and entertainment ticketing, were facing intense competition from niche websites. eBay's growth in the high priced category was also below expectations. Though eBay's community had been the source of its suc-

cess, it had, according to analysts become a hindrance to its growth in the early 21st century. Many of Whitman's strategic business moves for making eBay more profitable were, in fact, being opposed by the company's community. Reportedly, other leading Internet companies such as AOL, Amazon, Microsoft and Yahoo! were taking advantage of the growing customer unrest at eBay and creating their own online malls to attract customers.

Marching Ahead

By early 2003, eBay was offering more product categories than ever before. Some of its new categories were computers, books, CDs, electronic goods and automobiles. According to reports, eBay accounted for nearly 1% of total used car sales in the US. Commenting on the growth of the eBay community, Whitman said that if eBay were a country, it would have been the fifteenth largest nation in the world since it had 75.3 million registered users (in mid- 2003).

In 2003, many major companies such as Home Depot, IBM, Dell Financial Services and Sharper Image were selling their excess inventory through eBay. Reportedly, such sales accounted for more than 4% of eBay's total sales in mid-2003.

Whitman continued with her expansion plans for eBay in 2003. Early that year, eBay entered into various alliances and signed partnership agreements with a diverse range of companies to sell their goods on eBay. During the same period, Whitman also roped in Accenture, a leading consultancy firm to help eBay design a strategy to gain more business from Fortune 50 companies.

In the early 2003, as part of its efforts to increase, eBay focused on the fastest growing areas on the site. For example, when eBay realized that apparel was one of the fastest selling categories, it launched a designer boutique which offered links to hundreds of designer labels. Reportedly, the boutique accounted for 40% of total apparel sales on eBay. During this period, eBay also promoted non-auction sales (by mid-2003, fixed-price sales on eBay accounted for 19% of total sales on site).

In August 2003, Amazon left the auction market. As a result eBay had only one formidable competitor to deal with—Yahoo! However, many small companies, which targeted niche markets, also gave tough competition to eBay in certain categories. For example, AutoTrader and Ticketmaster competed with eBay in the car and tickets (selling tickets for sports events etc.) categories, respectively. During mid-2003, the leading search engine Google's paid service, which allowed sellers to place their items (on the site) for sale, also attracted small traders.

In August 2003, eBay, which was the undisputed leader in the online auction market, ranked eighth on Fortune magazine's list of '100 Fastest Growing Companies.' In the light of eBay's continuing success in mid 2003,

Whitman expressed full confidence on eBay's growth and said that her team of 5,000 employees and senior executives was fully prepared to achieve $3 billion in annual revenues by 2005.

However, analysts felt that this over-confidence could prove to be one of the biggest pitfalls for eBay. According to Useem, Whitman and her team needed "to be vigilant not to make an error in the euphoria of success; they must stay ahead of the curve."[38]

Questions for Discussion:

1. Discuss Whitman's ascent up the corporate ladder before joining eBay. Critically comment on her management style and examine the impact of the changes she made to build the eBay brand. Also comment on the 'success secrets' of Whitman as a manager.

2. Analyze Whitman's community building efforts. To what extent did the decision to involve customers in managing the business help eBay? Discuss the various advantages and disadvantages of allowing customers to guide a company's strategies.

3. Examine the strategies formulated by Whitman to make eBay a global online marketplace. Do you think Whitman should have run the risk of alienating the eBay community by encouraging big sellers and high priced items on eBay? Justify your answer.

4. Briefly comment on the criticisms leveled against Whitman. Examine the problems Whitman will have to deal with when leading eBay towards its goal of $3 billion in annual revenues by 2005. Do you think Whitman will succeed in this attempt? Why/Why not?

Chapter 1

1. D. Bunnell and R. Luecke, *The EBay Phenomenon* (New York: John Wiley & Sons, 2000).

2. R. E. Stross, *Eboys* (New York: Random House, 2000).

3. L. F. Kaiser, M. B. Kaiser, and P. Omidyar, "Foreword," in *The Official EBay Guide* (New York: Fireside Books, 1999).

4. Bunnell and Luecke, *The EBay Phenomenon.*

5. P. D. Reynolds, W. D. Bygrave, and E. Autio, "Global Entrepreneurship Monitor 2003 Executive Report" (Kansas City, Mo.: Kauffman Foundation Center for Entrepreneurship Leadership, 2003).

6. Small Business Administration, *The State of Small Business* (Washington, D.C.: U.S. Government Printing Office, 1999).

7. B. Bolton and J. Thompson, *Entrepreneurs* (Oxford: Butterworth-Heinemann, 2002).

8. P. Sharma and J. J. Chrisman, "Toward a Reconciliation of the Definitional Issues in the Field of Corporate Entrepreneurship," *Entrepreneurship Theory and Practice* 23, no. 3 (1999): 11–27.

9. H. H. Stevenson and J. C. Jarillo, "A Paradigm for Entrepreneurship: Entrepreneurial Management," *Strategic Management Journal* 11 (1990): 17–27.

10. R. D. Ireland, M. A. Hitt, and D. G. Sirmon, "A Model of Strategic Entrepreneurship," *Journal of Management* 29 (2003): 963–89.

11. D. Hussey, *The Innovative Challenge* (New York: John Wiley & Sons, 1997).

12. D. Bunnell, *Making the Cisco Connection* (New York: John Wiley & Sons, 2000).

13. J. G. Covin and D. P. Slevin, "A Conceptual Model of Entrepreneurship as Firm Behavior," *Entrepreneurship Theory and Practice* 16 (1991): 7–25.

14. B. R. Barringer and A. C. Bluedorn, "The Relationship Between Corporate Entrepreneurship and Strategic Management," *Strategic Management Journal* 20 (1999): 421–44.

15. R. Branson, *Losing My Virginity* (New York: Time Warner, 1999).

16. R. D. Jager and R. Ortiz, *In the Company of Giants* (New York: McGraw-Hill, 1997).

17. R. Jennings, C. Cox, and C. Cooper, *Business Elites* (London: Routledge, 1994).

18. C. M. Christensen, *The Innovator's Dilemma* (Boston: Harvard Business School Press, 1997).

19. Office of Advocacy, *The State of Small Business* (Washington, D.C.: U.S. Government Printing Office, 1998).

20. S. Hamm, "The Education of Marc Andreessen," *BusinessWeek,* April 13, 1998, 92, Industrial/Technology edition.

21. D. Carnoy, "Richard Branson," *Success,* April 1998, 62–63.

22. L. C. Farrell, *Entrepreneurial Age* (New York: Allworth Press, 2001).

23. R. Adams, *A Good Hard Kick in the Ass* (New York: Crown Business, 2002).

24. Farrell, *Entrepreneurial Age.*

25. P. Krass, *The Book of Entrepreneurs' Wisdom* (New York: John Wiley & Sons, 1999).

26. Jager and Ortiz, *In the Company of Giants.*

27. S. Baillie, "High Tech Heroes," *Profit,* December 2000/January 2001.

28. E. A. Locke, *The Prime Movers* (New York: AMACOM Books, 2000).

29. A. Grove, *Only The Paranoid Survive* (New York: Bantam Books, 1999).

30. Adams, *A Good Hard Kick in the Ass.*

31. L. Hazleton, "Profile: Jeff Bezos," *Success,* July 1998, 60.

32. N. Koehn, *Brand New: How Entrepreneurs Earned Consumers' Trust from Wedgwood to Dell* (Boston: Harvard Business School Press, 2001).

33. Koehn, *Brand New.*

34. Baillie, "High Tech Heroes."

35. M. Treacy and J. Sims, "Take Command of Your Growth," *Harvard Business Review* 82, no. 4 (2004): 127–33.
36. M. Morris, *Entrepreneurial Intensity* (Westport, Conn.: Quorum Books, 1998).
37. P. Davidsson and B. Honig, "The Role of Social and Human Capital among Nascent Entrepreneurs," *Journal of Business Venturing* 18 (2003): 301–31.
38. E. B. Roberts, *Entrepreneurs in High Technology* (New York: Oxford University Press, 1991).
39. P. D. Reynolds, W. D. Bygrave, E. Autio, L. Cox, and M. Hay, "Global Entrepreneurship Monitor 2002 Executive Report" (Kansas City, Mo: Kauffman Foundation Center for Entrepreneurship Leadership, 2002).
40. Morris, *Entrepreneurial Intensity.*
41. P. J. Bearse, "A Study of Entrepreneurship by Region and SMSA Size," in *Frontiers of Entrepreneurship Research* 78–112 (Wellesley, Mass.: Babson College, 1982).
42. T. Siebel, "Betting It All," in *Title*, ed. M. S. Malone (New York: John Wiley & Sons, 2002), 84.
43. C. Williams, *Lead, Follow, or Get Out of the Way* (New York: Times Books, 1981), 111.
44. J. H. Boyett and J. T. Boyett, *The Guru Guide to Entrepreneurship* (New York: John Wiley & Sons, 2001), 16.
45. S. Walton, *Made in America: My Story* (New York: Doubleday, 1992).
46. Farrell, *Entrepreneurial Age.*
47. R. Quindlen, *Confessions of a Venture Capitalist* (New York: Warner Books, 2000).
48. G. Singh, "Work after Early Retirement" (PhD diss.,University of Toronto, 1998).
49. Reynolds et al., "Global Entrepreneurship Monitor 2002 Executive Report."
50. Reynolds et al., "Global Entrepreneurship Monitor 2002 Executive Report."
51. J. A. Schumpeter, *The Theory of Economic Development* (Cambridge, Mass.: Harvard University Press, 1994).
52. M. Hammer, "Deep Change: How Operational Innovation Can Transform Your Company," *Harvard Business Review* 82, no. 4 (2004): 84–93.
53. Global Entrepreneurship Monitor, "National Entrepreneurship Assessment—United States of America" (Kansas City, Mo.: Kauffman Center for Entrepreneurial Leadership, July 1999), 4.
54. J. A. Timmons, *America's Entrepreneurial Revolution: The Demise of Brontosaurus Capitalism* (Babson Park, Mass.: Babson College, 1999).
55. B. Carlsson, "Small Business, Entrepreneurship, and Industrial Dynamics," in *Are Small Firms Important?*, ed. Z. Acts, 99–110 (Boston: Kluwer Academic Publishers, 1999).
56. R. D. Atkison and R. H. Court, *The New Economy Index: Understanding America's Economic Transformation* (Washington, D.C.: Progressive Policy Institute, November 1998), 13.
57. C. A. Purrington and K. E. Bettcher, *From the Garage to the Boardroom: The Entrepreneurial Roots of America's Largest Corporations* (Washington, D.C.: National Commission on Entrepreneurship, 2001), 1.
58. Export Data Base, U.S. Department of Commerce, Office of Trade and Economic Analysis, Trade Development/International Trade Agency, Washington, D.C., November 1999.
59. "Amgen," *Standard & Poor's Stock Report*, www.standardandpoors.com (accessed April 3, 2004).
60. B. Bygrave, "The Entrepreneurial Process," in *The Portable MBA in Entrepreneurship* (New York: John Wiley & Sons, 1997).

Chapter 2

1. J. R. Aspatore and A. Abell, *Digital Rush* (New York: AMACOM Books, 2000), 90.
2. Internet.com, "BuyAndHold.com's New Accounts Jump 500%," September 19, 2001.
3. Time, "Amazing Person.com," December 27, 1999.

4. J. A. Timmons, "Opportunity Recognition," in *The Portable MBA in Entrepreneurship*, ed. William D. Bygrave (New York: John Wiley & Sons, 1997), 27.

5. J. A. Timmons, *New Venture Creation: Entrepreneurship in the 21st Century*, 4th ed. (Burr Ridge, Ill.: Irwin, 1994).

6. *New Webster's Dictionary* (New York: Delair Publishing, 1981).

7. A. Ardichvili, R. Cardozo, and S. Ray, "A Theory of Entrepreneurial Opportunity Identification and Development," *Journal of Business Venturing* 18, no. 1: (2003): 105–23.

8. PricewaterhouseCoopers, "Fast Growth Companies Have Two Big Priorities, PricewaterhouseCoopers Finds," in *Trendsetter Barometer* (New York: PricewaterhouseCoopers, 2000).

9. S. H. Diorio, *Beyond "e": 12 Ways Technology Is Transforming Sales and Marketing Strategy* (New York: McGraw-Hill, 2002).

10. RealNetwork home page, www.realnetworks.com (accessed May 30, 2002).

11. C. M. Gaglio and P. Taub, "Entrepreneurs and Opportunity Recognition," in *Frontiers of Entrepreneurship Research* 136–47 (Wellesley, Mass.: Babson College, 1992).

12. P. Kotler, *Marketing Insights from A to Z* (New York: John Wiley & Sons, 2003), 128.

13. Hoovers, www.hoovers.com (accessed June 24, 2004).

14. C. M. Crawford and C. A. Di Benedetto, *Product Management*, 6th ed. (Boston: Irwin McGraw-Hill, 2000).

15. R. Adams, *A Good Hard Kick in the Ass* (New York: Crown Business, 2002), 76.

16. K. Vesper, *New Venture Experience*, rev. ed. (Seattle: Vector Books, 1996).

17. J. Case, "The Origins of Entrepreneurship," *Inc.*, June 1989.

18. A. C. Cooper, W. Dunkelberg, C. Woo, and W. Dennis, *New Business in America: The Firms and Their Owners* (Washington, D.C.: National Federation of Independent Business, 1990).

19. R. Ronstadt, "The Educated Entrepreneurs: A New Era of Entrepreneurial Education Is Beginning," *American Journal of Small Business* 10, no. 1 (1985): 7–23.

20. Gaglio and Taub, "Entrepreneurs and Opportunity Recognition."

21. I. M. Kirzner, *Perception, Opportunity, and Profit: Studies in the Theory of Entrepreneurship* (Chicago: University of Chicago Press, 1979).

22. G. E. Hills, G. T. Lumpkin, and R. Singh, "Opportunity Recognition: Perceptions and Behaviors of Entrepreneurs," in *Frontiers of Entrepreneurship Research* 168–72 (Wellesley, Mass.: Babson College, 1997)

23. C. M. Gaglio and J. A. Katz, "The Psychological Basis of Opportunity Identification: Entrepreneurial Alertness," *Small Business Economics* 16, no. 2 (2001): 95–111.

24. I. M. Kirzner, "The Primacy of Entrepreneurial Discovery," in *The Prime Mover of Progress*, ed. A. Seldon, 5–30 (London: Institute of Economic Affairs, 1980).

25. G. Kingsley and E. J. Malecki, "Networking for Competitiveness," *Small Business Economics* 23, no. 1 (2004): 71–84.

26. A. Hansen, *Fast Growth Strategies* (New York: McGraw-Hill, 1987).

27. P. Davidsson and B. Honig, "The Role of Social and Human Capital among Nascent Entrepreneurs," *Journal of Business Venturing* 18, no. 3 (2003): 301–31.

28. R. H. Koller, "On the Source of Entrepreneurial Ideas," in *Frontiers of Entrepreneurship Research* 194–207 (Wellesley, Mass.: Babson College, 1988).

29. Hills et al., "Opportunity Recognition," 168–72.

30. R. P. Singh, G. E. Hills, R. C. Hybels, and G. T. Lumpkin, "Opportunity Recognition through Social Network Characteristics of Entrepreneurs," in *Frontiers of Entrepreneurship* Research 228–238 (Wellesley, Mass.: Babson College, 1999).

31. M. Granovetter, "The Strength of Weak Ties," *American Journal of Sociology* 78 no. 6 (1973): 1360–80.

32. A. Ardichvili, R. Cardozo, and S. Ray, "A Theory of Entrepreneurial Opportunity Identification and Development," *Journal of Business Venturing* 18, no. 1: (2003): 105–23.

33. W. Long and W. E. McMullan, "Mapping the New Venture Opportunity Identification Process," in *Frontiers of Entrepreneurship Research* 567–90 (Wellesley, Mass.: Babson College, 1984).

34. J. J. Kao, *Entrepreneurship, Creativity, and Organization* (Englewood Cliffs, N.J.: Prentice Hall, 1989).

35. G. E. Hills, R. C. Shrader, and G. T. Lumpkin, "Opportunity Recognition as a Creative Process," in *Frontiers of Entrepreneurship Research* 216–27 (Wellesley, Mass.: Babson College, 1999).

36. W. Bygrave, "The Entrepreneurial Process," in *The Portable MBA in Entrepreneurship*, ed. William B. Bygrave (New York: John Wiley & Sons, 1997), 1–26.

37. M. Csikszentmihalyi, *Creativity* (New York: HarperCollins, 1996).

38. Csikszentmihalyi, *Creativity*.

39. R. P. Singh, *Entrepreneurial Opportunity Recognition* (New York: Garland Publishing, 2000).

40. J. Patrick, *How to Develop Successful New Products* (Lincolnwood, Ill.: NTC Business Books, 1997).

41. R. G. Cooper, Winning at New Products: Accelerating the Process from Idea to Launch, 2nd ed. (Reading, Mass.: Addison-Wesley, 1993).

42. R. G. Cooper and S. J. Edgett, *Product Development for the Service Sector* (Cambridge, Mass.: Perseus Books, 1999).

43. American Statistical Association, *What Are Focus Groups?* (Alexandria, Va.: American Statistical Association,1997), 1.

44. American Statistical Association, Web site section on survey research methods, www.bios.unc.edu/~kalsbeek/asa/survpamphlet.html (accessed June 3, 2002).

45. Cooper and Edgett, *Product Development for the Service Sector*.

46. T. S. Foster, *Managing Quality: An Integrative Approach* (Upper Saddle, N.J.: Prentice Hall, 2001).

47. Cooper and Edgett, *Product Development for the Service Sector*.

48. B. Leister, "How to Kill Creativity," *Harvard Business Review*, 76, no. 5 (1998), 76–87.

49. A. Cummings and G. R. Oldham, "Enhancing Creativity: Managing Work Contexts for the High Potential Employee," *California Management Review* 40, no. 1 (1997): 22–38.

50. United States Patent and Trademark Office, "Disclosure Document Program," www.uspto.gov/web/offices/pac/disdo.html (accessed June 4, 2002).

Chapter 3

1. R. D. Jager and R. Ortiz, *In the Company of Giants* (New York: McGraw-Hill, 1997), 76.

2. Jager and Ortiz, *In the Company of Giants*, 75.

3. R. Adams, *A Good Hard Kick in the Ass* (New York: Crown Business, 2002).

4. A. V. Bhide, *The Origin and Evolution of New Businesses* (Oxford: University Press, 2000).

5. D. Lovallo and G. Gosi, "Overconfidence and Excess Entry: An Experimental Approach." California Institute of Technology Work Paper No. 975, Pasadena, California: California Institute of Technology, 1996.

6. M. A. Hitt, R. D. Ireland, and R. E. Hoskisson, *Strategic Management* (Mason, Ohio: South-Western College Publishing, 2005).

7. "Info You'll Want to Know," *Sports Illustrated*, February 5, 2001.

8. M. Hiestand, "NHL Hoping Graphics Key to Better Television Image," *USA Today*, February 2, 2002.

9. K. Tan, "Interactive Technology Boosts Sports Business," *Wall Street Journal*, January 31, 2000.

10. L. M. Lodish, H. L. Morgan, and A. Kallianpur, *Entrepreneurial Marketing: Lessons from Wharton's Pioneering MBA Course* (New York: John Wiley & Sons, 2001).

11. R. G. Cooper, *Product Leadership: Creating and Launching Superior New Products* (Reading, Mass.: Perseus Books, 1998).

12. Cooper, *Product Leadership*, 99.

13. R. G. Cooper and S. J. Edgett, *Product Development for the Service Sector* (Cambridge, Mass.: Perseus Books, 1999).

14. Cheskin Web site, www.cheskin.com/who/pepsi/pepsi.html (accessed July 5, 2002).

15. C. M. Crawford and C. A. De Benedetto, *New Products Management* (Boston: Irwin McGraw-Hill, 2000).

16. S. T. Foster, *Managing Quality* (Upper Saddle River, N.J.: Prentice Hall, 2001).

17. The Usability Company home page, www.theuseabilitycompany.com (accessed July 9, 2002).

18. T. K. McKnight, *Will It Fly?* (London: Financial Times Prentice Hall, 2004).

19. P. A. Gompers and J. Lerner, *The Money of Invention: How Venture Capital Creates New Wealth* (Boston: Harvard Business School Press, 2001).

20. S. C. Wheelwright and K. B. Clark, *Leading Product Development* (New York: Free Press, 1995).

21. Marketing Terms home page, www.marketingterms.com (accessed July 5, 2002).

22. Tuck School of Business, "Note on First Mover Advantage," http://mba.tuck.dartmouth.edu/sats2001/fma/first_mover_advantage.htm (accessed July 5, 2002).

23. M. Coutler, *Strategic Management in Action* (Upper Saddle River, N.J.: Prentice Hall, 2002).

24. J. I. Rigdon, "The Second-Mover Advantage," *Red Herring*, September, 2000.

25. D. Hall, *In the Company of Heroes: An Insider's Guide to Entrepreneurs at Work* (London: Kogan Page, 1999).

26. J. L. Nesheim, *High Tech Start Up: The Corporate Handbook for Creating Successful New High Tech Companies* (New York: Free Press, 2000).

27. *Inc.,* "Inc. 500 List," January 2004, 64.

28. G. A. Benjamin and J. Margulis, *Angel Financing: How to Find and Invest in Private Equity* (New York: John Wiley & Sons, 2000).

29. M. Vivarelli, "Are All the Potential Entrepreneurs So Good?," *Small Business Economics* 23, no. 1 (2004): 41–49.

30. Jager and Ortiz, *In the Company of Giants.*

31. M. Rogers, "Networks, Firm Size and Innovation," *Small Business Economics* 22, no. 2 (2004): 141–53.

32. J. R. Van Slyke, H. H. Stevenson, and M. J. Roberts, "How to Write a Winning Business Plan," in *The Entrepreneurial Venture,* ed. William A. Sahlman and Howard H. Stevenson, 127–37 (Boston: Harvard Business School Press, 1992).

33. Van Slyke et al., "How to Write a Winning Business Plan."

Chapter 4

1. "JetBlue Skies Ahead," *CIO,* July 1, 2002.

2. "JetBlue Skies Ahead."

3. "JetBlue Skies Ahead."

4. Sun-tzu *The Art of War,* chap. 7 (Dover Publications, 2002).

5. R. P. Rumelt, "How Much Does Industry Matter?," *Strategic Management Journal* 12, no. 3 (1991): 167–85.

6. B. Eriksen and T. Knudsen, "Industry and Firm Level Interaction: Implications for Profitability," *Journal of Business Research* 56, no. 3 (2003): 191–99.

7. Rumelt, "How Much Does Industry Matter?"

8. A. McGahan, "The Performance of U.S. Corporations 1981–1994," *Journal of Industrial Economy* 47 (1999): 373–98.

9. A. M. McGahan and M. Porter, "How Much Does Industry Matter, Really?" *Strategic Management Journal* 18, special issue (1997): 15–30.

10. M. Porter, *Competitive Strategy: Techniques for Analyzing Industries and Competitors* (New York: Free Press, 1980).

11. Porter, *Competitive Strategy.*

12. G. Keighley, "Could This Be the Next Disney?," *Business 2.0,* December 2002.

13. S. McNealy, "A Winning Business Model," in *The Book of Entrepreneurs' Wisdom,* ed. Peter Krass, 171–89 (New York: John Wiley & Sons, 1999).

14. M. Porter, "How Competitive Forces Shape Strategy," *Harvard Business Review* 57, no. 2, 137-145.

15. J. A. Barney and W. Hesterly, "Organizational Economics: Understanding the Relationship Between Organizations and Economic Analysis," in *Handbook of Organization Studies,* ed. Steward R. Clegg, Cynthia Hardy, and Walter R. Nord, 115–147 (London: Sage, 1996).

16. Marketing Terms home page, www.marketingterms.com (accessed June 15, 2004).
17. J. Rodengen, *The Legend of Nucor Corporation* (Ft. Lauderdale, Fla.: Write Stuff Enterprises, 1997).
18. T. Levitt, *The Marketing Imagination* (New York: Free Press, 1986).
19. M-J. Chen, "Competitor Analysis and Inter-Firm Rivalry: Toward a Theoretical Integration," *Academy of Management Review* 21, no. 1 (1996): 100–34.
20. Kotler, *Marketing Insights from A to Z* (New York: Wiley, 2003), 23.
21. Activision 2002 10-K, 8.

Chapter 5

1. J. Magretta, *What Management Is* (New York: Free Press, 2002).
2. M. Dell, "Building the Perfect Machine," *Forbes Small Business*, October 2002, 80.
3. P. B. Seybold, *Customers.com* (New York: Random House, 1998).
4. Dell, "Building the Perfect Machine," 82.
5. J. Magretta, "Why Business Models Matter," *Harvard Business Review* 80, no. 5, 86–94
6. H. W. Chesbrough, *Open Innovation* (Boston: Harvard Business School Press, 2003).
7. G. Hamel, *Leading the Revolution* (New York: Plume, 2002).
8. M. Ragas, *Lessons from the E-Front* (Roseville, Calif.: Prima Venture, 2001).
9. N. Wingfield, "New Battlefield for Priceline Is Diapers, Tuna," *Wall Street Journal*, September 20, 1999, B1.
10. R. Hawkins, *The "Business Model" as a Research Problem in Electronic Commerce* (Delft: TNO Institute for Strategy, Technology and Policy, 2001).
11. M. Porter, *Competitive Advantage: Creating and Sustaining Superior Performance* (New York: Free Press, 1985).
12. C. B. Stabell and O. D. Fjeldstad, "Configuring Value for Competitive Advantage: On Chains, Shops and Networks," *Strategic Management Journal* 19, no. 5 (1998): 413–37.
13. N. Venkatraman and J. C. Henderson, "Real Strategies for Virtual Organizations," *Sloan Management Review* 40, no. 1 (1998): 33–48.
14. Hamel, *Leading the Revolution.*
15. M. E. Porter, *On Competition* (Boston: Harvard Business School Press, 1996).
16. R. D. Ireland and M. A. Hitt, "Mission Statements: Importance, Challenge, and Recommendations for Development," *Business Horizons* 35, no. 3 (1992): 34–42.
17. Hamel, *Leading the Revolution.*
18. D. Bovet and J. Martha, *Value Nets* (New York: John Wiley & Sons, 2000).
19. M. Dell, *Direct from Dell* (New York: HarperBusiness, 1999), 57.
20. Porter, *Competitive Advantage.*
21. C. K. Prahalad, "A New View of Strategy," in *Business: The Ultimate Resource*, 140–141 (Cambridge, Mass.: Perseus, 2002).
22. Hamel, *Leading the Revolution.*
23. C. Zook and J. Allen, *Profit from the Core* (Boston: Harvard Business School Press, 2001).
24. J. Nesheim, *High Tech Start Up: The Complete Handbook for Creating Successful New High Tech Companies* (New York: Free Press, 2000).
25. J. Barney, "Firm Resources and Sustained Competitive Advantage," *Journal of Management* 17, no. 1 (1991): 99–120.
26. G. S. Day and R. Wensley, "Assessing Advantage: A Framework for Diagnosing Competitive Superiority," *Journal of Marketing* 52, no. 2 (1988): 1–20.
27. G. Moore, *Living on the Fault Line* (New York: HarperBusiness, 2002).
28. E. Pinchot and G. Pinchot, "Leading Organizations into Partnerships," in *Partnering*, ed. L. Segil, M. Goldsmith, and J. Belasco, 41–55 (New York: AMACOM Books, 2002).
29. B. Barringer, "The Effects of Relational Channel Exchange on the Small Firm: A Conceptual Framework," *Journal of Small Business Management* 35, no. 2 (1997): 65–79.

30. Magretta, *What Management Is.*

31. Bovet and Martha, *Value Nets.*

32. i2 Technologies, "Configuring a 500 Percent ROI for Dell," www.i2Technologies.com (accessed November 15, 2002).

33. PricewaterhouseCoopers, "Partnerships Have Big Payoffs for Fast-Growth Companies," *Trendsetter Barometer*, August 26, 2002.

34. Dell, *Direct from Dell*, 173.

35. B. Barringer and J. Harrison, "Walking a Tightrope: Creating Value through Interorganizational Relationships," *Journal of Management* 26, no. 3 (2000): 367–403.

36. Coopers & Lybrand Consulting, *Alliances* (New York: Coopers & Lybrand Consulting, 1997).

37. G. Kok and L. Widleman, "High Touch Partnering: Beyond Traditional Selection Perspectives" (white paper published by KPMG, Amsterdam, 1999).

38. Barringer and Harrison, "Walking a Tightrope."

39. Hamel, *Leading the Revolution.*

40. W. M. Pride and O. C. Ferrell, *Marketing Concepts and Strategies* (Boston: Houghton Mifflin, 1999).

Chapter 6

1. R. Adams, *A Good Hard Kick in the Ass* (New York: Crown Business, 2002).

2. Adams, *A Good Hard Kick in the Ass*, 29

3. Waveset home page, www.waveset.com (accessed April 10, 2003).

4. PR Newswire, "Waveset Secures $13 Million in New Funding: Significant Up Round Underscores Waveset's Leadership in Rapidly Growing Identity Management Market," September 3, 2002.

5. A. Stinchcombe, "Social Structure and Organization," in *Handbook of Organizations*, ed. James G. March, 142–93 (Chicago: Rand McNally, 1965).

6. C. Read, J. Ross, J. Dunleavy, D. Schulman, and J. Bramante, *eCFO* (Chichester: John Wiley & Sons, 2001), 117.

7. S. Nance-Nash, "How to Impress a Venture Capitalist, Part 1: Assembling Your Management Team," *Fortune Small Business*, January 25, 1999.

8. H. Fesser and G. Willard, "Founding Strategy and Performance: A Comparison of High and Low Growth Tech Firms," *Strategic Management Journal* 11, no. 2 (1990): 87–98.

9. Fesser and Willard, "Founding Strategy and Performance."

10. K. Eisenhardt and C. Schoonhoven, "Organizational Growth: Linking Founding Team, Strategy, Environment, and Growth among U.S. Semiconductor Ventures, 1978–1988," *Administrative Science Quarterly* 35, no. 3 (1990): 504–29.

11. T. Zenger and B. Lawrence, "Organizational Demography: The Differential Effects of Age and Tenure Distribution on Technical Communication," *Academy of Management Journal* 32, no. 2 (1989): 353–76.

12. Eisenhardt and Schoonhoven, "Organizational Growth."

13. B. Clarysee and N. Moray, "A Process Study of Entrepreneurial Team Formation: The Case of a Research-Based Spin-Off," *Journal of Business Venturing* 19, no. 1 (2004): 55–79.

14. A. C. Cooper, F. J. Gimeno-Gascon, and C. Y. Woo, "Initial Human and Financial Capital as Predictors of New Venture Performance," *Journal of Business Venturing* 9, no. 5 (1994): 371–95.

15. B. Singer, "Contours of Development." *Journal of Business Venturing* 10, no.4 (1995): 303–29.

16. Clarysee and Moray, "A Process Study of Entrepreneurial Team Formation."

17. I. MacMillian, L. Zemann, and P. N. S. Narasimha, "Criteria Distinguishing Successful from Unsuccessful Ventures in the Venture Screening Process," *Journal of Business Venturing* 2, no. 2 (1987): 123–37.

18. A. Ardichvili, R. Cardozo, and S. Ray, "A Theory of Entrepreneurial Opportunity Recognition and Development," *Journal of Business Venturing* 18, no. 1 (2004): 105–23.

19. J. E. McGee, M. J. Dowling, and W. L. Meggison, "Co-Operative Strategy and New Venture Performance: The Role of Business Strategy and Management Experience," *Strategic Management Journal* 16, no. 7 (1995): 565–80.

20. Adams, *A Good Hard Kick in the Ass*, 240.

21. H. Schultz, *Pour Your Heart into It* (New York: Hyperion, 1997), 82.

22. Investorwords.com home page, www.investorwords.com (accessed June 1, 2004).

23. R. Charan, *Boards at Work* (San Francisco: Jossey-Bass, 1998), 29.

24. Charan, *Boards at Work*, 73.

25. S. Certo, C. Daily, and D. Dalton, "Signaling Firm Value through Board Structure: An Investigation of Initial Public Offerings," *Entrepreneurship Theory and Practice* 26, no. 2 (2001): 33–50.

26. A. Sherman, *Fast-Track Business Growth* (Washington, D.C.: Kiplinger Books, 2001).

27. Akamai home page, www.akamai.com (accessed June 23, 2004).

28. R. Kenny, "Rediscovering Advisory Boards," *IEEE Engineering Management Review* Fourth Quarter (2000): 24–27.

29. Sherman, *Fast-Track Business Growth*.

30. J. Lerner, "Venture Capitalists and the Oversight of Private Firms," *Journal of Finance* 50, no. 1 (1995): 301–18.

31. M. Gorman and W. A. Sahlman, "What Do Venture Capitalists Do?," *Journal of Business Venturing* 4, no. 4 (1989): 231–48.

32. A. Davila, G. Foster, and M. Gupta, "Venture Capital Financing and the Growth of Startup Firms," *Journal of Business Venturing* 18, no. 6 (2004): 689–708.

33. R. Stross, *eBoys* (New York: Crown Books, 2000), 29.

34. Adams, *A Good Hard Kick in the Ass*, 173.

35. C. James, "Some Evidence on the Uniqueness of Bank Loans," *Journal of Financial Economics* 19, no. 2 (1987): 217–35.

36. H. H. Stevenson and W. A. Sahlman, "How Small Companies Should Handle Advisors," in *The Entrepreneurial Venture*, ed. William A. Sahlman and Howard H. Stevenson, 295–302. (Boston: Harvard Business School Publications, 1992).

37. SCORE home page, www.score.org (accessed June 1, 2004).

Chapter 7

1. LeapFrog home page, www.leapfrog.com (accessed July 3, 2003).

2. B. Breen, "Leapfrog's Great Leap," *Fast Company*, June 2003, 88–96.

3. Breen, "Leapfrog's Great Leap."

4. Breen, "Leapfrog's Great Leap," 94.

5. LeapFrog 10-K (2003).

6. P. G. Bergeron, *Finance: Essentials for the Successful Professional* (New York: South-Western, 2002).

7. Bergeron, *Finance*.

8. J. H. Gittell, *The Southwest Airlines Way* (New York: McGraw-Hill, 2003), 7.

9. M. J. Lane, *Advising Entrepreneurs* (New York: John Wiley & Sons, 2001).

10. D. E. Vance, *Financial Analysis and Decision Making* (New York: McGraw-Hill, 2003).

11. B. Gates, *Business @ the Speed of Thought* (New York: Time Warner, 1999).

12. SEC home page, www.sec.gov (accessed July 22, 2003).

13. *Finance for Managers* (Boston: Harvard Business School Press, 2002).

14. A. K. Arrow, "Managing IP Financial Assets," in *From Ideas to Assets*, ed. B. Berman, 111–37 (New York: John Wiley & Sons, 2002).

15. E. F. Brigham and J. F. and Houston, *Fundamentals of Financial Management* (Fort Worth, TX,: Harcourt College Publishers, 1999).

16. R. Reider and P. B. Heyler, *Managing Cash Flow: An Operational Focus* (Hoboken, NJ: John Wiley & Sons, 2003).

17. J. V. Crosby, *Cycles, Trends, and Turning Points: Marketing and Sales Forecasting Techniques* (Chicago: NTC Business Books, 1997).

18. Brigham and Houston *Fundamentals of Financial Management* (Cincinnati: South-Western College, 2003).

Chapter 8

1. C. A. Brown, C. H.. Colbourne, and W. E. McMullen, "Legal Issues in New Venture Development," *Journal of Business Venturing* 3, no. 4 (1988): 273–86.
2. R. T. Peterson, "Small Retailers and Service Company Accuracy in Evaluating the Legality of Specified Practices," *Journal of Small Business Management* 39, no. 4 (2001): 312–19.
3. *Black's Law Dictionary*, 6th ed. (St. Paul, Minn.: West, 340).
4. R. P. Mandel, "Legal and Tax Issues," in *The Portable MBA in Entrepreneurship*, ed. William D. Bygrave, 285–326 (New York: John Wiley & Sons, 1997).
5. *Black's Law Dictionary*.
6. K. W. Clarkson, R. L. Miller, G. A. Jentz, and F. B. Cross, *West's Business Law* (New York: West Educational Publishing, 1998).
7. J. A. Fraser, "Cash Flow: When a Cash Crisis Strikes," *Inc.*, February 1, 1996, 104.
8. A. J. Sherman, *Fast-Track Business Growth* (Washington, D.C.: Kiplinger Washington Editors, 2001).
9. "Code of Ethics," in *Business: The Ultimate Resource*, exec. ed. Nick Philipson, 456–457 (New York: Bloomsbury Publishing, 2002).
10. TManage home page, www.tmanage.com (accessed February 15, 2003).
11. D. T. LeClair and L. Ferrell, "Innovation in Experiential Business Ethics Training," *Journal of Business Ethics* 23, no. 3 (2000): 313–22.
12. L. Trevino and K. Nelson, *Managing Ethics*, 2nd ed. (New York: John Wiley & Sons, 1999).
13. American Bar Association, *The American Bar Association Legal Guide for Small Business* (New York: Random House, 2000).
14. M. C. Ehrhardt and E. F. Brigham, *Corporate Finance* (Cincinnati: South-Western, 2003).
15. A. J. Sherman, *The Complete Guide to Running and Growing Your Business* (New York: Random House, 1997).
16. *Black's Law Dictionary*.
17. Sherman, *The Complete Guide to Running and Growing Your Business*.
18. R. A. Brealty and S. C. Myers, *Financing and Risk Management* (New York: McGraw-Hill, 2003).
19. *Black's Law Dictionary*.
20. Clarkson et al., *West's Business Law*.
21. Investorwords.com, www.investorwords.com (accessed February 1, 2003).
22. Investorwords.com, www.investorwords.com (accessed February 1, 2003).
23. J. T. Rich, "The Growth Imperative," *Journal of Business Strategy*, March/April 1999, 27–31.
24. P. K. Zingheim and J. R. Schuster, *Pay People Right!* (San Francisco: Jossey-Bass, 2000).
25. J. Stainman and K. Thompson, "Designing and Implementing a Broad-Based Stock Option Plan," *Compensation and Benefits Review* 30, no. 4 (1998): 23–40.
26. C. E. Bagley and C. E. Dauchy, *The Entrepreneur's Guide to Business Law* (New York: West Educational Publishing, 1998).
27. Ehrhardt and Brigham, *Corporate Finance*.
28. Sherman, *The Complete Guide to Running and Growing Your Business*.
29. "Legal Issues in E-Commerce," in *Business: The Ultimate Resource*, exec. ed. Nick Philipson, 648–649 (New York: Bloomsbury Publishing, 2002).
30. "Legal Issues in E-Commerce."
31. P. B. Seybold, *Customers.com* (New York: Random House, 1998).
32. "Legal Issues in E-Commerce."
33. D. E. Bouchoux, *Intellectual Property* (New York: AMACOM Books).
34. Webopedia home page, www.webopedia.com (accessed January 14, 2002).
35. FindLaw home page, www.findlaw.com (accessed February 7, 2003).

Chapter 9

1. Electronic Arts, Annual Report, 2002.
2. R. Demari and J. I. Wilson, *High Score: The Illustrated History of Computer Games* (Berkeley, Calif.: McGraw-Hill, 2002), 164.
3. Demari and Wilson, *High Score*, 165.
4. G. Hamel, *Leading the Revolution* (New York: Penguin, 2002), 268.
5. S. Barlett, "Seat of the Pants," *Inc.*, October 15, 2002, 38–40.
6. G. A. Benjamin and J. Margulis, *Angel Financing: How to Find and Invest in Private Equity* (New York: John Wiley & Sons, 2000).
7. Ernst & Young, *Outline for a Business Plan* (New York: Ernst & Young, 1997).
8. D. E. Gumpert and J. Mass, *How to Really Create a Successful Business Plan* (New York: Inc Publishing, 1994).
9. Deloitte & Touche, *Writing an Effective Business Plan* (New York: Deloitte & Touche, 2003).
10. B. Boulton and J. Thompson, *Entrepreneurs: Talent, Temperament, Technique* (Oxford: Butterworth Heinemann, 2000).
11. D. Valentine, "Don Valentine: Sequoia Capital," in *Done Deals: Venture Capitalists Tell Their Stories*, ed. U. Gupta (Boston: Harvard Business School Press, 2000), 173.
12. S. R. Rich and D. E. Gumpert, "How to Write a Winning Business Plan," in *The Entrepreneurial Venture*, ed. W. A. Sahlman and H. H. Stevenson, 127–37 (New York: McGraw-Hill, 1992).
13. Deloitte & Touche, *Writing an Effective Business Plan*.
14. Personal conversation with Michael Heller, January 20, 2002.
15. U. Looser and B. Schlapfer, *The New Venture Adventure* (New York: Texere, 2001).
16. S. Rogers, *The Entrepreneur's Guide to Finance and Business* (New York: McGraw-Hill, 2003).
17. E. S. Siegel, B. R. Ford, and J. M. Bornstein, *The Business Plan Guide* (New York: John Wiley & Sons, 1987).
18. Primus Venture Partners home page, www.primus.com (accessed March 3, 2003).
19. R. Abrams, *The Successful Business Plan* (Palo Alto, Calif.: Running 'R' Media, 2000).
20. Investorwords.com, www.investorwords.com (accessed March 3, 2003).
21. T. Abate, *The Biotech Investor* (New York: Times Books, 2003).
22. Abrams, *The Successful Business Plan*.
23. Looser and Schlapfer, *The New Venture Adventure*.
24. J. L. Nesheim, *High-Tech Start Up* (New York: Free Press, 2000).
25. Abrams, *The Successful Business Plan*.
26. S. Eng, "Impress Investors with Your Firm's Endgame," www.startup.wsj.com (accessed November 28, 2001).
27. Nesheim, *High-Tech Start Up*.
28. Nesheim, *High-Tech Start Up*.
29. R. Adams, *A Good Hard kick In the Ass* (New York: Crown Books, 2002), 150.

Chapter 10

1. "Cisco Systems," *Standard & Poor's Stock Report*, www.standardpoors.com (accessed May 19, 2004).
2. Hoovers Online, www.hoovers.com (accessed March 19, 2003).
3. D. Bunnell, *Making the Cisco Connection* (New York: John Wiley & Sons, 2000), 1.
4. J. Waters, *John Chambers and the Cisco Way* (New York: John Wiley & Sons, 2002).
5. Waters, *John Chambers and the Cisco Way*.
6. Waters, *John Chambers and the Cisco Way*.
7. B. Gibson, "Financial Information for Decision Making: An Alternative Small Firm Perspective," *Journal of Small Business Finance* 1 (1992): 221–32.
8. J. Timmons, *New Venture Creation*, 4th ed. (Chicago: Irwin Publishers, 1997).
9. G. N. Chandler and S. H. Hanks, "An Examination of the Substitutability of Founders Human and Financial Capital in Emerging Business Ventures," *Journal of Business Venturing* 13, No. 5 (1998): 353–69.

10. G. Keighley, "Could This Be the Next Disney?," *Business 2.0,* December, 2002, 110–118.

11. T. Abate, *The Biotech Investor* (New York: Times Books, 2003).

12. H. Van Auken and R. Carter, "Acquisition of Capital by Small Business," *Journal of Small Business Management* 27, no. 2 (1989): 1–9.

13. A. Riding, "Financing Entrepreneurial Firms: Research Paper for the Task Force on the Future of the Canadian Financial Services Sector," Carleton University, September 1998.

14. J. Freear, J. Sohl, and W. Wetzel, "Angels: Personal Investors in the Venture Capital Market," *Entrepreneurship and Regional Development* 7 (1995): 85–94.

15. G. Benjamin and J. Margulis, *Angel Financing* (New York: John Wiley & Sons, 2000).

16. A. Bhide, "Bootstrap Finance: The Art of Start-Ups," *Harvard Business Review,* 70, no. 6, November–December 1992, 109–17.

17. R. Stross, *eBoys* (New York: Crown Business, 2000), 25.

18. I. Smith, "Money: The Truth about Financing a Growing Small Business," in *The Book of Entrepreneurs' Wisdom,* ed. P. Krass, 121–29 (New York: John Wiley & Sons, 1999).

19. Riding, "Financing Entrepreneurial Firms."

20. S. Rogers, *The Entrepreneur's Guide to Finance and Business* (New York: McGraw-Hill, 2003).

21. Benjamin and Margulis, *Angel Financing.*

22. *Forbes,* ASAP, June 1, 1998, 24.

23. Rogers, *The Entrepreneur's Guide to Finance and Business.*

24. Rogers, *The Entrepreneur's Guide to Finance and Business.*

25. O. Strauss, "Toughed by an Angel," Entrepreneur's Byline, www.entreworld.org (accessed March 20, 2003).

26. Silicon Valley Biz Ink, "Viewpoint: Band of Angels Flying Despite Slowdown," www.svbizink.com (accessed March 20, 2003).

27. Investorwords, www.investorwords.com (accessed March 20, 2003).

28. A. Grimes, "Darwin Was Right: Venture Deals Are Off 50% in a Selective Market," *Wall Street Journal,* January 28, 2003, C5.

29. Hale and Dorr, LLP. *2003 Venture Capital Report.* (New York: Hale and Dorr, 2003).

30. PricewaterhouseCoopers, *Three Keys to Obtaining Venture Capital* (New York: PricewaterhouseCoopers, 2001).

31. PricewaterhouseCoopers, *Three Keys to Obtaining Venture Capital.*

32. Grimes, "Darwin Was Right."

33. D. Laurie, *Venture Catalyst* (Cambridge, Mass.: Perseus, 2001).

34. Rogers, *The Entrepreneur's Guide to Finance and Business.*

35. F. Lipman, *The Complete Going Public Handbook* (Roseville, Calif.: Prima Publishing, 2000).

36. Rogers, *The Entrepreneur's Guide to Finance and Business.*

37. Investorwords, www.investorwords.com (accessed March 20, 2003).

38. Lipman, *The Complete Going Public Handbook.*

39. K. Kelly, "Optimism Raises for Resurgence of Tech IPOs," *Wall Street Journal,* January 2, 2003, C1.

40. Renaissance Capital Analysts. (2003). *Renaisance Capital' 2003 Annual IPO Review.* New York: Renaissance Capital.

41. R. Hennessey. (2004). Volume, types of new issues shift in periods of rising interest rates. *Wall Street Journal Online,* www.wsj.com (accessed July 19, 2004).

42. Rogers, *The Entrepreneur's Guide to Finance and Business.*

43. G. Haines and L. Riding, "Loan Guarantee Programs for Small Firms: Recent Canadian Experience on Risk, Economic Impacts, and Incrementally," *Frontiers of Entrepreneurship Research* 16 (1995): 422–36.

44. Riding, "Financing Entrepreneurial Firms."

45. Rogers, *The Entrepreneur's Guide to Finance and Business.*

46. Small Business Administration home page, www.sba.gov (accessed March 24, 2003).

47. J. Nesheim, *High Tech Start Up: The Complete Handbook for Creating Successful New High Tech Companies* (New York: Free Press, 2000).

48. A. Sherman, *Raising Capital* (Washington, D.C.: Kiplinger Books, 2000).

49. M. Cardullo, *Technological Entrepreneurism* (Baldock: Research Studies Press, 1999).

50. Abate, *The Biotech Investor*.
51. B. Barringer and J. Harrison, "Walking a Tightrope: Creating Value through Interorganizational Relationship," *Journal of Management* 26 (2000): 367–403.

Chapter 11

1. H. W. Tesoriero, (2003). "A Slim Gym's Fat Success," *Time*, June.
2. H. W. Tesoriero, (2003). "A Slim Gym's Fat Success," *Time*, June.
3. P. Kufahl, "Get into the Niche," *Club Industry*, December 1, 2002.
4. M. E. McGrath, *Product Strategy for High-Technology Companies* (Burr Ridge, Ill.: Irwin, 1995).
5. O. Walker, H. Boyd, J. Mullins, and J. Larreche, *Marketing Strategy: A Decision-Focused Approach* (Boston: McGraw-Hill, 2003).
6. A. Hesseldahl, "Palm Goes Low," *Forbes*, October 6, 2002.
7. P. Kotler, *Marketing Insights from A to Z* (New York: John Wiley & Sons, 2003), 65.
8. K. J. Clancy and P. C. Krieg, *Counterintuitive Marketing: Achieve Great Results Using Uncommon Sense* (New York: Free Press, 2000).
9. L. M. Lodish, H. L. Morgan, and A. Kallianpur, *Entrepreneurial Marketing* (New York: John Wiley & Sons, 2001).
10. Lodish et al., *Entrepreneurial Marketing*.
11. S. Bedbury, *A New Brand World* (New York: Penguin, 2002).
12. R. M. McMath, *What Were They Thinking?* (New York: Times Books, 1999).
13. Lodish et al., *Entrepreneurial Marketing*.
14. Kotler, *Marketing Insights from A to Z*, 65.
15. P. B. Seybold, *The Customer Revolution* (New York: Crown Business, 2001).
16. S. Zyman, *Building Brandwidth: Closing the Sale Online* (New York: HarperCollins, 2000).
17. M. Salzman, R. Matathia, and A. O'Reilly, *Buzz: Harness the Power of Influence and Create Demand* (New York: John Wiley & Sons, 2003).
18. M. W. Ragas, *Lessons from the eFront* (New York: Prima Publishing, 2001), 181.
19. N. J. Hicks, "From Ben Franklin to Branding: The Evolution of Health Services Marketing," in *Branding Health Services*, ed. G. Bashe, N. J. Hicks, and A. Ziegenfuss, 1–18 (Gaithersburg, Md.: Aspen Publishers, 2000).
20. Hicks, "From Ben Franklin to Branding."
21. D. A. Aaker, *Managing Brand Equity: Capitalizing on the Value of a Brand Name* (New York: Free Press, 1991).
22. P. Kotler and G. Armstrong, *Principles of Marketing* (Upper Saddle River, N.J.: Prentice Hall, 1999).
23. H. W. Chesbrough, *Open Innovation* (Boston: Harvard Business School Press, 2003).
24. Kotler and Armstrong, *Principles of Marketing*.
25. Kotler and Armstrong, *Principles of Marketing*.
26. J. H. Boyett and J. T. Boyett, *The Guru Guide to Marketing* (New York: John Wiley & Sons, 2003).
27. T. Foster, *Managing Quality* (Upper Saddle River, N.J.: Prentice Hall, 2001).
28. Lodish et al., *Entrepreneurial Marketing*, 60–61.
29. R. A. Nykiel, *Marketing Your Business: A Guide to Developing a Strategic Marketing Plan* (New York: Best Business Books, 2003).
30. Kotler, *Marketing Insights from A to Z*, 2.
31. B. Barton, "Integrating Advertising with Other Campaigns," in *Business: The Ultimate Resource* (New York: Bloomsbury Publishing, 2003).
32. A. Ries and L. Ries, *The Fall of Advertising and the Rise of PR* (New York: HarperBusiness, 2002).

Chapter 12

1. D. E. Bouchoux, *Intellectual Property* (New York: AMACOM Books, 2001).
2. J. Pereira, "Etoys Returns to the Internet after Collapse," *Wall Street Journal*, December 12, 2001, B1.

3. KBToys, "About Us." KBToys Home Page, www.kbtoys.com (accessed July 20, 2004).
4. A. Gove, "Safeguarding Intellectual Property," *Red Herring*, December 1997, 54.
5. C. E. Bagley and C. E. Dauchy, *The Entrepreneur's Guide to Business Law* (Cincinnati: West, 1998).
6. Bouchoux, *Intellectual Property*.
7. H. J. Knight, "Intellectual Property "101," in *From Ideas to Assets*, ed. B. Berman, 3–25 (New York: John Wiley & Sons, 2002).
8. Knight, "Intellectual Property "101."
9. G. Wolff, *The Biotech Investor's Bible* (New York: John Wiley & Sons, 2001).
10. U.S. Patent and Trademark Office, www.uspto.gov (accessed October 21, 2003).
11. U.S. Patent and Trademark Office,www.uspto.gov (accessed January 10, 2002).
12. Bouchoux, *Intellectual Property*.
13. Gove, "Safeguarding Intellectual Property."
14. Bouchoux, *Intellectual Property*.
15. Bagley and Dauchy, *The Entrepreneur's Guide to Business Law* (Cincinnati: South-Western College, 2nd edition, 2002).
16. Bagley and Dauchy, *The Entrepreneur's Guide to Business Law* (Cincinnati: South-Western College, 2nd edition, 2002).
17. *Los Angeles Times*, November 20, 2001.

Chapter 13

1. H. Schultz, *Pour Your Heart into It* (New York: Hyperion, 1997).
2. R. Gulati, S. Huffman, and G. Neilson, "The Barista Principle: Starbucks and the Rise of Relational Capital," *Strategy and Business*, no. 28 (2002).
3. Starbucks, www.starbucks.com (accessed August 11, 2002).
4. Schultz, *Pour Your Heart into It*.
5. News.com, "Starbucks Celebrates Its First Decade as a Public Company," http://news.cnet.com (accessed August 11, 2002).
6. Schultz, *Pour Your Heart into It*, 276
7. C. Zook, and J. Allen, *The Facts about Growth* (New York: Bain & Company, 1999).
8. National Commission on Entrepreneurship, High Growth Companies: Mapping America's Entrepreneurial Landscape, July 2001.
9. D. Packard, *The HP Way: How Bill Hewlett and I Built Our Company*, ed. D. Kirby with Karen Lewis (New York: HarperBusiness, 1996).
10. Packard, *The HP Way*.
11. G. Hubbard, and P. Bromiley, "What Organizational Theories Say about How Firms Measure Performance" (paper Presented at the Strategic Management Society Annual Meeting, Mexico City, Mexico, 1995).
12. C. E. Lucier and A. Astin, "Toward a New Theory of Growth," *Strategy and Business*, first quarter (1996).
13. A. V. Bhide, *The Origin and Evolution of New Businesses* (Oxford: Oxford University Press, 2000).
14. C. Zook, J. Allen, and J. Smith, "Strategies for Corporate Growth," *European Business Journal* 12, no. 2 (2000).
15. J. Welch, "Growth Initiatives," *Executive Excellence* 16, no. 6 (1999): 8–9.
16. "Strategic HR Intelligence Key to Employee Retention," *The Biotech HR Pulse* 1, no. 14 (November 12, 2003): 1–4.
17. PricewaterhouseCoopers, "One-Third of Fast Growth CEOs Grapple with Self Doubt, PricewaterhouseCoopers Finds," *Trendsetter Barometer*, May 22, 2000.
18. E. T. Penrose, *The Theory of the Growth of the Firm*, 3rd ed. (Oxford: Oxford University Press, 1995).
19. E. T. Penrose, *The Theory of the Growth of the Firm* (New York: John Wiley & Sons, 1959).
20. C. Zook, *Profit from the Core* (Boston: Harvard Business School Press, 2001).
21. D. C. Hambrick and L. M. Crozier, "Stumblers and Stars in the Management of Rapid Growth," *Journal of Business Venturing* 1 (1985): 31–45.
22. M. Hay and K. Kamshad, "Small Firm Growth: Intentions, Implementation and Impediments," *Business Strategy Review* 5, no. 3 (1994): 49–68.

23. Penrose, *The Theory of the Growth of the Firm* (1959).

24. W. P. Barrett, "The Perils of Success," *Fortune*, November 3, 1997, 129–42.

25. B. Jaruzelski, K. Volkholz, and G. Horkan, *The High-Tech Challenge: Sustaining Rapid and Profitable Growth* (New York: Booz-Allen & Hamilton, 2002), 4.

26. "America's Fastest-Growing 500 Private Companies," *Inc.*, 2003, 28.

27. T. Ahrens, *High Growth Companies: Driving the Tiger* (Hampshire: Gower, 1999)

28. A. J. Sherman, *Fast-Track Business Growth* (Washington, D.C.: Kiplinger Books, 2001).

29. T. L. Doorley and J. M. Donovan, *Value-Creating Growth* (San Francisco: Jossey-Bass, 1999).

30. Doorley and Donovan, *Value-Creating Growth.*

31. Vondafone, www.vondafone.com (accessed August 21, 2002).

32. A. T. Kearney, Inc., *Sustaining Corporate Growth* (Boca Raton, Fla.: St. Lucie Press, 2000).

33. Ahrens, *High Growth Companies.*

34. PricewaterhouseCoopers, "Trendsetter CEOs Reveal Factors Empowering Sustained Growth—and Doppelgangers That Need Fixing," *Trendsetter Barometer*, February 20, 2002.

35. T. L. Doorley, quoted in *Value-Creating Growth: Goals, Strategies, Foundations* (New York: The Conference Board, Inc., 1997), 6.

36. Sherman, *Fast-Track Business Growth.*

37. G. C. Reid and J. A. Smith, "What Makes a New Business Start-Up Successful?," *Small Business Economics* 14 (2000): 165–82.

38. B. R. Barringer and J. S. Harrison, "Walking a Tightrope: Creating Value through Interorganizational Relationships," *Journal of Management* 26 (2000): 367–403.

39. A. Jaffe, M. Trajtenberg and R. Henderson, "Geographic Location of Knowledge Spillovers as Evidence by Patent Citations," *Quarterly Journal of Economics* 108, no. 3 (1993): 577–98.

Chapter 14

1. Ask Jeeves Annual Report, 2001.

2. Ask Jeeves Annual Report, 2003.

3. PricewaterhouseCoopers, "Partnerships Have Big Payoffs for Fast-Growth Companies," *Trendsetter Barometer*, August 26, 2000.

4. PricewaterhouseCoopers, "Most Fast Growth CEOs Planning Corporate Acquisitions, PricewaterhouseCoopers Finds," *Trendsetter Barometer*, April 10, 2001.

5. P. Killing, "Maximizing a New Strategic Alliance," in *Business: The Ultimate Resource*, 85–86 (Boston: Bloomsbury Publishing, 2002).

6. E. Gundling, *The 3M Way to Innovation* (Tokyo: Kodansha International, 2000).

7. Boston Consulting Group, *Winning the New Product War* (Boston: Boston Consulting Group, 2002).

8. PricewaterhouseCoopers, "Innovation Is the Leading Competitive Advantage of Fast Growth Companies," *Trendsetter Barometer*, June 24, 2004.

9. Sketchers Annual Report, 2001.

10. F. M. Stone, *The Oracle of Oracle* (New York: AMACOM Books, 2002), 125.

11. Office of Advocacy, U.S. Small Business Administration, *Exporting by Firm Size* (Washington, D.C.: U.S. Government Printing Office, 1998).

12. B. M. Oviatt and P. P. McDougall, "Toward a Theory of International New Ventures," *Journal of International Business Studies* 25, no. 1 (1994): 45–64.

13. "Worldwide Growth for Amazon.com," *NASDAQ Magazine*, September/October 2002.

14. S. Zahra and D. Garvis, "International Corporate Entrepreneurship and Firm Performance: The Moderating Effect of International Environmental Hostility," *Journal of Business Venturing* 15, no. 4–5 (2000): 469–92.

15. A. J. Sherman, *Fast-Track Business Growth* (Washington, D.C.: Kiplinger Washington Editors, 2001).

16. S. Chaudhuri and B. Tabrizi, "Capturing the Real Value in High-Tech Acquisitions," *Harvard Business Review*, September–October 1999: 123–30.

17. D. L. Laurie, *Venture Catalyst* (Cambridge, Mass.: Perseus, 2001).

18. PricewaterhouseCoopers, "What Successful Acquirers Know," *Growing Your Business*, September/October 2002.

19. P. E. Cardullo, *Technological Entrepreneurism* (Badlock: Research Studies Press, 1999).

20. Sherman, *Fast-Track Business Growth*.

21. PricewaterhouseCoopers, "Strategic Alliances Come Up 7's for Technology Businesses: 77% Involved; Average Participant Active in 7, PricewaterhouseCoopers Finds," *Trendsetter Barometer*, February 14, 2001.

22. S. Das, P. K. Sen and S. Sengupta, "Impact of Strategic Alliances on Firm Valuation," *Academy of Management Journal* 41 (1998): 27–41.

23. D. L. Deeds and C. W. L. Hill, "Strategic Alliances and the Rate of New Product Development: An Empirical Study of Entrepreneurial Biotechnology Firms," *Journal of Business Venturing* 11 (1996): 41–55.

24. M. Dell, *Direct from Dell* (New York: HarperBusiness, 1999).

25. A. Inkpen and M. M. Crossan, "Believing Is Seeing: Joint Ventures and Organizational Learning," *Journal of Management Studies* 32 (1995): 595–618.

26. A. C. Inkpen and K. O. Li, Joint Venture Formation: Planning and Knowledge-Gathering for Success," *Organizational Dynamics* 27, no. 4 (1999): 33–47.

27. G. T. Geis and G. S. Geis, *Digital Deals* (New York: McGraw-Hill, 2001).

28. J. F. Hennart, "A Transaction Cost Theory of Equity Joint Ventures," *Strategic Management Journal* 9 (1988): 361–74.

29. C. Rosen, "Companies and Their Technology Vendors Are Joining Forces to Start New Ventures," *Information Week,* June 4 , 2001.

30. S. H. Park and M. V. Russo, "When Competition Eclipses Cooperation: An Event History Analysis of Joint Venture Failure," *Management Science* 42, no. 6 (1996): 875–90.

31. Geis and Geis, *Digital Deals*.

Chapter 15

1. Tam, Pui-Wing (2004). Fill'er Up, With Color. *Wall Street Journal,* August 3, 2004, p. B1.

2. V. K. Jolly, *Commercializing New Technologies* (Cambridge, Mass.: Harvard Business School Press, 1997).

3. I. Alon, "The Use of Franchising by U.S.-Based Retailers," *Journal of Small Business Management* 39, no. 2 (2001): 111–22.

4. S. Shane, "Factors for New Franchise Success," *Sloan Management Review* 39, no. 3 (1998): 43–50.

5. Shane, "Factors for New Franchise Success."

6. "Wikipedia Encyclopedia," www.wikpedia.com (accessed February 12, 2004).

7. www.seniorjournal.com (accessed May 25, 2004).

8. Start Your Own Business, "It Pays to Care," *Small Business Opportunities,* spring 2002.

9. "Comfort Keepers Franchise Facts," www.comfortkeepers.com (accessed May 25, 2004).

10. P. H. Rubin, "The Theory of the Firm and the Structure of the Franchise Contract," *Journal of Law and Economics* 21 (1978): 223–33.

11. J. L. Bradach, *Franchise Organizations* (Boston: Harvard Business School Press, 1998).

12. "McDonald's Corporation," *Standard & Poor's Stock Report,* www.standardandpoors.com (accessed May 22, 2004).

13. A. Sherman, *Raising Capital* (Washington, D.C.: Kiplinger Books, 2000).

14. P. Birkeland, *Franchising Dreams* (Chicago: University of Chicago Press, 2002).

15. A. Oxenfeldt and A. Kelly, "Will Successful Franchise Systems Ultimately Become Wholly-Owned Chains?," *Journal of Retailing* 44 (1969): 69–83.

16. R. Bennett, "To Franchise or Not: How to Decide," in *Franchising Today: 1966–1967*, ed. C. L. Vaughn and D. B. Slater (New York: Matthew Bender and Company, 1967), 20.

17. J. Brickley and F. Dark, "The Choice of Organizational Form: The Case of Franchising," *Journal of Financial Economics* 18 (1987): 401–20.

18. "Darden Restaurants, Inc.," *Standard & Poor's Stock Report,* www.standardandpoors .com (accessed May 22, 2004).

19. A. Sherman, *Fast-Track Business Growth* (Washington, D.C.: Kiplinger Books, 2001).

20. International Franchising Association, "What Is Franchising?," www.franchise.org (accessed May 27, 2004).

21. Federal Trade Commission, *Consumers Guide to Buying a Franchise* (Washington, D.C.: U.S. Government Printing Office, 2002).

22. American Bar Association, *The American Bar Association Legal Guide for Small Business* (New York: Three Rivers Press, 2000).

23. Bradach, *Franchise Organizations.*

24. Federal Trade Commission, "Guide to the FTC Franchise Rule," www.ftc.gov/bcp/ franchise/netrule.html (accessed March 29, 2002).

25. R. L. Purvin, *The Franchise Fraud* (New York: John Wiley & Sons, 1994).

26. American Bar Association, *Legal Guide for Small Business* (New York: Random House, 2000).

27. Econo Lodge, www.econolodge.com (accessed April 1, 2002).

28. Federal Trade Commission, "Guide to the FTC Franchise Rule."

29. N. Aydin and M. Kacker, "International Outlook of US-Based Franchisors," *International Marketing Review* 7, no. 2 (1990): 43–53.

30. Federal Trade Commission, "Guide to the FTC Franchise Rule."

31. International Franchise Association, "How Widespread Is Franchising?," www.franchise.org (accessed March 29, 2002).

Case 1

1. Cavender 1998

2. Ibid.

3. Segaller 1999, p 106

4. Bronson 2000, p, 83

5. Bronson 2000, p. 79

6. Bronson 1998

7. Besser 1994

8. Jurvetson and Draper 1999

9. Hatlestad 1999

10. Ibid.

11. Ibid.

12. Ibid.

13. Ibid.

14. Smith 2001

15. Ibid.

16. Ibid.

17. PR Newswire 1997

18. Smith 2001

19. Bronson 1995

20. Gimein 1998

21. EMMS 1998

22. Hatlestadt 1999

23. Ibid.

24. Wilson 1998

25. Harbrecht 2000

26. Parker 2000

Case 2

1. In this context, *spam* is unsolicited commercial e-mail. *Spamming* is the act of sending such e-mail.

2. Banner advertising on the Internet is usually discussed in terms of CPMs or cost per 1,000 ad impressions. An ad impression occurs whenever a banner ad is served, which may occur, for example, every time a particular Web page containing the banner ad is accessed. In AllAdvantage's case, AllAdvantage members were shown a constant stream of ads, and an impression represented approximately 20 seconds of display time on a user's computer screen.

Case 6

1. "Meg Whitman eBay Inc.," www.allperson.com, in August 2000.
2. Plastic dessert holders bearing pictures of cartoon characters such as Spiderman and Snoopy.
3. Under eBay's business model, a seller placed an item on eBay, set a minimum bid, and specified the duration of the auction (last date for ending the auction). eBay charged a listing fee and a final fee (specific percentage of the item's sale price) when the listed item was sold.
4. "Meg Muscles eBay uptown," www.pathfinder.com, June 05, 1999.
5. "Meg Whitman," www.business2.com, June 1999 Issue.
6. In 1997, Hasbro was a leading toymaker in the US with $600 million in revenues and 600 employees.
7. "Face Time With Meg Whitman," www.fastcompany.com, May 2001.
8. In early 1998, Whitman's husband was appointed as the head of the Neurosurgery Department at Stanford University Medical Center. Thereafter, the whole family shifted to California.
9. "Behind the scenes at eBay," www.cnn.com, January 13, 2000.
10. "Q&A with eBay's Meg Whitman," www.business.cisco.com, July/August 2001.
11. "Q&A with eBay's Meg Whitman," www.business.cisco.com, July/August 2001.
12. "Behind the scenes at eBay," www.cnn.com, January 13, 2000.
13. "Meg and the Machine," *Fortune*, September 01, 2003.
14. "Meg and the Machine," *Fortune*, September 01, 2003.
15. "Q&A with eBay's Meg Whitman," www.business.cisco.com, July/August 2001.
16. "EBay's Whitman richest woman CEO," www.businessjournal.net, July 07, 1999
17. "Meg Whitman," www.archive.salon.com, November 27, 2001.
18. 'Buy It Now' feature allowed bidders to end an auction at a preset price. In early 2003, more than 40% of the auction listings on eBay used the feature.
19. "How Meg Whitman and eBay rule the world," www.creatingcustomerevangelists.com, 2002.
20. "No mere mega mall for Meg@eBay," www.guardian.co.uk, April 12, 2003.
21. "The People's Company," www.businessweek.com, December 03, 2001.
22. "Q&A with eBay's Meg Whitman," www.business.cisco.com, July/August 2001.
23. "EBay's Whitman richest woman CEO," www.businessjournal.net, July 07, 1999.
24. "Behind the scenes at eBay," www.cnn.com, January 13, 2000.
25. "Meet eBay's Auctioneer-in-Chief," www.businessweek.com, May 29, 2003.
26. NetMind technology allowed the company to track Web-based information and notified it of changes made via email, pager or cell phone.
27. "EBay's Whitman richest woman CEO," www.businessjournal.net, July 07, 1999.
28. "Meet eBay's Auctioneer-in-Chief," www.businessweek.com, May 29, 2003.
29. "Behind the scenes at eBay," www.cnn.com, January 13, 2000.
30. "EBay's Whitman richest woman CEO," www.businessjournal.net, July 07, 1999.
31. "eBay: Last man standing," www.msn-cnet.com.com, April 20, 2002.
32. "Meg Muscles eBay Uptown," www.pathfinder.com, June 05, 1999.
33. "The People's Company," www.businessweek.com, December 03, 2001.
34. The price was increased from 1.25%-to-5% of sales to 1.5%-to-5.25% of sales in January 2001.
35. The House Financial Services Committee (US) is a government committee, which oversees the entire financial services industry, including the securities, banking, insurance and housing industries. The committee also supervises the work of the Federal Reserve, the SEC, the Treasury and other financial regulatory authorities in the US.

36. Spinning is a practice, where investment banking firms offered senior executives at their top clients, a chance to buy into IPOs arranged them, as a way to win additional investment banking business from those clients. Though the practice is not illegal, analysts said that it artificially inflated the stock price.

37. Other top executives who were reported to have benefited from Goldman Sach's practice of spinning included Dennis Kozlowski, former CEO of Tyco, and Jerry Yang, co-founder of Yahoo.

38. "eBay: Last man standing," www.msn-cnet.com.com, April 20, 2002.

7(A) loan guaranty program The main Small Business Administration (SBA) program available to small businesses operating through private-sector lenders providing loans that are guaranteed by the SBA; loans guarantees reserved for small businesses that are unable to secure financing through normal lending channels.

10-K A report that is similar to the annual report, except that it contains more detailed information about the company's business.

accounts receivable The money owed to a firm by its customers.

acquirer The surviving firm in an acquisition.

acquisition The outright purchase of one firm by another.

adverse selection The challenge a firm must face as it grows that as the number of employees a firm needs increases, it becomes more difficult to find the right employees, place them in appropriate positions, and provide adequate supervision.

advertising Making people aware of a product or service in hopes of persuading them to buy it.

advisory board A panel of experts who are asked by a firm's managers to provide counsel and advice on an ongoing basis; unlike a board of directors, an advisory board possesses no legal responsibility for the firm and gives nonbinding advice.

Anticybersquatting Consumer Protection Act Act passed in 1999 that strengthened trademark laws to permit injured parties to sue for bad faith registration of domain names.

area franchise agreement Agreement that allows a franchisee to own and operate a specific number of outlets in a particular geographic area.

articles of incorporation Documents forming a legal corporation that are filed with the secretary of state's office in the state of incorporation; typically include the corporation's name, purpose, authorized number of stock shares, classes of stock, and other conditions of operation.

assignment of invention agreement A document signed by an employee as part of the employment agreement that assigns the employer the right to apply for the patent of an invention made by the employee during the course of his or her employment.

assumption sheet An explanation in a new firm's business plan of the sources of the numbers for its financial forecast and the assumptions used to generate them.

balance sheet A snapshot of a company's assets, liabilities, and owner's equity at a specific point in time.

barriers to entry Conditions that create disincentives for a new firm to enter an industry.

benchmarking The idea that a firm can improve the quality of an activity by identifying and copying the methods of other firms that have been successful in that area.

board of directors A panel of individuals who are elected by a corporation's shareholders to oversee the management of the firm.

bootstrapping Using creativity, ingenuity, or any means possible to obtain resources other than borrowing money or raising capital from traditional sources.

brainstorming A technique used to quickly generate a large number of ideas and solutions to problems; conducted to generate ideas that might represent product or business opportunities.

brand The set of attributes—positive or negative—that people associate with a company.

brand equity The set of assets and liabilities that is linked to a brand and enables it to raise a firm's valuation.

brand loyalty A valuable asset for a particular company wherein customers become loyal to its product or service and will buy its product or service time and time again.

brand management A program that protects the image and value of an organization's brand in consumers' minds.

breakthrough products and services New products and services that establish new markets or new market segments.

budgets Itemized forecasts of a company's income, expenses, and capital needs that are also important tools for financial planning and control.

burn rate The rate at which a company is spending its capital until it reaches profitability.

business angels Individuals who invest their personal capital directly in new ventures.

business concept blind spot An overly narrow focus that prevents a firm from seeing an opportunity that might fit its business model.

business format franchise By far the more popular approach to franchising in which the franchisor provides a formula for doing business to the franchisee along with training, advertising, and other forms of assistance.

business growth planning The process of setting growth-related goals and objectives and then mapping out a plan to achieve those goals and objectives.

business method patent A patent that protects an invention that is or facilitates a method of doing business.

business model A company's plan for how it competes, uses its resources, structures its relationships, interfaces with customers, and creates value to sustain itself on the basis of the profits it generates.

business model innovation Initiative that revolutionizes how products are sold in an industry.

business plan A written document describing all the aspects of a business venture, which is usually necessary to raise money and attract high-quality business partners.

buy-back clause A clause found in most founders' agreements that legally obligates the departing founder to sell to the remaining founders his or her interest in the firm if the remaining founders are interested.

buzz An awareness and a sense of anticipation about a company and its offerings.

c corporation A legal entity that in the eyes of the law is separate from its owners.

carry The percentage of profits that the venture capitalist gets from a specific venture capital fund.

certification marks Marks, words, names, symbols, or devices used by a person other than its owner to certify a particular quality about a product or service.

channel conflict A problem that occurs when two or more separate marketing channels (e.g., online sales and retail sales) are in conflict over their roles in selling a firm's products or services.

closely held corporation A corporation in which the voting stock is held by a small number of individuals and is very thinly or infrequently traded.

clusters Collections of similar firms in a specific geographic area (i.e., there is a "cluster" of semiconductor firms in the Silicon Valley near San Jose, California).

co-branding A relationship between two or more firms in which the firms' brands promote each other.

code of ethics Document that describes the firm's general value system, moral principles, and specific ethical rules providing guidance to managers and employees regarding what is expected of them in terms of ethical behavior.

collective marks Trademarks or service marks used by the members of a cooperative, association, or other collective group, including marks indicating membership in a union or similar organization.

commitment to growth The extent to which a firm's owners and managers have made a deliberate choice to pursue growth.

common stock Stock that is issued more broadly than preferred stock and that gives stockholders voting rights to elect the board of directors of the firm.

competitive analysis grid A tool for organizing the information a firm collects about its competitors that can help a firm see how it stacks up against its competitors, provide ideas for markets to pursue, and identify its primary sources of competitive advantage.

competitive intelligence The information that is gathered by a firm to learn about its competitors.

competitor analysis A detailed analysis of a firm's competition that helps a firm understand the positions of its major competitors and the opportunities that are available to obtain a competitive advantage in one or more areas.

concept statement A preliminary description of a business that includes descriptions of the product or service being offered, the intended target market, the benefits of the product or service, the product's position in the market, and how the product or service will be sold and distributed.

concept test A representation of the product or service to prospective users to gauge customer interest, desirability, and purchase intent.

constant ratio method of forecasting A forecasting approach using the percent of sales method in which expense items on a firm's income statement are expected to grow at the same rate as sales.

consultant An individual who gives professional or expert advice. Consultants fall into two categories: paid consultants and consultants who are made available for free or at a reduced rate through a non-profit or governmental agency.

copyright A form of intellectual property protection that grants to the owner of a work of authorship the legal right to determine how the work is used and to obtain the economic benefits from the work.

copyright bug The letter *c* inside a circle with the first year of publication and the author or copyright owner (e.g., © 2005 Dell Inc).

copyright infringement Violation of another's copyright that occurs when one work derives from another work or is an exact copy or shows substantial similarity to the original copyrighted work.

core competency A unique skill or capability that transcends products or markets, makes a significant contribution to the customer's perceived benefit, is difficult to imitate, and serves as a source of a firm's competitive advantage over its rivals.

core strategy The overall manner in which a firm competes relative to its rivals.

corporate entrepreneurship Behavior orientation exhibited by established firms with an entrepreneurial emphasis that is proactive, innovative, and risk taking.

corporate opportunity doctrine Legal principle that states that key employees (such as officers, directors, and managers) and skilled employees (such as software engineers, accountants, and marketing specialists) owe a special duty of loyalty to their employer.

corporate venture capital A type of capital similar to traditional venture capital, except that the money comes from corporations that invest in new ventures related to their areas of interest.

corporation A separate legal entity organized under the authority of a state.

corridor principle States that once an entrepreneur starts a firm and becomes immersed in an industry, "corridors" leading to new venture opportunities become more apparent to the entrepreneur than to someone looking in from the outside.

cost-based pricing A pricing method in which the list price is determined by adding a markup percentage to the product's cost.

cost leadership strategy Generic strategy in which firms strive to have the lowest costs in the industry relative to competitors' costs and typically attract customers on that basis.

cost of sales All of the direct costs associated with producing or delivering a product or service, including the material costs and direct labor (*also* cost of goods sold).

creative destruction The process by which new products and technologies developed by entrepreneurs over time make current products and technologies obsolete; stimulus of economic activity.

creativity The process of generating a novel or useful idea.

current assets Cash plus items that are readily convertible to cash, such as accounts receivable, inventories, and marketable securities.

current liabilities Obligations that are payable within a year, including accounts payable, accrued expenses, and the current portion of long-term debt.

current ratio A ratio that equals the firm's current assets divided by its current liabilities.

customer advisory boards Panel of individuals set up by some companies to meet regularly to discuss needs, wants, and problems that may lead to new product, service, or customer service ideas.

customer interface The way in which a firm interacts with its customers.

cybersquatting The act of registering a popular Internet address with the intent of reselling it to its rightful owner.

day-in-the-life research A form of anthropological research used by companies to make sure customers are satisfied and to probe for new product ideas by sending researchers to the customers' homes or businesses.

debt financing Getting a loan; most common sources of debt financing are commercial banks and the Small Business Administration (SBA) guaranteed loan program.

debt to equity ratio A ratio calculated by dividing the firm's long-term debt by its shareholders' equity.

declining industry An industry that is experiencing a reduction in demand.

derivative works Works that are new renditions of something that is already copyrighted, which are also copyrightable.

design patents The second most common type of patent covering the invention of new, original, and ornamental designs for manufactured products.

differentiation strategy Firms that strive to provide unique or different products and typically compete on the basis of quality, service, timeliness, or some other important dimension.

digital signature A computer-generated block of text that accurately identifies both the signer and the content, which helps ensure the authenticity and integrity of electronic documents.

disintermediation The process of eliminating layers of intermediaries, such as distributors and retailers, to sell directly to customers.

distribution channel The route a product takes from the place it is made to the customer who is the end user.

domain name A company's Internet address.

double taxation Form of taxation in which a corporation is taxed on its net income, and when the same income is distributed to shareholders in the form of dividends, it is taxed again on shareholders' personal income tax returns.

due diligence The process of investigating the merits of a potential venture and verifying the key claims made in the business plan.

Economic Espionage Act Passed in 1996, an act that makes the theft of trade secrets a crime.

economies of scale Phenomena that occurs when mass producing a product results in lower average costs.

efficiency How productively a firm utilizes its assets relative to its rate of return.

Electronic Signatures in Global and International Commerce Act Law enacted October 1, 2000, which states electronic contracts and electronic signatures are just as legal as traditional paper contracts signed in ink.

elevator speech A brief, carefully constructed statement that outlines the merits of a business opportunity.

emerging industry A new industry in which standard operating procedures have yet to be developed.

entrepreneurial alertness The ability to notice things without engaging in deliberate search.

entrepreneurial firms Companies that bring new products and services to market by creating and seizing opportunities.

entrepreneurial intensity The position of a firm on a conceptual continuum that ranges from highly conservative to highly entrepreneurial.

entrepreneurial services Those services that generate new market, product, and service ideas.

entrepreneurship The process by which individuals pursue opportunities without regard to resources they currently control.

equity financing A means of raising funds by exchanging partial ownership in a firm, which is usually in the form of stock, for funding.

ethics training programs Programs designed to teach employees how to respond to the types of ethical dilemmas that might arise on their jobs.

exclusive distribution arrangements An agreement that gives a retailer or other intermediary the exclusive rights to sell a company's products in a specific area for a specific period of time.

execution intelligence The ability to fashion a solid business idea into a viable business; a key characteristic of successful entrepreneurs.

executive search firm A company that specializes in helping other companies recruit and select key personnel.

executive summary A quick overview of the entire business plan that provides a busy reader everything that he or she needs to know about the distinctive nature of the new venture.

exit strategy A plan that details how the owners of a firm will sell their interest in the firm, and convert their stock to cash.

external growth strategies Growth strategies that rely on establishing relationships with third parties, such as mergers, acquisitions, strategic alliances, joint ventures, licensing, and franchising.

fair use The limited use of copyrighted material for purposes such as criticism, comment, news reporting, teaching, or scholarship.

fast track program A provision in the SBIR Program in which some applicants can simultaneously submit Phase I and Phase II grant applications.

feasibility analysis A preliminary evaluation of a business idea to determine if it is worth pursuing.

fiduciary obligation The obligation to always act in another's best interest; it is a mistake to assume that a franchisor has a fiduciary obligation to its franchisees.

final prospectus Document issued by the investment bank after the Securities and Exchange Commission (SEC) has approved the offering that sets a date and issuing price for the offering.

financial feasibility analysis A financial assessment that considers a business idea's capital requirements, financial rate of return, and overall attractiveness of investment.

financial management The process of raising money and managing a company's finances in a way that achieves the highest rate of return.

financial ratios Ratios showing the relationships between items on a firm's financial statements that are used to discern whether a firm is meeting its financial objectives and how it stacks up against its industry peers.

financial statements Written reports that quantitatively describe a firm's financial health.

financing activities Activities that raise cash during a certain period by borrowing money or selling stock, and/or use cash during a certain period by paying dividends, buying back outstanding stock, or buying back outstanding bonds.

first-mover advantage A sometimes significant advantage gained by the first company to move into a new market because of the opportunity to establish brand recognition and market power.

fixed assets Assets used over a longer time frame, such as real estate, buildings, equipment, and furniture.

Fixed costs The costs that a company incurs in operating a business whether it sells something or not (e.g., overhead).

focus group A gathering of five to ten people who have been selected based on their common characteristics relative to the issue being discussed; conducted to generate ideas that might represent product or business opportunities.

follow-me-home testing A product testing methodology in which a company sends teams of testers to the homes or businesses of users to see how its products are working.

follow-on funding Additional funding for a firm following the initial investment made by investors.

forecasts Estimates of a firm's future income and expenses, based on its past performance, its current circumstances, and its future plans.

founders' agreement A written document that deals with issues such as the relative split of the equity among the founders of a firm, how individual founders will be compensated for the cash or the "sweat equity" they put into the firm, and how long the founders will have to remain with the firm for their shares to fully vest (*also* shareholders' agreement).

founding team Team of individuals chosen to start a new venture that has an advantage over those started by an individual because a team brings more talent, resources, ideas, and professional contacts to a new venture than does a sole entrepreneur.

fragmented industry An industry characterized by a large number of firms approximately equal in size.

franchise agreement The document that consummates the sale of a franchise, which typically contains two sections: (1) the purchase agreement and (2) the franchise or license agreement.

franchise association A franchise advisory council that represents the franchisees' collective interests and provides a forum for franchisees to communicate with one another.

franchisee A firm that enters into a franchising agreement and pays an initial fee and an ongoing royalty in order to license another firm's successful product or service.

franchising A form of business organization in which a firm that already has a successful product or service (franchisor), licenses its trademark and method of doing businesses to other businesses (franchisees) in exchange for an initial franchise fee and an ongoing royalty.

franchisor A firm with a successful product or service that enters into a franchising agreement to license its trademark and method of doing business to other businesses in exchange for fee and royalty payments.

fulfillment and support The way a firm's product or service "goes to market" or how it reaches its customers; also the channels a company uses and the level of customer support it provides.

full business plan A document that spells out a company's operations and plans in much more detail than a summary business plan; the format that is usually used to prepare a business plan for an investor.

gazelles Fast-growth young companies.

general partnership A form of business organization in which two or more people pool their skills, abilities, and resources to run a business.

geographic expansion An internal growth strategy in which an entrepreneurial business grows by simply expanding from its original location to additional geographical sites.

global industry An industry that is experiencing significant international sales.

global strategy An international expansion strategy in which firms compete for market share by using the same basic approach in all foreign markets.

group support system (GSS) software Software that allows participants to submit ideas anonymously during electronic brainstorming sessions.

growth-oriented vision A plan that helps a firm crystallize the importance of growth for its stakeholders and ensures that its major decisions are made with growth in mind.

heterogeneous team A team whose individual members are diverse in terms of their abilities and experiences.

historical financial statements Financial statements of a firm that reflect past performance and are usually prepared on a quarterly and annual basis.

homogenous team A team whose individual members' areas of expertise are very similar to one another.

idea A thought, impression, or notion.

idea bank A physical or digital repository for storing ideas

idea–expression dichotomy The legal principle describing the concept that although an idea is not able to be copyrighted, the specific expression of an idea is.

illiquid Describes stock in both closely held and private corporations, meaning that it typically isn't easy to find a buyer for the stock.

improving an existing product or service Enhancing a product or service's quality by making it larger or smaller, making it easier to use, or making it more up-to-date, thereby increasing its value and price potential.

income statement Financial statement that reflects the results of the operations of a firm over a specified period of time prepared on a monthly, quarterly, or annual basis.

individual franchise agreement The most common type of franchise arrangement, which involves the sale of a single franchise for a specific location.

industry A group of firms producing a similar product or service, such as airlines, fitness drinks, or electronic games.

industry analysis Business research that focuses on the potential of an industry.

industry consolidation The primary opportunity existing for start-ups in fragmented industries to establish leadership when smaller companies are typically acquired or go out of business to give way to a handful of larger companies that take over the majority of the business.

industry/market feasibility analysis An assessment of the overall appeal of the market for the product or service being proposed.

initial public offering (IPO) The first sale of a company's stock to the public and an important milestone for a firm for four reasons: It is a way to raise equity capital; it raises a firm's public profile; it is a liquidity event; and it creates another form of currency (company stock) that can be used to grow the company.

innovation The process of creating something new, which is central to the entrepreneurial process.

inside director A person on a firm's board of directors who is also an officer of the firm.

intellectual property Any product of human intellect, imagination, creativity, or inventiveness that is intangible but has value in the marketplace and can be protected through tools such as patents, trademarks, copyrights, and trade secrets.

intellectual property audit A firm's assessment of the intellectual property it owns.

intent-to-use trademark application An application based on the applicant's intention to register and use a trademark.

internal growth strategies Growth strategies that rely on efforts generated within the firm itself, such as new product development, other product-related strategies, or international expansion.

international new ventures Businesses that, from inception, seek to derive significant competitive advantage by using their resources to sell their products or services in multiple countries.

intranet A privately maintained Internet site that can be accessed only by authorized users.

invention log book Documentation of the dates and activities related to the development of a particular invention.

inventory A company's merchandise, raw materials, and products waiting to be sold.

investing activities Activities that include the purchase, sale, or investment in fixed assets, such as real estate and buildings.

investment bank A financial institution that acts as an underwriter or agent for a firm issuing securities.

joint venture An entity created when two or more firms pool a portion of their resources to create a separate, jointly owned organization.

leadership strategy A competitive strategy in which the firm tries to become the dominant player in the industry.

lease A written agreement in which the owner of a piece of property allows an individual or business to use the property for a specified period of time in exchange for regular payments.

liability of newness Situation that often causes new firms to falter because the people who start the firms can't adjust quickly enough to their new roles, and because the firm lacks a "track record" with customers and suppliers.

licensee A company that purchases the right to use another company's intellectual property.

licensing The granting of permission by one company to another company to use a specific form of its intellectual property under clearly defined conditions.

licensing agreement The formal contract between a licensor and a licensee.

licensor The company that owns the intellectual property in a licensing agreement.

lifestyle firms Businesses that provide their owners the opportunity to pursue a particular lifestyle and earn a living while doing so (e.g., ski instructors, golf pros, and tour guides).

limited liability company (LLC) A form of business organization that combines the limited liability advantage of the corporation with the tax advantages of the partnership.

limited partnership A modified form of a general partnership that includes two classes of owners: general partners and limited partners. Similar to a general partnership, the general partners are liable for the debts and obligations of the partnership, but the limited partners are liable only up to the amount of their investment. The limited partners may not exercise any significant control over the organization without jeopardizing their limited liability status.

link joint venture A joint venture in which the position of the parties is not symmetrical and the objectives of the partners may diverge.

liquidity The ability to sell a business or other asset quickly at a price that is close to its market value; also a company's ability to meet its short-term financial obligations.

liquidity event An occurrence such as a new venture going public, finding a buyer, or being acquired by another company that converts some or all of a company's stock into cash.

liquid market Describes a market in which stock can be bought and sold fairly easily through an organized exchange.

long-term liabilities Notes or loans that are repayable beyond one year, including liabilities associated with purchasing real estate, buildings, and equipment.

love money Contributions by friends and family for new ventures, which can consist of outright gifts, loans, or investments but often are in the form of forgone or delayed compensation or reduced or free rent.

managerial capacity problem The problem that arises when the growth of a firm is limited by the managerial capacity (i.e., personnel, expertise, and intellectual resources) that a firm has available to implement new business ideas.

managerial services The routine functions of the firm that facilitate the profitable execution of new opportunities.

marketing alliances Alliances that typically match a company with a distribution system in order to increase sales of a product or service.

marketing mix The set of controllable, tactical marketing tools that a firm uses to produce the response it wants in the target market; typically organized around the four Ps—product, price, promotion, and place (or distribution).

market leadership The position of a firm when it is the number-one or the number-two firm in an industry or niche market in terms of sales volume.

market penetration strategy A strategy designed to increase the sales of a product or service through greater marketing efforts or through increased production capacity and efficiency.

market segmentation The process of studying the industry in which a firm intends to compete to determine the different potential target markets in that industry.

master franchise agreement Similar to an area franchise agreement, but in addition to having the right to operate a specific number of locations in a particular area, the franchisee also has the right to offer and sell the franchise to other people in the area.

mature industry An industry that is experiencing slow or no increase in demand, has numerous repeat (rather than new) customers, and has limited product innovation.

media coverage Mention of a firm in either print media, such as newspapers or magazines, or broadcast media, such as radio or television.

merchandise and character licensing The licensing of a recognized trademark or brand, which the licensor typically controls through a registered trademark or copyright.

merger The pooling of interests to combine two or more firms into one.

milestone In a business plan context, a noteworthy event in the past or future development of a business.

mission statement A statement that describes why a firm exists and what its business model is supposed to accomplish.

moderate risk takers Entrepreneurs who are often characterized as willing to assume a moderate amount of risk in business, being neither overly conservative nor likely to gamble.

moral hazard A problem a firm faces as it grows and adds personnel that new hires typically will not have the same ownership incentives or be as motivated to work hard as the original founders.

multidomestic strategy An international expansion strategy in which firms compete for market share on a country-by-country basis and vary their product or services offerings to meet the demands of the local market.

multiple unit franchisee An individual who owns and operates more than one outlet of the same franchisor, whether through an area or a master franchise agreement.

net sales Total sales minus allowances for returned goods and discounts.

network entrepreneurs Entrepreneurs who identified their idea through social contacts.

networking Building and maintaining relationships with people whose interests are similar or whose relationship could bring advantages to a firm.

new product development The creation and sale of new products (or services) as a means of increasing a firm's revenues.

news conference The live dissemination of new information by a firm to invited media.

new venture team The group of founders, key employees, and advisors that moves a new venture from an idea to a fully functioning firm.

niche market A place within a large market segment that represents a narrow group of customers with similar interests.

niche strategy A marketing strategy that focuses on a narrow segment of the industry that might be encouraged to grow through product or process innovation.

noncompete agreement Agreement that prevents an individual from competing against a former employer for a specific period of time.

nondisclosure agreement A promise made by an employee or another party (such as a supplier) to not disclose a company's trade secrets.

operating activities Activities that affect net income (or loss), depreciation, and changes in current assets and current liabilities other than cash and short-term debt.

operating expenses Marketing, administrative costs, and other expenses not directly related to producing a product or service.

operational business plan A blueprint for a company's operations primarily meant for an internal audience.

opportunity A favorable set of circumstances that creates a need for a new product, service, or business.

opportunity recognition The process of perceiving the possibility of a profitable new business or a new product or service.

organic growth Internally generated growth within a firm that does not rely on outside intervention.

organizational chart A graphic representation of how authority and responsibility are distributed within a company.

organizational feasibility analysis A study conducted to determine whether a proposed business has sufficient management expertise, organizational competence, and resources to be successful.

other assets Miscellaneous assets including accumulated goodwill.

outside director Someone on a firm's board of directors who is not employed by the firm.

outsourcing Work that is done for a company by people other than the company's full-time employees.

owner's equity The equity invested in the business by its owner(s) plus the accumulated earnings retained by the business after paying dividends.

pace of growth The rate at which a firm is growing on an annual basis.

partnership agreement A document that details the responsibilities and the ownership shares of the partners involved with an organization.

passion for the business An entrepreneur's belief that his or her business will positively influence people's lives; one of the characteristics of successful entrepreneurs

patent A grant from the federal government conferring the rights to exclude others from making, selling, or using an invention for the term of the patent.

percent of sales method A method for expressing each expense item as a percentage of sales.

piercing the corporate veil The chain of effects that occurs if the owners of a corporation don't file their yearly paperwork, neglect to pay their annual fees, or commit fraud, so that a court could ignore the fact that a corporation has been established, and the owners could be held personally liable for actions of the corporation.

place The marketing mix category that encompasses all of the activities that move a firm's product from its place of origin to the consumer (*also* distribution).

plant patents Patents that protect new varieties of plants that can be reproduced asexually by grafting or cross-breeding rather than by planting seeds.

position How the entire company is situated relative to its competitors.

preferred stock Stock that is typically issued to conservative investors, who have preferential rights over common stockholders in regard to dividends and to the assets of the corporation in the event of liquidation.

preliminary prospectus A document issued by an investment bank that describes the potential offering to the general public while the SEC is conducting an investigation of the offering (*also* red herring).

press kit A folder typically distributed to journalists and made available online that contains background information about a company and includes a list of the company's most recent accomplishments.

press release An announcement made by a firm that is circulated to the press.

price The amount of money consumers pay to buy a product; one of the four Ps in a company's marketing mix.

price/earnings (P/E) ratio A simple ratio that measures the price of a company's stock against its earnings.

price–quality attribution The assumption consumers naturally make that the higher-priced product is also the better-quality product.

primary research Research that is original and is collected firsthand by the entrepreneur by, for example, talking to potential customers and key industry participants.

prior entrepreneurial experience Prior start-up experience found to be one of the most consistent predictors of future entrepreneurial performance.

private corporation A corporation in which all the shares are held by a few shareholders, such as management or family members, and the stock is not publicly traded.

private placement A variation of the IPO in which there is a direct sale of an issue of securities to a large institutional investor.

product The element of the marketing mix that is the good or service a company offers to its target market; often thought of as something having physical form.

product and trademark franchise An arrangement under which the franchisor grants to the franchisee the right to buy its products and use its trade name.

product/customer focus A defining characteristic of successful entrepreneurs that emphasizes producing good products with the capability to satisfy customers.

productive opportunity set The set of opportunities the firm feels it is capable of pursuing.

product line extension strategy A strategy that involves making additional versions of a product so it will appeal to different clientele.

product/market scope A range that defines the products and markets on which a firm will concentrate.

product opportunity gap A gap between what is currently on the market and the possibility for a new or significantly improved product, service, or business that results from emerging trends.

product/service feasibility analysis An assessment of the overall appeal of the product or service being proposed.

profitability The ability to earn a profit.

profit margin A measure of a firm's return on sales that is computed by dividing net income by average net sales.

pro forma balance sheet Financial statement that shows a projected snapshot of a company's assets, liabilities, and owner's equity at a specific point in time.

pro forma financial statements Projections for future periods, based on a firm's forecasts, and are typically completed for two to three years in the future.

pro forma income statement Financial statement that shows the projected results of the operations of a firm over a specific period.

pro forma statement of cash flows Financial statement that shows the projected flow of cash into and out of a company for a specific period.

promotion The marketing mix category that includes the activities planned by a company to communicate the merits of its product to its target market with the goal of persuading people to buy the product.

prototyping An iterative process in which the prototype as a model of the product or service is continually refined until the customer and designer agree on the final design.

public corporation A corporation that is listed on a major stock exchange, such as the New York Stock Exchange or the NASDAQ, in which owners can sell their shares at almost a moment's notice.

public relations The efforts a company makes to establish and maintain a certain image with the public through networking with journalists and others to try to interest them in saying or writing good things about the company and its products.

rapid-growth firm A firm that maintains a growth rate of at least 20 percent per year for five consecutive years.

reference account An early user of a firm's product who is willing to give a testimonial regarding his or her experience with the product.

regression analysis A statistical technique used to find relationships between variables for the purpose of predicting future values.

relevant industry experience Experience in the same industry as an entrepreneur's current venture that includes a network of industry contacts and an understanding of the subtleties of the industry.

resource leverage The process of adapting a company's core competencies to exploit new opportunities.

road show A whirlwind tour taken by the top management team of a firm wanting to go public that consists of meetings in key cities where the firm presents its business plan to groups of investors.

rounds Stages of subsequent investments made in a firm by investors.

salary-substitute firms Small firms that afford their owners a level of income similar to what they would earn in a conventional job (e.g., dry cleaners, convenience stores, restaurants, accounting firms, retail stores, and hair styling salons).

sales forecast A projection of a firm's sales for a specified period (such as a year), although most firms forecast their sales for two to five years into the future.

SBA Guaranteed Loan Program An important source of funding for small businesses in general in which approximately 50 percent of the 9,000 banks in the United States participate.

SBIR program Small Business Innovation Research (SBIR) competitive grant program that provides over $1 billion per year to small businesses for early-stage and development projects.

SBTT program Small Business Technology Transfer (SBTT) competitive grant program for collaborative research projects.

scalable business model A business model in which increased revenues cost less to deliver than current revenues, so profit margins increase as sales go up.

scale joint venture A joint venture in which the partners collaborate at a single point in the value chain to gain economies of scale in production or distribution.

secondary research Data collected previously by someone else for a different purpose.

second-mover advantage The advantage the second company has in entering a market because of the opportunity to study the mistakes that were made by the first mover.

seed money The initial investment made in a firm.

self-selected opinion poll A survey whose participants have not been chosen by random but who have selected themselves to be respondents often because they have either strong positive or negative feelings about a particular product or topic; data may not be representative of the larger population.

serendipitous discovery A chance discovery made by someone with a prepared mind.

service An activity or benefit that is intangible and does not take on a physical form, such as an airplane trip or advice from an attorney.

service marks Similar to ordinary trademarks but used to identify the services or intangible activities of a business rather than a business's physical product.

shareholders Owners of a corporation who are shielded from personal liability for the debts and obligations of the corporation.

signaling The act of a high-quality individual agreeing to serve on a company's board of directors, which indicates that the individual believes that the company has the potential to be successful.

"skin in the game" The amount of money the management team has invested in a new venture.

solo entrepreneurs Entrepreneurs who identified their business idea on their own.

sole proprietorship The simplest form of business organization involving one person, in which the owner maintains complete control over the business and business losses can be deducted against the owner's personal tax return.

sources and uses of funds statement The explanation within the financial section of a business plan of the funding that will be needed by the business during the next three to five years, along with details of how the funds will be used.

spin-in An investment made by a larger firm with a small equity stake by acquiring a smaller firm.

spin-out The opposite of a spin-in that occurs when a larger company divests itself of one of its smaller divisions.

stability The strength and vigor of the firm's overall financial posture.

statement of cash flows A financial statement summarizing the changes in a firm's cash position for a specified period of time and detailing why the changes occurred. Similar to a month-end bank statement, it reveals how much cash is on hand at the end of the month as well as how the cash was acquired and spent during the month.

stealth mode Formulating initial business plans in secret.

stock options Special form of incentive compensation providing employees the option or right to buy a certain number of shares of their company's stock at a stated price over a certain period of time.

strategic alliance A partnership between two or more firms developed to achieve a specific goal.

strategic assets Anything rare and valuable that a firm owns, including plant and equipment, location, brands, patents, customer data, a highly qualified staff, and distinctive partnerships.

strong-tie relationships Relationships characterized by frequent interaction that form between like-minded individuals such as co-workers, friends, and spouses, which tend to reinforce insights and ideas the individuals already have and, therefore, are not likely to introduce new ideas.

subchapter S corporation A form of business organization that combines the advantages of a partnership and a C corporation; similar to a partnership, in that the profits and losses of the business are not subject to double taxation, and similar to a corporation, in that the owners are not subject to personal liability for the behavior of the business.

subfranchisees The people who buy franchises from master franchisees.

summary business plan A business plan 10 to 15 pages long that works best for companies very early in their development that are not prepared to write a full plan.

supplier A company or vendor that provides parts or services to another company.

supply chain A network of all the companies that participate in the production of a product, from the acquisition of raw materials to the final sale.

supply chain management The coordination of the flow of all information, money, and material that moves through a product's supply chain.

survey A method of gathering information from a sample of individuals usually representing just a fraction of the population being studied.

sustainable competitive advantage A combination of a company's core competencies and strategic assets achieved by implementing a unique value-creating strategy.

sustained growth Growth in both revenues and profits over an extended period of time.

sweat equity The value of the time and effort that a founder puts into a new firm.

tagline A phrase that is used consistently in a company's literature, advertisements, promotions, stationary, and even invoices to develop and to reinforce the position the company has staked out in its market.

target In an acquisition, the firm that is acquired.

target market The limited group of individuals or businesses that a firm goes after or tries to appeal to at a certain point in time.

technological alliances Business alliances that cooperate in R&D, engineering, and manufacturing.

technology licensing The licensing of proprietary technology, which the licensor typically controls by virtue of a utility patent.

trademark Any word, name, symbol, or device used to identify the source or origin of products or services and to distinguish those products and services from others.

trade secret Any formula, pattern, physical device, idea, process, or other information that provides the owner of the information with a competitive advantage in the marketplace.

trade show An event at which the goods or services in a specific industry are exhibited and demonstrated.

triggering event The event that prompts an individual to become an entrepreneur (e.g., losing a job, inheriting money, accommodating a certain lifestyle).

typosquatting A form of domain name abuse in which people making a common typographical error when typing in a domain name of a legitimate organization are redirected to another site.

Uniform Franchise Offering Circular (UFOC) Accepted in all 50 states and parts of Canada, a lengthy document that contains 23 categories of information giving a prospective franchisee a broad base of information about the background and financial health of the franchisor.

Uniform Trade Secrets Act Drafted in 1979 by a special commission in an attempt to set nationwide standards for trade secret legislation; although the majority of states have adopted the act, most revised it, resulting in a wide disparity among states in regard to trade secret legislation and enforcement.

usability testing Testing that requires the user of a product to perform certain tasks in order to measure the product's ease of use and the user's perception of the experience.

utility patents The most common type of patent covering what we generally think of as new inventions that must be useful, must be novel in relation to prior arts in the field, and must not be obvious to a person of ordinary skill in the field.

value Relative worth, importance, or utility.

value-based pricing A pricing method in which the list price is determined by estimating what consumers are willing to pay for a product and then backing off a bit to provide a cushion.

value chain The string of activities that moves a product from the raw material stage, through manufacturing and distribution, and ultimately to the end user.

variable costs The costs that are not fixed that a company incurs as it makes sales.

venture capital The money that is invested by venture capital firms in start-ups and small businesses with exceptional growth potential.

venture-leasing firms Firms that act as brokers, bringing the parties involved in a lease together (e.g., firms acquainted with the producers of specialized equipment match these producers with new ventures that are in need of the equipment).

viral marketing A new marketing technique that facilitates and encourages people to pass along a marketing message about a particular product or service.

weak-tie relationships Relationships characterized by infrequent interaction that form between casual acquaintances who do not have a lot in common and, therefore, may be the source of completely new ideas.

window of opportunity The time period in which a firm or an entrepreneur can realistically enter a new market.

working capital A firm's current assets minus its current liabilities.

Aaker, D. A., 262*n*, 452
Abate, T., 216*n*, 232*n*, 246*n*, 450, 451, 452
Abell, A., 28*n*, 442
Abrams, R., 215*n*, 218*n*, 450
Adams, R., 222*n*, 450
Adams, Rob, 8*n*, 10, 35*n*, 52*n*, 125*n*, 126*n*, 132*n*, 138*n*, 441, 443, 444, 447, 448
Adams, Rod, 34
Ahrens, T., 320*n*, 321*n*, 454
Akers, David, 203–204
Allen, J., 111*n*, 309*n*, 312*n*, 446, 453
Alon, I., 356*n*, 455
Anderson, Carl, 409
Anderson, Philip, 439
Andreessen, Marc, 7
Anton, Maria, 254
Ardichvili, A., 30*n*, 37*n*, 129*n*, 443, 447
Armstrong, G., 263*n*, 264*n*, 265*n*, 452
Aronson, Adam, 47
Arrow, A. K., 155*n*, 448
Aspatore, J. R., 28*n*, 442
Astin, A., 311*n*, 453
Atkison, R. D., 16*n*, 442
Auken, H. Van, 232*n*, 451
Autio, E., 4*n*, 11*n*, 14*n*, 441, 442
Aydin, N., 376*n*, 456

Backman-Robertson, David, 411
Bagley, C. E., 190*n*, 279*n*, 289*n*, 290*n*, 449, 453
Bailey, J., 257*n*
Baillie, S., 10*n*, 441, 442
Bajarin, Tim, 435
Bannick, Matt, 434
Baran, Paul, 385
Barger, David, 80
Barlett, S., 206*n*, 450
Barney, J. A., 85*n*, 111*n*, 445, 446
Barrett, W. P., 316*n*, 454
Barringer, B. R., 5*n*, 112*n*, 114*n*, 246*n*, 321*n*, 345*n*, 441, 446, 447, 452, 454
Barry, John, 290
Barton, B., 267*n*, 452
Baylis, Trevor, 351
Bearse, P. J., 12*n*, 442
Beasley, John, 24
Bedbury, S., 259*n*, 452
Behar, Howard, 308
Beirne, David, 432, 433
Belasco, J., 112*n*, 446
Benjamin, G. A., 64*n*, 206*n*, 235*n*, 237*n*, 445, 450, 451
Bennett, J., 377*n*
Bennett, R., 363*n*, 455
Bergeron, P. G., 148*n*, 149*n*, 448
Bermingham, Dick, 97
Bertiger, Bary, 53
Besser, H., 388*n*, 456
Bettcher, K. E., 16*n*, 442
Bezos, Jeff, 10, 28, 302–303, 430
Bhatia, Sabeer, 386, 387, 388, 389, 390
Bhide, A. V., 53*n*, 235*n*, 311*n*, 444, 451, 453
Bichara, Axel, 422–429

Birkeland, P., 360*n*, 455
Bluedorn, A. C., 5*n*, 441
Bolton, B., 5*n*, 441
Bond, Rodney, 97
Bornstein, J. M., 214*n*, 450
Bosack, Leonard, 34, 229–230, 233
Bouchoux, D. E., 194*n*, 278*n*, 282*n*, 283*n*, 285*n*, 449, 452, 453
Boulton, B., 208*n*, 450
Bovet, D., 109*n*, 112*n*, 446, 447
Bowie, N. E., 201
Boyce, Dick, 432
Boyd, H., 255*n*, 452
Boyett, J. H., 12*n*, 265*n*, 442, 452
Boyett, J. T., 12*n*, 265*n*, 442, 452
Bradach, J. L., 360*n*, 368*n*, 455, 456
Bramante, J., 128*n*, 447
Brandt, Gary, 351
Branson, Jim, 175–176
Branson, Richard, 4–6, 7, 441
Brealty, R. A., 188*n*, 449
Breen, B., 147*n*, 148*n*, 448
Breen, Peter, 27
Brickley, J., 363*n*, 456
Briggs, Gary, 434
Brigham, E. F., 161*n*, 162*n*, 184*n*, 190*n*, 448, 449
Brock, Oliver, 409
Bromiley, P., 310*n*, 453
Bronson, G., 386*n*, 387*n*, 389*n*, 456
Brown, C. A., 177*n*, 449
Brown, Roger, 120
Bunnell, D., 3*n*, 4*n*, 5*n*, 230*n*, 441, 450
Burns, Tim, 238
Bygrave, Bill, 406
Bygrave, W. D., 4*n*, 11*n*, 14*n*, 18*n*, 28*n*, 37*n*, 441, 442, 443, 444

Callahan, T. J., 95
Cardozo, R., 30*n*, 37*n*, 129*n*, 443, 447
Cardullo, M., 246*n*, 451
Cardullo, P. E., 343*n*, 455
Carlsson, B, 16*n*, 442
Carnoy, D., 7*n*, 441
Carter, R., 232*n*, 451
Case, J., 36*n*, 443
Cavender, S., 385*n*, 456
Certo, S., 134*n*, 448
Chan, Y. P., 11
Chandler, G. N., 231*n*, 450
Charan, R., 133*n*, 134*n*, 448
Charm, Maximilian, 403
Chase, Robin, 199
Chaudhuri, S., 340*n*, 454
Cheeseman, H. R., 294*n*
Chen, M.-J., 89*n*, 446
Chesbrough, H. W., 100*n*, 264, 446, 452
Chishti, Zia, 48
Chrisman, J. J., 5*n*, 441
Christensen, C. M., 7*n*, 441
Clancy, K. J., 258*n*, 452
Clark, D., 294*n*
Clark, K. B., 62*n*, 445

Clarkson, K. W., 180*n*, 449
Clarysee, B., 129*n*, 447
Clegg, Steward R., 85*n*, 445
Clum, Kristina, 357
Cohen, Jake, 398
Colbourne, C. H., 177*n*, 449
Collin, Jim, 435
Collins, Ed, 23
Cook, Scott, 35, 51, 52, 64
Cooper, A. C., 36*n*, 42*n*, 129*n*, 443, 444, 447
Cooper, C., 7*n*, 441
Cooper, R. G., 41*n*, 57*n*, 444
Cornish, Darryl, 96
Court, R. H., 16*n*, 442
Coutler, M., 63*n*, 445
Covin, J. G., 5*n*, 441
Cox, C., 7*n*, 441
Cox, L., 11*n*, 14*n*, 442
Crawford, C. M., 34*n*, 58*n*, 443, 444
Crosby, J. V., 162*n*, 448
Cross, F. B., 180*n*, 449
Crossan, M. M., 347*n*, 455
Crozier, L. M., 315*n*, 453
Csikszentmihalyi, M., 37*n*, 39*n*, 444
Cummings, A., 43*n*, 444

Daily, C., 134*n*, 448
DalleMolle, Daniel, 157
Dalton, D., 134*n*, 448
D'Amore, Rich, 428
Dark, F., 363*n*, 456
Darlin, D., 318*n*
Das, S., 346*n*, 455
Dauchy, C. E., 190*n*, 279*n*, 289*n*, 290*n*, 449, 453
Davidsson, P., 11*n*, 37*n*, 442, 443
Davila, A., 138*n*, 448
Day, G. S., 111*n*, 446
De Benedetto, C. A., 58*n*, 444
Deeds, D. L., 346*n*, 455
Dell, M., 7, 8, 9, 13, 35, 99–100, 102, 106, 109–110, 113*n*, 347*n*, 446, 447, 455
Demaria, R., 204, 450
Demos, Steve, 87
Dennis, W., 36*n*, 443
Desio, Anthony, 35
Di Benedetto, C. A., 34*n*, 443
Diorio, S. H., 31*n*, 443
Donovan, J. M., 320*n*, 321*n*, 454
Doorley, Thomas L., III, 320*n*, 321, 454
Dorr, 239*n*, 451
Dowling, M. J., 131*n*, 448
Draper, Tim, 288, 456
Drebes, Larry, 387
Dubinsky, Donna, 23
Dunkelberg, W., 36*n*, 443
Dunleavy, J., 128*n*, 447
DuPont, Ben, 297
Dutta, Rajiv, 438

Easton, J., 326
Edgett, S. J., 41*n*, 42*n*, 57*n*, 444
Ehrhardt, M. C., 184*n*, 190*n*, 449

Eisenhardt, K., 128n, 129n, 447
Ellison, Larry, 8
Eng, S., 220n, 450
Eriksen, B., 77n, 445
Everett-Church, Ray, 412
Eyler, John, 322

Fanning, Shawn, 293, 294
Farmian, John, 402
Farrell, L., 8n, 12n, 182n, 441, 442, 449
Ferrell, O. C., 116n, 447
Fesser, H., 128n, 447
Fields, Debbie, 12
Filo, David, 35, 208, 286
Finkelstein, Sydney, 53
Fiorina, Carly, 430
Fjeldstad, O. D., 105n, 446
Flint, Jon, 428
Ford, B. R., 214n, 450
Forelle, C., 334n
Foster, G., 138n, 448
Foster, S. T., 58n, 445
Foster, T., 42n, 265n, 444, 452
Fowler, W. B., 365
Fraser, J. A., 182n, 449
Freear, J., 233n, 451
Freivald, Matt, 437

Gaglio, C. M., 33n, 36n, 443
Gardner, John, 33
Garvis, D., 337n, 454
Gates, Bill, 8, 13, 152n, 389, 448
Geffen, David, 190
Geis, G. S., 347n, 348n, 455
Geis, G. T., 347n, 348n, 455
Gibson, B., 231n, 450
Gimein, M., 389n, 456
Gimeno-Gascon, F. J., 129n, 447
Gittell, J. H., 150n, 448
Glaser, Rob, 35
Goizueta, Roberto, 89
Goldman, Seth, 186
Goldsmith, M., 112n, 446
Gompers, P. A., 60n, 445
Goodman, Edwin A., 220
Gorman, M., 138n, 448
Gosi, G., 53n, 444
Gove, A., 279n, 285n, 453
Granovetter, M., 37n, 443
Greenberg, Robert, 318
Griffith, Jimmy, 430–431
Grimes, A., 239n, 240n, 451
Grottanelli, Ron, 304
Grove, Andy, 10, 441
Gulati, R., 308n, 453
Gumpert, D. E., 207n, 209n, 450
Gundling, E., 331n, 454
Gupta, M., 138n, 448

Haines, G., 243n, 451
Hale, D., 239n, 451
Hall, D., 64n, 445
Hall, Jay, 24
Hambrick, D. C., 315n, 453
Hamel, G., 102n, 108, 111n, 115n, 206n, 446, 447, 450
Hamm, S., 7n, 441
Hammer, M., 15n, 442
Hanks, S. H., 231n, 450

Hanlin, Russell, 160
Hansell, S., 303n
Hansen, A., 37n, 443
Harami, Chris, 400–408
Harbrecht, D., 390n, 456
Hardy, Cynthia, 85n, 445
Harris, Scott, 426–427
Harrison, J. S., 246n, 345n, 452
Harvey, Kevin, 326
Haseltine, William, 282
Hastings, Reed, 121
Hatlestad, L., 388n, 390n, 456
Hawkins, Jeff, 23
Hawkins, R., 104n, 446
Hawkins, Trip, 204, 206
Hay, M., 11n, 14n, 315n, 442, 453
Hazleton, L., 10n, 441
Heavin, Diane, 253
Heavin, Gary, 253, 254–255
Hein, K., 217n
Heller, Michael, 111n, 450
Henderson, J. C., 108n, 446
Henderson, R., 322n, 454
Hennart, J. F., 347n, 455
Hennessey, R., 241n, 451
Hesseldahl, A., 256n, 452
Hesterly, W., 85n, 445
Hewlett, Bill, 309
Heyler, P. B., 161n, 448
Hicks, N. J., 262n, 452
Hiestand, M., 55n, 444
Hill, C. W. L., 346n, 455
Hills, G. E., 36n, 37n, 443, 444
Hirschtick, Jon, 422–429
Hitt, M. A., 5n, 55n, 108n, 441, 444, 446
Honig, B., 11n, 37n, 442, 443
Hopkins, Samuel, 182
Horkan, G., 317n, 454
Hoskisson, R. E., 55n, 444
Houston, J. F., 161n, 162n, 448
Howland, Bill, 154
Hubbard, G., 310n, 453
Huffman, S., 308n, 453
Hussey, D., 5n, 441
Huston, Chad, 96
Hybels, R. C., 37n, 443
Hyman, J., 186n

Inkpen, A., 347n, 455
Ireland, R. D., 5n, 55n, 108n, 441, 444, 446

Jaffe, A., 322n, 454
Jager, R. D., 7n, 9n, 52n, 64n, 441, 444, 445
James, C., 138n, 448
Jarillo, J. C., 5n, 441
Jaruzelski, B., 317n, 454
Jennings, R., 7n, 441
Jentz, G. A., 180n, 449
Jobs, S., 8, 9, 13, 233, 386
Jolly, V. K., 356n, 455
Jones, Mike, 413
Jorgensen, Jim, 409–420, 414
Joyce, W., 318n
Jurvetson, Steve, 206, 388n, 456

Kacker, M., 376n, 456
Kaiser, L. F., 4n, 441
Kaiser, M. B., 4n, 441
Kallery, David, 88

Kallianpur, A., 56n, 258n, 444, 452
Kamer, Dean, 208
Kamshad, K., 315n, 453
Kao, J. J., 37n, 444
Kapor, Mitch, 237
Katz, J. A., 36n, 443
Katzenberg, Jeffrey, 190
Kaufman, L., 303n
Kearney, A. T., 321n, 454
Keighley, G., 79n, 232n, 445, 451
Kelly, A., 363n, 455
Kelly, K., 241n, 451
Kenny, R., 135n, 448
Killing, P., 330n, 454
Kingsley, G., 37n, 443
Kirzner, I. M., 36n, 443
Kirzner, L., 37n, 443
Knight, H. J., 282n, 453
Knudsen, T., 77n, 445
Koehn, N., 10n, 441, 442
Kok, G., 114n, 447
Koller, R. H., 37n, 443
Kollock, Peter, 430
Kotler, P., 33, 33n, 89n, 90, 257, 260n, 263n, 264n, 265n, 267n, 443, 446, 452
Kozlowski, Dennis, 438n, 458
Kramer, Stephen, 393–399
Krass, P., 9n, 80n, 441, 445
Krieg, P. C., 258n, 452
Kufahl, P., 255n, 452
Kuratko, D. F., 5n, 441

LaMacchia, John, 325
Lane, M. J., 150n, 448
Lane, Ray, 317
Larreche, J., 255n, 452
Laurie, D., 240n, 340n, 451, 455
Lawrence, B., 129n, 447
LeClair, D. T., 182n, 449
Leister, B., 43n, 444
Leonard, S., 201
Lerner, J., 60n, 138n, 445, 448
Lerner, Sandra, 33, 229–230, 233
Levitt, T., 89n, 446
Li, K. O., 347n, 455
Lipman, F., 241n, 451
Locke, E. A., 10n, 441
Lodish, L. M., 56n, 258n, 260n, 266n, 444, 452
London, Michael, 393–399
Long, W., 37n, 443
Looser, U., 214n, 218n, 450
Lougheed, Kirk, 230
Lovallo, D., 53n, 444
Lucier, C. E., 311n, 453
Luecke, R., 3n, 4n, 441
Lumpkin, G. T., 36n, 37n, 443, 444
Lynch, Kevin, 15

Macaluso, N., 322
MacMillian, I., 129n, 447
Madegarian, Kay, 88
Magretta, J., 99n, 100n, 112n, 446, 447
Malecki, E. J., 37n, 443
Malone, M. S., 12n, 442
Malugen, Joe, 326
Mandel, R. P., 177n, 449
March, James G., 127n, 447
Margulis, J., 64n, 206n, 235n, 237n, 445, 450, 451
Markkula, Mike, 237

Martha, J., 109n, 112n, 446, 447
Martin, Daniel, 383
Mason, Linda, 120
Mass, J., 207n, 450
Matathia, R., 262n, 452
Mateschitz, Dietrich, 217
Mathews, A., 294n
McCall, Burton, 351
McCue, Mike, 325
McDougall, P. P., 336n, 454
McGahan, A., 77n, 445
McGee, J. E., 131n, 448
McGrath, M. E., 255n, 452
McKnight, T. K., 60n, 445
McMath, R. M., 260n, 452
McMullan, W. E., 37n, 177n, 143, 149
McNealy, S., 7, 79–80, 386, 437, 445
Meggison, W. L., 131n, 448
Melmon, Rich, 204
Miller, R. L., 180n, 449
Mills, D., 242n
Moore, G., 112n, 446
Moray, N., 129n, 447
Morgan, H. L., 56n, 258n, 444, 452
Morgridge, John P., 230
Morita, Akio, 83
Morris, M., 11n, 442
Morrison, D. J., 234
Mullins, J., 255n, 452
Myers, S. C., 188n, 449

Nadkarni, Shirish, 390
Nalebuff, Barry, 186
Nance-Nash, S., 128n, 447
Narasimha, P. N. S., 129n, 447
Neeleman, David, 75, 80
Neilson, G., 308n, 453
Nelson, K., 183n, 449
Nelson, Zach, 262
Nesheim, J. L., 64n, 111n, 218n, 221n, 222n, 244n, 445, 446, 450, 451
Nicholson, Sean, 181
Nickerson, Nick, 9–10
Nohria, N., 318n
Nord, Walter R., 85n, 445
Nykiel, R. A., 267n, 452

Ochs, E., 327n
Oldham, G. R., 43n, 444
Omidyar, Pierre, 3–4, 5, 7, 430–432, 433, 436, 441
O'Reilly, A., 262n, 452
Ortiz, R., 7n, 9n, 52n, 64n, 441, 444, 445
Oviatt, B. M., 336n, 454
Oxenfeldt, A., 363n, 455

Packard, D., 309, 309n, 453
Park, S. H., 347n, 455
Parker, P., 390n, 456
Parker, Sean, 293, 294
Parrish, Harrison, 326
Patrick, J., 40n, 444
Payne, Michael, 427–428
Penrose, Edith T., 315, 315n, 316, 453, 454
Pereira, J., 279n, 452
Peterson, R. T., 177n, 449
Pinchot, E., 112n, 446
Pinchot, G., 112n, 446
Pohle, Johannes, 409

Porfeli, Joe, 238
Porter, M. E., 77, 78n, 82n, 104n, 108n, 110n, 445, 446
Prado, A. A., 297n
Prahalad, C. K., 111n, 446
Preiser, David, 182
Pride, W. M., 116n, 447
Proulx, Tom, 51, 52
Pui-Wing, Tam, 256n, 455
Purrington, C. A., 16n, 442
Purvin, R. L., 374, 456

Quindlen, R., 12n, 442
Quinn, Bob, 435

Ragas, M. W., 102n, 262n, 446, 452
Ray, S., 30n, 37n, 129n, 443, 447
Read, C., 128n, 447
Reed, C., 97
Reid, G. C., 321n, 454
Reider, R., 161n, 448
Reynolds, P. D., 4n, 11n, 14n, 441, 442
Rich, J. T., 189n, 449
Rich, S. R., 209n, 450
Riding, A., 232n, 237n, 451
Riding, L., 243n, 451
Ries, A., 268, 452
Ries, L., 268, 268n, 452
Riessenback, Jim, 213
Rigdon, J. I., 63n, 445
Roberson, B., 318n
Roberts, E. B., 11n, 442
Roberts, Julie, 194
Roberts, Larry, 385
Roberts, M. J., 67n, 445
Roddick, Anita, 35
Rodengen, J., 87n, 446
Rogers, M., 65n, 445
Rogers, S., 214n, 237n, 241n, 243n, 244n, 450, 451
Rogers, T. J., 6–7
Ronstadt, R., 36n, 443
Rosen, C., 347n, 455
Ross, J., 128n, 447
Rovner, Michael, 8, 222
Rubin, P. H., 358n, 455
Rumelt, R. P., 77n, 445
Russo, M. V., 347n, 455

Sahlman, W. A., 138n, 139n, 448
Salzman, M., 262n, 452
Santullo, Mike, 387
Schlapfer, B., 214n, 218n, 450
Schoonhoven, C., 128n, 129n, 447
Schulman, D., 128n, 447
Schultz, Charles, 35
Schultz, H., 10, 132n, 307–309, 448, 453
Schultz, Sheri, 307
Schumpeter, Joseph, 14, 442
Schuster, J. R., 189n, 449
Schwartz, M. S., 201
Segaller, S., 385n, 456
Segil, L., 112n, 446
Selz, M., 181n
Sen, P. K., 346n, 455
Sengupta, S., 346n, 455
Setz, Greg, 230
Seybold, P. B., 100n, 192n, 260n, 446, 449, 452
Shane, S., 356n, 455

Sharma, P., 5n, 441
Sherman, A. J., 134n, 137n, 182n, 187n, 191n, 244n, 320n, 321n, 340n, 343n, 360n, 366n, 448, 449, 451, 454, 455, 456
Shrader, R. C., 37n, 444
Siebel, Tom, 12, 442
Siegel, E. S., 214n, 450
Silverman, S., 326
Sims, J., 10n, 442
Singer, B., 129n, 447
Singh, G., 13n, 37n, 442, 443
Singh, R. P., 36n, 39n, 443, 444
Sirmon, D. G., 5n, 441
Skoll, Jeff, 4, 431–432, 433
Slevin, D. P., 5n, 441
Slywotzky, A. J., 234
Smith, Fred, 35
Smith, I., 237, 237n, 451
Smith, J., 312n, 321n, 386, 387, 388, 389, 389n, 453, 454, 456
Sohl, J., 233n, 451
Souza, Aaron, 181
Spiegel, Arlene, 398, 403, 407, 408
Spielberg, Steven, 190
Stabell, C. B., 105n, 446
Stainman, J., 189n, 449
Steiner, David, 438
Stevenson, H. H., 5n, 67n, 139n, 441, 445, 448
Stinchcombe, A., 127n, 447
Stone, F. M., 335n, 454
Strauss, Oron, 238, 238n, 451
Streeter, Ron, 413
Stross, R. E., 3n, 138n, 236, 441, 448, 451
Sun-tzu, 77, 77n, 445

Tabrizi, B., 340n, 454
Tan, K., 55n, 444
Tapiro, Michael, 400
Taub, P., 33n, 36n, 443
Taylor, R., 209n
Tesoriero, H. W., 253n, 254n, 452
Thomas, P., 365n
Thompson, J., 5n, 208n, 441, 450
Thompson, K., 189n, 449
Thurm, S., 303n
Timmons, J. A., 15n, 28n, 231n, 442, 443, 450
Tomlinson, Ray, 385
Trajtenberg, M., 322n, 454
Treacy, M., 10n, 442
Tregoe, Benjamin, 7–8
Trevino, L., 183n, 449
Tudisco, Geoffrey M., 27–28, 36
Turner, Ted, 12

Useem, Michael, 438

Valentine, D., 60, 208, 230, 237, 450
Vance, D. E., 150n, 448
Van Slyke, J. R., 67n, 445
Venkatraman, N., 108n, 446
Vesper, K., 36n, 443
Vivarelli, M., 64n, 445
Volkholz, K., 317n, 454

Waaden, Mark von, 95–96
Waitt, Ted, 233
Walker, Jay, 103
Walker, O., 255n, 452
Walsh, Michael, 64

Walton, Luke, 318
Walton, Sam, 12, 442
Washington, George, 282
Waters, J., 230n, 450
Watson, Carlos, 394
Webb, Maynard, 434
Welch, Jack, 312, 453
Wensley, R., 111n, 446
Westfield, Bill, 130
Westly, Steve, 437
Wetzel, W., 233n, 451
Wheelwright, S. C., 62n, 445
Whitman, Meg, 7, 211, 430–440, 457

Widleman, L., 114n, 447
Willard, G., 128n, 447
Williams, C., 12n, 442
Wilson, D. L., 390n, 456
Wilson, J. I., 204, 450
Winfrey, Oprah, 430
Wingfield, N., 102n, 446
Wirth, Kelsey, 48
Wodehouse, P.G., 329
Wolff, G., 282n, 453
Woo, C. Y., 36n, 129n, 443, 447
Wozniak, Steve, 233
Wrubel, Rob, 347

Yang, J., 35, 186n, 208, 286, 438n, 458
Yang, Jerry, 7
Yarkin, Burt, 356
Young, Bob, 10

Zahra, S., 337n, 454
Zamani, Payam, 88
Zemann, L., 129n, 447
Zenger, T., 129n, 447
Zingheim, P. K., 189n, 449
Zook, C., 111n, 309n, 312n, 315n, 446, 453
Zuffante, Robert, 426–427
Zyman, S., 261n, 452

Access to distribution channels, 79
Accountability, demonstrating to investors and
    shareholders, 183
Accounts receivable, 149
Acquirer, 340
Acquisitions, 340–343
    finding appropriate candidate, 340–341
    steps involved in, 341–342
Adverse selection, 315
Advertising, 266–267
Advisory board, 134. *See also* Board of directors
    attorney on, 180
    members of, 180
    online meetings for, 137
Agency theory, 363
Alliances, 246, 250–251
Alphanumeric marks, protection of, under
    trademark law, 288
American Association of Franchisees and Dealers,
    375
American Franchise Association, 375
Anticybersquatting Consumer Protection Act
    (1999), 194
Appendix in business plan, 220
Area franchise agreement, 359–360
Articles of incorporation, 188
Assets
    current, 155
    fixed, 155
    strategic, 111
Assignment of invention agreement, 284
Assumption sheet, 161
Attorney
    choosing, for new firm, 178–180
    patent, 285

Backward integration, threat of, 83
Balance sheet, 155–157
    consolidated, 155
    pro forma, 165–166
Band of Angels, 238
Banks
    commercial, 243–244
    investment, 241
Bar-code scanner technology, 16
Bargaining power
    of buyers, 82–83
    of suppliers, 82
Barrier to entry, 79
Benchmarking, 314
    steps in program, 214
Benefits, selling, 259–260
Beta tests, 59
Biotechnology, 246
Board of directors. *See also* Advisory board
    roles of, 132–134
Bootstrapping, 233, 234
Brainstorming, 39–41
Brand equity, 262
Brands
    building, 273–274
    defined, 260

establishing, 260–262
    loyalty to, 111
    management of, 260
Breakthrough products and services, 62
Brochureware, 192
Budgets, 150
Burn rate, 231
Business angels, 237–238
Business concepts
    blind spot in, 108
    research in, 125
Business ethics, promoting, 182
Business format franchise, 358–359
Business growth planning, 321
Business ideas, development of successful, 18–19
Business method patent, 283
Business model, 19, 100–117
    components of effective, 107–117
    emergence of, 104–106
    importance of, 102–104
    innovation, 102
    potential fatal flows of, 106–107
Business organization, 184
    comparison of forms of, 185*t*
    corporations as, 187–190
    limited liability company as, 190–191
    partnerships as, 186–187
    sole proprietorship as, 184–186
Business partnerships, participation in, 321
Business plan, 19, 205–222
    appendix in, 220
    business in, 214
    company structure in, 215
    confidentiality of, 207–208
    content of, 210–211
    cover letter for, 212
    cover page for, 214
    critical risk factors and, 220
    defined, 204
    executive summary for, 214
    financial plan in, 218–220
    flawed, 209
    format of, 211–212
    full, 111
    guidelines for writing, 209–212
    importance of, 203–204
    industry analysis in, 216
    intellectual property in, 215
    managed team in, 215
    marketing plan in, 217–218
    operational, 111
    operations plan in, 218
    oral presentation of, 221–222
    outline of, 212–214
    ownership in, 215
    presenting, to investors, 221–222
    reading, 207–208
    reasons for importance of, 206–207
    structure of, 210
    style of, 211–212
    summary, 211
    table of contents for, 214

Business practices, developing and maintaining
    professional, 317
Business-to-business (B2B) exchange, 164
Buyback clause, 180–181
Buyers, bargaining power of, 82–83
Buyout funding, 240

Capital constraints, 317
Capital investments, 232
Capital requirements, 79
Carry, 239
Cash flow, funding and, 231–232
Cash flow management, 317
C corporation, 188
    advantages of, 190
    disadvantages of, 190
Certification marks, 287
Channel conflict, 270
Character licensing, 344–345
Chat, 70
Chief executive officer (CEO), 156
    for new venture team, 129
Choreographic works, copyright protection of,
    291
Closely held corporation, 188
Clusters, 65
Cobranding, 262–263
    component, 263
Code of ethics, 182
Cognitive factors, 36–37
Collective marks, 287
Colors, protection of, under trademark law, 288
Commercial banks, 243–244
Commitment to growth, 321
Common stock, 188
Competitive analysis grid, completing, 91–92
Competitive intelligence, sources of, 90–91
Competitors
    analysis, 76, 89–92
    identifying, 89–90
Component cobranding, 263
Composite marks, protection of, under trademark
    law, 288
Concept statement, 56
Concept test, 57–58
Confidentiality of business firm, 207–208
Conflicts of interests, 183
Consolidated balance sheet, 155
Consortia, 114
Constant ratio method of forecasting, 162
Consultant, 139–140
Contracts, electronic, 194
Contractual obligations, meeting, 182
Contributed content Websites, 192–193
Copyright Act (1976), 290
Copyright bug, 291
Copyrights, 20, 290–293. *See also* Intellectual
    property
    conducting intellectual property audit for, 298
    exclusions from protection, 291
    infringemen oft, 292–293
    Internet and, 293

materials protected by, 290–291
   obtaining, 291–292
Core competencies, 55, 111
Core strategy, 108–111
Corporate entrepreneurship, 5
Corporate opportunity doctrine, 177
Corporate resources, inappropriate use of, 183
Corporate venture capital, 141
Corporations, 187–190
Corridor principle, 36
Cost advantages independent of size, 79
Cost-based pricing, 265
Cost leadership strategy, 110–111
Cost of sales, 154
Cost reduction strategy, 87
Costs
   fixed, 311
   switching, 82
   variable, 311
Cover letter for business plan, 212
Cover page for business plan, 214
Creativity, 37–39
   encouraging, at firm level, 42–43
Critical risk factors in business plan, 220
Current assets, 155
Current liabilities, 155
Current ratio, 155–156
Customer advisory boards, 42
Customer confidence, 183
Customer interface, 114–117
Customers, growth of key, 312
Cybersquatting, 193, 194

Data, 70
Day-in-the-life research, 42
Debt financing, 235
   preparing to raise, 233–237
   sources of, 243–244
Debt ratio, 168
Debt-to-equity ratio, 150, 168
Deceptive matter, 288
Declining industry, 87
Delaware, incorporation in, 189
Derivative works, copyright protection of, 291
Descriptive marks, 288–289
Design patents, 283–284
Designs, protection of, under trademark law, 288
Differentiation strategy, 110
Digital signatures, 194, 195
Digitization, power of, 313
Direct competitors, 89
Direct franchising arrangement, 377–378
Disintermediation, 270
Distribution, 269–270
Distribution channel, 169
Documents, labeling, 296
Domain names, 193–194
Double taxation, 188
Dramatic works, copyright protection of, 291
Due diligence, 240, 244

Econo Lodge Franchise Association, 375
Economic Espionage Act (1996), 295
Economic forces, 31
Economic impact of entrepreneurial firms,
   14–16
Economies of scale, 79, 311
Efficiency, 149
Elaboration, 39

Electronic contracts, 194
Electronic Signatures in Global and International
   Commerce Act (2000), 194
Elevator speech, 236
Emerging industry, 86
Employees
   attracting and retaining, 312
   reading of business plan by, 207–208
   recruiting and selecting key, 131–132
Employer, ethics in leaving, 177–178
Employment agreements, honoring, 178
Entrants, threat of new, 79–80
Entrepreneurial alertness, 36
Entrepreneurial firms, 14
   economic impact of, 14–16
   impact on larger firms, 16–17
   impact on society, 16
   managing and growing, 20
   moving from an idea to an, 19–20
Entrepreneurial intensity, 5
Entrepreneurial process, 17–20
Entrepreneurial services, 315
Entrepreneurs
   characteristics of successful, 7–10
   common myths about, 10–14
   decision to become, 18
   personal characteristics of, 35–39
   reasons for becoming, 6–7
Entrepreneurships
   defined, 4–6
   importance of, 14–17
Equity financing, 234–235
   preparing to raise, 233–237
   sources of, 237–243
Ethics
   franchise, 375–376
   human resources and, 183
   issues facing new firm, 176–183
Ethics training programs, 182–183
   usefulness of, 200
Evaluation, 39
Event sponsorships, 269
Exclusive distribution arrangements, 270
Execution intelligence, 10
Executive-search firm, 131
Executive summary for business plan, 214
Existing firms, rivalry among, 80–82
Exit strategy, 220
Export markets, 16
External growth strategies, 339–348
   advantages of, emphasizing, 341t
   disadvantages of, emphasizing, 341t
External stakeholders, reading of business plan by,
   208

Fair use, 293
Fast-track programs, 245
Feasibility analysis, 52–60, 62–65, 67, 102
   financial, 65, 67
   industry/market, 60, 62–64
   organizational, 64–65
   product/service, 57–60
Fiduciary obligation, 374
Field trials, 59
Final prospectus, 241
Financial feasibility analysis, 65, 67
   capital requirements, 65
   overall attractiveness of investment, 67
   rate of return, 67

Financial management, 148–152
   process of, 150–152
Financial objectives of firm, 149–150
Financial plan in business plan, 218–220
Financial rate of return, 67
Financial ratios, 151
Financial statements, 150, 152–164
   historical, 152, 153–154
   pro forma, 153, 160, 164–168
Financing
   activities in, 158
   creative sources of, 244–246
   importance of getting, 231–243
   need for, 231–232
   sources of personal, 132–233
Firms. *See also* Entrepreneurial firms
   benchmarking against successful growth, 314
   challenges of growing, 316–317
   choosing attorney for new, 178–180
   comparing financial results to industry norms,
     159–160
   encouraging creativity at level of, 42–43
   entrepreneurial firms' impact on larger, 16–17
   ethical and legal issues facing new, 176–183
   financial objectives of, 149–150
   growthul, 320–322
   lifestyle, 14
   rapid-growth, 309
   salary-substitute, 13–14
   start-up, 13–14, 106
   venture-leasing, 244
First-mover advantage, 63, 320
First-stage funding, 240
Five competitive forces, determining industry
   profitability, 78–83
Five forces model, value of, 83
Fixed assets, 155
Fixed costs, 311
Focal point, establishing, for ideas, 42
Focus groups, 41
Follow-me-home testing, 52, 59
Follow-on funding, 240
Forecasts, 150, 160–163
Foreign market entry strategies, 337–338
Forward integration, threat of, 82
Founders, 128–129, 131
   qualities of, 129
Founders' agreement, 176
   drafting, 180–181
Founding team, size of, 128–129
Fragmented industry, 87
Fragrance, protection of, under trademark law,
   288
Franchise
   advantages of buying, 368–369
   business format, 358–359
   buying, 366–371
   cost of, 366–367
   disadvantages of buying, 368–369
   finding, 367–368
   product, 358
   steps in purchasing, 370–371
   trademark, 358
Franchise agreement, 372
Franchise association, 375
Franchisees, 357
   selecting and developing effective, 362–363
Franchise ethics, 375–376
Franchise outlets, opening overseas, 377

Franchise relationship, legal aspects of, 372–374
Franchise system
	advantages of establishing, 363–365
	disadvantages of establishing, 363–365
	establishing, 360–365
Franchising
	defined, 357–358
	future of, 378
	international, 376–378
	misconceptions about, 371
	steps to, 361–362
	timing and, 360–361
Franchisor, 357
Free samples, 268
Free trials, 268
Fulfillment and support, 115–116
Full business plan, 211
Full e-commerce Websites, 193
Funding. See Financing
Future competitors, 89

Gazelles, 16
General partnership, 187
	advantages of, 187
	disadvantages of, 187
Geographic expansion, 335
Geographic location, that facilitates knowledge
	absorption, 322
Global Entrepreneurship Monitor (GEM), 4
Global industries, 87, 89
Globalization, 16
Global sales, 338–339
Global start-ups, 336
Global strategy, 87
Good Housekeeping Seal of Approval, 187
Government and legal barriers, 79
Graphic works, copyright protection of, 291
Group support system (or GSS) software, 40
Growth
	challenges of, 314–317, 319–320
	myths about, 319–320
	preparing for, 310–312, 314
Growth firms, attributes of successful, 320–322
Growth-oriented vision, 320–321
Growth-related firm attributes, 320–321
Growth strategies
	external, 339–348
	internal, 330–339
Guidance, providing, 133–134

Heterogeneous members, 129
Historical financial statements, 152, 153–154
Homogeneous members, 129
Human resource ethical problems, 183
Human resource management, outsourcing, 219
Hyperlink, 192

Idea bank, 42
Idea-expression dichotomy, 291
Ideas
	encouraging and protecting new, 42–44
	establishing focal point for, 42
	moving from, to an entrepreneurial firm,
		19–20
	protecting, from being lost or stolen, 43–44
	suggestion program or, 42
	techniques for generating, 39–42
Illiquid, 189
Images, 70

Immoral matter, 288
Inbound logistics, 104
Income statement, 154
	pro forma, 165
Incubator, 66
Indirect competitors, 89
Individual franchise agreement, 359
Industry analysis, 76
	in business plan, 216
	importance of industry-versus firm-specific
		factors, 77–87, 89
Industry attractiveness, 60
Industry consolidation, 87
Industry/market feasibility analysis, 60, 62–64
	attractiveness, 60
	identifying niche market, 64
	market timeliness, 62–63
Industry norms, comparing firm's financial results
	to, 159–160
Industry profitability, five competitive forces
	determining, 78–83
Industry trade associations, importance of, 38
Industry types, opportunities they offer, 85–87, 89
Initial public offering (IPO), 241–243
Innovation, 15
Inside director, 132
Instant messages, 70–71
Intellectual property. See also Copyrights
	in business plan, 215
	creating path between owners of, and those
		benefiting from, 297
	defined, 278
	importance of, 278–282
	key forms of, 282
	protecting, 281
Intellectual property audit, 298–299
	process of conducting, 299
	reasons for conducting, 298
Intent-to-use trademark application, 290
Intermediaries, selling through, 270
Internal growth strategies, 330–339
	advantages and disadvantages of, 332
International expansion, 335–337
International Franchise Association (IFA), 375,
	378
International franchising, 376–378
International markets, assessing firm's suitability
	for growth through, 336–337
International new ventures, 335–336
Internet
	copyrights and, 293
	legal environment of, 192–194
Invention logbook, 285
Inventory, 149
Investing activities, 158
Investment bank, 241
Investors
	presenting business plan to, 221–222
	questions and feedback to expect from, 222
	reading of business plan by, 208
	vested interest in companies financials, 138
Iridium, 54

Job creation, 16
Joint ventures, 114, 347–348
	advantages of participating in, 345t
	disadvantages of participating in, 345t
	link, 347
	scale, 347

Knowledge absorption, geographic location that
	facilitates, 322

Leadership strategy, 87
Leasing, 244
Legal aspects of franchise relationship, 372–374
Legal disputes, avoiding, 181–183
Legal environment of Internet, 192–194
Legal issues, facing new firm, 176–183
Legitimacy, role of board of directors in lending,
	134
Lenders, vested interest in companies financials,
	138
Letters, protection of, under trademark law,
	288
Liability of newness, 127
Licensee, 343
Licensing, 343–345
	character, 344–345
	merchandise, 344–345
	technology, 343–344
Licensing agreement, 343
Licensor, 343
Lifestyle firms, 14
Limited liability company (LLC), 189, 190–191
	advantages of, 191
	disadvantages of, 191
Limited partnership, 187
Link joint venture, 347
Liquidity, 149, 184
Liquidity event, 219–220
Liquidity ratios, 168
Liquid market, 188
Literary works, copyright protection of, 290
Logbooks, maintaining
	for access to sensitive material, 196
	for visitors, 296
Logos, protection of, under trademark law, 288
Long-term liabilities, 155
Love money, 233

Managerial capacity, 315–316
Managerial services, 315
Marketing
	key issues for new ventures, 259–262
	for online retailer, 274–275
	place in, 269–270
	price in, 265–266
	product in, 264–265
	promotion in, 266–269
	viral, 169
Marketing alliances, 346–347
Marketing mix, 263–270
Marketing plan in business plan, 217–218
Marketing strategy, 259–260
Market leadership, 312
Market penetration, increasing, of existing
	product or service, 333–334
Markets
	establishing position, 254–259
	export, 16
	international, 336–337
	liquid, 188
	niche, 64, 256
	selecting position, 254–259
	target, 114–115, 255–257
Market segmentation, 255–256
Market timeliness, 62–63
Master franchise agreement, 360, 378

Mature industry, 87
Media coverage, 268
Merchandise licensing, 344–345
Mergers, 340–343
Mezzanine financing, 240
Milestone, 214
Mission statement, 108
Moderate risk takers, 11
Moral hazard, 315
Multidomestic strategy, 87
Multiple-unit franchisee, 360
Musical compositions, copyright protection of, 290–291

National Association of Security Dealers Automated Quotation (NASDAQ), 5, 188
National Franchise Council, 375
Need-to-know basis, 153
Negative cash flow, 231
Net sales, 154
Network, 114
Network entrepreneurs, 37
Networking, 38, 131
New product development, 331–333
News conference, 268
New ventures
    key marketing issues for, 259–262
    marketing mix for, 263–270
New venture team, 64, 126
    board of directors on, 132–134
    creating, 127–129, 131–134
    founders of, 128–129, 131
    professional advisers on, 134–140
    recruiting and selecting key employees, 131–132
New York Stock Exchange (NYSE), 188
Niche market, 64, 256
Niche strategy, 87
Noncompete agreement, 178
Nondisclosure agreement, 178
North American Association of Subway Franchisees, 375
North American Free Trade Agreement (NAFTA), 376
Numbers, protection of, under trademark law, 288

Online meetings, 137
Online retailer, marketing for, 274–275
Operating activities, 158
Operating expenses, 154
Operational business plan, 211
Operations, 104
Operations plan in business plan, 218
Opportunities
    defined, 28
    identifying and recognizing, 28–39
    recognition of, 35
Oral presentation of business plan, 221–222
Organic growth, 331
Organizational chart, 215
Organizational feasibility analysis, 64–65
    management prowess, 64–65
    resource sufficiency, 65
Outbound logistics, 104
Outside director, 132
Outsourcing, 334
    human resource management, 219
Owners' equity, 155

Pace of growth, 311
Pantomimes, copyright protection of, 291
Partnership agreement, 187
Partnership network, 112–114
Partnerships, 186–187
    general, 187
    limited, 187
Password protecting confidential computer files, 296
Patent attorney, 285
Patents, 20, 282–286
    applying for, 284
    business method, 283
    conducting intellectual property audit for, 298
    design, 283–284
    filing application, 285
    plant, 284
    process of obtaining, 284–286
    search for, 285
    utility, 283
Peer groups, 127
Percent-of-sales method, 162
Personal financial management software, 52
Personal financing, sources of, 232–233
Pictorial works, copyright protection of, 291
Piercing corporate evil, 188
Place, 269–270
Plant patents, 284
Political action, 32–33
Position, 77
    establishing unique, 258
Positioning strategy, 259–260
Preferred stock, 188
Preliminary prospectus, 241
Press kit, 268
Press release, 268
Price, 265–266
Price-quality attribution, 265
Price stability, 317
Price-to-earnings ratio (P/E ratio), 155
Pricing
    cost-based, 265
    value-based, 265
Pricing models, 116
Pricing structure, 116–117
Primary research, 60
Prior entrepreneurial experience, 129
Prior experience, 36
Private corporation, 188–189
Private placement, 243
Problem, solving, 33–35
Product, 264–265
    improving existing, 333
    increasing market penetration of existing, 333–334
Product/customer focus, 8–9
Product development cycles, 232
Product differentiation, 79
Product franchise, 358
Productive opportunity set, 315
Product line extension strategy, 334–335
Product lines, extending, 334–335
Product/market scope, 108–110
Product-related strategies, 333
Product/service feasibility analysis, 57–60
    benefits of conducting, 57t
    concept test, 57–58
    usability testing, 58–60
Professional advisers, role of, 134–140

Profitability, 149
Profitability ratios, 168
Profit margin, 154–155
Pro forma balance sheet, 165–166
Pro forma financial statements, 153, 160, 164–168
Pro forma income statement, 165
Pro forma statement of cash flows, 166–167
Promotion, 266–269
Prospectus
    final, 141
    preliminary, 241
Prototyping, 58
Public corporations, 188
Public relations, 268

Quality control, 317

Rapid-growth firm, 209
Rapid-growth industries, 319
Ratio analysis, 159, 168
Reference account, 264–265
Regression analysis, 162
Regulatory changes, 32–33
Relevant industry experience, 129
Resource leverage, 111
Resource sufficiency, 65
Restricting access, 296
Road show, 241
Rounds, 240

Salary-substitute firms, 13–14
Sales forecast, 161–162
Scalable business model, 311–312
Scale joint venture, 347
Scandalous matter, 288
Sculptural works, copyright protection of, 291
Secondary research, 60–61
Second-mover advantage, 63
Second-stage funding, 240
Securities and Exchange Commission (SEC), 152
Security measures, maintaining adequate overall, 196
Seed funding, 240
Seed money, 54
Self-selected opinion poll, 41
Selling direct, 269–270
Selling through intermediaries, 270
Service, 264
    improving existing, 333
    increasing market penetration of existing, 333–334
Service marks, 287
7(A) Guaranty Program, 244
Shapes, protection of, under trademark law, 288
Shareholders, 188
    agreement of, 180
Shop window Websites, 192
Signaling, 134
Signatures, digital, 194, 195
Skin in game, 215
Small Business Administration (SBA). *See* Equity financing
    guaranteed loans of, 244
Small Business Innovation Research (SBIR) program, 245
Small Business Technology Transfer (SBTT) program, 245
Social forces, 31–32
Social networks, 37

Society, entrepreneurial firms99 impact on, 16
Sole proprietorship, 184–186
    advantages of, 185
    disadvantages of, 186
Solo entrepreneurs, 37
Sounds, 70
    protection of, under trademark law, 288
Sources and uses of funds statement, 218
Spin-ins, 348
Stability, 150
Start-up firms, 106
    types of, 13–14, 14*f*
Start-up funding, 240, 249–250
Statement of cash flows, 157–159
Stealth mode, 208
Stock
    common, 188
    preferred, 188
Stock options, 189
Strategic alliances, 114, 345–347
    advantages of participating in, 345*t*
    disadvantages of participating in, 345*t*
Strategic assets, 111
Strategic partners, 246
Strategic resources, 111
Strong-tie relationships, 37
Subchapter S corporation, 190
Subfranchisees, 360
Substitutes
    attractiveness of, 82
    threat of, 78–79
Summary business plan, 211
Supplier concentration, 82
Suppliers, 112
    bargaining power of, 82

Supply chain, 112
Supply chain management, 112
Surnames, 289
Surveys, 41–42
Sustainable competitive advantage, 111
Sustained growth, 309
Sweat equity, 232
Switching costs, 82

Table of contents for business plan, 214
Tagline, 258–259
Target, 340
Target market, 114–115, 255
    selecting, 256–257
Technological advances, 32
Technological alliances, 346
Technology licensing, 343–344
10-K, 152
Trade associations, 114
Trade dress, protection of, under trademark law, 288
Trademark franchise, 358
Trademark law, items covered under, 288
Trademarks, 20, 193–194, 286–290
    conducting intellectual property audit for, 298
    exclusions from protection, 288–289
    process of obtaining, 289–290
    search for, 289–290
    types of, 287
Trade secrets, 20, 178, 293, 295–297
    conducting intellectual property audit for, 298
    defined, 295
    disputes on, 295–296
    protection methods, 296–297
    qualification for protection, 295

Trade show, 268
Trends, observing, 30–33
Triggering event, 18
Two Pesos, Inc. v. *Cabana International Inc.*, 288
Typosquatting, 194

Undercapitalization, avoiding, 182
Uniform Franchise Offering Circular (UFOC), 372, 374
Uniform Trade Secrets Act (1979), 295
U.S. Patent and Trademark Office, 281, 282, 284, 285–286, 289, 290, 291
Usability testing, 58–60
User tests, 59
Utility patents, 283

Value, 14
Value-based pricing, 265
Value chain, 104
    analysis of, 104–106
    emergence of, 104–106
Variable costs, 311
V-commerce, 325–326
Venture capital, 139–241
Venture-leasing firms, 244
Viral marketing, 269

Weak-tie relationships, 37
Web links, 70
Window of opportunity, 28
Words, protection of, under trademark law, 288
Working capital, 155
World Wide Web (WWW), 192–193
Writing, importance of agreements in, 182

Abercrombie & Fitch, 110, 110*f*, 114, 115, 269–270, 270, 335,
Achieva, 394
Activision, 59*f*, 79, 91–92, 92*n*, 446
Agilent Technologies, 15
Airbus, 112
Air-Grid Networks, 70
Akamai Technologies, 135, 242
Align Technology, 48–49
AllAdvantage.com, 409–420
Alloy Ventures, 411
Alpine Lace, 403
AltaVista, 29
Amazon.com, 10, 14, 28, 89, 108, 114, 115*f*, 117, 193, 241, 270, 279–280, 283, 287, 302–303, 310, 321, 322, 430, 438, 439
AMD, 143
Amerada Hess, 151
American Airlines Admirals Clubs, 107
American Express, 390
American Golf Inc., 97
American Greetings, 346
American International Group (AIG), 397
America Online (AOL), 249, 278, 313, 346, 353, 386, 439
Ameritrade, 287
Amgen, 16*n*, 310, 319, 331, 442
Amway, 269
AOL Time Warner, 437
Apogent Technologies, 340
Apple Computer, 8, 9, 13, 23, 61, 204, 233, 288, 386
Arnold & Henderson, 423
ARPANET, 385
Arthur D. Little, 393
Ask Jeeves, 329–330, 343, 347
Asset Management/Alloy Ventures, 410
Atlas Venture, 422, 425, 427
AT&T, 288, 326
Au Bon Pain Co., 95, 404
AuctionBytes.com, 438
Auction Web, 430–432
Austin Ventures, 125
Avis, 16
AV Labs, 8, 10, 222
Avon, 269

BabyGap, 115
Bahama Breeze, 363
Bain & Company, 140, 309, 432
Banana Republic, 115
Barnes & Noble, 38, 89, 262, 263, 303, 308
Baskin-Robbins, 383
Bass Hotels and Resorts, 376
Batteries Plus, 358, 359
Baxter Healthcare, 15
Bayer, 297
Bearing Point, 140
BeautyBuys.com, 136–137
Benchmark Venture Capital, 138, 181, 236, 249, 432
Ben & Jerry's, 383

Beranek & Newman, 385
Bertucci's, 406
Best Buy, 11, 85*n*, 143, 270
BillPoint, 438
Biogen Idec, Inc., 250–251, 315
Blimpie Subs and Salads, 150, 151
Blockbuster, 317
BMW, 258
Boeing, 112, 113
Bolt, 385
Borders, 38
Boston Consulting Group, 34, 331, 434
Boston Market, 404, 406
Braxton Associates, 321
Bright Horizons Family Solutions, 120–121, 126
British Petroleum-Amoco (BP), 24, 151, 358
Broadview, 287
Budweiser, 376
Burger King, 357, 361, 366, 377, 403, 404, 408
Burr, Egan, Deleage & Co., 422, 428
Burton McCall, 351
The Business Center, 237
Butterfield & Butterfield, 436
BuyandHold.com, 28, 31, 64

Cambridge Child Development Centers, 376
Canadian Standards Association, 287
Capital Vision Group, 136
Carmax, 117
Carneros Wines, 287
Cartidge World, 355–356, 360, 363, 371
Caufield & Byers, 249, 326
CD Warehouse, 31, 360
Chaparral Steel, 42
Character Training International (CTI), 200
Charles Schwab, 28, 64
Chase Manhattan Bank, 408
ChemConnect, 24–25, 31, 164
Cheskin, 58
CHH Incorporated, 32
Chock Full O'Nuts, 408
ChromeaDex, 297
Cingular, 116, 270
Circuit City, 11, 85*n*, 270
Cisco Systems, 5, 16, 33–34, 120, 172, 229–230, 231, 233, 234, 236, 239, 288, 319
CleanSleeves, 88
CNET Networks, 337–338
CNN, 288
CNNSI.com, 253
Coca-Cola, 79, 89, 288, 312, 347, 376, 408
Cold Fusion Foods, 94
Coleman, 351
College Coach, 393–399
Columbia Sussex Hotels, 107
COMDEX, 268
Comfort Keepers, 357–358, 360, 363
Common Cause, 33
Compaq Computer, 63, 85*n*, 100, 309
Computervision, 422, 423–424, 425, 426
Continental Airlines, 80
Convey Software, 16

Coopers & Lybrand Consulting, 114*n*, 447
Creative Croissants, 383
Creative Strategies, 435
Credit Suisse First Boston, 47, 241
Cross Creek System, 145
CTH Consumer Plastic, 143
Curves Fitness Center, 253–256, 258, 260, 368, 376
CVS Pharmacy, 238
Cypress Semiconductor, 6–7

Daedalus Corporation, 353
Daimler-Benz, 273
DaimlerChrysler, 273, 330
Darden Restaurants Inc., 363
Dell Computers, Inc., 7, 8, 13, 16, 63, 85*n*, 99–101, 102, 104, 105, 109, 111, 112, 113, 114, 116, 171–172, 234, 244, 246, 264, 290, 291, 347, 437
Dell Financial Services, 439
Deloitte & Touche Consulting, 24, 321, 401–402
Delta Airlines, 193–194
Delta Semiconductor, 193
DFJ, 389
Digital Equipment Corporation, 393
Digital Home Working Group, 90
Domino's Pizza, 117, 325, 326
DoubleClick system, 412, 413
Double Delight Ice Cream, 289
Dow Chemical, 14
Draper Fisher Jurvetson, 387, 388
DreamWorks SKG, 121, 190
Dryers, 331
DuPont & Co, 297

eBags, 274–275
eBay, 3–4, 5, 7, 119, 138, 172, 194, 211, 239, 287, 344, 430–440
eBay Motors, 437
Eckerd, 238
Eclipse Aviation, 198
Eddie Bauer, 35
Electronic Arts (EA), 79, 203–204, 287
EMC, 33
Enesco Group, 257
Enron, 132
Epogen, 331
Ericsson, 115, 344
eShop, 3
E-Stamps, 29
eToys, 278–279
ETrade, 14, 28, 287, 326
Eve.com, 101
Excite, 29
Expedia.com, 193, 348
Exxon, 151, 289

Facilitate.com, 137
Federal Express, 14, 88, 112, 171, 207, 320
Fidelity Ventures, 64, 393
FINOVA Group, 133
Firepower Systems, 386

Florida Oranges, 287
Florists' Transworld Delivery (FTD), 432–433
Ford Motor Company, 314, 334
Forrester Research, 30, 62
Four, 11, 387, 388, 389
Freeplay Energy, 351–352
Fresh Fields, 186
Furniture.com, 225–226

Gap Store, 13, 115, 310, 335
Garden.com, 130
Gartner Group, 30
Gateway Computers, Inc., 90, 100, 109, 233, 287, 434
GE Financial Services, 319
General Electric, 16, 120, 149, 312
General Magic, 3
General Mills, 15, 103
General Motors, 358
General Nutrition Centers, 367, 383
Georgia Pacific, 15
GMA, 281
Gold Gym, 258
Goldman Sachs, 438
GolfWeb, 353
Google, 13, 14, 29, 101, 102, 239, 249–250
Green Planet Juicery, 181
GRID Systems, 23
Gym Children's Fitness Center, 256

Hammarplast, 307–309
Hardee's, 363
Harley-Davidson, 304–305, 312, 344
Harte-Hanks Direct Marketing, 393
Hasbro, 257, 433, 435, 436
Healthy Choice, 403
Hewlett-Packard, 63, 85n, 90, 100, 114, 172, 233, 309, 312, 430
Hilton Hotels, 107
Holiday Inn, 376, 408
Hollister, 335
Home Depot, 149, 439
Honest Tea, 186
Hotmail, 10, 269, 385–392
H & R Block, 357
Human Genome Sciences, 282
HydroPoint, 225

iBinary, 10
IBM, 85n, 114, 120, 125, 149, 172, 347, 408, 437, 439
IBM Foodservice Consulting Consortium, 408
IBM Global Services, 140
IFX International, 382–383
Informatics, 376
Information Technology Industry Council, 187
Infoseek, 387
Ink Development, 3
In-N-Out Burger, 282
Insitu, 113
Intel, 10, 90, 347–348, 387
International Franchise Association, 287
Intuit, 51, 64, 310
IQNavigator, 17
Iridium LLC, 53
Ivey Consulting, 193

J. Crew, 35
Jackson Hewitt, 105

Jack Sprat's Restaurant, 400–408
Jamba Juice, 181, 363
JetBlue, 75–76, 79, 80
Johnson & Johnson, 16
Juno, 389
Jupiter Communications, 313
Jupiter Media Metrix, 30
Just Do It, 288
J & W Seligman's New Technology Funds, 411

Kaplan, 394
KB Toys, 278–279
Kellogg's, 15, 103
Kentucky Fried Chicken (KFC), 357, 376, 408
Kinko's, 330, 335
Kleiner Perkins Caufield & Byers, 249, 326, 423
KnowledgePoints, 365
Kodak, 16, 41, 289
Kohl's, 335
Kopf Zimmerman Schultheis Advertising, 136
KPMG, 114, 140
Krispy Kreme, 80n
Kroger, 238
Kruse International, 436
KZS Advertising, 136

LA Gear, 318
Lane, 15, 132, 138
LeapFrog, 147–148
Lexus, 258
LifeStyle, 381–382
Li & Fung Limited, 351
Lightspeed Venture Partners, 126
Liz Claiborne, 270, 344–345, 345
Lost Children's Network, 143
Lotus Development, 237
LSI Logic, 143
Lycos, 29

Magic Plan, 401
MapQuest, 312, 313
Market Discoveries, Inc., 407
Marriott, 377, 408
Mary Kay, 269
Mattel, 157, 312
McAfee, 33
McAfee ASaP, 262
McDonald's, 10, 95, 260, 289, 308, 335, 356, 357, 359, 360, 366, 371, 376, 404, 408
McKinsey & Company, 394, 434
Merck & Company, 17, 312
Merrill Lynch, 16, 28, 64, 326
MGM, 288
Microsoft, 5, 8, 13, 16, 90, 152, 204, 246, 279, 290, 303, 310, 311, 346, 347, 348, 387, 389, 439
Microsoft Network, 10
Microsoft Windows, 278
Midas Muffler, 357, 377–378
Milestone Venture Partners, 220
Mitsubishi, 24
Mobil, 151
MobileStar, 107
Mobira, 273
Momentum Marketing Services, 319–320
Morris Air, 75
Motorola, 53, 115, 344, 351
Movie Gallery, 326–327
Mrs. Fields Chocolate Chippery, 13f

Mrs. Fields Cookies, 12
mvp.com, 193
MyCIO.com, 262

Napster, 293, 294
National Semiconductor, 116
Nestlé, 15, 347
NetCreations, 416
Netflix, 121–122
NetMind Technologies, 437
Netscape, 7, 325, 386, 387
Network Solutions, 193
Neupogen, 331
Newgistics, 34–35
NFL.com, 253
Nike, 258, 278, 312, 330
Nintendo, 204
Nistevo, 15
Nokia, 13, 63, 90, 115, 175–176, 177, 178, 270, 273–274, 344
Nordstrom, 101
Nortel Networks, 144
North American Coffee Partnership, 309
North Bridge Venture Capital Partners, 422, 428
Northern Michigan Apples, 290
Nucor Steel, 87, 320
NYNEX, 387

Oakley, 258, 259, 265
Old Navy, 115
Olive Garden, 363
1-800-FLOWERS, 89, 288, 345, 346
Open Skies, 76
Oracle, 5, 8, 287, 288, 317, 335
Outback Steakhouse, 335, 336

Palm Pilots, 23, 41–42, 63, 437
PalmSource, 23
Panera Bread, 85n, 95–96
Parametric Technology Corp., 424–425
ParentWatch, 47
Partech International, 411
PayPal, 436, 438
Pegasus Computing, 175–176
PepsiCo, 58, 79, 331
Perkins, 249, 326
Pets.com, 106
PetSmart, 106
Pfizer, 17, 283, 347
Pixar, 173, 340
Pizzeria Uno, 404
Playskool, 433
Premise, Inc., 422, 423
Priceline.com, 103, 283, 303
PricewaterhouseCoopers, 31, 113, 114, 314, 321, 330, 331, 341, 443, 447
Primus Venture Partners, 215
Princeton Review, 394
PRINTDreams, 302
Procter & Gamble, 51, 390, 432, 435
Prometheus Laboratories, 64
Protect-Data.com, 23
Providian Financial Corp., 416
Prudential, 120
PurpleTie Company, 87, 88

Qualcomm, 5, 343, 344
Quantum Computer services, 385
Quicken, 287

R. R. Donnelley & Sons, 313
Radar Golf, 22
RadioShack, 273
RAND Corporation, 385
RealNetworks, 32, 237
Red Bull, 117
Red Lobster, 363
Retailing Insights, 54
RMS System, 22
RocketMail, 389
Rotary International, 187
Roxio, 294

S2io Technologies, 144–145
Safety First, 316
Saks, 101
SAP, 24
SAS Institute, 266
Scios, 232
Sears Roebuck, 85n, 437
Sequoia Capital, 60, 230, 236, 249
Shareholder Communication Corporation (SCC), 27
Sharper Image, 439
Siebel Systems, 12
Singer Sewing Machine, 357
Singing Machine, 11
Sirf, 143
Sketchers, 333
Skinny Cow Inc., 403, 407
Smart Safety Systems, Inc., 142
Smith Computer Emporium, 289
Smokey Bones BBQ, 363
SOFTBANK Capital Partners, 411
Softbank Interactive Marketing, 389
SolidWorks, 422–429
Sony Corporation, 16, 83, 90, 204
Sony Walkman, 31
Sound Safety Products, 288
Southwest Airlines, 75–76, 108, 109, 149–150, 260–261, 320
SpencerTrask, 237, 238
Spiegel, 35
SportsLine.com, 252–353
Sprint, 116

Stamps.com, 29
Staples, 14
Starbucks, 5, 10, 14, 41, 79, 83, 107, 109, 132, 260, 262, 263, 287, 290, 307–309, 310, 330, 331, 333, 344, 363
Staybridge Suites, 376
Stilton Cheese, 287
StorageNetworks, 334
StrideRite, 432
Subway, Inc., 358, 367, 371, 383
SUN, 386
Sunkist Growers, 260
Sun Microsystems, 7, 79–80, 112, 126, 287, 434, 436, 437
SunTrust Bank, 330
Switchboard, 277–278
Sylvan Learning Centers, 365
Symantec Corporation, 33
Synergenix, 325

TCBY, 377
TechRx, 238
Tellme Networks, 325–326
Teoma Technologies, 330
Texas Pacific Group, 432
The Hog Farm, 204–305
3Com, 23
3M Corporation, 5, 288, 331
Ticketmaster, 439
Tivoli, 125
TManage, 182
Tosco, 151
Toysrus.com, 221, 322
TradeOut.com, 438
Trakus, Inc., 54, 55n
Travelocity, 270, 330
20th Century Fox, 121
Twin Cities Consulting, 290
Two Men and a Truck, 383
Ty, Inc., 281

Underwriters Laboratories, 287
United Parcel Service (UPS), 106, 112, 171, 246

U.S. Lawns, 383
U.S. Navy, 330
U.S. Robotics, 23
Universal Studios, 120, 121
UpLink, 96–97
Upromise, 226–227
USWEST, 387

ValuePay.com, 415
Verizon, 116, 278
ViewBar, 409, 410, 411, 413, 415
Virgin Group, 5–6
Virgin Music, 6
Virgin Records, 7
VISA, 330
Vondafone, 321

Walden Media and Information Technology Fun, 411
Wal-Mart, 257, 361
Walt Disney, 173, 288, 340, 432, 437
Waterboys, 393
Waveset Technologies, 125–126
WebHouse Club, 103, 106
WebTV, 279, 387
Wells Fargo, 244
Wendy's, 359
Wessels, 423
Wherify Wireless, 143–144
White Wave, 87
William Express, 151
William's Fresh Fish, 289
WorldCom, 132

Xerox, 9, 108, 289

Yahoo!, 7, 29, 62, 63, 108, 239, 278, 281, 286, 287, 320, 344, 346, 386, 387, 389, 439
Yankee Group, 30
Yet, 2, 297
Young Entrepreneurs Organization (YEO), 127

Zephyrhill, 188
Zipcar, 199

PHOTO CREDITS

Chapter 1

2 Photodisc **3** Nathaniel Welch/Corbis NY **6** Michael L. Abramson/Michael L. Abramson Photography **9** Stephen Simpson/Getty Images, Inc.—Taxi **13** Arizona Daily Star

Chapter 2

26 Stone **27** Corbis/Bettmann **33** Bob Daemmrich/Bob Daemmrich Photography, Inc. **36** Kim Kulish/Corbis/Bettmann **40** Ronnie Kaufman/Corbis NY

Chapter 3

50 BrandX **51** Michael Keller/Corbis/Stock Market **55** Doug Mills/AP Wide World Photos **59** Susan Goldman/The Image Works **63** Bruce Barringer

Chapter 4

74 Photodisc **75** Syracuse Newspapers/The Image Works **80** Arnold Gold/New Haven Register/The Image Works **85** AP Wide World Photos

Chapter 5

98 Photodisc **99** AP Wide World Photos **106** Getty Images, Inc—Liaison **110** Getty Images **115** Paul Souders

Chapter 6

124 Taxi **125** Sun Microsysytems, Inc **133** Shell Oil Co **136** Stephen Derr/Getty Images Inc.—Image Bank **139** AP Wide World Photos

Chapter 7

146 Photodisc **147** AP Wide World Photos **150** Ed Young/Science Photo Library/Photo Researchers, Inc. **153** Henry Sims/Getty Images Inc.—Image Bank

Chapter 8

174 Photodisc **175** Bonnie Kamin/PhotoEdit **183** Brian Smale/Brian Smale Photography **191** Esbin/Anderson/Omni-Photo Communications, Inc.

Chapter 9

202 Taxi **203** Digital Vision Ltd. **206** Stockbyte **216** Jonathan Nourok/PhotoEdit

Chapter 10

228 Photodisc **229** Paul Sakuma/AP Wide World Photos **232** Allan H. Shoemake/Getty Images, Inc.—Taxi **239** EyeWire Collection/Getty Images—Photodisc

Chapter 11

252 Image Bank **253** Curves International **256** Steve Marcus/Reuters/NewMedia/Corbis/Bettmann **261** iRobot Corporation;

Chapter 12

276 Stone **277** InfoSpace Inc. **279** Frank LaBua/Pearson Education/PH College **286** Paul Sakuma/AP Wide World Photos **292** Knut Mueller/Das Fotoarchiv/Peter Arnold, Inc.

Chapter 13

306 Stone **307** Alex Wong/Getty Images, Inc—Liaison **310** Evan Kafka **319** Nucor Corporation

Chapter 14

328 Photodisc **329** Ask Jeeves, Inc. **339** Paul Sakuma/AP Wide World Photos **344** Tony Freeman Photographs

Chapter 15

354 Stone **355** Cartridge World **357** Simon Smith/Dorling Kindersley Media Library **372** SW Productions/Getty Images, Inc.—Photodisc